FINANCIAL REPORTING AND ANALYSIS

CFA® Program Curriculum
2016 • LEVEL II • VOLUME 2

CFA Institute | **WILEY**

Photography courtesy of Hector Emanuel.

ISBN 978-1-942471-04-2 (paper)
ISBN 978-1-942471-25-7 (ebk)

10 9 8 7 6 5 4 3 2 1

Please visit our website at
www.WileyGlobalFinance.com.

WILEY

CONTENTS

indicates an optional segment

◙ indicates an optional segment

◙ indicates an optional segment

How to Use the CFA Program Curriculum

Congratulations on reaching Level II of the Chartered Financial Analyst (CFA®) Program. This exciting and rewarding program of study reflects your desire to become a serious investment professional. You are embarking on a program noted for its high ethical standards and the breadth of knowledge, skills, and abilities it develops. Your commitment to the CFA Program should be educationally and professionally rewarding.

The credential you seek is respected around the world as a mark of accomplishment and dedication. Each level of the program represents a distinct achievement in professional development. Successful completion of the program is rewarded with membership in a prestigious global community of investment professionals. CFA charterholders are dedicated to life-long learning and maintaining currency with the ever-changing dynamics of a challenging profession. The CFA Program represents the first step toward a career-long commitment to professional education.

The CFA examination measures your mastery of the core skills required to succeed as an investment professional. These core skills are the basis for the Candidate Body of Knowledge (CBOK™). The CBOK consists of four components:

- A broad outline that lists the major topic areas covered in the CFA Program (www.cfainstitute.org/cbok);
- Topic area weights that indicate the relative exam weightings of the top-level topic areas (www.cfainstitute.org/level_II);
- Learning outcome statements (LOS) that advise candidates about the specific knowledge, skills, and abilities they should acquire from readings covering a topic area (LOS are provided in candidate study sessions and at the beginning of each reading); and
- The CFA Program curriculum, which contains the readings and end-of-reading questions, that candidates receive upon exam registration.

Therefore, the key to your success on the CFA examinations is studying and understanding the CBOK. The following sections provide background on the CBOK, the organization of the curriculum, and tips for developing an effective study program.

CURRICULUM DEVELOPMENT PROCESS

The CFA Program is grounded in the practice of the investment profession. Beginning with the Global Body of Investment Knowledge (GBIK), CFA Institute performs a continuous practice analysis with investment professionals around the world to determine the knowledge, skills, and abilities (competencies) that are relevant to the profession. Regional expert panels and targeted surveys are conducted annually to verify and reinforce the continuous feedback from the GBIK collaborative website. The practice analysis process ultimately defines the CBOK. The CBOK reflects the competencies that are generally accepted and applied by investment professionals. These competencies are used in practice in a generalist context and are expected to be demonstrated by a recently qualified CFA charterholder.

The Education Advisory Committee, consisting of practicing charterholders, in conjunction with CFA Institute staff, designs the CFA Program curriculum in order to deliver the CBOK to candidates. The examinations, also written by charterholders, are designed to allow you to demonstrate your mastery of the CBOK as set forth in the CFA Program curriculum. As you structure your personal study program, you should emphasize mastery of the CBOK and the practical application of that knowledge. For more information on the practice analysis, CBOK, and development of the CFA Program curriculum, please visit www.cfainstitute.org.

ORGANIZATION OF THE CURRICULUM

The Level II CFA Program curriculum is organized into 10 topic areas. Each topic area begins with a brief statement of the material and the depth of knowledge expected.

Each topic area is then divided into one or more study sessions. These study sessions—18 sessions in the Level II curriculum—should form the basic structure of your reading and preparation.

Each study session includes a statement of its structure and objective and is further divided into specific reading assignments. An outline illustrating the organization of these 18 study sessions can be found at the front of each volume of the curriculum.

The readings and end-of-reading questions are the basis for all examination questions and are selected or developed specifically to teach the knowledge, skills, and abilities reflected in the CBOK. These readings are drawn from content commissioned by CFA Institute, textbook chapters, professional journal articles, research analyst reports, and cases. All readings include problems and solutions to help you understand and master the topic areas.

Reading-specific Learning Outcome Statements (LOS) are listed at the beginning of each reading. These LOS indicate what you should be able to accomplish after studying the reading. The LOS, the reading, and the end-of-reading questions are dependent on each other, with the reading and questions providing context for understanding the scope of the LOS.

You should use the LOS to guide and focus your study because each examination question is based on the assigned readings and one or more LOS. The readings provide context for the LOS and enable you to apply a principle or concept in a variety of scenarios. The candidate is responsible for the entirety of the required material in a study session, which includes the assigned readings as well as the end-of-reading questions and problems.

We encourage you to review the information about the LOS on our website (www. cfainstitute.org/programs/cfaprogram/courseofstudy/Pages/study_sessions.aspx), including the descriptions of LOS "command words" (www.cfainstitute.org/programs/Documents/cfa_and_cipm_los_command_words.pdf).

FEATURES OF THE CURRICULUM

OPTIONAL
SEGMENT

Required vs. Optional Segments   You should read all of an assigned reading. In some cases, though, we have reprinted an entire chapter or article and marked certain parts of the reading as "optional." The CFA examination is based only on the required segments, and the optional segments are included only when it is determined that they might help you to better understand the required segments (by seeing the required material in its full context). When an optional segment begins, you will see an icon and a dashed vertical bar in the outside margin that will continue until the optional segment ends, accompanied by another icon. *Unless the material is specifically marked as optional, you should assume it is required.* You should rely on the required segments and the reading-specific LOS in preparing for the examination.

END OPTIONAL
SEGMENT

End-of-Reading Problems/Solutions *All problems in the readings as well as their solutions (which are provided directly following the problems) are part of the curriculum and are required material for the exam.* When appropriate, we have included problems within and after the readings to demonstrate practical application and reinforce your understanding of the concepts presented. The problems are designed to help you learn these concepts and may serve as a basis for exam questions. Many of these questions are adapted from past CFA examinations.

Glossary and Index For your convenience, we have printed a comprehensive glossary in each volume. Throughout the curriculum, a **bolded** word in a reading denotes a term defined in the glossary. The curriculum eBook is searchable, but we also publish an index that can be found on the CFA Institute website with the Level II study sessions.

Source Material The authorship, publisher, and copyright owners are given for each reading for your reference. We recommend that you use the CFA Institute curriculum rather than the original source materials because the curriculum may include only selected pages from outside readings, updated sections within the readings, and problems and solutions tailored to the CFA Program.

LOS Self-Check We have inserted checkboxes next to each LOS that you can use to track your progress in mastering the concepts in each reading.

DESIGNING YOUR PERSONAL STUDY PROGRAM

Create a Schedule An orderly, systematic approach to exam preparation is critical. You should dedicate a consistent block of time every week to reading and studying. Complete all reading assignments and the associated problems and solutions in each study session. Review the LOS both before and after you study each reading to ensure that you have mastered the applicable content and can demonstrate the knowledge, skill, or ability described by the LOS and the assigned reading. Use the LOS self-check to track your progress and highlight areas of weakness for later review.

As you prepare for your exam, we will e-mail you important exam updates, testing policies, and study tips. Be sure to read these carefully. Curriculum errata are periodically updated and posted on the study session page at www.cfainstitute.org. You can also sign up for an RSS feed to alert you to the latest errata update.

Successful candidates report an average of more than 300 hours preparing for each exam. Your preparation time will vary based on your prior education and experience. For each level of the curriculum, there are 18 study sessions. So, a good plan is to devote 15–20 hours per week for 18 weeks to studying the material. Use the final four to six weeks before the exam to review what you have learned and practice with topic and mock exams. This recommendation, however, may underestimate the hours needed for appropriate examination preparation depending on your individual circumstances, relevant experience, and academic background. You will undoubtedly adjust your study time to conform to your own strengths and weaknesses and to your educational and professional background.

You will probably spend more time on some study sessions than on others, but on average you should plan on devoting 15–20 hours per study session. You should allow ample time for both in-depth study of all topic areas and additional concentration on those topic areas for which you feel the least prepared.

An interactive study planner is available in the candidate resources area of our website to help you plan your study time. The interactive study planner recommends completion dates for each topic of the curriculum. Dates are determined based on study time available, exam topic weights, and curriculum weights. As you progress through the curriculum, the interactive study planner dynamically adjusts your study plan when you are running off schedule to help you stay on track for completion prior to the examination.

CFA Institute Topic Exams The CFA Institute topic exams are intended to assess your mastery of individual topic areas as you progress through your studies. After each test, you will receive immediate feedback noting the correct responses and indicating the relevant assigned reading so you can identify areas of weakness for further study. For more information on the topic tests, please visit www.cfainstitute.org.

CFA Institute Mock Exams The three-hour mock exams simulate the morning and afternoon sessions of the actual CFA examination, and are intended to be taken after you complete your study of the full curriculum so you can test your understanding of the curriculum and your readiness for the exam. You will receive feedback at the end of the mock exam, noting the correct responses and indicating the relevant assigned readings so you can assess areas of weakness for further study during your review period. We recommend that you take mock exams during the final stages of your preparation for the actual CFA examination. For more information on the mock examinations, please visit www.cfainstitute.org.

Preparatory Providers After you enroll in the CFA Program, you may receive numerous solicitations for preparatory courses and review materials. When considering a prep course, make sure the provider is in compliance with the CFA Institute Prep Provider Guidelines Program (www.cfainstitute.org/utility/examprep/Pages/index.aspx). Just remember, there are no shortcuts to success on the CFA examinations; reading and studying the CFA curriculum is the key to success on the examination. The CFA examinations reference only the CFA Institute assigned curriculum—no preparatory course or review course materials are consulted or referenced.

SUMMARY

Every question on the CFA examination is based on the content contained in the required readings and on one or more LOS. Frequently, an examination question is based on a specific example highlighted within a reading or on a specific end-of-reading question and/or problem and its solution. To make effective use of the CFA Program curriculum, please remember these key points:

1 All pages of the curriculum are required reading for the examination except for occasional sections marked as optional. You may read optional pages as background, but you will not be tested on them.

2 All questions, problems, and their solutions—found at the end of readings—are part of the curriculum and are required study material for the examination.

3 You should make appropriate use of the topic and mock examinations and other resources available at www.cfainstitute.org.

4 Use the interactive study planner to create a schedule and commit sufficient study time to cover the 18 study sessions, review the materials, and take topic and mock examinations.

5 Some of the concepts in the study sessions may be superseded by updated rulings and/or pronouncements issued after a reading was published. Candidates are expected to be familiar with the overall analytical framework contained in the assigned readings. Candidates are not responsible for changes that occur after the material was written.

FEEDBACK

At CFA Institute, we are committed to delivering a comprehensive and rigorous curriculum for the development of competent, ethically grounded investment professionals. We rely on candidate and member feedback as we work to incorporate content, design, and packaging improvements. You can be assured that we will continue to listen to your suggestions. Please send any comments or feedback to info@cfainstitute.org. Ongoing improvements in the curriculum will help you prepare for success on the upcoming examinations and for a lifetime of learning as a serious investment professional.

Financial Reporting and Analysis

STUDY SESSIONS

Study Session 5	Inventories and Long-lived Assets
Study Session 6	Intercorporate Investments, Post-Employment and Share-Based Compensation, and Multinational Operations
Study Session 7	Quality of Financial Reports and Financial Statement Analysis

TOPIC LEVEL LEARNING OUTCOME

The candidate should be able to analyze the effects of financial reporting choices on financial statements and ratios. The candidate also should be able to analyze and interpret financial statements and accompanying disclosures and to evaluate financial reporting quality.

FINANCIAL RATIO LIST

Candidates should be aware that certain ratios may be defined differently. Such differences are part of the nature of practical financial analysis. For examination purposes, when alternative ratio definitions exist and no specific definition is given in the question, candidates should use the definition provided in this list of ratios.

1   Current ratio = Current assets ÷ Current liabilities
2   Quick ratio = (Cash + Short-term marketable investments + Receivables) ÷ Current liabilities

Note: In 2009, the Financial Accounting Standards Board (FASB) released the FASB Accounting Standards Codification™. The Codification is the single source of authoritative nongovernmental US generally accepted accounting principles (US GAAP) effective for periods ending after 15 September 2009. The Codification supersedes all previous US GAAP standards. We have attempted to update the readings to reference or cross-reference the Codification as appropriate. Candidates are responsible for the content of international and US accounting standards, not the reference numbers.

3   Cash ratio = (Cash + Short-term marketable investments) ÷ Current liabilities

4   Defensive interval ratio = (Cash + Short-term marketable investments + Receivables) ÷ Daily cash expenditures

5   Receivables turnover ratio = Total revenue ÷ Average receivables

6   Days of sales outstanding (DSO) = Number of days in period ÷ Receivables turnover ratio

7   Inventory turnover ratio = Cost of goods sold ÷ Average inventory

8   Days of inventory on hand (DOH) = Number of days in period ÷ Inventory turnover ratio

9   Payables turnover ratio = Purchases ÷ Average trade payables

10 Number of days of payables = Number of days in period ÷ Payables turnover ratio

11 Cash conversion cycle (net operating cycle) = DOH + DSO − Number of days of payables

12 Working capital turnover ratio = Total revenue ÷ Average working capital

13 Fixed asset turnover ratio = Total revenue ÷ Average net fixed assets

14 Total asset turnover ratio = Total revenue ÷ Average total assets

15 Gross profit margin = Gross profit ÷ Total revenue

16 Operating profit margin = Operating profit ÷ Total revenue

17 Pretax margin = Earnings before tax but after interest ÷ Total revenue

18 Net profit margin = Net income ÷ Total revenue

19 Operating return on assets = Operating income ÷ Average total assets

20 Return on assets = Net income ÷ Average total assets

21 Return on equity = Net income ÷ Average shareholders' equity

22 Return on total capital = Earnings before interest and taxes ÷ (Interest bearing debt + Shareholders' equity)

23 Return on common equity = (Net income − Preferred dividends) ÷ Average common shareholders' equity

24 Tax burden = Net income ÷ Earnings before taxes

25 Interest burden = Earnings before taxes ÷ Earnings before interest and taxes

26 EBIT margin = Earnings before interest and taxes ÷ Total revenue

27 Financial leverage ratio (equity multiplier) = Average total assets ÷ Average shareholders' equity

28 Total debt = The total of interest-bearing short-term and long-term debt, excluding liabilities such as accrued expenses and accounts payable

29 Debt-to-assets ratio = Total debt ÷ Total assets

30 Debt-to-equity ratio = Total debt ÷ Total shareholders' equity

31 Debt-to-capital ratio = Total debt ÷ (Total debt + Total shareholders' equity)

32 Interest coverage ratio = Earnings before interest and taxes ÷ Interest payments

33 Fixed charge coverage ratio = (Earnings before interest and taxes + Lease payments) ÷ (Interest payments + Lease payments)

34 Dividend payout ratio = Common share dividends ÷ Net income attributable to common shares

35 Retention rate = (Net income attributable to common shares − Common share dividends) ÷ Net income attributable to common shares = 1 − Payout ratio

36 Sustainable growth rate = Retention rate × Return on equity

37 Earnings per share = (Net income − Preferred dividends) ÷ Weighted average number of ordinary shares outstanding

38 Book value per share = Common stockholders' equity ÷ Total number of common shares outstanding

39 Free cash flow to equity (FCFE) = Cash flow from operating activities − Investment in fixed capital + Net borrowing

40 Free cash flow to the firm (FCFF) = Cash flow from operating activities + Interest expense × (1 − Tax rate) − Investment in fixed capital *(Interest expense should be added back only if it was subtracted in determining cash flow from operating activities. This may not be the case for companies electing an alternative treatment under IFRS.)*

Financial Reporting and Analysis

Inventories and Long-lived Assets

The readings in this study session focus on the effects that different accounting methods can have on financial statements and ratios. Comparing the performance of companies is challenging due to the variety of allowable accounting choices. Analysts must identify and understand any accounting differences and make appropriate adjustments to reported financial statements to achieve comparability.

If inventory price levels change over time, the choice of inventory valuation method affects a company's financial statements and ratios. Analysts must know the effects of different inventory valuation methods and be able to compare financial statements prepared using the same or different methods.

Analysts also must understand how the following affect financial statements and ratios:

1 capitalizing versus expensing costs,

2 the choice of depreciation method,

3 asset impairment and revaluation,

4 leasing versus purchasing an asset, and

5 recording a lease as a finance lease versus an operating lease.

Note: New rulings and/or pronouncements issued after the publication of the readings in financial reporting and analysis may cause some of the information in these readings to become dated. Candidates are expected to be familiar with the overall analytical framework contained in the study session readings, as well as the implications of alternative accounting methods for financial analysis and valuation, as provided in the assigned readings. Candidates are not responsible for changes that occur after the material was written.

READING ASSIGNMENTS

Inventories: Implications for Financial Statements and Ratios

by Michael A. Broihahn, CPA, CIA, CFA

Michael A. Broihahn, CPA, CIA, CFA, is at Barry University (USA).

LEARNING OUTCOMES

Mastery	The candidate should be able to:
☐	**a.** calculate and explain how inflation and deflation of inventory costs affect the financial statements and ratios of companies that use different inventory valuation methods;
☐	**b.** explain LIFO reserve and LIFO liquidation and their effects on financial statements and ratios;
☐	**c.** convert a company's reported financial statements from LIFO to FIFO for purposes of comparison;
☐	**d.** describe the implications of valuing inventory at net realisable value for financial statements and ratios;
☐	**e.** analyze and compare the financial statements and ratios of companies, including those that use different inventory valuation methods;
☐	**f.** explain issues that analysts should consider when examining a company's inventory disclosures and other sources of information.

Note: New rulings and/or pronouncements issued after the publication of the readings in financial reporting and analysis may cause some of the information in these readings to become dated. Candidates are expected to be familiar with the overall analytical framework contained in the study session readings, as well as the implications of alternative accounting methods for financial analysis and valuation, as provided in the assigned readings. Candidates are not responsible for changes that occur after the material was written.

INTRODUCTION

Inventories and cost of sales (cost of goods sold) are significant items in the financial statements of many companies. Comparing the performance of these companies is challenging because of the allowable choices for valuing inventories: Differences in the choice of inventory valuation method can result in significantly different amounts being assigned to inventory and cost of sales. Financial statement analysis would be much easier if all companies used the same inventory valuation method or if inventory price levels remained constant over time. If there was no inflation or deflation with respect to inventory costs and thus unit costs were unchanged, the choice of inventory valuation method would be irrelevant. However, inventory price levels typically do change over time.

International Financial Reporting Standards (IFRS) permit the assignment of inventory costs (costs of goods available for sale) to inventories and cost of sales by three cost formulas: specific identification, first-in, first-out (FIFO), and weighted average cost.[1] US generally accepted accounting principles (US GAAP) allow the same three inventory valuation methods, referred to as cost flow assumptions in US GAAP, but also include a fourth method called last-in, first-out (LIFO).[2] The choice of inventory valuation method affects the allocation of the cost of goods available for sale to ending inventory and cost of sales.

To evaluate a company's performance over time and relative to industry peers, analysts must clearly understand the various inventory valuation methods that companies use and the related impact on financial statements and financial ratios. This reading is organised as follows: Section 2 explains the effects of changing price levels on the financial statements of companies that use different inventory valuation methods. Section 3 discusses the LIFO method, LIFO reserve, and the effects of LIFO liquidations, and demonstrates the adjustments required to compare a company that uses LIFO with one that uses FIFO. Section 4 discusses the financial statement effects of a change in inventory valuation method. Section 5 demonstrates the financial statement effects of a decline in inventory value. Section 6 discusses issues analysts should consider when evaluating companies that carry inventory. A summary and practice problems in the CFA Institute item set format complete the reading.

INVENTORY AND CHANGING PRICE LEVELS

Each of the allowable inventory valuation methods involves a different assumption about cost flows. The choice of cost formula (IFRS terminology) or cost flow assumption (US GAAP terminology) determines how the cost of goods available for sale during a period is allocated between inventory and cost of sales. Specific identification assumes that inventory items are not ordinarily interchangeable and that the cost flows match the actual physical flows of the inventory items. Cost of sales and inventory reflect the actual costs of the specific items sold and unsold (remaining in inventory).

First-in, first-out (FIFO) assumes that the inventory items purchased or manufactured first are sold first. The items remaining in inventory are assumed to be those most recently purchased or manufactured. In periods of rising inventory prices (inflation), the costs assigned to the units in ending inventory are higher than the costs assigned to the units sold. Conversely, in periods of declining inventory prices (deflation), the

---

1 International Accounting Standard (IAS) 2 [Inventories].
2 Financial Accounting Standards Board *Accounting Standards Codification* (FASB ASC) Topic 330 [Inventory].

costs assigned to the units in ending inventory using FIFO are lower than the costs assigned to the units sold. In periods of changing prices, ending inventory values determined using FIFO more closely reflect current costs than do the cost of sales.

Weighted average cost assumes that the inventory items sold and those remaining in inventory are the same average age and cost. In other words, a mixture of older and newer inventory items is assumed to be sold and remaining in inventory. Weighted average cost assigns the average cost of the goods available for sale (beginning inventory plus purchases, conversion, and other costs) during the accounting period to the units that are sold as well as to the units in ending inventory. Weighted average cost per unit is calculated as total cost of goods available for sale divided by total units available for sale.

Companies typically record changes to inventory using either a periodic inventory system or a perpetual inventory system. Under a **periodic inventory system**, inventory values and costs of sales are determined at the end of the accounting period. Under a **perpetual inventory system**, inventory values and cost of sales are continuously updated to reflect purchases and sales. Under either system, the allocation of goods available for sale to cost of sales and ending inventory is the same if the inventory valuation method used is either specific identification or FIFO. This is not generally true for the weighted average cost method. Under a periodic inventory system, the amount of cost of goods available for sale allocated to cost of sales and ending inventory may be quite different using the FIFO method compared to the weighted average cost method. Under a perpetual inventory system, inventory values and cost of sales are continuously updated to reflect purchases and sales. As a result, the amount of cost of goods available for sale allocated to cost of sales and ending inventory is similar under the FIFO and weighted average cost methods. Because of lack of disclosure and the dominance of perpetual inventory systems, analysts typically do not make adjustments when comparing a company using the weighted average cost method with a company using the FIFO method.

Last-in, first-out (LIFO), which is allowed under US GAAP but not allowed under IFRS, assumes that the inventory items purchased or manufactured most recently are sold first. The items remaining in inventory are assumed to be the oldest items purchased or manufactured. In periods of rising prices, the costs assigned to the units in ending inventory are lower than the costs assigned to the units sold. Similarly, in periods of declining prices, the costs assigned to the units in ending inventory are higher than the costs assigned to the units sold. In periods of changing prices and using LIFO, cost of sales more closely reflects current costs than do ending inventory values.

Using the LIFO method, the periodic and perpetual inventory systems will generally result in different allocations to cost of sales and ending inventory. Under either a perpetual or periodic inventory system, the use of the LIFO method will generally result in significantly different allocations to cost of sales and ending inventory compared to other inventory valuation methods. When inventory costs are increasing and inventory unit levels are stable or increasing, using the LIFO method will result in higher cost of sales and lower inventory carrying amounts than using the FIFO method. The higher cost of sales under LIFO will result in lower gross profit, operating income, income before taxes, and net income. Income tax expense will be lower under LIFO, causing the company's net operating cash flow to be higher. On the balance sheet, the lower inventory carrying amount will result in lower reported current assets, working capital, and total assets. Analysts must carefully assess the financial statement implications of the choice of inventory valuation method when comparing companies that use the LIFO method with companies that use the FIFO method.

The choice of inventory valuation method would be largely irrelevant if inventory unit costs remained relatively constant over time. The allocation of cost of goods available for sale to items sold and inventory items would be very similar regardless of the choice of inventory valuation method. However, inventory unit costs typically change over time and the choice of inventory valuation method does in fact result in potentially different allocations of cost of goods available for sale to inventory sold in the period and inventory on hand at the end of the period. The financial results of two essentially similar companies can look very different if the companies choose different inventory valuation methods. Cost of sales (cost of goods sold) on the income statement and inventory on the balance sheet will differ depending upon the inventory valuation method chosen.

An inventory valuation method that allocates more of the cost of goods available for sale to cost of sales and a corresponding lower amount to inventory will result in lower gross profit, net income, current assets, and total assets than an inventory method that allocates more of the cost of goods available for sale to inventory and a correspondingly lower amount to cost of sales. Therefore, the choice of inventory valuation method can have a direct impact on a company's financial statements and many of the financial ratios that are derived from them.

EXAMPLE 1

Impact of Inflation Using LIFO Compared to FIFO

Company L and Company F are identical in all respects except that Company L uses the LIFO method and Company F uses the FIFO method. Each company has been in business for five years and maintains a base inventory of 2,000 units each year. Each year, except the first year, the number of units purchased equaled the number of units sold. Over the five-year period, unit sales increased 10 percent each year and the unit purchase and selling prices increased at the beginning of each year to reflect inflation of 4 percent per year. In the first year, 20,000 units were sold at a price of $15.00 per unit and the unit purchase price was $8.00.

1   What was the end of year inventory, sales, cost of sales, and gross profit for each company for each of the five years?

2   Compare the inventory turnover ratios (based on ending inventory carrying amounts) and gross profit margins over the five-year period and between companies.

Solution to 1:

Company L using LIFO	Year 1	Year 2	Year 3	Year 4	Year 5
Ending inventory[a]	$16,000	$16,000	$16,000	$16,000	$16,000
Sales[b]	$300,000	$343,200	$392,621	$449,158	$513,837
Cost of sales[c]	160,000	183,040	209,398	239,551	274,046
Gross profit	$140,000	$160,160	$183,223	$209,607	$239,791

[a] Inventory is unchanged at $16,000 each year (2,000 units × $8). 2,000 of the units acquired in the first year are assumed to remain in inventory.

[b] Sales Year X = $(20,000 \times \$15)(1.10)^{X-1}(1.04)^{X-1}$. The quantity sold increases by 10 percent each year and the selling price increases by 4 percent each year.

[c] Cost of sales Year X = $(20{,}000 \times \$8)(1.10)^{X-1}(1.04)^{X-1}$. In Year 1, 20,000 units are sold with a cost of \$8. In subsequent years, the number of units purchased equals the number of units sold and the units sold are assumed to be those purchased in the year. The quantity purchased increases by 10 percent each year and the purchase price increases by 4 percent each year.

Note that if the company sold more units than it purchased in a year, inventory would decrease. This is referred to as LIFO liquidation. The cost of sales of the units sold in excess of those purchased would reflect the inventory carrying amount. In this example, each unit sold in excess of those purchased would have a cost of sales of \$8 and a higher gross profit.

Company F using FIFO	Year 1	Year 2	Year 3	Year 4	Year 5
Ending inventory[a]	\$16,000	\$16,640	\$17,306	\$17,998	\$18,718
Sales[b]	\$300,000	\$343,200	\$392,621	\$449,158	\$513,837
Cost of sales[c]	160,000	182,400	208,732	238,859	273,326
Gross profit	\$140,000	\$160,800	\$183,889	\$210,299	\$240,511

[a] Ending inventory Year X = 2,000 units × Cost in Year X = 2,000 units [$\$8 \times (1.04)^{X-1}$]. 2,000 units of the units acquired in Year X are assumed to remain in inventory.

[b] Sales Year X = $(20{,}000 \times \$15)(1.10)^{X-1}(1.04)^{X-1}$

[c] Cost of sales Year 1 = \$160,000 (= 20,000 units × \$8). There was no beginning inventory.

Cost of sales Year X (where X ≠ 1) = Beginning inventory plus purchases less ending inventory

= (Inventory at Year X−1) + $[(20{,}000 \times \$8)(1.10)^{X-1}(1.04)^{X-1}]$ − (Inventory at Year X)

= $2{,}000(\$8)(1.04)^{X-2}$ + $[(20{,}000 \times \$8)(1.10)^{X-1}(1.04)^{X-1}]$ − $[2{,}000 (\$8)(1.04)^{X-1}]$

For example, Cost of sales Year 2 = $2{,}000(\$8)$ + $[(20{,}000 \times \$8)(1.10)(1.04)]$ − $[2{,}000 (\$8)(1.04)]$ = \$16,000 + 183,040 − 16,640 = \$182,400

Solution to 2:

	Company L					Company F				
Year	1	2	3	4	5	1	2	3	4	5
Inventory turnover	10.0	11.4	13.1	15.0	17.1	10.0	11.0	12.1	13.3	14.6
Gross profit margin (%)	46.7	46.7	46.7	46.7	46.7	46.7	46.9	46.8	46.8	46.8

Inventory turnover ratio = Cost of sales ÷ Ending inventory. The inventory turnover ratio increased each year for both companies because the units sold increased, whereas the units in ending inventory remained unchanged. The increase in the inventory turnover ratio is higher for Company L because Company L's cost of sales is increasing for inflation, but the inventory carrying amount is unaffected by inflation. It might appear that a company using the LIFO method manages its inventory more effectively, but this is deceptive. Both companies have identical quantities and prices of purchases and sales and only differ in the inventory valuation method used.

Gross profit margin = Gross profit ÷ Sales. The gross profit margin is stable under LIFO because both sales and cost of sales increase at the same rate of inflation. The gross profit margin is slightly higher under the FIFO method after the first year because a proportion of the cost of sales reflects an older purchase price.

THE LIFO METHOD

In the United States, the LIFO method is widely used (approximately 36 percent of US companies use the LIFO method). The potential income tax savings are a benefit of using the LIFO method when inventory costs are increasing. The higher cash flows due to lower income taxes may make the company more valuable because the value of a company is based on the present value of its future cash flows. Under the "LIFO conformity rule," the US tax code requires that companies using the LIFO method for tax purposes must also use the LIFO method for financial reporting. Under the LIFO method, ending inventory is assumed to consist of those units that have been held the longest. This generally results in ending inventories with carrying amounts lower than current replacement costs because inventory costs typically increase over time. Cost of sales will more closely reflect current replacement costs.

If the purchase prices (purchase costs) or production costs of inventory are increasing, the income statement consequences of using the LIFO method compared to other methods will include higher cost of sales, and lower gross profit, operating profit, income tax expense, and net income. The balance sheet consequences include lower ending inventory, working capital, total assets, retained earnings, and shareholders' equity. The lower income tax paid will result in higher net cash flow from operating activities. Some of the financial ratio effects are a lower current ratio, higher debt-to-equity ratios, and lower profitability ratios.

If the purchase prices or production costs of inventory are decreasing, it is unlikely that a company will use the LIFO method for tax purposes (and therefore for financial reporting purposes due to the LIFO conformity rule) because this will result in lower cost of sales, and higher taxable income and income taxes. However, if the company had elected to use the LIFO method and cannot justify changing the inventory valuation method for tax and financial reporting purposes when inventory costs begin to decrease, the income statement, balance sheet, and ratio effects will be opposite to the effects during a period of increasing costs.

The US Securities Exchange Commission (SEC) has proposed the full adoption of IFRS by all US reporting companies beginning in 2014. An important consequence of this proposal would be the complete elimination of the LIFO inventory method for financial reporting and, due to the LIFO conformity rule, tax reporting by US companies. As a consequence of the restatement of financial statements to the FIFO or weighted average cost method, significant immediate income tax liabilities may arise in the year of transition from the LIFO method to either the FIFO or weighted average cost method.

3.1 LIFO Reserve

For companies using the LIFO method, US GAAP requires disclosure, in the notes to the financial statements or on the balance sheet, of the amount of the LIFO reserve. The **LIFO reserve** is the difference between the reported LIFO inventory carrying amount and the inventory amount that would have been reported if the FIFO method had been used (in other words, the FIFO inventory value less the LIFO inventory value). The disclosure provides the information that analysts need to adjust a company's cost of sales (cost of goods sold) and ending inventory balance based on the LIFO method, to the FIFO method.

To compare companies using LIFO with companies not using LIFO, inventory is adjusted by adding the disclosed LIFO reserve to the inventory balance that is reported on the balance sheet. The reported inventory balance, using LIFO, plus the LIFO reserve equals the inventory that would have been reported under FIFO. Cost of sales is adjusted by subtracting the increase in the LIFO reserve during the period from the cost of sales amount that is reported on the income statement. If the LIFO reserve has declined during the period,[3] the decrease in the reserve is added to the cost of sales amount that is reported on the income statement. The LIFO reserve disclosure can be used to adjust the financial statements of a US company using the LIFO method to make them comparable with a similar company using the FIFO method.

EXAMPLE 2

Inventory Conversion from LIFO to FIFO

Caterpillar Inc. (NYSE: CAT), based in Peoria, Illinois, USA, is the largest maker of construction and mining equipment, diesel and natural gas engines, and industrial gas turbines in the world. Excerpts from CAT's consolidated financial statements are shown in Exhibits 1 and 2; notes pertaining to CAT's inventories are presented in Exhibit 3. Assume tax rates of 20 percent for 2008 and 30 percent for earlier years. The assumed tax rates are based on the provision for taxes as a percentage of consolidated profits before taxes rather than the US corporate statutory tax rate of 35 percent.

1 What inventory values would CAT report for 2008, 2007, and 2006 if it had used the FIFO method instead of the LIFO method?

2 What amount would CAT's cost of goods sold for 2008 and 2007 be if it had used the FIFO method instead of the LIFO method?

3 What net income (profit) would CAT report for 2008 and 2007 if it had used the FIFO method instead of the LIFO method?

4 By what amount would CAT's 2008 and 2007 net cash flow from operating activities decline if CAT used the FIFO method instead of the LIFO method?

5 What is the cumulative amount of income tax savings that CAT has generated through 2008 by using the LIFO method instead of the FIFO method?

6 What amount would be added to CAT's retained earnings (profit employed in the business) at 31 December 2008 if CAT had used the FIFO method instead of the LIFO method?

---

3 This typically results from a reduction in inventory units and is referred to as LIFO liquidation. LIFO liquidation is discussed in Section 3.2.

7 What would be the change in Cat's cash balance if CAT had used the FIFO method instead of the LIFO method?

8 Calculate and compare the following for 2008 under the LIFO method and the FIFO method: inventory turnover ratio, days of inventory on hand, gross profit margin, net profit margin, return on assets, current ratio, and total liabilities-to-equity ratio.

Exhibit 1	Caterpillar Inc. Consolidated Results of Operation (US$ Millions)		
For the Years Ended 31 December	**2008**	**2007**	**2006**
Sales and revenues:			
Sales of Machinery and Engines	48,044	41,962	38,869
Revenue of Financial Products	3,280	2,996	2,648
Total sales and revenues	51,324	44,958	41,517
Operating costs:			
Cost of goods sold	38,415	32,626	29,549
⋮	⋮	⋮	⋮
Interest expense of Financial Products	1,153	1,132	1,023
⋮	⋮	⋮	⋮
Total operating costs	46,876	40,037	36,596
Operating profit	4,448	4,921	4,921
Interest expense excluding Financial Products	274	288	274
Other income (expense)	299	320	214
Consolidated profit before taxes	4,473	4,953	4,861
Provision for income taxes	953	1,485	1,405
Profit of consolidated companies	3,520	3,468	3,456
Equity in profit of unconsolidated affiliated companies	37	73	81
Profit	3,557	3,541	3,537

Exhibit 2	Caterpillar Inc. Consolidated Financial Position (US$ Millions)		
31 December	**2008**	**2007**	**2006**
Assets			
Current assets:			
Cash and short-term investments	2,736	1,122	530
⋮	⋮	⋮	⋮
Inventories	8,781	7,204	6,351
Total current assets	31,633	25,477	23,663
⋮			

Exhibit 2	(Continued)			

31 December	2008	2007	2006
Total assets	67,782	56,132	51,449
Liabilities			
Total current liabilities	26,069	22,245	19,822
⋮	⋮	⋮	⋮
Total liabilities	61,171	47,249	44,590
Redeemable noncontrolling interest (Note 25)[a]	524		
Stockholders' equity			
Common stock of $1.00 par value:			
Authorized shares: 900,000,000			
Issued shares (2008, 2007 and 2006—814,894,624) at paid-in amount	3,057	2,744	2,465
Treasury stock (2008—213,367,983 shares; 2007—190,908,490 shares and 2006—169,086,448 shares) at cost	(11,217)	(9,451)	(7,352)
Profit employed in the business	19,826	17,398	14,593
Accumulated other comprehensive income	(5,579)	(1,808)	(2,847)
Total stockholders' equity	6,087	8,883	6,859
Total liabilities and stockholders' equity	67,782	56,132	51,449

[a] US GAAP permitted the reporting of non-controlling interest as a liability or mezzanine account between liabilities and equity.

Exhibit 3	Caterpillar Inc. Selected Notes to Consolidated Financial Statements

Note 1. Operations and Summary of Significant Accounting Policies
D. Inventories

Inventories are stated at the lower of cost or market. Cost is principally determined using the last-in, first-out (LIFO) method. The value of inventories on the LIFO basis represented about 70% of total inventories at December 31, 2008 and about 75% of total inventories at December 31, 2007 and 2006.

If the FIFO (first-in, first-out) method had been in use, inventories would have been $3,183 million, $2,617 million and $2,403 million higher than reported at December 31, 2008, 2007 and 2006, respectively.

Note 9. Inventories

31 December (Millions of Dollars)	2008	2007	2006
Raw Materials	3,356	2,990	2,698
Work-in-process	1,107	863	591
Finished goods	4,022	3,066	2,785

(continued)

Exhibit 3   (Continued)

31 December (Millions of Dollars)	2008	2007	2006
Supplies	296	285	277
Total inventories	8,781	7,204	6,351

We had long-term material purchase obligations of approximately $363 million at December 31, 2008.

Solution to 1:

31 December (Millions of Dollars)	2008	2007	2006
Total inventories (LIFO method)	8,781	7,204	6,351
From Note 1. D (LIFO reserve)	3,183	2,617	2,403
Total inventories (FIFO method)	11,964	9,821	8,754

Solution to 2:

31 December (Millions of Dollars)	2008	2007
Cost of goods sold (LIFO method)	38,415	32,626
Less: Increase in LIFO reserve*	−566	−214
Cost of goods sold (FIFO method)	37,849	32,412

*From Note 1. D, the increase in LIFO reserve for 2008 is 566 (3,183 − 2,617) and for 2007 is 214 (2,617 − 2,403).

Solution to 3:

31 December (Millions of Dollars)	2008	2007
Net income (LIFO method)	3,557	3,541
Reduction in cost of goods sold (increase in operating profit)	566	214
Taxes on increased operating profit*	−113	−64
Net income (FIFO method)	4,010	3,691

*The taxes on the increased operating profit are assumed to be 113 (566 × 20%) for 2008 and 64 (214 × 30%) for 2007.

Solution to 4:

The effect on a company's net cash flow from operating activities is limited to the impact of the change on income taxes paid; changes in allocating inventory costs to ending inventory and cost of goods sold does not change any cash flows except income taxes. Consequently, the effect of using FIFO on CAT's net operating cash flow from operating activities would be a decline of $113 million in 2008 and a decline of $64 million in 2007. These are the approximate incremental increases in income taxes that CAT would have incurred if the FIFO method were used instead of the LIFO method (see solution to 3 above).

Solution to 5:

Assuming tax rates of 20 percent for 2008 and 30 percent for earlier years, the cumulative amount of income tax savings that CAT has generated by using the LIFO method instead of FIFO is approximately $898 million (566 × 20% + 2,617 × 30%). Note 1.D indicates a LIFO reserve of $2,617 million at the end of 2007 and an increase in the LIFO reserve of $566 million in 2008. Therefore, under the FIFO method, cumulative gross profits would have been $2,617 million higher as of the end of 2007 and an additional $566 million higher as of the end of 2008. The estimated tax savings would be higher (lower) if income tax rates were assumed to be higher (lower).

Solution to 6:

The amount that would be added to CAT's retained earnings is $2,285 million (3,183 − 898) or (566 × 80% + 2,617 × 70%). This represents the cumulative increase in operating profit due to the decrease in cost of goods sold (LIFO reserve of $3,183 million) less the assumed taxes on that profit ($898 million, see solution to 5 above).

Solution to 7:

Under the FIFO method, an additional $898 million is assumed to have been paid in taxes and cash would be reduced accordingly. If CAT switched to FIFO, it would have an additional tax liability of $898 million as a consequence of the restatement of financial statements to the FIFO method. This illustrates the significant immediate income tax liabilities that may arise in the year of transition from the LIFO method to the FIFO method.

Solution to 8:

CAT's ratios for 2008 under the LIFO and FIFO methods are as follows:

	LIFO	FIFO
Inventory turnover	4.81	3.47
Days of inventory on hand	76.1 days	105.5 days
Gross profit margin	20.04%	21.22%
Net profit margin	6.93%	7.81%
Return on assets	5.74%	6.26%
Current ratio	1.21	1.30
Total liabilities-to-equity ratio	10.05	7.31

Inventory turnover ratio = cost of goods sold ÷ Average inventory

LIFO = 4.81 = 38,415 ÷ [(8,781 + 7,204) ÷ 2]

FIFO = 3.47 = 37,849 ÷ [(11,964 + 9,821) ÷ 2]

The ratio is higher under LIFO because, given rising inventory costs, cost of goods sold will be higher and inventory carrying amounts will be lower under LIFO. If an analyst made no adjustment for the difference in inventory methods, it might appear that a company using the LIFO method manages its inventory more effectively.

Days of inventory on hand = Number of days in period ÷ Inventory turnover ratio

LIFO = 76.1 days = (366 days* ÷ 4.81)

FIFO = 105.5 days = (366 days ÷ 3.47)

*2008 was a leap year.

Without adjustment, a company using the LIFO method might appear to manage its inventory more effectively. This is primarily the result of the lower inventory carrying amounts under LIFO.

Gross profit margin = Gross profit ÷ Total revenue

LIFO = 20.04 percent = [(48,044 − 38,415) ÷ 48,044]

FIFO = 21.22 percent = [(48,044 − 37,849) ÷ 48,044]

Revenue of financial products is excluded from the calculation of gross profit. Gross profit is sales of machinery and engines less cost of goods sold. The gross profit margin is lower under LIFO because the cost of goods sold is higher given rising inventory costs.

Net profit margin = Net income ÷ Total revenue

LIFO = 6.93 percent = (3,557 ÷ 51,324)

FIFO = 7.81 percent = (4,010 ÷ 51,324)

The net profit margin is lower under LIFO because the cost of goods sold is higher. The absolute percentage difference is less than that of the gross profit margin because of income taxes on the increased income reported under FIFO and because net income is divided by total revenue including sales of machinery and engines and revenue of financial products. The company appears to be less profitable under LIFO.

Return on assets = Net income ÷ Average total assets

LIFO = 5.74 percent = 3,557 ÷ [(67,782 + 56,132) ÷ 2]

FIFO = 6.26 percent = 4,010 ÷ [(67,782 + 3,183 − 898) + (56,132 + 2,617 − 785) ÷ 2]

The total assets under FIFO are the LIFO total assets increased by the LIFO reserve and decreased by the cash paid for the additional income taxes. The return on assets is lower under LIFO because the lower net income due to the higher cost of goods sold has a greater impact on the ratio than the lower total assets, which are the result of lower inventory carrying amounts. The company appears to be less profitable under LIFO.

Current ratio = Current assets ÷ Current liabilities

LIFO = 1.21 = (31,633 ÷ 26,069)

FIFO = 1.30 = [(31,633 + 3,183 − 898) ÷ 26,069]

The current ratio is lower under LIFO primarily because of lower inventory carrying amount. The company appears to be less liquid under LIFO.

Total liabilities-to-equity ratio = Total liabilities ÷ Total shareholder's equity

LIFO = 10.05 = (61,171 ÷ 6,087)

FIFO = 7.31 = [61,171 ÷ (6,087 + 2,285)]

The ratio is higher under LIFO because the addition to retained earnings under FIFO reduces the ratio. The company appears to be more highly leveraged under LIFO.

In summary, the company appears to be less profitable, less liquid, and more highly leveraged under LIFO. Yet, because a company's value is based on the present value of future cash flows, LIFO will increase the company's value because the cash flows are higher in earlier years due to lower taxes. LIFO is primarily used for the tax benefits it provides.

3.2 LIFO Liquidations

In periods of rising inventory unit costs, the carrying amount of inventory under FIFO will always exceed the carrying amount of inventory under LIFO. The LIFO reserve may increase over time as the result of the increasing difference between the older costs used to value inventory under LIFO and the more recent costs used to value inventory under FIFO. Also, when the number of inventory units manufactured or purchased exceeds the number of units sold, the LIFO reserve may increase as the result of the addition of new LIFO layers (the quantity of inventory units is increasing and each increase in quantity creates a new LIFO layer).

When the number of units sold exceeds the number of units purchased or manufactured, the number of units in ending inventory is lower than the number of units in beginning inventory and a company using LIFO will experience a LIFO liquidation (some of the older units held in inventory are assumed to have been sold). If inventory unit costs have been rising from period to period and LIFO liquidation occurs, this will produce an inventory-related increase in gross profits. The increase in gross profits occurs because of the lower inventory carrying amounts of the liquidated units. The lower inventory carrying amounts are used for cost of sales and the sales are at the current prices. The gross profit on these units is higher than the gross profit that would be recognised using more current costs. These inventory profits caused by a LIFO liquidation, however, are one-time events and are not sustainable.

LIFO liquidations can occur for a variety of reasons. The reduction in inventory levels may be outside of management's control; for example, labour strikes at a supplier may force a company to reduce inventory levels to meet customer demands. In periods of economic recession or when customer demand is declining, a company may choose to reduce existing inventory levels rather than invest in new inventory. Analysts should be aware that management can potentially manipulate and inflate their company's reported gross profits and net income at critical times by intentionally reducing inventory quantities and liquidating older layers of LIFO inventory (selling some units of beginning inventory). During economic downturns, LIFO liquidation may result in higher gross profit than would otherwise be realised. If LIFO layers of inventory are temporarily depleted and not replaced by fiscal year-end, LIFO liquidation will occur resulting in unsustainable higher gross profits. Therefore, it is imperative to review the LIFO reserve footnote disclosures to determine if LIFO liquidation has occurred. A decline in the LIFO reserve from the prior period may be indicative of LIFO liquidation.

EXAMPLE 3

LIFO Liquidation: Financial Statement Impact and Disclosure

The following excerpts are from the 2007 10-K of Sturm Ruger & Co., Inc. (NYSE:RGR):

> Item 7 — Management's Discussion and Analysis of Financial Condition and Results of Operations

Reduction in inventory generated positive cash flow for the Company, partially offset by the tax impact of the consequent LIFO liquidation, which generated negative cash flow as it created taxable income, resulting in higher tax payments.

Balance Sheets
(In thousands, except per share data)

December 31	2007	2006
Assets		
Current Assets		
⋮	⋮	⋮
Gross inventories:	64,330	87,477
Less LIFO reserve	(46,890)	(57,555)
Less excess and obsolescence reserve	(4,143)	(5,516)
Net inventories	13,297	24,406
⋮	⋮	⋮
Total Current Assets	73,512	81,785
⋮	⋮	⋮
Total Assets	$101,882	$117,066

Statements of Income
(In thousands, except per share data)

Year ended December 31	2007	2006
⋮	⋮	⋮
Total net sales	156,485	167,620
Cost of products sold	117,186	139,610
Gross profit	39,299	28,010
Expenses:		
⋮	⋮	⋮
Total expenses	30,184	27,088
Operating income	9,115	922
⋮	⋮	⋮
Total other income, net	7,544	921
Income before income taxes	16,659	1,843
Income taxes	6,330	739
Net income	$ 10,329	$ 1,104
Basic and Diluted Earnings Per Share	$ 0.46	$ 0.04
Cash Dividends Per Share	$ 0.00	$ 0.00

Notes to Financial Statements
1. Significant Accounting Policies
⋮
Inventories

Inventories are stated at the lower of cost, principally determined by the last-in, first-out (LIFO) method, or market. If inventories had been valued using the first-in, first-out method, inventory values would have been higher by approximately $46.9 million and $57.6 million at December 31, 2007 and

2006, respectively. During 2007 and 2006, inventory quantities were reduced. This reduction resulted in a liquidation of LIFO inventory quantities carried at lower costs prevailing in prior years as compared with the current cost of purchases, the effect of which decreased costs of products sold by approximately $12.1 million and $7.1 million in 2007 and 2006, respectively. There was no LIFO liquidation in 2005.

1 What is the decrease in the LIFO reserve on the balance sheet? How much less was cost of products sold in 2007, due to LIFO liquidation, according to the note disclosure?

2 How did the decreased cost of products sold compare to operating income in 2007?

3 How did the LIFO liquidation affect cash flows?

Solution to 1:

The LIFO reserve decreased by $10,665 thousand (57,555 − 46,890) in 2007. The LIFO liquidation decreased costs of products sold by approximately $12.1 million in 2007. The decrease in the LIFO reserve is indicative of a LIFO liquidation but is not sufficient to determine the exact amount of the LIFO liquidation.

Solution to 2:

The decreased cost of products sold of approximately $12.1 million exceeds the operating income of approximately $9 million.

Solution to 3:

The LIFO liquidation (reduction in inventory) generated positive cash flow. The positive cash flow effect of the LIFO liquidation was reduced by its tax impact. The LIFO liquidation resulted in higher taxable income and higher tax payments.

EXAMPLE 4

LIFO Liquidation Illustration

Reliable Fans, Inc. (RF), a hypothetical company, sells high-quality fans and has been in business since 2006. Exhibit 4 provides relevant data and financial statement information about RF's inventory purchases and sales of fan inventory for the years 2006 through 2009. RF uses the LIFO method and a periodic inventory system. What amount of RF's 2009 gross profit is due to LIFO liquidation?

Exhibit 4	RF Financial Statement Information under LIFO			
	2006	**2007**	**2008**	**2009**
Fans units purchased	12,000	12,000	12,000	12,000
Purchase cost per fan	$100	$105	$110	$115
Fans units sold	10,000	12,000	12,000	13,000
Sales price per fan	$200	$205	$210	$215
LIFO Method				
Beginning inventory	$0	$200,000	$200,000	$200,000
Purchases	1,200,000	1,260,000	1,320,000	1,380,000

(continued)

Exhibit 4   (Continued)

	2006	2007	2008	2009
Goods available for sale	1,200,000	1,460,000	1,520,000	1,580,000
Ending inventory*	(200,000)	(200,000)	(200,000)	(100,000)
Cost of goods sold	$1,000,000	$1,260,000	$1,320,000	$1,480,000
Income Statement				
Sales	$2,000,000	$2,460,000	$2,520,000	$2,795,000
Cost of goods sold	1,000,000	1,260,000	1,320,000	1,480,000
Gross profit	$1,000,000	$1,200,000	$1,200,000	$1,315,000
Balance Sheet				
Inventory	$200,000	$200,000	$200,000	$100,000

*Ending inventory 2006, 2007, and 2008 = (2,000 × $100).
 Ending inventory 2009 = (1,000 × $100).

Solution:

RF's reported gross profit for 2009 is $1,315,000. RF's 2009 gross profit due to LIFO liquidation is $15,000. If RF had purchased 13,000 fans in 2009 rather than 12,000 fans, the cost of goods sold under the LIFO method would have been $1,495,000 (13,000 fans sold at $115.00 purchase cost per fan), and the reported gross profit would have been $1,300,000 ($2,795,000 less $1,495,000). The gross profit due to LIFO liquidation is $15,000 ($1,315,000 reported gross profit less the $1,300,000 gross profit that would have been reported without the LIFO liquidation). The gross profit due to LIFO liquidation may also be determined by multiplying the number of units liquidated times the difference between the replacement cost of the units liquidated and their historical purchase cost. For RF, 1,000 units times $15 ($115 replacement cost per fan less the $100 historical cost per fan) equals the $15,000 gross profit due to LIFO liquidation.

4   INVENTORY METHOD CHANGES

Companies on rare occasion change inventory valuation methods. Under IFRS, a change in method is acceptable only if the change "results in the financial statements providing reliable and more relevant information about the effects of transactions, other events, or conditions on the business entity's financial position, financial performance, or cash flows."[4] If the change is justifiable, then it is applied retrospectively.

This means that the change is applied to comparative information for prior periods as far back as is practicable. The cumulative amount of the adjustments relating to periods prior to those presented in the current financial statements is made to the opening balance of each affected component of equity (i.e., retained earnings or comprehensive income) of the earliest period presented. For example, if a company changes its inventory method in 2009 and it presents three years of comparative financial statements (2007, 2008, and 2009) in its annual report, it would retrospectively

---

4 IAS 8 [Accounting Policies, Changes in Accounting Estimates and Errors].

reflect this change as far back as possible. The change would be reflected in the three years of financial statements presented; the financial statements for 2007 and 2008 would be restated as if the new method had been used in these periods, and the cumulative effect of the change on periods prior to 2007 would be reflected in the 2007 opening balance of each affected component of equity. An exemption to the restatement applies when it is impracticable to determine either the period-specific effects or the cumulative effect of the change.

Under US GAAP, the conditions to make a change in accounting policy and the accounting for a change in inventory policy are similar to IFRS.[5] US GAAP, however, requires companies to thoroughly explain why the newly adopted inventory accounting method is superior and preferable to the old method. If a company decides to change from LIFO to another inventory method, US GAAP requires a retrospective restatement as described above. However, if a company decides to change to the LIFO method, it must do so on a prospective basis and retrospective adjustments are not made to the financial statements. The carrying amount of inventory under the old method becomes the initial LIFO layer in the year of LIFO adoption.

Analysts should carefully evaluate changes in inventory valuation methods. Although the stated reason for the inventory change may be to better match inventory costs with sales revenue (or some other plausible business explanation), the real underlying (and unstated) purpose may be to reduce income tax expense (if changing to LIFO from FIFO or average cost), or to increase reported profits (if changing from LIFO to FIFO or average cost). As always, the choice of inventory valuation method can have a significant impact on financial statements and the financial ratios that are derived from them. As a consequence, analysts must carefully consider the impact of the change in inventory valuation methods and the differences in inventory valuation methods when comparing a company's performance with that of its industry or its competitors.

INVENTORY ADJUSTMENTS

Significant financial risk can result from the holding of inventory. The cost of inventory may not be recoverable due to spoilage, obsolescence, or declines in selling prices. IFRS state that inventories shall be measured (and carried on the balance sheet) at the lower of cost and net realisable value.[6] **Net realisable value** is the estimated selling price in the ordinary course of business less the estimated costs necessary to make the sale and estimated costs to get the inventory in condition for sale. The assessment of net realisable value is typically done item by item or by groups of similar or related items. In the event that the value of inventory declines below the carrying amount on the balance sheet, the inventory carrying amount must be written down to its net realisable value[7] and the loss (reduction in value) recognised as an expense on the income statement. This expense may be included as part of cost of sales or reported separately.

---

5 FASB ASC Topic 250 [Accounting Changes and Error Corrections].
6 IAS 2 paragraphs 28–33 [Inventories–Net realisable value].
7 Frequently, rather than writing inventory down directly, an inventory valuation allowance account is used. The allowance account is netted with the inventory accounts to arrive at the carrying amount that appears on the balance sheet.

In each subsequent period, a new assessment of net realisable value is made. Reversal (limited to the amount of the original write-down) is required for a subsequent increase in value of inventory previously written down. The reversal of any write-down of inventories is recognised as a reduction in cost of sales (reduction in the amount of inventories recognised as an expense).

US GAAP specify the lower of cost or market to value inventories.[8] This is broadly consistent with IFRS with one major difference: US GAAP prohibit the reversal of write-downs. Market is defined as current replacement cost subject to upper and lower limits. Market cannot exceed net realisable value (selling price less reasonably estimated costs of completion and disposal). The lower limit of market is net realisable value less a normal profit margin. Any write-down reduces the value of the inventory, and the loss in value (expense) is generally reflected in the income statement in cost of goods sold.

An inventory write-down reduces both profit and the carrying amount of inventory on the balance sheet and thus has a negative effect on profitability, liquidity, and solvency ratios. However, activity ratios (for example, inventory turnover and total asset turnover) will be positively affected by a write-down because the asset base (denominator) is reduced. The negative impact on some key ratios, due to the decrease in profit, may result in the reluctance by some companies to record inventory write-downs unless there is strong evidence that the decline in the value of inventory is permanent. This is especially true under US GAAP where reversal of a write-down is prohibited.

Analysts should consider the possibility of an inventory write-down because the impact on a company's financial ratios may be substantial. The potential for inventory write-downs can be high for companies in industries where technological obsolescence of inventories is a significant risk. Analysts should carefully evaluate prospective inventory impairments (as well as other potential asset impairments) and their potential effects on the financial ratios when debt covenants include financial ratio requirements. The breaching of debt covenants can have a significant impact on a company.

Companies that use specific identification, weighted average cost, or FIFO methods are more likely to incur inventory write-downs than companies that use the LIFO method. Under the LIFO method, the *oldest* costs are reflected in the inventory carrying amount on the balance sheet. Given increasing inventory costs, the inventory carrying amounts under the LIFO method are already conservatively presented at the oldest and lowest costs. Thus, it is far less likely that inventory write-downs will occur under LIFO—and if a write-down does occur, it is likely to be of a lesser magnitude.

EXAMPLE 5

Effect of Inventory Write-downs on Financial Ratios

The Volvo Group (OMX Nordic Exchange: VOLV B), based in Göteborg, Sweden, is a leading supplier of commercial transport products such as construction equipment, trucks, busses, and drive systems for marine and industrial applications as well as aircraft engine components.[9] Excerpts from Volvo's consolidated financial statements are shown in Exhibits 5 and 6. Notes pertaining to Volvo's inventories are presented in Exhibit 7.

1   What inventory values would Volvo have reported for 2008, 2007, and 2006 if it had no allowance for inventory obsolescence?

---

8 FASB ASC Section 330-10-35 [Inventory–Overall–Subsequent Measurement].
9 As of this writing, the Volvo line of automobiles is not under the control and management of the Volvo Group.

2 Assuming that any changes to the allowance for inventory obsolescence are reflected in the cost of sales, what amount would Volvo's cost of sales be for 2008 and 2007 if it had not recorded inventory write-downs in 2008 and 2007?

3 What amount would Volvo's profit (net income) be for 2008 and 2007 if it had not recorded inventory write-downs in 2008 and 2007? Assume tax rates of 28.5 percent for 2008 and 30 percent for 2007.

4 What would Volvo's 2008 profit (net income) have been if it had reversed all past inventory write-downs in 2008? This question is independent of 1, 2, and 3. Assume a tax rate of 28.5 percent for 2008.

5 Compare the following for 2008 based on the numbers as reported and those assuming no allowance for inventory obsolescence as in questions 1, 2, and 3: inventory turnover ratio, days of inventory on hand, gross profit margin, and net profit margin.

6 CAT (Example 2) has no disclosures indicative of either inventory write-downs or a cumulative allowance for inventory obsolescence in its 2008 financial statements. Provide a conceptual explanation as to why Volvo incurred inventory write-downs for 2008 but CAT did not.

Exhibit 5	Volvo Group Consolidated Income Statements (Swedish Krona in Millions, except per Share Data)		
For the years ended 31 December	**2008**	**2007**	**2006**
Net sales	303,667	285,405	258,835
Cost of sales	(237,578)	(219,600)	(199,054)
Gross income	66,089	65,805	59,781
	⋮	⋮	⋮
Operating income	15,851	22,231	20,399
Interest income and similar credits	1,171	952	666
Income expenses and similar charges	(1,935)	(1,122)	(585)
Other financial income and expenses	(1,077)	(504)	(181)
Income after financial items	14,010	21,557	20,299
Income taxes	(3,994)	(6,529)	(3,981)
Income for the period	10,016	15,028	16,318
Attributable to:			
Equity holders of the parent company	9,942	14,932	16,268
Minority interests	74	96	50
Profit	10,016	15,028	16,318

Exhibit 6	Volvo Group Consolidated Balance Sheets (Swedish Krona in Millions)		
31 December	**2008**	**2007**	**2006**
Assets			
Total non-current assets	196,381	162,487	124,039

(continued)

Exhibit 6   (Continued)

31 December	2008	2007	2006
Current assets:			
Inventories	55,045	43,645	34,211
⋮	⋮	⋮	⋮
Cash and cash equivalents	17,712	14,544	10,757
Total current assets	176,038	159,160	134,388
Total assets	372,419	321,647	258,427
Shareholders' equity and liabilities			
Shareholders' equity:			
Share capital	2,554	2,554	2,554
Reserves	5,078	2,146	1,664
Retained earnings	66,436	62,570	66,418
Income for the period	9,942	14,932	16,268
Equity attributable to equity holders of the parent company	84,010	82,202	86,904
Minority interests	630	579	284
Total shareholders' equity	84,640	82,781	87,188
Total non-current provisions	29,031	26,202	19,864
Total non-current liabilities	92,608	71,729	45,457
Total current provisions	11,750	10,656	9,799
Total current liabilities	154,390	130,279	96,119
Total shareholders' equity and liabilities	372,419	321,647	258,427

Exhibit 7   Volvo Group Selected Notes to Consolidated Financial Statements

Note 1. Accounting Principles
Inventories

Inventories are reported at the lower of cost, in accordance with the first-in, first-out method (FIFO), or net realisable value. The acquisition value is based on the standard cost method, including costs for all direct manufacturing expenses and the apportionable share of the capacity and other related manufacturing costs. The standard costs are tested regularly and adjustments are made based on current conditions. Costs for research and development, selling, administration and financial expenses are not included. Net realisable value is calculated as the selling price less costs attributable to the sale.

Note 2. Key Sources of estimation uncertainty
Inventory obsolescence

Inventories are reported at the lower of cost, in accordance with the first-in, first-out method (FIFO), or net realisable value. The estimated net realisable value includes management consideration of out-dated articles, over-stocking, physical damages, inventory-lead-time, handling

Exhibit 7   (Continued)

and other selling costs. If the estimated net realisable value is lower than cost, a valuation allowance is established for inventory obsolescence. The total inventory value, net of inventory obsolescence allowance, is per 31 December 2008, SEK (in millions) 55,045.

Note 18. Inventories

31 December (Millions of Krona)	2008	2007	2006
Finished products	39,137	28,077	20,396
Production materials, etc.	15,908	15,568	13,815
Total	**55,045**	**43,645**	**34,211**

Increase (decrease) in allowance for inventory obsolescence

31 December (Millions of Krona)	2008	2007	2006
Balance sheet, 31 December, preceding year	2,837	2,015	2,401
Increase in allowance for inventory obsolescence charged to income	1,229	757	186
Scrapping	(325)	(239)	(169)
Translation differences	305	2	(130)
Reclassifications, etc	(524)	302	(273)
Balance sheet, 31 December	3,522	2,837	2,015

Solution to 1:

31 December (Swedish Krona in Millions)	2008	2007	2006
Total inventories, net	55,045	43,645	34,211
From Note 18. (Allowance for obsolescence)	3,522	2,837	2,015
Total inventories (without allowance)	58,567	46,482	36,226

Solution to 2:

31 December (Swedish Krona in Millions)	2008	2007
Cost of sales	237,578	219,600
Less: Increase in allowance for obsolescence*	−685	−822
Cost of sales (without allowance)	236,893	218,778

*From Note 18, the increase in allowance for obsolescence for 2008 is 685 (3,522 − 2,837) and for 2007 is 822 (2,837 − 2,015).

Solution to 3:

31 December (Swedish Krona in Millions)	2008	2007
Profit (Net income)	10,016	15,028
Reduction in cost of sales (increase in operating profit)	685	822
Taxes on increased operating profit*	−195	−247
Profit (without allowance)	10,506	15,603

*Taxes on the increased operating profit are assumed to be 195 (685 × 28.5%) for 2008 and 247 (822 × 30%) for 2007.

Solution to 4:

31 December (Swedish Krona in Millions)	2008
Profit (Net income)	10,016
Reduction in cost of sales (increase in operating profit)	3,522
Taxes on increased operating profit*	−1,004
Profit (after recovery of previous write-downs)	12,534

*Taxes on the increased operating profit are assumed to be 1,004 (3,522 × 28.5%) for 2008.

Solution to 5:

The Volvo Group's financial ratios for 2008 with the allowance for inventory obsolescence and without the allowance for inventory obsolescence are as follows:

	With Allowance (As Reported)	Without Allowance (Adjusted)
Inventory turnover ratio	4.81	4.51
Days of inventory on hand	76.1	81.2
Gross profit margin	21.76%	21.99%
Net profit margin	3.30%	3.46%

Inventory turnover ratio = Cost of sales ÷ Average inventory

With allowance (as reported) = 4.81 = 237,578 ÷ [(55,045 + 43,645) ÷ 2]

Without allowance (adjusted) = 4.51 = 236,893 ÷ [(58,567 + 46,482) ÷ 2]

Inventory turnover is higher based on the numbers as reported because cost of sales will be higher (assuming inventory write-downs are reported as part of cost of sales) and inventory carrying amounts will be lower with an allowance for inventory obsolescence. The company appears to manage its inventory more efficiently when it has inventory write-downs.

Days of inventory on hand = Number of days in period ÷ Inventory turnover ratio

With allowance (as reported) = 76.1 days = (366 days* ÷ 4.81)

Without allowance (adjusted) = 81.2 days = (366 days ÷ 4.51)

*2008 was a leap year.

Days of inventory on hand are lower based on the numbers as reported because the inventory turnover is higher. A company with inventory write-downs might appear to manage its inventory more effectively. This is primarily the result of the lower inventory carrying amounts.

Gross profit margin = Gross income ÷ Net sales

With allowance (as reported) = 21.76 percent = [66,089 ÷ 303,667]

Without allowance (adjusted) = 21.99 percent = [(66,089 + 685) ÷ 303,667]

The gross profit margin is lower with inventory write-downs because the cost of sales is higher. This assumes that inventory write-downs are reported as part of cost of sales.

Net profit margin = Profit ÷ Net sales

With allowance (as reported) = 3.30 percent = (10,016 ÷ 303,667)

Without allowance (adjusted) = 3.46 percent = (10,506 ÷ 303,667)

The net profit margin is lower with inventory write-downs because the cost of sales is higher (assuming the inventory write-downs are reported as part of cost of sales). The absolute percentage difference is less than that of the gross profit margin because of income taxes on the increased income without write-downs.

The profitability ratios (gross profit margin and net profit margin) for Volvo Group would have been slightly better (higher) for 2008 if the company had not recorded inventory write-downs. The activity ratio (inventory turnover ratio) would appear less attractive without the write-downs. The inventory turnover ratio is slightly better (higher) with inventory write-downs because inventory write-downs increase cost of sales (numerator) and decrease the average inventory (denominator), making inventory management appear more efficient with write-downs.

Solution to 6:

CAT uses the LIFO method whereas Volvo uses the FIFO method. Given increasing inventory costs, companies that use the FIFO inventory method are far more likely to incur inventory write-downs than those companies that use the LIFO method. This is because under the LIFO method, the inventory carrying amounts reflect the *oldest* costs and therefore the *lowest* costs given increasing inventory costs. Because inventory carrying amounts under the LIFO method are already conservatively presented, it is less likely that inventory write-downs will occur.

IAS 2 [Inventories] does not apply to the inventories of producers of agricultural and forest products and minerals and mineral products, nor to commodity broker–traders. These inventories may be measured at net realisable value (fair value less costs to sell and complete) according to well-established industry practices. If an active market exists for these products, the quoted market price in that market is the appropriate basis for determining the fair value of that asset. If an active market does not exist, a company may use market determined prices or values (such as the most recent market transaction price) when available for determining fair value. Changes in the value of inventory (increase or decrease) are recognised in profit or loss in the period of the change. US GAAP is similar to IFRS in its treatment of inventories of agricultural and forest products and mineral ores. Mark-to-market inventory accounting is allowed for bullion.

6   FINANCIAL STATEMENT ANALYSIS ISSUES

IFRS and US GAAP require companies to disclose, either on the balance sheet or in the notes to the financial statements, the carrying amounts of inventories in classifications suitable to the company. For manufacturing companies, these classifications might include production supplies, raw materials, work in progress, and finished goods. For a retailer, these classifications might include significant categories of merchandise or the grouping of inventories with similar attributes. These disclosures may provide signals about a company's future sales and profits.

For example, a significant increase (attributable to increases in unit volume rather than increases in unit cost) in raw materials and/or work-in-progress inventories may signal that the company expects an increase in demand for its products. This suggests an anticipated increase in sales and profit. However, a substantial increase in finished goods inventories while raw materials and work-in-progress inventories are declining may signal a decrease in demand for the company's products and hence lower future sales and profit. This may also signal a potential future write-down of finished goods inventory. Irrespective of the signal, an analyst should thoroughly investigate the underlying reasons for any significant changes in a company's raw materials, work-in-progress, and finished goods inventories.

Analysts also should compare the growth rate of a company's sales to the growth rate of its finished goods inventories, because this could also provide a signal about future sales and profits. For example, if the growth of inventories is greater than the growth of sales, this could indicate a decline in demand and a decrease in future earnings. The company may have to lower (mark down) the selling price of its products to reduce its inventory balances, or it may have to write down the value of its inventory because of obsolescence, both of which would negatively affect profits. Besides the potential for mark-downs or write-downs, having too much inventory on hand or the wrong type of inventory can have a negative financial effect on a company because it increases inventory-related expenses such as insurance, storage costs, and taxes. In addition, it means that the company has less cash and working capital available to use for other purposes.

Inventory write-downs may have a substantial impact on a company's activity, profitability, liquidity, and solvency ratios. It is critical for the analyst to be aware of industry trends toward product obsolescence and to analyze the financial ratios for their sensitivity to potential inventory impairment. Companies can minimise the impact of inventory write-downs by better matching their inventory composition and growth with prospective customer demand. To obtain additional information about a company's inventory and its future sales, a variety of sources of information are available. Analysts should consider the Management Discussion and Analysis (MD&A) or similar sections of the company's financial reports, industry-related news and publications, and industry economic data.

When conducting comparisons, differences in the choice of inventory valuation method can significantly affect the comparability of financial ratios between companies. A restatement from the LIFO method to the FIFO method is critical to make a valid comparison with companies using a method other than the LIFO method such as those companies reporting under IFRS.

EXAMPLE 6

Comparative Illustration

1   Using CAT's LIFO numbers as reported and FIFO adjusted numbers (Example 2) and Volvo's numbers as reported (Example 5), compare the following for 2008: inventory turnover ratio, days of inventory on hand, gross profit margin, net profit margin, return on assets, current ratio, total liabilities-to-equity ratio, and return on equity. For the current ratio, include current provisions as part of current liabilities. For the total liabilities-to-equity ratio, include provisions in total liabilities.

2   How much do inventories represent as a component of total assets for CAT using LIFO numbers as reported and FIFO adjusted numbers, and for Volvo using reported numbers in 2007 and 2008? Discuss any changes that would concern an analyst.

3   Using the reported numbers, compare the 2007 and 2008 growth rates of CAT and Volvo for sales, finished goods inventory, and inventories other than finished goods.

Solution to 1:

The comparisons between Caterpillar and Volvo for 2008 are as follows:

	CAT(LIFO)	CAT(FIFO)	Volvo
Inventory turnover ratio	4.81	3.47	4.81
Days of inventory on hand	76.1 days	105.5 days	76.1 days
Gross profit margin	20.04%	21.22%	21.76%
Net profit margin	6.93%	7.81%	3.30%
Return on assets[a]	5.74%	6.26%	2.89%
Current ratio[b]	1.21	1.30	1.06
Total liabilities-to-equity ratio[c]	10.05	7.31	3.40
Return on equity[d]	47.5%	42.0%	12.0%

Note: Calculations for ratios previously calculated (see Examples 2 and 5) are not shown again.

[a] Return on assets = Net income ÷ Average total assets
Volvo = 2.89 percent = 10,016 ÷ [(372,419 + 321,647) ÷ 2]

[b] Current ratio = Current assets ÷ Current liabilities
Volvo = 1.06 = [176,038 ÷ (11,750 + 154,390)]
The question indicates to include current provisions in current liabilities.

[c] Total liabilities-to-equity ratio = Total liabilities ÷ Total shareholders' equity
Volvo = 3.40 = [(29,031 + 92,608 + 11,750 + 154,390) ÷ 84,640]
The question indicates to include provisions in total liabilities.

[d] Return on equity = Net income ÷ Average shareholders' equity
CAT (LIFO) = 47.5 percent = 3,557 ÷ [(6,087 + 8,883) ÷ 2]

(continued)

CAT (FIFO) = 42.0 percent = 4,010 ÷ {[(6,087 + 3,183 − 898) + (8,883 + 2,617 − 785)] ÷ 2}

Volvo = 12.0 percent = 10,016 ÷ [(84,640 + 82,781) ÷ 2]

Comparing CAT (FIFO) and Volvo, it appears that Volvo manages its inventory more effectively. It has higher inventory turnover and less days of inventory on hand. CAT appears to have superior profitability based on net profit margins. CAT did report some losses as other comprehensive income in the balance sheet (see Exhibit 2) as indicated by the absolute increase in the negative accumulated other comprehensive income. The absolute increase in the negative accumulated other comprehensive income results in a reduction of shareholders' equity which makes CAT's return on equity higher. The higher leverage of CAT also increases the return on equity. The sources of CAT's higher return on equity (reporting losses through other comprehensive income and higher leverage) should be of concern to an analyst. An analyst should investigate further, rather than reaching a conclusion based on ratios alone (in other words, try to identify the underlying causes of changes or differences in ratios).

Solution to 2:

The 2008 and 2007 inventory to total assets ratios for CAT using LIFO and adjusted to FIFO and for Volvo as reported, are as follows:

	CAT (LIFO)	CAT (FIFO)	Volvo
2008	12.95%	17.08%	14.78%
2007	12.83%	16.94%	13.57%

Inventory to total assets

CAT (LIFO) 2008 = 12.95 percent = 8,781 ÷ 67,782

CAT (LIFO) 2007 = 12.83 percent = 7,204 ÷ 56,132

CAT (FIFO) 2008 = 17.08 percent = 11,964 ÷ (67,782 + 3,183 − 898)

CAT (FIFO) 2007 = 16.94 percent = 9,821 ÷ (56,132 + 2,617 − 785)

Volvo 2008 = 14.78 percent = 55,045 ÷ 372,419

Volvo 2007 = 13.57 percent = 43,645 ÷ 321,647

Based on the numbers as reported, CAT appears to have a lower percentage of assets tied up in inventory than Volvo. However, when CAT's inventory is adjusted to FIFO, it has a higher percentage of its assets tied up in inventory than Volvo.

The increase in Volvo's inventory as a percentage of total assets is cause for some concern. Higher inventory typically results in higher maintenance costs (for example, storage and financing costs). In addition, Volvo may be building up slow moving or obsolete inventories that may result in future inventory write-downs for 2009. In Volvo's Note 18, the breakdown by inventory classification shows a small increase in the inventory of production materials. It appears that Volvo is planning on reducing production until it reduces its finished goods inventory. Looking at CAT's Note 9, all classifications of inventory seem to be increasing, and because these are valued using the LIFO method, there is some cause for concern. The company must be increasing inventory quantities and adding LIFO layers.

Solution to 3:

CAT's and Volvo's 2008 and 2007 growth rates for sales (for CAT use Sales of machinery and engines and for Volvo use Net sales), finished goods, and inventories other than finished goods are as follows:

2008	CAT (%)	Volvo (%)
Sales	14.5	6.4
Finished goods	31.2	39.4
Inventories other than finished goods	15.0	2.2

2007		
Sales	8.0	10.3
Finished goods	10.1	37.7
Inventories other than finished goods	16.0	12.7

Growth rate = (Value for year – Value for previous year)/Value for previous year

2008 CAT

Sales = 14.5 percent = (48,044 – 41,962) ÷ 41,962

Finished goods = 31.2 percent = (4,022 – 3,066) ÷ 3,066

Inventories other than finished goods = 15.0 percent = [(3,356 + 1,107 + 296) – (2,990 + 863 + 285)] ÷ (2,990 + 863 + 285)

2008 Volvo

Sales = 6.4 percent = (303,667 – 285,405) ÷ 285,405

Finished products = 39.4 percent = (39,137 – 28,077) ÷ 28,077

Inventories other than finished products = 2.2 percent = (15,908 – 15,568) ÷ 15,568

2007 CAT

Sales = 8.0 percent = (41,962 – 38,869) ÷ 38,869

Finished goods = 10.1 percent = (3,066 – 2,785) ÷ 2,785

Inventories other than finished goods = 16.0 percent = [(2,990 + 863 + 285) – (2,698 + 591 + 277)] ÷ (2,698 + 591 + 277)

2007 Volvo

Sales = 10.3 percent = (285,405 – 258,835) ÷ 258,835

Finished products = 37.7 percent = (28,077 – 20,396) ÷ 20,396

Inventories other than finished products = 12.7 percent = (15,568 – 13,815) ÷ 13,815

For both companies, the growth rates in finished goods inventory exceeds the growth rate in sales; this could be indicative of accumulating excess inventory. Volvo's growth rate in finished goods compared to its growth rate in sales is significantly higher but the lower growth rates in finished goods inventory for CAT is potentially a result of using the LIFO method versus the FIFO method. It appears Volvo is aware that an issue exists and is planning on cutting back production given the relatively small increase in inventories other than finished products. Regardless, an analyst should do further investigation before reaching any conclusion about a company's future prospects for sales and profit.

EXAMPLE 7

Management Discussion and Analysis

The following excerpts commenting on inventory management are from the Volvo Group Annual Report, 2008:

> **From the CEO Comment**: In a declining economy, it is extremely important to act quickly to reduce the Group's cost level and ensure we do not build inventories, since large inventories generally lead to pressure on prices. ... During the second half of the year, we implemented sharp production cutbacks to lower inventories of new trucks and construction equipment as part of efforts to maintain our product prices, which represent one of the most important factors in securing favorable profitability in the future. We have been successful in these efforts. During the fourth quarter, inventories of new trucks declined 13% and of new construction equipment by 19%. During the beginning of 2009, we have continued to work diligently and focused to reduce inventories to the new, lower levels of demand that prevail in most of our markets, and for most of our products.

> **From the Board of Directors' Report 2008**: Inventory reduction contributed to positive operating cash flow of SEK 1.8 billion in Industrial Operations. ... The value of inventories increased during 2008 by SEK 11.4 billion. Adjusted for currency changes, the increase amounted to SEK 5.8 billion. The increase is mainly related to the truck operations and to construction equipment and is an effect of the rapidly weakening demand during the second half of the year. ... In order to reduce the capital tied-up in inventory, a number of shutdown days in production were carried out during the end of year. Measures aimed at selling primarily trucks and construction equipment in inventory were prioritized. These measures have continued during the beginning of 2009 ... Overcapacity within the industry can occur if there is a lack of demand, potentially leading to increased price pressure.

> **From Business Areas 2008 (Ambitions 2009)**: Execute on cost reduction and adjust production to ensure inventory levels in line with demand.

Assume inventory write-downs are reported as part of cost of sales. Based on the excerpts above, discuss the anticipated direction of the following for 2009 compared to 2008:

1 Inventory carrying amounts
2 Inventory turnover ratio
3 Sales
4 Gross profit margin
5 Return on assets
6 Current ratio

Solution to 1:

Inventory carrying amounts are expected to decrease as the company cuts back on inventory levels and pressures are exerted on costs and prices.

Solution to 2:

Inventory turnover ratio is expected to increase. Any potential change in cost of sales will be more than offset by the decline in inventory carrying amounts. The company is expecting to reduce both inventories and sales, but sales and cost of sales are expected to decline by a lesser percentage than inventory.

Solution to 3:

Unit sales and sales revenues are expected to decline due to decrease in demand and pressure on prices.

Solution to 4:

Gross profit margin is difficult to predict. Sales revenues are expected to decline but cost of sales as a percentage of sales revenue may decline if cost controls are effective, stay the same if cost controls are offset by increased inventory write-downs, or increase if inventory write-downs more than offset cost controls. In this case, an analyst might use 2008's gross profit margin of 21.8 percent as a reasonable prediction. It is less than the 2006 and 2007 gross profit margin of 23.1 percent and may already reflect cost controls, price pressures, and inventory write-downs.

Solution to 5:

Return on assets is expected to decline. The positive effects of cost controls and reduction in assets is likely to be offset by decreased net income due to the declining sales revenues.

Solution to 6:

The direction of change in the current ratio is difficult to predict. Current assets are expected to be reduced but current liabilities are also expected to be reduced as costs are controlled and purchases are reduced resulting in lower accounts payable.

Analysts should seek out as much information as feasible when analyzing the performance of companies.

SUMMARY

Inventories and cost of sales (cost of goods sold) are significant items in the financial statements of many companies. Comparing the performance of these companies is challenging due to the allowable choices for valuing inventories; differences in the choice of inventory valuation method can result in significantly different amounts being assigned to inventory and the cost of sales. To evaluate a company's performance over time and relative to industry peers, analysts must clearly understand the various inventory valuation methods that companies use and the related impact on financial statements and financial ratios.

Key concepts in this reading are as follows:

- The allowable inventory valuation methods implicitly involve different assumptions about cost flows. The choice of inventory valuation method determines how the cost of goods available for sale during the period is allocated between inventory and cost of sales.

- Under IFRS, the cost of inventories is typically assigned by using either the first-in, first-out (FIFO) or weighted average cost formula. The specific identification method is required for inventories of items that are not ordinarily interchangeable and for goods or services produced and segregated for specific projects.

- Under US GAAP, in addition to specific identification, FIFO and weighted average cost, last-in first-out (LIFO) is an accepted inventory valuation method. The LIFO method is widely used in the United States for both tax and financial reporting purposes because of potential income tax savings.

- The choice of inventory method affects the financial statements and any financial ratios that are based on them. As a consequence, the analyst must carefully consider inventory valuation method differences when evaluating a company's performance over time or in comparison to industry data or industry competitors.

- Under US GAAP, companies that use the LIFO method must disclose in their financial notes the amount of the LIFO reserve or the amount that would have been reported in inventory if the FIFO method had been used. This information can be used to adjust reported LIFO inventory and cost of goods sold balances to the FIFO method for comparison purposes.

- LIFO liquidation occurs when the number of units in ending inventory declines from the number of units that were present at the beginning of the year. If inventory unit costs have generally risen from year to year, this will produce an inventory-related increase in gross profits.

- Consistency of inventory costing is required under both IFRS and US GAAP. If a company changes an accounting policy, the change must be justifiable and applied retrospectively to the financial statements. An exception to the retrospective restatement is when a company reporting under US GAAP changes to the LIFO method.

- Inventories are measured at the lower of cost and net realisable value under IFRS and the lower of cost and market under US GAAP. Any write-down of inventory to net realisable value or market reduces the carrying amount of inventory on the balance sheet and profit on the income statement.

- Reversals of inventory write-downs may occur under IFRS but are not allowed under US GAAP.

- Changes in the carrying amounts within inventory classifications (such as raw materials, work-in-process, and finished goods) may provide signals about a company's future sales and profits. Relevant information with respect to inventory management and future sales may be found in the Management Discussion and Analysis or similar items within the annual or quarterly reports, industry news and publications, and industry economic data.

- Inventory management may have a substantial impact on a company's activity, profitability, liquidity, and solvency ratios. It is critical for the analyst to be aware of industry trends and management's intentions.

PRACTICE PROBLEMS

The following information relates to Questions 1–6

John Martinson, CFA, is an equity analyst with a large pension fund. His supervisor, Linda Packard, asks him to write a report on Karp Inc. Karp prepares its financial statements in accordance with US GAAP. Packard is particularly interested in the effects of the company's use of the LIFO method to account for its inventory. For this purpose, Martinson collects the financial data presented in Exhibits 1 and 2.

Exhibit 1 Balance Sheet Information (US$ Millions)		
As of 31 December	**2009**	**2008**
Cash and cash equivalents	172	157
Accounts receivable	626	458
Inventories	620	539
Other current assets	125	65
Total current assets	1,543	1,219
Property and equipment, net	3,035	2,972
Total assets	4,578	4,191
Total current liabilities	1,495	1,395
Long-term debt	644	604
Total liabilities	2,139	1,999
Common stock and paid in capital	1,652	1,652
Retained earnings	787	540
Total shareholders' equity	2,439	2,192
Total liabilities and shareholders' equity	4,578	4,191

Exhibit 2 Income Statement Information (US$ Millions)		
For the Year Ended 31 December	**2009**	**2008**
Sales	4,346	4,161
Cost of goods sold	2,211	2,147
Depreciation and amortisation expense	139	119
Selling, general, and administrative expense	1,656	1,637
Interest expense	31	18
Income tax expense	62	48
Net income	247	192

Martinson finds the following information in the notes to the financial statements:

■ The LIFO reserves as of 31 December 2009 and 2008 are $155 million and $117 million respectively, and

■ The effective income tax rate applicable to Karp for 2009 and earlier periods is 20 percent.

1 If Karp had used FIFO instead of LIFO, the amount of inventory reported as of 31 December 2009 would have been *closest* to:

A $465 million.

B $658 million.

C $775 million.

2 If Karp had used FIFO instead of LIFO, the amount of cost of goods sold reported by Karp for the year ended 31 December 2009 would have been *closest* to:

A $2,056 million.

B $2,173 million.

C $2,249 million.

3 If Karp had used FIFO instead of LIFO, its reported net income for the year ended 31 December 2009 would have been higher by an amount *closest to*:

A $30 million.

B $38 million.

C $155 million.

4 If Karp had used FIFO instead of LIFO, Karp's retained earnings as of 31 December 2009 would have been higher by an amount *closest to*:

A $117 million.

B $124 million.

C $155 million.

5 If Karp had used FIFO instead of LIFO, which of the following ratios computed as of 31 December 2009 would *most likely* have been lower?

A Cash ratio.

B Current ratio.

C Gross profit margin.

6 If Karp had used FIFO instead of LIFO, its debt to equity ratio computed as of 31 December 2009 would have:

A increased.

B decreased.

C remained unchanged.

The following information relates to Questions 7–12

Robert Groff, an equity analyst, is preparing a report on Crux Corp. As part of his report, Groff makes a comparative financial analysis between Crux and its two main competitors, Rolby Corp. and Mikko Inc. Crux and Mikko report under US GAAP and Rolby reports under IFRS.

Groff gathers information on Crux, Rolby, and Mikko. The relevant financial information he compiles is in Exhibit 1. Some information on the industry is in Exhibit 2.

Exhibit 1 Selected Financial Information (US$ Millions)			
	Crux	**Rolby**	**Mikko**
Inventory valuation method	LIFO	FIFO	LIFO
From the Balance Sheets			
As of 31 December 2009			
Inventory, gross	480	620	510
Valuation allowance	20	25	14
Inventory, net	460	595	496
Total debt	1,122	850	732
Total shareholders' equity	2,543	2,403	2,091
As of 31 December 2008			
Inventory, gross	465	602	401
Valuation allowance	23	15	12
Inventory, net	442	587	389
From the Income Statements			
Year Ended 31 December 2009			
Revenues	4,609	5,442	3,503
Cost of goods sold[a]	3,120	3,782	2,550
Net income	229	327	205
[a]Charges included in cost of goods sold for inventory write-downs*	13	15	15

*This does not match the change in the inventory valuation allowance because the valuation allowance is reduced to reflect the valuation allowance attached to items sold and increased for additional necessary write-downs.

LIFO Reserve			
As of 31 December 2009	55	0	77
As of 31 December 2008	72	0	50
As of 31 December 2007	96	0	43
Tax Rate			
Effective tax rate	30%	30%	30%

Exhibit 2	Industry Information		
	2009	2008	2007
Raw materials price index	112	105	100
Finished goods price index	114	106	100

To compare the financial performance of the three companies, Groff decides to convert LIFO figures into FIFO figures, and adjust figures to assume no valuation allowance is recognized by any company.

After reading Groff's draft report, his supervisor, Rachel Borghi, asks him the following questions:

Question 1   Which company's gross profit margin would best reflect current costs of the industry?

Question 2   Would Rolby's valuation method show a higher gross profit margin than Crux's under an inflationary, a deflationary, or a stable price scenario?

Question 3   Which group of ratios usually appears more favorable with an inventory write-down?

7   Crux's inventory turnover ratio computed as of 31 December 2009, after the adjustments suggested by Groff, is *closest* to:

   A   5.67.

   B   5.83.

   C   6.13.

8   Rolby's net profit margin for the year ended 31 December 2009, after the adjustments suggested by Groff, is *closest* to:

   A   6.01%.

   B   6.20%.

   C   6.28%.

9   Compared with its unadjusted debt-to-equity ratio, Mikko's debt-to-equity ratio as of 31 December 2009, after the adjustments suggested by Groff, is:

   A   lower.

   B   higher.

   C   the same.

10   The *best* answer to Borghi's Question 1 is:

   A   Crux's.

   B   Rolby's.

   C   Mikko's.

11   The *best* answer to Borghi's Question 2 is:

   A   Stable.

   B   Inflationary.

   C   Deflationary.

12   The *best* answer to Borghi's Question 3 is:

   A   Activity ratios.

B Solvency ratios.

C Profitability ratios.

The following information relates to Questions 13–20

ZP Corporation is a (hypothetical) multinational corporation headquartered in Japan that trades on numerous stock exchanges. ZP prepares its consolidated financial statements in accordance with US GAAP. Excerpts from ZP's 2009 annual report are shown in Exhibits 1–3.

Exhibit 1	Consolidated Balance Sheets (¥ Millions)	
31 December	**2008**	**2009**
Current Assets		
Cash and cash equivalents	¥542,849	¥814,760
⋮	⋮	⋮
Inventories	608,572	486,465
⋮	⋮	⋮
Total current assets	4,028,742	3,766,309
⋮	⋮	⋮
Total assets	**¥10,819,440**	**¥9,687,346**
⋮	⋮	⋮
Total current liabilities	¥3,980,247	¥3,529,765
⋮	⋮	⋮
Total long-term liabilities	2,663,795	2,624,002
Minority interest in consolidated subsidiaries	218,889	179,843
Total shareholders' equity	3,956,509	3,353,736
Total liabilities and shareholders' equity	**¥10,819,440**	**¥9,687,346**

Exhibit 2	Consolidated Statements of Income (¥ Millions)		
For the years ended 31 December	**2007**	**2008**	**2009**
Net revenues			
Sales of products	¥7,556,699	¥8,273,503	¥6,391,240
Financing operations	425,998	489,577	451,950
	7,982,697	8,763,080	6,843,190
Cost and expenses			
Cost of products sold	6,118,742	6,817,446	5,822,805
Cost of financing operations	290,713	356,005	329,128

(continued)

Exhibit 2	(Continued)			

For the years ended 31 December	2007	2008	2009
Selling, general and administrative	827,005	832,837	844,927
⋮	⋮	⋮	⋮
Operating income (loss)	746,237	756,792	−153,670
⋮	⋮	⋮	⋮
Net income	¥548,011	¥572,626	−¥145,646

Exhibit 3	Selected Disclosures in the 2009 Annual Report

Management's Discussion and Analysis of Financial Condition and Results of Operations

Cost reduction efforts were offset by increased prices of raw materials, other production materials and parts ... Inventories decreased during fiscal 2009 by ¥122.1 billion, or 20.1%, to ¥486.5 billion. This reflects the impacts of decreased sales volumes and fluctuations in foreign currency translation rates.

Management & Corporate Information

Risk Factors

Industry and Business Risks

The worldwide market for our products is highly competitive. ZP faces intense competition from other manufacturers in the respective markets in which it operates. Competition has intensified due to the worldwide deterioration in economic conditions. In addition, competition is likely to further intensify because of continuing globalization, possibly resulting in industry reorganization. Factors affecting competition include product quality and features, the amount of time required for innovation and development, pricing, reliability, safety, economy in use, customer service and financing terms. Increased competition may lead to lower unit sales and excess production capacity and excess inventory. This may result in a further downward price pressure.

ZP's ability to adequately respond to the recent rapid changes in the industry and to maintain its competitiveness will be fundamental to its future success in maintaining and expanding its market share in existing and new markets.

Notes to Consolidated Financial Statements

2. Summary of significant accounting policies:

Inventories. Inventories are valued at cost, not in excess of market. Cost is determined on the "average-cost" basis, except for the cost of finished products carried by certain subsidiary companies which is determined "last-in, first-out" ("LIFO") basis. Inventories valued on the LIFO basis totaled ¥94,578 million and ¥50,037 million at December 31, 2008 and 2009, respectively. Had the "first-in, first-out" basis been used for those companies using the LIFO basis, inventories would have been ¥10,120 million and ¥19,660 million higher than reported at December 31, 2008 and 2009, respectively.

9. Inventories:

Inventories consist of the following:

31 December (¥ Millions)	2008	2009
Finished goods	¥ 403,856	¥ 291,977
Raw materials	99,869	85,966
Work in process	79,979	83,890
Supplies and other	24,868	24,632
	¥ 608,572	¥ 486,465

13 The MD&A indicated that the prices of raw material, other production materials, and parts increased. Based on the inventory valuation methods described in Note 2, which inventory classification would *least accurately* reflect current prices?

   A   Raw materials.

   B   Finished goods.

   C   Work in process.

14 The 2008 inventory value as reported on the 2009 Annual Report if the company had used the FIFO inventory valuation method instead of the LIFO inventory valuation method for a portion of its inventory would be *closest* to:

   A   ¥104,698 million.

   B   ¥506,125 million.

   C   ¥618,692 million.

15 What is the *least likely* reason why ZP may need to change its accounting policies regarding inventory at some point after 2009?

   A   The US SEC is likely to require companies to use the same inventory valuation method for all inventories.

   B   The US SEC is likely to prohibit the use of one of the methods ZP currently uses for inventory valuation.

   C   One of the inventory valuation methods used for US tax purposes may be repealed as an acceptable method.

16 If ZP had prepared its financial statement in accordance with IFRS, the inventory turnover ratio (using average inventory) for 2009 would be:

   A   lower.

   B   higher.

   C   the same.

17 Inventory levels decreased from 2008 to 2009 for all of the following reasons *except*:

    A   LIFO liquidation.

    B   decreased sales volume.

    C   fluctuations in foreign currency translation rates.

18 Which observation is *most likely* a result of looking only at the information reported in Note 9?

    A   Increased competition has led to lower unit sales.

    B   There have been significant price increases in supplies.

    C   Management expects a further downturn in sales during 2010.

19 Note 2 indicates that, "Inventories valued on the LIFO basis totaled ¥94,578 million and ¥50,037 million at December 31, 2008 and 2009, respectively." Based on this, the LIFO reserve should *most likely*:

    A   increase.

    B   decrease.

    C   remain the same.

20 The Industry and Business Risk excerpt states that, "Increased competition may lead to lower unit sales and excess production capacity and excess inventory. This may result in a further downward price pressure." The downward price pressure could lead to inventory that is valued above current market prices or net realisable value. Any write-downs of inventory are *least likely* to have a significant effect on the inventory valued using:

    A   weighted average cost.

    B   first-in, first-out (FIFO).

    C   last-in, first-out (LIFO).

SOLUTIONS

1 C is correct. Karp's inventory under FIFO equals Karp's inventory under LIFO plus the LIFO reserve. Therefore, as of 31 December 2009, Karp's inventory under FIFO equals:

Inventory (FIFO method) = Inventory (LIFO method) + LIFO reserve

= $620 million + 155 million

= $775 million

2 B is correct. Karp's cost of goods sold (COGS) under FIFO equals Karp's cost of goods sold under LIFO minus the increase in the LIFO reserve. Therefore, for the year ended 31 December 2009, Karp's cost of goods sold under FIFO equals:

COGS (FIFO method) = COGS (LIFO method) − Increase in LIFO reserve

= $2,211 million − (155 million − 117 million)

= $2,173 million

3 A is correct. Karp's net income (NI) under FIFO equals Karp's net income under LIFO plus the after-tax increase in the LIFO reserve. For the year ended 31 December 2009, Karp's net income under FIFO equals:

NI (FIFO method) = NI (LIFO method) + Increase in LIFO reserve × (1 − Tax rate)

= $247 million + 38 million × (1 − 20%)

= $277.4 million

Therefore, the increase in net income is:

Increase in NI = NI (FIFO method) − NI (LIFO method)

= $277 million − 247 million

= $30.4 million

4 B is correct. Karp's retained earnings (RE) under FIFO equals Karp's retained earnings under LIFO plus the after-tax LIFO reserve. Therefore, for the year ended 31 December 2009, Karp's retained earnings under FIFO equals:

RE (FIFO method) = RE (LIFO method) + LIFO reserve × (1 − Tax rate)

= $787 million + 155 million × (1 − 20%)

= $911 million

Therefore, the increase in retained earnings is:

Increase in RE = RE (FIFO method) − RE (LIFO method)

= $911 million − 787 million

= $124 million

5 A is correct. The cash ratio (cash and cash equivalents ÷ current liabilities) would be lower because cash would have been less under FIFO. Karp's income before taxes would have been higher under FIFO, and consequently taxes paid by Karp would have also been higher and cash would have been lower. There is no impact on current liabilities. Both Karp's current ratio and gross profit margin would have been higher if FIFO had been used. The current ratio would have been higher because inventory under FIFO increases by a larger amount than the cash decreases for taxes paid. Because the cost of goods sold under FIFO is lower than under LIFO, the gross profit margin would have been higher.

6   B is correct. If Karp had used FIFO instead of LIFO, the debt-to-equity ratio would have decreased. No change in debt would have occurred, but shareholders' equity would have increased as a result of higher retained earnings.

7   B is correct. Crux's adjusted inventory turnover ratio must be computed using cost of goods sold (COGS) under FIFO and excluding charges for increases in valuation allowances.

COGS (adjusted) = COGS (LIFO method) – Charges included in
cost of goods sold for inventory write-downs – Change
in LIFO reserve

= $3,120 million – 13 million – (55 million – 72 million)

= $3,124 million

Note: Minus the change in LIFO reserve is equivalent to plus the decrease in LIFO reserve. The adjusted inventory turnover ratio is computed using average inventory under FIFO.

Ending inventory (FIFO) = Ending inventory (LIFO) + LIFO reserve

Ending inventory 2009 (FIFO) = $480 + 55 = $535

Ending inventory 2008 (FIFO) = $465 + 72 = $537

Average inventory = ($535 + 537)/2 = $536

Therefore, adjusted inventory turnover ratio equals:

Inventory turnover ratio = COGS/Average inventory = $3,124/$536 = 5.83

8   B is correct. Rolby's adjusted net profit margin must be computed using net income (NI) under FIFO and excluding charges for increases in valuation allowances.

NI (adjusted) = NI (FIFO method) + Charges, included in cost of goods
sold for inventory write-downs, after tax

= $327 million + 15 million × (1 – 30%)

= $337.5 million

Therefore, adjusted net profit margin equals:

Net profit margin = NI/Revenues = $337.5/$5,442 = 6.20%

9   A is correct. Mikko's adjusted debt-to-equity ratio is lower because the debt (numerator) is unchanged and the adjusted shareholders' equity (denominator) is higher. The adjusted shareholders' equity corresponds to shareholders' equity under FIFO, excluding charges for increases in valuation allowances. Therefore, adjusted shareholders' equity is higher than reported (unadjusted) shareholders' equity.

10   C is correct. Mikko's and Crux's gross margin ratios would better reflect the current gross margin of the industry than Rolby because both use LIFO. LIFO recognizes as cost of goods sold the cost of the most recently purchased units, therefore, it better reflects replacement cost. However, Mikko's gross margin

ratio best reflects the current gross margin of the industry because Crux's LIFO reserve is decreasing. This could reflect a LIFO liquidation by Crux which would distort gross profit margin.

11 B is correct. The FIFO method shows a higher gross profit margin than the LIFO method in an inflationary scenario, because FIFO allocates to cost of goods sold the cost of the oldest units available for sale. In an inflationary environment, these units are the ones with the lowest cost.

12 A is correct. An inventory write-down increases cost of sales and reduces profit and reduces the carrying value of inventory and assets. This has a negative effect on profitability and solvency ratios. However, activity ratios appear positively affected by a write-down because the asset base, whether total assets or inventory (denominator), is reduced. The numerator, sales, in total asset turnover is unchanged, and the numerator, cost of sales, in inventory turnover is increased. Thus, turnover ratios are higher and appear more favorable as the result of the write-down.

13 B is correct. Finished goods least accurately reflect current prices because some of the finished goods are valued under the "last-in, first-out" ("LIFO") basis. The costs of the newest units available for sale are allocated to cost of goods sold, leaving the oldest units (at lower costs) in inventory. ZP values raw materials and work in process using the weighted average cost method. While not fully reflecting current prices, some inflationary effect will be included in the inventory values.

14 C is correct. FIFO inventory = Reported inventory + LIFO reserve = ¥608,572 + 10,120 = ¥618,692. The LIFO reserve is disclosed in Note 2 of the notes to consolidated financial statements.

15 A is correct. The SEC does not require companies to use the same inventory valuation method for all inventories, so this is the *least likely* reason to change accounting policies regarding inventory. The SEC is currently evaluating whether all US companies should be required to adopt IFRS. If the SEC requires companies to adopt IFRS, the LIFO method of inventory valuation would no longer be allowed.

16 A is correct. The inventory turnover ratio would be lower. The average inventory would be higher under FIFO and cost of products sold would be lower by the increase in LIFO reserve. LIFO is not permitted under IFRS.

Inventory turnover ratio = Cost of products sold ÷ Average inventory

2009 inventory turnover ratio as reported = 10.63 = ¥5,822,805/[(608,572 + 486,465)/2].

2009 inventory turnover ratio adjusted to FIFO as necessary = 10.34 = [¥5,822,805 − (19,660 − 10,120)]/[(608,572 + 10,120 + 486,465 + 19,660)/2].

17 A is correct. No LIFO liquidation occurred during 2009; the LIFO reserve increased from ¥10,120 million in 2008 to ¥19,660 million in 2009. Management stated in the MD&A that the decrease in inventories reflected the impacts of decreased sales volumes and fluctuations in foreign currency translation rates.

18 C is correct. Finished goods and raw materials inventories are lower in 2009 when compared to 2008. Reduced levels of inventory typically indicate an anticipated business contraction.

19 B is correct. The decrease in LIFO inventory in 2009 would typically indicate that more inventory units were sold than produced or purchased. Accordingly, one would expect a liquidation of some of the older LIFO layers and the LIFO reserve to decrease. In actuality, the LIFO reserve *increased* from

¥10,120 million in 2008 to ¥19,660 million in 2009. This is not to be expected and is likely caused by the increase in prices of raw materials, other production materials, and parts of foreign currencies as noted in the MD&A. An analyst should seek to confirm this explanation.

20 B is correct. If prices have been decreasing, write-downs under FIFO are least likely to have a significant effect because the inventory is valued at closer to the new, lower prices. Typically, inventories valued using LIFO are less likely to incur inventory write-downs than inventories valued using weighted average cost or FIFO. Under LIFO, the *oldest* costs are reflected in the inventory carrying value on the balance sheet. Given increasing inventory costs, the inventory carrying values under the LIFO method are already conservatively presented at the oldest and lowest costs. Thus, it is far less likely that inventory write-downs will occur under LIFO; and if a write-down does occur, it is likely to be of a lesser magnitude.

Long-lived Assets: Implications for Financial Statements and Ratios

by Elaine Henry, PhD, CFA, and Elizabeth A. Gordon

Elaine Henry, PhD, CFA, is at Fordham University (USA). Elizabeth A. Gordon (USA).

LEARNING OUTCOMES

Mastery	The candidate should be able to:
☐	a. explain and evaluate how capitalising versus expensing costs in the period in which they are incurred affects financial statements and ratios;
☐	b. explain and evaluate how the different depreciation methods for property, plant, and equipment affect financial statements and ratios;
☐	c. explain and evaluate how impairment and revaluation of property, plant, and equipment and intangible assets affect financial statements and ratios;
☐	d. analyze and interpret financial statement disclosures regarding long-lived assets;
☐	e. explain and evaluate how leasing rather than purchasing assets affects financial statements and ratios;
☐	f. explain and evaluate how finance leases and operating leases affect financial statements and ratios from the perspectives of both the lessor and the lessee.

Note: New rulings and/or pronouncements issued after the publication of the readings in financial reporting and analysis may cause some of the information in these readings to become dated. Candidates are expected to be familiar with the overall analytical framework contained in the study session readings, as well as the implications of alternative accounting methods for financial analysis and valuation, as provided in the assigned readings. Candidates are not responsible for changes that occur after the material was written.

INTRODUCTION

Long-lived assets include tangible assets such as property, plant, and equipment; identifiable intangible assets such as patents and trademarks; and goodwill. In this reading, we focus on the implications for financial statements and ratios of accounting choices involved in the financial reporting of tangible and identifiable intangible long-lived assets. Further, this reading considers both assets that a company owns and assets that a company leases.

Although companies must follow accounting standards, companies make numerous choices and decisions within what is allowed by those standards. In general, accounting choices related to long-lived assets affect the timing of expense recognition, which in turn affects the company's profitability for the current period and trends in profitability. Choices resulting in lower profits for the current period, such as expensing rather than capitalising expenditures, generally result in higher profits in a subsequent period and thus a more favorable trend. The choices may impact cash flows through taxes.

This reading is organised as follows: Section 2 describes and illustrates the implications for financial statements and ratios of capitalising versus expensing expenditures related to long-lived assets. Section 3 describes and illustrates the implications for financial statements and ratios of using different depreciation methods, depreciation periods, and residual value assumptions in allocating the cost of long-lived assets over time. Section 4 describes and illustrates the implications for financial statements and ratios of periodically estimating the recoverable value of long-lived assets which can give rise to impairments and/or revaluations.

Section 5 describes the analysis and interpretation of financial statement disclosures about long-lived assets. In Section 6, we turn to leased assets and examine the issues involved in lease accounting, along with the financial statement effects of different kinds of leases. A summary and practice problems in the CFA Institute item set format complete the reading.

CAPITALISING VERSUS EXPENSING

This section discusses the implications for financial statements and ratios of capitalising versus expensing costs in the period in which they are incurred. In general, when a company acquires a long-lived tangible or intangible asset, the company records an asset in an amount equal to the acquisition cost plus the cost, if any, to get the asset ready for its intended use. When a company acquires a long-lived asset in a business combination, the accounting treatment differs.

To be recognised as a long-lived asset, tangible or intangible, future economic benefits must flow to the entity from the use of the asset. International Financial Reporting Standards (IFRS) specify that "The cost of an item of property, plant and equipment shall be recognised as an asset if, and only if: a) it is probable that future economic benefits associated with the item will flow to the entity; and b) the cost of the item can be measured reliably."[1] US generally accepted accounting principles (US GAAP), as contained in the Financial Accounting Standards Board (FASB) Accounting Standards Codification™ (ASC),[2] are similar.[3] Examples of property, plant, and equipment (PPE) include land, buildings, machinery, furniture, fixtures, and vehicles. Major

---

1 IAS 16 [Property, Plant and Equipment], paragraph 7.
2 The Codification is the single source of authoritative nongovernmental US GAAP and supersedes previous US GAAP standards. The Codification is effective for periods ending after 15 September 2009.
3 FASB ASC Topic 360 [Property, Plant, and Equipment].

spare parts that are expected to be used during more than one period or spare parts that can be used only in connection with an item of PPE are treated as part of the PPE asset. (Minor spare parts and spare parts that are not specific to an item of PPE are usually expensed as consumed.) Examples of expenditures to get an asset ready for its intended use include purchase price, delivery, and installation.

Intangible assets lack physical substance. IFRS require that intangible assets be identifiable, under the control of the entity, and generators of future economic benefits.[4] Requirements under US GAAP are similar.[5] Examples of identifiable intangible long-lived assets include patents, licenses, trademarks, brands, copyrights, and mailing lists. When assets are acquired as part of a business combination, a company records for each identifiable tangible and intangible asset acquired and each liability assumed an amount equal to the estimated fair value of the asset or the liability. If the purchase price exceeds the sum of the amounts allocated to identifiable assets and liabilities, the excess is recorded as goodwill.

Before turning to specific instances, we will consider the general financial statement impact of capitalising versus expensing and two analytical issues related to the decision—namely the effect on an individual company's trend analysis and on comparability across companies.

In the period of the expenditure, an expenditure that is capitalised increases the amount of assets on the balance sheet and appears as an investing cash outflow on the statement of cash flows. In subsequent periods, a company allocates the capitalised amount over the asset's useful life as depreciation or amortisation expense (except assets that are not depreciated, i.e., land, or amortised, e.g., intangible assets with indefinite lives). This expense reduces net income on the income statement and reduces the value of the asset on the balance sheet. Depreciation and amortisation are non-cash expenses and therefore, apart from their effect on taxable income and taxes payable, have no impact on the cash flow statement. In the section of the statement of cash flows that reconciles net income to operating cash flow, depreciation and amortisation expenses are added back to net income.

Alternatively, an expenditure that is expensed reduces net income by the after-tax amount of the expenditure in the period it is made. No asset is recorded on the balance sheet and thus no depreciation or amortisation occurs in subsequent periods. The lower amount of net income is reflected in lower retained earnings on the balance sheet. An expenditure that is expensed appears as an operating cash outflow in the period it is made. There is no effect on the financial statements of subsequent periods.

Example 1 illustrates the impact on the financial statements of capitalising versus expensing an expenditure.

EXAMPLE 1

Financial Statement Impact of Capitalising versus Expensing

Assume two identical (hypothetical) companies, CAP Inc. (CAP) and NOW Inc. (NOW), start with €1,000 cash and €1,000 common stock. Each year the companies recognise total revenues of €1,500 cash and make cash expenditures, excluding an equipment purchase, of €500. At the beginning of operations, each company pays €900 to purchase equipment. CAP estimates the equipment will have a useful life of three years and an estimated salvage value of €0 at the end of the three years. NOW estimates a much shorter useful life and expenses

---

4 IAS 38 [Intangible Assets].
5 FASB ASC Topic 350 [Intangibles–Goodwill and Other].

the equipment immediately. The companies have no other assets and make no other asset purchases during the three-year period. Assume the companies pay no dividends, earn zero interest on cash balances, have a tax rate of 30 percent, and use the same accounting method for financial and tax purposes.

The left side of Exhibit 1 shows CAP's financial statements; i.e., with the expenditure capitalised and depreciated at €300 per year based on the straight-line method of depreciation (€900 cost minus €0 salvage value equals €900, divided by a three-year life equals €300 per year). The right side of the exhibit shows NOW's financial statements, with the entire €900 expenditure treated as an expense in the first year. All amounts are in euro.

Exhibit 1   Capitalising versus Expensing

CAP Inc.

Capitalise €900 as Asset and Depreciate

For Year	1	2	3
Revenue	1,500	1,500	1,500
Cash expenses	500	500	500
Depreciation	300	300	300
Income before tax	700	700	700
Tax at 30%	210	210	210
Net income	490	490	490
Cash from operations	790	790	790
Cash used in investing	(900)	0	0
Total change in cash	(110)	790	790

As of	Time 0	End of Year 1	End of Year 2	End of Year 3
Cash	1,000	890	1,680	2,470
PP & E (net)	—	600	300	—
Total assets	1,000	1,490	1,980	2,470
Retained earnings	0	490	980	1,470

NOW Inc.

Expense €900 Immediately

For Year	1	2	3
Revenue	1,500	1,500	1,500
Cash expenses	1,400	500	500
Depreciation	0	0	0
Income before tax	100	1,000	1,000
Tax at 30%	30	300	300
Net income	70	700	700
Cash from operations	70	700	700
Cash used in investing	0	0	0
Total change in cash	70	700	700

Time	Time 0	End of Year 1	End of Year 2	End of Year 3
Cash	1,000	1,070	1,770	2,470
PP & E (net)	—	—	—	—
Total Assets	1,000	1,070	1,770	2,470
Retained earnings	0	70	770	1,470

As of	Time 0	End of Year 1	End of Year 2	End of Year 3	Time	Time 0	End of Year 1	End of Year 2	End of Year 3
Common stock	1,000	1,000	1,000	1,000	Common stock	1,000	1,000	1,000	1,000
Total shareholders' equity	1,000	1,490	1,980	2,470	Total shareholders' equity	1,000	1,070	1,770	2,470

Exhibit 1   (Continued)

1 Which company reports higher net income over the three years? Total cash flow? Cash from operations?

2 Based on ROE and net profit margin, how does the profitability of the two companies compare?

3 Why does NOW report change in cash of €70 in Year 1, while CAP reports total change in cash of (€110)?

Solution to 1:

Neither company reports higher total net income or cash flow over the three years. The sum of net income over the three years is identical (€1,470 total) whether the €900 is capitalised or expensed. Also, the sum of the change in cash (€1,470 total) is identical under either scenario. CAP reports higher cash from operations by an amount of €900 because, under the capitalisation scenario, the €900 purchase is treated as an investing cash flow.

Note: Because the companies use the same accounting method for both financial and taxable income, absent the assumption of zero interest on cash balances, expensing the €900 would have resulted in higher income and cash flow for NOW because the lower taxes paid in the first year (€30 versus €210) would have allowed NOW to earn interest income on the tax savings.

Solution to 2:

In general, Ending shareholders' equity = Beginning shareholders' equity + Net income + Other comprehensive income − Dividends + Net capital contributions from shareholders. Because the companies in this example do not have other comprehensive income, did not pay dividends, and reported no capital contributions from shareholders, Ending retained earnings = Beginning retained earnings + Net income, and Ending shareholders' equity = Beginning shareholders' equity + Net income.

ROE is calculated as net income ÷ by average shareholders' equity, and net profit margin is calculated as net income ÷ by total revenue. For example, CAP had Year 1 ROE of 39 percent (€490/[(€1,000 + €1,490)/2]), and Year 1 net profit margin of 33 percent (€490 ÷ €1,500).

CAP Inc.				NOW Inc.			
Capitalise €900 as Asset and Depreciate				Expense €900 Immediately			
For year	1	2	3	For year	1	2	3
ROE	39%	28%	22%	ROE	7%	49%	33%
Net profit margin	33	33	33	Net profit margin	5	47	47

As shown, capitalising results in higher profitability ratios (ROE and net profit margin) in the first year, and lower profitability ratios in subsequent years. For example, CAP's Year 1 ROE of 39 percent was higher than NOW's Year 1 ROE of 7 percent, but in Years 2 and 3, NOW reports superior profitability.

Note also that NOW's superior growth in net income between Year 1 and Year 2 is not attributable to superior performance compared to CAP but rather to the accounting decision to recognise the expense sooner than CAP. In general, all else equal, accounting decisions that result in recognising expenses sooner will give the appearance of greater subsequent growth. Comparison of the growth of the two companies' net incomes without an awareness of the difference in accounting methods would be misleading. As a corollary, NOW's income and profitability exhibit greater volatility across the three years, not because of more volatile performance but rather because of the different accounting decision.

Solution to 3:

NOW reports an increase in cash of €70 in Year 1, while CAP reports a decrease in cash of €110 because NOW's taxes were €180 lower than CAP's taxes (€30 versus €210).

Note that this problem assumes the accounting method used by each company for its tax purposes is identical to the accounting method used by the company for its financial reporting. In many countries, companies are allowed to use different depreciation methods for financial reporting and taxes, which may give rise to deferred taxes.

As shown, discretion regarding whether to expense or capitalise expenditures can impede comparability across companies. Example 1 assumes the companies purchase a single asset in one year. Because the sum of net income over the three-year period is identical whether the asset is capitalised or expensed, it illustrates that although capitalising results in higher profitability compared to expensing in the first year, it results in lower profitability ratios in the subsequent years. Conversely, expensing results in lower profitability in the first year but higher profitability in later years, indicating a favorable trend.

Similarly, shareholders' equity for a company that capitalises the expenditure will be higher in the early years because the initially higher profits result in initially higher retained earnings. Example 1 assumes the companies purchase a single asset in one year and report identical amounts of total net income over the three-year period, so shareholders' equity (and retained earnings) for the firm that expenses will be identical to shareholders' equity (and retained earnings) for the capitalising firm at the end of the three-year period.

Although Example 1 shows companies purchasing an asset only in the first year, if a company continues to purchase similar or increasing amounts of assets each year, the profitability-enhancing effect of capitalising continues if the amount of the expenditures in a period continues to be more than the depreciation expense. Example 2 illustrates this point.

EXAMPLE 2

Impact of Capitalising versus Expensing for Ongoing Purchases

A company buys a £300 computer in Year 1 and capitalises the expenditure. The computer has a useful life of three years and an expected salvage value of £0, so the annual depreciation expense using the straight-line method is £100 per year. Compared to expensing the entire £300 immediately, the company's pre-tax profit in Year 1 is £200 greater.

1   Assume that the company continues to buy an identical computer each year at the same price. If the company uses the same accounting treatment for each of the computers, when does the profit-enhancing effect of capitalising versus expensing end?

2   If the company buys another identical computer in Year 4, using the same accounting treatment as the prior years, what is the effect on Year 4 profits of capitalising versus expensing these expenditures?

Solution to 1:

The profit-enhancing effect of capitalising versus expensing would end in Year 3. In Year 3, the depreciation expense on each of the three computers bought in Years 1, 2, and 3 would total £300 (£100 + £100 + £100). Therefore, the total depreciation expense for Year 3 will be exactly equal to the capital expenditure in Year 3. The expense in Year 3 would be £300, regardless of whether the company capitalised or expensed the annual computer purchases.

Solution to 2:

There is no impact on Year 4 profits. As in the previous year, the depreciation expense on each of the three computers bought in Years 2, 3, and 4 would total £300 (£100 + £100 + £100). Therefore, the total depreciation expense for Year 4 will be exactly equal to the capital expenditure in Year 4. Pre-tax profits would be reduced by £300, regardless of whether the company capitalised or expensed the annual computer purchases.

Compared to expensing an expenditure, capitalising the expenditure typically results in greater amounts reported as cash from operations. Capitalised expenditures are typically treated as an investment cash outflow whereas expenses reduce operating cash flows. Because cash flow from operating activities is an important consideration in some valuation models, companies may try to maximise reported cash flow from operations by capitalising expenditures that should be expensed. Valuation models that use free cash flow will consider not only operating cash flows but also investing cash flows. Analysts should be alert to evidence of companies manipulating reported cash flow from operations by capitalising expenditures that should be expensed.

In summary, holding all else constant, capitalising an expenditure enhances current profitability and increases reported cash flow from operations. The profitability-enhancing effect of capitalising continues so long as capital expenditures exceed the depreciation expense. Profitability-enhancing motivations for decisions to capitalise should be considered when analyzing performance. For example, a company may choose to capitalise more expenditures (within the allowable bounds of accounting standards) to achieve earnings targets for a given period. Expensing a cost in the period reduces current period profits but enhances future profitability and thus enhances the profit trend. Profit trend-enhancing motivations should also be considered when analyzing performance. If the company is in a reporting environment which requires identical accounting methods for financial reporting and taxes (unlike the United States, which permits companies to use depreciation methods for reporting purposes that differ from the depreciation method required by tax purposes), then expensing will have a more favorable cash flow impact because paying lower taxes in an earlier period creates an opportunity to earn interest income on the cash saved.

In contrast with the relatively simple examples above, it is generally neither possible nor desirable to identify individual instances involving discretion about whether to capitalise or expense expenditures. An analyst can, however, typically identify significant items of expenditure treated differently across companies. The items of expenditure giving rise to the most relevant differences across companies will vary by industry. This cross-industry variation is apparent in the following discussion of the capitalisation of expenditures.

2.1 Capitalisation of Interest Costs

Companies generally must capitalise interest costs associated with acquiring or constructing an asset that requires a long period of time to get ready for its intended use.[6] For example, constructing a building to sell or for a company's own use typically requires a substantial amount of time; any interest cost incurred, prior to completion, to finance construction is capitalised as part of the cost of the asset. The company determines the interest rate to use based on its existing borrowings or, if applicable, on a borrowing specifically incurred for constructing the asset. If a company takes out a loan specifically to construct a building, the interest cost on that loan during the time of construction would be capitalised as part of the building's cost.

As a consequence of this accounting treatment, a company's interest costs for a period can appear either on the balance sheet (to the extent they are capitalised) or on the income statement (to the extent they are expensed).

If the interest expenditure is incurred in connection with constructing an asset for the company's own use, the capitalised interest appears on the balance sheet as a part of the relevant long-lived asset. The capitalised interest is expensed over time as the property is depreciated—and is thus part of depreciation expense rather than interest expense. If the interest expenditure is incurred in connection with constructing an asset to sell, for example by a real estate construction company, the capitalised interest appears on the company's balance sheet as part of inventory. The capitalised interest is then expensed as part of the cost of sales when the asset is sold.

The treatment of capitalised interest poses certain issues that analysts should consider. First, capitalised interest appears as part of investing cash outflows, whereas expensed interest reduces operating cash flow. Although the treatment is consistent with accounting standards, an analyst may want to examine the impact on reported cash flows. Second, interest coverage ratios are solvency indicators measuring the extent to which a company's earnings (or cash flow) in a period covered its interest costs. To provide a true picture of a company's interest coverage, the entire amount of interest expenditure, both the capitalised portion and the expensed portion, should be used in calculating interest coverage ratios. Additionally, if a company is depreciating interest that it capitalised in a previous period, income should be adjusted to eliminate the effect of that depreciation. Example 3 illustrates the calculation.

---

6 IAS 23 [Borrowing Costs] and FASB ASC Subtopic 835-20 [Interest–Capitalization of Interest] specify respectively IFRS and US GAAP for capitalisation of interest costs. Although the standards are not completely converged, the standards are in general agreement.

EXAMPLE 3

Effect of Capitalised Interest Costs on Coverage Ratios and Cash Flow

MTR Gaming Group, Inc. (NASDAQGS: MNTG) disclosed the following information in one of the footnotes to its financial statements: "Interest is allocated and capitalized to construction in progress by applying our cost of borrowing rate to qualifying assets. Interest capitalized in 2007 and 2006 was $2.2 million and $6.0 million, respectively. There was no interest capitalized during 2008." (Form 10-K filed 13 March 2009).

Exhibit 2	MTR Gaming Group Selected Data, as Reported (Dollars in Thousands)		
	2008	**2007**	**2006**
EBIT (from income statement)	432,686	389,268	268,800
Interest expense (from income statement)	40,764	34,774	17,047
Interest capitalised (from footnote)	0	2,200	6,000
Net cash provided by operating activities	14,693	14,980	42,206
Net cash from (used) in investing activities	41,620	(144,824)	(162,415)

1 Calculate and interpret MTR's interest coverage ratio with and without capitalised interest. Assume that capitalised interest increases depreciation expense by $475 thousand in 2008 and 2007, and by $365 thousand in 2006.

2 Calculate MTR's percentage change in operating cash flow from 2006 to 2007 and from 2007 to 2008. Assuming the financial reporting does not affect reporting for income taxes, what were the effects of capitalised interest on operating and investing cash flows?

Solution to 1:

MTR did not capitalise any interest during 2008, so the interest coverage ratio for this year is affected only by depreciation expense related to previously capitalised interest. The interest coverage ratio, measured as earnings before interest and taxes (EBIT) divided by interest expense, was as follows for 2008:

10.61 ($432,686 ÷ $40,764) for 2008 without adjusting for capitalised interest; and

10.63 [($432,686 + $475) ÷ $40,764] including an adjustment to EBIT for depreciation of previously capitalised interest.

For the years 2007 and 2006, interest coverage ratios with and without capitalised interest were as follows:

For 2007

11.19 ($389,268 ÷ $34,774) without adjusting for capitalised interest; and

10.54 [($389,268 + $475) ÷ ($34,774 + $2,200)] including an adjustment to EBIT for depreciation of previously capitalised interest and an adjustment to interest expense for the amount of interest capitalised in 2007.

For 2006

15.77 ($268,800 ÷ $17,047) without adjusting for capitalised interest; and

11.68 [($268,800 + $365) ÷ ($17,047 + $6,000)] including an adjustment to EBIT for depreciation of previously capitalised interest and an adjustment to interest expense for the amount of interest capitalised in 2006.

Because MTR capitalises interest in previous years, EBIT is adjusted by adding in depreciation expense due to capitalised interest costs.

The above calculations indicate that MTR's interest coverage deteriorated over the three-year period from 2006 to 2008, even with no adjustments for capitalised interest. In both 2006 and 2007, the coverage ratio is lower when adjusted for capitalised interest. For 2006, the interest coverage ratio of 11.68 that includes capitalised interest is substantially lower than the ratio without capitalised interest.

Solution to 2:

If the interest had been expensed rather than capitalised, operating cash flows would have been substantially lower in 2006, slightly lower in 2007, but unchanged in 2008. If the interest had been expensed rather than capitalised, the trend—at least in the last two years—would have been more favorable; operating cash flows would have increased rather than decreased over the 2007 to 2008 period. On an unadjusted basis, for 2008 compared with 2007, MTR's operating cash flow declined by 1.9 percent [($14,693 ÷ $14,980) −1]. If the $2,200 of interest had been expensed rather than capitalised in 2007, the change in operating cash flow would have been positive, 15.0 percent {[$14,693 ÷ ($14,980 − $2,200)] − 1}.

If interest had been expensed rather than capitalised, the amount of cash outflow for investing activities would have been lower in 2006 and 2007 but unaffected in 2008. The percentage decline in cash outflows for investing activities from 2006 to 2007 would have been slightly smaller excluding capitalised interest from investing activities, 8.8 percent {[$144,824 − $2,200) ÷ ($162,415 − $6,000)] − 1}.

Generally, including capitalised interest in the calculation of interest coverage ratios provides a better assessment of a company's solvency. In assigning credit ratings, rating agencies include capitalised interest in coverage ratios. For example, Standard & Poor's calculates the EBIT interest coverage ratio as EBIT divided by gross interest (defined as interest prior to deductions for capitalised interest or interest income).

Maintaining a minimum interest coverage ratio is a financial covenant often included in lending agreements, e.g., bank loans and bond indentures. The definition of the coverage ratio can be found in the company's credit agreement. The definition is relevant because treatment of capitalised interest in calculating coverage ratios would affect an assessment of how close a company's actual ratios are to the levels specified by its financial covenants and thus the probability of breaching those covenants.

2.2 Capitalisation of Internal Development Costs

Costs to internally develop intangible assets are generally expensed when incurred, although there are exceptions, some of which are described in this section.

IFRS require that expenditures on *research* (or during the research phase of an internal project) be expensed rather than capitalised as an intangible asset. Research is defined as "original and planned investigation undertaken with the prospect of gaining new scientific or technical knowledge and understanding."[7] An example of an internal project is the search for alternative materials or systems to use in a production process. The research phase of an internal project refers to the period during which a company cannot demonstrate that an intangible asset will be created. IFRS allow companies to recognise an internal asset arising from *development* (or the development phase of an internal project) if certain criteria are met, including a demonstration of the technical feasibility of completing the intangible asset and the intent to use or sell the asset. Development is defined in IAS 38 as "the application of research findings or other knowledge to a plan or design for the production of new or substantially improved materials, devices, products, processes, systems, or services before the start of commercial production or use."

Generally, US GAAP require that research and development costs be expensed, although there are certain exceptions.[8] For example, certain costs related to software development must be capitalised. Costs incurred to develop a software product for sale are expensed until the product's feasibility is established, and capitalised after the product's feasibility has been established. In addition, companies capitalise costs related directly to developing software for internal use, such as the costs of employees who help build and test the software. Even though standards require companies to capitalise software development costs after a product's feasibility is established, judgment in determining feasibility means that companies' capitalisation practices differ. For example, if only a short period elapses between the time a company establishes feasibility and the time that a company markets its products, it may conclude that the amount of development costs to be capitalised are immaterial and should be expensed. Exhibit 3 illustrates this concept.

Exhibit 3   Disclosure on Software Development Costs

Excerpt from Notes to Consolidated Financial Statements—Note 1 of Apple Inc. (NASDAQGS: AAPL):

> Research and development costs are expensed as incurred. Development costs of computer software to be sold, leased, or otherwise marketed are subject to capitalization beginning when a product's technological feasibility has been established and ending when a product is available for general release to customers. In most instances, the Company's products are released soon after technological feasibility has been established. Therefore, costs incurred subsequent to achievement of technological feasibility are usually not significant, and generally most software development costs have been expensed.
>
> In 2009 and 2008, the Company capitalized $71 million and $11 million, respectively, of costs associated with the development of Mac OS X Version 10.6 Snow Leopard ("Mac OS X Snow Leopard"), which was released during the fourth quarter of 2009. During 2007, the Company capitalized $75 million of costs associated with the development of Mac OS X Version 10.5 Leopard ("Mac OS X Leopard")

(continued)

---

7 IAS 38 [Intangible Assets].
8 FASB ASC Topic 730 [Research and Development]; FASB ASC Subtopic 350-40 [Intangibles–Internal-Use Software]; FASB ASC Subtopic 985-20 [Software–Costs of Software to be Sold, Leased, or Marketed].

Exhibit 3   (Continued)

and iPhone software. The capitalized costs are being amortized to cost of sales on a straight-line basis over a three year estimated useful life of the underlying technology.

Source: Apple's Form 10-K for the year ended 26 September 2009.

As with other types of expenditures, expensing rather than capitalising development costs results in lower net income in the current period. The cumulative effect will also reduce net income so long as the amount of the current period development costs is higher than the expense that would have resulted from amortising prior periods' capitalised development costs—the typical situation when a company's development costs are increasing. On the statement of cash flows, expensing rather than capitalising development costs results in an operating cash outflow rather than an investing cash outflow.

In comparing the financial performance of a company that expenses most or all software development costs, such as Apple, with another company that capitalises software development costs, adjustments can be made to make the two comparable. For the company that capitalises software development costs, an analyst can adjust a) the income statement to include software development costs as an expense and to exclude amortisation of prior years' software development costs; b) the balance sheet to exclude capitalised software (decrease assets and equity); and c) the statement of cash flows to decrease operating cash flows and decrease cash used in investing by the amount of the current period development costs. Any ratios that include income, long-lived assets, or cash flow from operations—such as return on equity—will also be affected.

EXAMPLE 4

Software Development Costs

You are working on a project involving the analysis of JHH Software, a (hypothetical) software development company that established technical feasibility for its first product in 2007. Part of your analysis involves computing certain market-based ratios, which you will use to compare JHH to another company that expenses all of its software development expenditures. Relevant data and excerpts from the company's annual report are included in Exhibit 4.

Exhibit 4 JHH Software (Dollars in Thousands, Except Per-Share Amounts)			
CONSOLIDATED STATEMENT OF EARNINGS—abbreviated			
For year ended 31 December:	**2009**	**2008**	**2007**
Total revenue	$91,424	$91,134	$96,293
Total operating expenses	78,107	78,908	85,624
Operating income	13,317	12,226	10,669
Provision for income taxes	3,825	4,232	3,172
Net income	9,492	7,994	7,497
Earnings per share (EPS)	$1.40	$0.82	$0.68

Exhibit 4 (Continued)

STATEMENT OF CASH FLOWS—abbreviated

For year ended 31 December:	2009	2008	2007
Net cash provided by operating activities	$15,007	$14,874	$15,266
Net cash used in investing activities*	(11,549)	(4,423)	(5,346)
Net cash used in financing activities	(8,003)	(7,936)	(7,157)
Net change in cash and cash equivalents	($4,545)	$2,515	$2,763
*Includes software development expenses of and includes capital	($6,000)	($4,000)	($2,000)
expenditures of	($2,000)	($1,600)	($1,200)

Additional information:

For year ended 31 December:	2009	2008	2007
Market value of outstanding debt	0	0	0
Amortisation of capitalised software development expenses	($2,000)	($667)	$0
Depreciation expense	($2,200)	($1,440)	($1,320)
Market price per share of common stock	$42	$26	$17
Shares of common stock outstanding (thousands)	6,780	9,765	10,999

Footnote disclosure of accounting policy for software development:
Expenses that are related to the conceptual formulation and design of software products are expensed to research and development as incurred. The company capitalises expenses that are incurred to produce the finished product after technological feasibility has been established.

1 Compute the following ratios for JHH based on the reported financial statements for fiscal year ended 31 December 2009, with no adjustments. Next, determine the approximate impact on these ratios if the company had expensed rather than capitalised its investments in software. (Assume the financial reporting does not affect reporting for income taxes. There would be no change in the effective tax rate.)

A P/E: Price/Earnings per share.

B P/CFO: Price/Operating cash flow per share.

C EV/EBITDA: Enterprise value/EBITDA, where enterprise value is defined as the total market value of all sources of a company's financing, including equity and debt, and EBITDA is earnings before interest, taxes, depreciation, and amortisation.

2 Interpret the changes in the ratios.

Solution to 1:

(Dollars are in thousands, except per-share amounts.) JHH's 2009 ratios are presented in the following table:

	Ratios	As Reported	As Adjusted
A.	P/E ratio	30.0	42.9
B.	P/CFO	19.0	31.6
C.	EV/EBITDA	16.3	24.7

A Based on the information as reported, the P/E ratio was 30.0 ($42 ÷ $1.40). Based on EPS adjusted to expense software development costs, the P/E ratio was 42.9 ($42 ÷ $0.98).

- Price: Assuming that the market value of the company's equity is based on its fundamentals, the price per share is $42, regardless of a difference in accounting.

- EPS: As reported, EPS was $1.40. Adjusted EPS was $0.98. Expensing software development costs would have reduced JHH's 2009 operating income by $6,000, but the company would have reported no amortisation of prior years' software costs, which would have increased operating income by $2,000. The net change of $4,000 would have reduced operating income from the reported $13,317 to $9,317. The effective tax rate for 2009 ($3,825 ÷ $13,317) is 28.72%, and using this effective tax rate would give an adjusted net income of $6,641 [$9,317 × (1 − 0.2872)], compared to $9,492 before the adjustment. The EPS would therefore be reduced from the reported $1.40 to $0.98 (adjusted net income of $6,641 divided by 6,780 shares).

B Based on information as reported, the P/CFO was 19.0 ($42 ÷ $2.21). Based on CFO adjusted to expense software development costs, the P/CFO was 31.6 ($42 ÷ $1.33).

- Price: Assuming that the market value of the company's equity is based on its fundamentals, the price per share is $42, regardless of a difference in accounting.

- CFO per share, as reported, was $2.21 (total operating cash flows $15,007 ÷ 6,780 shares).

- CFO per share, as adjusted, was $1.33. The company's $6,000 expenditure on software development costs was reported as a cash outflow from investing activities, so expensing those costs would reduce cash from operating activities by $6,000, from the reported $15,007 to $9,007. Dividing adjusted total operating cash flow of $9,007 by 6,780 shares results in cash flow per share of $1.33.

C Based on information as reported, the EV/EBITDA was 16.3 ($284,760 ÷ $17,517). Based on EBITDA adjusted to expense software development costs, the EV/EBITDA was 24.7 ($284,760 ÷ $11,517).

- Enterprise Value: Enterprise value is the sum of the market value of the company's equity and debt. JHH has no debt, and therefore the enterprise value is equal to the market value of its equity. The market value of its equity is $284,760 ($42 per share × 6,780 shares).

- EBITDA, as reported, was $17,517 (earnings before interest and taxes of $13,317 plus $2,200 depreciation plus $2,000 amortisation).

- EBITDA, adjusted for expensing software development costs by the inclusion of $6,000 development expense and the exclusion of $2,000 amortisation of prior expense, would be $11,517 (earnings before interest and taxes of $9,317 plus $2,200 depreciation plus $0 amortisation).

Solution to 2:

Expensing software development costs would decrease historical profits, operating cash flow, and EBITDA, and would thus increase all market multiples. So JHH's stock would appear more expensive if it expensed rather than capitalised the software development costs.

If the unadjusted market-based ratios were used in the comparison of JHH to its competitor that expenses all software development expenditures, then JHH might appear to be under-priced when the difference is solely related to accounting factors. JHH's adjusted market-based ratios provide a better basis for comparison.

For the company in Example 4, current period software development expenditures exceed the amortisation of prior periods' capitalised software development expenditures. As a result, expensing rather than capitalising software development costs would have the effect of lowering income. If, however, software development expenditures slowed such that current expenditures were lower than the amortisation of prior periods' capitalised software development expenditures, then expensing software development costs would have the effect of increasing income relative to capitalising it.

This section illustrated how decisions about capitalising versus expensing impact financial statements and ratios. Earlier expensing lowers current profits but enhances trends, whereas capitalising now and expensing later enhances current profits. The next section illustrates how decisions about depreciation methods can impact financial statements and ratios.

DEPRECIATION

Capitalised costs of long-lived tangible assets (other than land which is not depreciated) and long-lived intangible assets with finite useful lives are allocated to subsequent periods via depreciation and amortisation expense, respectively. From this point forward, the term *depreciation* should be read as though it refers to depreciation or amortisation as appropriate. This section first examines the financial statement impact of choices about depreciation methods and judgments about useful lives and residual values. We then illustrate one use of financial disclosures to analyze long-lived assets.

3.1 Depreciation Methods

This section compares the financial statement impact of various depreciation methods. The method chosen should reflect the pattern in which the asset's future economic benefits are consumed. Accelerated depreciation methods, such as the double-declining balance method, result in higher depreciation expense (lower income) in earlier years and lower depreciation expense (higher income) in later years. Straight-line methods result in an even depreciation expense over the life of an asset. Production-based methods such as the units-of-production method can potentially result in variable depreciation expense.

EXAMPLE 5

Financial Statement Impact of Alternative Depreciation Methods

You are analyzing three (hypothetical) companies: EVEN-LI Co., SOONER Inc., and AZUSED Co. Each of the companies buys an identical piece of box-manufacturing equipment at a cost of $2,300, and each estimates the equipment's salvage value of $100. However, each company uses a different method of depreciation, as disclosed in the footnotes to their financial statements (including relevant assumptions).

Depreciation Method and Relevant Assumptions

- EVEN-LI uses the straight-line method and estimates the useful life of the equipment at 4 years.

- SOONER uses the double-declining balance method for the first year, switching to straight-line for the remaining years and estimates the useful life of the equipment at 4 years.

- AZUSED uses units-of-production method, assuming total productive capacity of 800 boxes. (Assume the following production: 200 boxes in Year 1; 300 boxes in Year 2; 200 boxes in Year 3; and 100 boxes in Year 4.)

Exhibit 5 presents the year-by-year book value, depreciation expense, and accumulated depreciation for each company.

Exhibit 5	Comparative Year-by-Year Book Value, Depreciation Expense, and Accumulated Depreciation			
	Beginning Net Book Value ($)	**Depreciation Expense ($)**	**Accumulated Year-End Depreciation ($)**	**Ending Net Book Value ($)**
EVEN-LI Co.				
Year 1	2,300	550	550	1,750
Year 2	1,750	550	1,100	1,200
Year 3	1,200	550	1,650	650
Year 4	650	550	2,200	100
SOONER Inc.				
Year 1	2,300	1,150	1,150	1,150
Year 2	1,150	350	1,500	800
Year 3	800	350	1,850	450
Year 4	450	350	2,200	100
AZUSED Co.				
Year 1	2,300	550	550	1,750
Year 2	1,750	825	1,375	925
Year 3	925	550	1,925	375
Year 4	375	275	2,200	100

Assume the following for each company: Revenues in each year were $3,000; expenses, other than depreciation and tax, were $1,000; and the tax rate is 32 percent.

1 Calculate each company's net profit margin (net income divided by sales) for each of the four years.

2 Assess the impact of the depreciation method on the comparative net profit margins.

Solution to 1:

Calculations in Exhibit 6 are as follows:

- Income before tax = Revenues of $3,000 – Expenses (other than depreciation) of $1,000 – Depreciation expense for each company
- Net income = Income before tax x (1 minus tax rate)
- Net profit margin = Net income ÷ Sales

Exhibit 6   Net Profit Margin

	Income before Tax ($)	Net Income ($)	Net Profit Margin (%)
EVEN-LI Co.			
Year 1	1,450	986	32.9
Year 2	1,450	986	32.9
Year 3	1,450	986	32.9
Year 4	1,450	986	32.9
SOONER Inc.			
Year 1	850	578	19.3
Year 2	1,650	1,122	37.4
Year 3	1,650	1,122	37.4
Year 4	1,650	1,122	37.4
AZUSED Co.			
Year 1	1,450	986	32.9
Year 2	1,175	799	26.6
Year 3	1,450	986	32.9
Year 4	1,725	1,173	39.1

Solution to 2:

Because revenues and expenses other than depreciation are assumed equal in each year, EVEN-LI, which uses straight-line depreciation, reports the same income before tax, net income, and net profit margin for each of the four years. SOONER, which uses an accelerated depreciation method in the first year, reports lower income before tax, net income, and net profit margin in the initial year because its depreciation expense is higher in that year. This company shows a positive trend in income and net profit margin, at least at the beginning of the asset's life. AZUSED, which employs a usage-based depreciation method, reports income before tax, net income, and a net profit margin that varies with the variations in usage of the asset.

Note, that the cumulative net income ($3,944) is the same over the 4-year period for all three companies. However, if a company's value is based on the present value of future cash flows. The company with higher cash flows in earlier years due to lower taxes may have a higher value.

3.2 Estimates Required for Depreciation Calculations

Estimates required for depreciation calculations include the useful life of the equipment (or its total lifetime productive capacity) and its expected residual value at the end of that useful life. A longer useful life and higher expected residual value decrease the amount of annual depreciation relative to a shorter useful life and lower expected residual value.

A company makes estimates used in the calculation of depreciation expense when depreciable assets are acquired or it may adopt estimates for major asset groups. The estimates are periodically reviewed. When a company determines that a change in an estimate is needed, the change is made going forward (prospectively). That is, the new estimate is applied to the current carrying amount going forward. Below is an example of how to incorporate a change in estimates to calculate depreciation expense and its effect on income.

EXAMPLE 6

Changing Estimates Used in the Depreciation Expense Calculation

Peacock Company, a (hypothetical) manufacturer of ornamental hardware, acquired a piece of machinery for $1,100,000 on 2 January Year 1. Originally, Peacock estimated the equipment would have a useful life of 5 years and $100,000 residual value. In December, Year three, Peacock determines that the useful life should be extended from five years to eight years. The residual value does not change. It uses the straight-line depreciation method.

1   What amount of depreciation expense is reported in Year 1 and Year 2?

2   What amount of depreciation expense is reported in Year 3?

3   What is the effect on income before taxes of the change in the useful life in Year 3?

Solution to 1:

In Year 1 and Year 2, Peacock's depreciation expense is $200,000 [(acquisition cost – residual value) ÷ estimated years of useful life = ($1,100,000 – $100, 000) ÷ 5].

Solution to 2:

The depreciation expense in Year 3 is $100,000. To estimate the amount of depreciation expense in Year 3, Peacock first determines the carrying amount of the machine (which is the amount of the machine remaining to be depreciated) and the machine's remaining useful life at the beginning of Year 3. The carrying amount of the machine is $700,000, determined as its acquisition cost of $1,100,000 less accumulated depreciation of $400,000 ($200,000 depreciation expense per year times two years). The remaining useful life of the machine is six years, determined as the new useful life of eight years less the two years the machine has already been used. The new depreciation expense of $100,000 is calculated as the carrying amount of $700,000 less the residual value of $100,000 divided by six years [($700,000 – $100,000)/6].

Solution to 3:

Income before taxes increases by $100,000 ($200,000 original depreciation expenses less $100,000 new depreciation expense) due to extending the machine's useful life.

In Exhibit 7, Franklin Towers Enterprises, Inc., a Chinese company listed on the OTCBB, discloses its increase in the useful lives used to estimate the depreciation of production equipment and its rationale for this change.

Exhibit 7   Disclosure of Changes in Estimates Used to Calculate Depreciation Expense

Franklin Towers Enterprises, Inc. (OTCBB: FRTW), disclosure of change in estimates used to calculate depreciation expense from its fiscal 2008 10-K filing.

NOTE 5—Property and Equipment

During the first quarter of 2008, management reviewed the useful lives and residual value of the Company's machinery and equipment and compared to industry standards. Management has determined the production equipment acquired in 2007, which were originally estimated to have 5–7 years useful lives should be increased to 10-years useful lives and with a residual value of 5% of their original cost. Accordingly, effective January 1, 2008, the Company has changed the depreciation lives for the production equipment and auxiliary equipment to 10 years.

Additional estimates are required to allocate depreciation expense between the cost of sales (cost of goods sold) and selling, general, and administrative expenses (SG&A). Footnotes to the financial statements often disclose some information regarding which income statement line item includes depreciation, although the exact amount of detail disclosed by individual companies varies. Including a higher proportion of depreciation expense in cost of sales lowers the gross margin and lowers the operating expenses, but does not affect the operating margin. When comparing two companies, apportionment of depreciation to cost of sales versus SG&A can contribute to explaining differences in gross margins and operating expenses.

The processes of depreciation and amortisation serve to allocate the cost of long-lived assets over the useful life of the asset, periodically reflecting a portion of the historical cost as depreciation or amortisation expense and correspondingly reducing the carrying amount of the asset. The next section focuses on two types of accounting processes that can change the carrying amount of an asset differently than the periodic allocation of the asset's cost: impairment and revaluation.

4   IMPAIRMENT AND REVALUATION OF LONG-LIVED ASSETS

Impairment charges reflect an unanticipated decline in the value of an asset. Both IFRS and US GAAP require companies to write down the carrying amount of impaired assets.[9] Impairment reversals—namely, writing the value of an asset back up if the value of the asset increases—is permitted under IFRS. Under US GAAP, however, reversing an impairment charge on an asset held for use is prohibited.

Another accounting process that can change the value of an asset differently than the periodic allocation of the asset's cost is the use of the revaluation model for valuing long-lived assets. Note the revaluation model is not allowed under US GAAP, and the discussion therefore pertains exclusively to IFRS.

4.1 Impairment of Long-lived Tangible Assets Held for Use

For long-lived tangible assets held for use, impairment losses are recognised when the asset's carrying amount is not recoverable and its carrying amount exceeds its fair value. Both of these concepts are based on the asset's carrying amount relative to its expected future cash flows. However, IFRS and US GAAP differ somewhat in both the guidelines for determining that impairment has occurred and in the measurement of any impairment loss. Under IAS 36, an impairment loss is measured as the excess of carrying amount over the recoverable amount of the asset. The recoverable amount is defined as "the higher of its fair value less costs to sell and its value in use." Value in use is a discounted measure of expected future cash flows. Under US GAAP, a two-step test is used to determine whether an asset is impaired. First, recoverability is assessed: An asset's carrying amount is considered not recoverable when the asset's carrying amount exceeds the undiscounted expected future cash flows. Second, if the asset's carrying amount is considered not recoverable, the impairment loss is measured as the difference between the asset's fair value and carrying amount.

The impairment loss will reduce the carrying amount of the asset on the balance sheet and will reduce net income on the income statement. The impairment loss is a non-cash item and will not affect cash flow from operations. As with any accounting estimate, management's estimate of an impairment loss may be affected by a motivation to manage earnings.

EXAMPLE 7

Implications of Impairment Charges in Financial Statement Analysis

Assume that OmeTech (a hypothetical company) owns one asset with a carrying amount of $2,000. The asset is manufacturing equipment that produces two products: the Ome-Gizmo and the Tech-Gizmo. An adverse event occurs that requires evaluation of the asset for impairment; one of OmeTech's competitors wins a lawsuit confirming its right to a patent on the technology underlying the Tech-Gizmo, leaving OmeTech with a single product. Because the equipment is highly specialised and can now only be used to manufacture a single product for

---

9 IAS 36 [Impairment of Assets] defines an impairment loss as "the amount by which the carrying amount of an asset or a cash-generating unit exceeds its recoverable amount." FASB ASC Glossary defines impairment as "the condition that exists when the carrying amount of a long-lived asset (asset group) exceeds its fair value."

which there is finite demand, OmeTech believes that this adverse event reduces the recoverable value of their manufacturing equipment to an amount below its carrying cost. Based on new estimates that the future cash flows from the equipment will total $300 per year for the next five years, and an assumed discount rate of 10 percent, the company estimates the fair value of the equipment is now $1,137 (calculated as the present value of a $300 per year cash flow for five years). The company thus determines it has an impairment loss of $863.

1   Where will the impairment loss appear in the company's financial statements?

2   How should the impairment loss be viewed in the context of evaluating past earnings and cash flow?

3   How should the impairment loss be viewed in the context of projecting future earnings and cash flow?

4   Compare and contrast the determination and reporting of any impairment loss under IFRS and US GAAP.

Solution to 1:

On the balance sheet, the impairment loss will reduce the carrying amount of the relevant long-lived asset, with detail on the impairment loss itself in the footnotes to the financial statements and the MD&A. On the income statement (and thus ultimately in the retained earnings account on the balance sheet), the impairment loss will reduce income. In the operating section of the statement of cash flows, the reconciliation of net income to cash flows from operating activities will add back the impairment charge because it represents a non-cash item.

Solution to 2:

Because the historical depreciation charge was insufficient to represent the full decline in the equipment's value, historical earnings may have been overstated. In evaluating past earnings, it should be understood that recognition and measurement of impairment charges are highly judgmental and thus can offer the potential for a company to manage its earnings. The direction of earnings management, to the extent that it exists, depends on what is motivating the management team. For example, a new management team might be motivated to show improvements in future performance, so recognising a substantial impairment charge in the current period will contribute to presenting a favorable trend. Alternatively, a management team that is close to missing a targeted earnings benchmark might be motivated to underestimate the impairment loss. In the context of evaluating past cash flow, an impairment charge does not affect cash flow. However, if the impairment loss relates to an asset that was relatively recently acquired, comparing the impairment loss to the amount invested to acquire the asset may offer some insight into management's ability to make successful acquisitions.

Solution to 3:

In projecting future earnings, impairment losses would typically be considered non-recurring and thus would not be included in future projections. In projecting future cash flows, the impairment loss can provide some guidance. In this hypothetical example with only a single machine, the disclosures would provide a fairly transparent picture of management's expectations about its future cash flows. If an analyst or other user of the financial statements made identical assumptions of a five year remaining life of the equipment and a 10 percent discount rate, the user could derive the expected future annual cash flows by calculating what annuity a present value of $1,137 would yield over five years at an interest rate of 10 percent, namely $300 per annum. The information from the impairment loss could be used as an input to an analyst's own future cash flow projections, based on his own expectations about the company's sales and profit margins, given information and assumptions about future demand for the product and competitive pressures.

Solution to 4:

In this example, an impairment loss of $863 will be reported under both IFRS and US GAAP. Under IFRS, the asset is considered impaired if its carrying amount is greater than its recoverable amount. The company thus determines it has an impairment loss of $863 ($2,000 carrying amount less the $1,137 present value of future cash flows). Under US GAAP, the first step in determining impairment is assessing recoverability by comparing the carrying amount to future undiscounted cash flows. Because the carrying amount of $2,000 is greater than the $1,500 future undiscounted cash flows (five years at $300 per year), the recoverability test is not satisfied. The second step under US GAAP then compares the carrying amount to fair value to determine the impairment loss of $863.

In practice, neither companies' businesses nor their disclosures are as simplistic as the above example. Nonetheless, impairment disclosures can provide similarly useful information. Exhibit 8 provides a footnote from the financial statements of Abitibi-Consolidated. The footnotes provide information about three properties assessed for potential impairment. Based on the information, we can estimate that the company forecasts undiscounted future cash flows on the three properties of around C$1,014 million (32 percent more than the book value of the three properties: C$250 million + C$174 million + C$344 million.) An assumption that the average remaining life of these assets is approximately the same as the estimated remaining life of the company's overall PPE asset base of 9.4 years, would indicate projected annual future cash flows from these three properties of C$108 million (C$1,014 million ÷ 9.4 years). While this cash flow projection is clearly a broad estimate, it could provide a useful basis of comparison for an analyst's own projections based on his own assumptions about the future cash flows of the company.

Exhibit 8   Disclosure of Impairment of Long-lived Assets

Excerpt from Financial Statement Footnotes of Abitibi-Consolidated Inc. (NYSE: ABY; TSX:A):

> IMPAIRMENT OF LONG-LIVED ASSETS
>
> During the fourth quarter of 2006, the Company conducted the initial step of the impairment tests on the Bridgewater, United Kingdom, paper mill and on the "Wood products" segment as a result of operating losses. The Company also conducted the initial step on the indefinitely idled Lufkin, Texas, paper mill. Estimates of future cash flows used to test the recoverability of a long-lived asset are mainly derived in the same manner as the projections of cash flows used in the initial step of the goodwill impairment test. In addition, the impairment test for the Lufkin paper mill was performed in light of a scenario of the mill's restart producing lightweight coated paper under a partnership structure.
>
> The Company concluded that the recognition of an impairment charge for the business units analyzed was not required, as the estimated undiscounted cash flows exceeded the book values by at least 32%. Certain paper mills and sawmills are particularly sensitive to the

Exhibit 8   (Continued)

key assumptions. Given the inherent imprecision and corresponding importance of the key assumptions used in the impairment test, it is reasonably possible that changes in future conditions may lead management to use different key assumptions, which could require a material change in the book value of these assets. The total book value of these assets was $250 million, $174 million and $344 million for the "Newsprint", "Commercial printing papers" and "Wood products" segments, respectively, as at December 31, 2006.

Source: Form 40-F for the year ended 31 December 2006, page 5, filed 15 March 2007.

Continuously testing the value of all these assets would obviously be impractical, so accounting standards set guidelines for when the tests must be done. For all long-lived assets, IFRS require that companies assess annually whether there are any indications that an asset might be impaired and then undertake an impairment test if such indications are present.[10] In contrast, US GAAP require that companies only undertake an impairment test for an asset group within property, plant, and equipment if "events or changes in circumstances indicate that its carrying amount may not be recoverable."[11] IFRS and US GAAP require that goodwill and identifiable intangible assets that are not amortised be tested for impairment annually, or more frequently when there are indications that impairment might have occurred. Examples of indicators that give rise to the need to test for impairment include a significant adverse change in an asset's physical condition, a significant adverse change in legal or economic factors, or a significant decrease in the market price among others.[12]

4.2 Revaluation of Long-lived Assets

The revaluation model of accounting for long-lived assets is an alternative to the historical cost model and is available under IFRS, but not under US GAAP. Only the historical cost model is available under US GAAP. Companies using IFRS have a choice of using the cost model or the revaluation model, although the majority uses the cost model.

Under the historical cost model, long-lived assets are reported at historical cost less accumulated depreciation or accumulated amortisation, adjusted for any impairment. Under the revaluation model, long-lived assets are reported at their fair value. IAS 16 states that the assets are to be reported at their fair value less any subsequent accumulated depreciation and subsequent impairment losses, but requires revaluations be made frequently enough that the carrying amount does not differ materially from fair value. Required frequency of revaluation depends on the significance of periodic changes. Fair value of tangible long-lived assets is usually determined by professional appraisal using market-based evidence, but can be based on a discounted cash flow or replacement cost analysis in the absence of market-based evidence, e.g., if the asset is very specialized and seldom sold.[13]

---

10 IAS 36, paragraph 9.
11 FASB ASC 360-10-35-21.
12 IAS 36, paragraph 12, FASB ASC 350-20-35-30, and FASB ASC 360-10-35-21.
13 For intangible long-lived assets, discounted cash flows and cost approach are typically used because market values are generally not obtainable.

IFRS allow a company to use the revaluation model for some classes of assets and the cost model for other classes, but the company must apply the same model to all assets within a particular class of assets. IFRS defines a class of assets as a "grouping of assets of a similar nature and use in an entity's operations."[14] Examples of separate classes include land, buildings, furniture and fixtures, office equipment, machinery, ships, aircraft, and motor vehicles. If an asset is revalued, the company must revalue all items within the class simultaneously to avoid selective revaluation.

Whether an asset revaluation affects earnings depends on whether the revaluation initially increases or decreases an asset's carrying amount. If an asset revaluation initially decreases the carrying amount, the decrease is recognised in profit or loss (similar to an asset impairment). Later, if the asset's carrying amount increases due to an increase in fair value, the increase is recognised in profit or loss to the extent that it reverses a revaluation decrease of the same asset previously recognised in profit or loss. In contrast, if an asset revaluation initially increases the carrying amount, the increase in the asset's carrying amount bypasses the income statement, is reported as other comprehensive income, and appears in equity under the heading of revaluation surplus. Any subsequent decrease in the asset's value first decreases the revaluation surplus, then goes to income. When an asset is retired or disposed of, any related amount of revaluation surplus included in equity is transferred directly to retained earnings.

Asset revaluations offer several considerations for financial statement analyses. First, an increase in the carrying amount of depreciable long-lived assets increases total assets and shareholders' equity, so asset revaluations that increase the carrying amount of an asset can be used to reduce reported leverage. Defining leverage as average total assets divided by average shareholders' equity, increasing both the numerator (assets) and denominator (equity) by the same amount, leads to a decline in the ratio. (Mathematically, when a ratio is greater than one, as in this case, an increase in both the numerator and the denominator by the same amount leads to a decline in the ratio.) Therefore, the leverage motivation for the revaluation should be considered in analysis. For example, a company may revalue assets up if it is seeking new capital or approaching leverage limitations set by financial covenants.

Second, assets revaluations that decrease the carrying amount of the assets reduce net income. In the year of the revaluation, profitability measures such as return on assets and return on equity decline. However, because total assets and shareholders' equity are also lower, the company may appear more profitable in future years. Additionally, reversals of downward revaluations also go through income, thus increasing earnings. Managers can then opportunistically time the reversals to manage earnings and increase income. Third, asset revaluations that increase the carrying amount of an asset initially increase depreciation expense, total assets, and shareholders' equity. Therefore, profitability measures, such as return on assets and return on equity, would decline. Although upward asset revaluations also generally decrease income (through higher depreciation expense), the increase in the value of the long-lived asset is presumably based on increases in the operating capacity of the asset, which will likely be evidenced in increased future revenues.

Finally, an analyst should consider who did the appraisal—i.e., an independent external appraiser or management—and how often revaluations are made. Appraisals of the fair value of long-lived assets involve considerable judgment and discretion. Presumably, appraisals of assets from independent external sources are more reliable. How often assets are revalued can provide an indicator of whether their reported value continues to be representative of their fair values.

---

14 IAS 36, paragraph 37.

EXAMPLE 8

Asset Revaluation

You are analyzing RevUp PLC, a (hypothetical) company which is planning to raise new debt in the coming year. Part of your analysis involves understanding the company's solvency to help determine its capacity to handle additional debt. You observe that in Year 2 RevUp made an asset revaluation that increased the reported value of its assets by €150 million and increased depreciation expense by €25 million. Other relevant data and excerpts from the company's annual report are included in Exhibit 9.

Exhibit 9 RevUp PLC Excerpts from Financial Statements		
Line Items (€ in Millions)	Year 1	Year 2
At 31 December:		
Property, plant, and equipment, net	700	750
Total assets	3,000	3,650
Total liabilities	1,400	1,900
Revaluation surplus (part of shareholders' equity)	—	150
Total shareholders' equity	1,600	1,750
For the year ended 31 December:		
Depreciation expense	100	125
Income before taxes	1,000	975
Tax expense	400	400
Net income	600	575

1 Compute the company's financial leverage (defined as average total assets ÷ average shareholders' equity) based on reported Year 2 financial statements, with no adjustments, and with adjustment for the impact of the asset revaluation on leverage. (Assume the asset revaluation is not taxable and any increases in depreciation expense related to the revaluation are not tax deductible, so there would be no change in taxes.)

2 Interpret the change in leverage.

Solution to 1:

RevUp's Year 2 ratios are as follows:

	With Asset Revaluation (as reported)	Without Asset Revaluation (as adjusted)
Leverage	1.99	2.02

Based on information as reported, leverage with the €150 million asset revaluation was 1.99 (average total assets ÷ average shareholders' equity).

- Average total assets: €3,325. [(beginning assets of €3,000 + ending assets of €3,650) ÷ 2]

- Average shareholders' equity: €1,675 [(beginning shareholders' equity of €1,600 + ending shareholders' equity of €1,750) ÷ 2]

Based on information as reported without the €150 million asset revaluation, leverage was 2.02.

- Average total assets: €3,263. [(beginning assets of €3,000 + ending assets of €3,525) ÷ 2].

  Ending assets = €3,650 – the €150 increase in the value of the asset surplus + €25 reversal of increased depreciation.

- Average shareholders' equity: €1,613. [(beginning shareholders' equity of €1,600 + ending shareholders' equity of €1,625) ÷ 2]

  Ending shareholders' equity = (€1,750 – €150 + €25).

Solution to 2:

Increasing the value of the assets through revaluation decreases leverage. Therefore, RevUp appears to have more capacity for any new debt issues.

5   FINANCIAL STATEMENT DISCLOSURES: ANALYSIS AND DISCLOSURE

In this section, we discuss analysis and interpretation of disclosures of long-lived assets. Disclosure of long-lived assets can be used to assess a company's usage of its assets, the average age of assets, and the average remaining useful life of assets. A company must disclose the depreciation method(s), the gross carrying amount, and the accumulated depreciation at the balance sheets dates for each class of property, plant, and equipment (ASC 360-10-50 and IAS 16). Under IFRS, the measurement bases, the useful lives (or equivalently the depreciation rate) used, and a reconciliation of the carrying amount at the beginning and end of the period also must be disclosed (IAS 16).[15]

As noted in Section 4.2, IFRS permit companies to measure PPE either under a cost model, i.e., historical cost (initially recognised acquisition cost) minus accumulated depreciation, or under a revaluation model, i.e., fair value.[16] Under the revaluation model, the relationship between carrying amount, accumulated depreciation, and depreciation expense will differ when the carrying amount differs significantly from the depreciated historical cost. Under US GAAP, only the cost model is permitted. The following discussion applies primarily to PPE reported under the cost model.

Disclosures about long-lived assets appear throughout the financial statements: in the balance sheet, the income statement, the statement of cash flows, and the notes. The balance sheet reports PPE at historical cost net of accumulated depreciation and net of any impairment charges. For the income statement, depreciation expense may or may not appear as a separate line item. Under IFRS, whether the income statement discloses depreciation expense separately depends on whether the company is using a "nature of expense" method or a "function of expense" method. Under the nature of expense method, a company aggregates expenses "according to their nature (for example, depreciation, purchases of materials, transport costs, employee benefits and

---

15 Most US companies disclose asset useful lives by asset class as part of the description of the depreciation method used.

16 Research indicates that revaluations of property, plant, and equipment permitted under IFRS but prohibited under US GAAP are an important cause of the lack of comparability of financial statements prepared under the two sets of standards. For example, see J.L. Haverty, "Are IFRS and US GAAP converging? Some evidence from People's Republic of China companies listed on the New York Stock Exchange," *Journal of International Accounting, Auditing and Taxes*, Volume 15, Issue 1 (2006): 48–71.

advertising costs), and does not reallocate them among functions within the entity."[17] Under the function of expense method, a company classifies expenses according to the function, for example as part of cost of sales or of SG&A (selling, general, and administrative expenses). At a minimum, a company using the function of expense method must disclose cost of sales, but the other line items vary.

The statement of cash flows reflects acquisitions and disposals of fixed assets in the investing section. In addition, when prepared using the indirect method, the statement of cash flows typically shows depreciation expense (or depreciation plus amortisation) as a line item in the adjustments of net income to cash flow from operations. The notes to the financial statements describe the company's accounting method(s), the range of estimated useful lives, historical cost by main category of fixed asset, accumulated depreciation, and annual depreciation expense.

The fixed asset turnover ratio (total revenue divided by average net fixed assets) reflects the relationship between total revenues and investment in PPE. The higher this ratio, the higher the amount of sales a company is able to generate with a given amount of investment in fixed assets.

Asset age and remaining useful life are important indicators of a company's need to reinvest in productive capacity. The older the assets and the shorter the remaining life, the more a company may need to reinvest to maintain productive capacity. The amount of depreciation expense and the amount of net PPE can be used to estimate the average remaining useful life of a company's asset base. Specifically, the average remaining useful life of a company's assets can be estimated as net PPE divided by depreciation expense. In this section, we discuss this analysis as well as the estimation of the average age of a company's depreciable assets. To estimate the average age of the asset base, divide accumulated depreciation by depreciation expense.

These estimates simply reflect the following relationships for assets accounted for on a historical cost basis: total historical cost minus accumulated depreciation equals net PPE; and, under straight-line depreciation, total historical cost less salvage value divided by estimated useful life equals annual depreciation expense. Equivalently, total historical cost less salvage value divided by annual depreciation expense equals estimated useful life. Assuming straight-line depreciation and no salvage value (for simplicity), we have the following:

Estimated total useful life	=	Time elapsed since purchase (age)	+	Estimated remaining life
Historical cost ÷ annual depreciation expense	=	Estimated total useful life		
Historical cost	=	Accumulated depreciation	+	Net PPE

Equivalently,

Estimated total useful life	=	Estimated age of equipment	+	Estimated remaining life
Historical cost ÷ annual depreciation expense	=	Accumulated depreciation ÷ annual depreciation expense	+	Net PPE ÷ annual depreciation expense

The application of these estimates can be illustrated by a hypothetical example of a company with a single depreciable asset. Assume the asset initially cost $100, had an estimated useful life of ten years, and an estimated salvage value of $0. Each year, the company records a depreciation expense of $10, so accumulated depreciation will

---

17 IAS 1 paragraph 102.

equal $10 times the number of years since the asset was acquired (when the asset is seven years old, accumulated depreciation will be $70). Equivalently, the age of the asset will equal accumulated depreciation divided by the annual depreciation expense.

In practice, such estimates are difficult to make with great precision. Companies use depreciation methods other than the straight-line method and have numerous assets with varying useful lives and salvage values, including some assets that are fully depreciated, so this approach produces an estimate only. Moreover, fixed asset disclosures are often quite general. Consequently, these estimates may be primarily useful to identify areas for further investigation.

One further measure compares a company's current reinvestment in productive capacity. Comparing annual capital expenditures to annual depreciation expense provides an indication of whether productive capacity is being maintained. It is a very general indicator of the rate at which a company is replacing its PPE relative to the rate at which PPE is being depreciated.

EXAMPLE 9

Using Fixed Asset Disclosure to Compare Companies' Fixed Asset Turnover and Average Age of Depreciable Assets

You are analyzing the property, plant, and equipment of three international paper and paper products companies:

- AbitibiBowater Inc. (NYSE: ABY) is a Canadian company that manufactures newsprint, commercial printing papers, and other wood products.

- International Paper Company (NYSE: IP) is a US paper and packaging company.

- UPM-Kymmene Corporation (UPM) is a Finnish company that manufactures fine and specialty papers, newsprint, magazine papers, and other related products. The company's common stock is listed on the Helsinki and New York stock exchanges.

Exhibit 10 presents selected information from the companies' financial statements.

Exhibit 10

	ABY	IP	UPM
Currency, Millions of:	Canadian $	US $	Euro €
Historical cost total PPE, end of year	9,013	29,815	16,382
Accumulated depreciation, end of year	4,553	15,613	10,694
Net PPE, end of year	4,460	14,202	5,688
Land included in PPE	161	Not separated	347
Average Net PPE	5,067	12,172	5,934
Net Sales	6,771	24,829	9,461
Annual depreciation expense (annual impairment)	726	1,347	745
			(182)
Capital expenditure	186	1,002	558
Accounting standards	Canadian GAAP	US GAAP	IFRS
PPE measurement	Historical cost	Historical cost	Historical cost

Exhibit 10 (Continued)			
	ABY	**IP**	**UPM**
Currency, Millions of:	**Canadian $**	**US $**	**Euro €**
Depreciation method	Straight-line	Units-of-production for pulp and paper mills;* straight-line for other	Straight-line
Useful life of assets, in years, except as noted	20–40 (buildings); 5–20 (machinery and equipment); 40 (power plants)	Straight-line depreciation rates are 2.5% to 8.5% (buildings), and 5% to 33% (machinery and equipment)	25–40 (buildings); 15–20 (heavy equip.); 5–15 (light equip.)

*Pulp and paper mills' historical cost as disclosed in a footnote totals $21,819 million. Depreciation expense and accumulated depreciation is not separately reported for mills.
Sources:
For ABY, Form 10-K for the year ended 31 December 2008, filed 31 March 2009.
For IP, Form 10-K for the year ended 31 December 2008, filed 20 February 2009.
For UPM, annual report for the year ended 31 December 2008.

1 Based on the above data for each company, estimate the total useful life, age, and remaining useful life of PPE.

2 Interpret the estimates. What items might affect comparisons across these companies?

3 How does each company's 2008 depreciation expense compare to its capital expenditures for the year?

4 Calculate and compare fixed asset turnover for each company.

Solution to 1:

The following table presents the estimated total useful life, estimated age, and estimated remaining useful life of PPE for each of the companies.

Estimates	ABY	IP	UPM
Estimated total useful life (years)	12.4	22.1	22.0
Estimated age (years)	6.3	11.6	14.4
Estimated remaining life (years)	6.1	10.5	7.6

The computations are explained using UPM's data. The estimated total useful life of PPE is total historical cost of PPE of €16,382 divided by annual depreciation expense of €745, giving 22.0 years. Estimated age and estimated remaining life are obtained by dividing accumulated depreciation of €10,694 and net PPE of €5,688 by the annual depreciation expense of €745, giving 14.4 years and 7.6 years, respectively.

Ideally, the estimates of asset lives illustrated in this example should exclude land, which is not depreciable, when the information is available; however, IP does not separately disclose land. We will use UPM, for which land appeared to be disclosed separately in the above table, to illustrate the estimates with adjusting for land. As an illustration of the calculations to exclude land, excluding UPM's land would give an estimated total useful life for the non-land PPE of 21.5 years [(total cost €16,382 minus land cost of €347) divided by annual depreciation expense of €745 million].

Solution to 2:

The estimated total useful life suggests that IP and UPM depreciate PPE over a much longer period than ABY: 22.1 and 22.0 years for IP and UPM, respectively, versus 12.4 years for ABY. This result can be compared, to an extent, to the useful life of assets noted by the companies, and the composition of fixed assets. For instance, ABY and UPM depreciate their buildings over similar periods and their equipment over the same period (5 to 20 years). That the estimated useful life of PPE overall differs so much between the companies suggests that equipment reflects a higher proportion of ABY's assets. An inspection of the companies' footnoted information (not shown above) on asset composition confirms that equipment accounts for a larger portion of ABY gross fixed assets (86 percent) compared to UPM (76 percent).

The estimated age of the equipment suggests that ABY has the newest PPE with an estimated age of 6.3 years. Additionally, the estimates suggest that around 50 percent of ABY's assets' useful lives have passed (6.3 years ÷ 12.4 years, or equivalently, C$4,553 million ÷ C$9,013 million). In comparison, around 67 percent of the useful lives of the PPE of UPM have passed. Items that can affect comparisons across the companies include business differences, such as differences in composition of the companies' operations and differences in acquisition and divestiture activity. In addition, the companies all report under different accounting standards, and IP discloses that it uses the units-of-production method for the largest component of its PPE. Differences in disclosures, e.g. in the categories of assets disclosed, also can affect comparisons.

Solution to 3:

Capital expenditure as a percentage of depreciation is 26 percent for ABY, 74 percent for IP, and 75 percent for UPM. Based on this measure, IP and UPM are replacing their PPE at rates closer to the rate PPE are being depreciated. ABY's measure suggests the company is replacing its PPE at a slower rate than the PPE is being depreciated, consistent with the company's apparently newer asset base.

Solution to 4:

Fixed asset turnover for each company is presented below, calculated as total revenues divided by average net PPE. Net sales is used as an approximation for total revenues, because differences like sales returns are not consistently disclosed by companies. We can see that IP's fixed asset turnover is highest, implying it is able to generate more sales from each unit of investment in fixed assets.

	ABY	IP	UPM
Fixed Asset Turnover	1.3	2.0	1.6
Currency, millions of:	*Canadian $*	*US $*	*Euro €*
Net Sales	6,771	24,829	9,461
Average Net PPE	5,067	12,172	5,934

6   LEASING

A lease is a contract between the owner of an asset—the **lessor**—and another party seeking use of the assets—the **lessee**. Through the lease, the lessor grants the right to use the asset to the lessee. The right to use the asset can be a long period, such as 20 years, or a much shorter period such as a month. In exchange for the right to use the asset, the lessee makes periodic lease payments to the lessor. A lease, then, is a form of financing to the lessee provided by the lessor that enables the lessee to purchase the *use* of the leased asset.

6.1 The Lease versus Buy Decision

There are several advantages to leasing an asset compared to purchasing it. Leases can provide less costly financing, usually require little, if any, down payment, and are often at fixed interest rates. The negotiated lease contract may contain less restrictive provisions than other forms of borrowing. A lease can also reduce the risks of obsolescence, residual value, and disposition to the lessee because the lessee does not own the asset. The lessor may be better positioned to manage servicing the asset and to take advantage of tax benefits of ownership. As a result, leasing the asset may be less costly than owning the asset for the lessee.

Leases also have perceived financial and tax reporting advantages. While providing a form of financing, certain types of leases are not reported as debt on the balance sheet. The items leased under these types of leases also do not appear as assets on the balance sheet. Therefore, no interest expense or depreciation expense is included in the income statement. Additionally, in some countries such as the United States, financial reporting standards may differ from reporting under tax regulations; thus, in some cases, a company may own an asset for tax purposes (and thus obtain deductions for depreciation expense for tax purposes) while not reflecting the ownership in its financial statements. A lease that is structured to provide a company with the tax benefits of ownership while not requiring the asset to be reflected on the company's financial statements is known as a **synthetic lease**.

6.2 Finance versus Operating Leases

Recall the differences in economic substance and accounting for the two main types of leases—finance and operating. The economic substance of a finance (or capital)[18] lease is different from an operating lease, as are the implications of each for the financial statements of the lessee and lessor. In substance, a **finance lease** is equivalent to the purchase of some asset (lease to own) by the buyer (lessee) that is directly financed by the seller (lessor). An **operating lease** is an agreement allowing the lessee to use the asset for a period of time, essentially a rental.

Under IFRS, if substantially *all* the risks and rewards incidental to ownership are transferred to the lessee, the lease is classified as a finance lease and the lessee reports a leased asset and a lease obligation on the balance sheet.[19] Otherwise, the lease is reported as an operating lease. While a similar principle of the transfer of benefits and risks guides US GAAP, US accounting standards are more prescriptive in their criteria for classifying finance and operating leases. Under US GAAP, a lease that meets any one of four specific requirements is classified as a finance lease.[20]

The following example illustrates and compares the accounting and financial statement effects of buying an asset using debt, leasing an asset under an operating lease, and leasing an asset under a finance lease.

---

18 Finance lease is IFRS terminology and capital lease is US GAAP terminology. IAS 17 [Leases] and FASB ASC Topic 840 [Leases].

19 International accounting for leases is prescribed under IAS 17 [Leases].

20 The four criteria are: (1) ownership of the leased asset transfers to lessee at end of lease, (2) the lease contains an option for the lessee to purchase the leased asset cheaply (bargain purchase option), (3) the lease term is 75 percent or more of the useful life of the leased asset, and (4) the present value of lease payments is 90 percent or more of the fair value of the leased asset (ASC 840-10-25-1).

EXAMPLE 10

Comparison of Accounting and Financial Statement Effects of the Buy versus Lease Decision

Bi-ly Company is considering the following alternatives in obtaining the use of a new piece of equipment at the beginning of Year 1:

Alternative 1	Buy the equipment and finance the purchase with new debt.
Alternative 2	Lease the equipment under an operating lease (the equipment is not reported as an asset, the lease payments each period are treated as an operating expense on the income statement).
Alternative 3	Lease the equipment under a finance lease (the equipment is reported as an asset and an obligation is recorded equal to the present value of future lease payments).

The fair value of the equipment, having a five-year useful life and no salvage value, is $1,000. If Bi-ly leases the equipment, annual lease payments would be $264 due at the end of each year. Bi-ly's discount rate is 10 percent. The company uses straight-line depreciation. (For illustration, assume the company can record the lease as either operating or financing.)

1 For each alternative under consideration, determine the effect on assets and liabilities at the beginning of Year 1.

2 For each alternative, determine the effect on the income statement in Year 1.

3 For each alternative, calculate Bi-ly's return on assets and debt-to-asset ratio at the end of Year 1. For simplicity, assume that—excluding any effects of Bi-ly's choice among the three alternatives for obtaining the assets—total assets at the beginning and end of the year are $4,500, total liabilities at the beginning and end of the year are $3,000, and net income for the year is $800.

Solution to 1:

At the beginning of Year 1, Bi-ly would show the following assets and debt:

Alternative	1	2	3
Buy/Lease	Buy	Lease	Lease
Finance/Accounting	Issue new debt	Operating	Finance*
Long-lived asset	$1,000		$1,000
Debt/lease obligation	$1,000		$1,000

*Under a finance lease, the present value of five future lease payments of $264 discounted at 10 percent is reported on the balance sheet as a lease obligation and an asset of $1,000 (rounded).

Solution to 2:

For Year 1, Bi-ly would show the following expenses related to the equipment:

Alternative	1	2	3
Rent expense		$264	
Depreciation expense	$200		$200
Interest expense	100		100
Total expenses	$300	$264	$300

For Alternatives 1 and 3, depreciation expense is the acquisition cost of $1,000 divided by the 5-year useful life. Salvage value is 0.

For Alternatives 1 and 3, interest expense is the beginning balance of debt, $1,000, times the discount rate of 10 percent. Each year the interest expense will decline.

For Alternative 2, rent expense is the lease payment of $264.

Solution to 3:

To calculate the return on assets:

Alternative	1	2	3
Net income, excluding new asset	$800	$800	$800
Subtract additional expenses (solution to 2 above)	300	264	300
Net income, adjusted	$500	$536	$500
Total assets, beginning, excluding new asset	$4,500	$4,500	$4,500
Add additional asset (solution to 1 above)	1,000		1,000
Total assets, beginning, adjusted	$5,500	$4,500	$5,500
Total assets, end, excluding new asset	$4,500	$4,500	$4,500
Add additional asset*	800		800
Total assets, end, adjusted	$5,300	$4,500	$5,300
Average total assets	$5,400	$4,500	$5,400
Return on assets, adjusted	9.3%	11.9%	9.3%

*The book value of the new asset at the end of the year is its beginning balance of $1,000 less $200 accumulated depreciation.

In this example, the highest return on assets is found when the equipment is leased under an operating lease which is expected because net income is highest and the asset base is lowest. Buying an asset and seeking to finance it with new debt and leasing it under a finance lease result in the same return on assets.

To calculate the debt-to-asset ratio at the end of the year:

Alternative	1	2	3
Total assets, end, excluding new asset	$4,500	$4,500	$4,500
Add additional asset	800		800
Total assets, end, adjusted	$5,300	$4,500	$5,300
Total liabilities, end, excluding new asset	$3,000	$3,000	$3,000
Add additional debt*	837		837
Total liabilities, end, adjusted	$3,837	$3,000	$3,837
Debt-to-asset ratio	0.724	0.667	0.724

*Additional debt at the end of the first year is the present value of the four remaining debt/lease payments of $264 discounted at 10 percent (and rounded).

In this example, the lowest debt-to-asset ratio is found when the equipment is financed through an operating lease. Buying an asset and seeking to finance it with new debt and leasing it under a finance lease result in the same return on assets.

6.2.1 *Accounting and Reporting by the Lessee*

A finance lease is economically similar to borrowing money and buying an asset; therefore, a company that enters into a finance lease as the lessee reports an asset (leased asset) and related debt (lease payable) on the balance sheet. The initial value of both the leased asset and the lease payable is the lower of the fair value of the leased asset or the present value of future lease payments. On the income statement, the company reports interest expense on the debt; and if the asset acquired is depreciable, the company reports depreciation expense. (The lessor, as we illustrate in Section 6.2.2, reports the sale of an asset and the lease as a receivable.)

Because an operating lease is economically similar to renting an asset, the lessee records a lease expense on its income statement during the period it uses the asset. No asset or liability is recorded on its balance sheet. The main accounting differences between a finance lease and an operating lease are that under a finance lease, reported debt and assets are higher and expenses are generally higher in the early years. Because of the higher reported assets, debt and expenses—and therefore the lower ROA, all else equal—lessees often prefer operating leases to finance leases. As we illustrate in the next section, lessors' preferences generally differ. Lessors would prefer a finance lease because, under an operating lease, lessors continue to show the asset and its associated financing on their balance sheets.

On the lessee's statement of cash flows, for an operating lease, the full lease payment is shown as an operating cash outflow. For a finance lease, only the portion of the lease payment relating to interest expense potentially reduces operating cash flows;[21] the portion of the lease payment that reduces the lease liability appears as a cash outflow in the financing section.

---

[21] Interest expense may be classified as a financing cash flow or an operating cash flow under IFRS (IAS 7, paragraph 33) but is classified as an operating cash flow under US GAAP (FASB ASC, paragraph 230-10-45-17).

A company reporting a lease as an operating lease will typically show higher profits in early years, higher return measures in early years, and a stronger solvency position than an identical company reporting an identical lease as a finance lease. However, the company reporting the lease as a finance lease will show higher operating cash flows because a portion of the lease payment will be reflected as a financing cash outflow rather than an operating cash outflow.

Example 11 illustrates the effect on a lessee's income, debt, and cash flows when reporting a lease as a finance lease versus an operating lease.

EXAMPLE 11

Financial Statement Impact of a Finance versus Operating Lease for the Lessee

Assume two similar (hypothetical) companies, CAPBS Inc. and OPIS Inc., enter into similar lease agreements for a piece of machinery on 1 January Year 1. The leases require four annual payments of €28,679 starting on 1 January Year 1. The useful life of the machine is four years and its salvage value is zero. CAPBS accounts for the lease as a finance lease and uses straight-line depreciation, while OPIS has determined the lease is an operating lease. For simplicity, this example assumes that the accounting rules governing these hypothetical companies do not mandate either type of lease. The present value of lease payments and fair value of the equipment is €100,000. (A reminder relevant for present value calculations: Lease payments are made at the beginning of each period.)

At the beginning of Year 1, before entering into the lease agreements, both companies reported liabilities of €100,000 and equity of €200,000. Each year the companies receive total revenues of €50,000, and all revenues are cash. Assume the companies have a tax rate of 30 percent, and use the same accounting for financial and tax purposes. Both companies' discount rate is 10 percent. In order to focus only on the differences in the type of lease, assume neither company incurs expenses other than those associated with the lease, and neither invests excess cash.

1 Which company reports higher expenses/net income in Year 1? Over the four years?

2 Which company reports higher total cash flow over the four years? Cash flow from operations?

3 Based on return on equity (ROE), how do the two companies' profitability measures compare?

4 Based on the ratio of debt-to-equity, how do the two companies' solvency positions compare?

Solution to 1:

In Year 1 and Year 2, CAPBS reports higher expenses because the depreciation expense and interest expense of its finance lease exceeds the lease expense of OPIS's operating lease. Therefore, OPIS reports higher net income in Year 1 and Year 2. The companies' total expense over the entire four-year period, however, is equal as is the companies' total net income.

Each year, OPIS reports lease expense of €28,679 associated with its operating lease. For CAPBS, its finance lease is treated as being economically similar to borrowing money and purchasing an asset. So, on its income statement, CAPBS reports depreciation expense on the leased asset acquired and interest expense on the lease liability.

The table below shows by year CAPBS's depreciation expense and book values on the leased asset.

Year	Acquisition Cost (a)	Depreciation Expense (b)	Accumulated Depreciation (c)	Carrying Amount (Year End) (d)
1	€100,000	€25,000	€25,000	€75,000
2	100,000	25,000	50,000	50,000
3	100,000	25,000	75,000	25,000
4	100,000	25,000	100,000	0
		€100,000		

- Column (a) is acquisition cost of €100,000 of the leased equipment.
- Column (b) is depreciation expense of €25,000 per year, calculated using the straight line convention, as the acquisition costs less salvage value divided by useful life [(€100,000 – €0)/4 years].
- Column (c) is the accumulated depreciation on the leased asset, calculated as the prior year's accumulated depreciation plus the current year's depreciation expense.
- Column (d) is the carrying amount at year end of the leased equipment, which is the difference between the acquisition cost and accumulated depreciation.

The table below shows CAPBS's lease payment, interest expense, and carrying amount for its lease liability by year.[22]

Year	Lease Liability, 1 January (a)	Annual Lease Payment, 1 January (b)	Interest (at 10%; Accrued in Previous Year) (c)	Reduction of Lease Liability, 1 January (d)	Lease Liability on 31 December after Lease Payment on 1 January Same Year (e)
1	€100,000	€28,679	€0	€28,679	€71,321
2	71,321	28,679	7,132	21,547	49,774
3	49,774	28,679	4,977	23,702	26,072
4	26,072	28,679	2,607	26,072	0
		€114,717	€14,717	€100,000	

- Column (a) is the lease liability at the beginning of the year.

    Year 1: €100,000

    Years thereafter: lease liability at end of previous year

- Column (b) is the annual lease payment made at the beginning of the year. Part of the lease payment pays any interest accrued in the previous year, and the remainder of the lease payment reduces the lease liability. For example, in Year 2, the €28,679 paid on 1 January reduces the interest payable of €7,132 that accrued in Year 1 (0.10 × 71,321) and then reduces the lease liability by €21,547.

---

22 The computations included throughout the example were made using an Excel worksheet; small discrepancies in the calculations are due to rounding.

- Column (c) is the interest portion of the 1 January lease payment made on that date. This amount of interest was accrued as interest payable during the *prior* year and is reported as the interest expense of the *prior* year.
- Column (d) is the reduction of the lease liability, which is the difference between the annual lease payment and the interest portion.
- Column (e) is the lease liability on 31 December of a given year just before the lease payment is made on the first day of the next year. It is equal to the lease liability on 1 January of the same year (column a) less the reduction of the lease liability (column d).

The table below summarizes and compares the income statement effects of the lease for CAPBS and OPIS. Notice that over the four-year lease, both companies report the same total amount of expense but CAPBS shows higher expenses earlier in the life of the lease.

| | CAPBS | | | OPIS | |
| | Depreciation | Interest | | Lease | |
Year	Expense	Expense	Total	Expense	Difference
1	€25,000	€7,132	€32,132	€28,679	€3,453
2	25,000	4,977	29,977	28,679	1,298
3	25,000	2,607	27,607	28,679	(1,072)
4	25,000	—	25,000	28,679	(3,679)
Total	€100,000	€14,717	€114,717	€114,717	€(0)

The complete income statements for CAPBS and OPIS are presented below. Notice under the assumption that the same accounting is used for financial and tax purposes, CAPBS's taxes are lower in Year 1 and Year 2. The lower taxes in the earlier years reflect the higher expenses in those years.

| Income Statements | CAPBS | | | | | OPIS | | | | |
	1	2	3	4	Total	1	2	3	4	Total
Sales	€50,000	€50,000	€50,000	€50,000	€200,000	€50,000	€50,000	€50,000	€50,000	€200,000
Depreciation expense	25,000	25,000	25,000	25,000	100,000					
Interest expense	7,132	4,977	2,607		14,717					
Lease expense	—	—	—	—	—	28,679	28,679	28,679	28,679	114,717
Income before taxes	17,868	20,023	22,393	25,000	85,283	21,321	21,321	21,321	21,321	85,283
Tax expense	5,360	6,007	6,718	7,500	25,585	6,396	6,396	6,396	6,396	25,585
Net income	€12,508	€14,016	€15,675	€17,500	€59,698	€14,925	€14,925	€14,925	€14,925	€59,698

Solution to 2:

On the statement of cash flows, observe that over the four years, both CAPBS and OPIS report the same total change in cash of €59,698. Operating cash flows reported by CAPBS are higher because a portion of the lease payment each year is categorised as a financing cash flow rather than an operating cash flow. In the first two years, CAPBS's change in cash is higher due to its lower taxes in those years.

Statements of Cash Flows	CAPBS					OPIS				
	1	2	3	4	Total	1	2	3	4	Total
Sales	€50,000	€50,000	€50,000	€50,000	€200,000	€50,000	€50,000	€50,000	€50,000	€200,000
Interest paid	—	7,132	4,977	2,607	14,717					
Taxes paid	5,360	6,007	6,718	7,500	25,585	6,396	6,396	6,396	6,396	25,585
Lease expense	—	—	—	—	—	28,679	28,679	28,679	28,679	114,717
Operating cash flows	44,640	36,861	38,305	39,893	159,698	14,925	14,925	14,925	14,925	59,698
Payment to reduce lease liability	(28,679)	(21,547)	(23,702)	(26,072)	(100,000)					
Financing cash flows	(28,679)	(21,547)	(23,702)	(26,072)	(100,000)	—	—	—	—	—
Total change in cash	€15,960	€15,314	€14,603	€13,821	€59,698	€14,925	€14,925	€14,925	€14,925	€59,698

Solution to 3:

Based on ROE, CAPBS looks less profitable than OPIS in the earlier years. Computing ROE requires forecasting shareholders' equity. In general, ending Shareholders' equity = Beginning shareholders' equity + Net income + Other comprehensive income – Dividends + Net capital contributions by shareholders. Because the companies in this example do not have other comprehensive income, did not pay dividends, and experienced no capital contributions from shareholders, Ending shareholders' equity = Beginning shareholders' equity + Net income. The forecasts are presented below.

CAPBS	0	1	2	3	4
Retained earnings	€0	€12,508	€26,523	€42,198	€59,698
Common stock	200,000	200,000	200,000	200,000	200,000
Total shareholders' equity	€200,000	€212,508	€226,523	€242,198	€259,698

OPIS	0	1	2	3	4
Retained earnings	€0	€14,925	€29,849	€44,774	€59,698
Common stock	200,000	200,000	200,000	200,000	200,000
Total shareholders' equity	€200,000	€214,925	€229,849	€244,774	€259,698

ROE is calculated as net income divided by average shareholders' equity. For example, CAPBS Inc. had Year 1 ROE of 6.1 percent: €12,508/ [(€200,000 + €212,508) ÷ 2].

	CAPBS				OPIS			
	1	2	3	4	1	2	3	4
ROE	6.1%	6.4%	6.7%	7.0%	7.2%	6.7%	6.3%	5.9%

Solution to 4:

Based on the ratio of debt-to-equity, the solvency position of CAPBS appears weaker than that of OPIS.

For the debt-to-equity ratio, take the total shareholders' equity from Part 3 above. Initially, both companies had reported liabilities of €100,000. For OPIS, the amount of total liabilities remains constant at €100,000. For CAPBS, add the lease liability at the end of the year and the amount of accrued interest payable at the end of each year from Part 1 above. So at the end of Year 1, CAPBS's total liabilities are €178,453 (€100,000 + €71,321 lease liability + €7,132 accrued interest payable at the end of the year), and its debt-to-equity ratio is 0.84 (€178,453 ÷ €212,508). At the end of Year 2, CAPBS total liabilities equal €154,751 (€100,000 + €49,774 lease liability + €4,977 accrued interest payable at the end of the year). The remaining years are computed in the same manner. The table below presents the ratios for each year.

	CAPBS				OPIS			
	1	2	3	4	1	2	3	4
Total debt	178,453	154,751	128,679	100,000	100,000	100,000	100,000	100,000
Shareholders' equity	212,508	226,523	242,198	259,698	214,925	229,849	244,774	259,698
Debt-to-equity ratio	0.84	0.68	0.53	0.39	0.47	0.44	0.41	0.39

In summary, a company reporting a lease as an operating lease will typically show higher profits in early years, higher return measures in early years, and a stronger solvency position than an identical company reporting an identical lease as a finance lease.[23] However, the company reporting the lease as a finance lease will show higher operating cash flows because a portion of the lease payment will be reflected as a financing cash outflow rather than an operating cash outflow.

The precisely defined accounting standards in the United States that determine when a company should report a capital (finance) versus an operating lease enable a company to structure a lease so as to avoid meeting any of the four capital lease criteria and thereby record an operating lease. Similar to debt disclosures, lease disclosures show payments under both capital and operating leases for the next five years and afterwards. Future payments under US GAAP are disclosed year by year for the first five years and then aggregated for all subsequent years. Under IFRS, future payments are disclosed for the first year, in aggregate for years 2–5, and then in aggregate for all subsequent years. These disclosures can help to estimate the extent of a company's off-balance sheet lease financing through operating leases. Example 12 illustrates the disclosures and how these disclosures can be used to determine the effect on the financial statements if all operating leases were capitalised.

---

23 Example 11 assumes the company uses the straight-line depreciation method, which is common under IFRS and US GAAP. If the company estimated depreciation expense based on the "economic" depreciation of the leased asset, there would be no difference in reported income under a finance lease and operating lease.

Financial Statement Impact of Treating Operating Leases as Finance Leases for the Lessee

CEC Entertainment, Inc. (NYSE: CEC) has significant commitments under capital (finance) and operating leases. Presented below is selected financial statement information and note disclosure to the financial statements for the company.

Commitments and Contingencies Footnote from CEC's Financial Statements:

8. Commitments and contingencies:

The company leases certain restaurants and related property and equipment under operating and capital leases. All leases require the company to pay property taxes, insurance, and maintenance of the leased assets. The leases generally have initial terms of 10 to 20 years with various renewal options.

Scheduled annual maturities of the obligations for capital and operating leases as of 28 December 2008 are as follows (US$ thousands):

Years	Capital	Operating
2009	$1,683	$66,849
2010	1,683	66,396
2011	1,683	66,558
2012	1,600	65,478
2013	1,586	63,872
Thereafter	9,970	474,754
Minimum future lease payments	$18,205	$803,907
Less amounts representing interest	(5,997)	
Present value of future minimum lease payments	$12,208	
Less current portion	(806)	
Long-term finance lease obligation	$11,402	

Selected Financial Statement Information for CEC:

	28 December 2008	30 December 2007
Total liabilities	$608,854	$519,900
Shareholders' equity	128,586	217,993

1 A Calculate the implicit interest rate used to discount the "scheduled annual maturities" under capital leases to obtain the "present value of future minimum lease payments" of $12,208 disclosed in the Commitments and Contingencies footnote. To simplify the calculation, assume that future minimum lease payments on the company's capital leases for the "thereafter" lump sum are as follows: $1,586 on 31 December of each year from 2014 to 2019, and $454 in 2020. Assume annual lease payments are made at the end of each year.

B Why is the implicit interest rate estimate in Part A important in assessing a company's leases?

2 If the operating lease agreements had been treated as capital leases, what additional amount would be reported as a lease obligation on the balance sheet at 28 December 2008? To simplify the calculation, assume that future minimum lease payments on the company's operating leases for the "thereafter" lump sum are as follows: $63,872 on 31 December each year from 2014 to 2020, and $27,650 in 2021. Based on the implicit interest rate obtained in Part 1A, use 7.245 percent to discount future cash flows on the operating leases.

3 What would be the effect on the debt-to-equity ratio of treating all operating leases as finance leases (i.e., the ratio of total liabilities to equity) at 28 December 2008?

Solution to 1A:

The implicit interest rate on finance leases is 7.245 percent. The implicit interest rate used to discount the finance lease payments is the internal rate of return on the stream of cash flows; i.e., the interest rate that will make the present value of the lease payments equal to $12,208. You can use an Excel spreadsheet or a financial calculator for the computations. Set the cash flow at time zero equal to $12,208 (note on Excel and on most financial calculators, you will input this amount as a negative number), input each of the annual payments on the finance leases, and solve for the internal rate of return.

To demonstrate how the internal rate of return corresponds to the individual present values, refer to the following schedule of the undiscounted minimum lease payments based on information from footnote 8 and the assumptions given. Exhibit 11 presents the present value computations.

Exhibit 11	Present Value Computations Implicit Interest Rate (Internal Rate of Return) based on Capital Leases (7.245%)			
Fiscal Year	**Years to Discount**	**Minimum Capital Lease Payment**	**Times Present Value Factor**	**Equals Present Value**
2009	1	1,683	$1/(1+\text{Interest rate})^1$	1,569
2010	2	1,683	$1/(1+\text{Interest rate})^2$	1,463
2011	3	1,683	$1/(1+\text{Interest rate})^3$	1,364
2012	4	1,600	$1/(1+\text{Interest rate})^4$	1,210
2013	5	1,586	$1/(1+\text{Interest rate})^5$	1,118
2014	6	1,586	$1/(1+\text{Interest rate})^6$	1,042
2015	7	1,586	$1/(1+\text{Interest rate})^7$	972
2016	8	1,586	$1/(1+\text{Interest rate})^8$	906
2017	9	1,586	$1/(1+\text{Interest rate})^9$	845
2018	10	1,586	$1/(1+\text{Interest rate})^{10}$	788
2019	11	1,586	$1/(1+\text{Interest rate})^{11}$	735
2020	12	454	$1/(1+\text{Interest rate})^{12}$	196
Undiscounted sum of minimum future lease payments		$18,205		
Present value of future minimum lease payments				$12,208

The interest rate of 7.245 percent approximately equates the future minimum lease payments with the present value of future minimum lease payments of $12,208 that CEC reports.

Solution to 1B:

The implicit interest rate is important because it will be used to estimate the present value of the lease obligations reported as a liability, the value of the leased assets on the balance sheet, the interest expense, and the lease amortisation on the income statement. For instance, by selecting a higher rate a company could, if desired, opportunistically reduce the present value of its finance leases and thus its reported debt. The reasonableness of the implicit interest rate can be gauged by comparing it to the interest rates of the company's other debt instruments outstanding, which are disclosed in financial statement footnotes, and by considering recent market conditions. Note, however, that the interest rate implicit in capitalisation of the finance lease obligations reflects the interest rate at the time the lease occurred and thus may differ from current rates.

Solution to 2:

If the operating leases had been treated as finance leases, the additional amount that would be reported as a lease obligation on the balance sheet at 28 December 2008, using a discount rate of 7.245 percent determined in Part 1 above, is $520,256. Exhibit 12 presents the present value computations. An alternative short cut approach is to divide the discounted finance lease cash flows of $12,208 by the undiscounted finance lease cash flows of $18,205 and then apply the resulting percentage of 67.06 percent to the undiscounted operating lease cash flows of $803,907. The shortcut approach estimates the present value of the operating lease payments as $539,100, which is close to the estimate obtained using the longer method. It is likely to be most accurate when the timing and relative quantities of the two sets of cash flows are similar.

Exhibit 12	Present Value Computations (Implicit Interest Rate: 7.245%)			
Fiscal Year	**Years to Discount**	**Operating Lease Payments**	**Times Present Value Factor**	**Equals Present Value**
2009	1	66,849	$1/(1+0.07245)^1$	$62,333
2010	2	66,396	$1/(1+0.07245)^2$	57,728
2011	3	66,558	$1/(1+0.07245)^3$	53,960
2012	4	65,478	$1/(1+0.07245)^4$	49,498
2013	5	63,872	$1/(1+0.07245)^5$	45,022
2014	6	63,872	$1/(1+0.07245)^6$	41,981
2015	7	63,872	$1/(1+0.07245)^7$	39,145
2016	8	63,872	$1/(1+0.07245)^8$	36,500
2017	9	63,872	$1/(1+0.07245)^9$	34,034
2018	10	63,872	$1/(1+0.07245)^{10}$	31,735
2019	11	63,872	$1/(1+0.07245)^{11}$	29,591
2020	12	63,872	$1/(1+0.07245)^{12}$	27,592
2021	13	27,650	$1/(1+0.07245)^{13}$	11,138

Exhibit 12	(Continued)			
Fiscal Year	Years to Discount	Operating Lease Payments	Times Present Value Factor	Equals Present Value
Undiscounted sum of future operating lease payment		$803,907		
Present value of future operating lease payments				$520,256

Solution to 3:

The debt-to-equity ratio almost doubles, increasing to 8.78x from 4.73x when capitalising the operating leases. The adjusted debt-to-equity ratio is computed as follows:

	Unadjusted for Operating Leases	Adjustment to Capitalise Operating Leases	Adjusted to Capitalise Operating Leases
Total liabilities	$608,854	$520,256	$1,129,110
Common shareholders' equity	128,586		128,586
Debt-to-equity ratio	4.73x		8.78x

6.2.2 Accounting and Reporting by the Lessor

Lessors that report under US GAAP determine whether a lease is a finance (also called "capital lease") or operating lease using the same four criteria as a lessee, plus additional revenue recognition criteria. If a lessor enters into an operating lease, the lessor records any lease revenue when earned. The lessor also continues to report the leased asset on the balance sheet and the asset's associated depreciation expense on the income statement.

Under a finance lease, the lessor reports a lease receivable based on the present value of future lease payments, and the lessor also reduces its assets by the carrying amount of the asset leased. Under US GAAP, the carrying amount of the asset leased relative to the present value of lease payments distinguishes a direct financing lease from a sales-type lease. The income statement will show interest revenue on the lease.

EXAMPLE 13

Financial Statement Impact of a Direct Financing Lease versus Operating Lease for the Lessor

Assume two similar (hypothetical) companies, DIRFIN Inc. and LOPER Inc., own a similar piece of machinery and make similar agreements to lease the machinery on 1 January Year 1. In the lease contract, each company requires four annual payments of €28,679 starting on 1 January Year 1. The useful life of the machine is four years and its salvage value is zero. DIRFIN Inc. accounts for the lease as a direct financing lease while LOPER has determined the lease is an operating lease. (For simplicity, this example assumes that the accounting rules governing these hypothetical companies do not mandate either type of lease.) The present value of lease payments and fair value of the equipment is €100,000.

At the beginning of Year 1, before entering into the lease agreement, both companies reported liabilities of €100,000 and equity of €200,000. Assets on hand include the asset about to be leased. Each year the companies receive total revenues of €50,000 cash, apart from any revenue earned on the lease. Assume the companies have a tax rate of 30 percent, and use the same accounting for financial and tax purposes. Both companies' discount rate is 10 percent. In order to focus only on the differences in the type of lease, assume that neither company incurs revenues or expenses other than those associated with the lease and that neither invests excess cash.

1   Which company reports higher expenses/net income in Year 1? Over the four years?

2   Which company reports higher total cash flow over the four years? Cash flow from operations?

3   Based on ROE, how do the two companies' profitability measures compare?

Solution to 1:

LOPER reports higher expenses in Year 1 because, under an operating lease, the lessor retains ownership of the asset and continues to report associated depreciation expense. DIRFIN, treating the lease as a finance lease, does not reflect ownership of the asset or the associated depreciation expense. DIRFIN has higher net income in Year 1 because the interest revenue component of the lease payment in that year exceeds the lease revenue net of depreciation reported by LOPER.

On its income statement, LOPER reports depreciation expense for the asset it has leased and lease revenue based on the lease payment received. The table below shows LOPER's depreciation and book values on leased equipment by year.[24]

Year	Cost (a)	Depreciation Expense (b)	Accumulated Depreciation (c)	Book Value (Year End) (d)
1	€100,000	€25,000	€25,000	€75,000
2	100,000	25,000	50,000	50,000
3	100,000	25,000	75,000	25,000
4	100,000	25,000	100,000	0
		€100,000		

■   Column (a) is the cost of €100,000 of the leased equipment.

■   Column (b) is depreciation expense of €25,000 per year, calculated using the straight-line method as the cost less the salvage value divided by the useful life [(€100,000 − €0) ÷ 4 years].

---

24 The computations included throughout the example were made using an Excel worksheet; small apparent discrepancies in the calculations are due to the rounding.

- Column (c) is the accumulated depreciation on the leased asset calculated as the prior year's accumulated depreciation plus the current year's depreciation expense.

- Column (d) is the ending book value of the leased equipment, which is the difference between the cost and accumulated depreciation.

DIRFIN, however, records the lease as a direct financing lease. It removes the leased asset from its assets and records a lease receivable. On its income statement, DIRFIN reports interest revenues earned from financing the lease. The table below shows DIRFIN's interest revenues and carrying amounts on the lease receivable.

Year	Lease Receivable, 1 January (a)	Annual Lease Payment Received, 1 January (b)	Interest (at 10%; Accrued in Previous Year) (c)	Reduction of Lease Receivable, 1 January (d)	Lease Receivable on 31 December after Lease Payment on 1 January of Same Year (e)
1	€100,000	€28,679	€0	€28,679	€71,321
2	71,321	28,679	7,132	21,547	49,774
3	49,774	28,679	4,977	23,702	26,072
4	26,072	28,679	2,607	26,072	0
		€114,717	€14,717	€100,000	

- Column (a) is the lease receivable at the beginning of the year.

- Column (b) is annual lease payment received at the beginning of the year, which is allocated to interest and reduction of the lease receivable.

- Column (c) is interest accrued in the previous year calculated as the lease receivable outstanding for the year times the interest rate.

- Column (d) is the reduction of the lease receivable, which is the difference between the annual lease payments received and interest. Because the lease payment is due on 1 January, this amount of interest is a receivable at the end of the *prior* year and is reported as interest revenue in the *prior* year.

- Column (e) is the lease receivable after the lease payment is received and at the end of the year. It is the lease receivable at 1 January (Column a) less the reduction of the lease receivable (Column d).

The table below summarises and compares the income statement effects of the lease for DIRFIN and LOPER. Notice that over the four-year lease, both companies report the same total amount of revenue, but DIRFIN's revenues in the earlier years of the lease are higher than the net of lease revenues less depreciation reported by LOPER in those years.

	DIRFIN	LOPER			
Year	Lease Revenue	Lease Revenue	Depreciation Expense	Total	Difference
1	€7,132	€28,679	€25,000	€3,679	€3,453
2	4,977	28,679	25,000	3,679	1,298
3	2,607	28,679	25,000	3,679	(1,072)
4	—	28,679	25,000	3,679	(−3,679)
Total	€14,717	€114,717	€100,000	€14,717	€0

The complete income statements for DIRFIN and LOPER are presented below. Notice that, under the assumption that the same accounting is used for financial and tax purposes, DIRFIN's taxes are higher than those of LOPER in Years 1 and 2.

Income Statements	DIRFIN					LOPER				
	1	2	3	4	Total	1	2	3	4	Total
Sales	€50,000	€50,000	€50,000	€50,000	€200,000	€50,000	€50,000	€50,000	€50,000	€200,000
Depreciation expense						(25,000)	(25,000)	(25,000)	(25,000)	(100,000)
Interest revenue	7,132	4,977	2,607		14,717					
Lease revenue	—	—	—	—	—	28,679	28,679	28,679	28,679	114,717
Income before taxes	€57,132	€54,977	€52,607	€50,000	€214,717	€53,679	€53,679	€53,679	€53,679	€214,717
Tax expense	17,140	16,493	15,782	15,000	64,415	16,104	16,104	16,104	16,104	64,415
Net income	€39,992	€38,484	€36,825	€35,000	€150,302	€37,575	€37,575	€37,575	€37,575	€150,302

Solution to 2:

Looking at the statement of cash flows, observe that operating cash flows reported by DIRFIN are lower, but investing cash flows are higher than LOPER. Over the four years, both DIRFIN and LOPER report the same total change in cash.

Statements of Cash Flows	DIRFIN					LOPER				
	1	2	3	4	Total	1	2	3	4	Total
Net income	€39,992	€38,484	€36,825	€35,000	€150,302	€37,575	€37,575	€37,575	€37,575	€150,302
Increase (decrease) in interest receivable	7,132	(2,155)	(2,370)	(2,607)	0					
Add back depreciation expense	—	—	—	—	—	25,000	25,000	25,000	25,000	100,000
Operating cash flows	€32,860	€40,639	€39,195	€37,607	€150,302	€62,575	€62,575	€62,575	€62,575	€250,302
Payments received on finance leases	28,679	21,547	23,702	26,072	100,000					
Investing cash flows	28,679	21,547	23,702	26,072	100,000	—	—	—	—	—
Change in cash	€61,540	€62,186	€62,897	€63,679	€250,302	€62,575	€62,575	€62,575	€62,575	€250,302

Solution to 3:

Based on ROE, DIRFIN appears more profitable than LOPER in the early years of the lease.

Computing ROE requires forecasting shareholders' equity. In general, Ending shareholders' equity = Beginning shareholders' equity + Net income + Other comprehensive income − Dividends + Net capital contributions by shareholders. Because the companies in this example do not have other comprehensive income, do not pay dividends, and have no capital contributions, Ending shareholders' equity = Beginning shareholders' equity + Net income. The forecasts are presented below.

DIRFIN	0	1	2	3	4
Retained earnings	€0	€39,992	€78,477	€115,302	€150,302
Common stock	200,000	200,000	200,000	200,000	200,000
Total shareholders' equity	€200,000	€239,992	€278,477	€315,302	€350,302

LOPER	0	1	2	3	4
Retained earnings	€0	€37,575	€75,151	€112,726	€150,302
Common stock	200,000	200,000	200,000	200,000	200,000
Total shareholders' equity	€200,000	€237,575	€275,151	€312,726	€350,302

ROE is calculated as net income divided by average shareholders' equity. For example, DIRFIN Inc. had Year 1 ROE of 18.2 percent: €39,992/[(€200,000 + €239,992)/2].

	DIRFIN				LOPER			
	1	2	3	4	1	2	3	4
ROE	18.2%	14.8%	12.4%	10.5%	17.2%	14.7%	12.8%	11.3%

From the comparisons above, DIRFIN looks more profitable in the early years of the lease, but less profitable in the later years.

US GAAP make a further distinction in defining two types of non-operating leases: 1) **direct financing leases**, and 2) **sales-type leases** from the lessor's perspective.[25] A direct financing lease results when the present value of lease payments (and thus the amount recorded as a lease receivable) equals the carrying amount of the leased asset. Because there is no "profit" on the asset itself, the lessor is essentially providing financing to the lessee, and the revenues earned by the lessor are financing in nature (i.e., interest revenue). If, however, the present value of lease payments (and thus the amount recorded as a lease receivable) exceeds the carrying value of the leased asset, the lease is treated as a sale.

When a company enters into a sales-type lease, a lease agreement in which the present value of lease payment is greater than the value of the leased asset to the lessor, it will show a profit on the transaction in the year of inception and interest revenue over the life of the lease.

---

25 IFRS does not make the distinction between a sales-type lease and a direct financing lease. However, a similar treatment to "sales-type" is allowed for finance leases originated by "manufacturer or dealer lessors," within the general provisions for finance leases.

EXAMPLE 14

Financial Statement Impact of a Sales-type Lease for the Lessor

Assume a (hypothetical) company, Selnow Inc., owns a piece of machinery and enters into an agreement to lease the machinery on 1 January Year 1. In the lease contract, the company requires four annual payments of €28,679 starting on 1 January Year 1. The present value of the lease payments (using a 10 percent discount rate) is €100,000, and the fair value of the equipment is €90,000. The useful life of the machinery is four years and its salvage value is zero.

1 Is the lease a direct financing or sales-type lease?

2 What is Selnow's income related to the lease in Year 1? In Year 2? Ignore taxes.

Solution to 1:

This is a sales-type lease: The present value of lease payments is more than the lessor's carrying amount of the leased asset. The difference between the present value of the lease payments and the carrying amount of the leased asset is the lessor's profit from selling the machinery. The lessor will record a profit of €10,000 on the sale of the leased equipment in Year 1 (€100,000 present value of lease payments receivable less €90,000 value of leased equipment).

Solution to 2:

In Year 1, Selnow shows income of €17,132 related to the lease. One part of this is the €10,000 gain on the sale of the lease equipment (sales revenues of €100,000 less costs of goods sold of €90,000). Selnow also shows interest revenue of €7,132 on its financing of the lease (lease receivable of €71,321 after the initial lease payment is received times the 10 percent discount rate). In Year 2, Selnow reports only the interest revenue of €4,977 (lease receivable of €49,774 after the 1 January lease payment is received times the 10 percent discount rate). The table below shows lease payments received, interest revenue, and reduction of the lease receivable for Selnow's sales-type lease. Note that this table is the same as DIRFIN's table in the previous example with the direct financing lease. They are the same because the present value of the lease payments in both cases is the same. It is the fair value of the equipment that differs between the two examples.

Year	Lease Receivable, 1 January (a)	Annual Lease Payment Received, 1 January (b)	Interest (at 10%; Accrued in Previous Year) (c)	Reduction of Lease Receivable, 1 January (d)	Lease Receivable on 31 December after Lease Payment on 1 January Same Year (e)
1	€100,000	€28,679	€0	€28,679	€71,321
2	71,321	28,679	7,132	21,547	49,774
3	49,774	28,679	4,977	23,702	26,072
4	26,072	28,679	2,607	26,072	0
		€114,717	€14,717	€100,000	

SUMMARY

This reading describes how companies' decisions about accounting for tangible and intangible long-lived assets affect their financial statements. Compared to expensing an expenditure in the current period, capitalising an expenditure results in higher profits and higher operating cash flows in the year of the expenditure. For capitalised amounts that are to be depreciated (or amortised), estimating a longer useful life and a higher salvage value results in higher profits in the earlier years of the asset's life.

After an asset is acquired, if its value declines such that its recoverable value is lower than its carrying amount, a company must record an impairment charge against income to reflect that change. Under IFRS, companies can subsequently revalue the asset if its value increases, but under US GAAP, revaluation is not permitted. Another key difference between IFRS and US GAAP reporting for long-lived assets is that IFRS (but *not* US GAAP) offer companies two distinct alternatives for reporting long-lived assets: the historical cost model or the revaluation model.

As an alternative to acquiring an asset, a company may choose to lease an asset. Leases are generally characterised as either operating leases, which is similar to renting the asset, or capital leases, which is similar to purchasing the asset. As a lessee, a capital lease increases both the company's reported assets and liabilities, generally increasing leverage. An operating lease does not change the company's balance sheet.

Key points include the following:

- Expenditures related to long-lived assets are included as part of the value of assets on the balance sheet, i.e., capitalised, if they are expected to provide future benefits, typically beyond one year.

- Although capitalising expenditures, rather than expensing, results in higher reported profit in the initial year, it results in lower profits in subsequent years; however, if a company continues to purchase similar or increasing amounts of assets each year, the profitability-enhancing effect of capitalising continues.

- Capitalising an expenditure rather than expensing it results in greater amounts reported as cash from operations.

- Including capitalised interest in the calculation of interest coverage ratios provides a better assessment of a company's solvency.

- If companies apply different approaches to capitalising software development costs, adjustments can be made to make the two comparable.

- Significant estimates required for depreciation calculations include the useful life of the equipment (or its total lifetime productive capacity) and its expected residual value at the end of that useful life. A longer useful life and higher expected residual value decrease the amount of annual depreciation relative to a shorter useful life and lower expected residual value.

- Intangible assets with finite useful lives are amortised over their useful lives.

- Intangible assets with indefinite useful lives are not amortised, but are tested for impairment whenever changes in events or circumstances indicate that the carrying amount of an asset may not be recoverable (and at least annually in the case of identifiable intangible assets with indefinite useful lives and goodwill).

- In contrast with depreciation and amortisation charges, which serve to allocate the cost of a long-lived asset over its useful life, impairment charges reflect a decline in the fair value of an asset to an amount lower than its carrying amount.

- Impairment disclosures can provide useful information about a company's expected cash flows.

- Under IFRS, companies can use the historical cost model or the revaluation model to report long-lived assets.

- Under US GAAP, the value of long-lived assets must be reported at depreciated historical cost. This value may be decreased by impairment charges, but cannot be increased. IFRS, however, permit impairment losses to be reversed.

- Estimates of average age and remaining useful life of a company's assets reflect the relationship between assets accounted for on a historical cost basis and depreciation amounts.

- The average remaining useful life of a company's assets can be estimated as net PPE divided by depreciation expense, although the accounting useful life may not necessarily correspond to the economic useful life.

- To estimate the average age of the asset base, divide accumulated depreciation by depreciation expense.

- Accounting standards generally define two types of leases: operating leases and finance (or capital) leases. US GAAP specify four criteria to determine when a lease is classified as a capital lease. IFRS are less prescriptive in determining the classification of a lease as a finance lease.

- When a lessee reports a lease as an operating lease rather than a finance lease, it usually appears more profitable in early years of the lease and less so later, and it appears more solvent over the whole period.

- When a company has a substantial amount of operating leases, adjusting reported financials to include the impact of capitalising these leases better reflects the company's solvency position.

- When a lessor reports a lease as a finance lease rather than an operating lease, it usually appears more profitable in early years of the lease.

- In direct financing leases under US GAAP, a lessor earns only interest revenue. In a sales-type lease under US GAAP, a lessor earns both interest revenue and a profit (or loss) on the sale of the leased asset.

PRACTICE PROBLEMS

The following information relates to Questions 1–6

Melanie Hart, CFA, is a transportation analyst. Hart has been asked to write a research report on Altai Mountain Rail Company (AMRC). Like other companies in the railroad industry, AMRC's operations are capital intensive, with significant investments in such long-lived tangible assets as property, plant, and equipment. In November of 2008, AMRC's board of directors hired a new team to manage the company. In reviewing the company's 2009 annual report, Hart is concerned about some of the accounting choices that the new management has made. These choices differ from those of the previous management and from common industry practice. Hart has highlighted the following statements from the company's annual report:

Statement 1   "In 2009, AMRC spent significant amounts on track replacement and similar improvements. AMRC expensed rather than capitalised a significant proportion of these expenditures."

Statement 2   "AMRC uses the straight-line method of depreciation for both financial and tax reporting purposes to account for plant and equipment."

Statement 3   "In 2009, AMRC recognized an impairment loss of €50 million on a fleet of locomotives. The impairment loss was reported as 'other income' in the income statement and reduced the carrying amount of the assets on the balance sheet."

Statement 4   "AMRC acquires the use of many of its assets, including a large portion of its fleet of rail cars, under long-term lease contracts. In 2009, AMRC acquired the use of equipment with a fair value of €200 million under 20-year lease contracts. These leases were classified as operating leases. Prior to 2009, most of these lease contracts were classified as finance leases."

Exhibits 1 and 2 contain AMRC's 2009 consolidated income statement and balance sheet. AMRC prepares its financial statements in accordance with International Financial Reporting Standards.

Exhibit 1 Consolidated Statement of Income				
	2009		**2008**	
For the Years Ended 31 December	**€ Millions**	**% Revenues**	**€ Millions**	**% Revenues**
Operating revenues	2,600	100.0	2,300	100.0
Operating expenses				
Depreciation	(200)	(7.7)	(190)	(8.3)
Lease payments	(210)	(8.1)	(195)	(8.5)
Other operating expense	(1,590)	(61.1)	(1,515)	(65.9)
Total operating expenses	(2,000)	(76.9)	(1,900)	(82.6)

(continued)

Exhibit 1   (Continued)

For the Years Ended 31 December	2009		2008	
	€ Millions	% Revenues	€ Millions	% Revenues
Operating income	600	23.1	400	17.4
Other income	(50)	(1.9)	—	0.0
Interest expense	(73)	(2.8)	(69)	(3.0)
Income before taxes	477	18.4	331	14.4
Income taxes	(189)	(7.3)	(125)	(5.4)
Net income	288	11.1	206	9.0

Exhibit 2   Consolidated Balance Sheet

As of 31 December	2009		2008	
Assets	€ Millions	% Assets	€ Millions	% Assets
Current assets	500	9.4	450	8.5
Property & equipment:				
Land	700	13.1	700	13.2
Plant & equipment	6,000	112.1	5,800	109.4
Total property & equipment	6,700	125.2	6,500	122.6
Accumulated depreciation	(1,850)	(34.6)	(1,650)	(31.1)
Net property & equipment	4,850	90.6	4,850	91.5
Total assets	5,350	100.0	5,300	100.0
Liabilities and Shareholders' Equity				
Current liabilities	480	9.0	430	8.1
Long-term debt	1,030	19.3	1,080	20.4
Other long-term provisions and liabilities	1,240	23.1	1,440	27.2
Total liabilities	2,750	51.4	2,950	55.7
Shareholders' equity				
Common stock and paid-in-surplus	760	14.2	760	14.3
Retained earnings	1,888	35.5	1,600	30.2
Other comprehensive losses	(48)	(0.9)	(10)	(0.2)
Total shareholders' equity	2,600	48.6	2,350	44.3
Total liabilities & shareholders' equity	5,350	100.0	5,300	100.0

1   With respect to Statement 1, which of the following is the *most likely* effect of management's decision to expense rather than capitalise these expenditures?

A   2009 net profit margin is higher than if the expenditures had been capitalised.

B   2009 total asset turnover is lower than if the expenditures had been capitalised.

C Future profit growth will be higher than if the expenditures had been capitalised.

2 With respect to Statement 2, what would be the *most likely* effect in 2010 if AMRC were to switch to an accelerated depreciation method for both financial and tax reporting?

A Net profit margin would increase.

B Total asset turnover would decrease.

C Cash flow from operating activities would increase.

3 With respect to Statement 3, what is the *most likely* effect of the impairment loss?

A Net income in years prior to 2009 was likely understated.

B Net profit margins in years after 2009 will likely exceed the 2009 net profit margin.

C Cash flow from operating activities in 2009 was likely lower due to the impairment loss.

4 Based on Exhibits 1 and 2, the *best estimate* of the average remaining useful life of the company's plant and equipment at the end of 2009 is:

A 20.75 years.

B 24.25 years.

C 30.00 years.

5 With respect to Statement 4, if AMRC had used its old classification method for its leases instead of its new classification method, its 2009 total asset turnover ratio would *most likely* be:

A lower.

B higher.

C the same.

6 With respect to Statement 4 and Exhibit 1, if AMRC had used its old classification method for its leases instead of its new classification method, the *most likely* effect on its 2009 ratios would be a:

A higher net profit margin.

B higher fixed asset turnover.

C higher total liabilities-to-total assets ratio.

The following information relates to Questions 7–13

Brian Jordan is interviewing for a junior equity analyst position at Orion Investment Advisors. As part of the interview process, Mary Benn, Orion's Director of Research, provides Jordan with information about two hypothetical companies, Alpha and Beta, and asks him to comment on the information on their financial statements and ratios. Both companies prepare their financial statements in accordance with International Financial Reporting Standards (IFRS) and are identical in all respects except for their accounting choices.

Jordan is told that at the beginning of the current fiscal year, both companies purchased a major new computer system and began building new manufacturing plants for their own use. Alpha capitalised and Beta expensed the cost of the computer system; Alpha capitalised and Beta expensed the interest costs associated with the construction of the manufacturing plants. In mid-year, both companies leased new office headquarters. Alpha classified the lease as an operating lease, and Beta classified it as a finance lease.

Benn asks Jordan, "What was the impact of these decisions on each company's current fiscal year financial statements and ratios?"

Jordan responds, "Alpha's decision to capitalise the cost of its new computer system instead of expensing it results in lower net income, lower total assets, and higher cash flow from operating activities in the current fiscal year. Alpha's decision to capitalise its interest costs instead of expensing them results in a lower fixed asset turnover ratio and a higher interest coverage ratio. Alpha's decision to classify its lease as an operating lease instead of a finance lease results in higher net income, higher cash flow from operating activities, and stronger solvency and activity ratios compared to Beta."

Jordan is told that Alpha uses the straight-line depreciation method and Beta uses an accelerated depreciation method; both companies estimate the same useful lives for long-lived assets. Many companies in their industry use the units-of-production method.

Benn asks Jordan, "What are the financial statement implications of each depreciation method, and how do you determine a company's need to reinvest in its productive capacity?"

Jordan replies, "All other things being equal, the straight-line depreciation method results in the least variability of net profit margin over time, while an accelerated depreciation method results in a declining trend in net profit margin over time. The units-of-production can result in a net profit margin trend that is quite variable. I use a three-step approach to estimate a company's need to reinvest in its productive capacity. First, I estimate the average age of the assets by dividing net property, plant, and equipment by annual depreciation expense. Second, I estimate the average remaining useful life of the assets by dividing accumulated depreciation by depreciation expense. Third, I add the estimates of the average remaining useful life and the average age of the assets in order to determine the total useful life."

Jordan is told that at the end of the current fiscal year, Alpha revalued a manufacturing plant; this increased its reported carrying amount by 15 percent. There was no previous downward revaluation of the plant. Beta recorded an impairment loss on a manufacturing plant; this reduced its carrying by 10 percent.

Benn asks Jordan "What was the impact of these decisions on each company's current fiscal year financial ratios?"

Jordan responds, "Beta's impairment loss increases its debt to total assets and fixed asset turnover ratios, and lowers its cash flow from operating activities. Alpha's revaluation increases its debt to capital and return on assets ratios, and reduces its return on equity."

At the end of the interview, Benn thanks Jordan for his time and states that a hiring decision will be made shortly.

7 Jordan's response about the financial statement impact of Alpha's decision to capitalise the cost of its new computer system is most likely *correct* with respect to:

A lower net income.

B lower total assets.

C higher cash flow from operating activities.

8 Jordan's response about the ratio impact of Alpha's decision to capitalise interest costs is most likely *correct* with respect to the:

A interest coverage ratio.

B fixed asset turnover ratio.

C interest coverage and fixed asset turnover ratios.

9 Jordan's response about the impact of Alpha's decision to classify its lease as an operating lease instead of finance lease is most likely *incorrect* with respect to:

A net income.

B solvency and activity ratios.

C cash flow from operating activities.

10 Jordan's response about the impact of the different depreciation methods on net profit margin is most likely *incorrect* with respect to:

A accelerated depreciation.

B straight-line depreciation.

C units-of-production depreciation.

11 Jordan's response about his approach to estimating a company's need to reinvest in its productive capacity is most likely *correct* regarding:

A estimating the average age of the asset base.

B estimating the total useful life of the asset base.

C estimating the average remaining useful life of the asset base.

12 Jordan's response about the effect of Beta's impairment loss is most likely *incorrect* with respect to the impact on its:

A debt to total assets.

B fixed asset turnover.

C cash flow from operating activities.

13 Jordan's response about the effect of Alpha's revaluation is most likely *correct* with respect to the impact on its:

A return on equity.

B return on assets.

C debt to capital ratio.

SOLUTIONS

1 C is correct. Expensing rather than capitalising an investment in long-term assets will result in higher expenses and lower net income and net profit margin in the current year. Future years' incomes will not include depreciation expense related to these expenditures. Consequently, year-to-year growth in profitability will be higher. If the expenses had been capitalised, the carrying amount of the assets would have been higher and the 2009 total asset turnover would have been lower.

2 C is correct. In 2010, switching to an accelerated depreciation method would increase depreciation expense and decrease income before taxes, taxes payable, and net income. Cash flow from operating activities would increase because of the resulting tax savings.

3 B is correct. 2009 net income and net profit margin are lower because of the impairment loss. Consequently, net profit margins in subsequent years are likely to be higher. An impairment loss suggests that insufficient depreciation expense was recognized in prior years, and net income was overstated in prior years. The impairment loss is a non-cash item and will not affect operating cash flows.

4 A is correct. The estimated average remaining useful life is 20.75 years.

Estimate of remaining useful life = Net plant and equipment ÷ Annual depreciation expense

Net plant and equipment = Gross P & E − Accumulated depreciation
= €6000 − €1850 = €4150

Estimate of remaining useful life = Net P & E ÷ Depreciation expense
= €4150 ÷ €200 = 20.75

5 A is correct. When leases are classified as finance leases, the lessee initially reports an asset and liability at a carrying amount equal to the lower of the fair value of the leased asset or the present value of the future lease payments. Under an operating lease, the lessee does not report an asset or liability. Therefore, total asset turnover (total revenue ÷ average total assets) would be lower if the leases were classified as finance leases.

6 C is correct. Total liabilities-to-assets would be higher. When leases are classified as finance leases, the lessee initially reports an asset and liability at a carrying amount equal to the lower of the fair value of the leased asset or the present value of the future lease payments. Both the numerator and denominator would increase by an equal amount, but the proportional increase in the numerator is higher and the ratio would be higher. The following exhibit shows what would happen to 2009 total liabilities, assets, and total liabilities-to-assets if €200 million, the fair value of the leased equipment, is added to AMRC's total liabilities and assets. This simple example ignores the impact of accounting for the 2009 lease payment.

	2009 Actual Under Operating Lease	2009 Hypothetical Under Finance Lease
Total liabilities	€2,750	€2,950
Total assets	€5,350	€5,550
Total liabilities-to-assets	51.4%	53.2%

The depreciation and interest expense under a finance lease tends to be higher than the operating lease payment in the early years of the lease. The finance lease would result in lower net income and net profit margin. Long-lived (fixed) assets are higher under a finance lease and fixed asset turnover is lower.

7   C is correct. The decision to capitalise the costs of the new computer system results in higher cash flow from operating activities; the expenditure is reported as an outflow of investing activities. The company allocates the capitalised amount over the asset's useful life as depreciation or amortisation expense rather than expensing it in the year of expenditure. Net income and total assets are higher in the current fiscal year.

8   B is correct. Alpha's fixed asset turnover will be lower because the capitalised interest will appear on the balance sheet as part of the asset being constructed. Therefore, fixed assets will be higher and the fixed asset turnover ratio (total revenue/average net fixed assets) will be lower than if it had expensed these costs. Capitalised interest appears on the balance sheet as part of the asset being constructed instead of being reported as interest expense in the period incurred. However, the interest coverage ratio should be based on interest payments, not interest expense (earnings before interest and taxes/interest payments), and should be unchanged. To provide a true picture of a company's interest coverage, the entire amount of interest expenditure, both the capital-ised portion and the expensed portion, should be used in calculating interest coverage ratios.

9   C is correct. The cash flow from operating activities will be lower, not higher, because the full lease payment is treated as an operating cash outflow. With a finance lease, only the portion of the lease payment relating to interest expense potentially reduces operating cash outflows. A company reporting a lease as an operating lease will typically show higher profits in early years, because the lease expense is less than the sum of the interest and depreciation expense. The company reporting the lease as an operating lease will typically report stronger solvency and activity ratios.

10 A is correct. Accelerated depreciation will result in an improving, not declin-ing, net profit margin over time, because the amount of depreciation expense declines each year. Under straight-line depreciation, the amount of depreciation expense will remain the same each year. Under the units-of-production method, the amount of depreciation expense reported each year varies with the number of units produced.

11 B is correct. The estimated average total useful life of a company's assets is calculated by adding the estimates of the average remaining useful life and the average age of the assets. The average age of the assets is estimated by divid-ing accumulated depreciation by depreciation expense. The average remaining useful life of the asset base is estimated by dividing net property, plant, and equipment by annual depreciation expense.

12 C is correct. The impairment loss is a non-cash charge and will not affect cash flow from operating activities. The debt to total assets and fixed asset turn-over ratios will increase, because the impairment loss will reduce the carrying amount of fixed assets and therefore total assets.

13 A is correct. In an asset revaluation, the carrying amount of the assets increases. The increase in the asset's carrying amount bypasses the income statement and is reported as other comprehensive income and appears in equity under the heading of revaluation surplus. Therefore, shareholders' equity will increase but net income will not be affected, so return on equity will decline. Return on assets and debt to capital ratios will also decrease.

Financial Reporting and Analysis

Intercorporate Investments, Post-Employment and Share-Based Compensation, and Multinational Operations

Intercorporate investments receive different accounting treatments depending on the percentage ownership, amount of control, and other variables that define the relation between the company making the investment (the investor) and the investee. An analysis of intercorporate investments is necessary to separate operating performance from investing performance and to understand the potential accounting distortions that arise as a result of accounting standards and/or earnings management.

Mergers and acquisitions can be an important strategic consideration that affects financial statements and ratios. The accounting standards that govern business combinations are the result of a joint project between the IASB and the FASB. IFRS and US GAAP require the use of the acquisition method. The structure and scope of business combinations create comparability challenges because the financial statements of the acquiring company may be radically changed. An analyst must understand how business combinations, including full consolidation and proportionate consolidation, affect the comparability of financial statements and ratios.

IFRS and US GAAP require the reporting of net obligations (or net assets) for pensions and other post-employment benefits on the balance sheet. IFRS and US GAAP may differ in their treatment of periodic pension costs and reporting of pension expenses. Analysts must also understand how the accounting treatment of employee stock options affects financial statements.

Multinational companies often have subsidiaries in different countries that maintain their books and records in currencies different from that of the parent company. Floating exchange rates present an additional challenge. Foreign currency transactions and translations in a parent company's financial statements must be analyzed to evaluate a company's performance and financial position.

Note: New rulings and/or pronouncements issued after the publication of the readings in financial reporting and analysis may cause some of the information in these readings to become dated. Candidates are expected to be familiar with the overall analytical framework contained in the study session readings, as well as the implications of alternative accounting methods for financial analysis and valuation, as provided in the assigned readings. Candidates are not responsible for changes that occur after the material was written.

READING ASSIGNMENTS

Reading 18	Intercorporate Investments
	by Susan Perry Williams, CPA, CMA, PhD
Reading 19	Employee Compensation: Post-Employment and Share-Based
	by Elaine Henry, PhD, CFA, and Elizabeth A. Gordon
Reading 20	Multinational Operations
	by Timothy S. Doupnik, PhD, and Elaine Henry, PhD, CFA

Intercorporate Investments

by Susan Perry Williams, CPA, CMA, PhD

Susan Perry Williams, CPA, CMA, PhD, is at the McIntire School of Commerce, University of Virginia (USA).

LEARNING OUTCOMES

Mastery	The candidate should be able to:
☐	**a.** describe the classification, measurement, and disclosure under International Financial Reporting Standards (IFRS) for 1) investments in financial assets, 2) investments in associates, 3) joint ventures, 4) business combinations, and 5) special purpose and variable interest entities;
☐	**b.** distinguish between IFRS and US GAAP in the classification, measurement, and disclosure of investments in financial assets, investments in associates, joint ventures, business combinations, and special purpose and variable interest entities;
☐	**c.** analyze how different methods used to account for intercorporate investments affect financial statements and ratios.

Note: New rulings and/or pronouncements issued after the publication of the readings in financial reporting and analysis may cause some of the information in these readings to become dated. Candidates are expected to be familiar with the overall analytical framework contained in the study session readings, as well as the implications of alternative accounting methods for financial analysis and valuation, as provided in the assigned readings. Candidates are not responsible for changes that occur after the material was written.

INTRODUCTION

Intercorporate investments (investments in other companies) can have a significant impact on an investing company's financial performance and position. Companies invest in the debt and equity securities of other companies to diversify their asset base, enter new markets, obtain competitive advantages, and achieve additional profitability. Debt securities include commercial paper, corporate and government bonds and notes, redeemable preferred stock, and asset-backed securities. Equity securities include common stock and non-redeemable preferred stock. The percentage of equity ownership a company acquires in an investee depends on the resources available, the ability to acquire the shares, and the desired level of influence or control.

The International Accounting Standards Board (IASB) and the US Financial Accounting Standards Board (FASB) have worked to reduce differences in accounting standards that apply to the classification, measurement, and disclosure of intercorporate investments. The resulting standards have improved the relevance, transparency, and comparability of information provided in financial statements. This reading includes accounting standards issued by IASB and FASB through 31 December 2012. References for US GAAP reflect the new FASB Accounting Standards Codification™ (FASB ASC).

Moving towards convergence, in December 2007, the FASB issued two new standards: SFAS 141(R), *Business Combinations*,[1] and SFAS 160, *Noncontrolling Interests in Consolidated Financial Statements*.[2] These statements introduced significant changes in the accounting for and reporting of business acquisitions and non-controlling interests in a subsidiary. In January 2008, the IASB revised IFRS 3, *Business Combinations* and amended IAS 27, *Consolidated and Separate Financial Statements*. In 2011, the IASB issued a revised IAS 27, *Separate Financial Statements*, and replaced portions of the earlier IAS 27 with IFRS 10, *Consolidated Financial Statements*. The new standards are effective for annual periods beginning on or after 1 January 2013.

Another convergence effort is the project on classification and measurement of financial assets and financial liabilities. The first phase of the project has been incorporated in IFRS 9, *Financial Instruments – Classification and Measurement*. This pronouncement initially required adoption for annual periods beginning on or after 1 January 2013. However, the effective date has been extended to annual periods beginning on or after 1 January 2018, with early adoption permitted. Phases two and three of the project will address financial instrument impairments and hedge accounting. When completed, this standard is expected to replace IAS 39, *Financial Instruments: Recognition and Measurement*. The FASB is working on a similar standard for classification and measurement but has not issued a pronouncement.

Convergence between IFRS and US GAAP makes it easier to compare financial reports because the accounting is the same or similar for many transactions. However, differences still remain. When differences exist, there is generally enough transparency in the disclosures to allow financial statement users to adjust for the differences. Understanding the appropriate accounting treatment for different intercorporate investments and the similarities and differences that exist between IFRS and US GAAP will enable analysts to make better comparisons between companies and improve investment decision making. The terminology used in this reading is IFRS oriented. US GAAP may not use identical terminology, but in most cases the terminology is similar.

This reading is organized as follows: Section 2 explains the basic categorization of corporate investments. Section 3 describes reporting for investments in debt and equity securities of other entities prior to IFRS 9 taking effect (hereafter referred to

---

1 FASB ASC Topic 805 [Business Combinations].
2 FASB ASC Topic 810 [Consolidations].

as current standards or reporting). Section 4 describes reporting under IFRS 9, the IASB standard for financial instruments that becomes effective in 2018 (hereafter referred to as new standard or reporting). Section 4 also illustrates the primary differences between the current and new standards. Section 5 describes equity method reporting for investments in associates where significant influence can exist including the reporting for joint ventures, a type of investment where control is shared. Section 6 describes reporting for business combinations, the parent/subsidiary relationship, and variable interest and special purpose entities. A summary and practice problems in the CFA Institute item set format complete the reading.

BASIC CORPORATE INVESTMENT CATEGORIES

In general, investments in marketable debt and equity securities can be categorized as 1) investments in financial assets in which the investor has no significant influence or control over the operations of the investee, 2) investments in associates in which the investor can exert significant influence (but not control) over the investee, 3) joint ventures where control is shared by two or more entities, and 4) business combinations, including investments in subsidiaries, in which the investor has control over the investee The distinction between investments in financial assets, investments in associates, and business combinations is based on the degree of influence or control rather than purely on the percent holding. However, lack of influence is generally presumed when the investor holds less than a 20% equity interest, significant influence is generally presumed between 20% and 50%, and control is presumed when the percentage of ownership exceeds 50%.

The following excerpt from Note 2 to the Financial Statements in the 2011 Annual Report of GlaxoSmithKline (London Stock Exchange: GSK), a British pharmaceutical and healthcare company, illustrates the categorization and disclosure in practice:

> Entities over which the Group has the power to govern the financial and operating policies are accounted for as subsidiaries. Where the Group has the ability to exercise joint control, the entities are accounted for as joint ventures, and where the Group has the ability to exercise significant influence, they are accounted for as associates. The results and assets and liabilities of associates and joint ventures are incorporated into the consolidated financial statements using the equity method of accounting.

A summary of the financial reporting and relevant standards for various types of corporate investment is presented in Exhibit 1 (the headings in Exhibit 1 use the terminology of IFRS; US GAAP categorizes intercorporate investments similarly but not identically). The reader should be alert to the fact that value measurement and/ or the treatment of changes in value can vary depending on the classification and whether IFRS or US GAAP is used. The alternative treatments are discussed in greater depth later in this reading.

Exhibit 1	Summary of Accounting Treatments for Investments			
	In Financial Assets	**In Associates**	**Business Combinations**	**In Joint Ventures**
Influence	Not significant	Significant	Controlling	Shared control
Typical percentage interest	Usually < 20%	Usually 20% to 50%	Usually > 50% or other indications of control	
Current Financial Reporting (prior to IFRS 9 taking effect)	Classified as: ▪ Held to maturity ▪ Available for sale ▪ Fair value through profit or loss (held for trading or designated as fair value) ▪ Loans and receivables	Equity method	Consolidation	IFRS: Equity method or proportionate consolidation
Applicable IFRS [a]	IAS 39	IAS 28	IAS 27	IAS 31 (replaced by IFRS 11)
US GAAP [b]	FASB ASC Topic 320	FASB ASC Topic 323	FASB ASC Topics 805 and 810	FASB ASC Topic 323
New Financial Reporting (post IFRS 9 taking effect)	Classified as: ▪ Fair value through profit or loss ▪ Fair value through other comprehensive income ▪ Amortized cost	Equity method	Consolidation	IFRS: Equity method
Applicable IFRS [a]	IFRS 9	IAS 28	IAS 27 IFRS 3 IFRS 10	IFRS 11 IFRS 12 IAS 28
US GAAP [b]	FASB ASC Topic 320	FASB ASC Topic 323	FASB ASC Topics 805 and 810	FASB ASC Topic 323

[a] IAS 39 Financial Instruments: Recognition and Measurement; IFRS 9 Financial Instruments; IAS 28 Investments in Associates; IAS 27 Separate Financial Statements (Previously, Consolidated and Separate Financial Statements); IFRS 3 Business Combinations; IAS 31 Interests in Joint Ventures; IFRS 10 Consolidated Financial Statements; IFRS 11 Joint Arrangements; IFRS 12, Disclosure of Interests in Other Entities.
[b] FASB ASC Topic 320 [Investments–Debt and Equity Securities]; FASB ASC Topic 323 [Investments– Equity Method and Joint Ventures]; FASB ASC Topics 805 [Business Combinations] and 810 [Consolidations].

3   INVESTMENTS IN FINANCIAL ASSETS: STANDARD IAS 39 (AS OF DECEMBER 2012)

When the investor cannot exert significant influence or control over the operations of the investee, investments in financial assets (debt and equity) are considered passive. IFRS and US GAAP are similar regarding the accounting for investments in financial assets. IFRS has four basic classifications of investments in financial assets: 1) held-to-maturity, 2) fair value through profit or loss, 3) available-for-sale, and 4) loans and receivables. Under IFRS, financial assets classified as fair value through profit or loss includes both financial assets held for trading and financial assets specifically designated as through profit or loss by management. These classifications determine the reporting for the investments.

Passive investments in financial assets are initially recognized at fair value. Dividend and interest income from investments in financial assets, regardless of categorization, are reported in the income statement. The reporting of subsequent changes in fair value, however, depends on the classification of the financial asset.

3.1 Held-to-Maturity

Held-to-maturity investments are investments in financial assets with fixed or determinable payments and fixed maturities (debt securities) that the investor has the positive intent and ability to hold to maturity. Held-to-maturity investments are exceptions from the general requirement (under both IFRS and US GAAP) that investments in financial assets are subsequently recognized at fair value. Therefore, strict criteria apply before this designation can be used. Under both IFRS and US GAAP, the investor must have a positive intent and ability to hold the security to maturity.

Reclassifications and sales prior to maturity may call into question the company's intent and ability. Under IFRS, a company is not permitted to classify any financial assets as held-to-maturity if it has, during the current or two preceding financial reporting years, sold or reclassified more than an insignificant amount of held-to-maturity investments before maturity unless the sale or reclassification meets certain criteria. Similarly, under US GAAP, a sale (and by inference a reclassification) is taken as an indication that intent was not truly present and use of the held-to-maturity category may be precluded for the company in the future.

IFRS require that held-to-maturity securities be initially recognized at fair value, whereas US GAAP require held-to-maturity securities be initially recognized at initial price paid. In most cases, however, initial fair value is equal to initial price paid so the treatment is identical. At each reporting date (subsequent to initial recognition), IFRS and US GAAP require that held-to-maturity securities are reported at amortized cost using the effective interest rate method,[3] unless objective evidence of impairment exists. Any difference—discount or premium—between maturity (par) value and fair value existing at the time of purchase is amortized over the life of the security. A discount (par value exceeds fair value) occurs when the stated interest rate is less than the effective rate, and a premium (fair value exceeds par value) occurs when the stated interest rate is greater than the effective rate. Amortization impacts the carrying value of the security. Any interest payments received are adjusted for amortization and are reported as interest income. If the security is sold before maturity (with the potential consequences described above), any realized gains or losses arising from the sale are recognized in profit or loss of the period. Transaction costs are included in initial fair value for investments that are not classified as fair value through profit or loss.

---

3 The effective interest method is a method of calculating the carrying value of a debt security and allocating the interest income to the period in which it is earned. It is based on the effective interest rate calculated at the time of purchase. Under US GAAP, the calculation of the effective interest rate is generally based on *contractual* cash flows over the asset's *contractual* life. Under IFRS, the effective rate is based on the *estimated* cash flows over the *expected* life of the asset. Contractual cash flows over the full contractual term of the security are only used if the expected cash flows over the expected life of the security cannot be reliably estimated.

3.2 Fair Value through Profit or Loss

Under IFRS, securities classified as fair value through profit or loss include securities held for trading and those designated by management as carried at fair value. US GAAP is similar; however, the classification is based on legal form and special guidance exists for some financial assets.

3.2.1 *Held for Trading*

Held for trading investments are debt or equity securities acquired with the intent to sell them in the near term. Held for trading securities are reported at fair value. At each reporting date, the held for trading investments are remeasured and recognized at fair value with any unrealized gains and losses arising from changes in fair value reported in profit or loss. Also included in profit or loss are interest received on debt securities and dividends received on equity securities.

3.2.2 *Designated at Fair Value*

Both IFRS and US GAAP allow entities to initially designate investments at fair value that might otherwise be classified as available-for-sale or held-to-maturity. The accounting treatment for investments designated at fair value is similar to that of held for trading investments. Initially, the investment is recognized at fair value. At each subsequent reporting date, the investments are remeasured at fair value with any unrealized gains and losses arising from changes in fair value as well as any interest and dividends received included in profit or loss.

3.3 Available-for-Sale

Available-for-sale investments are debt and equity securities not classified as held-to-maturity or fair value through profit or loss. Under both IFRS and US GAAP, investments classified as available-for-sale are initially measured at fair value. At each subsequent reporting date, the investments are remeasured and recognized at fair value. Unrealized gain or loss at the end of the reporting period is the difference between fair value and the carrying amount at that date. Other comprehensive income (in shareholder's equity) is adjusted to reflect the cumulative unrealized gain or loss. The amount reported in other comprehensive income is net of taxes. When these investments are sold, the cumulative gain or loss previously recognized in other comprehensive income is reclassified (i.e., reversed out of other comprehensive income) and reported as a reclassification adjustment on the statement of profit or loss. Interest (calculated using the effective interest method) from debt securities and dividends from equity securities are included in profit or loss.

IFRS and US GAAP differ on the treatment of foreign exchange gains and losses on available-for-sale debt securities.[4] Under IFRS, for the purpose of recognizing foreign exchange gains and losses, a debt security is treated as if it were carried at amortized cost in the foreign currency. Exchange rate differences arising from changes in amortized cost are recognized in profit or loss, and other changes in the carrying amount are recognized in other comprehensive income. In other words, the total exchange gain or loss in fair value of an available-for-sale debt security is divided into two components. The portion attributable to foreign exchange gains and losses is recognized on the income statement (in profit or loss), and the remaining portion is recognized in other comprehensive income. Under US GAAP, the total change in

---

4 Under IAS 21, a debt security is defined as a monetary item, because the holder (investor) has the right to receive a fixed or determinable number of units of currency in the form of contractual interest payments. An equity instrument is not considered a monetary item.

fair value of available-for-sale debt securities (including foreign exchange rate gains or losses) is included in other comprehensive income. For equity securities, under IFRS and US GAAP, the gain or loss that is recognized in other comprehensive income arising from changes in fair value includes any related foreign exchange component. There is no separate recognition of foreign exchange gains or losses.

3.4 Loans and Receivables

Loans and receivables are broadly defined as non-derivative financial assets with fixed or determinable payments. Loans and receivables that meet the more specific IFRS definition in the current standard are carried at amortized cost unless designated as either fair value through profit or loss or available for sale. IFRS does not rely on a legal form, whereas US GAAP relies on the legal form for the classification of debt securities. Loans and receivables that meet the definition of a debt security under US GAAP are typically classified as held for trading, available-for-sale, or held-to-maturity. Held for trading and available-for-sale securities are measured at fair value.

The accounting treatment for investments in financial assets under IFRS is illustrated in Exhibit 2. This excerpt from the 2011 Annual Report of Volvo Group (OMX Nordic exchange: VOLV B),[5] a manufacturer of trucks, buses and construction equipment, discloses how its investments are classified, measured, and reported on its financial statements.

Exhibit 2   Volvo 2011 Annual Report

NOTES TO THE CONSOLIDATED FINANCIAL STATEMENTS RECOGNITION OF FINANCIAL ASSETS ...

The fair value of assets is determined based on valid market prices, when available. If market prices are unavailable, the fair value is determined for each asset using various measurement techniques. Transaction expenses are included in the asset's fair value, except in cases in which the change in value is recognized in profit and loss. The transaction costs that arise in conjunction with the assumption of financial liabilities are amortized over the term of the loan as a financial cost.

Embedded derivatives are detached from the related main contract, if applicable. Contracts containing embedded derivatives are valued at fair value in profit and loss if the contracts' inherent risk and other characteristics indicate a close relation to the embedded derivative.

FINANCIAL ASSETS AT FAIR VALUE THROUGH PROFIT OR LOSS

All of Volvo's financial assets that are recognized at fair value in profit and loss are classified as held for trading. This includes derivatives to which Volvo has decided not to apply hedge accounting as well as derivatives that are not part of an evidently effective hedge accounting policy pursuant to IAS 39. Gains and losses on these assets are recognized in profit and loss.

FINANCIAL ASSETS CLASSIFIED AS AVAILABLE FOR SALE

This category includes assets available for sale and assets that have not been classified in any of the other categories. These assets are initially measured at fair value including transaction costs. Any change in value is recognized directly

(continued)

---

5 As of this writing, the Volvo line of automobiles is not under the control and management of the Volvo Group.

Exhibit 2   (Continued)

in other comprehensive income. The cumulative gain or loss recognized in other comprehensive income is reversed in profit and loss on the sale of the asset. Unrealized declines in value are recognized in other comprehensive income, unless the decline is significant or prolonged. Then the impairment is recognized in profit and loss. If the event that caused the impairment no longer exists, impairment can be reversed in profit and loss if it does not involve an equity instrument.

Earned or paid interest attributable to these assets is recognized in profit and loss as part of net financial items in accordance with the effective interest method. Dividends received attributable to these assets are recognized in profit and loss as Income from other investments.

If assets available for sale are impaired, the impaired amount is the difference between the asset's cost (adjusted for any accrued interest if applicable) and its fair value. However, if equity instruments, such as shares, are involved, a completed impairment is not reversed in profit and loss. On the other hand, impairments performed on debt instruments (interest-bearing instruments) are wholly or partly reversible in profit and loss, in those instances where an event, proven to have occurred after the impairment was performed, is identified and impacts the valuation of that asset.

3.5 Reclassification of Investments

Under the current standard, both IFRS and US GAAP permit entities to reclassify their intercorporate investments. However, there are certain restrictions and criteria that must be met. Reclassification may result in changes in how the asset value is measured and how unrealized gains or losses are recognized.

IFRS generally prohibits the reclassification of securities into or out of the designated at fair value category,[6] and reclassification out of the held for trading category is severely restricted. Held-to-maturity (debt) securities can be reclassified as available-for-sale if a change in intention or a change in ability to hold the security until maturity occurs. At the time of reclassification to available-for-sale, the security is remeasured at fair value with the difference between its carrying amount (amortized cost) and fair value recognized in other comprehensive income. Recall that the reclassification has implications for the use of the held-to-maturity category for existing debt securities and new purchases. A mandatory reclassification and a prohibition from future use may result from the reclassification.

Debt securities initially designated as available-for-sale may be reclassified to held-to-maturity if a change in intention or ability has occurred. The fair value carrying amount of the security at the time of reclassification becomes its new (amortized) cost. Any previous gain or loss that had been recognized in other comprehensive income is amortized to profit or loss over the remaining life of the security using the effective interest method. Any difference between the new amortized cost of the security and its maturity value is amortized over the remaining life of the security using the effective interest method. If the definition is met, debt instruments may be reclassified from held for trading or available-for-sale to loans and receivables if the company expects to hold them for the foreseeable future.

---

6 In rare circumstances, IFRS permits reclassification of a financial asset if it is no longer held for the purpose of selling it in the near term. The financial asset is reclassified at its fair value with any gain or loss recognized in profit or loss, and the fair value on the date of its reclassification becomes its new cost or amortized cost.

Financial assets classified as available-for-sale may be measured at cost, where there is no longer a reliable measure of fair value and no evidence of impairment. However, if a reliable fair value measure becomes available, the financial asset must be remeasured at fair value with changes in value recognized in other comprehensive income.

US GAAP allows reclassifications (transfers) of securities between all categories when justified. Fair value of the security is determined at the date of transfer. However, recall that the reclassification of securities from the held-to-maturity category has implications for the use of this category for other securities. The treatment of unrealized holding gains and losses on the transfer date depends on the initial classification of the security.

1 If a security initially classified as held for trading is reclassified as available-for-sale, any unrealized gains and losses (arising from the difference between its carrying value and current fair value) are recognized in profit and loss.

2 If a security is reclassified as held for trading, the unrealized gains or losses are recognized immediately in profit and loss. In the case of reclassification from available-for-sale, the cumulative amount of gains and losses previously recognized in other comprehensive income is recognized in profit and loss on the date of transfer.

3 If a debt security is reclassified as available-for-sale from held-to-maturity, the unrealized holding gain or loss at the date of the reclassification (i.e., the difference between the fair value and amortized cost) is reported in other comprehensive income.

4 If a debt security is reclassified as held-to-maturity from available-for-sale, the cumulative amount of gains or losses previously reported in other comprehensive income will be amortized over the remaining life of the security as an adjustment of yield (interest income) in the same manner as a premium or discount.

3.6 Impairments

A financial asset (in this case, debt or equity securities) becomes impaired whenever its carrying amount is expected to permanently exceed its recoverable amount. There are key differences in the approaches taken by the IFRS and US GAAP to determine if a financial asset is impaired and how the impairment loss is measured and reported.

Under IFRS, at the end of each reporting period, financial assets not carried at fair value (individually or as a group) need to be reviewed for any objective evidence that the assets are impaired. Any current impairment will be recognized in profit or loss immediately. For investments measured and reported at fair value through profit or loss (designated as fair value through profit or loss, and held-for-trading), any prior impairment loss will have already been recognized in profit or loss.

A debt security is impaired if one or more events (loss events) occur that have a reliably estimated impact on its future cash flows. Although it may not be possible to identify a single specific event that caused the impairment, the combined effect of several events may cause the impairment. Losses expected as a result of future (anticipated) events, no matter how likely, are not recognized. Examples of loss events causing impairment are:

■ The issuer experiences significant financial difficulty;

■ Default or delinquency in interest or principal payments;

- The borrower encounters financial difficulty and receives a concession from the lender as a result; and
- It becomes probable that the borrower will enter bankruptcy or other financial reorganization.

The disappearance of an active market because an entity's financial instruments are no longer publicly traded is not evidence of impairment. A downgrade of an entity's credit rating or a decline in fair value of a security below its cost or amortized cost is also not by itself evidence of impairment. However, it may be evidence of impairment when considered with other available information.

For equity securities, objective evidence of a loss event includes:

- Significant changes in the technological, market, economic, and/or legal environments that adversely affect the investee and indicate that the initial cost of the equity investment may not be recovered.
- A significant or prolonged decline in the fair value of an equity investment below its cost.

For held-to-maturity (debt) investments and loans and receivables that have become impaired, the amount of the loss is measured as the difference between the security's carrying value and the present value of its estimated future cash flows discounted at the security's original effective interest rate (the effective interest rate computed at initial recognition). The carrying amount of the investment is reduced either directly or through the use of an allowance account, and the amount of the loss is recognized in profit or loss. If, in a subsequent period, the amount of the impairment loss decreases and the decrease can be objectively related to an event occurring after the impairment was recognized (for example, the debtor's credit rating improves), the previously recognized impairment loss can be reversed either directly (by increasing the carrying value of the security) or by adjusting the allowance account. The amount of this reversal is then recognized in profit or loss.

For available-for-sale securities that have become impaired, the cumulative loss that had been recognized in other comprehensive income is reclassified from equity to profit or loss as a reclassification adjustment. The amount of the cumulative loss to be reclassified is the difference between acquisition cost (net of any principal repayment and amortization) and current fair value, less any impairment loss that has previously been recognized in profit or loss. Impairment losses on available-for-sale equity securities cannot be reversed through profit or loss. However, impairment losses on available-for-sale debt securities can be reversed if a subsequent increase in fair value can be objectively related to an event occurring after the impairment loss was recognized in profit or loss. In this case, the impairment loss is reversed with the amount of the reversal recognized in profit or loss.

Exhibit 3 contains an excerpt from the 2011 Annual Report of Deutsche Bank (Deutsche Börse: DBK) that describes how impairment losses for its financial assets are determined, measured, and recognized on its financial statements.

Exhibit 3   Excerpt from Deutsche Bank 2011 Annual Report

IMPAIRMENT OF FINANCIAL ASSETS

At each balance sheet date, the Group assesses whether there is objective evidence that a financial asset or a group of financial assets is impaired. A financial asset or group of financial assets is impaired and impairment losses are incurred if:

- there is objective evidence of impairment as a result of a loss event that occurred after the initial recognition of the asset and up to the balance sheet date ("a loss event");
- the loss event had an impact on the estimated future cash flows of the financial asset or the group of financial assets; and
- a reliable estimate of the amount can be made.

IMPAIRMENT OF FINANCIAL ASSETS CLASSIFIED AS AVAILABLE FOR SALE

For financial assets classified as AFS, management assesses at each balance sheet date whether there is objective evidence that an asset is impaired.

In the case of equity investments classified as AFS, objective evidence includes a significant or prolonged decline in the fair value of the investment below cost. In the case of debt securities classified as AFS, impairment is assessed based on the same criteria as for loans.

If there is evidence of impairment, any amounts previously recognized in other comprehensive income are recognized in the consolidated statement of income for the period, reported in net gains (losses) on financial assets available for sale. This amount is determined as the difference between the acquisition cost (net of any principal repayments and amortization) and current fair value of the asset less any impairment loss on that investment previously recognized in the consolidated statement of income.

When an AFS debt security is impaired, any subsequent decreases in fair value are recognized in the consolidated statement of income as it is considered further impairment. Any subsequent increases are also recognized in the consolidate statement of income until the asset is no longer considered impaired. When the fair value of the AFS debt security recovers to at least amortized cost it is no longer considered impaired and subsequent changes in fair value are reported in other comprehensive income.

Reversals of impairment losses on equity investments classified as AFS are not reversed through the consolidated statement of income; increases in their fair value after impairment are recognized in other comprehensive income.

Under US GAAP, the determination of impairment and the calculation of the impairment loss are different than under IFRS. For securities classified as available-for-sale or held-to-maturity, the investor is required to determine at each balance sheet date whether the decline in value is other than temporary. For debt securities classified as held-to-maturity, this means that the investor will be unable to collect all amounts due according to the contractual terms existing at acquisition. If the decline in fair value is deemed to be other than temporary, the cost basis of the security is written down to its fair value, which then becomes the new cost basis of the security. The amount of the write-down is treated as a realized loss and reported on the income statement.

For available-for-sale securities (both debt and equity), if the decline in fair value is other than temporary, the cost basis of the security is written down to its fair value. This value becomes the new cost basis, and the amount of the write-down is treated as a realized loss. However, the new cost basis cannot be increased for subsequent increases in fair value. Instead, subsequent increases in fair value (and decreases, if other than temporary) are treated as unrealized gains or losses and included in other comprehensive income.

EXAMPLE 1

Accounting for Investments in Debt Securities

In this example, two fictitious companies are used. On 1 January 2011, Baxter Inc. invested £300,000 in Cartel Co. debt securities (with a 6% stated rate on par value, payable each 31 December). The par value of the securities was £275,000. On 31 December 2011, the fair value of Baxter's investment in Cartel is £350,000.

Assume that the market interest rate in effect when the bonds were purchased was 4.5%.[7] If the investment is designated as held-to-maturity, the investment is reported at amortized cost using the effective interest method. A portion of the amortization table is as follows:

End of Year	Interest Payment (£)	Interest Income (£)	Amortization (£)	Amortized Cost (£)
0				300,000
1*	16,500	13,500	3,000	297,000
2	16,500	13,365	3,135	293,865
3	16,500	13,224	3,276	290,589

* (6% × par value of £275,000 = £16,500) and (4.5% × carrying value of £300,000 = £13,500)

---

1   How would this investment be reported on the balance sheet, income statement, and statement of shareholders' equity at 31 December 2011, under either IFRS or US GAAP (accounting is essentially the same in this case), if Baxter designated the investment as 1) held-to-maturity, 2) held for trading, 3) available-for-sale, or 4) designated at fair value?

2   How would the gain be recognized if the debt securities were sold on 1 January 2012 for £352,000?

3   How would this investment appear on the balance sheet at 31 December 2012?

4   How would the classification and reporting differ if Baxter had invested in Cartel's equity securities instead of its debt securities?

Solution to 1:

The amount received each period (£16,500) is based on the par value (£275,000) and the stated 6% rate. The interest income is calculated using the effective interest method (4.5% market rate times the beginning amortized cost each period). The difference between the amount received and the interest income is the amortization.

---

[7] The effective interest rate method applies the market rate in effect when the bonds were purchased to the current amortized cost (book value) of the bonds to obtain interest income for the period. Assume that the debt securities' contractual cash flows are equal to estimated cash flows and that its contractual life is equal to its expected life.

The initial fair value (£300,000) is reduced by amortization resulting in a £297,000 amortized cost. This represents the carrying value reported on the balance sheet if the security is classified as held-to-maturity. If the security is reported at fair value, remeasurement to fair value (£350,000 at the end of Year 1) results in an unrealized gain of £53,000 (£350,000 – £297,000).

	Income Statement	Balance Sheet	Statement of Shareholders' Equity
Held-to-maturity	Interest income £13,500 (£16,500 – £3,000 or £300,000 × 4.5%)	Reported at amortized cost of £297,000	
Held for trading security	Interest income £13,500. £53,000 unrealized gain is recognized through profit	Reported at fair value £350,000	
Designated at fair value	Interest income £13,500. £53,000 unrealized gain is recognized through profit	Reported at fair value £350,000	
Available-for-sale	Interest income of £13,500	Reported at fair value £350,000	£53,000 unrealized gain (net of tax) is reported as other comprehensive income

Solution to 2:

If the debt securities were sold on 1 January 2012 for £352,000, the amount of the realized gain would be as follows:

- Held-to-maturity: The selling price less the carrying value results in a gain on income statement of £55,000 (£352,000 – £297,000).

- Assets held for trading and designated fair value through profit or loss: The security is fair valued on the balance sheet at 31 December 2011 at £350,000. The appreciation was previously recognized in profit and loss. The gain on income statement (profit and loss) of £2,000 (£352,000 – £350,000) reflects the difference between the selling price and the recorded fair value.

- Available-for-sale: The security is fair valued on the balance sheet at 31 December 2011 at £350,000. Because it is designated as available-for-sale, the appreciation was reflected in other comprehensive income in the equity section of the balance sheet. Upon sale in 2012, the cumulative unrealized gain or loss is removed from other comprehensive income and the entire gain is recognized in the profit and loss statement £55,000 = (£352,000 – £350,000) + £53,000 (removed from other comprehensive income).

Solution to 3:

If the investment was classified as held-to-maturity, the reported amount at amortized cost at the end of Year 2 on the balance sheet would be £293,865. If the investment was classified as either held for trading, available-for-sale, or designated at fair value, it would be measured at its fair value at the end of Year 2.

Solution to 4:

If the investment had been in Cartel Co. equity securities rather than debt securities, the analysis would change in the following ways:

- There would not be a held-to-maturity option.
- Dividend income (if any) would replace interest income and there would be no amortization.

4 INVESTMENTS IN FINANCIAL ASSETS: IFRS 9 (AS OF DECEMBER 2012)

Both IASB and FASB have been working on new standards for financial investments. The IASB has issued the first phase of their project dealing with classification and measurement of financial instruments by including relevant chapters in IFRS 9, *Financial Instrument*. This updated standard initially was to take effect 1 January 2013; however, the effective date has been extended to 1 January 2018, with early adoption permitted. Phases two and three of the project will address financial instrument impairments and hedging accounting. When completed, this standard is expected to replace IAS 39. The FASB has yet to issue a pronouncement and their deliberations have yielded tentative decisions. Although requirements are not finalized, it appears there will be significant (but not total) convergence with IFRS. In this section, differences between the current standard (IAS 39) and the new standard (IFRS 9) are discussed. The new standard is based on an approach that considers the contractual characteristic of cash flows as well as the management of the financial assets. The portfolio approach of the current standard (i.e., designation of held for trading, available-for-sale, and held-to-maturity) is no longer appropriate and the terms *available-for-sale* and *held-to-maturity* no longer appear in IFRS 9.

The criteria to use amortized cost are similar to those of the current "management intent to hold-to-maturity" classification. To be measured at amortized cost, financial assets must meet two criteria:

1. A business model test: The financial assets are being held to collect contractual cash flows; and
2. A cash flow characteristic test: The contractual cash flows are solely payments of principal and interest on principal.

4.1 Classification and Measurement

All financial assets are measured at fair value when initially acquired. Subsequently, financial assets are measured at either fair value or amortized cost. Financial assets that meet the two criteria above are generally measured at amortized cost. However, management may choose the "fair value through profit or loss" option to avoid an accounting mismatch. An "accounting mismatch" refers to an inconsistency resulting from different measurement bases for assets and liabilities. Debt instruments are measured either at amortized cost or fair value through profit or loss.

Equity instruments are measured at fair value through profit or loss (FVPL) or at fair value through other comprehensive income (FVOCI). Equity investments held-for-trading must be measured at fair value through profit or loss (FVPL). Other equity investments can be measured at FVPL or FVOCI; however, the choice is irrevocable.

Exhibit 4   Financial Assets Classification and Measurement Model, IFRS 9

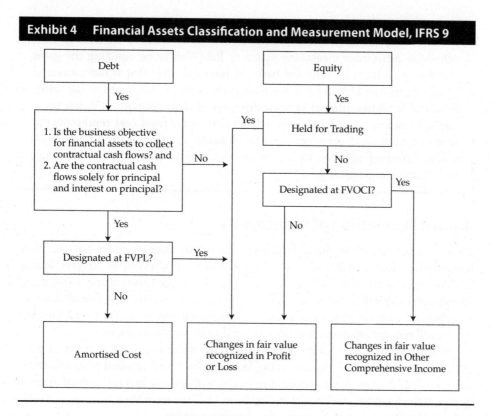

Financial assets that are derivatives are measured at fair value through profit or loss (except for hedging instruments). Embedded derivatives are not separated from the hybrid contract if the asset falls within the scope of this standard.

Exhibit 5 contains an excerpt from a report by Nortel Inversora S.A. (NYSE: NTL) that describes how financial assets and financial liabilities are determined, measured, and recognized on its financial statements.

Exhibit 5   Excerpt from Nortel Inversora S.A. Notes to Unaudited Condensed Consolidated Financial Statements at 30 September 2012

FINANCIAL ASSETS

Upon acquisition, in accordance with IFRS 9, financial assets are subsequently measured at either amortized cost, or fair value, on the basis of both:

a the Company's business model for managing the financial assets; and

b the contractual cash flow characteristics of the financial asset.

A financial asset shall be measured at amortized cost if both of the following conditions are met:

a the asset is held within a business model whose objective is to hold assets in order to collect contractual cash flows, and

b the contractual terms of the financial asset give rise on specified dates to cash flows that are solely payments of principal and interest on the principal amount outstanding.

Additionally, for assets that meet the abovementioned conditions, IFRS provides for an option to designate, at inception, those assets as measured at fair value if doing so eliminates or significantly reduces a measurement or recognition inconsistency (sometimes referred to as an 'accounting mismatch') that would

(continued)

Exhibit 5   (Continued)

otherwise arise from measuring assets or liabilities or recognizing the gains and losses on them on different bases. A financial asset that is not measured at amortized cost according to the paragraphs above is measured at fair value. Financial liabilities other than derivatives are initially recognized at fair value and subsequently measured at amortized cost. Amortized cost represents the initial amount net of principal repayments made, adjusted by the amortization of any difference between the initial amount and the maturing amount using the effective interest method.

4.2 Reclassification of Investments

Under the new standard, the reclassification of equity instruments is not permitted because the initial classification of FVPL and FVOCI is irrevocable. Reclassification of debt instruments from FVPL to amortized cost (or vice versa) is only permitted if the business model for the financial assets (objective for holding the financial assets) has changed in a way that significantly affects operations. Changes to the business model will require judgment and are expected to be very infrequent.

When reclassification is deemed appropriate, there is no restatement of prior periods at the reclassification date. If the financial asset is reclassified from amortized cost to FVPL, the asset is measured at fair value with gain or loss recognized in profit or loss. If the financial asset is reclassified from FVPL to amortized cost, the fair value at the reclassification date becomes the carrying amount.

In summary, the major changes made by phase one of IFRS 9 are:

■ A business model approach to classification of debt instruments.

■ Three classifications for financial assets: Fair value through profit or loss (FVPL), fair value through other comprehensive income (FVOCI), and amortized cost.

■ Reclassifications of debt instruments are permitted only when the business model changes. The choice to measure equity investments at FVOCI or FVPL is irrevocable.

The convergence between IFRS and US GAAP in the classification and reporting standards for investments in financial assets should make it easier for analysts to evaluate investment returns. Analysts typically evaluate performance separately for operating and investing activities. Analysis of operating performance should exclude items related to investing activities such as interest income, dividends, and realized and unrealized gains and losses. For comparative purposes, analysts should exclude non-operating assets in the determination of return on net operating assets. IFRS and US GAAP[8] require disclosure of fair value of each class of investment in financial assets. Using market values and adjusting pro forma financial statements for consistency improves assessments of performance ratios across companies.

---

8 IFRS 7 Financial Instruments: Disclosures and FASB ASC Section 320-10-50 [Investments–Debt and Equity Securities–Overall–Disclosure].

INVESTMENTS IN ASSOCIATES AND JOINT VENTURES

In 2011, the IASB amended IAS 28 to include investments in associates and joint ventures. This revised standard is effective for annual periods beginning on or after 1 January 2013.

Under both IFRS and US GAAP, when a company (investor) holds 20 to 50% of the voting rights of an associate (investee), either directly or indirectly (i.e., through subsidiaries), it is presumed (unless circumstances demonstrate otherwise) that the company has (or can exercise) significant influence, but not control, over the investee's business activities.[9] Conversely, if the investor holds, directly or indirectly, less than 20% of the voting power of the associate (investee), it is presumed that the investor does not have (or cannot exercise) significant influence, unless such influence can be demonstrated. IAS 28 (IFRS) and FASB ASC Topic 323 (US GAAP) apply to most investments in which an investor has significant influence; they also provide guidance on accounting for investments in associates using the equity method.[10] These standards note that significant influence may be evidenced by

- representation on the board of directors;
- participation in the policy-making process;
- material transactions between the investor and the investee;
- interchange of managerial personnel; or
- technological dependency.

The ability to exert significant influence means that the financial and operating performance of the investee is partly influenced by management decisions and operational skills of the investor. The equity method of accounting for the investment reflects the economic reality of this relationship and provides a more objective basis for reporting investment income.

Joint ventures—ventures undertaken and controlled by two or more parties—can be a convenient way to enter foreign markets, conduct specialized activities, and engage in risky projects. They can be organized in a variety of different forms and structures. Some joint ventures are primarily contractual relationships, whereas others have common ownership of assets. They can be partnerships, limited liability companies (corporations), or other legal forms (unincorporated associations, for example). IFRS identify the following common characteristics of joint ventures: 1) A contractual arrangement exists between two or more venturers, and 2) the contractual arrangement establishes joint control. Both IFRS and US GAAP require the equity method of accounting for joint ventures.[11]

Only under rare circumstances will joint ventures be allowed to use proportionate consolidation under IFRS and US GAAP. On the venturer's financial statements, proportionate consolidation requires the venturer's share of the assets, liabilities, income, and expenses of the joint venture to be combined or shown on a line-by-line basis

---

9 The determination of significant influence under IFRS also includes currently exercisable or convertible warrants, call options, or convertible securities that the investor owns, which give it additional voting power or reduce another party's voting power over the financial and operating policies of the investee. Under US GAAP, the determination of an investor's voting stock interest is based only on the voting shares outstanding at the time of the purchase. The existence and effect of securities with potential voting rights are not considered.

10 IAS 28 Investments in Associates and Joint Ventures and FASB ASC Topic 323 [Investments–Equity Method and Joint Ventures].

11 IFRS 11, Joint Arrangements classifies joint arrangements as either a joint operation or a joint venture. Joint ventures are arrangements wherein parties with joint control have rights to the net assets of the arrangement. Joint ventures are required to use equity method under IAS 28.

with similar items under its sole control. In contrast, the equity method results in a single line item (equity in income of the joint venture) on the income statement and a single line item (investment in joint venture) on the balance sheet.

Because the single line item on the income statement under the equity method reflects the net effect of the sales and expenses of the joint venture, the total income recognized is identical under the two methods. In addition, because the single line item on the balance sheet item (investment in joint venture) under the equity method reflects the investors' share of the net assets of the joint venture, the total net assets of the investor is identical under both methods. There can be significant differences, however, in ratio analysis between the two methods because of the differential effects on values for total assets, liabilities, sales, expenses, etc.

5.1 Equity Method of Accounting: Basic Principles

Under the equity method of accounting, the equity investment is initially recorded on the investor's balance sheet at cost. In subsequent periods, the carrying amount of the investment is adjusted to recognize the investor's proportionate share of the investee's earnings or losses, and these earnings or losses are reported in income. Dividends or other distributions received from the investee are treated as a return of capital and reduce the carrying amount of the investment and are not reported in the investor's profit or loss. The equity method is often referred to as "one-line consolidation" because the investor's proportionate ownership interest in the assets and liabilities of the investee is disclosed as a single line item (net assets) on its balance sheet, and the investor's share of the revenues and expenses of the investee is disclosed as a single line item on its income statement. (Contrast these disclosures with the disclosures on consolidated statements in Section 6.) Equity method investments are classified as non-current assets on the balance sheet. The investor's share of the profit or loss of equity method investments, and the carrying amount of those investments, must be separately disclosed on the income statement and balance sheet.

EXAMPLE 2

Equity Method: Balance in Investment Account

Branch (a fictitious company) purchases a 20% interest in Williams (a fictitious company) for €200,000 on 1 January 2010. Williams reports income and dividends as follows:

	Income	Dividends
2010	€200,000	€50,000
2011	300,000	100,000
2012	400,000	200,000
	€900,000	€350,000

Calculate the investment in Williams that appears on Branch's balance sheet as of the end of 2012.

Solution:

Investment in Williams at 31 December 2012:

Initial cost	€200,000	
Equity income 2010	€40,000	= (20% of €200,000 Income)
Dividends received 2010	(€10,000)	= (20% of €50,000 Dividends)

Equity income 2011	€60,000	= (20% of €300,000 Income)
Dividends received 2011	(€20,000)	= (20% of €100,000 Dividends)
Equity income 2012	€80,000	= (20% of €400,000 Income)
Dividends received 2012	(€40,000)	= (20% of €200,000 Dividends)
Balance-Equity Investment	€310,000	= [€200,000 + 20% × (€900,000 – €350,000)]

This simple example implicitly assumes that the purchase price equals the purchased equity (20%) in the book value of Williams' net assets. Sections 5.2 and 5.3 will cover the more common case in which the purchase price does not equal the proportionate share of the book value of the investee's net assets.

Using the equity method, the investor includes its share of the investee's profit and losses on the income statement. The equity investment is carried at cost, plus its share of post-acquisition income, less dividends received. The recorded investment value can decline as a result of investee losses or a permanent decline in the investee's market value (see Section 5.5 for treatment of impairments). If the investment value is reduced to zero, the investor usually discontinues the equity method and does not record further losses. If the investee subsequently reports profits, the equity method is resumed after the investor's share of the profits equals the share of losses not recognized during the suspension of the equity method. Exhibit 6 contains excerpts from Deutsche Bank's 2011 annual report that describes its accounting treatment for investments in associates.

Exhibit 6   Excerpt from Deutsche Bank 2011 Annual Report

[From Note 01] ASSOCIATES AND JOINTLY CONTROLLED ENTITIES

An associate is an entity in which the Group has significant influence, but not a controlling interest, over the operating and financial management policy decisions of the entity. Significant influence is generally presumed when the Group holds between 20% and 50% of the voting rights. The existence and effect of potential voting rights that are currently exercisable or convertible are considered in assessing whether the Group has significant influence. Among the other factors that are considered in determining whether the Group has significant influence are representation on the board of directors (supervisory board in the case of German stock corporations) and material intercompany transactions. The existence of these factors could require the application of the equity method of accounting for a particular investment even though the Group's investment is for less than 20% of the voting stock.

A jointly controlled entity exists when the Group has a contractual arrangement with one or more parties to undertake activities through entities which are subject to joint control.

[From Note 17] EQUITY METHOD INVESTMENTS

Investments in associates and jointly controlled entities are accounted for using the equity method of accounting. As of December 31, 2011, the following investees were significant, representing 75% of the carrying value of equity method investments.

(continued)

Exhibit 6   (Continued)

Investment[1]	Ownership Percentage
Actavis Equity S.a r.l., Munscach[2]	0.00
BrisConnections Investment Trust, Kedron	35.59
Huamao Property Holdings, Ltd. George Town[3]	0.00
Hua Xia Bank Company Limited, Beijing	19.99
Rongde Asset Management Company Limited, Beijing	40.70
Station Holdco LLC, Wilmington	25.00

[1] All significant equity method investments are investments in associates.
[2] Equity method accounting based on subordinated financial arrangement.
[3] The Group has significant influence over the investee through board seats or other measures.

Summarized aggregated financial information of significant equity method investees follows:

In € m	Dec 31, 2011	Dec 31, 2010
Total assets	147,793	131,002
Total liabilities	137,862	128,745
Revenues	5,478	4,988
Net income/loss	696	(709)

The following are the components of the net income (loss) from all equity method investments:

In € m	2011	2010
Net income (loss) from equity method investments:		
Pro rata share of investees' net income (loss)	222	457
Net gains (losses) on disposal of equity method investments	29	14
Impairments	(515)	(2,475)
Total net income (loss) from equity method investments	**(264)**	**(2,004)**

2011 included an impairment of €457 million related to Actavis Group, a generic pharmaceutical group.

In 2010 a charge of approximately €2.3 billion attributable to the equity method investment in Deutsche Postbank AG prior to consolidation was included. On December 3, 2010, Deutsche gained a controlling majority in Postbank shares and commenced consolidation of the Postbank Group as of that date. As a consequence the Group ceased equity method accounting for its investment in Postbank. Further detail is included in Note 4 "Acquisitions and Dispositions".

There was no unrecognized share of losses of an investee, neither for the period, or cumulatively.

Equity method investments for which there were published price quotations had a carrying value of €2.2 billion and a fair value of €2.1 billion as of December 31, 2011 and a carrying value of €280 million and a fair value of €561 million as of December 31, 2010. In 2011 Hua Xia Bank is included for the first time.

It is interesting to note the explanations for the treatment as associates when the ownership percentage is less than 20% or is greater than 50%. The equity method reflects the strength of the relationship between the investor and its associates. In the instances where the percentage ownership is less than 20%, Deutsche Bank uses the equity method because it has significant influence over these associates' operating and financial policies either through its representation on their boards of directors and/ or other measures. The equity method provides a more objective basis for reporting investment income than the accounting treatment for investments in financial assets, because the investor can potentially influence the timing of dividend distributions.

5.2 Investment Costs That Exceed the Book Value of the Investee

The cost (purchase price) to acquire shares of an investee is often greater than the book value of those shares. This is because, among other things, many of the investee's assets and liabilities reflect historical cost rather than fair values. IFRS allow a company to measure its property, plant, and equipment using either historical cost or fair value (less accumulated depreciation).[12] US GAAP, however, require the use of historical cost (less accumulated depreciation) to measure property, plant, and equipment.[13]

When the cost of the investment exceeds the investor's proportionate share of the book value of the investee's (associate's) net identifiable tangible and intangible assets (e.g., inventory, property, plant and equipment, trademarks, patents), the difference is first allocated to specific assets (or categories of assets) using fair values. These differences are then amortized to the investor's proportionate share of the investee's profit or loss over the economic lives of the assets whose fair values exceeded book values. It should be noted that the allocation is not recorded formally; what appears initially in the investment account on the balance sheet of the investor is the cost. Over time, as the differences are amortized, the balance in the investment account will come closer to representing the ownership percentage of the book value of the net assets of the associate.

IFRS and US GAAP both treat the difference between the cost of the acquisition and investor's share of the fair value of the net identifiable assets as goodwill. Therefore, any remaining difference between the acquisition cost and the fair value of net identifiable assets that cannot be allocated to specific assets is treated as goodwill and is not amortized. Instead, it is reviewed for impairment on a regular basis, and written down for any identified impairment. Goodwill, however, is included in the carrying amount of the investment, because investment is reported as a single line item on the investor's balance sheet.[14]

---

12 After initial recognition, an entity can choose to use either a cost model or a revaluation model to measure its property, plant, and equipment. Under the revaluation model, property, plant, and equipment whose fair value can be measured reliably can be carried at a revalued amount. This revalued amount is its fair value at the date of the revaluation less any subsequent accumulated depreciation.

13 Successful companies should be able to generate, through the productive use of assets, economic value in excess of the resale value of the assets themselves. Therefore, investors may be willing to pay a premium in anticipation of future benefits. These benefits could be a result of general market conditions, the investor's ability to exert significant influence on the investee, or other synergies.

14 If the investor's share of the fair value of the associate's net assets (identifiable assets, liabilities, and contingent liabilities) is greater than the cost of the investment, the difference is excluded from the carrying amount of the investment and instead included as income in the determination of the investor's share of the associate's profit or loss in the period in which the investment is acquired.

EXAMPLE 3

Equity Method Investment in Excess of Book Value

Assume that the hypothetical Blake Co. acquires 30% of the outstanding shares of the hypothetical Brown Co. At the acquisition date, book values and fair values of Brown's recorded assets and liabilities are as follows:

	Book Value	Fair Value
Current assets	€10,000	€10,000
Plant and equipment	190,000	220,000
Land	120,000	140,000
	€320,000	€370,000
Liabilities	100,000	100,000
Net assets	€220,000	€270,000

Blake Co. believes the value of Brown Co. is higher than the fair value of its identifiable net assets. They offer €100,000 for a 30% interest in Brown, which represents a 34,000 excess purchase price. The difference between the fair value and book value of the net identifiable assets is €50,000 (€370,000 – 320,000). Based on Blake Co.'s 30% ownership, €15,000 of the excess purchase price is attributable to the net identifiable assets, and the residual is attributable to goodwill. Calculate goodwill.

Solution:

Purchase price	€100,000
30% of book value of Brown (30% × €220,000)	66,000
Excess purchase price	€34,000
Attributable to net assets	
Plant and equipment (30% × €30,000)	€9,000
Land (30% × €20,000)	6,000
Goodwill (residual)	19,000
	€34,000

As illustrated above, goodwill is the residual excess not allocated to identifiable assets or liabilities. The investment is carried as a non-current asset on the Blake's book as a single line item (Investment in Brown, €100,000) on the acquisition date.

5.3 Amortization of Excess Purchase Price

The excess purchase price allocated to the assets and liabilities is accounted for in a manner that is consistent with the accounting treatment for the specific asset or liability to which it is assigned. Amounts allocated to assets and liabilities that are expensed (such as inventory) or periodically depreciated or amortized (plant, property, and intangible assets) must be treated in a similar manner. These allocated amounts are not reflected on the financial statements of the investee (associate), and the investee's income statement will not reflect the necessary periodic adjustments. Therefore, the investor must directly record these adjustment effects by reducing the carrying amount of the investment on its balance sheet and by reducing the investee's profit recognized on its income statement. Amounts allocated to assets or liabilities that are not systematically amortized (e.g., land) will continue to be reported at their fair value as of the date the investment was acquired. As stated above, goodwill is included in the carrying amount of the investment instead of being separately recognized. It is not amortized because it is considered to have an indefinite life.

Using the example above and assuming a 10-year useful life for plant, property, and equipment and using straight-line depreciation, the annual amortization is as follows:

Account	Excess Price (€)	Useful Life	Amortization/Year (€)
Plant and equipment	9,000	10 years	900
Land	6,000	Indefinite	0
Goodwill	19,000	Indefinite	0

Annual amortization would reduce the investor's share of the investee's reported income (equity income) and the balance in the investment account by €900 for each year over the 10-year period.

EXAMPLE 4

Equity Method Investments with Goodwill

On 1 January 2011, Parker Company acquired 30% of Prince Inc. common shares for the cash price of €500,000 (both companies are fictitious). It is determined that Parker has the ability to exert significant influence on Prince's financial and operating decisions. The following information concerning Prince's assets and liabilities on 1 January 2011 is provided:

Prince, Inc.

	Book Value	Fair Value	Difference
Current assets	€100,000	€100,000	€0
Plant and equipment	1,900,000	2,200,000	300,000
	€2,000,000	€2,300,000	€300,000
Liabilities	800,000	800,000	0
Net assets	€1,200,000	€1,500,000	€300,000

The plant and equipment are depreciated on a straight-line basis and have 10 years of remaining life. Prince reports net income for 2011 of €100,000 and pays dividends of €50,000. Calculate the following:

1 Goodwill included in the purchase price.

2 Investment in associate (Prince) at the end of 2011.

Solution to 1:

Purchase price	€500,000
Acquired equity in book value of Prince's net assets (30% × €1,200,000)	360,000
Excess purchase price	€140,000
Attributable to plant and equipment (30% × €300,000)	(90,000)
Goodwill (residual)	€50,000

Solution to 2:

Investment in associate

Purchase price	€500,000
Parker's share of Prince's net income (30% × €100,000)	30,000
Dividends received (30% of €50,000)	(15,000)
Amortization of excess purchase price attributable to plant and equipment (€90,000 ÷ 10 years)	(9,000)
31 December 2011 balance in investment in Prince	€506,000

An alternate way to look at the balance in the investment account is that it reflects the basic valuation principle of the equity method. At any point in time, the investment account balance equals the investor's (Parker) proportionate share of the net equity (net assets at book value) of the investee (Prince) plus the unamortized balance of the original excess purchase price. Applying this principle to this example:

2011 Beginning net assets =	€1,200,000
Plus: Net income	100,000
Less: Dividends	(50,000)
2011 Ending net assets	€1,250,000
Parker's proportionate share of Prince's recorded net assets (30% × €1,250,000)	€375,000
Unamortized excess purchase price (€140,000 − 9,000)	131,000
Investment in Prince	€506,000

Note that the unamortized excess purchase price is a cost incurred by Parker, not Prince. Therefore, the total amount is included in the investment account balance.

5.4 Fair Value Option

Both IFRS and US GAAP give the investor the option to account for their equity method investment at fair value.[15] Under US GAAP, this option is available to all entities; however, under IFRS, its use is restricted to venture capital organizations, mutual funds, unit trusts, and similar entities, including investment-linked insurance funds.

Both standards require that the election to use the fair value option occur at the time of initial recognition and is irrevocable. Subsequent to initial recognition, the investment is reported at fair value with unrealized gains and losses arising from changes in fair value as well as any interest and dividends received included in the investor's profit or loss (income). Under the fair value method, the investment account on the investor's balance sheet does not reflect the investor's proportionate share of the investee's profit or loss, dividends, or other distributions. In addition, the excess of cost over the fair value of the investee's identifiable net assets is not amortized, nor is goodwill created.

---

15 IAS 39 Financial Instruments: Recognition and Measurement. FASB ASC Section 825-10-25 [Financial Instruments–Overall–Recognition].

5.5 Impairment

Both IFRS and US GAAP require periodic reviews of equity method investments for impairment. If the fair value of the investment is below its carrying value and this decline is deemed to be other than temporary, an impairment loss must be recognized.

Under IFRS, there must be objective evidence of impairment as a result of one or more (loss) events that occurred after the initial recognition of the investment, and that loss event has an impact on the investment's future cash flows, which can be reliably estimated. Because goodwill is included in the carrying amount of the investment and is not separately recognized, it is not separately tested for impairment. Instead, the entire carrying amount of the investment is tested for impairment by comparing its recoverable amount with its carrying amount.[16] The impairment loss is recognized on the income statement, and the carrying amount of the investment on the balance sheet is either reduced directly or through the use of an allowance account.

US GAAP takes a different approach. If the fair value of the investment declines below its carrying value *and* the decline is determined to be permanent, US GAAP[17] requires an impairment loss to be recognized on the income statement and the carrying value of the investment on the balance sheet is reduced to its fair value.

Both IFRS and US GAAP prohibit the reversal of impairment losses even if the fair value later increases.

Section 6.4.4 of this reading discusses impairment tests for the goodwill attributed to a controlling investment (consolidated subsidiary). Note the distinction between the disaggregated goodwill impairment test for consolidated statements and the impairment test of the total fair value of for equity method investments.

5.6 Transactions with Associates

Because an investor company can influence the terms and timing of transactions with its associates, profits from such transactions cannot be realized until confirmed through use or sale to third parties. Accordingly, the investor company's share of any unrealized profit must be deferred by reducing the amount recorded under the equity method. In the subsequent period(s) when this deferred profit is considered confirmed, it is added to the equity income. At that time, the equity income is again based on the recorded values in the associate's accounts.

Transactions between the two affiliates may be **upstream** (associate to investor) or **downstream** (investor to associate). In an upstream sale, the profit on the intercompany transaction is recorded on the associate's income (profit or loss) statement. The investor's share of the unrealized profit is thus included in equity income on the investor's income statement. In a downstream sale, the profit is recorded on the investor's income statement. Both IFRS and US GAAP require that the unearned profits be eliminated to the extent of the investor's interest in the associate.[18] The result is an adjustment to equity income on the investor's income statement.

---

16 Recoverable amount is the higher of "value in use" or net selling price. Value in use is equal to the present value of estimated future cash flows expected to arise from the continuing use of an asset and from its disposal at the end of its useful life. Net selling price is equal to fair value less cost to sell.

17 FASB ASC Section 323-10-35 [Investments–Equity Method and Joint Ventures–Overall–Subsequent Measurement].

18 IAS 28 Investments in Associates and Joint Ventures; FASB ASC Topic 323 [Investments–Equity Method and Joint Ventures].

EXAMPLE 5

Equity Method with Sale of Inventory: Upstream Sale

On 1 January 2011, Wicker Company acquired a 25% interest in Foxworth Company (both companies are fictitious) for €1,000,000 and used the equity method to account for its investment. The book value of Foxworth's net assets on that date was €3,800,000. An analysis of fair values revealed that all fair values of assets and liabilities were equal to book values except for a building. The building was undervalued by €40,000 and has a 20-year remaining life. The company used straight-line depreciation for the building. Foxworth paid €3,200 in dividends in 2011. During 2011, Foxworth reported net income of €20,000. During the year, Foxworth sold inventory to Wicker. At the end of the year, there was €8,000 profit from the upstream sale in Foxworth's net income. The inventory sold to Wicker by Foxworth had not been sold to an outside party.

1 Calculate the equity income to be reported as a line item on Wicker's 2011 income statement.

2 Calculate the balance in the investment in Foxworth to be reported on the 31 December 2011 balance sheet.

Purchase price	€1,000,000
Acquired equity in book value of Foxworth's net assets (25% × €3,800,000)	950,000
Excess purchase price	€50,000
Attributable to:	
Building (25% × €40,000)	€10,000
Goodwill (residual)	40,000
	€50,000

Solution to 1:

Equity Income

Wicker's share of Foxworth's reported income (25% × €20,000)	€5,000
Amortization of excess purchase price attributable to building, (€10,000 ÷ 20)	(500)
Unrealized profit (25% × €8,000)	(2,000)
Equity income 2011	€2,500

Solution to 2:

Investment in Foxworth:

Purchase price	€1,000,000
Equity income 2011	2,500
Dividends received (25% × €3,200)	(800)
Investment in Foxworth, 31 Dec 2011	€1,001,700
Composition of investment account:	
Wicker's proportionate share of Foxworth's net equity (net assets at book value) [25% × (€3,800,000 + (20,000 − 8,000) − 3,200)]	€952,200

Unamortized excess purchase price (€50,000 – 500)	49,500
	€1,001,700

EXAMPLE 6

Equity Method with Sale of Inventory: Downstream Sale

Jones Company owns 25% of Jason Company (both fictitious companies) and appropriately applies the equity method of accounting. Amortization of excess purchase price, related to undervalued assets at the time of the investment, is €8,000 per year. During 2011 Jones sold €96,000 of inventory to Jason for €160,000. Jason resold €120,000 of this inventory during 2011. The remainder was sold in 2012. Jason reports income from its operations of €800,000 in 2011 and €820,000 in 2012.

1 Calculate the equity income to be reported as a line item on Jones's 2011 income statement.

2 Calculate the equity income to be reported as a line item on Jones's 2012 income statement.

Solution to 1:

Equity Income 2011

Jones's share of Jason's reported income (25% × €800,000)	€200,000
Amortization of excess purchase price	(8,000)
Unrealized profit (25% × €16,000)	(4,000)
Equity income 2011	€188,000

Jones's profit on the sale to Jason = €160,000 – 96,000 = €64,000

Jason sells 75% (€120,000/160,000) of the goods purchased from Jones; 25% is unsold.

Total unrealized profit = €64,000 × 25% = €16,000

Jones's share of the unrealized profit = €16,000 × 25% = €4,000

Alternative approach:

Jones's profit margin on sale to Jason: 40% (€64,000/€160,000)

Jason's inventory of Jones's goods at 31 Dec 2011: €40,000

Jones's profit margin on this was 40% × 40,000 = €16,000

Jones's share of profit on unsold goods = €16,000 × 25% = €4,000

Solution to 2:

Equity Income 2012

Jones's share of Jason's reported income (25% × €820,000)	€205,000
Amortization of excess purchase price	(8,000)
Realized profit (25% × €16,000)	4,000
Equity income 2012	€201,000

Jason sells the remaining 25% of the goods purchased from Jones.

5.7 Disclosure

The notes to the financial statements are an integral part of the information necessary for investors. Both IFRS and US GAAP require disclosure about the assets, liabilities, and results of equity method investments. For example, in their 2011 annual report, Deutsche Bank reports that:

> Investments in associates and jointly controlled entities are accounted for under the equity method of accounting. The Group's share of the results of associates and jointly controlled entities is adjusted to conform to the accounting policies of the Group and are reported in the consolidated statement of income as net income (loss) from equity method investments. The Group's share in the associate's profit and losses resulting from inter-company sales is eliminated on consolidation.
>
> Under the equity method of accounting, the Group's investments in associates and jointly controlled entities are initially recorded at cost including any directly related transaction costs incurred in acquiring the associate, and subsequently increased (or decreased) to reflect both the Group's pro-rata share of the post-acquisition net income (or loss) of the associate or jointly controlled entity and other movements included directly in the equity of the associate or jointly controlled entity. Goodwill arising on the acquisition of an associate or a jointly controlled entity is included in the carrying value of the investment (net of any accumulated impairment loss). As goodwill is not reported separately it is not specifically tested for impairment. Rather, the entire equity method investment is tested for impairment.

For practical reasons, associated companies' results are sometimes included in the investor's accounts with a certain time lag, normally not more than one quarter. Dividends from associated companies are not included in investor income because it would be a double counting. Applying the equity method recognizes the investor's full share of the associate's income. Dividends received involve exchanging a portion of equity interest for cash. In the consolidated balance sheet, the book value of shareholdings in associated companies is increased by the investor's share of the company's net income and reduced by amortization of surplus values and the amount of dividends received.

5.8 Issues for Analysts

Equity method accounting presents several challenges for analysis. First, analysts should question whether the equity method is appropriate. For example, an investor holding 19% of an associate may in fact exert significant influence but may attempt to avoid using the equity method to avoid reporting associate losses. On the other hand, an investor holding 25% of an associate may be unable to exert significant influence and may be unable to access cash flows, and yet may prefer the equity method to capture associate income.

Second, the investment account represents the investor's percentage ownership in the net assets of the investee company through "one-line consolidation." There can be significant assets and liabilities of the investee that are not reflected on the investor's balance sheet, which will significantly affect debt ratios. Net margin ratios could be overstated because income for the associate is included in investor net income but is not specifically included in sales. An investor may actually control the investee with less than 50% ownership but prefer the financial results using the equity method. Careful analysis can reveal financial performance driven by accounting structure.

Finally, the analyst must consider the quality of the equity method earnings. The equity method assumes that a percentage of each dollar earned by the investee company is earned by the investor (i.e., a fraction of the dollar equal to the fraction of the company owned), even if cash is not received. Analysts should, therefore, consider potential restrictions on dividend cash flows (the statement of cash flows).

BUSINESS COMBINATIONS

6

Business combinations (controlling interest investments) involve the combination of two or more entities into a larger economic entity. Business combinations are typically motivated by expectations of added value through synergies, including potential for increased revenues, elimination of duplicate costs, tax advantages, coordination of the production process, and efficiency gains in the management of assets.[19]

Under IFRS, there is no distinction among business combinations based on the resulting structure of the larger economic entity. For all business combinations, one of the parties to the business combination is identified as the acquirer. Under US GAAP, an acquirer is identified, but the business combinations are categorized as merger, acquisition, or consolidation based on the legal structure after the combination. Each of these types of business combinations has distinctive characteristics that are described in Exhibit 7. Features of variable interest and special purpose entities are also described in Exhibit 7 because these are additional instances where control is exerted by another entity. Under both IFRS and US GAAP, business combinations are accounted for using the *acquisition method*.

Exhibit 7   Types of Business Combinations

Merger

The distinctive feature of a merger is that only one of the entities remains in existence. One hundred percent of the target is absorbed into the acquiring company. Company A may issue common stock, preferred stock, bonds, or pay cash to acquire the net assets. The net assets of Company B are transferred to Company A. Company B ceases to exist and Company A is the only entity that remains.

Company A + Company B = Company A

(continued)

---

19 IAS 3, *Business Combinations*, revised in 2008 and FASB ASC Topic 805 [*Business Combinations*] provide guidance on business combinations.

> | Exhibit 7   (Continued) |
>
> ## Acquisition
>
> The distinctive feature of an acquisition is the legal continuity of the entities. Each entity continues operations but is connected through a parent–subsidiary relationship. Each entity is an individual that maintains separate financial records, but the parent (the acquirer) provides consolidated financial statements in each reporting period. Unlike a merger or consolidation, the acquiring company does not need to acquire 100% of the target. In fact, in some cases, it may acquire less than 50% and still exert control. If the acquiring company acquires less than 100%, non-controlling (minority) shareholders' interests are reported on the consolidated financial statements.
>
> Company A + Company B = (Company A + Company B)
>
> ## Consolidation
>
> The distinctive feature of a consolidation is that a new legal entity is formed and none of the predecessor entities remain in existence. A new entity is created to take over the net assets of Company A and Company B. Company A and Company B cease to exist and Company C is the only entity that remains.
>
> Company A + Company B = Company C
>
> ## Special Purpose or Variable Interest Entities
>
> The distinctive feature of a special purpose (variable interest) entity is that control is not usually based on voting control, because equity investors do not have a sufficient amount at risk for the entity to finance its activities without additional subordinated financial support. Furthermore, the equity investors may lack a controlling financial interest. The sponsoring company usually creates a special purpose entity (SPE) for a narrowly defined purpose. IFRS require consolidation if the substance of the relationship indicates control by the sponsor.

In May 2011, the IASB issued IFRS 10, *Consolidated Financial Statements*, which replaces IAS 27, *Consolidated and Separate Financial Statements* and SIC-12, *Consolidation-Special Purpose Entities*. The standard applies to annual periods beginning on or after 1 January 2013. The underlying framework is based on a new definition of control and achieves consistency in the consolidation criteria for all entities. The definition of control extends to a broad range of activities. The control concept requires judgment and evaluation of relevant factors to determine whether control exists. Control is present when 1) the investor has the ability to exert influence on the financial and operating policy of the entity; and 2) is exposed, or has rights, to variable returns from its involvement with the investee. Consolidation criteria apply to all entities that meet the definition of control.

US GAAP uses a two-component consolidation model that includes both a variable interest component and a voting interest (control) component. Under the variable interest component, US GAAP[20] requires the primary beneficiary of a variable interest entity (VIE) to consolidate the VIE regardless of its voting interests (if any) in the VIE or its decision-making authority. The primary beneficiary is defined as the party that will absorb the majority of the VIE's expected losses, receive the majority of the VIE's expected residual returns, or both.

---

20 FASB ASC Topic 810 [Consolidation].

In the past, business combinations could be accounted for either as a purchase transaction or as a uniting (or pooling) of interests. The accounting standards that currently govern business combinations are reflective of the joint project between IASB and FASB to converge on a single set of high-quality accounting standards. The first phase of the project prohibited the use of the pooling of interests (uniting of interests) method, required the use of the purchase method, and prohibited the amortization of goodwill.

Since that time, the FASB and IASB have further reduced differences between IFRS and US GAAP and ensured that the standards would be applied consistently. IFRS and US GAAP now require that all business combinations be accounted for in a similar manner. The *acquisition method* developed by the IASB and the FASB replaces the purchase method, and substantially reduces any differences between IFRS and US GAAP for business combinations.[21]

These standards are expected to improve the relevance, representational faithfulness, transparency, and comparability of information provided in financial statements about business combinations and their effects on the reporting entity. This reporting consistency should make it easier for analysts to evaluate how the operations of the acquirer and the target business (the acquiree) will combine and the effect of this transaction on the combined entity's subsequent financial performance.

6.1 Pooling of Interests and Purchase Methods

Prior to June 2001, under US GAAP, combining companies that met twelve strict criteria could use the **pooling of interests method** for the business combination. Companies not meeting these criteria used the purchase method. In a pooling of interests, the combined companies were portrayed as if they had always operated as a single economic entity. Consequently, assets and liabilities were recorded at book values, and the pre-combination retained earnings were included in the balance sheet of the combined entity. This treatment was consistent with the view that there was a continuity of ownership and no new basis of accounting existed. Similar rules applied under IFRS, which used the term uniting of interests in reference to the same concept. IFRS permitted use of the **uniting of interests method** until March 2004. Currently, neither IFRS nor US GAAP allows use of the pooling/uniting of interests method.

In contrast, a combination accounted for as a purchase was viewed as a purchase of net assets (tangible and intangible assets minus liabilities), and those net assets were recorded at fair values. An increase in the value of depreciable assets resulted in additional depreciation expense. As a result, for the same level of revenue, the purchase method resulted in lower reported income than the pooling of interests method. For this reason, managers had a tendency to favor the pooling of interests method.

Although the pooling of interests method is no longer allowed, companies may continue to use pooling of interests accounting for business combinations that occurred prior to its disallowance as a method. We describe the method because pooling of interests accounting was commonly used and will have an impact on financial statements for the foreseeable future. Because of the ongoing effect, an understanding of pooling of interests will facilitate the analyst's assessment of the performance and financial position of the company.

---

21 IFRS 10, Consolidated Financial Statements; IFRS 3, Business Combinations; FASB ASC Topic 805 [Business Combinations]; FASB ASC Topic 810 [Consolidations].

6.2 Acquisition Method

IFRS and US GAAP currently require the acquisition method of accounting for business combinations, although both have a few specific exemptions.

Fair value of the consideration given by the acquiring company is the appropriate measurement for acquisitions and includes the acquisition-date fair value of contingent consideration. Direct costs of the business combination, such as professional and legal fees, valuation experts, and consultants, are expensed as incurred.

The acquisition method (which replaces the purchase method) addresses three major accounting issues that often arise in business combinations and the preparation of consolidated (combined) financial statements:

- The recognition and measurement of the assets and liabilities of the combined entity;
- The initial recognition and subsequent accounting for goodwill; and
- The recognition and measurement of any non-controlling interest.

6.2.1 Recognition and Measurement of Identifiable Assets and Liabilities

IFRS and US GAAP require that the acquirer measure the identifiable tangible and intangible assets and liabilities of the acquiree (acquired entity) at fair value as of the date of the acquisition. The acquirer must also recognize any assets and liabilities that the acquiree had not previously recognized as assets and liabilities in its financial statements. For example, identifiable intangible assets (for example, brand names, patents, technology) that the acquiree developed internally would be recognized by the acquirer.

6.2.2 Recognition and Measurement of Contingent Liabilities[22]

On the acquisition date, the acquirer must recognize any contingent liability assumed in the acquisition if 1) it is a present obligation that arises from past events, and 2) it can be measured reliably. Costs that the acquirer expects (but is not obliged) to incur, however, are not recognized as liabilities as of the acquisition date. Instead, the acquirer recognizes these costs in future periods as they are incurred. For example, expected restructuring costs arising from exiting an acquiree's business will be recognized in the period in which they are incurred.

There is a difference between IFRS and US GAAP in their inclusion of contingent liabilities. IFRS include contingent liabilities if their fair values can be reliably measured. US GAAP includes only those contingent liabilities that are probable and can be reasonably estimated.

6.2.3 Recognition and Measurement of Indemnification Assets

On the acquisition date, the acquirer must recognize an indemnification asset if the seller (acquiree) contractually indemnifies the acquirer for the outcome of a contingency or an uncertainty related to all or part of a specific asset or liability of the acquiree. The seller may also indemnify the acquirer against losses above a specified amount on a liability arising from a particular contingency. For example, the seller guarantees that an acquired contingent liability will not exceed a specified amount. In this situation, the acquirer recognizes an indemnification asset at the same time it recognizes the indemnified liability, with both measured on the same basis. If the

---

22 A contingent liability must be recognized even if it is not probable that an outflow of resources or economic benefits will be used to settle the obligation.

indemnification relates to an asset or a liability that is recognized at the acquisition date and measured at its acquisition date fair value, the acquirer will also recognize the indemnification asset at the acquisition date at its acquisition date fair value.

6.2.4 Recognition and Measurement of Financial Assets and Liabilities

At the acquisition date, identifiable assets and liabilities acquired are classified in accordance with IASB (or US GAAP) standards. The acquirer reclassifies the financial assets and liabilities of the acquiree based on the contractual terms, economic conditions, and the acquirer's operating or accounting policies, as they exist at the acquisition date.

6.2.5 Recognition and Measurement of Goodwill

IFRS allows two options for recognizing goodwill at the transaction date. The goodwill option is on a transaction-by-transaction basis. "Partial goodwill" is measured as the fair value of the acquisition (fair value of consideration given) less the acquirer's share of the fair value of all identifiable tangible and intangible assets, liabilities, and contingent liabilities acquired. "Full goodwill" is measured as the fair value of the entity as a whole less the fair value of all identifiable tangible and intangible assets, liabilities, and contingent liabilities. US GAAP views the entity as a whole and requires full goodwill.[23] Because goodwill is considered to have an indefinite life, it is not amortized. Instead, it is tested for impairment annually or more frequently if events or circumstances indicate that goodwill might be impaired.

EXAMPLE 7

Recognition and Measurement of Goodwill

Acquirer contributes $800,000 for an 80% interest in Acquiree. The identifiable net assets have a fair value of $900,000. The fair value of the entire entity is determined to be $1 million.

	IFRS Partial Goodwill
Fair value of consideration	$800,000
80% of Fair value of identifiable net assets	720,000
Goodwill recognized	$80,000

	IFRS and US GAAP Full Goodwill
Fair value of entity	$1,000,000
Fair value of identifiable assets	900,000
Goodwill recognized	$100,000

---

23 FASB ASC Topic 805 [Business Combinations].

6.2.6 *Recognition and Measurement when Acquisition Price Is Less than Fair Value*

Occasionally, a company faces adverse circumstances such that its market value drops below the fair value of its net assets. In an acquisition of such a company, where the purchase price is less than the fair value of the target's (acquiree's) net assets, the acquisition is considered to be a bargain acquisition. IFRS and US GAAP require the difference between the fair value of the acquired net assets and the purchase price to be recognized immediately as a gain in profit or loss. Any contingent consideration must be measured and recognized at fair value at the time of the business combination. Any subsequent changes in value of the contingent consideration are recognized in profit or loss.

6.3 Impact of the Acquisition Method on Financial Statements, Post-Acquisition

Example 8 shows the consolidated balance sheet of an acquiring company after the acquisition.

EXAMPLE 8

Acquisition Method Post-Combination Balance Sheet

Franklin Company, headquartered in France, acquired 100% of the outstanding shares of Jefferson, Inc. by issuing 1,000,000 shares of its €1 par common stock (€15 market value). Immediately before the transaction, the two companies compiled the following information:

	Franklin Book Value (000)	Jefferson Book Value (000)	Jefferson Fair Value (000)
Cash and receivables	€10,000	€300	€300
Inventory	12,000	1,700	3,000
PP&E (net)	27,000	2,500	4,500
	€49,000	€4,500	€7,800
Current payables	8,000	600	600
Long-term debt	16,000	2,000	1,800
	24,000	2,600	2,400
Net assets	€25,000	€1,900	€5,400
Shareholders' equity:			
Capital stock (€1 par)	€5,000	€400	
Additional paid in capital	6,000	700	
Retained earnings	€14,000	€800	

Jefferson has no identifiable intangible assets. Show the balances in the post-combination balance sheet using the acquisition method.

Solution:

Under the acquisition method, the purchase price allocation would be as follows:

Fair value of the stock issued	
(1,000,000 shares at market value of €15)	€15,000,000
Book value of Jefferson's net assets	1,900,000

Excess purchase price	€13,100,000
Fair value of the stock issued	€15,000,000
Fair value allocated to identifiable net assets	5,400,000
Goodwill	€9,600,000

Allocation of excess purchase price (based on the differences between fair values and book values):

Inventory	€1,300,000
PP&E (net)	2,000,000
Long-term debt	200,000
Goodwill	9,600,000
	€13,100,000

Both IFRS and US GAAP record the fair value of the acquisition at the market value of the stock issued, or €15,000,000. In this case, the purchase price exceeds the book value of Jefferson's net assets by €13,100,000. Inventory, PP&E (net), and long-term debt are adjusted to fair values. The excess of the purchase price over the fair value of identifiable net assets results in goodwill recognition of €9,600,000.

The post-combination balance sheet of the combined entity would appear as follows:[24]

Franklin Consolidated Balance Sheet (Acquisition Method) (000)	
Cash and receivables	€10,300
Inventory	15,000
PP&E (net)	31,500
Goodwill	9,600
Total assets	€66,400
Current payables	€8,600
Long-term debt	17,800
Total liabilities	€26,400
Capital stock (€1 par)	€6,000
Additional paid in capital	20,000
Retained earnings	14,000
Total stockholders' equity	€40,000
Total liabilities and stockholders' equity	€66,400

Assets and liabilities are combined using book values of Franklin plus fair values for the assets and liabilities acquired from Jefferson. For example, the book value of Franklin's inventory (€12,000,000) is added to the fair value of inventory acquired from Jefferson (€3,000,000) for a combined inventory of €15,000,000.

---

24 Under the uniting (pooling) of interests method (which required an exchange of common shares), the shares issued by Franklin would be measured at their par value. In addition, the assets and liabilities of both companies would be combined at their book values resulting in no goodwill being recognized. The retained earnings of Jefferson would also be combined with that of Franklin on the consolidated balance sheet. Uniting (pooling) of interests method is not allowed for transactions initiated after 2004.

Long-term debt has a book value of €16,000,000 on Franklin's pre-acquisition statements, and Jefferson's fair value of debt is €1,800,000. The combined long-term debt is recorded as €17,800,000.

Franklin's post-merger financial statement reflects in stockholders' equity the stock issued by Franklin to acquire Jefferson. Franklin issues stock with a par value of €1,000,000; however, the stock is measured at fair value under both IFRS and US GAAP. Therefore, the consideration exchanged is 1,000,000 shares at market value of €15, or €15,000,000. Prior to the transaction, Franklin had 5,000,000 shares of €1 par stock outstanding (€5,000,000). The combined entity reflects the Franklin capital stock outstanding of €6,000,000 (€5,000,000 plus the additional 1,000,000 shares of €1 par stock issued to effect the transaction). Franklin's additional paid in capital of €6,000,000 is increased by the €14,000,000 additional paid in capital from the issuance of the 1,000,000 shares (€15,000,000 less par value of €1,000,000) for a total of €20,000,000. At the acquisition date, only the acquirer's retained earnings are carried to the combined entity. Earnings of the target are included on the consolidated income statement and retained earnings only in post-acquisition periods.

In the periods subsequent to the business combination, the financial statements continue to be affected by the acquisition method. Net income reflects the performance of the combined entity. Under the acquisition method, amortization/depreciation is based on historical cost of Franklin's assets and the fair value of Jefferson's assets. Using Example 8, as Jefferson's acquired inventory is sold, the cost of goods sold would be €1,300,000 higher and depreciation on PP&E would be €2,000,000 higher over the life of the asset than under the pooling of interests method or if the companies had not combined.[25]

6.4 The Consolidation Process

Consolidated financial statements combine the separate financial statements for distinct legal entities, the parent and its subsidiaries, as if they were one economic unit. Consolidation combines the assets, liabilities, revenues, and expenses of subsidiaries with the parent company. Transactions between the parent and subsidiary (intercompany transactions) are eliminated to avoid double counting and premature income recognition. Consolidated statements are presumed to be more meaningful in terms of representational faithfulness. It is important for the analyst to consider the differences in IFRS and US GAAP, valuation bases, and other factors that could impair the validity of comparative analyses.

6.4.1 Business Combination with Less than 100% Acquisition

The acquirer purchases 100% of the equity of the target company in a transaction structured as a merger or consolidation. For a transaction structured as an acquisition, however, the acquirer does not have to purchase 100% of the equity of the target in order to achieve control. The acquiring company may purchase less than 100% of the target because it may be constrained by resources or it may be unable to acquire all the outstanding shares. As a result, both the acquirer and the target remain separate

---

25 Under the pooling method, cost of goods sold and depreciation expense would be lower, because both would be based on the book value of the Jefferson's assets. Therefore, analysts must be aware of companies that used the uniting (pooling) of interests prior to the method being disallowed. This is because in the periods after pooling was disallowed, the assets of an entity that had used uniting of interests (pooling) may be understated and income overstated relative to companies that used the acquisition method. These differences will affect the comparability of return on investment ratios.

legal entities. Both IFRS and US GAAP presume a company has control if it owns more than 50% of the voting shares of an entity. In this case, the acquiring company is viewed as the parent, and the target company is viewed as the subsidiary. Both the parent and the subsidiary typically prepare their own financial records, but the parent also prepares consolidated financial statements at each reporting period. The consolidated financial statements are the primary source of information for investors and analysts.

6.4.2 Non-controlling (Minority) Interests: Balance Sheet

A non-controlling (minority) interest is the portion of the subsidiary's equity (residual interest) that is held by third parties (i.e., not owned by the parent). Non-controlling interests are created when the parent acquires less than a 100% controlling interest in a subsidiary. IFRS and US GAAP have similar treatment for how non-controlling interests are classified.[26] Non-controlling interests in consolidated subsidiaries are presented on the consolidated balance sheet as a separate component of stockholders' equity. IFRS and US GAAP differ, however, on the measurement of non-controlling interests. Under IFRS, the parent can measure the non-controlling interest at either its fair value (full goodwill method) or at the non-controlling interest's proportionate share of the acquiree's identifiable net assets (partial goodwill method). Under US GAAP, the parent must use the full goodwill method and measure the non-controlling interest at fair value.

Example 9 illustrates the differences in reporting requirements.

EXAMPLE 9

Non-controlling Asset Valuation

On 1 January 2012, the hypothetical Parent Co. acquired 90% of the outstanding shares of the hypothetical Subsidiary Co. in exchange for shares of Parent Co.'s no par common stock with a fair value of €180,000. The fair market value of the subsidiary's shares on the date of the exchange was €200,000. Below is selected financial information from the two companies immediately prior to the exchange of shares (before the parent recorded the acquisition):

	Parent Book Value	Subsidiary Book Value	Subsidiary Fair Value
Cash and receivables	€40,000	€15,000	€15,000
Inventory	125,000	80,000	80,000
PP&E (net)	235,000	95,000	155,000
	€400,000	€190,000	€250,000
Payables	55,000	20,000	20,000
Long-term debt	120,000	70,000	70,000
	175,000	90,000	90,000
Net assets	€225,000	€100,000	€160,000
Shareholders' equity:			

(continued)

---

26 IFRS 10, Consolidated Financial Statements and FASB ASC Topic 810 [Consolidation].

	Parent Book Value	Subsidiary	
		Book Value	Fair Value
Capital stock (no par)	€87,000	€34,000	
Retained earnings	€138,000	€66,000	

1 Calculate the value of PP&E (net) on the consolidated balance sheet under both IFRS and US GAAP.

2 Calculate the value of goodwill and the value of the non-controlling interest at the acquisition date under the full goodwill method.

3 Calculate the value of goodwill and the value of the non-controlling interest at the acquisition date under the partial goodwill method.

Solution to 1:

Relative to fair value, the PP&E of the subsidiary is understated by €60,000. Under the acquisition method (IFRS and US GAAP), as long as the parent has control over the subsidiary (i.e., regardless of whether the parent had purchased 51% or 100% of the subsidiary's stock), it would include 100% of the subsidiary's assets and liabilities at fair value on the consolidated balance sheet. Therefore, PP&E on the consolidated balance sheet would be valued at €390,000.

Solution to 2:

Under the full goodwill method (mandatory under US GAAP and optional under IFRS), goodwill on the consolidated balance sheet would be the difference between the total fair value of the subsidiary and the fair value of the subsidiary's identifiable net assets.

Fair value of the subsidiary	€200,000
Fair value of subsidiary's identifiable net assets	160,000
Goodwill	€40,000

The value of the non-controlling interest is equal to the non-controlling interest's proportionate share of the subsidiary's fair value. The non-controlling interest's proportionate share of the subsidiary is 10% and the fair value of the subsidiary is €200,000 on the acquisition date. Under the full goodwill method, the value of the non-controlling interest would be €20,000 (10% × €200,000).

Solution to 3:

Under the partial goodwill method (IFRS only), goodwill on the parent's consolidated balance sheet would be €36,000, the difference between the purchase price and the parent's proportionate share of the subsidiary's identifiable assets.

Acquisition price	€180,000
90% of fair value	144,000
Goodwill	€36,000

The value of the non-controlling interest is equal to the non-controlling interest's proportionate share of the fair value of the subsidiary's identifiable net assets. The non-controlling interest's proportionate share is 10%, and the fair value of the subsidiary's identifiable net assets on the acquisition date is €160,000. Under the partial goodwill method, the value of the non-controlling interest would be €16,000 (10% × €160,000).

Regardless of which method is used, goodwill is not amortized under either IFRS or US GAAP but it is tested for impairment at least annually.

For comparative purposes, below is the balance sheet at the acquisition date under the full goodwill and partial goodwill methods.

Comparative Consolidated Balance Sheet at Acquisition Date: Acquisition Method

	Full Goodwill	Partial Goodwill
Cash and receivables	€55,000	€55,000
Inventory	205,000	205,000
PP&E (net)	390,000	390,000
Goodwill	40,000	36,000
Total assets	€690,000	€686,000
Payables	€75,000	€75,000
Long-term debt	190,000	190,000
Total liabilities	€265,000	€265,000
Shareholders' equity:		
Noncontrolling interests	€20,000	€16,000
Capital stock (no par)	€267,000	€267,000
Retained earnings	138,000	138,000
Total equity	€425,000	€421,000
Total liabilities and shareholders' equity	€690,000	€686,000

6.4.3 Non-controlling (Minority) Interests: Income Statement

On the income statement, non-controlling (minority) interests are presented as a line item reflecting the allocation of profit or loss for the period. Intercompany transactions, if any, are eliminated in full.

Using assumed data consistent with the facts in Example 9, the amounts included for the subsidiary in the consolidated income statements under IFRS and US GAAP are presented below:

	Full Goodwill	Partial Goodwill
Sales	€250,000	€250,000
Cost of goods sold	137,500	137,500
Interest expense	10,000	10,000
Depreciation expense	39,000	39,000
Income from continuing operations	€63,500	€63,500
Non-controlling interest (10%)	(6,350)	(6,350)
Consolidated net income to parent's shareholders	€57,150	€57,150

Income to the parent's shareholders is €57,150 using either method. This is because the fair value of the PP&E is allocated to non-controlling shareholders as well as to the controlling shareholders under the full goodwill and the partial goodwill methods. Therefore, the non-controlling interests will share in the adjustment for excess depreciation resulting from the €60,000 increase in PP&E. Because depreciation expense is the same under both methods, it results in identical net income to all shareholders, whichever method is used to recognize goodwill and to measure the non-controlling interest.

Although net income to parent's shareholders is the same, the impact on ratios would be different because total assets and stockholders' equity would differ.

Impact on Ratios		
	Full Goodwill (%)	Partial Goodwill (%)
Return on assets	8.28	8.33
Return on equity	13.45	13.57

Over time, the value of the subsidiary will change as a result of net income and changes in equity. As a result, the value of the non-controlling interest on the parent's consolidated balance sheet will also change.

6.4.4 *Goodwill Impairment*

Although goodwill is not amortized, it must be tested for impairment at least annually or more frequently if events or changes in circumstances indicate that it might be impaired. If it is probable that some or all of the goodwill will not be recovered through the profitable operations of the combined entity, it should be partially or fully written off by charging it to an expense. Once written down, goodwill cannot be later restored.

IFRS and US GAAP differ on the definition of the levels at which goodwill is assigned and how goodwill is tested for impairment.

Under IFRS, at the time of acquisition, the total amount of goodwill recognized is allocated to each of the acquirer's cash-generating units that will benefit from the expected synergies resulting from the combination with the target. A cash-generating unit represents the lowest level within the combined entity at which goodwill is monitored for impairment purposes.[27] Goodwill impairment testing is then conducted under a one-step approach. The recoverable amount of a cash-generating unit is calculated and compared with the carrying value of the cash-generating unit.[28] An impairment loss is recognized if the recoverable amount of the cash-generating unit is less than its carrying value. The impairment loss (the difference between these two amounts) is first applied to the goodwill that has been allocated to the cash-generating unit. Once this has been reduced to zero, the remaining amount of the loss is then allocated to all of the other non-cash assets in the unit on a pro rata basis.

Under US GAAP, at the time of acquisition, the total amount of goodwill recognized is allocated to each of the acquirer's reporting units. A reporting unit is an operating segment or component of an operating segment that is one level below the operating segment as a whole. Goodwill impairment testing is then conducted under a two-step approach: identification of impairment and then measurement of the loss. First, the carrying amount of the reporting unit (including goodwill) is compared to its fair value. If the carrying value of the reporting unit exceeds its fair value, potential

---

27 A cash-generating unit is the smallest identifiable group of assets that generates cash inflows that are largely independent of the cash inflows from other assets or groups of assets.

28 The recoverable amount of a cash-generating unit is the higher of net selling price (i.e., fair value less costs to sell) and its value in use. Value in use is the present value of the future cash flows expected to be derived from the cash-generating unit. The carrying value of a cash-generating unit is equal to the carrying value of the unit's assets and liabilities including the goodwill that has been allocated to that unit.

impairment has been identified. The second step is then performed to measure the amount of the impairment loss. The amount of the impairment loss is the difference between the implied fair value of the reporting unit's goodwill and its carrying amount. The implied fair value of goodwill is determined in the same manner as in a business combination (it is the difference between the fair value of the reporting unit and the fair value of the reporting unit's assets and liabilities). The impairment loss is applied to the goodwill that has been allocated to the reporting unit. After the goodwill of the reporting unit has been eliminated, no other adjustments are made automatically to the carrying values of any of the reporting unit's other assets or liabilities. However, it may be prudent to test other asset values for recoverability and possible impairment.

Under both IFRS and US GAAP, the impairment loss is recorded as a separate line item in the consolidated income statement.

EXAMPLE 10

Goodwill Impairment: IFRS

The cash-generating unit of a French company has a carrying value of €1,400,000, which includes €300,000 of allocated goodwill. The recoverable amount of the cash-generating unit is determined to be €1,300,000, and the estimated fair value of its identifiable net assets is €1,200,000. Calculate the impairment loss.

Solution:

Recoverable amount of unit	€1,300,000
Carrying amount of unit	1,400,000
Impairment loss	€100,000

The impairment loss of €100,000 is reported on the income statement, and the goodwill allocated to the cash-generating unit would be reduced by €100,000 to €200,000.

If the recoverable amount of the cash-generating unit had been €800,000 instead of €1,300,000, the impairment loss recognized would be €600,000. This would first be absorbed by the goodwill allocated to the unit (€300,000). Once this has been reduced to zero, the remaining amount of the impairment loss (€300,000) would then be allocated on a pro rata basis to the other non-cash assets within the unit.

EXAMPLE 11

Goodwill Impairment: US GAAP

A reporting unit of a US corporation (e.g., a division) has a fair value of $1,300,000 and a carrying value of $1,400,000 that includes recorded goodwill of $300,000. The estimated fair value of the identifiable net assets of the reporting unit at the impairment test date is $1,200,000. Calculate the impairment loss.

Solution:

Step 1 – Determination of an Impairment Loss

Because the fair value of the reporting unit is less than its carrying book value, a potential impairment loss has been identified.

Fair value of unit: $1,300,000 < $1,400,000

Step 2 – Measurement of the Impairment Loss

Fair value of reporting unit	$1,300,000
Less: net assets	1,200,000
Implied goodwill	$100,000
Current carrying value of goodwill	$300,000
Less: implied goodwill	100,000
Impairment loss	$200,000

The impairment loss of $200,000 is reported on the income statement, and the goodwill allocated to the reporting unit would be reduced by $200,000 to $100,000.

If the fair value of the reporting unit was $800,000 (instead of $1,300,000), the implied goodwill would be a negative $400,000. In this case, the maximum amount of the impairment loss recognized would be $300,000, the carrying amount of goodwill.

6.5 Financial Statement Presentation Subsequent to the Business Combination

The presentation of consolidated financial statements is similar under IFRS and US GAAP. For example, selected financial statements for GlaxoSmithKline are shown in Exhibits 8 and 9. GlaxoSmithKline is a leading pharmaceutical company headquartered in the United Kingdom.

The consolidated balance sheet in Exhibit 8 combines the operations of GlaxoSmithKline and its subsidiaries. The analyst can observe that in 2011 GlaxoSmithKline had investments in financial assets (other investments of £590,000,000 and liquid investments of £184,000,000), and investments in associates and joint ventures of £560,000,000. In 2011 GlaxoSmithKline acquired 100% interests in four companies. The increase in goodwill on the balance sheet reflects the fact that GlaxoSmithKline paid an amount in excess of the fair value of the identifiable net assets in these acquisitions. The analyst can also note that GlaxoSmithKline is the parent company in a less than 100% acquisition. The minority interest of £795,000,000 in the equity section is the portion of the combined entity that accrues to non-controlling shareholders.

Exhibit 8   GlaxoSmithKline Consolidated Balance Sheet at 31 December 2011

	Notes	2011 £m	2010 £m
Non-current assets			
Property, plant and equipment	17	**8,748**	9,045
Goodwill	18	**3,754**	3,606
Other intangible assets	19	**7,802**	8,532
Investments in associates and joint ventures	20	**560**	1,081
Other investments	21	**590**	711
Deferred tax assets	14	**2,849**	2,566
Derivative financial instruments	41	**85**	97

Exhibit 8 (Continued)			
	Notes	**2011 £m**	**2010 £m**
Other non-current assets	22	525	556
Total non-current assets		24,913	26,194
Current assets			
Inventories	23	3,873	3,837
Current tax recoverable	14	85	56
Trade and other receivables	24	5,576	5,793
Derivative financial instruments	41	70	93
Liquid investments	32	184	184
Cash and cash equivalents	25	5,714	6,057
Assets held for sale	26	665	16
Total current assets		16,167	16,036
Total assets		41,080	42,230
Current liabilities			
Short-term borrowings	32	(2,698)	(291)
Trade and other payables	27	(7,359)	(6,888)
Derivative financial instruments	41	(175)	(188)
Current tax payable	14	(1,643)	(1,047)
Short-term provisions	29	(3,135)	(4,380)
Total current liabilities		(15,010)	(12,794)
Non-current liabilities			
Long-term borrowings	32	(12,203)	(14,809)
Deferred tax liabilities	14	(822)	(707)
Pensions and other post-employment benefits	28	(3,091)	(2,672)
Other provisions	29	(499)	(904)
Derivative financial instruments	41	(2)	(5)
Other non-current liabilities	30	(626)	(594)
Total non-current liabilities		(17,243)	(19,691)
Total liabilities		(32,253)	(32,485)
Net assets		8,827	9,745
Equity			
Share capital	33	1,387	1,418
Share premium account	33	1,673	1,428
Retained earnings	34	3,370	4,779
Other reserves	34	1,602	1,262
Shareholders' equity		8,032	8,887
Non-controlling interests		795	858
Total equity		8,827	9,745

The consolidated income statement for GlaxoSmithKline is presented in Exhibit 9. IFRS and US GAAP have similar formats for consolidated income statements. Each line item (e.g., turnover [sales], cost of sales, etc.) includes 100% of the parent and the subsidiary transactions after eliminating any **upstream** (subsidiary sells to parent) or **downstream** (parent sells to subsidiary) intercompany transactions. The portion of income accruing to non-controlling shareholders is presented as a separate line item on the consolidated income statement. Note that net income would be the same under IFRS and US GAAP.[29] The analyst will need to make adjustments for any analysis comparing specific line items that might differ between IFRS and US GAAP.

| Exhibit 9 | GlaxoSmithKline Consolidated Income Statement for the Year Ended 31 December 2011 |

	Notes	Results before major restructuring business performance £m	Major Restructuring £m	2011 Total £m	2010 £m	2009 £m
Turnover	6	27,387	—	**27,387**	28,392	28,368
Cost of sales		(7,259)	(73)	**(7,332)**	(7,592)	(7,380)
Gross profit		20,128	(73)	**20,055**	20,800	20,988
Selling, general and administration		(8,429)	(397)	**(8,826)**	(13,053)	(9,592)
Research and development		(3,912)	(97)	**(4,009)**	(4,457)	(4,106)
Other operating income	8	610	(23)	**587**	493	1,135
Operating profit	9	8,397	(590)	**7,807**	3,783	8,425
Finance income	11	90	—	**90**	116	70
Finance costs	12	(797)	(2)	**(799)**	(831)	(783)
Profit on disposal of interests in Associates		585		**585**	8	115
Share of after tax profits of associates and joint ventures	13	15	—	**15**	81	64
Profit before taxation		8,290	(592)	**7,698**	3,157	7,891
Taxation	14	(2,354)	114	**(2,240)**	(1,304)	(2,222)
Profit after taxation for the year		5,936	(478)	**5,458**	1,853	5,669
Profit attributable to non-controlling interests		197	—	**197**	219	138
Profit attributable to shareholders		5,739	(478)	**5,261**	1,634	5,531
		5,936	(478)	**5,458**	1,853	5,669

---

29 It is possible, however, for differences to arise through the application of different accounting rules (e.g., valuation of fixed assets).

Exhibit 9	**(Continued)**					

	Notes	Results before major restructuring business performance £m	Major Restructuring £m	2011 Total £m	2010 £m	2009 £m
Basic earnings per share (pence)	15			**104.6p**	32.1p	109.1p
Diluted earnings per share (pence)	15			**103.2p**	31.9p	108.2p

6.6 Variable Interest and Special Purpose Entities

Special purpose entities (SPEs) are enterprises that are created to accommodate specific needs of the sponsoring entity.[30] The sponsoring entity (on whose behalf the SPE is created) frequently transfers assets to the SPE, obtains the right to use assets held by the SPE, or performs services for the SPE, while other parties (capital providers) provide funding to the SPE. SPEs can be a legitimate financing mechanism for a company to segregate certain activities and thereby reduce risk. SPEs may take the form of a limited liability company (corporation), trust, partnership, or unincorporated entity. They are often created with legal arrangements that impose strict and sometimes permanent limits on the decision-making powers of their governing board or management.

Beneficial interest in an SPE may take the form of a debt instrument, an equity instrument, a participation right, or a residual interest in a lease. Some beneficial interests may simply provide the holder with a fixed or stated rate of return, while beneficial interests give the holder the rights or the access to future economic benefits of the SPE's activities. In most cases, the creator/sponsor of the entity retains a significant beneficial interest in the SPE even though it may own little or none of the SPE's voting equity.

In the past, sponsors were able to avoid consolidating SPEs on their financial statements because they did not have "control" (i.e., own a majority of the voting interest) of the SPE. SPEs were structured so that the sponsoring company had financial control over their assets or operating activities, while third parties held the majority of the voting interest in the SPE.

These outside equity participants often funded their investments in the SPE with debt that was either directly or indirectly guaranteed by the sponsoring companies. The sponsoring companies, in turn, were able to avoid the disclosure of many of these guarantees as well as their economic significance. In addition, many sponsoring companies created SPEs to facilitate the transfer of assets and liabilities from their own balance sheets. As a result, they were able to recognize large amounts of revenue and gains, because these transactions were accounted for as sales. By avoiding consolidation, sponsoring companies did not have to report the assets and the liabilities of the SPE; financial performance as measured by the unconsolidated financial statements was potentially misleading. The benefit to the sponsoring company was improved asset turnover, lower operating and financial leverage metrics, and higher profitability.

---

30 The term "special purpose entity" is used by IFRS and "variable interest entity" and "special purpose entity" is used by US GAAP.

Enron, for example, used SPEs to obtain off-balance sheet financing and artificially improve its financial performance. Its subsequent collapse was partly attributable to its guarantee of the debt of the SPEs it had created.

To address the accounting issues arising from the misuse and abuse of SPEs, the IASB and the FASB have worked to improve the consolidation models to take into account financial arrangements where parties other than the holders of the majority of the voting interests exercise financial control over another entity. IFRS 10, *Consolidated Financial Statements*, revised the definition of control to encompass many special purpose entities. This standard is effective for annual periods beginning on or after 1 January 2013, with early application permitted. Special purpose entities involved in a structured financial transaction will require an evaluation of the purpose, design, and risks.

In developing new accounting standards to address this consolidation issue, the FASB used the more general term variable interest entity (VIE) to more broadly define an entity that is financially controlled by one or more parties that do not hold a majority voting interest. Therefore, under US GAAP, a VIE includes other entities besides SPEs. FASB ASC Topic 810 [*Consolidation*] provides guidance for US GAAP, which classifies special purpose entities as variable interest entities if:

1   total equity at risk is insufficient to finance activities without financial support from other parties, or

2   equity investors lack any one of the following:

   a   the ability to make decisions;

   b   the obligation to absorb losses; or

   c   the right to receive returns.

Common examples of variable interests are entities created to lease real estate or other property, entities created for the securitization of financial assets, or entities created for R&D activity.

Under FASB ASC Topic 810 [*Consolidation*], the primary beneficiary of a VIE must consolidate it as its subsidiary regardless of how much of an equity investment it has in the VIE. The primary beneficiary (which is often the sponsor) is the entity that is expected to absorb the majority of the VIE's expected losses, receive the majority of the VIE's residual returns, or both. If one entity will absorb a majority of the VIE's expected losses and another unrelated entity will receive a majority of the VIE's expected residual returns, the entity absorbing a majority of the losses must consolidate the VIE. If there are non-controlling interests in the VIE, these would also be shown in the consolidated balance sheet and consolidated income statement of the primary beneficiary.

6.6.1 *Illustration of an SPE for a Leased Asset*

Consider the situation in which a sponsoring company creates a special purpose entity with minimal and independent third party equity. The SPE borrows from the debt market and acquires or constructs an asset. The asset may be acquired from the sponsoring company or from an outside source. The sponsoring company then leases the asset, and the cash flow from lease payments is used to repay the debt and provide a return to equity holders. Because the asset is pledged as collateral, risk is reduced and a lower interest rate may be offered by the financing organization. In addition, because equity investors are not exposed to all the business risks of the sponsoring company but only those of the restricted SPE, they may be more willing to invest in this relatively safe investment. The sponsor retains the risk of default and receives the benefits of ownership of the leased asset through a residual value guarantee. Under these conditions, the sponsor is the primary beneficiary and consolidates the SPE.

Exhibit 10   Special Purpose Entity

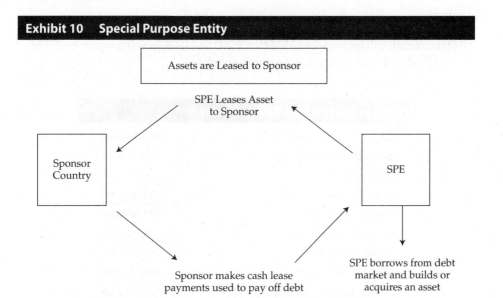

6.6.2 *Securitization of Assets*

Example 12 shows the effects of securitizing assets on companies' balance sheets.

EXAMPLE 12

Receivables Securitization

Odena, a (fictional) Italian auto manufacturer, wants to raise €55M in capital by borrowing against its financial receivables. To accomplish this objective, Odena can choose between two alternatives:

Alternative 1	Borrow directly against the receivables; or
Alternative 2	Create a special purpose entity, invest €5M in the SPE, have the SPE borrow €55M, and then use the funds to purchase €60M of receivables from Odena.

Using the financial statement information provided below, describe the effect of each Alternative on Odena, assuming that Odena meets the definition of control and will consolidate the SPE.

Odena Balance Sheet	
Cash	€30,000,000
Accounts receivable	60,000,000
Other assets	40,000,000
Total assets	€130,000,000
Current liabilities	€27,000,000
Noncurrent liabilities	20,000,000
Total liabilities	€47,000,000
Shareholder equity	€83,000,000
Total liabilities and equity	€130,000,000

Alternative 1:

Odena's cash will increase by €55M (to €85M) and its debt will increase by €55M (to €75M). Its sales and net income will not change.

Odena: Alternative 1 Balance Sheet	
Cash	€85,000,000
Accounts receivable	60,000,000
Other assets	40,000,000
Total assets	€185,000,000
Current liabilities	€27,000,000
Noncurrent liabilities	75,000,000
Total liabilities	€102,000,000
Shareholder equity	€83,000,000
Total liabilities and equity	€185,000,000

Alternative 2:

Odena's accounts receivable will decrease by €60M and its cash will increase by €55 (it invests €5M in cash in the SPE). However, if Odena is able to sell the receivables to the SPE for more than their carrying value (for example, €65), it would also report a gain on the sale in its profit and loss. Equally important, the SPE may be able to borrow the funds at a lower rate than Odena, since they are bankruptcy remote from Odena (i.e., out of reach of Odena's creditors), and the lenders to the SPE are the claimants on its assets (i.e., the purchased receivables).

SPE Balance Sheet	
Accounts receivable	€60,000,000
Total assets	€60,000,000
Long-term debt	€55,000,000
Equity	5,000,000
Total liabilities and equity	€60,000,000

Because Odena consolidates the SPE, its financial balance sheet would look like the following:

Odena: Alternative 2 Consolidated Balance Sheet	
Cash	€85,000,000
Accounts receivable	60,000,000
Other assets	40,000,000
Total assets	€185,000,000
Current liabilities	€27,000,000
Noncurrent liabilities	75,000,000

(Continued)	
Total liabilities	€102,000,000
Shareholder equity	€83,000,000
Total liabilities and equity	€185,000,000

Therefore, the consolidated balance sheet of Odena would look exactly the same as if it borrowed directly against the receivables. In addition, as a result of the consolidation, the transfer (sale) of the receivables to the SPE would be reversed along with any gain Odena recognized on the sale.

6.7 Additional Issues in Business Combinations That Impair Comparability

Accounting for business combinations is a complex topic. In addition to the basics covered so far in this reading, we briefly mention some of the more common issues that impair comparability between IFRS and US GAAP.

6.7.1 Contingent Assets and Liabilities

Under IFRS, the cost of an acquisition is allocated to the fair value of assets, liabilities, and contingent liabilities. Contingent liabilities are recorded separately as part of the cost allocation process, provided that their fair values can be measured reliably. Subsequently, the contingent liability is measured at the higher of the amount initially recognized or the best estimate of the amount required to settle. Contingent assets are not recognized under IFRS.

Under US GAAP, contractual contingent assets and liabilities are recognized and recorded at their fair values at the time of acquisition. Non-contractual contingent assets and liabilities must also be recognized and recorded only if it is "more likely than not" they meet the definition of an asset or a liability at the acquisition date. Subsequently, a contingent liability is measured at the higher of the amount initially recognized or the best estimate of the amount of the loss. A contingent asset, however, is measured at the lower of the acquisition date fair value or the best estimate of the future settlement amount.

6.7.2 Contingent Consideration

Contingent consideration may be negotiated as part of the acquisition price. For example, the acquiring company (parent) may agree to pay additional money to the acquiree's (subsidiary's) former shareholders if certain agreed upon events occur. These can include achieving specified sales or profit levels for the acquiree and/or the combined entity. Under both IFRS and US GAAP, contingent consideration is initially measured at fair value. IFRS and US GAAP classify contingent consideration as an asset, liability or equity. In subsequent periods, changes in the fair value of liabilities (and assets, in the case of US GAAP) are recognized in the consolidated income statement. Both IFRS and US GAAP do not remeasure equity classified contingent consideration; instead, settlement is accounted for within equity.

6.7.3 In-Process R&D

IFRS and US GAAP recognize in-process research and development acquired in a business combination as a separate intangible asset and measure it at fair value (if it can be measured reliably). In subsequent periods, this research and development is subject to amortization if successfully completed (a marketable product results) or to impairment if no product results or if the product is not technically and/or financially viable.

6.7.4 *Restructuring Costs*

IFRS and US GAAP do not recognize restructuring costs that are associated with the business combination as part of the cost of the acquisition. Instead, they are recognized as an expense in the periods the restructuring costs are incurred.

SUMMARY

Intercompany investments play a significant role in business activities and create significant challenges for the analyst in assessing company performance. Investments in other companies can take five basic forms: investments in financial assets, investments in associates, joint ventures, business combinations, and investments in special purpose and variable interest entities. Key concepts are as follows:

- Investments in financial assets are those in which the investor has no significant influence. They can be measured and reported as
  - Fair value through profit or loss.
  - Fair value through other comprehensive income.
  - Amortized cost.

  IFRS and US GAAP treat investments in financial assets in a similar manner.

- Investments in associates and joint ventures are those in which the investor has significant influence, but not control, over the investee's business activities. Because the investor can exert significant influence over financial and operating policy decisions, IFRS and US GAAP require the equity method of accounting because it provides a more objective basis for reporting investment income.
  - The equity method requires the investor to recognize income as earned rather than when dividends are received.
  - The equity investment is carried at cost, plus its share of post-acquisition income (after adjustments) less dividends received.
  - The equity investment is reported as a single line item on the balance sheet and on the income statement.

- Current IFRS and US GAAP accounting standards require the use of the acquisition method to account for business combinations. Fair value of the consideration given is the appropriate measurement for identifiable assets and liabilities acquired in the business combination.

- Goodwill is the difference between the acquisition value and the fair value of the target's identifiable net tangible and intangible assets. Because it is considered to have an indefinite life, it is not amortized. Instead, it is evaluated at least annually for impairment. Impairment losses are reported on the income statement. IFRS use a one-step approach to determine and measure the impairment loss, whereas US GAAP uses a two-step approach.

- If the acquiring company acquires less than 100%, non-controlling (minority) shareholders' interests are reported on the consolidated financial statements. IFRS allows the non-controlling interest to be measured at either its fair value (full goodwill) or at the non-controlling interest's proportionate share of the acquiree's identifiable net assets (partial goodwill). US GAAP requires the non-controlling interest to be measured at fair value (full goodwill).

- Consolidated financial statements are prepared in each reporting period.

- Special purpose (SPEs) and variable interest entities (VIEs) are required to be consolidated by the entity which is expected to absorb the majority of the expected losses or receive the majority of expected residual benefits.

PRACTICE PROBLEMS

The following information relates to Questions 1–6

Cinnamon, Inc. is a diversified manufacturing company headquartered in the United Kingdom. It complies with IFRS. In 2009, Cinnamon held a 19 percent passive equity ownership interest in Cambridge Processing that was classified as available-for-sale. During the year, the value of this investment rose by £2 million. In December 2009, Cinnamon announced that it would be increasing its ownership interest to 50 percent effective 1 January 2010 through a cash purchase. Cinnamon and Cambridge have no intercompany transactions.

Peter Lubbock, an analyst following both Cinnamon and Cambridge, is curious how the increased stake will affect Cinnamon's consolidated financial statements. He asks Cinnamon's CFO how the company will account for the investment, and is told that the decision has not yet been made. Lubbock decides to use his existing forecasts for both companies' financial statements to compare the outcomes of alternative accounting treatments.

Lubbock assembles abbreviated financial statement data for Cinnamon (Exhibit 1) and Cambridge (Exhibit 2) for this purpose.

Exhibit 1	Selected Financial Statement Information for Cinnamon, Inc. (£ Millions)		
Year ending 31 December		**2009**	**2010***
Revenue		1,400	1,575
Operating income		126	142
Net income		62	69
31 December		**2009**	**2010***
Total assets		1,170	1,317
Shareholders' equity		616	685

*Estimates made prior to announcement of increased stake in Cambridge.

Exhibit 2	Selected Financial Statement Information for Cambridge Processing (£ Millions)		
Year ending 31 December		**2009**	**2010***
Revenue		1,000	1,100
Operating income		80	88
Net income		40	44
Dividends paid		20	22
31 December		**2009**	**2010***

Exhibit 2 (Continued)		
Year ending 31 December	**2009**	**2010***
Total assets	800	836
Shareholders' equity	440	462

*Estimates made prior to announcement of increased stake by Cinnamon.

1 In 2009, Cinnamon's earnings before taxes includes a contribution (in £ millions) from its investment in Cambridge Processing that is *closest* to:

   A £3.8.

   B £5.8.

   C £7.6.

2 In 2010, if Cinnamon is deemed to have control over Cambridge, it will *most likely* account for its investment in Cambridge using:

   A the equity method.

   B the acquisition method.

   C proportionate consolidation.

3 At 31 December 2010, Cinnamon's shareholders' equity on its balance sheet would *most likely* be:

   A highest if Cinnamon is deemed to have control of Cambridge.

   B independent of the accounting method used for the investment in Cambridge.

   C highest if Cinnamon is deemed to have significant influence over Cambridge.

4 In 2010, Cinnamon's net profit margin would be *highest* if:

   A it is deemed to have control of Cambridge.

   B it had not increased its stake in Cambridge.

   C it is deemed to have significant influence over Cambridge.

5 At 31 December 2010, assuming control and recognition of goodwill, Cinnamon's reported debt to equity ratio will *most likely* be highest if it accounts for its investment in Cambridge using the:

   A equity method.

   B full goodwill method.

   C partial goodwill method.

6 Compared to Cinnamon's operating margin in 2009, if it is deemed to have control of Cambridge, its operating margin in 2010 will *most likely* be:

   A lower.

   B higher.

   C the same.

The following information relates to Questions 7–12

Zimt, AG is a consumer products manufacturer headquartered in Austria. It complies with IFRS. In 2009, Zimt held a 10 percent passive stake in Oxbow Limited that was classified as held for trading securities. During the year, the value of this stake declined by €3 million. In December 2009, Zimt announced that it would be increasing its ownership to 50 percent effective 1 January 2010.

Franz Gelblum, an analyst following both Zimt and Oxbow, is curious how the increased stake will affect Zimt's consolidated financial statements. Because Gelblum is uncertain how the company will account for the increased stake, he uses his existing forecasts for both companies' financial statements to compare various alternative outcomes.

Gelblum gathers abbreviated financial statement data for Zimt (Exhibit 1) and Oxbow (Exhibit 2) for this purpose.

Exhibit 1	Selected Financial Statement Estimates for Zimt AG (€ Millions)	
Year ending 31 December	2009	2010*
Revenue	1,500	1,700
Operating income	135	153
Net income	66	75
31 December	2009	2010*
Total assets	1,254	1,421
Shareholders' equity	660	735

*Estimates made prior to announcement of increased stake in Oxbow.

Exhibit 2	Selected Financial Statement Estimates for Oxbow Limited (€ Millions)	
Year ending 31 December	2009	2010*
Revenue	1,200	1,350
Operating income	120	135
Net income	60	68
Dividends paid	20	22
31 December	2009	2010*
Total assets	1,200	1,283
Shareholders' equity	660	706

*Estimates made prior to announcement of increased stake by Zimt.

7   In 2009, Zimt's earnings before taxes includes a contribution (in € millions) from its investment in Oxbow Limited *closest* to:

A   (€0.6) million.

B   (€1.0) million.

C €2.0 million.

8 At 31 December 2010, Zimt's total assets balance would *most likely* be:

    A highest if Zimt is deemed to have control of Oxbow.

    B highest if Zimt is deemed to have significant influence over Oxbow.

    C unaffected by the accounting method used for the investment in Oxbow.

9 Based on Gelblum's estimates, if Zimt is deemed to have significant influence over Oxbow, its 2010 net income (in € millions) would be *closest* to:

    A €75.

    B €109.

    C €143.

10 Based on Gelblum's estimates, if Zimt is deemed to have joint control of Oxbow, and Zimt uses the proportionate consolidation method, its 31 December 2010 total liabilities (in € millions) will *most likely* be *closest* to:

    A €686.

    B €975.

    C €1,263.

11 Based on Gelblum's estimates, if Zimt is deemed to have control over Oxbow, its 2010 consolidated sales (in € millions) will be *closest* to:

    A €1,700.

    B €2,375.

    C €3,050.

12 Based on Gelblum's estimates, Zimt's net income in 2010 will *most likely* be:

    A highest if Zimt is deemed to have control of Oxbow.

    B highest if Zimt is deemed to have significant influence over Oxbow.

    C independent of the accounting method used for the investment in Oxbow.

The following information relates to Questions 13–18

Burton Howard, CFA, is an equity analyst with Maplewood Securities. Howard is preparing a research report on Confabulated Materials, SA, a publicly traded company based in France that complies with IFRS. As part of his analysis, Howard has assembled data gathered from the financial statement footnotes of Confabulated's 2009 Annual Report and from discussions with company management. Howard is concerned about the effect of this information on Confabulated's future earnings.

Information about Confabulated's investment portfolio for the years ended 31 December 2008 and 2009 is presented in Exhibit 1. As part of his research, Howard is considering the possible effect on reported income of Confabulated's accounting classification for fixed income investments.

Exhibit 1   Confabulated's Investment Portfolio (€ Thousands)

Characteristic	Bugle AG	Cathay Corp	Dumas SA
Classification	Available-for-sale	Held-to-maturity	Held-to-maturity
Cost*	€25,000	€40,000	€50,000
Market value, 31 December 2008	29,000	38,000	54,000
Market value, 31 December 2009	28,000	37,000	55,000

*All securities were acquired at par value.

In addition, Confabulated's annual report discusses a transaction under which receivables were securitized through a special purpose entity (SPE) for Confabulated's benefit.

13 The balance sheet carrying value of Confabulated's investment portfolio (in € thousands) at 31 December 2009 is *closest* to:

   A   112,000.

   B   115,000.

   C   118,000.

14 The balance sheet carrying value of Confabulated's investment portfolio at 31 December 2009 would have been higher if which of the securities had been reclassified as a held for trading security?

   A   Bugle.

   B   Cathay.

   C   Dumas.

15 Compared to Confabulated's reported interest income in 2009, if Dumas had been classified as available-for-sale, the interest income would have been:

   A   lower.

   B   the same.

   C   higher.

16 Compared to Confabulated's reported earnings before taxes in 2009, if Bugle had been classified as a held for trading security, the earnings before taxes (in € thousands) would have been:

   A   the same.

   B   €1,000 lower.

   C   €3,000 higher.

17 Confabulated's reported interest income would be lower if the cost was the same but the par value (in € thousands) of:

   A   Bugle was €28,000.

   B   Cathay was €37,000.

   C   Dumas was €55,000.

18 Confabulated's special purpose entity is *most likely* to be:

   A   held off-balance sheet.

   B   consolidated on Confabulated's financial statements.

   C   consolidated on Confabulated's financial statements only if it is a "qualifying SPE."

The following information relates to Questions 19–24

BetterCare Hospitals, Inc. operates a chain of hospitals throughout the United States. The company has been expanding by acquiring local hospitals. Its largest acquisition, that of Statewide Medical, was made in 2001 under the pooling of interests method. BetterCare complies with US GAAP.

BetterCare is currently forming a 50/50 joint venture with Supreme Healthcare under which the companies will share control of several hospitals. BetterCare plans to use the equity method to account for the joint venture. Supreme Healthcare complies with IFRS and will use the proportionate consolidation method to account for the joint venture.

Erik Ohalin is an equity analyst who covers both companies. He has estimated the joint venture's financial information for 2010 in order to prepare his estimates of each company's earnings and financial performance. This information is presented in Exhibit 1.

Exhibit 1	Selected Financial Statement Forecasts for Joint Venture ($ Millions)	
Year ending 31 December		**2010**
Revenue		1,430
Operating income		128
Net income		62
31 December		**2010**
Total assets		1,500
Shareholders' equity		740

Supreme Healthcare recently announced it had formed a special purpose entity through which it plans to sell up to $100 million of its accounts receivable. Supreme Healthcare has no voting interest in the SPE, but it is expected to absorb any losses that it may incur. Ohalin wants to estimate the impact this will have on Supreme Healthcare's consolidated financial statements.

19 Compared to accounting principles currently in use, the pooling method BetterCare used for its Statewide Medical acquisition has *most likely* caused its reported:

A revenue to be higher.

B total equity to be lower.

C total assets to be higher.

20 Based on Ohalin's estimates, the amount of joint venture revenue (in $ millions) included on BetterCare's consolidated 2010 financial statements should be *closest* to:

A $0.

B $715.

C $1,430.

21 Based on Ohalin's estimates, the amount of joint venture net income included on the consolidated financial statements of each venturer will *most likely* be:

   A   higher for BetterCare.

   B   higher for Supreme Healthcare.

   C   the same for both BetterCare and Supreme Healthcare.

22 Based on Ohalin's estimates, the amount of the joint venture's 31 December 2010 total assets (in $ millions) that will be included on Supreme Healthcare's consolidated financial statements will be *closest* to:

   A $0.

   B $750.

   C $1,500.

23 Based on Ohalin's estimates, the amount of joint venture shareholders' equity at 31 December 2010 included on the consolidated financial statements of each venturer will *most likely* be:

   A   higher for BetterCare.

   B   higher for Supreme Healthcare.

   C   the same for both BetterCare and Supreme Healthcare.

24 If Supreme Healthcare sells its receivables to the SPE, its consolidated financial results will *most likely* show:

   A   a higher revenue for 2010.

   B   the same cash balance at 31 December 2010.

   C   the same accounts receivable balance at 31 December 2010.

The following information relates to Questions 25–30

Percy Byron, CFA, is an equity analyst with a UK-based investment firm. One firm Byron follows is NinMount PLC, a UK-based company. On 31 December 2008, NinMount paid £320 million to purchase a 50 percent stake in Boswell Company. The excess of the purchase price over the fair value of Boswell's net assets was attributable to previously unrecorded licenses. These licenses were estimated to have an economic life of six years. The fair value of Boswell's assets and liabilities other than licenses was equal to their recorded book values. NinMount and Boswell both use the pound sterling as their reporting currency and prepare their financial statements in accordance with IFRS.

Byron is concerned whether the investment should affect his "buy" rating on NinMount common stock. He knows NinMount could choose one of several accounting methods to report the results of its investment, but NinMount has not announced which method it will use. Byron forecasts that both companies' 2009 financial results (excluding any merger accounting adjustments) will be identical to those of 2008.

NinMount's and Boswell's condensed income statements for the year ended 31 December 2008, and condensed balance sheets at 31 December 2008, are presented in Exhibits 1 and 2, respectively.

Exhibit 1	NinMount PLC and Boswell Company Income Statements for the Year Ended 31 December 2008 (£ millions)

	NinMount	Boswell
Net sales	950	510
Cost of goods sold	(495)	(305)
Selling expenses	(50)	(15)
Administrative expenses	(136)	(49)
Depreciation & amortization expense	(102)	(92)
Interest expense	(42)	(32)
Income before taxes	125	17
Income tax expense	(50)	(7)
Net income	75	10

Exhibit 2	NinMount PLC and Boswell Company Balance Sheets at 31 December 2008 (£ millions)

	NinMount	Boswell
Cash	50	20
Receivables—net	70	45
Inventory	130	75
Total current assets	250	140
Property, plant, & equipment—net	1,570	930
Investment in Boswell	320	—
Total assets	2,140	1,070
Current liabilities	110	90
Long-term debt	600	400
Total liabilities	710	490
Common stock	850	535
Retained earnings	580	45
Total equity	1,430	580
Total liabilities and equity	2,140	1,070

Note: Balance sheets reflect the purchase price paid by NinMount, but do not yet consider the impact of the accounting method choice.

25 NinMount's current ratio on 31 December 2008 *most likely* will be highest if the results of the acquisition are reported using:

A the equity method.

B consolidation with full goodwill.

C consolidation with partial goodwill.

26 NinMount's long-term debt to equity ratio on 31 December 2008 *most likely* will be lowest if the results of the acquisition are reported using:

    A the equity method.

    B consolidation with full goodwill.

    C consolidation with partial goodwill.

27 Based on Byron's forecast, if NinMount deems it has acquired control of Boswell, NinMount's consolidated 2009 depreciation and amortization expense (in £ millions) will be *closest* to:

    A 102.

    B 148.

    C 204.

28 Based on Byron's forecast, NinMount's net profit margin for 2009 *most likely* will be highest if the results of the acquisition are reported using:

    A the equity method.

    B consolidation with full goodwill.

    C consolidation with partial goodwill.

29 Based on Byron's forecast, NinMount's 2009 return on beginning equity *most likely* will be the same under:

    A either of the consolidations, but different under the equity method.

    B the equity method, consolidation with full goodwill, and consolidation with partial goodwill.

    C none of the equity method, consolidation with full goodwill, or consolidation with partial goodwill.

30 Based on Byron's forecast, NinMount's 2009 total asset turnover ratio on beginning assets under the equity method is *most likely*:

    A lower than if the results are reported using consolidation.

    B the same as if the results are reported using consolidation.

    C higher than if the results are reported using consolidation.

SOLUTIONS

1 A is correct. Dividends from equity securities that are classified as available-for-sale are included in income when earned. Cinnamon would record its 19 percent share of the dividends paid by Cambridge; this is £3.8 million (£20 × 0.19). Though the value of Cinnamon's stake in Cambridge Processing rose by £2 million during the year, under IFRS any unrealized gains or losses for available-for-sale securities are reported in the equity section of the balance sheet as part of other comprehensive income until the securities are sold.

2 B is correct. If Cinnamon is deemed to have control over Cambridge, it would use the acquisition method to account for Cambridge and prepare consolidated financial statements. Proportionate consolidation is used for joint ventures; the equity method is used for some joint ventures and when there is significant influence but not control.

3 A is correct. If Cinnamon is deemed to have control over Cambridge, consolidated financial statements would be prepared and Cinnamon's shareholders' equity would increase and include the amount of the noncontrolling interest. If Cinnamon is deemed to have significant influence, the equity method would be used and there would be no change in the shareholders' equity of Cinnamon.

4 C is correct. If Cinnamon is deemed to have significant influence, it would report half of Cambridge's net income as a line item on its income statement, but no additional revenue is shown. Its profit margin is thus higher than if it consolidated Cambridge's results, which would impact revenue and income, or if it only reported 19 percent of Cambridge's dividends (no change in ownership).

5 C is correct. The full and partial goodwill method will have the same amount of debt; however, shareholders' equity will be higher under full goodwill (and the debt to equity ratio will be lower). Therefore, the debt to equity will be higher under partial goodwill. If control is assumed, Cinnamon cannot use the equity method.

6 A is correct. Cambridge has a lower operating margin (88/1,100 = 8.0%) than Cinnamon (142/1,575 = 9.0%). If Cambridge's results are consolidated with Cinnamon's, the consolidated operating margin will reflect that of the combined company, or 230/2,675 = 8.6%.

7 B is correct. Oxbow was classified as a held for trading security. Held for trading securities are reported at fair value, with unrealized gains and losses included in income. The income statement also includes dividends from equity securities that are classified as held for trading. The €3 million decline in the value of Zimt's stake would reduce income by that amount. Zimt would record its share of the dividends paid (0.1 × €20 million = €2 million). The net effect of Zimt's stake in Oxbow Limited would be to reduce Zimt's income before taxes by €1 million for 2009.

8 A is correct. When a company is deemed to have control of another entity, it records all of the other entity's assets on its own consolidated balance sheet.

9 B is correct. If Zimt is deemed to have significant influence, it would use the equity method to record its ownership. Under the equity method, Zimt's share of Oxbow's net income would be recorded as a single line item. Net income of Zimt = 75 + 0.5(68) = 109.

10 B is correct. Under the proportionate consolidation method, Zimt's balance sheet would show its own total liabilities of €1,421 – 735 = €686 plus half of Oxbow's liabilities of €1,283 – 706 = €577. €686 + (0.5 × 577) = €974.5.

11 C is correct. Under the assumption of control, Zimt would record its own sales plus 100 percent of Oxbow's. €1,700 + 1,350 = €3,050.

12 C is correct. Net income is not affected by the accounting method used to account for active investments in other companies. "One-line consolidation" and consolidation result in the same impact on net income; it is the disclosure that differs.

13 C is correct. Held for trading and available-for-sale securities are carried at market value, whereas held-to-maturity securities are carried at historical cost. €28,000 + 40,000 + 50,000 = €118,000.

14 C is correct. If Dumas had been classified as a held for trading security, its carrying value would have been the €55,000 fair value rather than the €50,000 historical cost.

15 B is correct. The coupon payment is recorded as interest income whether securities are held-to-maturity or available-for-sale. No adjustment is required for amortization since the bonds were bought at par.

16 B is correct. Unrealized gains and losses are included in income when securities are classified as held for trading securities. During 2009 there was an unrealized loss of €1,000.

17 B is correct. The difference between historical cost and par value must be amortized under the effective interest method. If the par value is less than the initial cost (stated interest rate is greater than the effective rate), the interest income would be lower than the interest received because of amortization of the premium.

18 B is correct. Under IFRS, SPEs must be consolidated if they are conducted for the benefit of the sponsoring entity. Further, under IFRS, SPEs cannot be classified as qualifying. Under US GAAP, qualifying SPEs (a classification which has been eliminated) do not have to be consolidated.

19 B is correct. Statewide Medical was accounted for under the pooling of interest method, which causes all of Statewide's assets and liabilities to be reported at historical book value. The excess of assets over liabilities generally is lower using the historical book value method than using the fair value method (this latter method must be used under currently required acquisition accounting). It would have no effect on revenue.

20 A is correct. Under the equity method, BetterCare would record its interest in the joint venture's net profit as a single line item, but would show no line-by-line contribution to revenues or expenses.

21 C is correct. Net income will be the same under the equity method and proportional consolidation. However, sales, cost of sales, and expenses are different because under the equity method the net effect of sales, cost of sales, and expenses is reflected in a single line.

22 B is correct. Under the proportionate consolidation method, Supreme Healthcare's consolidated financial statements will include its 50 percent share of the joint venture's total assets.

23 C is correct. The choice of equity method or proportionate consolidation does not affect reported shareholders' equity.

24 C is correct. Although Supreme Healthcare has no voting interest in the SPE, it is expected to absorb any losses that the SPE incurs. Therefore, Supreme Healthcare "in substance" controls the SPE and would consolidate it. On the consolidated balance sheet, the accounts receivable balance will be the same since the sale to the SPE will be reversed upon consolidation.

25 A is correct. The current ratio using the equity method of accounting is Current assets/Current liabilities = £250/£110 = 2.27. Using consolidation (either full or partial goodwill), the current ratio = £390/£200 = 1.95. Therefore, the current ratio is highest using the equity method.

26 A is correct. Using the equity method, long-term debt to equity = £600/£1,430 = 0.42. Using the consolidation method, long-term debt to equity = long-term debt/equity = £1,000/£1,750 = 0.57. Equity includes the £320 non-controlling interest under either consolidation. It does not matter if the full or partial goodwill method is used since there is no goodwill.

27 C is correct. The projected depreciation and amortization expense will include NinMount's reported depreciation and amortization (£102), Boswell's reported depreciation and amortization (£92), and amortization of Boswell's licenses (£10 million). The licenses have a fair value of £60 million. £320 purchase price indicates a fair value of £640 for the net assets of Boswell. The net book (fair) value of the recorded assets is £580. The previously unrecorded licenses have a fair value of £60 million. The licenses have a remaining life of six years; the amortization adjustment for 2008 will be £10 million. Therefore, Projected depreciation and amortization = £102 + £92 + £10 = £204 million.

28 A is correct. Net income is the same using any of the methods but under the equity method, net sales are only £950; Boswell's sales are not included in the net sales figure. Therefore, net profit margin is highest using the equity method.

29 A is correct. Net income is the same using any of the choices. Beginning equity under the equity method is £1,430. Under either of the consolidations, beginning equity is £1,750 since it includes the £320 noncontrolling interest. Return on beginning equity is highest under the equity method.

30 A is correct. Using the equity method, Total asset turnover = Net sales/Beginning total assets = £950/£2,140 = 0.444. Total asset turnover on beginning assets using consolidation = £1,460/£2,950 = 0.495. Under consolidation, Assets = £2,140 − 320 + 1,070 + 60 = £2,950. Therefore, total asset turnover is lowest using the equity method.

READING

19

Employee Compensation: Post-Employment and Share-Based

by Elaine Henry, PhD, CFA, and Elizabeth A. Gordon

Elaine Henry, PhD, CFA, is at Fordham University (USA). Elizabeth A. Gordon (USA).

LEARNING OUTCOMES

Mastery	The candidate should be able to:
☐	a. describe the types of post-employment benefit plans and implications for financial reports;
☐	b. explain and calculate measures of a defined benefit pension obligation (i.e., present value of the defined benefit obligation and projected benefit obligation) and net pension liability (or asset);
☐	c. describe the components of a company's defined benefit pension costs;
☐	d. explain and calculate the effect of a defined benefit plan's assumptions on the defined benefit obligation and periodic pension cost;
☐	e. explain and calculate how adjusting for items of pension and other post-employment benefits that are reported in the notes to the financial statements affects financial statements and ratios;
☐	f. interpret pension plan note disclosures including cash flow related information;
☐	g. explain issues associated with accounting for share-based compensation;
☐	h. explain how accounting for stock grants and stock options affects financial statements, and the importance of companies' assumptions in valuing these grants and options.

INTRODUCTION

This reading covers two complex aspects of employee compensation: post-employment (retirement) benefits and share-based compensation. Retirement benefits include pensions and other post-employment benefits, such as health insurance. Examples of share-based compensation are stock options and stock grants.

A common issue underlying both of these aspects of employee compensation is the difficulty in measuring the value of the compensation. One factor contributing to the difficulty is that employees earn the benefits in the periods that they provide service but typically receive the benefits in future periods, so measurement requires a significant number of assumptions.

This reading provides an overview of the methods companies use to estimate and measure the benefits they provide to their employees and how this information is reported in financial statements. There has been some convergence between International Financial Reporting Standards (IFRS) and US generally accepted accounting principles (US GAAP) in the measurement and accounting treatment for pensions, other post-employment benefits, and share-based compensation, but some differences remain. Although this reading focuses on IFRS as the basis for discussion, instances where US GAAP significantly differ are discussed.

The reading is organized as follows: Section 2 addresses pensions and other post-employment benefits, and Section 3 covers share-based compensation with a primary focus on the accounting for and analysis of stock options. A summary and practice problems conclude the reading.

PENSIONS AND OTHER POST-EMPLOYMENT BENEFITS

This section discusses the accounting and reporting of pensions and other post-employment benefits by the companies that provide these benefits (accounting and reporting by pension and other retirement funds are not covered in this reading). Under IFRS, IAS 19, *Employee Benefits*, provides the principal source of guidance in accounting for pensions and other post-employment benefits.[1] Under US GAAP, the guidance is spread across several sections of the FASB Codification.[2]

The discussion begins with an overview of the types of benefits and measurement issues involved, including the accounting treatment for defined contribution plans. It then continues with financial statement reporting of pension plans and other post-employment benefits, including an overview of critical assumptions used to value these benefits. The section concludes with a discussion of evaluating defined benefit pension plan and other post-employment benefit disclosures.

---

1 This reading describes IFRS requirements contained in IAS 19 as updated in June 2011 and effective beginning January 2013.
2 Guidance on pension and other post-employment benefits is included in FASB ASC Topic 712 [Compensation-Nonretirement Postemployment Benefits], FASB ASC Topic 715 [Compensation-Retirement Benefits], FASB ASC Topic 960 [Plan Accounting-Defined Benefit Pension Plans], and FASB ASC Topic 965 [Plan Accounting-Health and Welfare Benefit Plans].

2.1 Types of Post-Employment Benefit Plans

Companies may offer various types of benefits to their employees following retirement, including pension plans, health care plans, medical insurance, and life insurance. Some of these benefits involve payments in the current period, but many are promises of future benefits. The objectives of accounting for employee benefits is to measure the cost associated with providing these benefits and to recognise these costs in the sponsoring company's financial statements during the employees' periods of service. Complexity arises because the sponsoring company must make assumptions to estimate the value of future benefits. The assumptions required to estimate and recognise these future benefits can have a significant impact on the company's reported performance and financial position. In addition, differences in assumptions can reduce comparability across companies.

Pension plans, as well as other post-employment benefits, may be either defined contribution plans or defined benefit plans. Under a **defined contribution** (DC) pension plan, specific (or agreed-upon) contributions are made to an employee's pension plan. The agreed upon amount is the pension expense. Typically, in a DC pension plan, an individual account is established for each participating employee. The accounts are generally invested through a financial intermediary, such as an investment management company or an insurance company. The employees and the employer may each contribute to the plan. After the employer makes its agreed-upon contribution to the plan on behalf of an employee—generally in the same period in which the employee provides the service—the employer has no obligation to make payments beyond this amount. The future value of the plan's assets depends on the performance of the investments within the plan. Any gains or losses related to those investments accrue to the employee. Therefore, in DC pension plans, the employee bears the risk that plan assets will not be sufficient to meet future needs. The impact on the company's financial statements of DC pension plans is easily assessed because the company has no obligations beyond the required contributions.

In contrast to DC pension plans, **defined benefit** (DB) pension plans are essentially promises by the employer to pay a defined amount of pension in the future. As part of total compensation, the employee works in the current period in exchange for a pension to be paid after retirement. In a DB pension plan, the amount of pension benefit to be provided is defined, usually by reference to age, years of service, compensation, etc. For example, a DB pension plan may provide for the retiree to be paid, annually until death, an amount equal to 1 percent of the final year's salary times the number of years of service. The future pension payments represent a liability or obligation of the employer (i.e., the sponsoring company). To measure this obligation, the employer must make various actuarial assumptions (employee turnover, average retirement age, life expectancy after retirement) and computations. It is important for an analyst to evaluate such assumptions for their reasonableness and to analyse the impact of these assumptions on the financial reports of the company.

Under IFRS and US GAAP, all plans for pensions and other post-employment benefits other than those explicitly structured as DC plans are classified as DB plans.[3] DB plans include both formal plans and those informal arrangements that create a constructive obligation by the employer to its employees.[4] The employer must estimate the total cost of the benefits promised and then allocate these costs to the periods in

---

3 Multi-employer plans are an exception under IFRS. These are plans to which many different employers contribute on behalf of their employees, such as an industry association pension plan. For multi-employer plans, the employer accounts for its proportionate share of the plan. If, however, the employer does not have sufficient information from the plan administrator to meet the reporting requirement for a defined benefit plan, IFRS allow the employer to account for the plan as if it were a defined contribution plan.

4 For example, a company has a constructive obligation if the benefits it promises are not linked solely to the amount of its contributions or if it indirectly or directly guarantees a specified return on pension assets.

which the employees provide service. This estimation and allocation further increases the complexity of pension reporting because the timing of cash flows (contributions into the plan and payments from the plan) can differ significantly from the timing of accrual-basis reporting. Accrual-basis reporting is based on when the services are rendered and the benefits are earned.

Most DB pension plans are funded through a separate legal entity, typically a pension trust, and the assets of the trust are used to make the payments to retirees. The sponsoring company is responsible for making contributions to the plan. The company also must ensure that there are sufficient assets in the plan to pay the ultimate benefits promised to plan participants. Regulatory requirements usually specify minimum funding levels for DB pension plans, but those requirements vary by country. The funded status of a pension plan—overfunded or underfunded—refers to whether the amount of assets in the pension trust is greater than or less than the estimated liability. If the amount of assets in the DB pension trust exceeds the present value of the estimated liability, the DB pension plan is said to be overfunded; conversely, if the amount of assets in the pension trust is less than the estimated liability, the plan is said to be underfunded. Because the company has promised a defined amount of benefit to the employees, it is obligated to make those pension payments when they are due regardless of whether the pension plan assets generate sufficient returns to provide the benefits. In other words, the company bears the investment risk. Many companies are reducing the use of DB pension plans because of this risk.

Similar to DB pension plans, **other post-employment benefits** (OPB) are promises by the company to pay benefits in the future, such as life insurance premiums and all or part of health care insurance for its retirees. OPB are typically classified as DB plans, with accounting treatment similar to DB pension plans. However, the complexity in reporting for OPB may be even greater than for DB pension plans because of the need to estimate future increases in costs, such as health care, over a long time horizon. Unlike DB pension plans, however, companies may not be required by regulation to fund an OPB in advance to the same degree as DB pension plans. This is partly because governments, through some means, often insure DB pension plans but not OPB, partly because OPB may represent a much smaller financial liability, and partly because OPB are often easier to eliminate should the costs become burdensome. It is important that an analyst determine what OPB are offered by a company and the obligation they represent.

Types of post-employment benefits offered by employers differ across countries. For instance, in countries where government-sponsored universal health care plans exist (such as Germany, France, Canada, Brazil, Mexico, New Zealand, South Africa, India, Israel, Bhutan, and Singapore), companies are less likely to provide post-retirement health care benefits to employees. The extent to which companies offer DC or DB pension plans also varies by country.

Exhibit 1 summarizes these three types of post-employment benefits.

Exhibit 1   Types of Post-Employment Benefits

Type of Benefit	Amount of Post-Employment Benefit to Employee	Obligation of Sponsoring Company	Sponsoring Company's Pre-funding of its Future Obligation
Defined contribution pension plan	Amount of future benefit is not defined. Actual future benefit will depend on investment performance of plan assets. Investment risk is borne by employee.	Amount of the company's obligation (contribution) is defined in each period. The contribution, if any, is typically made on a periodic basis with no additional future obligation.	Not applicable.
Defined benefit pension plan	Amount of future benefit is defined, based on the plan's formula (often a function of length of service and final year's compensation). Investment risk is borne by company.	Amount of the future obligation, based on the plan's formula, must be estimated in the current period.	Companies typically pre-fund the DB plans by contributing funds to a pension trust. Regulatory requirements to pre-fund vary by country.
Other post-employment benefits (e.g., retirees' health care)	Amount of future benefit depends on plan specifications and type of benefit.	Eventual benefits are specified. The amount of the future obligation must be estimated in the current period.	Companies typically do not pre-fund other post-employment benefit obligations.

The following sections provide additional detail on how DB pension plan liabilities and periodic costs are measured, the financial statement impact of reporting pension and other post-employment benefits, and how disclosures in the notes to the financial statements can be used to gain insights about the underlying economics of a company's defined benefit plans. Section 2.2 describes how a DB pension plan's obligation is estimated and the key inputs into and assumptions behind the estimate. Section 2.3 describes financial statement reporting of pension and OPB plans and demonstrates the calculation of defined benefit obligations and current costs and the effects of assumptions. Section 2.4 describes disclosures in financial reports about pension and OPB plans. These include disclosures about assumptions that can be useful in analysing and comparing pension and OPB plans within and among companies.

2.2 Measuring a Defined Benefit Pension Plan's Obligations

Both IFRS and US GAAP measure the **pension obligation** as the present value of future benefits earned by employees for service provided to date. The obligation is called the present value of the defined benefit obligation (PVDBO) under IFRS and the projected benefit obligation (PBO) under US GAAP.[5] This measure is defined as

---

5 In addition to the projected benefit obligation, US GAAP identify two other measures of the pension liability. The **vested benefit obligation** (VBO) is the "actuarial present value of vested benefits" (FASB ASC Glossary). The **accumulated benefit obligation** (ABO) is "the actuarial present value of benefits (whether vested or non-vested) attributed, generally by the pension benefit formula, to employee service rendered before a specified date and based on employee service and compensation (if applicable) before that date. The accumulated benefit obligation differs from the projected benefit obligation in that it includes no assumption about future compensation levels" (FASB ASC Glossary). Both the vested benefit obligation and the accumulated benefit obligation are based on the amounts promised as a result of an employee's service up to a specific date. Thus, both of these measures will be less than the projected benefit obligation (VBO < ABO < PBO).

"the present value, without deducting any plan assets, of expected future payments required to settle the obligation arising from employee service in the current and prior periods" under IFRS and "the actuarial present value as of a date of all benefits attributed by the pension benefit formula to employee service rendered prior to that date" under US GAAP. In the remainder of this reading, the term "pension obligation" will be used to generically refer to PVDBO and PBO.

In determining the pension obligation, a company estimates the future benefits it will pay. To estimate the future benefits, the company must make a number of assumptions[6] such as future compensation increases and levels, discount rates, and expected vesting. For instance, an estimate of future compensation is made if the pension benefit formula is based on future compensation levels (examples include pay-related, final-pay, final-average-pay, or career-average-pay plans). The expected annual increase in compensation over the employee service period can have a significant impact on the defined benefit obligation. The determination of the benefit obligation implicitly assumes that the company will continue to operate in the future (the "going concern assumption") and recognises that benefits will increase with future compensation increases.

Another key assumption is the discount rate—the interest rate used to calculate the present value of the future benefits. This rate is based on current rates of return on high-quality corporate bonds (or government bonds in the absence of a deep market in corporate bonds) with currency and durations consistent with the currency and durations of the benefits.

Under both DB and DC pension plans, the benefits that employees earn may be conditional on remaining with the company for a specified period of time. "Vesting" refers to a provision in pensions plans whereby an employee gains rights to future benefits only after meeting certain criteria, such as a pre-specified number of years of service. If the employee leaves the company before meeting the criteria, he or she may be entitled to none or a portion of the benefits earned up until that point. However, once the employee has met the vesting requirements, he or she is entitled to receive the benefits earned in prior periods (i.e., once the employee has become vested, benefits are not forfeited if the employee leaves the company). In measuring the defined benefit obligation, the company considers the probability that some employees may not satisfy the vesting requirements (i.e., may leave before the vesting period) and uses this probability to calculate the current service cost and the present value of the obligation. Current service cost is the increase in the present value of a defined benefit obligation as a result of employee service in the current period. Current service cost is not the only cause of change in the present value of a defined benefit obligation.

The estimates and assumptions about future salary increases, the discount rate, and the expected vesting can change. Of course, any changes in these estimates and assumptions will change the estimated pension obligation. If the changes increase the obligation, the increase is referred to as an actuarial loss. If the changes decrease the obligation, the change is referred to as an actuarial gain. Section 2.3.3 further discusses estimates and assumptions and the effect on the pension obligation and expense.

---

6 These assumptions are referred to as "actuarial assumptions." Thus, losses or gains due to changes in these assumptions, or due to differences between these assumptions and what actually occurs, are referred to as "actuarial gains or losses."

2.3 Financial Statement Reporting of Pension Plans and Other Post-Employment Benefits

Sections 2.3.1 to 2.3.3 describe how pension plans and other post-employment benefits are reported in the financial statements of the sponsoring company and how assumptions affect the amounts reported. Disclosures related to pensions plans and OPB are described in Section 2.4.

2.3.1 Defined Contribution Pension Plans

The accounting treatment for defined contribution pension plans is relatively simple. From a financial statement perspective, the employer's obligation for contributions into the plan, if any, is recorded as an expense on the income statement. Because the employer's obligation is limited to a defined amount that typically equals its contribution, no significant pension-related liability accrues on the balance sheet. An accrual (current liability) is recognised at the end of the reporting period only for any unpaid contributions.

2.3.2 Defined Benefit Pension Plans

The accounting treatment for defined benefit pension plans is more complex, primarily because of the complexities of measuring the pension obligation and expense.

2.3.2.1 Balance Sheet Presentation Both IFRS and US GAAP require a pension plan's funded status to be reported on the balance sheet. The funded status is determined by netting the pension obligation against the fair value of the pension plan assets. If the pension obligation exceeds the pension plan assets, the plan has a deficit. If the plan assets exceed the pension obligation, the plan has a surplus. Summarizing this information in equation form gives

Funded status = Fair value of the plan assets − PV of the Defined benefit obligation

If the plan has a deficit, an amount equal to the net underfunded pension obligation is reported on the balance sheet as a net pension liability. If the plan has a surplus, an asset equal to the overfunded pension obligation is reported on the balance sheet as a net pension asset (except that the amount of reported assets is subject to a ceiling defined as the present value of future economic benefits, such as refunds from the plan or reductions of future contributions). Disclosures in the notes provide additional information about the net pension liability or asset reported on the balance sheet.

EXAMPLE 1

Determination of Amounts to be Reported on the Balance Sheet

The following information pertains to two hypothetical companies' defined benefit pension plans as of 31 December 2010:

- For company ABC, the present value of the company's defined benefit obligation is €6,723 and the fair value of the pension plan's assets is €4,880.

- For company DEF, the present value of the company's defined benefit obligation is €5,485 and the fair value of the pension plan assets is €5,998. In addition, the present value of available future refunds and reductions in future contributions is €326.

Calculate the amount each company would report as a pension asset or liability on its 2010 balance sheet.

Solution:

Company ABC would report the full underfunded status of its pension plan (i.e., the amount by which the present value of the defined benefit obligation exceeds the fair value of plan assets) as a liability. Specifically, the company would report a pension liability of €1,843.

Present value of defined benefit obligation	€6,723
Fair value of plan assets	(4,880)
Net pension liability	€1,843

Company DEF's pension plan is overfunded by €513, which is the amount by which the fair value of the plan's assets exceed the defined benefit obligation (€5,998 – €5,485). However, when a company has a surplus in a defined benefit plan, the amount of asset that can be reported is the lower of the surplus and the asset ceiling (the present value of future economic benefits, such as refunds from the plan or reductions of future contributions). In this case, the asset ceiling is given as €326, so the amount of company DEF's reported net pension asset would be limited to €326.

2.3.2.2 Periodic Pension Cost   The periodic cost of a company's DB pension plan is the change in the net pension liability or asset adjusted for the employer's contributions. Each period, the periodic pension cost is recognised in profit or loss (P&L) and/or in other comprehensive income (OCI). (In some cases, amounts of pension costs may qualify for inclusion as part of the costs of such assets as inventories and thus be included in P&L as part of cost of goods sold when those inventories are later sold. The focus here is on the amounts not capitalised.) IFRS and US GAAP differ in the way that the periodic pension cost is divided between P&L and OCI.

Under IFRS, the periodic pension cost is viewed as having three components, two of which are recognised in P&L and one of which is recognised in OCI.

1 *Service costs.* The first component of periodic pension cost is service cost. Current service cost is the amount by which a company's pension obligation increases as a result of employees' service in the current period. Past service cost is the amount by which a company's pension obligation relating to employees' service in prior periods changes as a result of plan amendments or a plan curtailment.[7] Under IFRS, service costs (including both current service costs and past service costs) are recognised as an expense in P&L.

2 *Net interest expense/income.* The second component of periodic pension cost is net interest expense or income, which we will refer to as "net interest expense/income." Net interest expense/income is calculated by multiplying the net pension liability or net pension asset by the discount rate used in determining the present value of the pension liability. A net interest expense represents

---

7 A curtailment occurs when there is a significant reduction by the entity either in the number of employees covered by a plan or in benefits.

the financing cost of deferring payments related to the plan, and a net interest income represents the financing income from prepaying amounts related to the plan. Under IFRS, the net interest expense/income is recognised in P&L.

3 *Remeasurement.* The third component of periodic pension cost is remeasurement of the net pension liability or asset. Remeasurement includes (a) actuarial gains and losses and (b) any differences between the actual return on plan assets and the amount included in the net interest expense/income calculation. Under IFRS, remeasurement amounts are recognised in OCI. Remeasurement amounts are not subsequently amortised to P&L.

Similar to IFRS, under US GAAP current service cost is recognised in P&L. However, under US GAAP, past service costs are reported in OCI in the period in which the change giving rise to the cost occurs. In subsequent periods, these past service costs are amortised to P&L over the average service lives of the affected employees.

Also similar to IFRS, under US GAAP the periodic pension cost for P&L includes interest expense on pension obligations (which increases the amount of the periodic cost) and returns on the pension plan assets (which reduce the amount of the periodic cost). Unlike IFRS, however, under US GAAP, the two components are not presented net. Also, under US GAAP, returns on plan assets included in the P&L recognition of pension costs (pension expense) use an expected return rather than the actual return. (Under IFRS, returns on plan assets included in the P&L recognition of pension costs (pension expense) use the discount rate as the expected return.) Thus, under US GAAP, differences between the expected return and the actual return on plan assets represent another source of actuarial gains or losses. As noted, actuarial gains and losses can also result from changes in the actuarial assumptions used in determining the benefit obligation. Under US GAAP, all actuarial gains and losses are included in the net pension liability or net pension asset and can be reported either in P&L or in OCI. Typically, companies report actuarial gains and losses in OCI and recognise gains and losses in P&L only when certain conditions are met under a so-called corridor approach.

Under the corridor approach, the net cumulative unrecognised actuarial gains and losses at the beginning of the reporting period are compared with the defined benefit obligation and the fair value of plan assets at the beginning of the period. If the cumulative amount of unrecognised actuarial gains and losses becomes too large (i.e., exceeds 10 percent of the greater of the defined benefit obligation or the fair value of plan assets), then the excess is amortised over the expected average remaining working lives of the employees participating in the plan and is included as a component of periodic pension cost in P&L. The term "corridor" refers to the 10 percent range, and only amounts in excess of the corridor must be amortised.

To illustrate the corridor approach, assume that the beginning balance of the defined benefit obligation is $5,000,000, the beginning balance of fair value of plan assets is $4,850,000, and the beginning balance of unrecognised actuarial losses is $610,000. The expected average remaining working lives of the plan employees is 10 years. In this scenario, the corridor is $500,000, which is 10 percent of the defined benefit obligation (selected as the greater of the defined benefit obligation or the fair value of plan assets). Because the balance of unrecognised actuarial losses exceeds the $500,000 corridor, amortisation is required. The amount of the amortisation is $11,000, which is the excess of the unrecognised actuarial loss over the corridor divided by the expected average remaining working lives of the plan employees [($610,000 – $500,000) ÷ 10 years]. Actuarial gains or losses can also be amortised more quickly than under the corridor method; companies may use a faster recognition method, provided the company applies the method of amortisation to both gains and losses consistently in all periods presented.

To summarize, under IFRS, the periodic pension costs recognised in P&L include service costs (both current and past) and net interest expense/income. The periodic pension costs recognised in OCI include remeasurements that comprise net return on plan assets and actuarial gains and losses. Under US GAAP, the periodic pension costs recognised in P&L include current service costs, interest expense on plan liabilities, expected returns on plan assets (which is a reduction of the cost), the amortisation of past service costs, and actuarial gains and losses to the extent not reported in OCI. The components of a company's defined benefit periodic pension costs are summarized in Exhibit 2.

Exhibit 2   Components of a Company's Defined Benefit Pension Periodic Costs

IFRS Component	IFRS Recognition	US GAAP Component	US GAAP Recognition
Service costs	Recognised in P&L.	Current service costs	Recognised in P&L.
		Past service costs	Recognised in OCI and subsequently amortised to P&L over the service life of employees.
Net interest income/ expense	Recognised in P&L as the following amount: Net pension liability or asset × interest rate[a]	Interest expense on pension obligation	Recognised in P&L.
		Expected return on plan assets	Recognised in P&L as the following amount: Plan assets × expected return.
Remeasurements: Net return on plan assets and actuarial gains and losses	Recognised in OCI and not subsequently amortised to P&L. ■ Net return on plan assets = Actual return − (Plan assets × Interest rate). ■ Actuarial gains and losses = Changes in a company's pension obligation arising from changes in actuarial assumptions.	Actuarial gains and losses including differences between the actual and expected returns on plan assets	Recognised immediately in P&L or, more commonly, recognised in OCI and subsequently amortised to P&L using the corridor or faster recognition method.[b] ■ Difference between expected and actual return on assets = Actual return − (Plan assets × Expected return). ■ Actuarial gains and losses = Changes in a company's pension obligation arising from changes in actuarial assumptions.

[a] The interest rate used is equal to the discount rate used to measure the pension liability (the yield on high-quality corporate bonds.)
[b] If the cumulative amount of unrecognised actuarial gains and losses exceeds 10 percent of the greater of the value of the plan assets or of the present value of the DB obligation (under US GAAP, the projected benefit obligation), the difference must be amortised over the service lives of the employees.

Reporting the Periodic Pension Cost.   As noted above, some amounts of pension costs may qualify for capitalisation as part of the costs of self-constructed assets, such as inventories. Pension costs included in inventories would thus be recognised in P&L as part of cost of goods sold when those inventories are sold. For pension costs that are not capitalised, IFRS do not specify where companies present the various components of periodic pension cost beyond differentiating between components included in P&L and in OCI. In contrast, for pension costs that are not capitalised, US GAAP require all components of periodic pension cost that are recognised in P&L to be aggregated and presented as a net amount within the same line item on the income statement. Both IFRS and US GAAP require total periodic pension cost to be disclosed in the notes to the financial statements.

2.3.3 *More on the Effect of Assumptions and Actuarial Gains and Losses on Pension and Other Post-Employment Benefits Costs*

As noted, a company's pension obligation for a DB pension plan is based on many estimates and assumptions. The amount of future pension payments requires assumptions about employee turnover, length of service, and rate of increase in compensation levels. The length of time the pension payments will be made requires assumptions about employees' life expectancy post-employment. Finally, the present value of these future payments requires assumptions about the appropriate discount rate (which is used as the rate at which interest expense or income will subsequently accrue on the net pension liability or asset).

Changes in any of the assumptions will increase or decrease the pension obligation. An increase in pension obligation resulting from changes in actuarial assumptions is considered an actuarial loss, and a decrease is considered an actuarial gain. The estimate of a company's pension liability also affects several components of periodic pension costs, apart from actuarial gains and losses. First, the service cost component of annual pension cost is essentially the amount by which the pension liability increases as a result of the employees' service during the year. Second, the interest expense component of annual pension cost is based on the amount of the liability. Third, the past service cost component of annual pension cost is the amount by which the pension liability increases because of changes to the plan.

Estimates related to plan assets can also affect annual pension cost reported in P&L (pension expense), primarily under US GAAP. Because a company's periodic pension cost reported in P&L under US GAAP includes the *expected* return on pension assets rather than the actual return, the assumptions about the expected return on plan assets can have a significant impact. Also, the expected return on plan assets requires estimating in which future period the benefits will be paid. As noted above, a divergence of actual returns on pension assets from expected returns results in an actuarial gain or loss.

Understanding the effect of assumptions on the estimated pension obligation and on periodic pension costs is important both for interpreting a company's financial statements and for evaluating whether a company's assumptions appear relatively conservative or aggressive.

The projected unit credit method is the IFRS approach to measuring the DB obligation. Under the projected unit credit method, each period of service (e.g., year of employment) gives rise to an additional unit of benefit to which the employee is entitled at retirement. In other words, for each period in which an employee provides service, they earn a portion of the post-employment benefits that the company has promised to pay. An equivalent way of thinking about this is that the amount of eventual benefit increases with each additional year of service. The employer measures each unit of service as it is earned to determine the amount of benefits it is obligated to pay in future reporting periods.

The objective of the projected unit credit method is to allocate the entire expected retirement costs (benefits) for an employee over the employee's service periods. The defined benefit obligation represents the actuarial present value of all units of benefit (credit) to which the employee is entitled (i.e., those that the employee has earned) as a result of prior and current periods of service. This obligation is based on actuarial assumptions about demographic variables, such as employee turnover and life expectancy, and on estimates of financial variables, such as future inflation and the discount rate. If the pension benefit formula is based on employees' future compensation levels, then the unit of benefit earned each period will reflect this estimate.

Under both IFRS and US GAAP, the assumed rate of increase in compensation—the expected annual increase in compensation over the employee service period—can have a significant impact on the defined benefit obligation. Another key assumption is the discount rate used to calculate the present value of the future benefits. It represents the rate at which the defined benefit obligation could be effectively settled. This rate is based on current rates of return on high quality corporate bonds with durations consistent with the durations of the benefit.

The following example illustrates the calculation of the defined benefit pension obligation and current service costs, using the projected unit credit method, for an individual employee under four different scenarios. Interest on the opening obligation also increases the obligation and is part of current costs. The fourth scenario is used to demonstrate the impact on a company's pension obligation of changes in certain key estimates. Examples 2 and 3 focus on the pension obligation. The change in pension obligation over the period is included in the calculation of pension expense (pension cost reported in P&L).

EXAMPLE 2

Calculation of Defined Benefit Pension Obligation for an Individual Employee

The following information applies to each of the four scenarios. Assume that a (hypothetical) company establishes a DB pension plan. The employee has a salary in the coming year of €50,000 and is expected to work five more years before retiring. The assumed discount rate is 6 percent, and the assumed annual compensation increase is 4.75 percent. For simplicity, assume that there are no changes in actuarial assumptions, all compensation increases are awarded on the first day of the service year, and no additional adjustments are made to reflect the possibility that the employee may leave the company at an earlier date.

Current salary	€50,000.00
Years until retirement	5
Annual compensation increases	4.75%
Discount rate	6.00%
Final year's estimated salary[a]	€60,198.56

[a] Final year's estimated salary = Current year's salary × [(1 + Annual compensation increase)$^{\text{Years until retirement}}$].

At the end of Year 1, the final year's estimated salary = €50,000 × [(1 + 0.0475)^4] = €60,198.56, assuming that the employee's salary increases by 4.75 percent each year. With no change in assumption about the rate of increase in compensation or the date of retirement, the estimate of the final year's salary will remain unchanged.

At the end of Year 2, assuming the employee's salary actually increased by 4.75 percent, the final year's estimated salary = €52,375 × [(1 + 0.0475)^3] = €60,198.56.

Scenario 1: Benefit is paid as a lump sum amount upon retirement.

The plan will pay a lump sum pension benefit equal to 1.5 percent of the employee's final salary for each year of service beyond the date of establishment. The lump sum payment to be paid upon retirement = (Final salary × Benefit formula) × Years of service = (€60,198.56 × 0.015) × 5 = €4,514.89.

Annual unit credit (benefit) per service year = Value at retirement/Years of service = €4,514.89/5 = €902.98.

If the discount rate (the interest rate at which the defined benefit obligation could be effectively settled) is assumed to be 0 percent, the amount of annual unit credit per service year is the amount of the company's annual obligation and the closing obligation each year is simply the annual unit credit multiplied by the number of past and current years of service. However, because the assumed discount rate must be based on the yield on high-quality corporate bonds and will thus not equal 0 percent, the future obligation resulting from current and prior service is discounted to determine the value of the obligation at any point in time.

The following table shows how the obligation builds up for this employee.

Year	1	2	3	4	5
Estimated annual salary	€50,000.00	€52,375.00	€54,862.81	€57,468.80	€60,198.56
Benefits attributed to:					
Prior years[a]	€0.00	€902.98	€1,805.96	€2,708.94	€3,611.92
Current year[b]	902.98	902.98	902.98	902.98	902.97*
Total benefits earned	€902.98	€1,805.96	€2,708.94	€3,611.92	€4,514.89
Opening obligation[c]	€0.00	€715.24	€1,516.31	€2,410.94	€3,407.47
Interest cost at 6 percent[d]	0.00	42.91	90.98	144.66	204.45
Current service costs[e]	715.24	758.16	803.65	851.87	902.97
Closing obligation[f]	€715.24	€1,516.31	€2,410.94	€3,407.47	€4,514.89

*Final amounts may differ slightly to compensate for rounding in earlier years.

[a] The benefit attributed to prior years = Annual unit credit × Years of prior service.
For Year 2, €902.98 × 1 = €902.98.
For Year 3, €902.98 × 2 = €1,805.96.

[b] The benefit attributed to current year = Annual unit credit based on benefit formula = Final year's estimated salary × Benefit formula = Value at retirement date/Years of service = (€60,198.56 × 1.5%) = €4,514.89/5 = €902.98.

[c] The opening obligation is the closing obligation at the end of the previous year, but can also be viewed as the present value of benefits earned in prior years:
Benefits earned in prior years/[(1 + Discount rate)$^{\text{Years until retirement}}$].
Opening obligation Year 1 = €0.
Opening obligation Year 2 = €902.98/[(1 + 0.06)^4] = €715.24.
Opening obligation Year 3 = €1,805.96/[(1 + 0.06)^3] = €1,516.32.

[d] The interest cost is the increase in the present value of the defined benefit obligation due to the passage of time:
Interest cost = Opening obligation × Discount rate.
For Year 2 = €715.24 × 0.06 = €42.91.
For Year 3 = €1,516.32 × 0.06 = €90.98.

[e] Current service costs are the present value of annual unit credits earned in the current period:
Annual unit credit/[(1 + Discount rate)$^{\text{Years until retirement}}$].
For Year 1 = €902.98/[(1 + 0.06)^4] = €715.24.
For Year 2 = €902.98/[(1 + 0.06)^3] = €758.16.

(continued)

Note: Given no change in actuarial assumptions and estimates of financial growth, the current service costs in any year (except the first) are the previous year's current service costs increased by the discount rate; the current service costs increase with the passage of time.

[f] The closing obligation is the opening obligation plus the interest cost and the current service costs but can also be viewed as the present value of benefits earned in prior and current years. There is a slight difference due to rounding.

Total benefits earned/$[(1 + \text{Discount rate})^{\text{Years until retirement}}]$.

Closing obligation Year 1 = €902.98/$[(1 + 0.06)^4]$ = €715.24.

Closing obligation Year 2 = €1,805.96/$[(1 + 0.06)^3]$ = €1,516.32.

Closing obligation Year 3 = €2,708.94/$[(1 + 0.06)^2]$ = €2,410.95.

Note: Assuming no past service costs or actuarial gains/losses, the closing obligation less the fair value of the plan assets represents both the funded status of the plan and the net pension liability/asset. The change in obligation is the amount of expense for pensions on the income statement.

Scenario 2: Prior years of service, and benefit paid as a lump sum upon retirement.

The plan will pay a lump sum pension benefit equal to 1.5 percent of the employee's final salary for each year of service beyond the date of establishment. In addition, at the time the pension plan is established, the employee is given credit for 10 years of prior service with immediate vesting. The lump sum payment to be paid upon retirement = (Final salary × Benefit formula) × Years of service = (€60,198.56 × 0.015) × 15 = €13,544.68.

Annual unit credit = Value at retirement date/Years of service = €13,544.68/15 = €902.98.

The following table shows how the obligation builds up for this employee.

Year	1	2	3	4	5
Benefits attributed to:					
Prior years[a]	€9,029.78	€9,932.76	€10,835.74	€11,738.72	€12,641.70
Current years	902.98	902.98	902.98	902.98	902.98
Total benefits earned	€9,932.76	€10,835.74	€11,738.72	€12,641.70	€13,544.68
Opening obligation[b]	€6,747.58	€7,867.67	€9,097.89	€10,447.41	€11,926.13
Interest at 6 percent	404.85	472.06	545.87	626.85	715.57
Current service costs	715.24	758.16	803.65	851.87	902.98
Closing obligation	€7,867.67	€9,097.89	€10,447.41	€11,926.13	€13,544.68

[a] Benefits attributed to prior years of service = Annual unit credit × Years of prior service. At beginning of Year 1 = (€60,198.56 × 0.015) × 10 = €9,029.78.

[b] Opening obligation is the present value of the benefits attributed to prior years = Benefits attributed to prior years/$(1 + \text{Discount rate})^{\text{Number of years to retirement}}$.
At beginning of Year 1 = €9,029.78/$(1.06)^5$ = €6,747.58. This is treated as past service costs in Year 1 because there was no previous recognition and there is immediate vesting.

Scenario 3: Employee to receive benefit payments for 20 years (no prior years of service).

Years of receiving pension = 20.

Estimated annual payment (end of year) for each of the 20 years = (Estimated final salary × Benefit formula) × Years of service = (€60,198.56 × 0.015) × 5 = €4,514.89.

Value at the end of Year 5 (retirement date) of the estimated future payments = PV of €4,514.89 for 20 years at 6 percent = €51,785.46.[8]

Annual unit credit = Value at retirement date/Years of service = €51,785.46/5 = €10,357.09.

Year	1	2	3	4	5
Benefit attributed to:					
Prior years	€0.00	€10,357.09	€20,714.18	€31,071.27	€41,428.36
Current year	10,357.09	10,357.09	10,357.09	10,357.09	10,357.10
Total benefits earned	€10,357.09	€20,714.18	€31,071.27	€41,428.36	€51,785.46
Opening obligation	€0.00	€8,203.79	€17,392.03	€27,653.32	€39,083.36
Interest at 6 percent	0.00	492.23	1,043.52	1,659.20	2,345.00
Current service costs	8,203.79	8,696.01	9,217.77	9,770.84	10,357.10
Closing obligation	€8,203.79	€17,392.03	€27,653.32	€39,083.36	€51,785.46

In this scenario, the pension obligation at the end of Year 3 is €27,653.32 and the portion of pension expense (pension costs reported in P&L) attributable to interest and current service costs for Year 3 is €10,261.29 (= €1,043.52 + €9,217.77). The total pension expense would include other items such as a reduction for return on plan assets.

Scenario 4: Employee to receive benefit payments for 20 years and is given credit for 10 years of prior service with immediate vesting.

Estimated annual payment (end of year) for each of the 20 years = (Estimated final salary × Benefit formula) × Years of service = (€60,198.56 × 0.015) × (10 + 5) = €13,544.68.

Value at the end of Year 5 (retirement date) of the estimated future payments = PV of €13,544.68 for 20 years at 6 percent = €155,356.41.

Annual unit credit = Value at retirement date/Years of service = €155,356.41/15 = €10,357.09.

Year	1	2	3	4	5
Benefit attributed to:					
Prior years	€103,570.94	€113,928.03	€124,285.12	€134,642.21	€144,999.30
Current year	10,357.09	10,357.09	10,357.09	10,357.09	10,357.11
Total benefits earned	€113,928.03	€124,285.12	€134,642.21	€144,999.30	€155,356.41
Opening obligation[a]	€77,394.23	€90,241.67	€104,352.18	€119,831.08	€136,791.79
Interest at 6 percent	4,643.65	5,414.50	6,261.13	7,189.87	8,207.51

(continued)

---

8 This is a simplification of the valuation process for illustrative purposes. For example, the actuarial valuation would use mortality rates, not just assumed life expectancy. Additionally, annualizing the present value of an ordinary annuity probably understates the liability because the actual benefit payments are usually made monthly or bi-weekly rather than annually.

Year	1	2	3	4	5
Current service costs	8,203.79	8,696.01	9,217.77	9,770.84	10,357.11
Closing obligation	€90,241.67	€104,352.18	€119,831.08	€136,791.79	€155,356.41

[a] This is treated as past service costs in Year 1 because there was no previous recognition and there is immediate vesting.

EXAMPLE 3

The Effect of a Change in Assumptions

Based on Scenario 4 of Example 2 (10 years of prior service and the employee receives benefits for 20 years after retirement):

1 What is the effect on the Year 1 closing pension obligation of a 100 basis point increase in the assumed discount rate—that is, from 6 percent to 7 percent? What is the effect on pension cost in Year 1?

2 What is the effect on the Year 1 closing pension obligation of a 100 basis point increase in the assumed annual compensation increase—that is, from 4.75 percent to 5.75 percent? Assume this is independent of the change in Question 1.

Solution to 1:

The estimated final salary and the estimated annual payments after retirement are unchanged at €60,198.56 and €13,544.68, respectively. However, the value at the retirement date is changed. Value at the end of Year 5 (retirement date) of the estimated future payments = PV of €13,544.68 for 20 years at 7 percent = €143,492.53. Annual unit credit = Value at retirement date/Years of service = €143,492.53/15 = €9,566.17.

Year	1
Benefit attributed to:	
Prior years	€95,661.69
Current year	9,566.17
Total benefits earned	€105,227.86
Opening obligation[a]	€68,205.46
Interest at 7 percent	4,774.38
Current service costs	7,297.99
Closing obligation	€80,277.83

[a] Opening obligation = Benefit attributed to prior years discounted for the remaining time to retirement at the assumed discount rate = $95,661.69/(1 + 0.07)^5$.

A 100 basis point increase in the assumed discount rate (from 6 percent to 7 percent) will *decrease* the Year 1 closing pension obligation by €90,241.67 − €80,277.83 = €9,963.84. The Year 1 pension cost declined from €12,847.44 (= 4,643.65 + 8,203.79) to €12,072.37 (= 4,774.38 + 7,297.99). The change in the interest component is a function of the decline in the opening obligation (which will decrease the interest component) and the increased discount rate (which will increase the interest component). In this case, the increase in the discount rate dominated and the interest component increased. The current service costs and the opening obligation both declined because of the increase in the discount rate.

Solution to 2:

The estimated final salary is $[€50,000 \times [(1 + 0.0575)^4] = €62,530.44$. Estimated annual payment for each of the 20 years = (Estimated final salary × Benefit formula) × Years of service = $(€62,530.44 \times 0.015) \times (10 + 5) = €14,069.35$. Value at the end of Year 5 (retirement date) of the estimated future payments = PV of €14,069.35 for 20 years at 6 percent = €161,374.33. Annual unit credit = Value at retirement date/Years of service = €161,374.33/15 = €10,758.29.

Year	1
Benefit attributed to:	
Prior years	€107,582.89
Current year	10,758.29
Total benefits earned	€118,341.18
Opening obligation	€80,392.19
Interest at 6 percent	4,823.53
Current service costs	8,521.57
Closing obligation	€93,737.29

A 100 basis point increase in the assumed annual compensation increase (from 4.75 percent to 5.75 percent) will *increase* the pension obligation by €93,737.29 − €90,241.67 = €3,495.62.

Example 3 illustrates that an increase in the assumed discount rate will *decrease* a company's pension obligation. In the Solution to 1, there is a slight increase in the interest component of the pension obligation and periodic pension cost (from €4,643.65 in Scenario 4 of Example 2 to €4,774.38 in Example 3). Depending on the pattern and duration of the annual benefits being projected, however, it is possible that the amount of the interest component could decrease because the decrease in the opening obligation may more than offset the effect of the increase in the discount rate.

Example 3 also illustrates that an increase in the assumed rate of annual compensation increase will *increase* a company's pension obligation when the pension formula is based on the final year's salary. In addition, a higher assumed rate of annual compensation increase will increase the service components and the interest component of a company's periodic pension cost because of an increased annual unit credit and the resulting increased obligation. An increase in life expectancy also will increase the pension obligation unless the promised pension payments are independent of life expectancy—for example, paid as a lump sum or over a fixed period.

Finally, under US GAAP, because the expected return on plan assets reduces periodic pension costs reported in P&L, a higher expected return will decrease pension cost reported in P&L (pension expense). Exhibit 3 summarizes the impact of some key estimates on the balance sheet and the periodic pension cost.

Exhibit 3	Impact of Key DB Pension Assumptions on Balance Sheet and Periodic Costs	
Assumption	**Impact of Assumption on Balance Sheet**	**Impact of Assumption on Periodic Cost**
Higher discount rate.	Lower obligation.	Periodic pension costs will typically be lower because of lower opening obligation and lower service costs.
Higher rate of compensation increase.	Higher obligation.	Higher service costs.
Higher expected return on plan assets.	No effect, because fair value of plan assets is used on balance sheet.	Not applicable for IFRS. Lower periodic pension expense under US GAAP.

Accounting for other post-employment benefits also requires assumptions and estimates. For example, assumed trends in health care costs are an important component of estimating costs of post-employment health care plans. A higher assumed medical expense inflation rate will result in a higher post-employment medical obligation. Companies also estimate various patterns of health care cost trend rates—for example, higher in the near term but becoming lower after some point in time. For post-employment health plans, an increase in the assumed inflationary trends in health care costs or an increase in life expectancy will increase the obligation and associated periodic expense of these plans.

The sections above have explained how the amounts to be reported on the balance sheet are calculated, how the various components of periodic pension cost are reflected in income, and how changes in assumptions can affect pension-related amounts. The next section evaluates disclosures of pension and other post-employment benefits, including disclosures about key assumptions.

2.4 Disclosures of Pension and Other Post-Employment Benefits

Several aspects of the accounting for pensions and other post-employment benefits described above can affect comparative financial analysis using ratios based on financial statements.

- Differences in key assumptions can affect comparisons across companies.

- Amounts disclosed in the balance sheet are net amounts (plan liabilities minus plan assets). Adjustments to incorporate gross amounts would change certain financial ratios.

- Periodic pension costs recognized in P&L (pension expense) may not be comparable. IFRS and US GAAP differ in their provisions about costs recognised in P&L versus in OCI.

- Reporting of periodic pension costs in P&L may not be comparable. Under US GAAP, all of the components of pension costs in P&L are reported in operating expense on the income statement even though some of the components are of a financial nature (specifically, interest expense and the expected return on assets). However, under IFRS, the components of periodic pension costs in P&L can be included in various line items.

- Cash flow information may not be comparable. Under IFRS, some portion of the amount of contributions might be treated as a financing activity rather than an operating activity; under US GAAP, the contribution is treated as an operating activity.

Information related to pensions can be obtained from various portions of the financial statement note disclosures, and appropriate analytical adjustments can be made. In the following sections, we examine pension plan note disclosures and highlight analytical issues related to each of the points listed above.

2.4.1 *Assumptions*

Companies disclose their assumptions about discount rates, expected compensation increases, medical expense inflation, and—for US GAAP companies—expected return on plan assets. Comparing these assumptions over time and across companies provides a basis to assess any conservative or aggressive biases. Some companies also disclose the effects of a change in their assumptions.

Exhibit 4 presents the assumed discount rates (Panel A) and assumed annual compensation increases (Panel B) to estimate pension obligations for four companies operating in the automotive and equipment manufacturing sector. Fiat S.p.A. (an Italy-based company) and the Volvo Group[9] (a Sweden-based company) use IFRS. General Motors and Ford Motor Company are US-based companies that use US GAAP. All of these companies have both US and non-US defined benefit pension plans, which facilitates comparison.

Exhibit 4

Panel A. Assumed discount rates used to estimate pension obligations (percent)

	2009	2008	2007	2006	2005
Fiat S.p.A. (Italy)	5.02	5.10	4.70	3.98	3.53
The Volvo Group (Sweden)	4.00	4.50	4.50	4.00	4.00
General Motors (non-US plans)	5.31	6.22	5.72	4.76	4.72
Ford Motor Company (non-US plans)	5.93	5.58	5.58	4.91	4.58
Fiat S.p.A. (US plans)	5.50	5.10	5.80	5.80	5.50
The Volvo Group (US plans)	4.00–5.75	5.75–6.25	5.75–6.25	5.50	5.75
General Motors (US plans)	5.52	6.27	6.35	5.90	5.70
Ford Motor Company (US plans)	6.50	6.25	6.25	5.86	5.61

Panel B. Assumed annual compensation increases used to estimate pension obligations (percent)

	2009	2008	2007	2006	2005
Fiat S.p.A. (Italy)	4.02	4.65	4.60	3.65	2.58
The Volvo Group (Sweden)	3.00	3.50	3.20	3.20	3.20

(continued)

---

[9] The Volvo Group primarily manufactures trucks, buses, construction equipment, and engines and engine components for boats, industry, and aircraft. The Volvo car division was sold to Ford Motor Company in 1999, and Ford sold Volvo Car Corporation to the Zhejiang Geely Holding Group in 2010.

Exhibit 4   (Continued)

Panel B. Assumed annual compensation increases used to estimate pension obligations (percent)

	2009	2008	2007	2006	2005
General Motors (non-US plans)	3.23	3.59	3.60	3.00	3.10
Ford Motor Company (non-US plans)	3.13	3.21	3.21	3.30	3.44
Fiat S.p.A. (US plans)*	na	na	na	na	na
The Volvo Group (US plans)	3.00	3.50	3.50	3.50	3.50
General Motors (US plans)	3.94	5.00	5.25	5.00	4.90
Ford Motor Company (US plans)	3.80	3.80	3.80	3.80	4.00

*In the United States, Fiat has obligations to former employees under DB pension plans but no longer offers DB plans. As a result, annual compensation increases are not applicable (na).

The assumed discount rates used to estimate pension obligations are generally based on the market interest rates of high-quality corporate fixed-income investments with a maturity profile similar to the timing of a company's future pension payments. The trend in discount rates across the companies (in both their non-US plans and US plans) is generally similar. In the non-US plans, discount rates increased from 2005 to 2008 and then decreased in 2009 except for Ford, which increased discount rates in 2009. In the US plans, discount rates increased from 2005 to 2007 and held steady or decreased in 2008. In 2009, Fiat and Ford's discount rates increased while Volvo and GM's discount rates decreased. Ford had the highest assumed discount rates for both its non-US and US plans in 2009. Recall that a higher discount rate assumption results in a lower estimated pension obligation. Therefore, the use of a higher discount rate compared with its peers may indicate a less conservative bias.

Explanations for differences in the level of the assumed discount rates, apart from bias, are differences in the regions/countries involved and differences in the timing of obligations (for example, differences in the percentage of employees covered by the DB pension plan that are at or near retirement). In this example, the difference in regions/countries might explain the difference in rates used for the non-US plans but would not explain the difference in the rates shown for the companies' US plans. The timing of obligations under the companies' DB pension plans likely varies, so the relevant market interest rates selected as the discount rate will vary accordingly. Because the timing of the pension obligations is not disclosed, differences in timing cannot be ruled out as an explanation for differences in discount rates.

An important consideration is whether the assumptions are internally consistent. For example, do the company's assumed discount rates and assumed compensation increases reflect a consistent view of inflation? For Volvo, both the assumed discount rates and the assumed annual compensation increases (for both its non-US and US plans) are lower than those of the other companies, so the assumptions appear internally consistent. The assumptions are consistent with plans located in lower-inflation regions. Recall that a lower rate of compensation increase results in a lower estimated pension obligation.

In Ford's US and non-US pension plans, the assumed discount rate is increasing and the assumed rate of compensation increase is decreasing or holding steady in 2009. Each of these will reduce the pension obligation. Therefore, holding all else equal, Ford's pension liability is decreasing because of the higher assumed discount rate and the reduced assumed rate of compensation increase.

Another relevant assumption—for US GAAP companies but not for IFRS companies—is the expected return on pension plan assets. Under US GAAP, a higher expected return on plan assets lowers the periodic pension cost. (Of course, a higher expected return on plan assets presumably reflects riskier investments, so it would not be advisable for a company to simply invest in riskier investments to reduce periodic pension expense.) Because companies are also required to disclose the target asset allocation for their pension plan assets, analysts can assess reasonableness of those assumptions by comparing companies' assumed expected return on plan assets in the context of the plans' asset allocation. For example, a higher expected return is consistent with a greater proportion of plan assets being allocated to riskier asset classes.

Companies with other post-employment benefits also disclose information about these benefits, including assumptions made to estimate the obligation and expense. For example, companies with post-employment health care plans disclose assumptions about increases in health care costs. The assumptions are typically that the inflation rate in health care costs will taper off to some lower, constant rate at some year in the future. That future inflation rate is known as the ultimate health care trend rate. Holding all else equal, each of the following assumptions would result in a higher benefit obligation and a higher periodic cost:

- A higher assumed near-term increase in health care costs,
- A higher assumed ultimate health care trend rate, and
- A later year in which the ultimate health care trend rate is assumed to be reached.

Conversely, holding all else equal, each of the following assumptions would result in a lower benefit obligation and a lower periodic cost:

- A lower assumed near-term increase in health care costs,
- A lower assumed ultimate health care trend rate, and
- An earlier year in which the ultimate health care trend rate is assumed to be reached.

Example 4 examines two companies' assumptions about trends in US health care costs.

EXAMPLE 4

Comparison of Assumptions about Trends in US Health Care Costs

In addition to disclosing assumptions about health care costs, companies also disclose information on the sensitivity of the measurements of both the obligation and the periodic cost to changes in those assumptions. Exhibit 5 presents information obtained from the notes to the financial statements for CNH Global N.V. (a Dutch manufacturer of construction and mining equipment) and Caterpillar Inc. (a US manufacturer of construction and mining equipment, engines, and turbines). Each company has US employees for whom they provide post-employment health care benefits.

Panel A shows the companies' assumptions about health care costs and the amounts each reported for post-employment health care benefit plans. For example, CNH assumes that the initial year's (2010) increase in health care costs will be 9 percent, and this rate of increase will decline to 5 percent over the next seven years to 2017. Caterpillar assumes a lower initial-year increase of 7 percent and a decline to the ultimate health care trend rate of 5 percent in 2016.

Panel B shows the effect of a 100 basis point increase or decrease in the assumed health care cost trend rates. A 1 percentage point increase in the assumed health care cost trend rates would increase Caterpillar's 2009 service and interest cost component of the other post-employment benefit costs by $23 million and the related obligation by $220 million. A 1 percentage point increase in the assumed health care cost trend rates would increase CNH Global's 2009 service and interest cost component of the other post-employment benefit costs by $8 million and the related obligation by $106 million.

Exhibit 5	Post-Employment Health Care Plan Disclosures

Panel A. Assumptions and Reported Amounts for US Post-Employment Health Care Benefit Plans

	Assumptions about Health Care Costs			Amounts Reported for Other Post-Employment Benefits ($ Millions)	
	Initial Health Care Trend Rate 2010	Ultimate Health Care Trend Rate	Year Ultimate Trend Rate Attained	Accumulated Benefit Obligation Year-End 2009	Periodic Expense for Benefits for 2009
CNH Global N.V.	9.0%	5%	2017	$1,152	$65
Caterpillar Inc.	7.0%	5%	2016	$4,537	$287

Panel B. Effect of 1 Percentage Point Increase (Decrease) in Assumed Health Care Cost Trend Rates on 2009 Total Accumulated Post-Employment Benefit Obligations and Periodic Expense

	1 Percentage Point Increase	1 Percentage Point Decrease
CNH Global N.V.	+$106 million (Obligation) +$8 million (Expense)	−$90 million (Obligation) −$6 million (Expense)
Caterpillar Inc.	+$220 million (Obligation) +$23 million (Expense)	−$186 million (Obligation) −$20 million (Expense)

Sources: Caterpillar information is from the company's Form 10-K filed 19 February 2010, Note 14 (pages A-36 and A-42). CNH Global information is from the company's 2009 Form 20-F, Note 12 (pages F-41, F-43, and F-45).

Based on the information in Exhibit 5, answer the following questions:

1 Which company's assumptions about health care costs appear less conservative?

2 What would be the effect of adjusting the post-employment benefit obligation and the periodic post-employment benefit expense of the less conservative company for a 1 percentage point increase in health care cost trend rates? Does this make the two companies more comparable?

3 What would be the change in each company's 2009 ratio of debt to equity assuming a 1 percentage point increase in the health care cost trend rate? Assume the change would have no impact on taxes. Total liabilities and total equity at 31 December 2009 are given below.

At 31 December 2009 (US$ millions)	CNH Global N.V.	Caterpillar Inc.
Total liabilities	$16,398	$50,738
Total equity	$6,810	$8,823

Solution to 1:

Caterpillar's assumptions about health care costs appear less conservative (the assumptions will result in lower health care costs) than CNH's. Caterpillar's initial assumed health care cost increase of 7 percent is significantly lower than CNH's assumed 9 percent. Further, Caterpillar assumes that the ultimate health care cost trend rate of 5 percent will be reached a year earlier than assumed by CNH.

Solution to 2:

The sensitivity disclosures indicate that a 1 percentage point increase in the assumed health care cost trend rate would increase Caterpillar's post-employment benefit obligation by $220 million and its periodic cost by $23 million. However, Caterpillar's initial health care cost trend rate is 2 percentage points lower than CNH's. Therefore, the impact of a 1 percentage point change for Caterpillar multiplied by 2 provides an approximation of the adjustment required for comparability to CNH. Note, however, that the sensitivity of the pension obligation and expense to a change of more than 1 percentage point in the assumed health care cost trend rate cannot be assumed to be exactly linear, so this adjustment is only an approximation. Further, there may be justifiable differences in the assumptions based on the location of their US operations.

Solution to 3:

A 1 percentage point increase in the health care cost trend rate increases CNH's ratio of debt to equity by about 2 percent, from 2.41 to 2.46. A 1 percentage point increase in the health care cost trend rate increases Caterpillar's ratio of debt to equity by about 3 percent, from 5.75 to 5.92.

CNH Global N.V. ($ millions)	Reported	Adjustment for 1 percentage point increase in health care cost trend rate	Adjusted
Total liabilities	$16,398	+ $106	$16,504
Total equity	$6,810	− $106	$6,704
Ratio of debt to equity	2.41		2.46

Caterpillar Inc. ($ millions)	Reported	Adjustment for 1 percentage point increase in health care cost trend rate	Adjusted
Total liabilities	$50,738	+ $220	$50,958
Total equity	$8,823	− $220	$8,603
Ratio of debt to equity	5.75		5.92

This section has explored the use of pension and other post-employment benefit disclosures to assess a company's assumptions and explore how the assumptions can affect comparisons across companies. The following sections describe the use of disclosures to further analyse a company's pension and other post-employment benefits.

2.4.2 *Net Pension Liability (or Asset)*

Under both IFRS and US GAAP standards, the amount disclosed in the balance sheet is a net amount. Analysts can use information from the notes to adjust a company's assets and liabilities for the gross amount of the benefit plan assets and the gross amount of the benefit plan liabilities. An argument for making such adjustments is that they reflect the underlying economic liabilities and assets of a company; however, it should be recognised that actual consolidation is precluded by laws protecting a pension or other benefit plan as a separate legal entity.

At a minimum, an analyst will compare the gross benefit obligation (i.e., the benefit obligation without deducting related plan assets) with the sponsoring company's total assets, including the gross amount of the benefit plan assets, shareholders' equity, and earnings. Although presumably infrequent in practice, if the gross benefit obligation is large relative to these items, a small change in the pension liability can have a significant financial impact on the sponsoring company.

2.4.3 Total Periodic Pension Costs

The total periodic cost of a company's DB pension plan is the change in the net pension liability or asset—excluding the effect of the employer's periodic contribution into the plan. To illustrate this point, assume a company has a completely new DB pension plan. At inception, the net pension liability equals $0 ($0 plan assets minus $0 obligations). In the first period, the plan obligation increases by $500 because of service costs. If the employer makes no contribution to the plan, then the net pension liability would increase to $500 ($0 plan assets minus $500 obligations) and the periodic service costs would be exactly equal to that change. If, however, the employer contributes $500 to the plan in that period, then the net pension liability would remain at $0 ($500 plan assets minus $500 obligations). In this situation, although the change in net pension liability is $0, the periodic pension cost is $500.

Thus, the total periodic pension cost in a given period is calculated by summing the periodic components of cost or, alternatively, by adjusting the change in the net pension liability or asset for the amount of employer contributions. The relationship between the periodic pension cost and the plan's funded status can be expressed as Periodic pension cost = Ending funded status − Employer contributions − Beginning funded status.[10]

Note that, unlike employer contributions into the plan's assets, the payment of cash out of a DB plan to a retiree does not affect the net pension liability or asset. Payment of cash out of a DB plan to a retiree reduces plan assets and plan obligations in an equal amount.

2.4.4 Periodic Pension Costs Recognised in P&L vs. OCI

Each period, the components of periodic pension cost—other than any amounts that qualify for capitalisation as part of the costs of such assets as inventories—are recognised either in P&L (an expense) or in OCI. To understand the total pension cost of the period, an analyst should thus consider the amounts shown both in P&L and in OCI.

IFRS and US GAAP differ in their provisions about which periodic pension costs are recognised in P&L versus in OCI. These differences can be relevant to an analyst in comparing the reported profitability of companies that use different sets of standards. Under IFRS, P&L for the period includes both current and past service costs; in contrast, under US GAAP, P&L for the period includes only current service costs (and any amortisation of past service costs.) Under IFRS, P&L incorporates a return on plan assets set equal to the discount rate used in estimating the pension obligation; in contrast, under US GAAP, P&L incorporates an expected return on plan assets. Under US GAAP, P&L may show the impact of amortising actuarial gains or losses that were recognised in previous periods' OCI. Under IFRS, P&L would not show any similar impact because amortising amounts from OCI into P&L is not permitted.

An analyst comparing an IFRS-reporting company with a US GAAP–reporting company could adjust the reported amounts of P&L to achieve comparability. For example, the analyst could adjust the US GAAP company's P&L to make it similar to an IFRS company by including past service costs arising during the period, excluding

---

10 Note that a net pension liability is treated as a negative funded status in this relationship.

amortisation of past service costs arising in previous periods, and including an amount of return on plan assets at the discount rate rather than the expected rate. Alternatively, the analyst could use comprehensive income (net income from P&L plus OCI) as the basis for comparison.

2.4.5 *Classification of Periodic Pension Costs Recognised in P&L*

Amounts of periodic pension costs recognised in P&L (pension expense) are generally treated as operating expenses. An issue with the reported periodic pension expense is that conceptually the components of this expense could be classified as operating and/or non-operating expenses. It can be argued that only the current service cost component is an operating expense, whereas the interest component and asset returns component are both non-operating. The interest expense component of pension expense is conceptually similar to the interest expense on any of the company's other liabilities. The pension liability is essentially equivalent to borrowing from employees, and the interest expense of that borrowing can be considered a financing cost. Similarly, the return on pension plan assets is conceptually similar to returns on any of the company's other financial assets. These classification issues apply equally to OPB costs.

To better reflect a company's operating performance, an adjustment can be made to operating income by adding back the full amount of pensions costs reported in the P&L (pension expense) and then subtracting only the service costs (or the total of service costs and settlements and curtailments). Note that this adjustment excludes from operating income the amortisation of past service costs and the amortisation of net actuarial gains and losses. This adjustment also eliminates the interest expense component and the return on plan assets component from the company's operating income. The interest expense component would be added to the company's interest expense, and the return on plan assets would be treated as non-operating income.

In addition to adjusting for the classification of different components of pension costs, an adjustment can be made to incorporate the *actual return* on plan assets. Recall that under IFRS, the net interest expense/income calculation effectively includes a return on plan assets calculated using the discount rate used to determine the present value of the pension liability and any difference from the actual return is shown as a component of OCI. Under US GAAP, the *expected* return on plan assets is included as a component of periodic pension cost in P&L and any difference between the actual and expected return is shown as a component of OCI. Under either set of standards, an adjustment can incorporate the actual return. This adjustment changes net income and potentially introduces earnings volatility. The reclassification of interest expense would not change net income. Example 5 illustrates adjustments to operating and non-operating incomes.

EXAMPLE 5

Adjusting Periodic Costs Expensed to P&L and Reclassifying Components between Operating and Non-Operating Income

SABMiller plc is a UK-based company that brews and distributes beer and other beverages. The following information was taken from the company's 2010 Annual Report. Note that in 2010, IFRS required the use of expected return on plan assets, similar to US GAAP. All amounts are in millions of US dollars.

Summary information from the Consolidated Income Statement
For the year ended 31 March 2010

Revenue	$18,020
Net operating expenses	(15,401)
Operating profit	2,619
Interest payable and similar charges*	(879)
Interest receivable and similar income*	316
Share of post-tax results of associates	873
Profit before taxation	$ 2,929

Note: This is the terminology used in the income statement. The solution to question 2 below uses *interest expense* and *interest and investment income*.

Excerpt from Note 31: Pensions and post-retirement benefits

	Pension	OPB	Total
Current service costs	$ (8)	$(3)	$(11)
Interest costs	(29)	(10)	(39)
Expected return on plan assets	14		14
Total	$(23)	$(13)	$(36)
Actual return (loss) on plan assets	$47		

(Components of the amount recognised in net operating expenses for pension and other post-retirement benefits.)

Based on the information above,

1 Adjust pre-tax income for the actual rather than expected return on plan assets.

2 Adjust the individual line items on the company's income statement to reclassify the components of the pension and other post-retirement benefits expense as operating expense, interest expense, or interest income.

Solution to 1:

The total amount of periodic pension cost reported in P&L as an expense is $23. If the actual return on plan assets of $47 is used instead of the expected return on plan assets, the total P&L expense (income) will be $(10) [(= 8 + 29 − 47) or (= 23 + 14 − 47)]. Use of the actual rather than expected return on plan assets provides an estimate of the economic expense (income) for the pension. Profit before taxation adjusted for actual rather than expected return on plan assets will be higher by $33 ($47 − $14) and will total $2,962.

Solution to 2:

All adjustments are summarized below.

	Reported	Adjustments	Adjusted
Revenue	$18,020		$18,020
Net operating expenses	−15,401	+ 36 − 11[a]	−15,376

	Reported	Adjustments	Adjusted
Operating profit	2,619		2,644
Interest expense	−879	− 39[b]	−918
Interest and investment income	316	+ 47[c]	363
Share of post-tax results of associates	873		873
Profit before taxation	$2,929	$33	$2,962

[a] Operating income is adjusted to include only the current service costs. The $36 total of pension and OPB expenses are excluded from operating expenses, and only the $11 current service cost component is included in operating expenses.

[b] The $39 interest cost component is reclassified as interest expense.

[c] The *actual* return on plan assets is added as investment income.

2.4.6 Cash Flow Information

For a sponsoring company, the cash flow impact of pension and other post-employment benefits is the amount of contributions that the company makes to fund the plan—or for plans without funding requirements, the amount of benefits paid. The amount of contributions a company makes to fund a pension or other post-employment benefit plan is partially determined by the regulations of the countries in which the company operates. In the United States, for example, the amount of contributions to DB pension plans is governed by ERISA (the Employee Retirement and Income Security Act) and depends on the funded status of the plan. Companies may choose to make contributions in excess of those required by regulation.

If a sponsoring company's periodic contributions to a plan exceed the total pension costs of the period, the excess can be viewed from an economic perspective as a reduction of the pension obligation. The contribution covers not only the pension obligation arising in the current period but also the pension obligations of another period. Such a contribution would be similar in concept to making a principal payment on a loan in excess of the scheduled principal payment. Conversely, a periodic contribution that is less than the total pension cost of the period can be viewed as a source of financing. Where the amounts of benefit obligations are material, an analyst may choose to adjust the cash flows that a company presents in its statement of cash flows. Example 6 describes such an adjustment.

EXAMPLE 6

Adjusting Cash Flow

Vassiliki Doukas is analysing the cash flow statement of a hypothetical company, GeoRace plc, as part of a valuation. Doukas suggests to her colleague, Dimitri Krontiras, that the difference between the company's contributions to the pension plan and the total pension costs incurred during a period is similar to a form of borrowing or a repayment of borrowing, depending on the direction of the difference; this affects the company's reported cash from operating activities and cash from financing activities. Based on information from the company's 2009 annual report (currency in £ millions), she determines that the company's total pension cost was £437; however, the company also disclosed that it made a contribution of £504. GeoRace reported cash inflow from operating activities of £6,161 and cash outflow from financing activities of £1,741. The company's effective tax rate was 28.7 percent.

Use the information provided to answer the following questions:

1 How did the company's 2009 contribution to the pension plan compare with the total pension cost for the year?

2 How would cash from operating activities and financing activities be adjusted to illustrate Doukas' interpretation of the difference between the company's contribution and the total pension cost?

Solution to 1:

The company's contribution to the pension plan in 2009 was £504, which was £67 more than the total pension cost of £437. The £67 difference is approximately £48 on an after-tax basis, using the effective tax rate of 28.7 percent.

Total pension costs	£437	
Company's contribution	£504	
Amount by which the sponsoring company's contribution exceeds total pension cost (pre-tax)	£ 67	
Tax rate	28.7%	
After-tax amount by which the sponsoring company's contribution exceeds total pension cost	£48	[= £67 × (1 − 0.2870)]

Solution to 2:

The company's contribution to the pension plan in 2009 was £67 (£48 after tax) greater than the 2009 total pension cost. Interpreting the excess contribution as similar to a repayment of borrowing (financing use of funds) rather than as an operating cash flow would increase the company's cash outflow from financing activities by £48, from £1,741 to £1,789, and increase the cash inflow from operations by £48, from £6,161 to £6,209.

3 SHARE-BASED COMPENSATION

In this section, we provide an overview of executive compensation other than pension plans and other post-retirement benefits, focusing on share-based compensation. First, we briefly discuss common components of executive compensation packages, their objectives, and advantages and disadvantages of share-based compensation. The discussion of share-based compensation then moves to accounting for and reporting of stock grants and stock options. The explanation includes a discussion of fair value accounting, the choice of valuation models, the assumptions used, common disclosures, and important dates in measuring and reporting compensation expense.

Employee compensation packages are structured to achieve varied objectives, including satisfying employees' needs for liquidity, retaining employees, and motivating employees. Common components of employee compensation packages are salary, bonuses, non-monetary benefits, and share-based compensation.[11] The salary component provides for the liquidity needs of an employee. Bonuses, generally in the form of cash, motivate and reward employees for short- or long-term performance or goal achievement by linking pay to performance. Non-monetary benefits, such as medical care, housing, and cars, may be provided to facilitate employees performing their jobs. Salary, bonuses, and non-monetary benefits are short-term employee benefits.

Share-based compensation is intended to align employees' interests with those of the shareholders and is typically a form of deferred compensation. Both IFRS and US GAAP[12] require a company to disclose in their annual report key elements of management compensation. Regulators may require additional disclosure. The disclosures enable analysts to understand the nature and extent of compensation, including the share-based payment arrangements that existed during the reporting period. Below are examples of descriptions of the components and objectives of executive compensation programs for companies that report under IFRS and under US GAAP. Exhibit 6 shows excerpts of the disclosure for the executive compensation program of SABMiller plc (London Stock Exchange: SAB); SABMiller plc reports under IFRS and includes a nine-page remuneration report as part of its annual report.

Exhibit 6

Excerpts from Remuneration Report of SABMiller plc

… On balance, the committee concluded that its policy of agreeing a total remuneration package for each executive director comprising an annual base salary, a short-term incentive in the form of an annual cash bonus, long-term incentives through participation in share incentive plans, pension contributions, other usual security and health benefits, and benefits in kind, continued to be appropriate….

The committee's policy continues to be to ensure that executive directors and members of the executive committee are rewarded for their contribution to the group's operating and financial performance at levels which take account of industry, market and country benchmarks, and that their remuneration is appropriate to their scale of responsibility and performance, and will attract, motivate and retain individuals of the necessary calibre. The committee takes account of the need to be competitive in the different parts of the world in which the company operates….

The committee considers that alignment with shareholders' interests and linkage to SABMiller's long-term strategic goals is best achieved through a twin focus on earnings per share and, from 2010 onwards, additional value created for shareholders, and a blend of absolute and relative performance.

Source: SABMiller plc, Annual Report 2010.

---

11 An extensive overview of different employee compensation mechanisms can be found in Lynch and Perry (2003).
12 IAS 24 *Related Party Disclosures*, paragraph 17; FASB ASC Section 718-10-50 [Compensation-Stock Compensation-Overall-Disclosure].

In the United States, similar disclosures are required in a company's proxy statement that is filed with the SEC. Exhibit 7 shows the disclosure of American Eagle Outfitters, Inc.'s (NYSE: AEO) executive compensation program, including a description of the key elements and objectives.

Exhibit 7   Excerpts from Executive Compensation Disclosures of American Eagle Outfitters, Inc.

Compensation Program Elements

Our executive compensation program is designed to place a sizeable amount of pay at risk for all executives and this philosophy is intended to cultivate a pay-for-performance environment. Our executive compensation plan design has six key elements:

- Base Salary
- Annual Incentive Bonus
- Long-term Incentive Cash Plan—in place for the Chief Executive Officer and Vice Chairman, Executive Creative Director only
- Restricted Stock ("RS")—issued as Units ("RSUs") and Awards ("RSAs")
- Performance Shares ("PS")
- Non-Qualified Stock Options ("NSOs")

Two of the elements (Annual Incentive Bonus and LTICP) were entirely "at risk" based on the Company's performance in Fiscal 2009 and were subject to forfeiture if the Company did not achieve threshold performance goals. Performance Shares are entirely "at risk" and subject to forfeiture if the Company does not achieve threshold performance goals by the close of Fiscal 2011, as described below. At threshold performance, the CEO's total annual compensation declines by 46% relative to target performance. The NEO's total annual compensation declines by an average of 33% relative to target performance. Company performance below threshold levels results in forfeiture of all elements of direct compensation other than base salary, RSUs and NSOs. NSOs provide compensation only to the extent that vesting requirements are satisfied and our share price appreciates.

We strategically allocate compensation between short-term and long-term components and between cash and equity in order to maximize executive performance and retention. Long-term compensation and equity awards comprise an increasingly larger proportion of total compensation as position level increases. The portion of total pay attributable to long-term incentive cash and equity compensation increases at successively higher levels of management. This philosophy ensures that executive compensation closely aligns with changes in stockholder value and achievement of performance objectives while also ensuring that executives are held accountable for results relative to position level.

Source: American Eagle Outfitters, Inc. Proxy Statement (Form Def 14A) filed 26 April 2010.

Share-based compensation, in addition to theoretically aligning the interests of employees (management) with shareholders, has the advantage of potentially requiring no cash outlay.[13] Share-based compensation arrangements can take a variety of

---

13 Although issuing employee stock options requires no initial cash outlay, the company implicitly forgoes issuing new shares of stock at the then-current market price (and receiving cash) when the options are exercised.

forms, including those that are equity-settled and those that are cash-settled. However, share-based compensation is treated as an expense and thus as a reduction of earnings even when no cash changes hands. In addition to decreasing earnings through compensation expense, stock options have the potential to dilute earnings per share.

Although share-based compensation is generally viewed as motivating employees and aligning managers' interests with those of the shareholders, there are several disadvantages of share-based compensation. One disadvantage is that the recipient of the share-based compensation may have limited influence over the company's market value (consider the scenario of overall market decline), so share-based compensation does not necessarily provide the desired incentives. Another disadvantage is that the increased ownership may lead managers to be risk averse. In other words, fearing a large market value decline (and loss in individual wealth), managers may seek less risky (and less profitable) projects. An opposite effect, excessive risk taking, can also occur with the awarding of options. Because options have skewed payouts that reward excessive risk taking, managers may seek more risky projects. Finally, when share-based compensation is granted to employees, existing shareholders' ownership is diluted.

For financial reporting, a company reports compensation expense during the period in which employees earn that compensation. Accounting for cash salary payments and cash bonuses is relatively straightforward. When the employee has earned the salary or bonus, an expense is recorded. Typically, compensation expense for managers is reported in sales, general, and administrative expenses on the income statement.

Share-based compensation is more varied and includes such items as stock, stock options, stock appreciation rights, and phantom shares. By granting shares or share options in addition to other compensation, companies are paying additional compensation for services rendered by employees. Under both IFRS and US GAAP, companies use the fair value of the share-based compensation granted to measure the value of the employees' services for purposes of reporting compensation expense. However, the specifics of the accounting depend on the type of share-based compensation given to the employee. Under both IFRS and US GAAP, the usual disclosures required for share-based compensation include (1) the nature and extent of share-based compensation arrangements during the period, (2) how the fair value of a share-based compensation arrangement was determined, and (3) the effect of share-based compensation on the company's income for the period and on its financial position.

Two common forms of equity-settled share-based compensation, stock grants and stock options, are discussed below.

3.1 Stock Grants

A company can grant stock to employees outright, with restrictions, or contingent on performance. For an outright stock grant, compensation expense is reported on the basis of the fair value of the stock on the grant date—generally the market value at grant date. Compensation expense is allocated over the period benefited by the employee's service, referred to as the service period. The employee service period is presumed to be the current period unless there are some specific requirements, such as three years service in the future, before the employee is vested (has the right to receive the compensation).

Another type of stock award is a restricted stock, which requires the employee to return ownership of those shares to the company if certain conditions are not met. Common restrictions include the requirements that employees remain with the company for a specified period or that certain performance goals are met. Compensation expense for restricted stock grants is measured as the fair value (usually market value) of the shares issued at the grant date. This compensation expense is allocated over the employee service period.

Shares granted contingent on meeting performance goals are called performance shares. The amount of the grant is usually determined by performance measures other than the change in stock price, such as accounting earnings or return on assets. Basing the grant on accounting performance addresses employees' potential concerns that the stock price is beyond their control and thus should not form the basis for compensation. However, performance shares can potentially have the unintended impact of providing incentives to manipulate accounting numbers. Compensation expense is equal to the fair value (usually market value) of the shares issued at the grant date. This compensation expense is allocated over the employee service period.

3.2 Stock Options

Like stock grants, compensation expense related to option grants is reported at fair value under both IFRS and US GAAP. Both require that fair value be estimated using an appropriate valuation model.

Whereas the fair value of stock grants is usually based on the market value at the date of the grant, the fair value of option grants must be estimated. Companies cannot rely on market prices of options to measure the fair value of employee stock options because features of employee stock options typically differ from traded options. To measure the fair value of employee stock options, therefore, companies must use a valuation model. The choice of valuation or option pricing model is one of the critical elements in estimating fair value. Several models are commonly used, such as the Black–Scholes option pricing model or a binomial model. Accounting standards do not prescribe a particular model. Generally, though, the valuation method should (1) be consistent with fair value measurement, (2) be based on established principles of financial economic theory, and (3) reflect all substantive characteristics of the award.

Once a valuation model is selected, a company must determine the inputs to the model, typically including exercise price, stock price volatility, estimated life of each award, estimated number of options that will be forfeited, dividend yield, and the risk-free rate of interest.[14] Some inputs, such as the exercise price, are known at the time of the grant. Other critical inputs are highly subjective—such as stock price volatility or the estimated life of stock options—and can greatly change the estimated fair value and thus compensation expense. Higher volatility, a longer estimated life, and a higher risk-free interest rate increase the estimated fair value, whereas a higher assumed dividend yield decreases the estimated fair value.

Combining different assumptions with alternative valuation models can significantly affect the fair value of employee stock options. Below is an excerpt from GlaxoSmithKline, plc explaining the assumptions and model used in valuing its stock options. (Although not discussed in the disclosure, from 2007 to 2009 the trends of decreasing interest rates, lower share price, and increasing dividend yield would decrease estimated fair values and thus lower option expense. In contrast, the trend of increasing volatility would increase the estimated fair values.)

Exhibit 8　Assumptions Used in Stock Option Pricing Models: Excerpts from Financial Statements of GlaxoSmithKline, plc

Note 42—Employee share schemes [excerpt]

Option pricing

---

[14] The estimated life of an option award incorporates such assumptions as employee turnover and is usually shorter than the expiration period.

Exhibit 8   (Continued)

For the purposes of valuing options and awards to arrive at the share based payment charge, the Black–Scholes option pricing model has been used. The assumptions used in the model for 2007, 2008 and 2009 are as follows:

	2009	2008	2007
Risk-free interest rate	1.4% – 2.9%	1.3% – 4.8%	4.7% – 5.3%
Dividend yield	5.20%	4.80%	4.00%
Volatility	23% – 29%	19% – 24%	17% – 25%
Expected lives of options granted under:			
Share option schemes	5 years	5 years	5 years
Savings-related share option and share award schemes	3–4 years	3 years	3 years
Weighted average share price for grants in the year:			
Ordinary Shares	£11.72	£11.59	£14.41
ADS*	$33.73	$45.02	$57.59

*American Depositary Shares

Volatility is determined based on the three and five year share price history where appropriate. The fair value of performance share plan grants take into account market conditions. Expected lives of options were determined based on weighted average historic exercises of options.

Source: GlaxoSmithKline Annual Report 2009.

In accounting for stock options, there are several important dates, including the grant date, the vesting date, the exercise date, and the expiration date. The **grant date** is the day that options are granted to employees. The **service period** is usually the period between the grant date and the vesting date.

The **vesting date** is the date that employees can first exercise the stock options. The vesting can be immediate or over a future period. If the share-based payments vest immediately (i.e., no further period of service is required), then expense is recognised on the grant date. If the share-based awards do not vest until a specified service period is completed, compensation expense is recognised and allocated over the service period. If the share-based awards are conditional upon the achievement of a performance condition or a market condition (i.e., a target share price), then compensation expense is recognised over the estimated service period. The **exercise date** is the date when employees actually exercise the options and convert them to stock. If the options go unexercised, they may expire at some pre-determined future date, commonly 5 or 10 years from the grant date.

The grant date is also usually the date that compensation expense is measured if both the number of shares and the option price are known. If facts affecting the value of options granted depend on events after the grant date, then compensation expense is measured at the exercise date. In the example below, Coca Cola, Inc. (NYSE: KO) reported, in the 2009 Form 10-K, $241 million of compensation expense from option grants.

EXAMPLE 7

Disclosure of Stock Options' Current Compensation Expense, Vesting, and Future Compensation Expense

Using information from Coca Cola, Inc.'s Note 9 to financial statements, given below, determine the following:

1   Total compensation expense relating to options already granted that will be recognised in future years as options vest.

2   Approximate compensation expense in 2010 and 2011 relating to options already granted.

> *Excerpts from Note 9: Stock Compensation Plans in the Notes to Financial Statements of Coca Cola, Inc.*
>
> NOTE 9: STOCK COMPENSATION PLANS
>
> Our Company grants stock options and restricted stock awards to certain employees of the Company. Total stock-based compensation expense was approximately $241 million in 2009, $266 million in 2008 and $313 million in 2007 and was included as a component of selling, general and administrative expenses in our consolidated statements of income. The total income tax benefit recognized in our consolidated statements of income for share-based compensation arrangements was approximately $68 million, $72 million and $91 million for 2009, 2008 and 2007, respectively.
>
> As of December 31, 2009, we had approximately $335 million of total unrecognised compensation cost related to nonvested share-based compensation arrangements granted under our plans. This cost is expected to be recognized over a weighted-average period of 1.7 years as stock-based compensation expense. This expected cost does not include the impact of any future stock-based compensation awards.
>
> *Source*: Coca Cola, Inc. Form 10-K filed 26 February 2010.

Solution to 1:

Coca Cola, Inc. discloses that unrecognised compensation expense relating to stock options already granted but not yet vested totals $335 million.

Solution to 2:

The options already granted will vest over the next 1.7 years. Compensation expense related to stock options already granted will be $197 million ($335/1.7 years) in 2010 and $138 million in 2011 ($335 total less $197 expensed in 2010). New options granted in the future will likely raise the total reported compensation expense.

As the option expense is recognised over the relevant vesting period, the impact on the financial statements is to ultimately reduce retained earnings (as with any other expense). The offsetting entry is an increase in paid-in capital. Thus, the recognition of option expense has no net impact on total equity.

3.3 Other Types of Share-Based Compensation

Both stock grants and stock options allow the employee to obtain direct ownership in the company. Other types of share-based compensation, such as stock appreciation rights (SARs) or phantom stock, compensate an employee on the basis of changes in the value of shares without requiring the employee to hold the shares. These are referred to as cash-settled share-based compensation. With SARs, an employee's compensation is based on increases in a company's share price. Like other forms of share-based compensation, SARs serve to motivate employees and align their interests with shareholders. The following are two additional advantages of SARs:

- The potential for risk aversion is limited because employees have limited downside risk and unlimited upside potential similar to employee stock options, and

- Shareholder ownership is not diluted.

A disadvantage is that SARs require a current-period cash outflow. Similar to other share-based compensation, SARs are valued at fair value and compensation expense is allocated over the service period of the employee. While phantom share plans are similar to other types of share-based compensation, they differ somewhat because compensation is based on the performance of hypothetical stock rather than the company's actual stock. Unlike SARs, phantom shares can be used by private companies or business units within a company that are not publicly traded or by highly illiquid companies.

SUMMARY

This reading discussed two different forms of employee compensation: post-employment benefits and share-based compensation. Although different, the two are similar in that they are forms of compensation outside of the standard salary arrangements. They also involve complex valuation, accounting, and reporting issues. Although IFRS and US GAAP are converging on accounting and reporting, it is important to note that differences in a country's social system, laws, and regulations can result in differences in a company's pension and share-based compensation plans that may be reflected in the company's earnings and financial reports.

Key points include the following:

- Defined contribution pension plans specify (define) only the amount of contribution to the plan; the eventual amount of the pension benefit to the employee will depend on the value of an employee's plan assets at the time of retirement.

- Balance sheet reporting is less analytically relevant for defined contribution plans because companies make contributions to defined contribution plans as the expense arises and thus no liabilities accrue for that type of plan.

- Defined benefit pension plans specify (define) the amount of the pension benefit, often determined by a plan formula, under which the eventual amount of the benefit to the employee is a function of length of service and final salary.

- Defined benefit pension plan obligations are funded by the sponsoring company contributing assets to a pension trust, a separate legal entity. Differences exist in countries' regulatory requirements for companies to fund defined benefit pension plan obligations.

- Both IFRS and US GAAP require companies to report on their balance sheet a pension liability or asset equal to the projected benefit obligation minus the fair value of plan assets. The amount of a pension asset that can be reported is subject to a ceiling.

- Under IFRS, the components of periodic pension cost are recognised as follows: Service cost is recognised in P&L, net interest income/expense is recognised in P&L, and remeasurements are recognised in OCI and are not amortised to future P&L.

- Under US GAAP, the components of periodic pension cost recognised in P&L include current service costs, interest expense on the pension obligation, and expected returns on plan assets (which reduces the cost). Other components of periodic pension cost—including past service costs, actuarial gains and losses, and differences between expected and actual returns on plan assets—are recognised in OCI and amortised to future P&L.

- Estimates of the future obligation under defined benefit pension plans and other post-employment benefits are sensitive to numerous assumptions, including discount rates, assumed annual compensation increases, expected return on plan assets, and assumed health care cost inflation.

- Employee compensation packages are structured to fulfill varied objectives, including satisfying employees' needs for liquidity, retaining employees, and providing incentives to employees.

- Common components of employee compensation packages are salary, bonuses, and share-based compensation.

- Share-based compensation serves to align employees' interests with those of the shareholders. It includes stocks and stock options.

- Share-based compensation has the advantage of requiring no current-period cash outlays.

- Share-based compensation expense is reported at fair value under IFRS and US GAAP.

- The valuation technique, or option pricing model, that a company uses is an important choice in determining fair value and is disclosed.

- Key assumptions and input into option pricing models include such items as exercise price, stock price volatility, estimated life of each award, estimated number of options that will be forfeited, dividend yield, and the risk-free rate of interest. Certain assumptions are highly subjective, such as stock price volatility or the expected life of stock options, and can greatly change the estimated fair value and thus compensation expense.

REFERENCES

Lynch, L.J., and S.E. Perry. 2003. "An Overview of Management Compensation." *Journal of Accounting Education*, vol. 21, no. 1 (1st Quarter):43–60.

PRACTICE PROBLEMS

The following information relates to Questions 1–7

Kensington plc, a hypothetical company based in the United Kingdom, offers its employees a defined benefit pension plan. Kensington complies with IFRS. The assumed discount rate that the company used in estimating the present value of its pension obligations was 5.48 percent. Information on Kensington's retirement plans is presented in Exhibit 1.

Exhibit 1 Kensington plc Defined Benefit Pension Plan	
(in millions)	**2010**
Components of periodic benefit cost	
Service cost	£228
Net interest (income) expense	273
Remeasurements	−18
Periodic pension cost	£483
Change in benefit obligation	
Benefit obligations at beginning of year	£28,416
Service cost	228
Interest cost	1,557
Benefits paid	−1,322
Actuarial gain or loss	0
Benefit obligations at end of year	£28,879
Change in plan assets	
Fair value of plan assets at beginning of year	£23,432
Actual return on plan assets	1,302
Employer contributions	693
Benefits paid	−1,322
Fair value of plan assets at end of year	£24,105
Funded status at beginning of year	−£4,984
Funded status at end of year	−£4,774

1 At year-end 2010, £28,879 million represents:

   A the funded status of the plan.

   B the defined benefit obligation.

   C the fair value of the plan's assets.

2 For the year 2010, the net interest expense of £273 represents the interest cost on the:

   A ending benefit obligation.

   B beginning benefit obligation.

   C beginning net pension obligation.

3 For the year 2010, the remeasurement component of Kensington's periodic pension cost represents:

   A the change in the net pension obligation.

   B actuarial gains and losses on the pension obligation.

   C actual return on plan assets minus the amount of return on plan assets included in the net interest expense.

4 Which of the following is *closest* to the actual rate of return on beginning plan assets and the rate of return on beginning plan assets that is included in the interest income/expense calculation?

   A The actual rate of return was 5.56 percent, and the rate included in interest income/expense was 5.48 percent.

   B The actual rate of return was 1.17 percent, and the rate included in interest income/expense was 5.48 percent.

   C Both the actual rate of return and the rate included in interest income/expense were 5.48 percent.

5 Which component of Kensington's periodic pension cost would be shown in OCI rather than P&L?

   A Service cost

   B Net interest (income) expense

   C Remeasurements

6 The relationship between the periodic pension cost and the plan's funded status is *best* expressed in which of the following?

   A Periodic pension cost of −£483 = Ending funded status of −£4,774 − Employer contributions of £693 − Beginning funded status of −£4,984.

   B Periodic pension cost of £1,322 = Benefits paid of £1,322.

   C Periodic pension cost of £210 = Ending funded status of −£4,774 − Beginning funded status of −£4,984.

7 An adjustment to Kensington's statement of cash flows to reclassify the company's excess contribution for 2010 would *most likely* entail reclassifying £210 million (excluding income tax effects) as an outflow related to:

   A investing activities rather than operating activities.

   B financing activities rather than operating activities.

   C operating activities rather than financing activities.

The following information relates to Questions 8–13

XYZ SA, a hypothetical company, offers its employees a defined benefit pension plan. Information on XYZ's retirement plans is presented in Exhibit 2. It also grants stock options to executives. Exhibit 3 contains information on the volatility assumptions used to value stock options.

Exhibit 2 XYZ SA Retirement Plan Information 2009	
Employer contributions	1,000
Current service costs	200
Past service costs	120
Discount rate used to estimate plan liabilities	7.00%
Benefit obligation at beginning of year	42,000
Benefit obligation at end of year	41,720
Actuarial loss due to increase in plan obligation	460
Plan assets at beginning of year	39,000
Plan assets at end of year	38,700
Actual return on plan assets	2,700
Expected rate of return on plan assets	8.00%

Exhibit 3 XYZ SA Volatility Assumptions Used to Value Stock Option Grants	
Grant Year	Weighted Average Expected Volatility
2009 valuation assumptions	
2005–2009	21.50%
2008 valuation assumptions	
2004–2008	23.00%

8   The retirement benefits paid during the year were *closest* to:

   A   280.

   B   3,000.

   C   4,000.

9   The total periodic pension cost is *closest* to:

   A   320.

   B   1,020.

   C   1,320.

10   The amount of periodic pension cost that would be reported in P&L under IFRS is *closest* to:

   A   20.

   B   530.

   C   1,020.

11 Assuming the company chooses not to immediately recognise the actuarial loss and assuming there is no amortisation of past service costs or actuarial gains and losses, the amount of periodic pension cost that would be reported in P&L under US GAAP is *closest* to:

A 20.

B 59.

C 530.

12 Under IFRS, the amount of periodic pension cost that would be reported in OCI is *closest* to:

A 20.

B 490.

C 1,020.

13 Compared to 2009 net income as reported, if XYZ had used the same expected volatility assumption for its 2009 option grants that it had used in 2008, its 2009 net income would have been:

A lower.

B higher.

C the same.

The following information relates to Questions 14–19

Stereo Warehouse is a US retailer that offers employees a defined benefit pension plan and stock options as part of its compensation package. Stereo Warehouse prepares its financial statements in accordance with US GAAP.

Peter Friedland, CFA, is an equity analyst concerned with earnings quality. He is particularly interested in whether the discretionary assumptions the company is making regarding compensation plans are contributing to the recent earnings growth at Stereo Warehouse. He gathers information from the company's regulatory filings regarding the pension plan assumptions in Exhibit 4 and the assumptions related to option valuation in Exhibit 5.

Exhibit 4 Assumptions Used for Stereo Warehouse Defined Benefit Plan			
	2009	2008	2007
Expected long-term rate of return on plan assets	6.06%	6.14%	6.79%
Discount rate	4.85	4.94	5.38
Estimated future salary increases	4.00	4.44	4.25
Inflation	3.00	2.72	2.45

Exhibit 5   Option Valuation Assumptions

	2009	2008	2007
Risk-free rate	4.6%	3.8%	2.4%
Expected life	5.0 yrs	4.5 yrs	5.0 yrs
Dividend yield	1.0%	0.0%	0.0%
Expected volatility	29%	31%	35%

14 Compared to the 2009 reported financial statements, if Stereo Warehouse had used the same expected long-term rate of return on plan assets assumption in 2009 as it used in 2007, its year-end 2009 pension obligation would *most likely* have been:

  A lower.

  B higher.

  C the same.

15 Compared to the reported 2009 financial statements, if Stereo Warehouse had used the same discount rate as it used in 2007, it would have *most likely* reported lower:

  A net income.

  B total liabilities.

  C cash flow from operating activities.

16 Compared to the assumptions Stereo Warehouse used to compute its periodic pension cost in 2008, earnings in 2009 were *most favorably* affected by the change in the:

  A discount rate.

  B estimated future salary increases.

  C expected long-term rate of return on plan assets.

17 Compared to the pension assumptions Stereo Warehouse used in 2008, which of the following pairs of assumptions used in 2009 is *most likely* internally inconsistent?

  A Estimated future salary increases, inflation

  B Discount rate, estimated future salary increases

  C Expected long-term rate of return on plan assets, discount rate

18 Compared to the reported 2009 financial statements, if Stereo Warehouse had used the 2007 expected volatility assumption to value its employee stock options, it would have *most likely* reported higher:

  A net income.

  B compensation expense.

  C deferred compensation liability.

19 Compared to the assumptions Stereo Warehouse used to value stock options in 2008, earnings in 2009 were most favorably affected by the change in the:

  A expected life.

  B risk-free rate.

  C dividend yield.

SOLUTIONS

1 B is correct. The £28,879 million year-end benefit obligation represents the defined benefit obligation.

2 C is correct. The net interest expense of £273 million represents the interest cost on the beginning net pension obligation (beginning funded status) using the discount rate that the company uses in estimating the present value of its pension obligations. This is calculated as −£4,984 million times 5.48 percent = −£273 million; this represents an interest expense on the amount that the company essentially owes the pension plan.

3 C is correct. The remeasurement component of periodic pension cost includes both actuarial gains and losses on the pension obligation and net return on plan assets. Because Kensington does not have any actuarial gains and losses on the pension obligation, the remeasurement component includes only net return on plan assets. In practice, actuarial gains and losses are rarely equal to zero. The net return on plan assets is equal to actual returns minus beginning plan assets times the discount rate, or £1,302 million − (£23,432 million × 0.0548) = £18 million.

4 A is correct. The actual return on plan assets was 1,302/23,432 = 0.0556, or 5.56 percent. The rate of return included in the interest income/expense is the discount rate, which is given in this example as 5.48 percent.

The rate of 1.17 percent, calculated as the net interest income divided by beginning plan assets, is not used in pension cost calculations.

5 C is correct. Under IFRS, the component of periodic pension cost that is shown in OCI rather than P&L is remeasurments.

6 A is correct. The relation between the periodic pension cost and the plan's funded status can be expressed as Periodic pension cost = Ending funded status − Employer contributions − Beginning funded status.

7 B is correct. Kensington's periodic pension cost was £483. The company's contributions to the plan were £693. The £210 difference between these two numbers can be viewed as a reduction of the overall pension obligation. To adjust the statement of cash flows to reflect this view, an analyst would reclassify the £210 million (excluding income tax effects) as an outflow related to financing activities rather than operating activities.

8 C is correct. The retirement benefits paid during the year were closest to 4,000. The beginning obligation plus current and past service costs plus interest expense plus increase in obligation due to actuarial loss less ending obligation equals benefits paid (= 42,000 + 200 + 120 + (42,000 × 0.07) + 460 − 41,720 = 4,000). Beginning plan assets plus contributions plus actual return on plan assets less ending plan assets equals benefits paid (= 39,000 + 1,000 + 2,700 − 38,700 = 4,000).

9 B is correct. The total periodic pension cost is the change in the net pension liability adjusted for the employer's contribution into the plan. The net pension liability increased from 3,000 to 3,020, and the employer's contribution was 1,000. The total periodic pension cost is 1,020. This will be allocated between P&L and OCI.

10 B is correct. Under IFRS, the components of periodic pension cost that would be reported in P&L are the service cost (composed of current service and past service costs) and the net interest expense or income, calculated by multiplying the net pension liability or net pension asset by the discount rate used to

measure the pension liability. Here, the service costs are 320 (= 200 + 120) and the net interest expense is 210 [= (42,000 − 39,000) × 7%]. Thus, the total periodic pension cost is equal to 530.

11 A is correct. Under US GAAP—assuming the company chooses not to immediately recognise the actuarial loss and assuming there is no amortisation of past service costs or actuarial gains and losses—the components of periodic pension cost that would be reported in P&L include the current service cost of 200, the interest expense on the pension obligation at the beginning of the period of 2,940 (= 7.0% × 42,000), and the expected return on plan assets, which is a reduction of the cost of 3,120 (= 8.0% × 39,000). Summing these three components gives 20.

12 B is correct. The component of periodic pension cost that would be reported in OCI is the remeasurements component. It consists of actuarial gains and losses on the pension obligation and net return on plan assets. Here, the actuarial loss was 460. In addition, the actual return on plan assets was 2,700, which was 30 lower than the return of 2,730 (= 39,000 × 0.07) incorporated in the net interest income/expense. Therefore, the total remeasurements are 490.

13 A is correct. In 2009, XYZ used a lower volatility assumption than it did in 2008. Lower expected volatility reduces the fair value of an option and thus the reported expense. Using the 2008 volatility estimate would have resulted in higher expense and thus lower net income.

14 C is correct. The assumed long-term rate of return on plan assets is not a component that is used in calculating the pension obligation, so there would be no change.

15 B is correct. A higher discount rate (5.38 percent instead of 4.85 percent) will reduce the present value of the pension obligation (liability). In most cases, a higher discount rate will decrease the interest cost component of the net periodic cost because the decrease in the obligation will more than offset the increase in the discount rate (except if the pension obligation is of short duration). Therefore, periodic pension cost would have been lower and reported net income higher. Cash flow from operating activities should not be affected by the change.

16 B is correct. In 2009, the three relevant assumptions were lower than in 2008. Lower expected salary increases reduce the service cost component of the periodic pension cost. A lower discount rate will increase the defined benefit obligation and increase the interest cost component of the periodic pension cost (the increase in the obligation will, in most cases, more than offset the decrease in the discount rate). Reducing the expected return on plan assets typically increases the periodic pension cost.

17 A is correct. The company's inflation estimate rose from 2008 to 2009. However, it lowered its estimate of future salary increases. Normally, salary increases will be positively related to inflation.

18 B is correct. A higher volatility assumption increases the value of the stock option and thus the compensation expense, which, in turn, reduces net income. There is no associated liability for stock options.

19 C is correct. A higher dividend yield reduces the value of the option and thus option expense. The lower expense results in higher earnings. Higher risk-free rates and expected lives result in higher call option values.

Multinational Operations

by Timothy S. Doupnik, PhD, and Elaine Henry, PhD, CFA

Timothy S. Doupnik, PhD, is at the University of South Carolina (USA). Elaine Henry, PhD, CFA, is at Fordham University (USA).

LEARNING OUTCOMES

Mastery	The candidate should be able to:
☐	**a.** distinguish among presentation (reporting) currency, functional currency, and local currency;
☐	**b.** describe foreign currency transaction exposure, including accounting for and disclosures about foreign currency transaction gains and losses;
☐	**c.** analyze how changes in exchange rates affect the translated sales of the subsidiary and parent company;
☐	**d.** compare the current rate method and the temporal method, evaluate how each affects the parent company's balance sheet and income statement, and determine which method is appropriate in various scenarios;
☐	**e.** calculate the translation effects and evaluate the translation of a subsidiary's balance sheet and income statement into the parent company's presentation currency;
☐	**f.** analyze how the current rate method and the temporal method affect financial statements and ratios;
☐	**g.** analyze how alternative translation methods for subsidiaries operating in hyperinflationary economies affect financial statements and ratios;
☐	**h.** describe how multinational operations affect a company's effective tax rate;
☐	**i.** explain how changes in the components of sales affect the sustainability of sales growth;
☐	**j.** analyze how currency fluctuations potentially affect financial results, given a company's countries of operation.

INTRODUCTION

According to the World Trade Organization, merchandise exports worldwide were nearly US$15 trillion in 2010.[1] The amount of worldwide merchandise exports in 2010 was more than twice the amount in 2003 (US$7.4 trillion) and more than four times the amount in 1993 (US$3.7 trillion). The top five exporting countries in 2010, in order, were China, the United States, Germany, Japan, and the Netherlands. In the United States alone, 293,131 companies were identified as exporters in 2010, but only 2.2% of those companies were large (more than 500 employees).[2] The vast majority of US companies with export activity were small or medium-sized entities.

The point illustrated by these statistics is that many companies engage in transactions that cross national borders. The parties to these transactions must agree on the currency in which to settle the transaction. Generally, this will be the currency of either the buyer or the seller. Exporters that receive payment in foreign currency and allow the purchaser time to pay must carry a foreign currency receivable on their books. Conversely, importers that agree to pay in foreign currency will have a foreign currency account payable. To be able to include them in the total amount of accounts receivable (payable) reported on the balance sheet, these foreign currency denominated accounts receivable (payable) must be translated into the currency in which the exporter (importer) keeps its books and presents financial statements.

The prices at which foreign currencies can be purchased or sold are called foreign exchange rates. Because foreign exchange rates fluctuate over time, the value of foreign currency payables and receivables also fluctuates. The major accounting issue related to foreign currency transactions is how to reflect the changes in value for foreign currency payables and receivables in the financial statements.

Many companies have operations located in foreign countries. For example, the Swiss food products company Nestlé SA reports that it has factories in 83 countries and a presence in almost every country in the world. US-based Procter & Gamble's annual filing discloses more than 400 subsidiaries located in more than 80 countries around the world. Foreign subsidiaries are generally required to keep accounting records in the currency of the country in which they are located. To prepare consolidated financial statements, the parent company must translate the foreign currency financial statements of its foreign subsidiaries into its own currency. Nestlé, for example, must translate the assets and liabilities its various foreign subsidiaries carry in foreign currency into Swiss francs to be able to consolidate those amounts with the Swiss franc assets and liabilities located in Switzerland.

A multinational company like Nestlé is likely to have two types of foreign currency activities that require special accounting treatment. Most multinationals (1) engage in transactions that are denominated in a foreign currency and (2) invest in foreign subsidiaries that keep their books in a foreign currency. To prepare consolidated financial statements, a multinational company must translate the foreign currency amounts related to both types of international activities into the currency in which the company presents its financial statements.

This reading presents the accounting for foreign currency transactions and the translation of foreign currency financial statements. The conceptual issues related to these accounting topics are discussed, and the specific rules embodied in International Financial Reporting Standards (IFRS) and US GAAP are demonstrated through examples. Fortunately, differences between IFRS and US GAAP with respect to foreign currency translation issues are minimal.

---

1 World Trade Organization, *International Trade Statistics 2011*, Table I4, page 21.
2 US Census Bureau, Department of Commerce. *A Profile of US Importing and Exporting Companies, 2009–2010*. Released 12 April 2012.

Analysts need to understand the effects of foreign exchange rate fluctuations on the financial statements of a multinational company and how a company's financial statements reflect foreign currency gains and losses, whether realized or not.

FOREIGN CURRENCY TRANSACTIONS

When companies from different countries agree to conduct business with one another, they must decide which currency will be used. For example, if a Mexican electronic components manufacturer agrees to sell goods to a customer in Finland, the two parties must agree whether the Finnish company will pay for the goods in Mexican pesos, euro, or perhaps even a third currency such as the US dollar. If the transaction is denominated in Mexican pesos, the Finnish company has a foreign currency transaction but the Mexican company does not. To account for the inventory being purchased and the account payable in Mexican pesos, the Finnish company must translate the Mexican peso amounts into euro using appropriate exchange rates. Although the Mexican company also has entered into an international transaction (an export sale), it does not have a foreign currency transaction and no translation is necessary. It simply records the sales revenue and account receivable in Mexican pesos, which is the currency in which it keeps its books and prepares financial statements.

The currency in which financial statement amounts are presented is known as the **presentation currency**. In most cases, a company's presentation currency will be the currency of the country where the company is located. Finnish companies are required to keep accounting records and present financial results in euro, US companies in US dollars, Chinese companies in Chinese yuan, and so on.

Another important concept in accounting for foreign currency activities is the **functional currency**, which is the currency of the primary economic environment in which an entity operates. Normally, the functional currency is the currency in which an entity primarily generates and expends cash. In most cases, an organization's functional currency will be the same as its presentation currency. And, because most companies primarily generate and expend cash in the currency of the country where they are located, the functional and presentation currencies are most often the same as the **local currency** where the company operates.

Because the local currency generally is an entity's functional currency, a multinational corporation with subsidiaries in a variety of different countries is likely to have a variety of different functional currencies. The Thai subsidiary of a Japanese parent company, for example, is likely to have the Thai baht as its functional currency, whereas the Japanese parent's functional currency is the Japanese yen. But in some cases, the foreign subsidiary could have the parent's functional currency as its own. For example, prior to its 2011 acquisition of McAfee, Intel Corporation had determined that the US dollar was the functional currency for all of its significant foreign subsidiaries. However, subsequent to the acquisition of McAfee, as stated in Intel Corporation's 2011 Annual Report, Note 1: Basis of Presentation, "Certain of the operations acquired from McAfee have a functional currency other than the US dollar."

By definition, a foreign currency is any currency other than a company's functional currency, and **foreign currency transactions** are those denominated in a currency other than the company's functional currency. Foreign currency transactions occur when a company (1) makes an import purchase or an export sale that is denominated in a foreign currency or (2) borrows or lends funds where the amount to be repaid or received is denominated in a foreign currency. In each of these cases, the company has an asset or a liability denominated in a foreign currency.

2.1 Foreign Currency Transaction Exposure to Foreign Exchange Risk

Assume that FinnCo, a Finland-based company, imports goods from Mexico in January under 45-day credit terms, and the purchase is denominated in Mexican pesos. By deferring payment until April, FinnCo runs the risk that from the date the purchase is made until the date of payment, the value of the Mexican peso might increase relative to the euro. FinnCo would then need to spend more euro to settle its Mexican peso account payable. In this case, FinnCo is said to have an **exposure to foreign exchange risk**. Specifically, FinnCo has a foreign currency **transaction exposure**. Transaction exposure related to imports and exports can be summarized as follows:

- *Import purchase.* A transaction exposure arises when the importer is obligated to pay in foreign currency and is allowed to defer payment until sometime after the purchase date. The importer is exposed to the risk that from the purchase date until the payment date the foreign currency might increase in value, thereby increasing the amount of functional currency that must be spent to acquire enough foreign currency to settle the account payable.

- *Export sale.* A transaction exposure arises when the exporter agrees to be paid in foreign currency and allows payment to be made sometime after the purchase date. The exporter is exposed to the risk that from the purchase date until the payment date, the foreign currency might decrease in value, thereby decreasing the amount of functional currency into which the foreign currency can be converted when it is received.

The major issue in accounting for foreign currency transactions is how to account for the foreign currency risk—that is, how to reflect in the financial statements the change in value of the foreign currency asset or liability. Both IFRS and US GAAP require the change in the value of the foreign currency asset or liability resulting from a foreign currency transaction to be treated as a gain or loss reported on the income statement.[3]

2.1.1 *Accounting for Foreign Currency Transactions with Settlement before Balance Sheet Date*

Example 1 demonstrates FinnCo's accounting, assuming that it purchased goods on account from a Mexican supplier that required payment in Mexican pesos, and that it made payment before the balance sheet date. The basic principle is that all transactions are recorded at the spot rate on the date of the transaction. The foreign currency risk on *transactions*, therefore, arises only when the transaction date and the payment date are different.

---

3 International standards are presented in International Accounting Standard (IAS) 21, "The Effects of Changes in Foreign Exchange Rates," and US GAAP standards are presented in FASB ASC Topic 830, "Foreign Currency Matters."

EXAMPLE 1

Accounting for Foreign Currency Transactions with Settlement before the Balance Sheet Date

FinnCo purchases goods from its Mexican supplier on 1 November 20X1; the purchase price is 100,000 Mexican pesos. Credit terms allow payment in 45 days, and FinnCo makes payment of 100,000 pesos on 15 December 20X1. FinnCo's functional and presentation currency is the euro. Spot exchange rates between the euro (EUR) and Mexican peso (MXN) are as follows:

1 November 20X1	MXN1 = EUR0.0684
15 December 20X1	MXN1 = EUR0.0703

FinnCo's fiscal year end is 31 December. How will FinnCo account for this foreign currency transaction, and what effect will it have on the 20X1 financial statements?

Solution:

The euro value of the Mexican peso account payable on 1 November 20X1 was EUR6,840 (MXN100,000 × EUR0.0684). FinnCo could have paid for its inventory on 1 November by converting 6,840 euro into 100,000 Mexican pesos. Instead, the company purchases 100,000 Mexican pesos on 15 December 20X1, when the value of the peso has increased to EUR0.0703. Thus, FinnCo pays 7,030 euro to purchase 100,000 Mexican pesos. The net result is a loss of 190 euro (EUR7,030 − EUR6,840).

Although the cash outflow to acquire the inventory is EUR7,030, the cost included in the inventory account is only EUR6,840. This cost represents the amount that FinnCo could have paid if it had not waited 45 days to settle its account. By deferring payment, and because the Mexican peso increased in value between the transaction date and settlement date, FinnCo has to pay an additional 190 euro. The company will report a foreign exchange loss of EUR190 in its net income in 20X1. This is a realized loss because FinnCo actually spent an additional 190 euro to purchase its inventory. The net effect on the financial statements, in EUR, can be seen as follows:

Balance Sheet				Income Statement	
Assets		**= Liabilities +**	**Stockholders' Equity**	**Revenues and Gains**	**Expenses and Losses**
Cash	−7,030		Retained		Foreign
Inventory	+6,840		earnings −190		exchange loss −190
	−190				

2.1.2 *Accounting for Foreign Currency Transactions with Intervening Balance Sheet Dates*

Another important issue related to the accounting for foreign currency transactions is what, if anything, should be done if a balance sheet date falls between the initial transaction date and the settlement date. For foreign currency transactions whose settlement dates fall in subsequent accounting periods, both IFRS and US GAAP require adjustments to reflect intervening changes in currency exchange rates. Foreign currency transaction gains and losses are reported on the income statement, creating one of the few situations in which accounting rules allow, indeed require, companies to include (recognize) a gain or loss in income before it has been realized.

Subsequent foreign currency transaction gains and losses are recognized from the balance sheet date through the date the transaction is settled. Adding together foreign currency transaction gains and losses for both accounting periods (transaction initiation to balance sheet date and balance sheet date to transaction settlement) produces an amount equal to the actual realized gain or loss on the foreign currency transaction.

EXAMPLE 2

Accounting for Foreign Currency Transaction with Intervening Balance Sheet Date

FinnCo sells goods to a customer in the United Kingdom for £10,000 on 15 November 20X1, with payment to be received in British pounds on 15 January 20X2. FinnCo's functional and presentation currency is the euro. Spot exchange rates between the euro (€) and British pound (£) are as follows:

15 November 20X1	£1 = €1.460
31 December 20X1	£1 = €1.480
15 January 20X2	£1 = €1.475

FinnCo's fiscal year end is 31 December. How will FinnCo account for this foreign currency transaction, and what effect will it have on the 20X1 and 20X2 financial statements?

Solution:

The euro value of the British pound account receivable at each of the three relevant dates is determined as follows:

		Account Receivable (£10,000)	
Date	€/£ Exchange Rate	Euro Value	Change in Euro Value
15 Nov 20X1	€1.460	14,600	N/A
31 Dec 20X1	€1.480	14,800	+ 200
15 Jan 20X2	€1.475	14,750	− 50

A change in the euro value of the British pound receivable from 15 November to 31 December would be recognized as a foreign currency transaction gain or loss on FinnCo's 20X1 income statement. In this case, the increase in the value of the British pound results in a transaction gain of €200 [£10,000 × (€1.48 − €1.46)]. Note that the gain recognized in 20X1 income is unrealized, and remember that this is one of few situations in which companies include an unrealized gain in income.

Any change in the exchange rate between the euro and British pound that occurs from the balance sheet date (31 December 20X1) to the transaction settlement date (15 January 20X2) will also result in a foreign currency transaction gain or loss. In our example, the British pound weakened slightly against the euro during this period, resulting in an exchange rate of €1.475/ £1 on 15 January 20X2. The £10,000 account receivable now has a value of €14,750, which is a decrease of €50 from 31 December 20X1. FinnCo will recognize a foreign currency transaction loss on 15 January 20X2 of €50 that will be included in the company's calculation of net income for the first quarter of 20X2.

From the transaction date to the settlement date, the British pound has increased in value by €0.015 (€1.475 − €1.460), which generates a realized foreign currency transaction gain of €150. A gain of €200 was recognized in 20X1 and

> a loss of €50 is recognized in 20X2. Over the two-month period, the net gain recognized in the financial statements is equal to the actual realized gain on the foreign currency transaction.

In Example 2, FinnCo's British pound account receivable resulted in a net foreign currency transaction gain because the British pound strengthened (increased) in value between the transaction date and the settlement date. In this case, FinnCo has an asset exposure to foreign exchange risk. This asset exposure benefited the company because the foreign currency strengthened. If FinnCo instead had a British pound account payable, a liability exposure would have existed. The euro value of the British pound account payable would have increased as the British pound strengthened, and FinnCo would have recognized a foreign currency transaction loss as a result.

Whether a change in exchange rate results in a foreign currency transaction gain or loss (measured in local currency) depends on (1) the nature of the exposure to foreign exchange risk (asset or liability) and (2) the direction of change in the value of the foreign currency (strengthens or weakens).

		Foreign Currency	
Transaction	**Type of Exposure**	**Strengthens**	**Weakens**
Export sale	Asset (account receivable)	Gain	Loss
Import purchase	Liability (account payable)	Loss	Gain

A foreign currency receivable arising from an export sale creates an asset exposure to foreign exchange risk. If the foreign currency strengthens, the receivable increases in value in terms of the company's functional currency and a foreign currency transaction gain arises. The company will be able to convert the foreign currency when received into more units of functional currency because the foreign currency has strengthened. Conversely, if the foreign currency weakens, the foreign currency receivable loses value in terms of the functional currency and a loss results.

A foreign currency payable resulting from an import purchase creates a liability exposure to foreign exchange risk. If the foreign currency strengthens, the payable increases in value in terms of the company's functional currency and a foreign currency transaction loss arises. The company must spend more units of functional currency to be able to settle the foreign currency liability because the foreign currency has strengthened. Conversely, if the foreign currency weakens, the foreign currency payable loses value in terms of the functional currency and a gain exists.

2.2 Analytical Issues

Both IFRS and US GAAP require foreign currency transaction gains and losses to be reported in net income (even if the gains and losses have not yet been realized), but neither standard indicates where on the income statement these gains and losses should be placed. The two most common treatments are either (1) as a component of other operating income/expense or (2) as a component of non-operating income/expense, in some cases as a part of net financing cost. The calculation of operating profit margin is affected by where foreign currency transaction gains or losses are placed on the income statement.

EXAMPLE 3

Placement of Foreign Currency Transaction Gains/Losses on the Income Statement—Effect on Operating Profit

Assume that FinnCo had the following income statement information in both 20X1 and 20X2, excluding a foreign currency transaction gain of €200 in 20X1 and a transaction loss of €50 in 20X2.

	20X1	20X2
Revenues	€20,000	€20,000
Cost of goods sold	12,000	12,000
Other operating expenses, net	5,000	5,000
Non-operating expenses, net	1,200	1,200

FinnCo is deciding between two alternatives for the treatment of foreign currency transaction gains and losses. Alternative 1 calls for the reporting of foreign currency transaction gains/losses as part of "Other operating expenses, net." Under Alternative 2, the company would report this information as part of "Non-operating expenses, net."

FinnCo's fiscal year end is 31 December. How will Alternatives 1 and 2 affect the company's gross profit margin, operating profit margin, and net profit margin for 20X1? For 20X2?

Solution:

Remember that a gain would serve to reduce expenses, whereas a loss would increase expenses.

20X1—Transaction Gain of €200		
	Alternative 1	**Alternative 2**
Revenues	€20,000	€20,000
Cost of goods sold	(12,000)	(12,000)
Gross profit	8,000	8,000
Other operating expenses, net	(4,800) incl. gain	(5,000)
Operating profit	3,200	3,000
Non-operating expenses, net	(1,200)	(1,000) incl. gain
Net profit	€2,000	€2,000

Profit margins in 20X1 under the two alternatives can be calculated as follows:

	Alternative 1	**Alternative 2**
Gross profit margin	€8,000/€20,000 = 40.0%	€8,000/€20,000 = 40.0%
Operating profit margin	3,200/20,000 = 16.0%	3,000/20,000 = 15.0%
Net profit margin	2,000/20,000 = 10.0%	2,000/20,000 = 10.0%

20X2—Transaction Loss of €50		
	Alternative 1	**Alternative 2**
Revenues	€20,000	€20,000
Cost of goods sold	(12,000)	(12,000)

20X2—Transaction Loss of €50		
	Alternative 1	**Alternative 2**
Gross profit	8,000	8,000
Other operating expenses, net	(5,050) incl. loss	(5,000)
Operating profit	2,950	3,000
Non-operating expenses, net	(1,200)	(1,250) incl. loss
Net profit	€1,750	€1,750

Profit margins in 20X2 under the two alternatives can be calculated as follows:

	Alternative 1	**Alternative 2**
Gross profit margin	€8,000/€20,000 = 40.0%	€8,000/€20,000 = 40.0%
Operating profit margin	2,950/20,000 = 14.75%	3,000/20,000 = 15.0%
Net profit margin	1,750/20,000 = 8.75%	1,750/20,000 = 8.75%

Gross profit and net profit are unaffected, but operating profit differs under the two alternatives. In 20X1, the operating profit margin is larger under Alternative 1, which includes the transaction gain as part of "Other operating expenses, net." In 20X2, Alternative 1 results in a smaller operating profit margin than Alternative 2. Alternative 2 has the same operating profit margin in both periods. Because exchange rates do not fluctuate by the same amount or in the same direction from one accounting period to the next, Alternative 1 will cause greater volatility in operating profit and operating profit margin over time.

Because accounting standards do not provide guidance on the placement of foreign currency transaction gains and losses on the income statement, companies are free to choose among the alternatives. Two companies in the same industry could choose different alternatives, which would distort the direct comparison of operating profit and operating profit margins between those companies.

A second issue that should be of interest to analysts relates to the fact that unrealized foreign currency transaction gains and losses are included in net income when the balance sheet date falls between the transaction and settlement dates. The implicit assumption underlying this accounting requirement is that the unrealized gain or loss as of the balance sheet date reflects the company's ultimate net gain or loss. In reality, though, the ultimate net gain or loss may vary dramatically because of the possibility for changes in trend and volatility of currency prices.

This effect was seen in the previous hypothetical Example 2 with FinnCo. Using given currency exchange rate data shows that the real-world effect can also be quite dramatic. Assume that a French company purchased goods from a Canadian supplier on 1 December 20X1, with payment of 100,000 Canadian dollars (C$) to be made on 15 May 20X2. Actual exchange rates between the Canadian dollar and euro (€) during the period 1 December 20X1 and 15 May 20X2, the euro value of the Canadian dollar account payable, and the foreign currency transaction gain or loss are shown below:

	€/C$	**Account Payable (C$100,000)**	
		€ Value	**Change in € Value (Gain/Loss)**
1 Dec X1	0.7285	72,850	N/A
31 Dec X1	0.7571	75,710	2,860 loss

(continued)

	€/C$	Account Payable (C$100,000)	
		€ Value	Change in € Value (Gain/Loss)
31 Mar X2	0.7517	75,170	540 gain
15 May X2	0.7753	77,530	2,360 loss

As the Canadian dollar strengthened against the euro in late 20X1, the French company would have recorded a foreign currency transaction loss of €2,860 in the fourth quarter of 20X1. The Canadian dollar reversed course by weakening over the first three months of 20X2, resulting in a transaction gain of €540 in the first quarter, and then strengthened against the euro in the second quarter of 20X2, resulting in a transaction loss of €2,360. At the time payment is made on 15 May 20X2, the French company realizes a net foreign currency transaction loss of €4,680 (€77,530 − €72,850).

2.3 Disclosures Related to Foreign Currency Transaction Gains and Losses

Because accounting rules allow companies to choose where they present foreign currency transaction gains and losses on the income statement, it is useful for companies to disclose both the amount of transaction gain or loss that is included in income and the presentation alternative they have selected. IFRS require disclosure of "the amount of exchange differences recognized in profit or loss," and US GAAP require disclosure of "the aggregate transaction gain or loss included in determining net income for the period," but neither standard specifically requires disclosure of the line item in which these gains and losses are located.

Exhibit 1 provides disclosures from BASF AG's 2011 annual report that the German company made related to foreign currency transaction gains and losses. Exhibit 2 presents similar disclosures found in the Netherlands-based Heineken NV's 2011 Annual Report. Both companies use IFRS to prepare their consolidated financial statements.

BASF's income statement in Exhibit 1 does not include a separate line item for foreign currency gains and losses. From Note 6 in Exhibit 1, an analyst can determine that BASF has chosen to include "Income from foreign currency and hedging transactions" in "Other operating income." Of the total amount of €2,008 million reported as "Other operating income" in 2011, €170 million is attributable to foreign currency and hedging transaction income. It is not possible to determine from BASF's financial statements whether or not these gains were realized in 2011, and any unrealized gain reported in 2011 income might or might not be realized in 2012.

Note 7 in Exhibit 1 indicates that "Expenses from foreign currency and hedging transactions as well as market valuation" in 2011 were €399 million, making up 15% of Other operating expenses. Combining foreign currency transaction gains and losses results in a net loss of €229 million, which is equal to 2.55% of BASF's "Income before taxes and minority interests."

Exhibit 1	Excerpts from BASF AG's 2011 Annual Report Related to Foreign Currency Transactions

Consolidated Statements of Income Million €	Explanation in Notes	2011	2010
Sales	(4)	73,497	63,873
Cost of sales		(53,986)	(45,310)
Gross profit on sales		**19,511**	**18,563**
Selling expenses		(7,323)	(6,700)

Exhibit 1   (Continued)

Consolidated Statements of Income Million €	Explanation in Notes	2011	2010
General and administrative expenses		(1,315)	(1,138)
Research and development expenses		(1,605)	(1,492)
Other operating income	(6)	2,008	1,140
Other operating expenses	(7)	(2,690)	(2,612)
Income from operations	(4)	**8,586**	**7,761**
(detail omitted)			
Financial result	(8)	**384**	**(388)**
Income before taxes and minority interests		**8,970**	**7,373**
Income taxes	(9)	(2,367)	(2,299)
Income before minority interests		**6,603**	**5,074**
Minority interests	(10)	(415)	(517)
Net income		**6,188**	**4,557**

Notes:

1   Summary of Accounting Policies

Foreign currency transactions: The cost of assets acquired in foreign currencies and revenues from sales in foreign currencies are recorded at the exchange rate on the date of the transaction. Foreign currency receivables and liabilities are valued at the exchange rates on the balance sheet date.

6   Other Operating Income

Million €	2011	2010
Reversal and adjustment of provisions	170	244
Revenue from miscellaneous revenue-generating activities	207	142
Income from foreign currency and hedging transactions	170	136
Income from the translation of financial statements in foreign currencies	42	76
Gains on the disposal of property, plant and equipment and divestitures	666	101
Reversals of impairments of property, plant and equipment	—	40
Gains on the reversal of allowance for doubtful business-related receivables	77	36
Other	676	365
	2,008	1,140

Income from foreign currency and hedging transactions concerned foreign currency transactions, the measurement at fair value of receivables and payables in foreign currencies, as well as currency derivatives and other hedging transactions.

7   Other Operating Expenses

(continued)

Exhibit 1   (Continued)

Million €	2011	2010
Restructuring measures	233	276
Environmental protection and safety measures, costs of demolition and removal, and planning expenses related to capital expenditures that are not subject to mandatory capitalization	203	98
Valuation adjustments on tangible and intangible assets	366	247
Costs from miscellaneous revenue-generating activities	220	180
Expenses from foreign currency and hedging transactions as well as market valuation	399	601
Losses from the translation of the financial statements in foreign currencies	56	63
Losses from the disposal of property, plant and equipment and divestitures	40	24
Oil and gas exploration expenses	184	190
Expenses from additions to allowances for business-related receivables	124	107
Expenses from the use of inventories measured at market value and the derecognition of obsolete inventory	233	188
Other	632	638
	2,690	2,612

Expenses from foreign currency and hedging transactions as well as market valuation concern foreign currency translations of receivables and payables as well as changes in the fair value of currency derivatives and other hedging transactions.

In Exhibit 2, Heineken's Note 2, Basis of Preparation, part (c) explicitly states that the euro is the company's functional currency. Note 3(b)*(i)* indicates that monetary assets and liabilities denominated in foreign currencies at the balance sheet date are translated to the functional currency and that foreign currency differences arising on the translation (i.e., translation gains and losses) are recognized on the income statement. Note 3(r) discloses that foreign currency gains and losses are included on a net basis in the other net finance income and expenses. Note 12, "Net finance income and expense," shows that a net foreign exchange loss of €107 million existed in 2011 and a net gain of €61 million arose in 2010. The net foreign currency transaction gain in 2010 amounted to 3.1% of Heineken's profit before income tax that year, and the net translation loss in 2011 represented 5.3% of the company's profit before income tax in that year. Note 12 also shows gains and losses related to changes in the fair value of derivatives, some of which related to foreign currency derivatives.

Exhibit 2   Excerpts from Heineken NV's 2011 Annual Report Related to Foreign Currency Transactions

Consolidated Income Statement for the Year Ended 31 December in Millions of EUR	Note	2011	2010
Revenue	5	17,123	16,133
Other income	8	64	239

Exhibit 2   (Continued)

Consolidated Income Statement for the Year Ended 31 December in Millions of EUR	Note	2011	2010
Raw materials, consumables, and services	9	(10,966)	(10,291)
Personnel expenses	10	(2,838)	(2,665)
Amortisation, depreciation, and impairments	11	(1,168)	(1,118)
Total expenses		**(14,972)**	**(14,074)**
Results from operating activities		**2,215**	**2,298**
Interest income	12	70	100
Interest expenses	12	(494)	(590)
Other net finance income/(expenses)	12	(6)	(19)
Net finance expenses		**(430)**	**(509)**
Share of profit of associates and joint ventures and impairments thereof (net of income tax)	16	240	193
Profit before income tax		**2,025**	**1,982**
Income tax expenses	13	(465)	(403)
Profit		**1,560**	**1,579**
Attributable to:			
Equity holders of the Company (net profit)		1,430	1,447
Minority interest		130	132
Profit		**1,560**	**1,579**

Notes:

2   Basis of preparation

   c   Functional and presentation currency

These consolidated financial statements are presented in euro, which is the Company's functional currency. All financial information presented in euro has been rounded to the nearest million unless stated otherwise.

3   Significant accounting policies

   b   Foreign currency

     i. Foreign currency transactions

Transactions in foreign currencies are translated to the respective functional currencies of Heineken entities at the exchange rates at the dates of the transactions. Monetary assets and liabilities denominated in foreign currencies at the reporting date are retranslated to the functional currency at the exchange rate at that date. . . . Foreign currency differences arising on retranslation are recognised in profit or loss, except for differences arising on the retranslation of available-for-sale (equity) investments and foreign currency differences arising on the retranslation of a financial liability designated as a hedge of a net investment, which are recognised in other comprehensive income.[4]

(continued)

---

4 Note that this excerpt uses "retranslation" in the same way that "translation" is used throughout the rest of this reading. The translation of currency for foreign subsidiaries will be covered in the next section.

Exhibit 2   (Continued)

r   Interest income, interest expenses and other net finance income and expenses

...Foreign currency gains and losses are reported on a net basis in the other net finance income and expenses.

12 Net finance income and expense

Recognised in profit or loss

In millions of EUR	2011	2010
Interest income	**70**	**100**
Interest expenses	**(494)**	**(590)**
Dividend income on available-for-sale investments	2	1
Dividend income on investments held for trading	11	7
Net gain/(loss) on disposal of available-for-sale investments	1	—
Net change in fair value of derivatives	96	(75)
Net foreign exchange gain/(loss)	(107)	61
Impairment losses on available-for-sale investments	—	(3)
Unwinding discount on provisions	(7)	(7)
Other net financial income/(expenses)	(2)	(3)
Other net finance income/(expenses)	**(6)**	**(19)**
Net finance income/(expenses)	**(430)**	**(509)**

Disclosures related to foreign currency are commonly found both in the Management Discussion & Analysis (MD&A) and the Notes to Financial Statements sections of an annual report. In applying US GAAP to account for its foreign currency transactions, Yahoo! Inc. reported the following in the Quantitative and Qualitative Disclosures about Market Risk section of its 2011 annual report:

> Our exposure to foreign currency transaction gains and losses is the result of assets and liabilities, (including inter-company transactions) that are denominated in currencies other than the relevant entity's functional currency.... We may enter into derivative instruments, such as foreign currency forward contracts or other instruments to minimize the short-term foreign currency fluctuations on such assets and liabilities. The gains and losses on the forward contracts may not offset any or more than a portion of the transaction gains and losses on certain foreign currency receivables, investments and payables recognized in earnings. Transaction gains and losses on these foreign exchange contracts are recognized each period in other income, net included on the consolidated statements of income. During the years ended December 31, 2011, 2010, and 2009, we recorded net realized and unrealized foreign currency transaction gains of $9 million and $13 million, and a transaction loss of $1 million, respectively.

Yahoo!'s disclosure clearly explains that both realized and unrealized foreign currency transaction gains and losses are reflected in income, specifically as a part of non-operating activities. The net foreign currency transaction gain in 2011 of $9 million represented only 1.1% of the company's pretax income ($827.5 million) for the year.

Some companies may choose not to disclose either the location or the amount of their foreign currency transaction gains and losses, presumably because the amounts involved are immaterial. There are several reasons why the amount of transaction gains and losses can be immaterial for a company:

1 The company engages in a limited number of foreign currency transactions that involve relatively small amounts of foreign currency.

2 The exchange rates between the company's functional currency and the foreign currencies in which it has transactions tend to be relatively stable.

3 Gains on some foreign currency transactions are naturally offset by losses on other transactions, such that the net gain or loss is immaterial. For example, if a US company sells goods to a customer in Canada with payment in Canadian dollars to be received in 90 days and at the same time purchases goods from a supplier in Canada with payment to be made in Canadian dollars in 90 days, any loss that arises on the Canadian dollar receivable due to a weakening in the value of the Canadian dollar will be exactly offset by a gain of equal amount on the Canadian dollar payable.

4 The company engages in foreign currency hedging activities to offset the foreign exchange gains and losses that arise from foreign currency transactions. Hedging foreign exchange risk is a common practice for many companies engaged in foreign currency transactions.

The two most common types of hedging instruments used to minimize foreign exchange transaction risk are foreign currency forward contracts and foreign currency options. Nokia Corporation describes its foreign exchange risk management approach in its 2011 Form 20-F annual report in Note 34, Risk Management. An excerpt from that note follows:

> Nokia operates globally and is thus exposed to foreign exchange risk arising from various currencies. Foreign currency denominated assets and liabilities together with foreign currency denominated cash flows from highly probable or probable purchases and sales contribute to foreign exchange exposure. These transaction exposures are managed against various local currencies because of Nokia's substantial production and sales outside the Euro zone.
>
> According to the foreign exchange policy guidelines of the Group, which remains the same as in the previous year, material transaction foreign exchange exposures are hedged unless hedging would be uneconomical due to market liquidity and/or hedging cost. Exposures are defined using nominal values of the transactions. Exposures are mainly hedged with derivative financial instruments such as forward foreign exchange contracts and foreign exchange options. The majority of financial instruments hedging foreign exchange risk have duration of less than a year. The Group does not hedge forecasted foreign currency cash flows beyond two years.

Elsewhere in its annual report, Nokia provides additional disclosures about the currencies to which it has exposure and the accounting for different types of hedges. The company also summarizes the effect of material exchange rate movements. For example, the 4.2% appreciation of the US dollar in 2011 had a positive effect on net sales expressed in euro (40% of Nokia's net sales are in US dollars or currencies closely following the US dollar) and a negative effect on product cost (60% of Nokia's components are sourced in US dollars); this resulted in a slightly negative effect on operating profit.

3 TRANSLATION OF FOREIGN CURRENCY FINANCIAL STATEMENTS

Many companies have operations in foreign countries. Most operations located in foreign countries keep their accounting records and prepare financial statements in the local currency. For example, the US subsidiary of German automaker BMW AG keeps its books in US dollars. IFRS and US GAAP require parent companies to prepare consolidated financial statements in which the assets, liabilities, revenues, and expenses of both domestic and foreign subsidiaries are added to those of the parent company. To prepare worldwide consolidated statements, parent companies must translate the foreign currency financial statements of their foreign subsidiaries into the parent company's presentation currency. BMW AG, for example, must translate both the US dollar financial statements of its US subsidiary and the South African rand financial statements of its South African subsidiary into euro to consolidate these foreign operations. If, for example, the US dollar and South African rand appreciate against the euro over the course of a given year, the amount of sales translated into euro will be greater than if the subsidiary's currencies weaken against the euro.

IFRS and US GAAP have similar rules for the translation of foreign currency financial statements. To fully understand the results from applying these rules, however, several conceptual issues must first be examined.

3.1 Translation Conceptual Issues

In translating foreign currency financial statements into the parent company's presentation currency, two questions must be addressed:

1 What is the appropriate exchange rate to use in translating each financial statement item?

2 How should the translation adjustment that inherently arises from the translation process be reflected in the consolidated financial statements? In other words, how is the balance sheet brought back into balance?

These issues and the basic concepts underlying the translation of financial statements are demonstrated through the following example.

Spanco is a hypothetical Spain-based company that uses the euro as its presentation currency. Spanco establishes a wholly owned subsidiary, Amerco, in the United States on 31 December 20X1 by investing €10,000 when the exchange rate between the euro and the US dollar is €1 = US$1. The equity investment of €10,000 is physically converted into US$10,000 to begin operations. In addition, Amerco borrows US$5,000 from local banks on 31 December 20X1. Amerco purchases inventory that costs US$12,000 on 31 December 20X1 and retains US$3,000 in cash. Amerco's balance sheet at 31 December 20X1 thus appears as follows:

Amerco Balance Sheet, 31 December 20X1 (in US Dollars)

Cash	$ 3,000	Notes payable	$ 5,000
Inventory	12,000	Common stock	10,000
Total	$15,000	Total	$15,000

To prepare a consolidated balance sheet in euro as of 31 December 20X1, Spanco must translate all of the US dollar balances on Amerco's balance sheet at the €1 = US$1 exchange rate. The translation worksheet as of 31 December 20X1 is as follows:

Translation Worksheet for Amerco, 31 December 20X1

	USD	Exchange Rate (€)	EUR
Cash	$ 3,000	1.00	€3,000
Inventory	12,000	1.00	12,000
Total	$15,000		€15,000
Notes payable	5,000	1.00	5,000
Common stock	10,000	1.00	10,000
Total	$15,000		€15,000

By translating each US dollar balance at the same exchange rate (€1.00), Amerco's translated balance sheet in euro reflects an equal amount of total assets and total liabilities plus equity and remains in balance.

During the first quarter of 20X2, Amerco engages in no transactions. During that period, however, the US dollar weakens against the euro such that the exchange rate on 31 March 20X2 is €0.80 = US$1.

To prepare a consolidated balance sheet at the end of the first quarter of 20X2, Spanco now must choose between the current exchange rate of €0.80 and the historical exchange rate of €1.00 to translate Amerco's balance sheet amounts into euro. The original investment made by Spanco of €10,000 is a historical fact, so the company wants to translate Amerco's common stock in such a way that it continues to reflect this amount. This goal is achieved by translating common stock of US$10,000 into euro using the historical exchange rate of €1 = US$1.

Two approaches for translating the foreign subsidiary's assets and liabilities are as follows:

1 All assets and liabilities are translated at the **current exchange rate** (the spot exchange rate on the balance sheet date).

2 Only **monetary assets and liabilities** are translated at the current exchange rate; **non-monetary assets and liabilities** are translated at **historical exchange rates** (the exchange rates that existed when the assets and liabilities were acquired). Monetary items are cash and receivables (payables) that are to be received (paid) in a fixed number of currency units. Non-monetary assets include inventory, fixed assets, and intangibles, and non-monetary liabilities include deferred revenue.

These two different approaches are demonstrated and the results analyzed in turn.

3.1.1 All Assets and Liabilities Are Translated at the Current Exchange Rate

The translation worksheet on 31 March 20X2, in which all assets and liabilities are translated at the current exchange rate (€0.80), is as follows:

Translation Worksheet for Amerco, 31 March 20X2

	US Dollar	Exchange Rate (€)	Euro	Change in Euro Value since 31 Dec 20X1
Cash	$ 3,000	0.80 C	€2,400	−€600
Inventory	12,000	0.80 C	9,600	−2,400
Total	$15,000		€12,000	−€3,000
Notes payable	5,000	0.80 C	4,000	−1,000
Common stock	10,000	1.00 H	10,000	0

(continued)

Translation Worksheet for Amerco, 31 March 20X2

	US Dollar	Exchange Rate (€)	Euro	Change in Euro Value since 31 Dec 20X1
Subtotal	$15,000		14,000	−1,000
Translation adjustment			(2,000)	−2,000
Total			€12,000	−€3,000

Note: C = current exchange rate; H = historical exchange rate

By translating all assets at the lower current exchange rate, total assets are written down from 31 December 20X1 to 31 March 20X2 in terms of their euro value by €3,000. Liabilities are written down by €1,000. To keep the euro translated balance sheet in balance, a *negative* translation adjustment of €2,000 is created and included in stockholders' equity on the consolidated balance sheet.

Those foreign currency balance sheet accounts that are translated using the current exchange rate are revalued in terms of the parent's functional currency. This process is very similar to the revaluation of foreign currency receivables and payables related to foreign currency transactions. The net translation adjustment that results from translating individual assets and liabilities at the current exchange rate can be viewed as the *net* foreign currency translation gain or loss caused by a change in the exchange rate:

(€600)	loss on cash
(€2,400)	loss on inventory
€1,000	gain on notes payable
(€2,000)	net translation loss

The negative translation adjustment (net translation loss) does not result in a cash outflow of €2,000 for Spanco and thus is unrealized. The loss could be realized, however, if Spanco were to sell Amerco at its book value of US$10,000. The proceeds from the sale would be converted into euro at €0.80 per US$1, resulting in a cash inflow of €8,000. Because Spanco originally invested €10,000 in its US operation, a *realized* loss of €2,000 would result.

The second conceptual issue related to the translation of foreign currency financial statements is whether the unrealized net translation loss should be included in the determination of consolidated net income currently or deferred in the stockholders' equity section of the consolidated balance sheet until the loss is realized through sale of the foreign subsidiary. There is some debate as to which of these two treatments is most appropriate. This issue is discussed in more detail after considering the second approach for translating assets and liabilities.

3.1.2 *Only Monetary Assets and Monetary Liabilities Are Translated at the Current Exchange Rate*

Now assume only monetary assets and monetary liabilities are translated at the current exchange rate. The worksheet at 31 March 20X2, in which only monetary assets and liabilities are translated at the current exchange rate (€0.80), is as follows:

Translation Worksheet for Amerco, 31 March 20X2

	US Dollar	Exchange Rate (€)	Euro	Change in Euro Value since 31 Dec 20X1
Cash	$ 3,000	0.80 C	€2,400	−€600
Inventory	12,000	1.00 H	12,000	0
Total	$15,000		€14,400	−€600
Notes payable	5,000	0.80 C	4,000	−1,000
Common stock	10,000	1.00 H	10,000	0
Subtotal	$15,000		14,000	−1,000
Translation adjustment			400	400
Total			€14,400	−€600

Note: C = current exchange rate; H = historical exchange rate

Using this approach, cash is written down by €600 but inventory continues to be carried at its euro historical cost of €12,000. Notes payable is written down by €1,000. To keep the balance sheet in balance, a positive translation adjustment of €400 must be included in stockholders' equity. The translation adjustment reflects the *net* translation gain or loss related to monetary items only:

(€600)	loss on cash
€1,000	gain on notes payable
€400	net translation gain

The positive translation adjustment (net translation gain) also is *unrealized*. The gain could be *realized*, however, if:

1 The subsidiary uses its cash (US$3,000) to pay as much of its liabilities as possible, and

2 The parent sends enough euro to the subsidiary to pay its remaining liabilities (US$5,000 − US$3,000 = US$2,000). As of 31 December 20X1, at the €1.00 per US$1 exchange rate, Spanco will have sent €2,000 to Amerco to pay liabilities of US$2,000. On 31 March 20X2, given the €0.80 per US$1 exchange rate, the parent needs to send only €1,600 to pay US$2,000 of liabilities. As a result, Spanco would enjoy a foreign exchange gain of €400.

The second conceptual issue again arises under this approach. Should the unrealized foreign exchange gain be recognized in current period net income or deferred on the balance sheet as a separate component of stockholders' equity? The answer to this question, as provided by IFRS and US GAAP, is described in Section 3.2, Translation Methods.

3.1.3 Balance Sheet Exposure

Those assets and liabilities translated at the *current* exchange rate are revalued from balance sheet to balance sheet in terms of the parent company's presentation currency. These items are said to be *exposed* to translation adjustment. Balance sheet items translated at *historical* exchange rates do not change in parent currency value and therefore are not exposed to translation adjustment. Exposure to translation adjustment is referred to as balance sheet translation exposure, or accounting exposure.

A foreign operation will have a **net asset balance sheet exposure** when assets translated at the current exchange rate are greater than liabilities translated at the current exchange rate. A **net liability balance sheet exposure** exists when liabilities translated at the current exchange rate are greater than assets translated at the current exchange rate. Another way to think about the issue is to realize that there is a net asset balance sheet exposure when exposed assets are greater than exposed liabilities and a net liability balance sheet exposure when exposed liabilities are greater than exposed assets. The sign (positive or negative) of the current period's translation adjustment is a function of two factors: (1) the nature of the balance sheet exposure (asset or liability) and (2) the direction of change in the exchange rate (strengthens or weakens). The relationship between exchange rate fluctuations, balance sheet exposure, and the current period's translation adjustment can be summarized as follows:

Balance Sheet Exposure	Foreign Currency (FC)	
	Strengthens	**Weakens**
Net asset	Positive translation adjustment	Negative translation adjustment
Net liability	Negative translation adjustment	Positive translation adjustment

These relationships are the same as those summarized in Section 2.2 with respect to foreign currency transaction gains and losses. In reference to the example in Section 3.1.2, for instance, the amount of exposed assets (the US$3,000 cash) was less than the amount of exposed liabilities (US$5,000 of notes payable), implying a net liability exposure. Further, in the example the foreign currency (US$) weakened, resulting in a positive translation adjustment.

The combination of balance sheet exposure and direction of exchange rate change determines whether the current period's translation adjustment will be positive or negative. After the initial period of operations, a cumulative translation adjustment is required to keep the translated balance sheet in balance. The cumulative translation adjustment will be the sum of the translation adjustments that arise over successive accounting periods. For example, assume that Spanco translates all of Amerco's assets and liabilities using the current exchange rate (a net asset balance sheet exposure exists), which, because of a weakening US dollar in the first quarter of 20X2, resulted in a negative translation adjustment of €2,000 on 31 March 20X2 (as shown in Section 3.1.1). Assume further that in the second quarter of 20X2, the US dollar strengthens against the euro and there still is a net asset balance sheet exposure, which results in a *positive* translation adjustment of €500 for that quarter. Although the current period translation adjustment for the second quarter of 2009 is positive, the cumulative translation adjustment as of 30 June 20X2 still will be negative, but the amount now will be only €1,500.

3.2 Translation Methods

The two approaches to translating foreign currency financial statements described in the previous section are known as (1) the **current rate method** (all assets and liabilities are translated at the current exchange rate), and (2) the **monetary/non-monetary method** (only monetary assets and liabilities are translated at the current exchange rate). A variation of the monetary/non-monetary method requires not only monetary assets and liabilities but also non-monetary assets and liabilities that are measured at their current value on the balance sheet date to be translated at the current exchange rate. This variation of the monetary/non-monetary method sometimes is referred to as the **temporal method**.

The basic idea underlying the temporal method is that assets and liabilities should be translated in such a way that the measurement basis (either current value or historical cost) in the foreign currency is preserved after translating to the parent's presentation currency. To achieve this objective, assets and liabilities carried on the foreign currency balance sheet at a current value should be translated at the current exchange rate, and assets and liabilities carried on the foreign currency balance sheet at historical costs should be translated at historical exchange rates. Although neither the IASB nor the FASB specifically refer to translation methods by name, the procedures specified by IFRS and US GAAP for translating foreign currency financial statements essentially require the use of either the current rate or the temporal method.

Which method is appropriate for an individual foreign entity depends on that entity's functional currency. As noted earlier, the functional currency is the currency of the primary economic environment in which an entity operates. A foreign entity's functional currency can be either the parent's presentation currency or another currency, typically the currency of the country in which the foreign entity is located. Exhibit 3 lists the factors that IFRS indicate should be considered in determining a foreign entity's functional currency. Although not identical, US GAAP provide similar indicators for determining a foreign entity's functional currency.

When the functional currency indicators listed in Exhibit 3 are mixed and the functional currency is not obvious, IFRS indicate that management should use its best judgment in determining the functional currency. In this case, however, indicators 1 and 2 should be given priority over indicators 3 through 9.

Exhibit 3   Factors Considered in Determining the Functional Currency

In accordance with IFRS, the following factors should be considered in determining an entity's functional currency:

1 The currency that mainly influences sales prices for goods and services.

2 The currency of the country whose competitive forces and regulations mainly determine the sales price of its goods and services.

3 The currency that mainly influences labour, material, and other costs of providing goods and services.

4 The currency in which funds from financing activities are generated.

5 The currency in which receipts from operating activities are usually retained.

Additional factors to consider in determining whether the foreign entity's functional currency is the same as the parent's functional currency are

6 Whether the activities of the foreign operation are an extension of the parent's or are carried out with a significant amount of autonomy.

7 Whether transactions with the parent are a large or a small proportion of the foreign entity's activities.

8 Whether cash flows generated by the foreign operation directly affect the cash flow of the parent and are available to be remitted to the parent.

9 Whether operating cash flows generated by the foreign operation are sufficient to service existing and normally expected debt or whether the foreign entity will need funds from the parent to service its debt.

The following three steps outline the functional currency approach required by accounting standards in translating foreign currency financial statements into the parent company's presentation currency:

1   Identify the functional currency of the foreign entity.

2   Translate foreign currency balances into the foreign entity's functional currency.

3   Use the current exchange rate to translate the foreign entity's functional currency balances into the parent's presentation currency, if they are different.

To illustrate how this approach is applied, consider a US parent company with a Mexican subsidiary that keeps its accounting records in Mexican pesos. Assume that the vast majority of the subsidiary's transactions are carried out in Mexican pesos, but it also has an account payable in Guatemalan quetzals. In applying the three steps, the US parent company first determines that the Mexican peso is the functional currency of the Mexican subsidiary. Second, the Mexican subsidiary translates its foreign currency balances (i.e., the Guatemalan quetzal account payable), into Mexican pesos using the current exchange rate. In step 3, the Mexican peso financial statements (including the translated account payable) are translated into US dollars using the current rate method.

Now assume, alternatively, that the primary operating currency of the Mexican subsidiary is the US dollar, which thus is identified as the Mexican subsidiary's functional currency. In that case, in addition to the Guatemalan quetzal account payable, all of the subsidiary's accounts that are denominated in Mexican pesos also are considered to be foreign currency balances (because they are not denominated in the subsidiary's functional currency, which is the US dollar). Along with the Guatemalan quetzal balance, each of the Mexican peso balances must be translated into US dollars as if the subsidiary kept its books in US dollars. Assets and liabilities carried at current value in Mexican pesos are translated into US dollars using the current exchange rate, and assets and liabilities carried at historical cost in Mexican pesos are translated into US dollars using historical exchange rates. After completing this step, the Mexican subsidiary's financial statements are stated in terms of US dollars, which is both the subsidiary's functional currency and the parent's presentation currency. As a result, there is no need to apply step 3.

The following two sections describe the procedures to be followed in applying the functional currency approach in more detail.

3.2.1 *Foreign Currency Is the Functional Currency*

In most cases, a foreign entity will operate primarily in the currency of the country where it is located, which will differ from the currency in which the parent company presents its financial statements. For example, the Japanese subsidiary of a French parent company is likely to have the Japanese yen as its functional currency, whereas the French parent company must prepare consolidated financial statements in euro. When a foreign entity has a functional currency that differs from the parent's presentation currency, the foreign entity's foreign currency financial statements are translated into the parent's presentation currency using the following procedures:

1   All assets and liabilities are translated at the current exchange rate at the balance sheet date.

2   Stockholders' equity accounts are translated at historical exchange rates.

3   Revenues and expenses are translated at the exchange rate that existed when the transactions took place. For practical reasons, a rate that approximates the exchange rates at the dates of the transactions, such as an average exchange rate, may be used.

These procedures essentially describe the *current rate method*.

When the current rate method is used, the cumulative translation adjustment needed to keep the translated balance sheet in balance is reported as a separate component of stockholders' equity.

The basic concept underlying the current rate method is that the entire investment in a foreign entity is exposed to translation gain or loss. Therefore, all assets and all liabilities must be revalued at each successive balance sheet date. The net translation gain or loss that results from this procedure is unrealized, however, and will be realized only when the entity is sold. In the meantime, the unrealized translation gain or loss that accumulates over time is deferred on the balance sheet as a separate component of stockholders' equity. When a specific foreign entity is sold, the cumulative translation adjustment related to that entity is reported as a realized gain or loss in net income.

The current rate method results in a net asset balance sheet exposure (except in the rare case in which an entity has negative stockholders' equity):

Items Translated at Current Exchange Rate

Total assets > Total liabilities → Net asset balance sheet exposure

When the foreign currency increases in value (i.e., strengthens), application of the current rate method results in an increase in the positive cumulative translation adjustment (or a decrease in the negative cumulative translation adjustment) reflected in stockholders' equity. When the foreign currency decreases in value (i.e., weakens), the current rate method results in a decrease in the positive cumulative translation adjustment (or an increase in the negative cumulative translation adjustment) in stockholders' equity.

3.2.2 *Parent's Presentation Currency Is the Functional Currency*

In some cases, a foreign entity might have the parent's presentation currency as its functional currency. For example, a Germany-based manufacturer might have a 100%-owned distribution subsidiary in Switzerland that primarily uses the euro in its day-to-day operations and thus has the euro as its functional currency. As a Swiss company, however, the subsidiary is required to record its transactions and keep its books in Swiss francs. In that situation, the subsidiary's Swiss franc financial statements must be translated into euro as if the subsidiary's transactions had originally been recorded in euro. US GAAP refer to this process as *remeasurement*. IFRS do not refer to this process as remeasurement but instead describe this situation as "reporting foreign currency transactions in the functional currency." To achieve the objective of translating to the parent's presentation currency as if the subsidiary's transactions had been recorded in that currency, the following procedures are used:

1 a Monetary assets and liabilities are translated at the current exchange rate.

b Non-monetary assets and liabilities measured at historical cost are translated at historical exchange rates.

c Non-monetary assets and liabilities measured at current value are translated at the exchange rate at the date when the current value was determined.

2 Stockholders' equity accounts are translated at historical exchange rates.

3 a Revenues and expenses, other than those expenses related to non-monetary assets (as explained in 3.b. below), are translated at the exchange rate that existed when the transactions took place (for practical reasons, average rates may be used).

b Expenses related to non-monetary assets, such as cost of goods sold (inventory), depreciation (fixed assets), and amortization (intangible assets), are translated at the exchange rates used to translate the related assets.

These procedures essentially describe the *temporal method*.

Under the temporal method, companies must keep record of the exchange rates that exist when non-monetary assets (inventory, prepaid expenses, fixed assets, and intangible assets) are acquired, because these assets (normally measured at historical cost) are translated at historical exchange rates. Keeping track of the historical exchange rates for these assets is not necessary under the current rate method. Translating these assets (and their related expenses) at historical exchange rates complicates application of the temporal method.

The historical exchange rates used to translate inventory (and cost of goods sold) under the temporal method will differ depending on the cost flow assumption—first in, first out (FIFO); last in, first out (LIFO); or average cost—used to account for inventory. Ending inventory reported on the balance sheet is translated at the exchange rate that existed when the inventory's acquisition is assumed to have occurred. If FIFO is used, ending inventory is assumed to be composed of the most recently acquired items and thus inventory will be translated at relatively recent exchange rates. If LIFO is used, ending inventory is assumed to consist of older items and thus inventory will be translated at older exchange rates. The weighted-average exchange rate for the year is used when inventory is carried at weighted-average cost. Similarly, cost of goods sold is translated using the exchange rates that existed when the inventory items assumed to have been sold during the year (using FIFO or LIFO) were acquired. If weighted-average cost is used to account for inventory, cost of goods sold will be translated at the weighted-average exchange rate for the year.

Under both international and US accounting standards, when the temporal method is used, the translation adjustment needed to keep the translated balance sheet in balance is reported as a gain or loss in net income. US GAAP refer to these as *remeasurement* gains and losses. The basic assumption underlying the recognition of a translation gain or loss in income relates to timing. Specifically, if the foreign entity primarily uses the parent company's currency in its day-to-day operations, then the foreign entity's monetary items that are denominated in a foreign currency generate translation gains and losses that will be realized in the near future and thus should be reflected in current net income.

The temporal method generates either a net asset or a net liability balance sheet exposure, depending on whether assets translated at the current exchange rate—that is, monetary assets and non-monetary assets measured on the balance sheet date at current value (exposed assets)—are greater than or less than liabilities translated at the current exchange rate—that is, monetary liabilities and non-monetary liabilities measured on the balance sheet date at current value (exposed liabilities):

Items Translated at Current Exchange Rate

Exposed assets > Exposed liabilities → Net asset balance sheet exposure

Exposed assets < Exposed liabilities → Net liability balance sheet exposure

Most liabilities are monetary liabilities. Only cash and receivables are monetary assets, and non-monetary assets generally are measured at their historical cost. As a result, liabilities translated at the current exchange rate (exposed liabilities) often exceed assets translated at the current exchange rate (exposed assets), which results in a net liability balance sheet exposure when the temporal method is applied.

3.2.3 *Translation of Retained Earnings*

Stockholders' equity accounts are translated at historical exchange rates under both the current rate and the temporal methods. This approach creates somewhat of a problem in translating retained earnings (R/E), which are the accumulation of previous years' income less dividends over the life of the company. At the end of the first year of operations, foreign currency (FC) retained earnings are translated into the parent's currency (PC) as follows:

Net income in FC	[Translated according to the method used to translate the income statement]	=	Net income in PC
− Dividends in FC			− Dividends in PC
R/E in FC ×	Exchange rate when dividends declared	=	R/E in PC

Retained earnings in parent currency at the end of the first year become the beginning retained earnings in parent currency for the second year, and the translated retained earnings in the second year (and subsequent years) are then calculated in the following manner:

Beginning R/E in FC	[From last year's translation]	→	Beginning R/E in PC
+ Net income in FC	[Translated according to method used to translate the income statement]	=	+ Net income in PC
− Dividends in FC			− Dividends in PC
Ending R/E in FC ×	Exchange rate when dividends declared	=	Ending R/E in PC

Exhibit 4 summarizes the translation rules as discussed in Sections 3.2.1, 3.2.2, and 3.2.3.

Exhibit 4   Rules for the Translation of a Foreign Subsidiary's Foreign Currency Financial Statements into the Parent's Presentation Currency under IFRS and US GAAP

	Foreign Subsidiary's Functional Currency	
	Foreign Currency	Parent's Presentation Currency
Translation method:	**Current Rate Method**	**Temporal Method**
Exchange rate at which financial statement items are translated from the foreign subsidiary's bookkeeping currency to the parent's presentation currency:		
Assets		
Monetary, such as cash and receivables	Current rate	Current rate
Non-monetary		
■ measured at current value (e.g., marketable securities and inventory measured at market value under the lower of cost or market rule)	Current rate	Current rate
■ measured at historical costs, (e.g., inventory measured at cost under the lower of cost or market rule; property, plant & equipment; and intangible assets)	Current rate	Historical rates

(continued)

Exhibit 4   (Continued)

	Foreign Subsidiary's Functional Currency	
	Foreign Currency	**Parent's Presentation Currency**
Translation method:	**Current Rate Method**	**Temporal Method**
Liabilities		
Monetary, such as accounts payable, accrued expenses, long-term debt, and deferred income taxes	Current rate	Current rate
Non-monetary		
▪ measured at current value	Current rate	Current rate
▪ not measured at current value, such as deferred revenue	Current rate	Historical rates
Equity		
Other than retained earnings	Historical rates	Historical rates
Retained earnings	Beginning balance plus translated net income less dividends translated at historical rate	Beginning balance plus translated net income less dividends translated at historical rate
Revenues	Average rate	Average rate
Expenses		
Most expenses	Average rate	Average rate
Expenses related to assets translated at historical exchange rate, such as cost of goods sold, depreciation, and amortization	Average rate	Historical rates
Treatment of the translation adjustment in the parent's consolidated financial statements	Accumulated as a separate component of equity	Included as gain or loss in net income

3.2.4 *Highly Inflationary Economies*

When a foreign entity is located in a highly inflationary economy, the entity's functional currency is irrelevant in determining how to translate its foreign currency financial statements into the parent's presentation currency. IFRS require that the foreign entity's financial statements first be restated for local inflation using the procedures outlined in IAS 29, "Financial Reporting in Hyperinflationary Economies." Then, the inflation-restated foreign currency financial statements are translated into the parent's presentation currency using the current exchange rate.

US GAAP require a very different approach for translating the foreign currency financial statements of foreign entities located in highly inflationary economies. US GAAP do not allow restatement for inflation but instead require the foreign entity's financial statements to be remeasured as if the functional currency were the reporting currency (i.e., the temporal method).

US GAAP define a highly inflationary economy as one in which the cumulative three-year inflation rate exceeds 100% (but note that the definition should be applied with judgment, particularly because the trend of inflation can be as important as the absolute rate). A cumulative three-year inflation rate of 100% equates to an average of approximately 26% per year. IAS 21 does not provide a specific definition of high inflation, but IAS 29 indicates that a cumulative inflation rate approaching or exceeding 100% over three years would be an indicator of hyperinflation. If a country in which a foreign entity is located ceases to be classified as highly inflationary, the functional currency of that entity must be identified to determine the appropriate method for translating the entity's financial statements.

The FASB initially proposed that companies restate for inflation and then translate the financial statements, but this approach met with stiff resistance from US multinational corporations. Requiring the temporal method ensures that companies avoid a "disappearing plant problem" that exists when the current rate method is used in a country with high inflation. In a highly inflationary economy, as the local currency loses purchasing power within the country, it also tends to weaken in value in relation to other currencies. Translating the historical cost of assets such as land and buildings at progressively weaker exchange rates causes these assets to slowly disappear from the parent company's consolidated financial statements. Example 4 demonstrates the effect of three different translation approaches when books are kept in the currency of a highly inflationary economy. Example 4 pertains to Turkey in the period 2000 to 2002, when it was recognized as one of the few highly inflationary countries. Turkey is no longer viewed as having a highly inflationary economy. (In 2010, the International Practices Task Force of the Center for Audit Quality SEC Regulations Committee indicated that Venezuela had met the thresholds for being considered highly inflationary.)

EXAMPLE 4

Foreign Currency Translation in a Highly Inflationary Economy

Turkey was one of the few remaining highly inflationary countries at the beginning of the 21st century. Annual inflation rates and selected exchange rates between the Turkish lira (TL) and US dollar during the 2000–2002 period were as follows:

Date	Exchange Rates	Year	Inflation Rate (%)
01 Jan 2000	TL542,700 = US$1		
31 Dec 2000	TL670,800 = US$1	2000	38
31 Dec 2001	TL1,474,525 = US$1	2001	69
31 Dec 2002	TL1,669,000 = US$1	2002	45

Assume that a US-based company established a subsidiary in Turkey on 1 January 2000. The US parent sent the subsidiary US$1,000 on 1 January 2000 to purchase a piece of land at a cost of TL542,700,000 (TL542,700/US$ × US$1,000 = TL542,700,000). Assuming no other assets or liabilities, what are the annual and cumulative translation gains or losses that would be reported under each of three possible translation approaches?

Solution:

Approach 1: Translate Using the Current Rate Method

The historical cost of the land is translated at the current exchange rate, which results in a new translated amount at each balance sheet date.

Date	Carrying Value	Current Exchange Rate	Translated Amount in US$	Annual Translation Gain (Loss)	Cumulative Translation Gain (Loss)
01 Jan 2000	TL542,700,000	542,700	$1,000	N/A	N/A
31 Dec 2000	542,700,000	670,800	809	($191)	($191)
31 Dec 2001	542,700,000	1,474,525	368	(441)	(632)
31 Dec 2002	542,700,000	1,669,000	325	(43)	(675)

At the end of three years, land that was originally purchased with US$1,000 would be reflected on the parent's consolidated balance sheet at US$325 (and remember that land is not a depreciable asset). A cumulative translation loss of US$675 would be reported as a separate component of stockholders' equity on 31 December 2002. Because this method accounts for adjustments in exchange rates but does not account for likely changes in the local currency values of assets, it does a poor job of accurately reflecting the economic reality of situations such as the one in our example. That is the major reason this approach is not acceptable under either IFRS or US GAAP.

Approach 2: Translate Using the Temporal Method (US GAAP ASC 830)

The historical cost of land is translated using the historical exchange rate, which results in the same translated amount at each balance sheet date.

Date	Carrying Value	Historical Exchange Rate	Translated Amount in US$	Annual Translation Gain (Loss)	Cumulative Translation Gain (Loss)
01 Jan 2000	TL542,700,000	542,700	$1,000	N/A	N/A
31 Dec 2000	542,700,000	542,700	1,000	N/A	N/A
31 Dec 2001	542,700,000	542,700	1,000	N/A	N/A
31 Dec 2002	542,700,000	542,700	1,000	N/A	N/A

Under this approach, land continues to be reported on the parent's consolidated balance sheet at its original cost of US$1,000 each year. There is no translation gain or loss related to balance sheet items translated at historical exchange rates. This approach is required by US GAAP and ensures that nonmonetary assets do not disappear from the translated balance sheet.

Approach 3: Restate for Inflation/Translate Using Current Exchange Rate (IAS 21)

The historical cost of the land is restated for inflation, and then the inflation-adjusted historical cost is translated using the current exchange rate.

Date	Inflation Rate (%)	Restated Carrying Value	Current Exchange Rate	Translated Amount in US$	Annual Translation Gain (Loss)	Cumulative Translation Gain (Loss)
01 Jan 00		TL542,700,000	542,700	$1,000	N/A	N/A
31 Dec 00	38	748,926,000	670,800	1,116	$116	$116
31 Dec 01	69	1,265,684,940	1,474,525	858	(258)	(142)
31 Dec 02	45	1,835,243,163	1,669,000	1,100	242	100

Under this approach, land is reported on the parent's 31 December 2002 consolidated balance sheet at US$1,100 with a cumulative, unrealized gain of US$100. Although the cumulative translation gain on 31 December 2002 is unrealized, it could have been realized if (1) the land had appreciated in TL value by the rate of local inflation, (2) the Turkish subsidiary sold the land for TL1,835,243,163, and (3) the sale proceeds were converted into US$1,100 at the current exchange rate on 31 December 2002.

This approach is required by IAS 21. It is the approach that, apart from doing an appraisal, perhaps best represents economic reality, in the sense that it reflects both the likely change in the local currency value of the land as well as the actual change in the exchange rate.

3.3 Illustration of Translation Methods (Excluding Hyperinflationary Economies)

To demonstrate the procedures required in translating foreign currency financial statements (excluding hyperinflationary economies), assume that Interco is a Europe-based company that has the euro as its presentation currency. On 1 January 20X1, Interco establishes a wholly owned subsidiary in Canada, Canadaco. In addition to Interco making an equity investment in Canadaco, a long-term note payable to a Canadian bank was negotiated to purchase property and equipment. The subsidiary begins operations with the following balance sheet in Canadian dollars (C$):

Canadaco Balance Sheet, 1 January 20X1	
Assets	
Cash	C$1,500,000
Property and equipment	3,000,000
	C$4,500,000
Liabilities and Equity	
Long-term note payable	C$3,000,000
Capital stock	1,500,000
	C$4,500,000

Canadaco purchases and sells inventory in 20X1, generating net income of C$1,180,000, out of which C$350,000 in dividends are paid. The company's income statement and statement of retained earnings for 20X1 and balance sheet at 31 December 20X1 follow:

Canadaco Income Statement and Statement of Retained Earnings, 20X1	
Sales	C$12,000,000
Cost of sales	(9,000,000)
Selling expenses	(750,000)
Depreciation expense	(300,000)
Interest expense	(270,000)
Income tax	(500,000)
Net income	C$1,180,000

(continued)

(Continued)

Less: Dividends, 1 Dec 20X1	(350,000)
Retained earnings, 31 Dec 20X1	C$830,000

Canadaco Balance Sheet, 31 December 20X1

Assets		Liabilities and Equity	
Cash	C$980,000	Accounts payable	C$450,000
Accounts receivable	900,000	Total current liabilities	450,000
Inventory	1,200,000	Long-term notes payable	3,000,000
Total current assets	C$3,080,000	Total liabilities	C$3,450,000
Property and equipment	3,000,000	Capital stock	1,500,000
Less: accumulated depreciation	(300,000)	Retained earnings	830,000
Total	C$5,780,000	Total	C$5,780,000

Inventory is measured at historical cost on a FIFO basis.

To translate Canadaco's Canadian dollar financial statements into euro for consolidation purposes, the following exchange rate information was gathered:

Date	€ per C$
1 January 20X1	0.70
Average, 20X1	0.75
Weighted-average rate when inventory was acquired	0.74
1 December 20X1 when dividends were declared	0.78
31 December 20X1	0.80

During 20X1, the Canadian dollar strengthened steadily against the euro from an exchange rate of €0.70 at the beginning of the year to €0.80 at year-end.

The translation worksheet that follows shows Canadaco's translated financial statements under each of the two translation methods. Assume first that Canadaco's functional currency is the Canadian dollar, and thus the current rate method must be used. The Canadian dollar income statement and statement of retained earnings are translated first. Income statement items for 20X1 are translated at the average exchange rate for 20X1 (€0.75), and dividends are translated at the exchange rate that existed when they were declared (€0.78). The ending balance in retained earnings as of 31 December 20X1 of €612,000 is transferred to the Canadian dollar balance sheet. The remaining balance sheet accounts are then translated. Assets and liabilities are translated at the current exchange rate on the balance sheet date of 31 December 20X1 (€0.80), and the capital stock account is translated at the historical exchange rate (€0.70) that existed on the date that Interco made the capital contribution. A positive translation adjustment of €202,000 is needed as a balancing amount, which is reported in the stockholders' equity section of the balance sheet.

If instead Interco determines that Canadaco's functional currency is the euro (the parent's presentation currency), the temporal method must be applied as shown in the far right columns of the table. The differences in procedure from the current rate method are that inventory, property, and equipment (and accumulated depreciation), as well as their related expenses (cost of goods sold and depreciation), are translated at the historical exchange rates that existed when the assets were acquired: €0.70 in the case of property and equipment, and €0.74 for inventory. The balance sheet is translated first, with €472,000 determined as the amount of retained earnings needed to keep the balance sheet in balance. This amount is transferred to the income statement and statement of retained earnings as the ending balance in retained earnings as of 31 December 20X1. Income statement items then are translated, with cost of goods sold and depreciation expense being translated at historical exchange rates. A negative translation adjustment of €245,000 is determined as the amount needed to arrive at the ending balance in retained earnings of €472,000, and this adjustment is reported as a translation loss on the income statement.

The positive translation adjustment under the current rate method can be explained by the facts that Canadaco has a net asset balance sheet exposure (total assets exceed total liabilities) during 20X1 and the Canadian dollar strengthened against the euro. The negative translation adjustment (translation loss) under the temporal method is explained by the fact that Canadaco has a net liability balance sheet exposure under this method (because the amount of exposed liabilities [accounts payable plus notes payable] exceeds the amount of exposed assets [cash plus receivables]) during 20X1 when the Canadian dollar strengthened against the euro.

Canadaco Income Statement and Statement of Retained Earnings, 20X1

Canadaco's Functional Currency Is:		Local Currency (C$)		Parent's Currency (€)	
		Current Rate		**Temporal**	
	C$	**Exch. Rate**	**€**	**Exch. Rate**	**€**
Sales	12,000,000	0.75 A	9,000,000	0.75 A	9,000,000
Cost of goods sold	(9,000,000)	0.75 A	(6,750,000)	0.74 H	(6,660,000)
Selling expenses	(750,000)	0.75 A	(562,500)	0.75 A	(562,500)
Depreciation expense	(300,000)	0.75 A	(225,000)	0.70 H	(210,000)
Interest expense	(270,000)	0.75 A	(202,500)	0.75 A	(202,500)
Income tax	(500,000)	0.75 A	(375,000)	0.75 A	(375,000)
Income before trans. gain (loss)	1,180,000		885,000		990,000
Translation gain (loss)	N/A		N/A	to balance	(245,000)
Net income	1,180,000		885,000		745,000
Less: Dividends, 12/1/20X1	(350,000)	0.78 H	(273,000)	0.78 H	(273,000)
Retained earnings, 12/31/20X1	830,000		612,000	from B/S	472,000

Note: C = current exchange rate; A = average-for-the-year exchange rate; H = historical exchange rate

Canadaco Balance Sheet, 31 December 20X1

| Canadaco's Functional Currency Is: | | Local Currency (C$) | | Parent's Currency (€) | |
| | | Current Rate | | Temporal | |
	C$	Exch. Rate	€	Exch. Rate	€
Assets					
Cash	980,000	0.80 C	784,000	0.80 C	784,000
Accounts receivable	900,000	0.80 C	720,000	0.80 C	720,000
Inventory	1,200,000	0.80 C	960,000	0.74 H	888,000
Total current assets	3,080,000		2,464,000		2,392,000
Property and equipment	3,000,000	0.80 C	2,400,000	0.70 H	2,100,000
Less: accumulated depreciation	(300,000)	0.80 C	(240,000)	0.70 H	(210,000)
Total assets	5,780,000		4,624,000		4,282,000
Liabilities and Equity					
Accounts payable	450,000	0.80 C	360,000	0.80 C	360,000
Total current liabilities	450,000		360,000		360,000
Long-term notes payable	3,000,000	0.80 C	2,400,000	0.80 C	2,400,000
Total liabilities	3,450,000		2,760,000		2,760,000
Capital stock	1,500,000	0.70 H	1,050,000	0.70 H	1,050,000
Retained earnings	830,000	from I/S	612,000	to balance	472,000
Translation adjustment	N/A	to balance	202,000		N/A
Total	5,780,000		4,624,000		4,282,000

Note: C = current exchange rate; A = average-for-the-year exchange rate; H = historical exchange rate

3.4 Translation Analytical Issues

The two different translation methods used to translate Canadaco's Canadian dollar financial statements into euro result in very different amounts to be included in Interco's consolidated financial statements. The chart below summarizes some of these differences:

| Canadaco's Functional Currency Is: | Local Currency (C$) | Parent's Currency (€) | |
| | Translation Method | | |
Item	Current Rate (€)	Temporal (€)	Difference (%)
Sales	900,000	900,000	0.0
Net income	885,000	745,000	+18.8
Income before translation gain (loss)	885,000	990,000	−10.6

Canadaco's Functional Currency Is:	Local Currency (C\$)	Parent's Currency (€)	
	Translation Method		
Item	**Current Rate (€)**	**Temporal (€)**	**Difference (%)**
Total assets	4,624,000	4,282,000	+8.0
Total equity	1,864,000	1,522,000	+22.5

In this particular case, the current rate method results in a significantly larger net income than the temporal method. This result occurs because under the current rate method, the translation adjustment is not included in the calculation of income. If the translation loss were excluded from net income, the temporal method would result in a significantly larger amount of net income. The combination of smaller net income under the temporal method and a positive translation adjustment reported on the balance sheet under the current rate method results in a much larger amount of total equity under the current rate method. Total assets also are larger under the current rate method because all assets are translated at the current exchange rate, which is higher than the historical exchange rates at which inventory and fixed assets are translated under the temporal method.

To examine the effects of translation on the underlying relationships that exist in Canadaco's Canadian dollar financial statements, several significant ratios are calculated from the original Canadian dollar financial statements and the translated (euro) financial statements and presented in the table below.

Canadaco's Functional Currency Is:			Local Currency (C\$)		Parent's Currency (€)
		C\$	**Current Rate (€)**		**Temporal (€)**
Current ratio		6.84	6.84		6.64
Current assets		3,080,000	2,464,000		2,392,000
Current liabilities	=	450,000 =	360,000	=	360,000
Debt-to-assets ratio		0.52	0.52		0.56
Total debt		3,000,000	2,400,000		2,400,000
Total assets	=	5,780,000 =	4,624,000	=	4,282,000
Debt-to-equity ratio		1.29	1.29		1.58
Total debt		3,000,000	2,400,000		2,400,000
Total equity	=	2,330,000 =	1,864,000	=	1,522,000
Interest coverage		7.22	7.22		7.74
EBIT		1,950,000	1,462,500		1,567,500
Interest payments	=	270,000 =	202,500	=	202,500
Gross profit margin		0.25	0.25		0.26
Gross profit		3,000,000	2,250,000		2,340,000
Sales	=	12,000,000 =	9,000,000	=	9,000,000
Operating profit margin		0.16	0.16		0.17
Operating profit		1,950,000	1,462,500		1,567,500
Sales	=	12,000,000 =	9,000,000	=	9,000,000
Net profit margin		0.10	0.10		0.08
Net income		1,180,000	885,000		745,000
Sales	=	12,000,000 =	9,000,000	=	9,000,000

(continued)

Canadaco's Functional Currency Is:			Local Currency (C$)		Parent's Currency (€)
		C$	Current Rate (€)		Temporal (€)
Receivables turnover		13.33	12.50		12.50
Sales		12,000,000	9,000,000		9,000,000
Accounts receivable	=	900,000	= 720,000	=	720,000
Inventory turnover		7.50	7.03		7.50
Cost of goods sold		9,000,000	6,750,000		6,660,000
Inventory	=	1,200,000	= 960,000	=	888,000
Fixed asset turnover		4.44	4.17		4.76
Sales		12,000,000	9,000,000		9,000,000
Property & equipment (net)	=	2,700,000	= 2,160,000	=	1,890,000
Return on assets		0.20	0.19		0.17
Net income		1,180,000	885,000		745,000
Total assets	=	5,780,000	= 4,624,000	=	4,282,000
Return on equity		0.51	0.47		0.49
Net income		1,180,000	885,000		745,000
Total equity	=	2,330,000	= 1,864,000	=	1,522,000

Comparing the current rate method (€) and temporal method (€) columns in the above table shows that financial ratios calculated from Canadaco's translated financial statements (in €) differ significantly depending on which method of translation is used. Of the ratios presented, only receivables turnover is the same under both translation methods. This is the only ratio presented in which there is no difference in the type of exchange rate used to translate the items that comprise the numerator and the denominator. Sales are translated at the average exchange rate and receivables are translated at the current exchange rate under both methods. For each of the other ratios, at least one of the items included in either the numerator or the denominator is translated at a different type of rate (current, average, or historical) under the temporal method than under the current rate method. For example, the current ratio has a different value under the two translation methods because inventory is translated at the current exchange rate under the current rate method and at the historical exchange rate under the temporal method. In this case, because the euro/Canadian dollar exchange rate on 31 December 20X1 (€0.80) is higher than the historical exchange rate when the inventory was acquired (€0.74), the current ratio is larger under the current rate method of translation.

Comparing the ratios in the Canadian dollar and current rate method (euro) columns of the above table shows that many of the underlying relationships that exist in Canadaco's Canadian dollar financial statements are preserved when the current rate method of translation is used (i.e., the ratio calculated from the Canadian dollar and euro translated amounts is the same). The current ratio, the leverage ratios (debt-to-assets and debt-to-equity ratios), the interest coverage ratio, and the profit margins (gross profit margin, operating profit margin, and net profit margin) are the same in the Canadian dollar and current rate method (euro) columns of the above table. This result occurs because each of the ratios is calculated using information from either the balance sheet or the income statement, but not both. Those ratios that compare amounts from the balance sheet with amounts from the income statement (e.g., turnover and return ratios) are different. In this particular case, each of the turnover and return ratios is larger when calculated from the Canadian dollar amounts than when calculated using the current rate (euro) amounts. The underlying Canadian dollar relationships are distorted when translated using the current rate method because the balance sheet amounts are translated using the current exchange rate while revenues and expenses are translated using the average exchange rate. (These distortions would not occur if revenues and expenses also were translated at the current exchange rate.)

Comparing the ratios in the Canadian dollar and temporal method (euro) columns of the table shows that translation using the temporal method distorts all of the underlying relationships that exist in the Canadian dollar financial statements, except inventory turnover. Moreover, it is not possible to generalize the direction of the distortion across ratios. In Canadaco's case, using the temporal method results in a larger gross profit margin and operating profit margin but a smaller net profit margin as compared with the values of these ratios calculated from the original Canadian dollar amounts. Similarly, receivables turnover is smaller, inventory turnover is the same, and fixed asset turnover is larger when calculated from the translated amounts.

In translating Canadaco's Canadian dollar financial statements into euro, the temporal method results in a smaller amount of net income than the current rate method only because IFRS and US GAAP require the resulting translation loss to be included in net income when the temporal method is used. The translation loss arises because the Canadian dollar strengthened against the euro and Canadaco has a larger amount of liabilities translated at the current exchange rate (monetary liabilities) than it has assets translated at the current exchange rate (monetary assets). If Canadaco had a net monetary asset exposure (i.e., if monetary assets exceeded monetary liabilities), a translation gain would arise and net income under the temporal method (including the translation gain) would be greater than under the current rate method. Example 5 demonstrates how different types of balance sheet exposure under the temporal method can affect translated net income.

EXAMPLE 5

Effects of Different Balance Sheet Exposures under the Temporal Method (*Canadaco's functional currency is the parent's functional currency*)

Canadaco begins operations on 1 January 20X1, with cash of C$1,500,000 and property and equipment of C$3,000,000. In Case A, Canadaco finances the acquisition of property and equipment with a long-term note payable and begins operations with net monetary liabilities of C$1,500,000 (C$3,000,000 long-term note payable less C$1,500,000 cash). In Case B, Canadaco finances the acquisition of property and equipment with capital stock and begins operations with net monetary assets of C$1,500,000. To isolate the effect that balance sheet exposure has on net income under the temporal method, assume that Canadaco continues to have C$270,000 in interest expense in Case B, even though there is no debt financing. This assumption is inconsistent with reality, but it allows us to more clearly see the effect of balance sheet exposure on net income. The only difference between Case A and Case B is the net monetary asset/liability position of the company, as shown in the following table:

Canadaco Balance Sheet, 1 January 20X1		
	Case A	**Case B**
Assets		
Cash	C$1,500,000	C$1,500,000
Property and equipment	3,000,000	3,000,000
	C$4,500,000	C$4,500,000
Liabilities and Equity		
Long-term note payable	C$3,000,000	C$ 0
Capital stock	1,500,000	4,500,000
	C$4,500,000	C$4,500,000

Canadaco purchases and sells inventory in 20X1, generating net income of C$1,180,000, out of which dividends of C$350,000 are paid. The company has total assets of C$5,780,000 as of 31 December 20X1. Canadaco's functional currency is determined to be the euro (the parent's presentation currency), and the company's Canadian dollar financial statements are translated into euro using the temporal method. Relevant exchange rates are as follows:

Date	€ per C$
1 January 20X1	0.70
Average, 20X1	0.75
Weighted-average rate when inventory was acquired	0.74
1 December 20X1 when dividends were declared	0.78
31 December 20X1	0.80

What effect does the nature of Canadaco's net monetary asset or liability position have on the euro translated amounts?

Solution:

Translation of Canadaco's 31 December 20X1 balance sheet under the temporal method in Case A and Case B is shown in the following table:

Canadaco Balance Sheet on 31 December 20X1 under the Temporal Method						
	Case A: Net Monetary Liabilities			**Case B: Net Monetary Assets**		
	C$	Exch. Rate	€	C$	Exch. Rate	€
Assets						
Cash	980,000	0.80 C	784,000	980,000	0.80 C	784,000
Accounts receivable	900,000	0.80 C	720,000	900,000	0.80 C	720,000
Inventory	1,200,000	0.74 H	888,000	1,200,000	0.74 H	888,000
Total current assets	3,080,000		2,392,000	3,080,000		2,392,000
Property and equipment	3,000,000	0.70 H	2,100,000	3,000,000	0.70 H	2,100,000
Less: accum. deprec.	(300,000)	0.70 H	(210,000)	(300,000)	0.70 H	(210,000)
Total assets	5,780,000		4,282,000	5,780,000		4,282,000
Liabilities and Equity						

(Continued)

	Case A: Net Monetary Liabilities			Case B: Net Monetary Assets		
	C$	Exch. Rate	€	C$	Exch. Rate	€
Accounts payable	450,000	0.80 C	360,000	450,000	0.80 C	360,000
Total current liabilities	450,000		360,000	450,000		360,000
Long-term notes payable	3,000,000	0.80 C	2,400,000	0		0
Total liabilities	3,450,000		2,760,000	450,000		360,000
Capital stock	1,500,000	0.70 H	1,050,000	4,500,000	0.70 H	3,150,000
Retained earnings	830,000		472,000	830,000		772,000
Total	5,780,000		4,282,000	5,780,000		4,282,000

Note: C = current exchange rate; A = average-for-the-year exchange rate; H = historical exchange rate.

To keep the balance sheet in balance, retained earnings must be €472,000 in Case A (net monetary liability exposure) and €772,000 in Case B (net monetary asset exposure). The difference in retained earnings of €300,000 is equal to the translation loss that results from holding a Canadian dollar–denominated note payable during a period in which the Canadian dollar strengthens against the euro. This difference is determined by multiplying the amount of long-term note payable in Case A by the change in exchange rate during the year [C$3,000,000 × (€0.80 − €0.70) = €300,000]. Notes payable are exposed to foreign exchange risk under the temporal method, whereas capital stock is not. Canadaco could avoid the €300,000 translation loss related to long-term debt by financing the acquisition of property and equipment with equity rather than debt.

Translation of Canadaco's 20X1 income statement and statement of retained earnings under the temporal method for Case A and Case B is shown in the following table:

Canadaco Income Statement and Statement of Retained Earnings for 20X1 under the Temporal Method

	Case A: Net Monetary Liabilities			Case B: Net Monetary Assets		
	C$	Exch. Rate	€	C$	Exch. Rate	€
Sales	12,000,000	0.75 A	9,000,000	12,000,000	0.75 A	9,000,000
Cost of goods sold	(9,000,000)	0.74 H	(6,660,000)	(9,000,000)	0.74 H	(6,660,000)
Selling expenses	(750,000)	0.75 A	(562,500)	(750,000)	0.75 A	(562,500)
Depreciation expense	(300,000)	0.70 H	(210,000)	(300,000)	0.70 H	(210,000)
Interest expense	(270,000)	0.75 A	(202,500)	(270,000)	0.75 A	(202,500)
Income tax	(500,000)	0.75 A	(375,000)	(500,000)	0.75 A	(375,000)
Income before translation gain (loss)	1,180,000		990,000	1,180,000		990,000
Translation gain (loss)	N/A		(245,000)	N/A		55,000
Net income	1,180,000		745,000	1,180,000		1,045,000

(continued)

(Continued)						
	Case A: Net Monetary Liabilities			**Case B: Net Monetary Assets**		
	C$	Exch. Rate	€	C$	Exch. Rate	€
Less: Dividends on 1 December 20X1	(350,000)	0.78 H	(273,000)	(350,000)	0.78 H	(273,000)
Retained earnings on 31 December 20X1	830,000		472,000	830,000		772,000

Note: C = current exchange rate; A = average-for-the-year exchange rate; H = historical exchange rate.

Income before translation gain (loss) is the same in both cases. To obtain the amount of retained earnings needed to keep the balance sheet in balance, a translation loss of €245,000 must be subtracted from net income in Case A (net monetary liabilities), whereas a translation gain of €55,000 must be added to net income in Case B (net monetary assets). The difference in net income between the two cases is €300,000, which equals the translation loss related to the long-term note payable.

When using the temporal method, companies can manage their exposure to translation gain (loss) more easily than when using the current rate method. If a company can manage the balance sheet of a foreign subsidiary such that monetary assets equal monetary liabilities, no balance sheet exposure exists. Elimination of balance sheet exposure under the current rate method occurs only when total assets equal total liabilities. This equality is difficult to achieve because it requires the foreign subsidiary to have no stockholders' equity.

For Canadaco, in 20X1, applying the current rate method results in larger euro amounts of total assets and total equity being reported in the consolidated financial statements than would result from applying the temporal method. The direction of these differences between the two translation methods is determined by the direction of change in the exchange rate between the Canadian dollar and the euro. For example, total exposed assets are greater under the current rate method because all assets are translated at the current exchange rate. The current exchange rate at 31 December 20X1 is greater than the exchange rates that existed when the non-monetary assets were acquired, which is the translation rate for these assets under the temporal method. Therefore, the current rate method results in a larger amount of total assets because the Canadian dollar strengthened against the euro. The current rate method would result in a smaller amount of total assets than the temporal method if the Canadian dollar had weakened against the euro.

Applying the current rate method also results in a much larger amount of stockholders' equity than the temporal method. A positive translation adjustment arises under the current rate method, which is included in equity, whereas a translation loss reduces total equity (through retained earnings) under the temporal method.

Example 6 shows the effect that the direction of change in the exchange rate has on the translated amounts. Canadaco's Canadian dollar financial statements are translated into euro, first assuming no change in the exchange rate during 20X1, and then assuming the Canadian dollar strengthens and weakens against the euro. Using the current rate method to translate the foreign currency financial statements into the parent's presentation currency, the foreign currency strengthening increases the revenues, income, assets, liabilities, and total equity reported on the parent company's consolidated financial statements. Likewise, smaller amounts of revenues, income, assets, liabilities, and total equity will be reported if the foreign currency weakens against the parent's presentation currency.

When the temporal method is used to translate foreign currency financial statements, foreign currency strengthening still increases revenues, assets, and liabilities reported in the parent's consolidated financial statements. Net income and stockholders' equity, however, translate into smaller amounts (assuming that the foreign subsidiary has a net monetary liability position) because of the translation loss. The opposite results are obtained when the foreign currency weakens against the parent's presentation currency.

EXAMPLE 6

Effect of Direction of Change in the Exchange Rate on Translated Amounts

Canadaco's Canadian dollar (C$) financial statements are translated into euro (€) under three scenarios: (1) the Canadian dollar remains stable against the euro, (2) the Canadian dollar strengthens against the euro, and (3) the Canadian dollar weakens against the euro. Relevant exchange rates are as follows:

Date	€ per C$		
	Stable	Strengthens	Weakens
1 January 20X1	0.70	0.70	0.70
Average, 20X1	0.70	0.75	0.65
Weighted-average rate when inventory was acquired	0.70	0.74	0.66
Rate when dividends were declared	0.70	0.78	0.62
31 December 20X1	0.70	0.80	0.60

What amounts will be reported on the parent's consolidated financial statements under the three different exchange rate assumptions if Canadaco's Canadian dollar financial statements are translated using the:

1 current rate method?
2 temporal method?

Solution to 1:

Current Rate Method: Using the current rate method, Canadaco's Canadian dollar financial statements would be translated into euro as follows under the three different exchange rate assumptions:

Canadaco Income Statement and Statement of Retained Earnings for 20X1 under the Current Rate Method							
		C$ Stable		C$ Strengthens		C$ Weakens	
	C$	Exch. Rate	€	Exch. Rate	€	Exch. Rate	€
Sales	12,000,000	0.70	8,400,000	0.75 A	9,000,000	0.65 A	7,800,000
Cost of goods sold	(9,000,000)	0.70	(6,300,000)	0.75 A	(6,750,000)	0.65 A	(5,850,000)

(continued)

(Continued)

	C$	C$ Stable Exch. Rate	C$ Stable €	C$ Strengthens Exch. Rate	C$ Strengthens €	C$ Weakens Exch. Rate	C$ Weakens €
Selling expenses	(750,000)	0.70	(525,000)	0.75 A	(562,500)	0.65 A	(487,500)
Deprec. expense	(300,000)	0.70	(210,000)	0.75 A	(225,000)	0.65 A	(195,000)
Interest expense	(270,000)	0.70	(189,000)	0.75 A	(202,500)	0.65 A	(175,500)
Income tax	(500,000)	0.70	(350,000)	0.75 A	(375,000)	0.65 A	(325,000)
Net income	1,180,000		826,000		885,000		767,000
Less: Dividends	(350,000)	0.70	(245,000)	0.78 H	(273,000)	0.62 H	(217,000)
Retained earnings	830,000		581,000		612,000		550,000

Note: C = current (period-end) exchange rate; A = average-for-the-year exchange rate; H = historical exchange rate.

Compared with the translated amount of sales and net income under a stable Canadian dollar, a stronger Canadian dollar results in a larger amount of sales and net income being reported in the consolidated income statement. A weaker Canadian dollar results in a smaller amount of sales and net income being reported in consolidated net income.

Canadaco Balance Sheet on 31 December 20X1 under the Current Rate Method

	C$	C$ Stable Exch. Rate	C$ Stable €	C$ Strengthens Exch. Rate	C$ Strengthens €	C$ Weakens Exch. Rate	C$ Weakens €
Assets							
Cash	980,000	0.70	686,000	0.80 C	784,000	0.60 C	588,000
Accounts receivable	900,000	0.70	630,000	0.80 C	720,000	0.60 C	540,000
Inventory	1,200,000	0.70	840,000	0.80 C	960,000	0.60 C	720,000
Total current assets	3,080,000		2,156,000		2,464,000		1,848,000
Property and equipment	3,000,000	0.70	2,100,000	0.80 C	2,400,000	0.60 C	1,800,000
Less: accum. deprec.	(300,000)	0.70	(210,000)	0.80 C	(240,000)	0.60 C	(180,000)
Total assets	5,780,000		4,046,000		4,624,000		3,468,000
Liabilities and Equity							
Accounts payable	450,000	0.70	315,000	0.80 C	360,000	0.60 C	270,000

(Continued)

	C$	C$ Stable Exch. Rate	C$ Stable €	C$ Strengthens Exch. Rate	C$ Strengthens €	C$ Weakens Exch. Rate	C$ Weakens €
Total current liabilities	450,000		315,000		360,000		270,000
Long-term notes pay	3,000,000	0.70	2,100,000	0.80 C	2,400,000	0.60 C	1,800,000
Total liabilities	3,450,000		2,415,000		2,760,000		2,070,000
Capital stock	1,500,000	0.70	1,050,000	0.70 H	1,050,000	0.70 H	1,050,000
Retained earnings	830,000		581,000		612,000		550,000
Translation adjustment	N/A		0		202,000		(202,000)
Total equity	2,330,000		1,631,000		1,864,000		1,398,000
Total	5,780,000		4,046,000		4,624,000		3,468,000

Note: C = current (period-end) exchange rate; A = average-for-the-year exchange rate; H = historical exchange rate.

The translation adjustment is zero when the Canadian dollar remains stable for the year; it is positive when the Canadian dollar strengthens and negative when the Canadian dollar weakens. Compared with the amounts that would appear in the euro consolidated balance sheet under a stable Canadian dollar assumption, a stronger Canadian dollar results in a larger amount of assets, liabilities, and equity being reported on the consolidated balance sheet, and a weaker Canadian dollar results in a smaller amount of assets, liabilities, and equity being reported on the consolidated balance sheet.

Solution to 2:

Temporal Method: Using the temporal method, Canadaco's financial statements would be translated into euro as follows under the three different exchange rate scenarios:

Canadaco Balance Sheet on 31 December 20X1

		Temporal Method					
	C$	C$ Stable Exch. Rate	C$ Stable €	C$ Strengthens Exch. Rate	C$ Strengthens €	C$ Weakens Exch. Rate	C$ Weakens €
Assets							
Cash	980,000	0.70	686,000	0.80 C	784,000	0.60 C	588,000
Accounts receivable	900,000	0.70	630,000	0.80 C	720,000	0.60 C	540,000
Inventory	1,200,000	0.70	840,000	0.74 H	888,000	0.66 H	792,000

(continued)

(Continued)

| | C$ | Temporal Method | | | | | | |
| | | C$ Stable | | C$ Strengthens | | C$ Weakens | | |
	C$	Exch. Rate	€	Exch. Rate	€	Exch. Rate	€
Total current assets	3,080,000		2,156,000		2,392,000		1,920,000
Property and equipment	3,000,000	0.70	2,100,000	0.70 H	2,100,000	0.70 H	2,100,000
Less: accum. deprec.	(300,000)	0.70	(210,000)	0.70 H	(210,000)	0.70 H	(210,000)
Total assets	5,780,000		4,046,000		4,282,000		3,810,000
Liabilities and Equity							
Accounts payable	450,000	0.70	315,000	0.80 C	360,000	0.60 C	270,000
Total current liabilities	450,000		315,000		360,000		270,000
Long-term notes pay	3,000,000	0.70	2,100,000	0.80 C	2,400,000	0.60 C	1,800,000
Total liabilities	3,450,000		2,415,000		2,760,000		2,070,000
Capital stock	1,500,000	0.70	1,050,000	0.70 H	1,050,000	0.70 H	1,050,000
Retained earnings	830,000		581,000		472,000		690,000
Total equity	2,330,000		1,631,000		1,522,000		1,740,000
Total	5,780,000		4,046,000		4,282,000		3,810,000

Note: C = current (period-end) exchange rate; A = average-for-the-year exchange rate; H = historical exchange rate.

Compared with the stable Canadian dollar scenario, a stronger Canadian dollar results in a larger amount of assets and liabilities but a smaller amount of equity reported on the consolidated balance sheet. A weaker Canadian dollar results in a smaller amount of assets and liabilities but a larger amount of equity reported on the consolidated balance sheet.

Canadaco Income Statement and Statement of Retained Earnings for 2008 under the Temporal Method

| | C$ | C$ Stable | | C$ Strengthens | | C$ Weakens | |
		Exch. Rate	€	Exch. Rate	€	Exch. Rate	€
Sales	12,000,000	0.70	8,400,000	0.75 A	9,000,000	0.65 A	7,800,000
Cost of sales	(9,000,000)	0.70	(6,300,000)	0.74 H	(6,660,000)	0.66 H	(5,940,000)
Selling expenses	(750,000)	0.70	(525,000)	0.75 A	(562,500)	0.65 A	(487,500)
Depreciation expense	(300,000)	0.70	(210,000)	0.70 H	(210,000)	0.70 H	(210,000)

(Continued)

| | C$ | C$ Stable | | C$ Strengthens | | C$ Weakens | |
		Exch. Rate	€	Exch. Rate	€	Exch. Rate	€
Interest expense	(270,000)	0.70	(189,000)	0.75 A	(202,500)	0.65 A	(175,500)
Income tax	(500,000)	0.70	(350,000)	0.75 A	(375,000)	0.65 A	(325,000)
Income before translation gain (loss)	1,180,000		826,000		990,000		662,000
Translation gain (loss)	N/A		0		(245,000)		245,000
Net income	1,180,000		826,000		745,000		907,000
Less: Dividends	(350,000)	0.70	(245,000)	0.78 H	(273,000)	0.62 H	(217,000)
Retained earnings	830,000		581,000		472,000		690,000

Note: C = current (period-end) exchange rate; A = average-for-the-year exchange rate; H = historical exchange rate.

No translation gain or loss exists when the Canadian dollar remains stable during the year. Because the subsidiary has a net monetary liability exposure to changes in the exchange rate, a stronger Canadian dollar results in a translation loss and a weaker Canadian dollar results in a translation gain. Compared with a stable Canadian dollar, a stronger Canadian dollar results in a larger amount of sales and a smaller amount of net income reported on the consolidated income statement. This difference in direction results from the translation loss that is included in net income. (As demonstrated in Example 5, a translation gain would have resulted if the subsidiary had a net monetary asset exposure.) A weaker Canadian dollar results in a smaller amount of sales but a larger amount of net income than if the Canadian dollar had remained stable.

Exhibit 5 summarizes the relationships illustrated in Examples 5 and 6, focusing on the typical effect that a strengthening or weakening of the foreign currency has on financial statement amounts compared with what the amounts would be if the foreign currency were to remain stable.

	Temporal Method, Net Monetary Liability Exposure	**Temporal Method, Net Monetary Asset Exposure**	**Current Rate Method**
Exhibit 5	**Effect of Currency Exchange Rate Movement on Financial Statements**		
Foreign currency strengthens relative to parent's presentation currency	↑ Revenues ↑ Assets ↑ Liabilities ↓ Net income ↓ Shareholders' equity Translation loss	↑ Revenues ↑ Assets ↑ Liabilities ↑ Net income ↑ Shareholders' equity Translation gain	↑ Revenues ↑ Assets ↑ Liabilities ↑ Net income ↑ Shareholders' equity Positive translation adjustment
Foreign currency weakens relative to parent's presentation currency	↓ Revenues ↓ Assets ↓ Liabilities ↑ Net income ↑ Shareholders' equity Translation gain	↓ Revenues ↓ Assets ↓ Liabilities ↓ Net income ↓ Shareholders' equity Translation loss	↓ Revenues ↓ Assets ↓ Liabilities ↓ Net income ↓ Shareholders' equity Negative translation adjustment

3.5 Translation when a Foreign Subsidiary Operates in a Hyperinflationary Economy

As noted earlier, IFRS and US GAAP differ substantially in their approach to translating the foreign currency financial statements of foreign entities operating in the currency of a hyperinflationary economy. US GAAP simply require the foreign currency financial statements of such an entity to be translated as if the parent's currency is the functional currency (i.e., the temporal method must be used with the resulting translation gain or loss reported in net income). IFRS require the foreign currency financial statements first to be restated for inflation using the procedures of IAS 29, and then the inflation-adjusted financial statements are translated using the current exchange rate.

IAS 29 requires the following procedures in adjusting financial statements for inflation:

Balance Sheet

- Monetary assets and monetary liabilities are not restated because they are already expressed in terms of the monetary unit current at the balance sheet date. Monetary items consist of cash, receivables, and payables.

- Non-monetary assets and non-monetary liabilities are restated for changes in the general purchasing power of the monetary unit. Most non-monetary items are carried at historical cost. In these cases, the restated cost is determined by applying to the historical cost the change in the general price index from the date of acquisition to the balance sheet date. Some non-monetary items are carried at revalued amounts; for example, property, plant, and equipment revalued according to the allowed alternative treatment in IAS 16, "Property, Plant and Equipment." These items are restated from the date of revaluation.

- All components of stockholders' equity are restated by applying the change in the general price level from the beginning of the period or, if later, from the date of contribution to the balance sheet date.

Income Statement

- All income statement items are restated by applying the change in the general price index from the dates when the items were originally recorded to the balance sheet date.

- The net gain or loss in purchasing power that arises from holding monetary assets and monetary liabilities during a period of inflation is included in net income.

The procedures for adjusting financial statements for inflation are similar in concept to the procedures followed when using the temporal method for translation. By restating non-monetary assets and liabilities along with stockholders' equity in terms of the general price level at the balance sheet date, these items are carried at their historical amount of purchasing power. Only the monetary items, which are not restated for inflation, are exposed to inflation risk. The effect of that exposure is reflected through the purchasing power gain or loss on the net monetary asset or liability position.

Holding cash and receivables during a period of inflation results in a **purchasing power loss**, whereas holding payables during inflation results in a **purchasing power gain**. This relationship can be demonstrated through the following examples.

Assume that the general price index (GPI) on 1 January 20X1 is 100; that is, a representative basket of goods and services can be purchased on that date for $100. At the end of 20X1, the same basket of goods and services costs $120; thus, the country has experienced an inflation rate of 20% [($120 − $100) ÷ $100]. Cash of $100 can be used to acquire one basket of goods on 1 January 20X1. One year later, however, when the GPI stands at 120, the same $100 in cash can now purchase only 83.3% of a basket of goods and services. At the end of 20X1, it now takes $120 to purchase the same amount as $100 could purchase at the beginning of the year. The difference between the amount of cash needed to purchase one market basket at year end ($120) and the amount actually held ($100) results in a purchasing power loss of $20 from holding cash of $100 during the year.

Borrowing money during a period of inflation increases purchasing power. Assume that a company expects to receive $120 in cash at the end of 20X1. If it waits until the cash is received, the company will be able to purchase exactly 1.0 basket of goods and services when the GPI stands at 120. If instead, the company borrows $120 on 1 January 20X1 when the GPI is 100, it can acquire 1.2 baskets of goods and services. This transaction results in a purchasing power gain of $20. Of course, there is an interest cost associated with the borrowing that offsets a portion of this gain.

A net purchasing power gain will arise when a company holds a greater amount of monetary liabilities than monetary assets, and a net purchasing power loss will result when the opposite situation exists. As such, purchasing power gains and losses are analogous to the translation gains and losses that arise when the currency is weakening in value and the temporal method of translation is applied.

Although the procedures required by IFRS and US GAAP for translating the foreign currency financial statements in high-inflation countries are fundamentally different, the results, in a rare occurrence, can be very similar. Indeed, if the exchange rate between two currencies changes by exactly the same percentage as the change in the general price index in the highly inflationary country, then the two methodologies produce the same results. Example 7 demonstrates this scenario.

EXAMPLE 7

Translation of Foreign Currency Financial Statements of a Foreign Entity Operating in a High Inflation Country

ABC Company formed a subsidiary in a foreign country on 1 January 20X1, through a combination of debt and equity financing. The foreign subsidiary acquired land on 1 January 20X1, which it rents to a local farmer. The foreign subsidiary's financial statements for its first year of operations, in foreign currency units (FC), are as follows:

Foreign Subsidiary Income Statement	
(in FC)	**20X1**
Rent revenue	1,000
Interest expense	(250)
Net income	750

Foreign Subsidiary Balance Sheets		
(in FC)	**1 Jan 20X1**	**31 Dec 20X1**
Cash	1,000	1,750
Land	9,000	9,000
Total	10,000	10,750
Note payable (5%)	5,000	5,000
Capital stock	5,000	5,000
Retained earnings	0	750
Total	10,000	10,750

The foreign country experienced significant inflation in 20X1, especially in the second half of the year. The general price index during the year was as follows:

1 January 20X1	100
Average, 20X1	125
31 December 20X1	200

The inflation rate in 20X1 was 100%, and the foreign country clearly meets the definition of a highly inflationary economy.

As a result of the high inflation rate in the foreign country, the FC weakened substantially during the year relative to other currencies. Relevant exchange rates between ABC's presentation currency (US dollars) and the FC during 20X1 were as follows:

	US$ per FC
1 January 20X1	1.00
Average, 20X1	0.80
31 December 20X1	0.50

What amounts will ABC Company include in its consolidated financial statements for the year ended 31 December 20X1 related to this foreign subsidiary?

Solution:

Assuming that ABC Company wishes to prepare its consolidated financial statements in accordance with IFRS, the foreign subsidiary's 20X1 financial statements will be restated for local inflation and then translated into ABC's presentation currency using the current exchange rate as follows:

	FC	Restatement Factor	Inflation-Adjusted FC	Exch. Rate	US$
Cash	1,750	200/200	1,750	0.50	875
Land	9,000	200/100	18,000	0.50	9,000
Total	10,750		19,750		9,875
Note payable	5,000	200/200	5,000	0.50	2,500
Capital stock	5,000	200/100	10,000	0.50	5,000
Retained earnings	750		4,750	0.50	2,375
Total	10,750		19,750		9,875
Revenues	1,000	200/125	1,600	0.50	800
Interest expense	(250)	200/125	(400)	0.50	(200)
Subtotal	750		1,200		600
Purchasing power gain/loss			3,550	0.50	1,775
Net income			4,750		2,375

All financial statement items are restated to the GPI at 31 December 20X1. The net purchasing power gain of FC3,550 can be explained as follows:

Gain from holding note payable	FC5,000 × (200 − 100)/100 =	FC5,000
Loss from holding beginning balance in cash	−1,000 × (200 − 100)/100 =	(1,000)
Loss from increase in cash during the year	−750 × (200 − 125)/125 =	(450)
Net purchasing power gain (loss)		FC3,550

Note that all inflation-adjusted FC amounts are translated at the current exchange rate, and thus no translation adjustment is needed.

Now assume alternatively that ABC Company wishes to comply with US GAAP in preparing its consolidated financial statements. In that case, the foreign subsidiary's FC financial statements are translated into US dollars using the temporal method, with the resulting translation gain/loss reported in net income, as follows:

	FC	Exch. Rate	US$
Cash	1,750	0.50 C	875
Land	9,000	1.00 H	9,000
Total	10,750		9,875
Note payable	5,000	0.50 C	2,500
Capital stock	5,000	1.00 H	5,000
Retained earnings	750		2,375
Total	10,750		9,875
Revenues	1,000	0.80 A	800
Interest expense	(250)	0.80 A	(200)
Subtotal	750		600
Translation gain*			1,775
Net income			2,375

*The dividend is US$0 and the increase in retained earnings is US$2,375 (from the balance sheet); so, net income is US$2,375, and thus the translation gain is US$1,775.
Note: C = current (period-end) exchange rate; A = average-for-the-year exchange rate; H = historical exchange rate

Application of the temporal method as required by US GAAP in this situation results in exactly the same US dollar amounts as were obtained under the restate/translate approach required by IFRS. The equivalence of results under the two approaches exists because of the exact one-to-one inverse relationship between the change in the foreign country's GPI and the change in the dollar value of the FC, as predicted by the theory of purchasing power parity. The GPI doubled and the FC lost half its purchasing power, which caused the FC to lose half its value in dollar terms. To the extent that this relationship does not hold, and it rarely ever does, the two different methodologies will generate different translated amounts. For example, if the 31 December 20X1 exchange rate had adjusted to only US$0.60 per FC1 (rather than US$0.50 per FC1), then translated net income would have been US$2,050 under US GAAP and US$2,850 under IFRS.

3.6 Companies Use Both Translation Methods at the Same Time

Under both IFRS and US GAAP, a multinational corporation may need to use both the current rate and the temporal methods of translation at a single point in time. This situation will apply when some foreign subsidiaries have a foreign currency as their functional currency (and therefore are translated using the current rate method) and other foreign subsidiaries have the parent's currency as their functional currency (and therefore are translated using the temporal method). As a result, a multinational corporation's consolidated financial statements can reflect simultaneously both a net translation gain or loss that is included in the determination of net income (from foreign subsidiaries translated using the temporal method) and a separate cumulative translation adjustment reported on the balance sheet in stockholders' equity (from foreign subsidiaries translated using the current rate method).

Exxon Mobil Corporation is an example of a company that has a mixture of foreign currency and parent currency functional currency subsidiaries, as evidenced by the following excerpt from its 2011 annual report, Note 1 Summary of Accounting Policies:

> **Foreign Currency Translation.** The Corporation selects the functional reporting currency for its international subsidiaries based on the currency of the primary economic environment in which each subsidiary operates. Downstream and Chemical operations primarily use the local currency. However, the US dollar is used in countries with a history of high inflation (primarily in Latin America) and Singapore, which predominantly sells into the US dollar export market. Upstream operations which are relatively self-contained and integrated within a particular country, such as Canada, the United Kingdom, Norway and continental Europe, use the local currency. Some upstream operations, primarily in Asia and Africa, use the US dollar because they predominantly sell crude and natural gas production into US dollar–denominated markets. For all operations, gains or losses from remeasuring foreign currency transactions into the functional currency are included in income.

Because of the judgment involved in determining the functional currency of foreign operations, two companies operating in the same industry might apply this judgment differently. For example, although Exxon Mobil has identified the local currency as the functional currency for many of its international subsidiaries, Chevron Corporation has designated the US dollar as the functional currency for substantially all of its overseas operations, as indicated in its 2011 annual report, Note 1 Summary of Significant Accounting Policies:

> **Currency Translation.** The US dollar is the functional currency for substantially all of the company's consolidated operations and those of its equity affiliates. For those operations, all gains and losses from currency remeasurement are included in current period income. The cumulative translation effects for those few entities, both consolidated and affiliated, using functional currencies other than the US dollar are included in "Currency translation adjustment" on the Consolidated Statement of Equity.

Evaluating net income reported by Exxon Mobil against net income reported by Chevron presents a comparability problem. This problem can be partially resolved by adding the translation adjustments reported in stockholders' equity to net income for both companies. The feasibility of this solution depends on the level of detail disclosed by multinational corporations with respect to the translation of foreign currency financial statements.

3.7 Disclosures Related to Translation Methods

Both IFRS and US GAAP require two types of disclosures related to foreign currency translation:

1 the amount of exchange differences recognized in net income, and

2 the amount of cumulative translation adjustment classified in a separate component of equity, along with a reconciliation of the amount of cumulative translation adjustment at the beginning and end of the period.

US GAAP also specifically require disclosure of the amount of translation adjustment transferred from stockholders' equity and included in current net income as a result of the disposal of a foreign entity.

The amount of exchange differences recognized in net income consists of

- foreign currency *transaction* gains and losses, and
- *translation* gains and losses resulting from application of the temporal method.

Neither IFRS nor US GAAP require disclosure of the two separate amounts that constitute the total exchange difference recognized in net income, and most companies do not provide disclosure at that level of detail. However, BASF AG (shown earlier in Exhibit 1) is an exception. Note 6 in BASF's annual report separately discloses gains from foreign currency and hedging transactions and gains from translation of financial statements, both of which are included in the line item "Other Operating Income" on the income statement, as shown below:

6. Other Operating Income		
Million €	**2011**	**2010**
Reversal and adjustment of provisions	170	244
Revenue from miscellaneous revenue-generating activities	207	142
Income from foreign currency and hedging transactions	170	136
Income from the translation of financial statements in foreign currencies	42	76
Gains on the disposal of property, plant and equipment and divestitures	666	101
Reversals of impairments of property, plant and equipment	—	40
Gains on the reversal of allowance for doubtful business-related receivables	77	36
Other	676	365
	2,008	1,140

The company provides a similar level of detail in Note 7 related to "Other Operating Expenses."

Disclosures related to foreign currency translation are commonly found in both the MD&A and the Notes to Financial Statements sections of an annual report. Example 8 uses the foreign currency translation–related disclosures made in 2011 by Yahoo! Inc.

EXAMPLE 8

Disclosures Related to Foreign Currency Translation: Yahoo! Inc. 2011 Annual Report

Yahoo! Inc. is a US-based digital media company that reports in US dollars and prepares financial statements in accordance with US GAAP.

The stockholders' equity section of Yahoo!'s consolidated balance sheets includes the following line items:

(in thousands)	31 December 2010	2011
Common stock	$1,306	$1,242
Additional paid-in capital	10,109,913	9,825,899
Treasury stock	—	(416,237)
Retained earnings	1,942,656	2,432,294
Accumulated other comprehensive income (loss)	504,254	697,869
Total Yahoo! Inc. stockholders' equity	12,558,129	12,541,067

The consolidated statement of stockholders' equity provides detail on the components comprising "Accumulated other comprehensive income." The relevant portion of that statement appears below:

	Years Ended 31 December		
	2009	2010	2011
Accumulated other comprehensive income			
Balance, beginning of year	120,276	369,236	504,254
Net change in unrealized gains/losses on available-for-sale securities, net of tax	(1,936)	3,813	(16,272)
Foreign currency translation adjustments, net of tax	250,896	131,205	209,887
Balance, end of year	369,236	504,254	697,869

Yahoo! reported the following net income in 2010 and 2011, as shown on the consolidated statement of income:

	2010	2011	% Change
Net income	$1,244,628	$1,062,699	−14.6%

Yahoo!'s disclosures for its three geographic segments are disclosed in a note to the financial statements. Revenue (excluding total acquisition costs) and direct segment operating costs are shown below:

	2009	2010	2011
Revenue ex-TAC by segment:			
Americas	3,656,752	3,467,850	3,142,879
EMEA	390,456	368,884	407,467
Asia Pacific	635,281	751,495	830,482
Total revenue ex-TAC	4,682,489	4,588,229	4,380,828
Direct costs by segment:			
Americas	620,690	568,017	560,016
EMEA	115,778	118,954	135,266
Asia Pacific	138,739	146,657	194,394

In the MD&A section of the 2011 annual report, Yahoo! describes the source of its translation exposure:

Translation Exposure

We are also exposed to foreign exchange rate fluctuations as we convert the financial statements of our foreign subsidiaries and our investments in equity interests into US dollars in consolidation. If there is a change in foreign currency exchange rates, the conversion of the foreign subsidiaries' financial statements into US dollars results in a gain or loss which is recorded as a component of accumulated other comprehensive income which is part of stockholders' equity.

Revenue ex-TAC (total acquisition costs) and related expenses generated from our international subsidiaries are generally denominated in the currencies of the local countries. Primary currencies include Australian dollars, British pounds, Euros, Japanese Yen, Korean won, and Taiwan dollars. The statements of income of our international operations are translated into US dollars at exchange rates indicative of market rates during each applicable period. To the extent the US dollar strengthens against foreign currencies, the translation of these foreign currency-denominated transactions results in reduced consolidated revenue and operating expenses. Conversely, our consolidated revenue and operating expenses will increase if the US dollar weakens against foreign currencies. Using the foreign currency exchange rates from the year ended December 31, 2010, revenue ex-TAC for the Americas segment for the year ended December 31, 2011 would have been lower than we reported by $6 million, revenue ex-TAC for the EMEA segment would have been lower than we reported by $16 million, and revenue ex-TAC for the Asia Pacific segment would have been lower than we reported by $59 million. Using the foreign currency exchange rates from the year ended December 31, 2010, direct costs for the Americas segment for the year ended December 31, 2011 would have been lower than we reported by $2 million, direct costs for the EMEA segment would have been lower than we reported by $5 million, and direct costs for the Asia Pacific segment would have been lower than we reported by $15 million.

Using the information above, address the following questions:

1 By how much did accumulated other comprehensive income change during the year ended 31 December 2011? Where can this information be found?

2 How much foreign currency translation adjustment was included in other comprehensive income for the year ended 31 December 2011? How does such an adjustment arise?

3 If foreign currency translation adjustment had been included in net income (rather than in other comprehensive income), how would the 2010/2011 change in income have been affected?

4 From what perspective does Yahoo! describe its foreign currency risk?

5 What percentage of total revenue ex-TAC was generated by the Asia-Pacific segment for the year ended 31 December 2011? What would this percentage have been if there had been no change in foreign currency exchange rates during the year?

Solutions:

1. Accumulated other comprehensive income increased by $193,615 thousand (from $504,254 thousand beginning balance to $697,869 thousand at the end of the year). This information can be found in two places: the stockholders' equity section of the balance sheet and the consolidated statement of stockholders' equity.

2. The amount of foreign currency translation adjustment included in other comprehensive income for 2011 was $209,887 thousand. The foreign currency translation adjustment arises from applying the current rate method to translate the foreign currency functional currency financial statements of foreign subsidiaries. Assuming that Yahoo!'s foreign subsidiaries have positive net assets, the positive translation adjustment in 2011 results from a strengthening in foreign currencies (weakening in the US dollar).

3. If foreign currency translation adjustment had been included in net income (rather than other comprehensive income), the percentage decrease in reported net income from 2010 to 2011 of 14.6% would have been smaller (7.5%).

	2010	2011	% Change
Net income	$1,244,628	$1,062,699	−14.6%
Foreign currency translation adjustment	131,205	209,887	
	$1,375,833	$1,272,586	−7.5%

4. Yahoo! describes its foreign currency risk from the perspective of how the US dollar fluctuates against foreign currencies because the dollar is the reporting currency. If the US dollar strengthens, then foreign currencies must weaken, which will result in reduced revenues, expenses, and income from foreign operations.

5. The Asia-Pacific segment represented 19.0% of total revenue ex-TAC. Information from the MD&A disclosure can be used to determine that if there had been no change in foreign currency exchange rates during the year, the segment would have represented a slightly lower percentage of total revenue (17.9%).

	2011, as reported			2011, if no change in exchange rates	
Revenue ex-TAC by segment:					
Americas	3,142,879	71.7%	6,000	3,136,879	73.0%
EMEA	407,467	9.3%	16,000	391,467	9.1%
Asia Pacific	830,482	19.0%	59,000	771,482	17.9%
Total revenue ex-TAC	4,380,828	100.0%		4,299,828	100.0%

As noted in the previous section, because of the judgment involved in determining the functional currency of foreign operations, two companies operating in the same industry might use different predominant translation methods. As a result, income reported by these companies may not be directly comparable. Exxon Mobil Corporation and Chevron Corporation, both operating in the petroleum industry, are an example of two companies for which this is the case. Whereas Chevron has identified the US dollar as the functional currency for substantially all of its foreign subsidiaries, Exxon Mobil indicates that its downstream and chemical operations, as well as some of its upstream operations, primarily use the local currency as the functional currency. As a result, Chevron primarily uses the temporal method with translation gains and losses included in income, while Exxon Mobil uses the current rate method to a much greater extent, with the resulting translation adjustments excluded from income. To make the income of these two companies more comparable, an analyst can use the disclosures related to translation adjustments to include these as gains and losses in determining an adjusted amount of income. Example 9 demonstrates this process for Exxon Mobil and Chevron.

EXAMPLE 9

Comparing Net Income for Exxon Mobil Corporation and Chevron Corporation

Exxon Mobil Corporation uses the current rate method to translate the foreign currency financial statements of a substantial number of its foreign subsidiaries and includes the resulting translation adjustments in the "Accumulated other non-owner changes in equity" line item in the stockholders' equity section of the consolidated balance sheet. Detail on the items composing "Accumulated other non-owner changes in equity," including "Foreign exchange translation adjustment," is provided in the consolidated statement of shareholders' equity.

Chevron Corporation uses the temporal method to translate the foreign currency financial statements of substantially all of its foreign subsidiaries. For those few entities using functional currencies other than the US dollar, however, the current rate method is used and the resulting translation adjustments are included in the "Accumulated other comprehensive loss" component of stockholders' equity. The consolidated statement of stockholders' equity provides detail on the changes in the component of stockholders' equity, including a "Currency translation adjustment."

Combining net income from the income statement and the change in the cumulative translation adjustment account from the statement of stockholders' equity, an adjusted net income in which translation adjustments are treated as gains and losses can be calculated for each company, as shown in the following table (amounts in millions of US dollars):

Exxon Mobil	2011	2010	2009
Reported net income	42,206	31,398	19,658
Translation adjustment	(867)	1,034	3,629
Adjusted net income	41,339	32,432	23,287

Chevron	2011	2010	2009
Reported net income	27,008	19,136	10,563
Translation adjustment	17	6	60
Adjusted net income	27,025	19,142	10,623

The direction, positive or negative, of the translation adjustment is the same for both companies in 2009 and 2010 but not in 2011. Overall, Exxon Mobil has significantly larger translation adjustments than Chevron because Exxon Mobil designates the local currency as functional currency for a substantially larger portion of its foreign operations.

A comparison of the relative amounts of net income generated by the two companies is different depending on whether reported net income or adjusted net income is used. Exxon Mobil's reported net income in 2009 is 1.90 times larger than Chevron's, whereas its adjusted net income is 2.2 times larger, as shown in the following table.

	2011	2010	2009
Exxon Mobil reported net income/ Chevron reported net income	1.6	1.6	1.9
Exxon Mobil adjusted net income/ Chevron adjusted net income	1.5	1.7	2.2

Including translation adjustments as gains and losses in the measurement of an adjusted net income provides a more comparable basis for evaluating the profitability of two companies that use different predominant translation methods. Bringing the translation adjustments into the calculation of adjusted net income still might not provide truly comparable measures, however, because of the varying effect that the different translation methods have on reported net income.

Some analysts believe that all non-owner changes in stockholders' equity, such as translation adjustments, should be included in the determination of net income. This approach is referred to as clean-surplus accounting, as opposed to dirty-surplus accounting, in which some income items are reported as part of stockholders' equity rather than as gains and losses on the income statement. One of the dirty-surplus items found in both IFRS and US GAAP financial statements is the translation adjustment that arises when a foreign currency is determined to be the functional currency of a foreign subsidiary. Disclosures made in accordance with IFRS and US GAAP provide analysts with the detail needed to calculate net income on a clean-surplus basis. In fact, both sets of standards now require companies to prepare a statement of comprehensive income in which unrealized gains and losses that have been deferred in stockholders' equity are included in a measure of comprehensive income.

MULTINATIONAL OPERATIONS AND A COMPANY'S EFFECTIVE TAX RATE

In general, multinational companies incur income taxes in the country in which the profit is earned. Transfer prices, the prices that related companies charge on intercompany transactions, affect the allocation of profit between the companies. An entity with operations in multiple countries with different tax rates could aim to set transfer prices such that a higher portion of its profit is allocated to lower tax rate jurisdictions. Countries have established various laws and practices to prevent aggressive transfer pricing practices. Transfer pricing has been defined as "the system of laws and practices used by countries to ensure that goods, services and intellectual property transferred between related companies are appropriately priced, based on market conditions, such that profits are correctly reflected in each jurisdiction."[5] Also, most countries are party to tax treaties that prevent double-taxation of corporate profits by granting a credit for taxes paid to another country.

Whether and when a company also pays income taxes in its home country depends on the specific tax regime. In the United States, for example, multinational companies are liable only for a residual tax on foreign income, after applying a credit for foreign taxes paid on that same income. The effect of the tax credit is that the multinational company owes taxes on the foreign income only to the extent that the US corporate tax rate exceeds the foreign rate of tax on that income. In addition, much of the foreign income earned by US multinationals is not taxed until it is repatriated.[6]

An analyst can obtain information about the effect of multinational operations from companies' disclosure on effective tax rates. Accounting standards require companies to provide an explanation of the relationship between tax expense and accounting profit. The explanation is presented as a reconciliation between the average effective tax rate (tax expense divided by pretax accounting profits) and the relevant statutory rate. The purpose of this disclosure is to enable users of financial statements to understand whether the relationship between tax expense and accounting profit in a particular fiscal period is unusual and to understand the significant factors—including the effect of foreign taxes—that could affect that relationship in the future.[7] Changes in the effective tax rate impact of foreign taxes could be caused by changes in the applicable tax rates and/or changes in the mix of profits earned in different jurisdictions.

EXAMPLE 10

Below are excerpts from the effective tax rate reconciliation disclosures by two companies: Heineken N.V., a Dutch brewer, and Colgate Palmolive, a US consumer products company. Use the disclosures to answer the following questions:

1 Which company's home country has a lower statutory tax rate?

2 What was the impact of multinational operations on each company's 2011 effective tax rate?

3 Changes in the tax rate impact of multinational operations can often be explained by changes of profit mix between countries with higher or lower marginal tax rates. What do Heineken's disclosures suggest about the geographic mix of its 2011 profit?

Heineken N.V. Annual Report 2011
Notes to the consolidated financial statements
13. Income tax expense (excerpt)

Reconciliation of the effective tax rate

In millions of EUR	2011	2010
Profit before income tax	2,025	1,982
Share of net profit of associates and joint ventures and impairments thereof	(240)	(193)

---

5 TP Analytics. http://www.tpanalytics.com.
6 United States Government Accountability Office (GAO) Report GAO-08-950. *US Multinational Corporations: Effective Tax Rates Are Correlated with Where Income Is Reported.* August 2008.
7 International Accounting Standard 12 *Income Taxes*, ¶84.

(Continued)

Reconciliation of the effective tax rate

In millions of EUR	2011	2010
Profit before income tax excluding share of profit of associates and joint ventures (inclusive impairments thereof)	1,785	1,789

	%	2011	%	2010
Income tax using the Company's domestic tax rate	25.0	446	25.5	456
Effect of tax rates in foreign jurisdictions	3.5	62	1.9	34
Effect of non-deductible expenses	3.2	58	4	72
Effect of tax incentives and exempt income	(6.0)	−107	−8.2	−146
Recognition of previously unrecognised temporary differences	(0.5)	−9	−0.1	−2
Utilisation or recognition of previously unrecognised tax losses	(0.3)	−5	−1.2	−21
Unrecognised current year tax losses	1.0	18	0.8	15
Effect of changes in tax rate	0.1	1	0.2	3
Withholding taxes	1.5	26	1.4	25
Under/(over) provided in prior years	(1.5)	−27	−2.3	−42
Other reconciling items	0.1	2	0.5	9
	26.1	465	22.5	403

COLGATE-PALMOLIVE COMPANY Annual Report 2011
Notes to Consolidated Financial Statements
10. Income Taxes (excerpt)

The difference between the statutory US federal income tax rate and the Company's global effective tax rate as reflected in the Consolidated Statements of Income is as follows:

Percentage of Income before income taxes	2011	2010	2009
Tax at United States statutory rate	35.0%	35.0%	35.0%
State income taxes, net of federal benefit	0.4	1.1	0.5
Earnings taxed at other than United States statutory rate	(1.7)	(4.6)	(2.5)
Venezuela hyperinflationary transition charge	—	2.8	—
Other, net	(1.1)	(1.7)	(0.8)
Effective tax rate	32.6%	32.6%	32.2%

Solution to 1:

Heineken's home country tax rate (25.0% in 2011) is lower than Colgate Palmolive's home country tax rate (35.0%).

Solution to 2:

The line item labeled "Effect of tax rates in foreign jurisdictions" indicates that multinational operations increased Heineken's effective tax rate by 3.5 percentage points. The line item labeled "Earnings taxed at other than United States statutory rate" indicates that multinational operations lowered Colgate Palmolive's effective tax rate by 1.7 percentage points in 2011.

Solution to 3:

Multinational operations increased Heineken's effective tax rate by 3.5 percentage points in 2011 but only 1.9 percentage points in 2010. This greater impact in 2011 could indicate that Heineken's profit mix in 2011 shifted to countries with higher marginal tax rates. (The change could also indicate that the marginal tax rates increased in the countries in which Heineken earns profits.)

5   ADDITIONAL DISCLOSURES ON THE EFFECTS OF FOREIGN CURRENCY

We turn now to the question of how an analyst can use multinational companies' disclosures to better understand the effects of foreign currency.

5.1 Disclosures Related to Sales Growth

Companies often make important disclosures about foreign currency effect on sales growth in the MD&A. Additional disclosures are also often made in financial presentations to the analyst community.

For a multinational company, sales growth is driven not only by changes in volume and price but also by changes in the exchange rates between the reporting currency and the currency in which sales are made. Arguably, growth in sales that comes from changes in volume or price is more sustainable than growth in sales that comes from changes in exchange rates. Further, management arguably has greater control over growth in sales resulting from greater volume or higher price than from changes in exchange rates. Thus, an analyst will consider the foreign currency effect on sales growth both for forecasting future performance and for evaluating a management team's historical performance.

Companies often include disclosures about the effect of exchange rates on sales growth in the MD&A. Such disclosures may also appear in other financial reports, such as company presentations to investors or earnings announcements. Exhibit 6 provides an example of disclosure from the MD&A, and Example 11 illustrates even more detailed disclosure from a company's report to analysts.

Exhibit 6

General Mills' 2011 annual report includes the following disclosures about the components of net sales growth in its international segment. The first excerpt is from the MD&A, and the second is from a supplementary schedule reconciling non-GAAP measures. Although the overall effect on international net sales growth was minimal "flat," the geographic detail provided in the supplementary schedule shows that the effects varied widely by region.

Excerpt from MD&A

Components of International Net Sales Growth

	Fiscal 2011 vs. 2010	Fiscal 2010 vs. 2009
Contributions from volume growth[a]	6 pts	Flat
Net price realization and mix	1 pt	3 pts
Foreign currency exchange	Flat	1 pt
Net sales growth	7 pts	4 pts

[a] Measured in tons based on the stated weight of our product shipments.

Excerpt from Supplementary Schedule on Non-GAAP Measures

International Segment and Region Sales Growth Rates Excluding Impact of Foreign Exchange

	Fiscal Year 2011		
	Percentage change in Net Sales as Reported	Impact of Foreign Currency Exchange	Percentage change in Net Sales on Constant Currency Basis
Europe	5%	−2%	7%
Canada	8	5	3
Asia/Pacific	14	5	9
Latin America	−5	−16	11
Total International segment	7%	Flat	7%

Use the information disclosed in Procter & Gamble Company's CAGNY [Consumer Analyst Group of New York] conference slides to answer the following questions:

1   Why does the company present "organic sales growth"?
2   On average, for the four quarters beginning October 2008 and ending September 2009, how did changes in foreign exchange rates affect P&G's reported sales growth?

The Procter & Gamble Company

2012 CAGNY CONFERENCE SLIDES

Reg G Reconciliation of Non-GAAP measures

In accordance with the SEC's Regulation G, the following provides definitions of the non-GAAP measures used in the earnings call and slides with the reconciliation to the most closely related GAAP measure.

1   *Organic Sales Growth:*

Organic sales growth is a non-GAAP measure of sales growth excluding the impacts of acquisitions, divestitures and foreign exchange from year-over-year comparisons. We believe this provides investors with a more complete understanding of underlying sales trends by providing sales growth on a consistent basis. "Organic sales" is also one of the measures used to evaluate senior management and is a factor in determining their at-risk compensation. The reconciliation of reported sales growth to organic sales is as follows:

Total P&G	Net Sales Growth	Foreign Exchange Impact	Acquisition/ Divestiture Impact	Organic Sales Growth
JAS 06	27%	−1%	−20%	6%
OND 06	8%	−3%	0%	5%
JFM07	8%	−2%	0%	6%
AMJ07	8%	−3%	0%	5%
JAS07	8%	−3%	0%	5%
OND07	9%	−5%	1%	5%
JFM08	9%	−5%	1%	5%
AMJ08	10%	−6%	1%	5%
JAS08	9%	−5%	1%	5%
Average–JAS 06–JAS 08	11%	−4%	−2%	5%
OND08	−3%	5%	0%	2%
JFM09	−8%	9%	0%	1%
AMJ09	−11%	9%	1%	−1%
JAS09	−6%	7%	1%	2%
Average–OND 08–JAS 09	−7%	8%	0%	1%
OND09	6%	−2%	1%	5%
JFM010	7%	−3%	0%	4%
AMJ010	5%	−1%	0%	4%
JAS010	2%	3%	−1%	4%
OND010	2%	2%	−1%	3%
JFM011	5%	−1%	0%	4%
AMJ011	10%	−5%	0%	5%
JAS011	9%	−5%	0%	4%
OND011	4%	0%	0%	4%
Average–OND 09–OND 11	5%	−1%	0%	4%
JFM 12 (Estimate)	0% to 2%	3%	0%	3% to 5%
AMJ 12(Estimate)	−1% to 2%	5% to 4%	0%	4% to 6%

Solution to 1:

According to its disclosures, Procter & Gamble presents "organic sales growth" because the company believes it provides investors with a better understanding of underlying sales trends and because it is one of the measures used for management evaluation and compensation.

Solution to 2:

The average effect of foreign exchange changes during the period was negative: Although organic sales grew by 1%, the company reported net sales growth of −7% as a result of a negative 8% foreign exchange effect In other words, if no foreign exchange effect had occurred, reported sales growth and organic sales growth would have been equal, both at 1%.

5.2 Disclosures Related to Major Sources of Foreign Exchange Risk

Disclosures about the effects of currency fluctuations often include sensitivity analyses. For example, a company might describe the major sources of foreign exchange risk given its countries of operations and then disclose the profit impact of a given change in exchange rates.

Exhibit 7 includes two excerpts from the 2011 BMW AG annual report. The first excerpt, from the management report, describes the source of the company's currency risks and its approach to measuring and managing those risks. The second excerpt, from the additional disclosures section of the notes, presents the results of the company's sensitivity analysis.

Exhibit 7

Excerpts from 2011 BMW AG Annual Report

Excerpt from the management report describing the source of the company's currency risks and its approach to measuring and managing those risks:

"The sale of vehicles outside the euro zone gives rise to exchange risks. Three currencies (the Chinese renminbi, the US dollar and the British pound) accounted for approximately two-thirds of the BMW Group's foreign currency exposures in 2011. We employ cash-flow-at-risk models and scenario analyses to measure exchange rate risks. These tools provide information which serves as the basis for decision-making in the area of currency management.

"We manage currency risks both at a strategic (medium and long term) and at an operating level (short and medium term). In the medium and long term, foreign exchange risks are managed by "natural hedging", in other words by increasing the volume of purchases denominated in foreign currency or increasing the volume of local production. In this context, the expansion of the plant in Spartanburg, USA, and the new plant under construction in Tiexi* at the Shenyang site in China are helping to reduce foreign exchange risks in two major sales markets. For operating purposes (short and medium term), currency risks are hedged on the financial markets. Hedging transactions are entered into only with financial partners of good credit standing. Counterparty risk management procedures are carried out continuously to monitor the creditworthiness of those partners."

Excerpt, from the additional disclosures section of the notes, presenting the results of the company's sensitivity analysis risks:

(continued)

Exhibit 7   (Continued)

"The BMW Group measures currency risk using a cash-flow-at-risk model. The starting point for analysing currency risk with this model is the identification of forecast foreign currency transactions or "exposures". At the end of the reporting period, the principal exposures for the coming year were as follows:

in € million	31.12.2011	31.12.2010
Euro/Chinese Renminbi	7,114	6,256
Euro/US Dollar	4,281	3,888
Euro/British Pound	3,266	3,056
Euro/Japanese Yen	1,334	1,086

"In the next stage, these exposures are compared to all hedges that are in place. The net cash flow surplus represents an uncovered risk position. The cash-flow-at-risk approach involves allocating the impact of potential exchange rate fluctuations to operating cash flows on the basis of probability distributions. Volatilities and correlations serve as input factors to assess the relevant probability distributions.

"The potential negative impact on earnings for the current period is computed on the basis of current market prices and exposures to a confidence level of 95% and a holding period of up to one year for each currency. Aggregation of these results creates a risk reduction effect due to correlations between the various portfolios.

"The following table shows the potential negative impact for the BMW Group—measured on the basis of the cash-flow-at-risk approach—attributable at the balance sheet date to unfavourable changes in exchange rates for the principal currencies."

in € million	31.12.2011	31.12.2010
Euro/Chinese Renminbi	180	265
Euro/US Dollar	121	103
Euro/British Pound	182	184
Euro/Japanese Yen	23	30

The level of detail varies in companies' disclosures about sensitivity of earnings to foreign currency fluctuations, with some companies providing information on the range of possible values of foreign exchange rates. An analyst can use sensitivity analysis disclosures in conjunction with his or her own forecast of exchange rates when developing forecasts of profit and cash flow. When detailed disclosures are provided, the analyst can explicitly incorporate foreign exchange impact. Alternatively, in the absence of detailed disclosures, the analyst can incorporate the sensitivity analysis when calibrating the downside risks to base-case profit and cash flow forecasts.

SUMMARY

The translation of foreign currency amounts is an important accounting issue for companies with multinational operations. Foreign exchange rate fluctuations cause the functional currency values of foreign currency assets and liabilities resulting from foreign currency transactions as well as from foreign subsidiaries to change over time. These changes in value give rise to foreign exchange differences that companies' financial statements must reflect. Determining how to measure these foreign exchange differences and whether to include them in the calculation of net income are the major issues in accounting for multinational operations.

- The local currency is the national currency of the country where an entity is located. The functional currency is the currency of the primary economic environment in which an entity operates. Normally, the local currency is an entity's functional currency. For accounting purposes, any currency other than an entity's functional currency is a foreign currency for that entity. The currency in which financial statement amounts are presented is known as the presentation currency. In most cases, the presentation currency will be the same as the local currency.

- When an export sale (import purchase) on an account is denominated in a foreign currency, the sales revenue (inventory) and foreign currency account receivable (account payable) are translated into the seller's (buyer's) functional currency using the exchange rate on the transaction date. Any change in the functional currency value of the foreign currency account receivable (account payable) that occurs between the transaction date and the settlement date is recognized as a foreign currency transaction gain or loss in net income.

- If a balance sheet date falls between the transaction date and the settlement date, the foreign currency account receivable (account payable) is translated at the exchange rate at the balance sheet date. The change in the functional currency value of the foreign currency account receivable (account payable) is recognized as a foreign currency transaction gain or loss in income. Analysts should understand that these gains and losses are unrealized at the time they are recognized and might or might not be realized when the transactions are settled.

- A foreign currency transaction gain arises when an entity has a foreign currency receivable and the foreign currency strengthens or it has a foreign currency payable and the foreign currency weakens. A foreign currency transaction loss arises when an entity has a foreign currency receivable and the foreign currency weakens or it has a foreign currency payable and the foreign currency strengthens.

- Companies must disclose the net foreign currency gain or loss included in income. They may choose to report foreign currency transaction gains and losses as a component of operating income or as a component of non-operating income. If two companies choose to report foreign currency transaction gains and losses differently, operating profit and operating profit margin might not be directly comparable between the two companies.

- To prepare consolidated financial statements, foreign currency financial statements of foreign operations must be translated into the parent company's presentation currency. The major conceptual issues related to this translation process are, What is the appropriate exchange rate for translating each financial statement item, and how should the resulting translation adjustment be reflected in the consolidated financial statements? Two different translation methods are used worldwide.

- Under the current rate method, assets and liabilities are translated at the current exchange rate, equity items are translated at historical exchange rates, and revenues and expenses are translated at the exchange rate that existed when the underlying transaction occurred. For practical reasons, an average exchange rate is often used to translate income items.

- Under the temporal method, monetary assets (and non-monetary assets measured at current value) and monetary liabilities (and non-monetary liabilities measured at current value) are translated at the current exchange rate. Non-monetary assets and liabilities not measured at current value and equity items are translated at historical exchange rates. Revenues and expenses, other than those expenses related to non-monetary assets, are translated at the exchange rate that existed when the underlying transaction occurred. Expenses related to non-monetary assets are translated at the exchange rates used for the related assets.

- Under both IFRS and US GAAP, the functional currency of a foreign operation determines the method to be used in translating its foreign currency financial statements into the parent's presentation currency and whether the resulting translation adjustment is recognized in income or as a separate component of equity.

- The foreign currency financial statements of a foreign operation that has a foreign currency as its functional currency are translated using the current rate method, and the translation adjustment is accumulated as a separate component of equity. The cumulative translation adjustment related to a specific foreign entity is transferred to net income when that entity is sold or otherwise disposed of. The balance sheet risk exposure associated with the current rate method is equal to the foreign subsidiary's net asset position.

- The foreign currency financial statements of a foreign operation that has the parent's presentation currency as its functional currency are translated using the temporal method, and the translation adjustment is included as a gain or loss in income. US GAAP refer to this process as remeasurement. The balance sheet exposure associated with the temporal method is equal to the foreign subsidiary's net monetary asset/liability position (adjusted for non-monetary items measured at current value).

- IFRS and US GAAP differ with respect to the translation of foreign currency financial statements of foreign operations located in a highly inflationary country. Under IFRS, the foreign currency statements are first restated for local inflation and then translated using the current exchange rate. Under US GAAP, the foreign currency financial statements are translated using the temporal method, with no restatement for inflation.

- Applying different translation methods for a given foreign operation can result in very different amounts reported in the parent's consolidated financial statements.

- Companies must disclose the total amount of translation gain or loss reported in income and the amount of translation adjustment included in a separate component of stockholders' equity. Companies are not required to separately disclose the component of translation gain or loss arising from foreign currency transactions and the component arising from application of the temporal method.

- Disclosures related to translation adjustments reported in equity can be used to include these as gains and losses in determining an adjusted amount of income following a clean-surplus approach to income measurement.

- Foreign currency translation rules are well established in both IFRS and US GAAP. Fortunately, except for the treatment of foreign operations located in highly inflationary countries, the two sets of standards have no major differences in this area. The ability to understand the impact of foreign currency translation on the financial results of a company using IFRS should apply equally well in the analysis of financial statements prepared in accordance with US GAAP.

- An analyst can obtain information about the tax impact of multinational operations from companies' disclosure on effective tax rates.

- For a multinational company, sales growth is driven not only by changes in volume and price but also by changes in the exchange rates between the reporting currency and the currency in which sales are made. Arguably, growth in sales that comes from changes in volume or price is more sustainable than growth in sales that comes from changes in exchange rates.

PRACTICE PROBLEMS

The following information relates to Questions 1–6

Pedro Ruiz is an analyst for a credit rating agency. One of the companies he follows, Eurexim SA, is based in France and complies with International Financial Reporting Standards (IFRS). Ruiz has learned that Eurexim used EUR220 million of its own cash and borrowed an equal amount to open a subsidiary in Ukraine. The funds were converted into hryvnia (UAH) on 31 December 20X1 at an exchange rate of EUR1.00 = UAH6.70 and used to purchase UAH1,500 million in fixed assets and UAH300 of inventories.

Ruiz is concerned about the effect that the subsidiary's results might have on Eurexim's consolidated financial statements. He calls Eurexim's Chief Financial Officer, but learns little. Eurexim is not willing to share sales forecasts and has not even made a determination as to the subsidiary's functional currency.

Absent more useful information, Ruiz decides to explore various scenarios to determine the potential impact on Eurexim's consolidated financial statements. Ukraine is not currently in a hyperinflationary environment, but Ruiz is concerned that this situation could change. Ruiz also believes the euro will appreciate against the hryvnia for the foreseeable future.

1 If Ukraine's economy becomes highly inflationary, Eurexim will *most likely* translate inventory by:

   A restating for inflation and using the temporal method.

   B restating for inflation and using the current exchange rate.

   C using the temporal method with no restatement for inflation.

2 Given Ruiz's belief about the direction of exchange rates, Eurexim's gross profit margin would be *highest* if it accounts for the Ukraine subsidiary's inventory using:

   A FIFO and the temporal method.

   B FIFO and the current rate method.

   C weighted-average cost and the temporal method.

3 If the euro is chosen as the Ukraine subsidiary's functional currency, Eurexim will translate its fixed assets using the:

   A average rate for the reporting period.

   B rate in effect when the assets were purchased.

   C rate in effect at the end of the reporting period.

4 If the euro is chosen as the Ukraine subsidiary's functional currency, Eurexim will translate its accounts receivable using the:

   A rate in effect at the transaction date.

   B average rate for the reporting period.

   C rate in effect at the end of the reporting period.

Practice Problems and Solutions: *International Financial Statement Analysis*, by Thomas R. Robinson, CFA, Jan Hendrik van Greuning, CFA, Elaine Henry, CFA, and Michael A. Broihahn, CFA. Copyright © 2013 by CFA Institute.

5 If the hryvnia is chosen as the Ukraine subsidiary's functional currency, Eurexim will translate its inventory using the:

A average rate for the reporting period.

B rate in effect at the end of the reporting period.

C rate in effect at the time the inventory was purchased.

6 Based on the information available and Ruiz's expectations regarding exchange rates, if the hryvnia is chosen as the Ukraine subsidiary's functional currency, Eurexim will *most likely* report:

A an addition to the cumulative translation adjustment.

B a translation gain or loss as a component of net income.

C a subtraction from the cumulative translation adjustment.

The following information relates to Questions 7–12

Consolidated Motors is a US-based corporation that sells mechanical engines and components used by electric utilities. Its Canadian subsidiary, Consol-Can, operates solely in Canada. It was created on 31 December 20X1, and Consolidated Motors determined at that time that it should use the US dollar as its functional currency.

Chief Financial Officer Monica Templeton was asked to explain to the board of directors how exchange rates affect the financial statements of both Consol-Can and the consolidated financial statements of Consolidated Motors. For the presentation, Templeton collects Consol-Can's balance sheets for the years ended 20X1 and 20X2 (Exhibit 1), as well as relevant exchange rate information (Exhibit 2).

Exhibit 1	Consol-Can Condensed Balance Sheet for Fiscal Years Ending 31 December (C$ millions)	
Account	**20X2**	**20X1**
Cash	135	167
Accounts receivable	98	—
Inventory	77	30
Fixed assets	100	100
Accumulated depreciation	(10)	—
Total assets	400	297
Accounts payable	77	22
Long-term debt	175	175
Common stock	100	100
Retained earnings	48	—
Total liabilities and shareholders' equity	400	297

Exhibit 2	Exchange Rate Information	
		US$/C$
Rate on 31 December 20X1		0.86
Average rate in 20X2		0.92
Weighted-average rate for inventory purchases		0.92
Rate on 31 December 20X2		0.95

Templeton explains that Consol-Can uses the FIFO inventory accounting method and that purchases of C$300 million and the sell-through of that inventory occurred evenly throughout 20X2. Her presentation includes reporting the translated amounts in US dollars for each item, as well as associated translation-related gains and losses. The board responds with several questions.

- Would there be a reason to change the functional currency to the Canadian dollar?

- Would there be any translation effects for Consolidated Motors if the functional currency for Consol-Can were changed to the Canadian dollar?

- Would a change in the functional currency have any impact on financial statement ratios for the parent company?

- What would be the balance sheet exposure to translation effects if the functional currency were changed?

7   After translating Consol-Can's inventory and long-term debt into the parent company's currency (US$), the amounts reported on Consolidated Motor's financial statements on 31 December 20X2 would be *closest* to (in millions):

   A $71 for inventory and $161 for long-term debt.

   B $71 for inventory and $166 for long-term debt.

   C $73 for inventory and $166 for long-term debt.

8   After translating Consol-Can's 31 December 20X2 balance sheet into the parent company's currency (US$), the translated value of retained earnings will be *closest* to:

   A $41 million.

   B $44 million.

   C $46 million.

9   In response to the board's first question, Templeton would *most likely* reply that such a change would be justified if:

   A   the inflation rate in the United States became hyperinflationary.

   B   management wanted to flow more of the gains through net income.

   C   Consol-Can were making autonomous decisions about operations, investing, and financing.

10   In response to the board's second question, Templeton should reply that if the change is made, the consolidated financial statements for Consolidated Motors would begin to recognize:

   A   realized gains and losses on monetary assets and liabilities.

   B   realized gains and losses on non-monetary assets and liabilities.

   C   unrealized gains and losses on non-monetary assets and liabilities.

11 In response to the board's third question, Templeton should note that the change will *most likely* affect:

  A the cash ratio.

  B fixed asset turnover.

  C receivables turnover.

12 In response to the board's fourth question, the balance sheet exposure (in C$ millions) would be *closest* to:

  A −19.

  B 148.

  C 400.

The following information relates to Questions 13–18

Romulus Corp. is a US-based company that prepares its financial statements in accordance with US GAAP. Romulus Corp. has two European subsidiaries: Julius and Augustus. Anthony Marks, CFA, is an analyst trying to forecast Romulus's 20X2 results. Marks has prepared separate forecasts for both Julius and Augustus, as well as for Romulus's other operations (prior to consolidating the results.) He is now considering the impact of currency translation on the results of both the subsidiaries and the parent company's consolidated financials. His research has provided the following insights:

- The results for Julius will be translated into US dollars using the current rate method.

- The results for Augustus will be translated into US dollars using the temporal method.

- Both Julius and Augustus use the FIFO method to account for inventory.

- Julius had year-end 20X1 inventory of €340 million. Marks believes Julius will report €2,300 in sales and €1,400 in cost of sales in 20X2.

Marks also forecasts the 20X2 year-end balance sheet for Julius (Exhibit 1). Data and forecasts related to euro/dollar exchange rates are presented in Exhibit 2.

Exhibit 1	Forecasted Balance Sheet Data for Julius, 31 December 20X2 (€ millions)
Cash	50
Accounts receivable	100
Inventory	700
Fixed assets	1,450
Total assets	2,300
Liabilities	700
Common stock	1,500
Retained earnings	100
Total liabilities and shareholder equity	2,300

Exhibit 2	Exchange Rates ($/€)
31 December 20X1	1.47
31 December 20X2	1.61
20X2 average	1.54
Rate when fixed assets were acquired	1.25
Rate when 20X1 inventory was acquired	1.39
Rate when 20X2 inventory was acquired	1.49

13 Based on the translation method being used for Julius, the subsidiary is *most likely:*

 A a sales outlet for Romulus's products.

 B a self-contained, independent operating entity.

 C using the US dollar as its functional currency.

14 To account for its foreign operations, Romulus has *most likely* designated the euro as the functional currency for:

 A Julius only.

 B Augustus only.

 C both Julius and Augustus.

15 When Romulus consolidates the results of Julius, any unrealized exchange rate holding gains on monetary assets should be:

 A reported as part of operating income.

 B reported as a non-operating item on the income statement.

 C reported directly to equity as part of the cumulative translation adjustment.

16 When Marks translates his forecasted balance sheet for Julius into US dollars, total assets as of 31 December 20X2 (dollars in millions) will be *closest* to:

 A $1,429.

 B $2,392.

 C $3,703.

17 When Marks converts his forecasted income statement data for Julius into US dollars, the 20X2 gross profit margin will be *closest* to:

 A 39.1%.

 B 40.9%.

 C 44.6%.

18 Relative to the gross margins the subsidiaries report in local currency, Romulus's consolidated gross margin *most likely:*

 A will not be distorted by currency translations.

 B would be distorted if Augustus were using the same translation method as Julius.

 C will be distorted because of the translation and inventory accounting methods Augustus is using.

The following information relates to Questions 19–24

Redline Products, Inc. is a US-based multinational with subsidiaries around the world. One such subsidiary, Acceletron, operates in Singapore, which has seen mild but not excessive rates of inflation. Acceletron was acquired in 2000 and has never paid a dividend. It records inventory using the FIFO method.

Chief Financial Officer Margot Villiers was asked by Redline's board of directors to explain how the functional currency selection and other accounting choices affect Redline's consolidated financial statements. Villiers gathers Acceletron's financial statements denominated in Singapore dollars (SGD) in Exhibit 1 and the US dollar/Singapore dollar exchange rates in Exhibit 2. She does not intend to identify the functional currency actually in use but rather to use Acceletron as an example of how the choice of functional currency affects the consolidated statements.

Exhibit 1	Selected Financial Data for Acceletron, 31 December 2007 (SGD millions)
Cash	SGD125
Accounts receivable	230
Inventory	500
Fixed assets	1,640
Accumulated depreciation	(205)
Total assets	SGD2,290
Accounts payable	185
Long-term debt	200
Common stock	620
Retained earnings	1,285
Total liabilities and equity	2,290
Total revenues	SGD4,800
Net income	SGD450

Exhibit 2	Exchange Rates Applicable to Acceletron
Exchange Rate in Effect at Specific Times	USD per SGD
Rate when first SGD1 billion of fixed assets were acquired	0.568
Rate when remaining SGD640 million of fixed assets were acquired	0.606
Rate when long-term debt was issued	0.588
31 December 2006	0.649
Weighted-average rate when inventory was acquired	0.654

(continued)

Exhibit 2 (Continued)	
Exchange Rate in Effect at Specific Times	**USD per SGD**
Average rate in 2007	0.662
31 December 2007	0.671

19 Compared with using the Singapore dollar as Acceletron's functional currency for 2007, if the US dollar were the functional currency, it is *most likely* that Redline's consolidated:

 A inventories will be higher.

 B receivable turnover will be lower.

 C fixed asset turnover will be higher.

20 If the US dollar were chosen as the functional currency for Acceletron in 2007, Redline could reduce its balance sheet exposure to exchange rates by:

 A selling SGD30 million of fixed assets for cash.

 B issuing SGD30 million of long-term debt to buy fixed assets.

 C issuing SGD30 million in short-term debt to purchase marketable securities.

21 Redline's consolidated gross profit margin for 2007 would be *highest* if Acceletron accounted for inventory using:

 A FIFO, and its functional currency were the US dollar.

 B LIFO, and its functional currency were the US dollar.

 C FIFO, and its functional currency were the Singapore dollar.

22 If the current rate method is used to translate Acceletron's financial statements into US dollars, Redline's consolidated financial statements will *most likely* include Acceletron's:

 A USD3,178 million in revenues.

 B USD118 million in long-term debt.

 C negative translation adjustment to shareholder equity.

23 If Acceletron's financial statements are translated into US dollars using the temporal method, Redline's consolidated financial statements will *most likely* include Acceletron's:

 A USD336 million in inventory.

 B USD956 million in fixed assets.

 C USD152 million in accounts receivable.

24 When translating Acceletron's financial statements into US dollars, Redline is *least likely* to use an exchange rate of USD per SGD:

 A 0.671.

 B 0.588.

 C 0.654.

SOLUTIONS

1 B is correct. IAS 21 requires that the financial statements of the foreign entity first be restated for local inflation using the procedures outlined in IAS 29, "Financial Reporting in Hyperinflationary Economies." Then, the inflation-restated foreign currency financial statements are translated into the parent's presentation currency using the current exchange rate. Under US GAAP, the temporal method would be used with no restatement.

2 B is correct. Ruiz expects the EUR to appreciate against the UAH and expects some inflation in the Ukraine. In an inflationary environment, FIFO will generate a higher gross profit than weighted-average cost. For either inventory choice, the current rate method will give higher gross profit to the parent company if the subsidiary's currency is depreciating. Thus, using FIFO and translating using the current rate method will generate a higher gross profit for the parent company, Eurexim SA, than any other combination of choices.

3 B is correct. If the parent's currency is chosen as the functional currency, the temporal method must be used. Under the temporal method, fixed assets are translated using the rate in effect at the time the assets were acquired.

4 C is correct. Monetary assets and liabilities such as accounts receivable are translated at current (end-of-period) rates regardless of whether the temporal or current rate method is used.

5 B is correct. When the foreign currency is chosen as the functional currency, the current rate method is used. All assets and liabilities are translated at the current (end-of-period) rate.

6 C is correct. When the foreign currency is chosen as the functional currency, the current rate method must be used and all gains or losses from translation are reported as a cumulative translation adjustment to shareholder equity. When the foreign currency decreases in value (weakens), the current rate method results in a negative translation adjustment in stockholders' equity.

7 B is correct. When the parent company's currency is used as the functional currency, the temporal method must be used to translate the subsidiary's accounts. Under the temporal method, monetary assets and liabilities (e.g., debt) are translated at the current (year-end) rate, non-monetary assets and liabilities measured at historical cost (e.g., inventory) are translated at historical exchange rates, and non-monetary assets and liabilities measured at current value are translated at the exchange rate at the date when the current value was determined. Because beginning inventory was sold first and sales and purchases were evenly acquired, the average rate is most appropriate for translating inventory and C\$77 million × 0.92 = \$71 million. Long-term debt is translated at the year-end rate of 0.95. C\$175 million × 0.95 = \$166 million.

8 B is correct. Translating the 20X2 balance sheet using the temporal method, as is required in this instance, results in assets of US\$369 million. The translated liabilities and common stock are equal to US\$325 million, meaning that the value for 20X2 retained earnings is US\$369 million – US\$325 million = US\$44 million.

Temporal Method (20X2)			
Account	C\$	Rate	US\$
Cash	135	0.95	128
Accounts receivable	98	0.95	93

(continued)

Temporal Method (20X2)			
Account	**C$**	**Rate**	**US$**
Inventory	77	0.92	71
Fixed assets	100	0.86	86
Accumulated depreciation	(10)	0.86	(9)
Total assets	400		369
Accounts payable	77	0.95	73
Long-term debt	175	0.95	166
Common stock	100	0.86	86
Retained earnings	48	to balance	44
Total liabilities and shareholders' equity	400		369

9   C is correct. The Canadian dollar would be the appropriate reporting currency when substantially all operating, financing, and investing decisions are based on the local currency. The parent country's inflation rate is never relevant. Earnings manipulation is not justified, and at any rate changing the functional currency would take the gains off of the income statement.

10   C is correct. If the functional currency were changed from the parent currency (US dollar) to the local currency (Canadian dollar), the current rate method would replace the temporal method. The temporal method ignores unrealized gains and losses on non-monetary assets and liabilities, but the current rate method does not.

11   B is correct. If the Canadian dollar is chosen as the functional currency, the current rate method will be used and the current exchange rate will be the rate used to translate all assets and liabilities. Currently, only monetary assets and liabilities are translated at the current rate. Sales are translated at the average rate during the year under either method. Fixed assets are translated using the historical rate under the temporal method but would switch to current rates under the current rate method. Therefore, there will most likely be an effect on sales/fixed assets. Because the cash ratio involves only monetary assets and liabilities, it is unaffected by the translation method. Receivables turnover pairs a monetary asset with sales and is thus also unaffected.

12   B is correct. If the functional currency were changed, then Consol-Can would use the current rate method and the balance sheet exposure would be equal to net assets (total assets − total liabilities). In this case, 400 − 77 − 175 = 148.

13   B is correct. Julius is using the current rate method, which is most appropriate when it is operating with a high degree of autonomy.

14   A is correct. If the current rate method is being used (as it is for Julius), the local currency (euro) is the functional currency. When the temporal method is being used (as it is for Augustus), the parent company's currency (US dollar) is the functional currency.

15   C is correct. When the current rate method is being used, all currency gains and losses are recorded as a cumulative translation adjustment to shareholder equity.

16   C is correct. Under the current rate method, all assets are translated using the year-end 20X2 (current) rate of $1.61/€1.00. €2,300 × 1.61 = $3,703.

17   A is correct. Under the current rate method, both sales and cost of goods sold would be translated at the 20X2 average exchange rate. The ratio would be the same as reported under the euro. €2,300 − €1,400 = €900, €900/€2,300 = 39.1%. Or, $3,542 − $2,156 = $1,386, $1,386/$3,542 = 39.1%.

18 C is correct. Augustus is using the temporal method in conjunction with FIFO inventory accounting. If FIFO is used, ending inventory is assumed to be composed of the most recently acquired items, and thus inventory will be translated at relatively recent exchange rates. To the extent that the average weight used to translate sales differs from the historical rate used to translate inventories, the gross margin will be distorted when translated into US dollars.

19 C is correct. If the US dollar is the functional currency, the temporal method must be used. Revenues and receivables (monetary asset) would be the same under either accounting method. Inventory and fixed assets were purchased when the US dollar was stronger, so at historical rates (temporal method), translated they would be lower. Identical revenues/lower fixed assets would result in higher fixed-asset turnover.

20 A is correct. If the US dollar is the functional currency, the temporal method must be used, and the balance sheet exposure will be the net monetary assets of 125 + 230 − 185 − 200 = −30, or a net monetary liability of SGD30 million. This net monetary liability would be eliminated if fixed assets (non-monetary) were sold to increase cash. Issuing debt, either short-term or long-term, would increase the net monetary liability.

21 A is correct. Because the US dollar has been consistently weakening against the Singapore dollar, cost of sales will be lower and gross profit higher when an earlier exchange rate is used to translate inventory, compared with using current exchange rates. If the Singapore dollar is the functional currency, current rates would be used. Therefore, the combination of the US dollar (temporal method) and FIFO will result in the highest gross profit margin.

22 A is correct. Under the current rate method, revenue is translated at the average rate for the year, SGD4,800 × 0.662 = USD3,178 million. Debt should be translated at the current rate, SGD200 × 0.671 = USD134 million. Under the current rate method, Acceletron would have a net asset balance sheet exposure. Because the Singapore dollar has been strengthening against the US dollar, the translation adjustment would be positive rather than negative.

23 B is correct. Under the temporal method, inventory and fixed assets would be translated using historical rates. Accounts receivable is a monetary asset and would be translated at year-end (current) rates. Fixed assets are found as (1,000 × 0.568) + (640 × 0.606) = USD 956 million.

24 B is correct. USD0.671/SGD is the current exchange rate. That rate would be used regardless of whether Acceletron uses the current rate or temporal method. USD0.654 was the weighted-average rate when inventory was acquired. That rate would be used if the company translated its statements under the temporal method but not the current rate method. USD0.588/SGD was the exchange rate in effect when long-term debt was issued. As a monetary liability, long-term debt is always translated using current exchange rates. Consequently, that rate is not applicable regardless of how Acceletron translates its financial statements.

7

Financial Reporting and Analysis

Quality of Financial Reports and Financial Statement Analysis

This study session focuses on evaluating the quality of financial reports and applying financial statement analysis techniques. The first reading shows the application of a conceptual framework to assessing the quality of a company's financial reports. The assessment includes identifying and evaluating potential problems. The second reading uses mini-cases to demonstrate the application of a framework for analyzing financial statements.

READING ASSIGNMENTS

Reading 21	Evaluating Quality of Financial Reports by Jack T. Ciesielski, Jr., CFA, Elaine Henry, PhD, CFA, and Thomas I. Selling, PhD, CPA
Reading 22	Integration of Financial Statement Analysis Techniques by Jack T. Ciesielski, Jr., CFA

Note: New rulings and/or pronouncements issued after the publication of the readings in financial reporting and analysis may cause some of the information in these readings to become dated. Candidates are expected to be familiar with the overall analytical framework contained in the study session readings, as well as the implications of alternative accounting methods for financial analysis and valuation, as provided in the assigned readings. Candidates are not responsible for changes that occur after the material was written.

READING

21

Evaluating Quality of Financial Reports

by Jack T. Ciesielski, Jr., CFA, Elaine Henry, PhD, CFA, and
Thomas I. Selling, PhD, CPA

*Jack T. Ciesielski, Jr., CFA (USA). Elaine Henry, PhD, CFA, is at Fordham University
(USA). Thomas I. Selling, PhD, CPA, is at the Cox School of Business, Southern Methodist
University (USA).*

LEARNING OUTCOMES

Mastery	The candidate should be able to:
☐	a. demonstrate the use of a conceptual framework for assessing the quality of a company's financial reports;
☐	b. explain potential problems that affect the quality of financial reports;
☐	c. describe how to evaluate the quality of a company's financial reports;
☐	d. evaluate the quality of a company's financial reports;
☐	e. describe the concept of sustainable (persistent) earnings;
☐	f. describe indicators of earnings quality;
☐	g. explain mean reversion in earnings and how the accruals component of earnings affects the speed of mean reversion;
☐	h. evaluate the earnings quality of a company;
☐	i. describe indicators of cash flow quality;
☐	j. evaluate the cash flow quality of a company;
☐	k. describe indicators of balance sheet quality;
☐	l. evaluate the balance sheet quality of a company;
☐	m. describe sources of information about risk.

INTRODUCTION

The ability to assess the quality of reported financial information can be a valuable skill. An analyst or investor who can recognize high-quality financial reporting can have greater confidence in analysis based on those financial reports and the resulting investment decisions. Similarly, an analyst or investor who can recognize poor financial reporting quality early—before deficiencies become widely known—is more likely to make profitable investment decisions or to reduce or even avoid losses.

An example of early recognition of an ultimate financial disaster is James Chanos's short position in Enron in November 2000 (Chanos 2002)—more than a year before Enron filed for bankruptcy protection (in December 2001). Despite Enron's high profile and reputation,[1] Chanos had a negative view of Enron based on both quantitative and qualitative factors. Chanos noted that Enron's return on capital was both lower than comparable companies' return on capital and lower than the company's own cost of capital. Qualitative factors contributing to Chanos's view included the company's aggressive revenue recognition policy, its complex and difficult-to-understand disclosures on related-party transactions, and one-time earnings-boosting gains. Later events that substantiated Chanos's perspective included sales of the company's stock by insiders and the resignation of senior executives.

Another example of early recognition of eventual financial troubles is June 2001 reports by analyst Enitan Adebonojo. These reports highlighted questionable accounting by Royal Ahold, a European food retailer. The questionable accounting included "claiming profits of acquired firms as 'organic growth,' booking capital gains from sale-and-leaseback deals as profit, and keeping billions in debt off its balance sheet."[2] In 2003, Royal Ahold announced that it had significantly overstated its profits in the prior two years. The CEO and CFO resigned, various regulators announced investigations, and Royal Ahold's market value dropped significantly.

This reading focuses on reporting quality and the interrelated attribute of results quality. *Reporting quality* pertains to the information disclosed in financial reports. High-quality reporting provides decision-useful information—information that is relevant and faithfully represents the economic reality of the company's activities during the reporting period and the company's financial condition at the end of the period. A separate, but interrelated, attribute of quality is *results* or *earnings quality*, which pertains to the earnings and cash generated by the company's actual economic activities and the resulting financial condition relative to expectations of current and future financial performance. Note that the term "earnings quality" is more commonly used in practice than "results quality," so throughout this reading, earnings quality is used broadly to encompass the quality of earnings, cash flow, and/or balance sheet items.

High-quality earnings reflect an adequate level of return on investment and are derived from activities that a company will likely be able to sustain in the future. Thus, high-quality earnings increase the value of a company more than low-quality earnings. When reported earnings are described as being high quality, it means that the company's underlying economic performance was good (i.e., value enhancing), and it also implies that the company had high reporting quality (i.e., that the information that the company calculated and disclosed was a good reflection of the economic reality).

Earnings can be termed "low quality" either because the reported information properly represents genuinely bad performance or because the reported information misrepresents economic reality. In theory, a company could have low-quality earnings while simultaneously having high reporting quality. Consider a company with

---

1 In October 2000, Enron was named in the top 25 on *Fortune* magazine's list of the World's Most Admired Companies.
2 "Ahold: Europe's Enron," *The Economist*, (27 February 2003).

low-quality earnings—for example, one whose only source of earnings in a period is a one-off settlement of a lawsuit without which the company would have reported huge losses. The company could nonetheless have high reporting quality if it calculated its results properly and provided decision-useful information. Although it is theoretically possible that a company could have low-quality earnings while simultaneously having high reporting quality, experiencing poor financial performance can motivate the company's management to misreport.

This reading begins in Section 2 with a description of a conceptual framework for and potential problems with financial reporting quality. This is followed in Section 3 with a discussion of how to evaluate financial reporting quality. Sections 4, 5, and 6 focus on the quality of reported earnings, cash flows, and balance sheets, respectively. Section 7 covers sources of information about risk. A summary and practice problems in the CFA Institute item set format complete the reading.

QUALITY OF FINANCIAL REPORTS

This section reviews a conceptual framework for assessing the quality of financial reports and then outlines potential problems that affect the quality of financial reports.

2.1 Conceptual Framework for Assessing the Quality of Financial Reports

As indicated in the introduction, financial reporting quality and results or earnings quality are related attributes of quality. Exhibit 1 illustrates this relationship and its implications. Low financial reporting quality can make it difficult or impossible to assess a company's results, and as a result, it is difficult to make investment and other decisions, such as lending and extending credit to the company.

Exhibit 1	Relationships between Financial Reporting Quality and Earnings Quality		

		Financial Reporting Quality	
		Low	**High**
Earnings (Results) Quality	High	LOW financial reporting quality impedes assessment of earnings quality and impedes valuation.	HIGH financial reporting quality enables assessment. HIGH earnings quality increases company value.
	Low		HIGH financial reporting quality enables assessment. LOW earnings quality decreases company value.

Financial reporting quality varies across companies. Financial reports can range from those that contain relevant and faithfully representational information to those that contain information that is pure fabrication. Earnings (results) quality can range from high and sustainable to low and unsustainable. The presence of high-quality financial reporting is a necessary condition for enabling investors to evaluate results quality. High-quality financial reporting alone is an insufficient condition to ensure the presence of high-quality results, but the existence of high-quality financial reporting allows the investor to make such an assessment.

Combining the two aspects of quality—financial reporting and earnings—the overall quality of financial reports from a user perspective can be thought of as spanning a continuum from the highest to the lowest. Exhibit 2 presents a spectrum that provides a basis for evaluating better versus poorer quality reports.

Exhibit 2   Quality Spectrum of Financial Reports

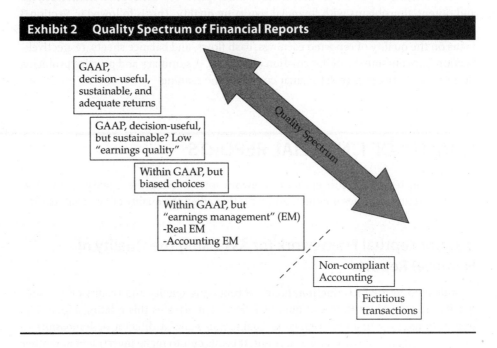

Essentially, the analyst needs to consider two basic questions:

1   Are the financial reports GAAP-compliant and decision-useful?

2   Are the results (earnings) of high quality? In other words, do they provide an adequate level of return, and are they sustainable?

These two questions provide a basic conceptual framework to assess the quality of a company's financial reports and to locate the company's financial reports along the quality spectrum. At the top of the spectrum, labeled in Exhibit 2 as "GAAP, decision-useful, sustainable, and adequate returns" are high-quality reports that provide decision-useful information about high-quality earnings. "GAAP" refers generically to the generally accepted accounting principles or the accepted accounting standards of the jurisdiction under which the company reports. Examples of GAAP are International Financial Reporting Standards (IFRS), US GAAP, and other home-country accounting standards. *Decision-useful* information embodies the characteristics of relevance and faithful representation.[3] High-quality earnings provide an *adequate level of return* on investment (i.e., a return equal to or in excess of the cost of capital) and are sustainable.

---

3 These characteristics are from the *Conceptual Framework for Financial Reporting* (IASB 2010). The characteristics of decision-useful information are identical under IFRS and US GAAP. Relevant information is defined as information that can affect a decision and encompasses the notion of materiality. Faithful representation of economic events is complete, neutral, and free from error. The *Framework* also identifies enhancing characteristics of useful information: comparability, verifiability, timeliness, and understandability. High-quality information results when necessary trade-offs among these characteristics are made in an unbiased, skillful manner.

Sustainable indicates that the earnings are derived from activities that a company will likely be able to sustain in the future. Sustainable earnings that provide a high return on investment contribute to a higher valuation of a company and its securities.

Any deviation from the highest point on the quality spectrum can be assessed in terms of the two-question conceptual framework. For example, a company that provides GAAP-compliant, decision-useful information about low-quality earnings (they can be of low quality because they do not provide an adequate level of return and/or they are not sustainable) would appear lower on the quality spectrum. Even lower on the spectrum would be companies that provide GAAP-compliant information, which is less decision-useful because of biased choices.

Biased accounting choices result in financial reports that do not faithfully represent economic phenomena. Biased choices can be made not only in the context of reported amounts but also in the context of how information is presented. For example, companies can disclose information transparently and in a manner that facilitates analysis, or they can disclose information in a manner that aims to obscure unfavorable information and/or to emphasize favorable information.

The problem with bias in accounting choices, as with other deficiencies in financial reporting quality, is that it impedes an investor's ability to correctly assess a company's past performance, to accurately forecast future performance, and thus to appropriately value the company. Choices are deemed to be "aggressive" if they increase the company's reported performance and financial position in the current period. Aggressive choices may decrease the company's reported performance and financial position in later periods. In contrast, choices are deemed to be "conservative" if they decrease the company's reported performance and financial position in the current period. Conservative choices may increase the company's reported performance and financial position in later periods.

Another type of bias is "earnings management." An example of this bias is earnings "smoothing" to understate earnings volatility relative to the volatility if earnings were faithfully represented. Earnings volatility is decreased by understating earnings in periods when a company's operations are performing well and overstating in periods when the company's operations are struggling.

The next levels down on the spectrum mark a departure from GAAP. Financial reports that depart from GAAP can generally be considered low quality; they are of poor financial reporting quality and cannot be relied on to assess earnings quality. The lowest-quality financial reports portray fictitious transactions or omit actual transactions; such financial reports are fabrications.

2.2 Potential Problems that Affect the Quality of Financial Reports

The basic choices that give rise to potential problems with quality of financial reports include reported amounts and timing of recognition and classification. Remember that even GAAP-compliant financial reports can diverge from economic reality if GAAP allows for biased choices. In addition to GAAP-compliant choices, a financial statement preparer may choose to present fraudulent reports. This choice represents a divergence from GAAP and economic reality.

2.2.1 *Reported Amounts and Timing of Recognition*

The choice of the reported amount and timing of recognition may focus on a single financial statement element (assets, liabilities, owners' equity, revenue and gains [income], or expenses and losses). However, this choice may affect other elements and more than one financial statement because financial statements are interrelated.[4] It is useful to think of the impact of accounting choices in terms of the basic accounting equation (Assets = Liabilities + Equity). This equation can be restated as Assets − Liabilities = Equity, which is also equivalent to Net Assets = Equity. Choices related to income statement elements will affect the balance sheet through equity, and if equity is affected, then another balance sheet element(s) has to be affected or the balance sheet will not balance.

Following are some examples of choices—accounting choices that comply with GAAP, accounting choices that depart from GAAP, and operating choices—and their effects in the current period:

- Aggressive, premature, and fictitious revenue recognition results in overstated income and thus overstated equity. Assets, usually accounts receivable, are also overstated.

- Conservative revenue recognition, such as deferred recognition of revenue, results in understated net income, understated equity, and understated assets.

- Omission and delayed recognition of expenses results in understated expenses and overstated income, overstated equity, overstated assets, and/or understated liabilities. An understatement of bad debt expense results in overstated accounts receivable. Understated depreciation or amortization expense results in the overstatement of the related long-lived asset. Understated interest, taxes, or other expenses result in the understatement of the related liability: accrued interest payable, taxes payable, or other payable.

- Understatement of contingent liabilities is associated with overstated equity resulting from understated expenses and overstated income or overstated other comprehensive income.

- Overstatement of financial assets and understatement of financial liabilities, reported at fair value, are associated with overstated equity resulting from overstated unrealized gains or understated unrealized losses.

- Cash flow from operations may be increased by deferring payments on payables, accelerating payments from customers, deferring purchases of inventory, and deferring other expenditures related to operations, such as maintenance and research.

Example 1 describes events and choices at Satyam Computer Services Limited, which resulted in the issuance of fraudulent reports.

EXAMPLE 1

Fictitious Reports

Satyam Computer Services Limited

Satyam Computer Services Limited, an Indian information technology company, was founded in 1987 and grew rapidly by providing business process outsourcing (BPO) on a global basis. In 2007, its CEO, Ramalinga Raju, was named "Entrepreneur of the Year" by Ernst & Young, and in 2008, the World Council for Corporate Governance recognized the company for "global excellence in corporate accountability." In 2009, the CEO submitted a letter of resignation that outlined a massive financial fraud at the company. The company's decline was so rapid and significant that it came to be referred to as "India's Enron."

---

4 Depending on management's motivation, poor-quality financial reports may either over-state or under-state results. Fraudulent financial reports almost always overstate results.

In late 2008, the World Bank terminated its relationship with the company after finding that Satyam gave kickbacks to bank staff and billed for services that were not provided. These initial revelations of wrongdoing had the effect of putting the company under increased scrutiny. Among other misconduct, the CEO eventually admitted that he created fictitious bank statements to inflate cash and to show interest income. The CEO also created fake salary accounts and took the money paid to those "employees." The company's head of internal auditing created fictitious customer accounts and invoices to inflate revenues.[5]

The external auditors did not independently verify much of the information provided by the company. Even when bank confirmations, which were sent to them directly as opposed to indirectly through Satyam, contained significantly different balances than those reported by Satyam, they did not follow up.

1 Based on the information provided, characterize Satyam's financial reports, with reference to the quality spectrum of financial reports.

2 Explain each of the following misconducts with reference to the basic accounting equation:

   A Transactions with World Bank

   B Fictitious interest income

   C CEO's embezzlement

   D Fictitious revenue

3 Based on the information provided, what documents were falsified to support the misconducts listed in Question 2?

Solution to 1:

Based on the information provided, Satyam's financial reports were of the lowest quality. They clearly are at the bottom of the quality spectrum of financial reports: reports based on fictitious information.

Solution to 2:

The effects on the basic accounting equation of the different acts of misconduct are as follows:

A Upon billing for fictitious services, the company would increase an asset, such as accounts receivable, and a revenue account, such as service revenues. The kickbacks to the customer's staff, if recorded, would increase an expense account, such as commissions paid, and increase a liability, such as commissions payable, or decrease an asset, such as cash. The net effect of this misconduct is the overstatement of income, net assets, and equity.

B Fictitious interest income would result in overstated income; overstated assets, such as cash and interest receivable; and overstated equity. These overstatements were hidden by falsifying revenue and cash balances.

C The embezzlement by creating fictitious employees would increase an expense account, such as wages and salaries, and decrease the asset, cash. The resulting understatement of income and equity was offset by a real but fraudulent decrease in cash, which was hidden by falsifying revenue and cash balances.

D Fictitious revenues would result in overstated revenues and income; overstated assets, such as cash and accounts receivable; and overstated equity.

---

5 See Bhasin (2012) for more information.

Solution to 3:

Based on the information provided, the documents that were falsified include

- invoices to the World Bank for services that were not provided,
- bank statements,
- employee records, and
- customer accounts and invoices.

The falsified documents were intended to mislead the external auditors.

An astute reader of financial statements may have identified a potential problem at Satyam by comparing the growth in revenue with the growth in assets on its balance sheet, such as short-term and long-term trade receivables and unbilled revenue. Long-term trade receivables and unbilled revenue accounts may have raised questions. Also, there was an account separate from cash, investments in bank deposits, which may have raised questions. However, fraudulent reports that are well constructed can be very challenging to identify.

2.2.2 *Classification*

Choices with respect to reported amounts and timing of recognition typically affect more than one financial element, financial statement, and financial period. Classification choices typically affect one financial statement and relate to how an item is classified within a particular financial statement. The balance sheet, the statement of comprehensive income, or the cash flow statement may be the primary focus of the choice.

With respect to the balance sheet, the concern may be to make the balance sheet ratios more attractive or to hide an issue. For example, a company may focus on accounts receivable because it wants to hide liquidity or revenue collection issues. Choices include removing the accounts receivable from the balance sheet by selling them externally or transferring them to a controlled entity, converting them to notes receivable, or reclassifying them within the balance sheet, such as by reporting them as long-term receivables. Although these amounts remain on the balance sheet as receivables of some sort, a result of their reclassification is a lower accounts receivable balance. This could imply to investors that a collection has taken place and also might favorably skew receivables measures, such as days' sales outstanding and receivables turnover.

In the 2003 Merck Annual Report, Merck & Co. reclassified a portion of its inventory to "Other assets," a long-term asset. This reclassification affects the balance sheet and financial ratios as demonstrated in Example 2.

EXAMPLE 2

Balance Sheet Reclassifications

Merck & Co., Inc. and Subsidiaries

In the 2002 Annual Report, inventory was reported at $3,411.8 million. In the 2003 Annual Report, the 2002 inventory value was reported at $2,964.3 million and $447.5 million of inventory was included in other assets. This information was contained in Note 6 to the financial statements, reproduced in Exhibit 3.

Exhibit 3   Note 6 to Consolidated Financial Statements

Exhibit 3   Note 6 to Consolidated Financial Statements

6. Inventories
Inventories at December 31 consisted of:

($ in millions)	2003	2002
Finished goods	$552.5	$1,262.3
Raw materials and work in process	2,309.8	2,073.8
Supplies	90.5	75.7
Total (approximate current cost)	$2,952.8	$3,411.8
Reduction to LIFO cost	—	—
	$2,952.8	$3,411.8
Recognized as:		
Inventories	$2,554.7	$2,964.3
Other assets	398.1	447.5

Inventories valued under the LIFO method comprised approximately 51% and 39% of inventories at December 31, 2003 and 2002, respectively. Amounts recognized as Other assets consist of inventories held in preparation for product launches and not expected to be sold within one year. The reduction in finished goods is primarily attributable to the spin-off of Medco Health in 2003.

1   The reclassification of a portion of inventory to other assets will *most likely* result in the days of inventory on hand:

   A   decreasing.

   B   staying the same.

   C   increasing.

2   As a result of the reclassification of a portion of inventory to other assets, the current ratio will *most likely*:

   A   decrease.

   B   stay the same.

   C   increase.

Solution to 1:

A is correct. The number of days of inventory on hand calculated using the reported inventory number will most likely decrease because the amount of inventory relative to cost of goods sold will decrease.

Solution to 2:

A is correct. The current ratio will decrease because current assets will decrease and current liabilities will stay the same.

From Exhibit 3, notice that the reclassification is described in the sentence, "Amounts recognized as Other assets consist of inventories held in preparation for product launches and not expected to be sold within one year." The reasoning behind the reclassification's explanation is logical: Current assets include assets to be consumed or converted into cash in a company's operating cycle, which is usually one year. The inventory items associated with product launches beyond one year are more appropriately classified as "other assets." Yet, the change in classification poses analytical problems. Inventory turnover is a key indicator of efficiency in managing inventory levels and is calculated as cost of sales divided by average inventory. Although the inventory turnover can be calculated for 2003, it cannot be calculated on a consistent basis for 2002, or any year before then, because the amount of inventory that would have been classified as "other assets" in those periods is not disclosed. An investor has to recognize that a time-series comparison of Merck's inventory turnover is going to produce an inconsistent history because of the lack of consistent information.

The classification of revenues as being derived from core, continuing operations could mislead financial statement users into considering inflated amounts of income as being sustainable. Similarly, the classification of expenses as non-operating could mislead financial statement users into considering inflated amounts of income as being sustainable. In non-GAAP metrics reported outside of the financial statements, the classification of income-reducing items as non-recurring could also mislead financial statement users into considering inflated amounts of income as being sustainable.

Classifications that result in an item being reported in other comprehensive income rather than on the income statement can affect analysis and comparison. For example, if two otherwise identical companies classify investments differently, net income may differ because the change in value of the investments may flow through net income for one company and through other comprehensive income for the other company.

Classification issues also arise specifically with the statement of cash flows for which management may have incentives to maximize the amount of cash flows that are classified as "operating." Management may be motivated to classify activities, such as the sale of long-term assets, as operating activities rather than investing activities. Operating activities are part of the day-to-day functioning of a company, such as selling inventory or providing services. For most companies, the sale of property or other long-term assets are not operating activities, and including them in operating activities overstates the company's ability to generate cash from its operations. Management may capitalize rather than expense operating expenditures. As a result, the outflow may be classified as an investing activity rather than an operating activity.

Exhibit 4 presents a selection of potential issues, possible actions, and warning signs of possible deviations from high-quality financial reports, some of which will be specifically discussed in later sections of this reading. The warning signs may be visible in the financial statements themselves, in the notes to the financial statements, or in ratios calculated by the analyst that are assessed over time or compared with those of peer companies. Frequently, the chosen actions bias net income upward. However, a new management or management of a company in financial difficulty may be motivated to bias current income downward to enhance future periods.

Exhibit 4	Accounting Warning Signs	
Potential Issues	**Possible Actions/Choices**	**Warning Signs**

■ Overstatement or non-sustainability of operating income and/or net income
 	
  ● Overstated or accelerated revenue recognition
 	
  ● Understated expenses
 	
  ● Misclassification of revenue, gains, expenses, or losses
	■ Contingent sales with right of return, "channel stuffing" (the practice of inducing customers to order products they would otherwise not order or order at a later date through generous terms), "bill and hold" sales (encouraging customers to order goods and retain them on seller's premises)
	
	■ Lessor use of finance (capital) leases
	
	■ Fictitious (fraudulent) revenue
	
	■ Capitalizing expenditures as assets
	
	■ Lessee use of operating leases
	
	■ Classifying non-operating income or gains as part of operations
	
	■ Classifying ordinary expenses as non-recurring or non-operating
	
	■ Reporting gains through net income and losses through other comprehensive income
		■ Growth in revenue higher than that of industry or peers
		
		■ Increases in discounts to and returns from customers
		
		■ Higher growth rate in receivables than revenue
		
		■ Large proportion of revenue in final quarter of year for a non-seasonal business
		
		■ Cash flow from operations is much lower than operating income
		
		■ Inconsistency over time in the items included in operating revenues and operating expenses
		
		■ Increases in operating margin
		
		■ Aggressive accounting assumptions, such as long, depreciable lives
		
		■ Losses in non-operating income or other comprehensive income and gains in operating income or net income
		
		■ Compensation largely tied to financial results

■ Misstatement of balance sheet items (may affect income statement)
 	
  ● Over- or understatement of assets
 	
  ● Over- or understatement of liabilities
 	
  ● Misclassification of assets and/or liabilities
	■ Choice of models and model inputs to measure fair value
	
	■ Classification from current to non-current
	
	■ Over- or understating reserves and allowances
	
	■ Understating identifiable assets and overstating goodwill
		■ Models and model inputs that bias fair value measures
		
		■ Inconsistency in model inputs when measuring fair value of assets compared with that of liabilities
		
		■ Typical current assets, such as accounts receivable and inventory, included in non-current assets
		
		■ Allowances and reserves that fluctuate over time or are not comparable with peers
		
		■ High goodwill value relative to total assets
		
		■ Use of special purpose vehicles
		
		■ Large changes in deferred tax assets and liabilities
		
		■ Significant off-balance-sheet liabilities

(continued)

Exhibit 4	(Continued)	
Potential Issues	**Possible Actions/Choices**	**Warning Signs**
■ Overstatement of cash flow from operations	■ Managing activities to affect cash flow from operations ■ Misclassifying cash flows to positively affect cash flow from operations	■ Increase in accounts payable and decrease in accounts receivable and inventory ■ Capitalized expenditures in investing activities ■ Sales and leaseback ■ Increases in bank overdrafts

2.2.3 Quality Issues and Mergers and Acquisitions

Quality issues with respect to financial reports often arise in connection with mergers and acquisitions. Mergers and acquisitions provide opportunities and motivations to manage financial results. For accounting purposes, the business combination is accounted for using the acquisition method, and one company is identified as the acquirer. The financial results of the combined companies are reported on a consolidated basis.

Companies with faltering cash-generating ability may be motivated to acquire other companies to increase cash flow from operations. The acquisition will be reported in the investing cash flows if paid in cash, or not even appear on the cash flow statement if paid for with equity. The consolidated cash flow from operations will include the cash flow of the acquired company, effectively concealing the acquirer's own cash flow problems. Such an acquisition can provide a one-time boost to cash from operations that may or may not be sustainable. There are no required post-acquisition "with and without acquisitions" disclosures, making it impossible for investors to reliably assess whether or not the acquirer's cash flow problems are worsening.

A potential acquisition may create an incentive for a company to report using aggressive choices or even misreport. For example, an acquirer's managers may be motivated to make choices to increase earnings to make an acquisition on more favorable terms. Evidence indicates that acquirers making an acquisition for stock may manipulate their reported earnings prior to the acquisition to inflate the value of shares being used to pay for the acquisition (Erickson and Wang 1999). Similarly, the target company's managers may be motivated to make choices to increase earnings to secure a more favorable price for their company. As another example, the acquiring managers may try to manipulate earnings upward after an acquisition if they want to positively influence investors' opinion of the acquisition.[6]

In other cases, misreporting can be an incentive to make an acquisition. Acquisitions complicate a company's financial statements and thus can conceal previous accounting misstatements. Some evidence indicates that companies engaged in intentional misreporting (specifically, companies that were subsequently accused of accounting fraud by the US SEC) are more likely than non-misreporting companies to make an acquisition. They are also more likely to acquire a company that would reduce the comparability and consistency of their financial statements, such as by targeting companies that have less public information and less similar operations (Erickson, Heitzman, and Zhang 2012).

There are also opportunities to make choices that affect the initial consolidated balance sheet and consolidated income statements in the future. When a business combination occurs, the acquirer must measure and recognize identifiable assets acquired

---

6 Findings consistent with this possibility are presented in Bens, Goodman, and Neamtiu (2012).

and liabilities assumed at their fair values as of the acquisition date. These may include assets and liabilities that the acquired company had not previously recognized as assets and liabilities in its financial statements. For example, identifiable intangible assets that the acquired company developed internally and some contingent liabilities would be recognized by the acquirer. The excess of the purchase price over the recognized value of the identified assets acquired and liabilities assumed is reported as goodwill. Unlike other long-lived assets, goodwill is not amortized; however, it is subject to impairment testing. Because goodwill is not amortized, unless appropriate impairment charges are recorded, the capitalized goodwill amount continues indefinitely.

The default accounting treatment for goodwill—no future amortization expense—provides an incentive to acquirers to understate the value of amortizable intangibles when recording an acquisition. Being a residual amount, more of the value of an acquisition will thus be classified as goodwill, with its future earnings-friendly accounting treatment. That bias may result in postponement of the recognition of an uneconomic acquisition until impairment charges on the goodwill are recorded, which may be long after the acquisition. Managements may be willing to take this chance because they may be able to convince analysts and investors that a goodwill impairment charge is a non-recurring, non-cash charge—something that many will overlook. Nevertheless, the presence of goodwill should make an investor more inquisitive about a company's record in recognizing impairments and should also motivate an investor to evaluate a company's impairment testing process for goodwill. Fair value measurement, except in the case of assets and liabilities with quoted prices in active markets for identical assets or liabilities, presents an opportunity for the acquirer's management to exercise judgment and affect reported values. For example, they could understate fair value of assets to avoid future charges to expense. Understating the fair value of assets will result in a higher goodwill amount. In the absence of impairment of goodwill, there will be no charges associated with the goodwill. Many analysts question whether reported goodwill reflects economic reality.

2.2.4 *Financial Reporting that Diverges from Economic Reality Despite Compliance with Accounting Rules*

Certain accounting standards may give rise to financial reporting that an analyst may find less useful because he or she does not view it as reflective of economic reality. Examples 3 and 4 illustrate these types of situations. When possible, an analyst should adjust the reported information to better reflect his or her view of economic reality. If an adjustment is not possible because the relevant data are not disclosed, an analyst can instead make a qualitative assessment of the effect.

Example 3 describes one of the earlier cases of creative consolidation accounting that raised the need for an in-depth consideration of consolidation accounting and the related issue of control. Many entities are governed by the votes of shareholders under which the majority rules. However, exceptions may exist and both US GAAP and IFRS have endeavored to create regimes under which consolidation is required when it is appropriate to depict economic substance.

EXAMPLE 3

Treatment of Variable Interest (Special Purpose) Entities

SEC enforcement action regarding the financial statements of Digilog, Inc.

In order to develop and introduce a new product, Digilog created a separate business entity, DBS, that was capitalized with $10 million of convertible debt issued to Digilog. Upon conversion, Digilog would end up owning nearly 100% of DBS. Initially, owners' equity of DBS consisted of a few thousand dollars of common stock issued to DBS's manager.

During the first two years of DBS's operations, Digilog did not consolidate DBS; it argued that DBS was controlled by its manager, who owned 100% of the outstanding common shares. Even though DBS generated substantial losses over its first two years of existence, Digilog reported interest income on its investment in the convertible debt. After two years, when DBS started to generate profits, Digilog exercised its conversion option and consolidated from that point forward.

Although DBS had been set up as an "independent" corporation, the SEC took the position that the contractual and operating relationships between the two companies were such that they should have been viewed as constituting a single enterprise for financial reporting purposes. The defendants in the enforcement action, Digilog's auditors, consented to a settlement. The settlement included the opinion by the SEC that consolidation would have provided a user of the financial statements with the most meaningful presentation in accordance with GAAP—even though no specific GAAP at that time directly addressed Digilog's "creative" accounting solution.

Eventually, after many more years of debate, and in the wake of the Enron scandal, which also involved abuse of subsequent consolidation rules, the concept of a "variable interest entity" (VIE) was created. A key aspect is control for consolidation purposes; even in the absence of voting control, consolidation is necessary if the investor has the ability to exert influence on the financial and operating policy of the entity and is exposed, or has rights, to variable returns from its investment in the entity. Although the term VIE is not employed by IFRS, its provisions are similar.

Given the facts above and the consolidation rules for a variable interest entity, Digilog is *most likely* to try to argue that it does not need to consolidate DBS because:

A   Digilog does not have voting control.

B   Digilog's interest income from DBS is not variable.

C   DBS's manager has operational and financial control.

Solution:

C is correct. Digilog is most likely to assert that operational and financial control rest with DBS's manager. However, the assertion is not likely to be accepted because the manager's investment is a few thousand dollars compared with $10 million by Digilog. Simply not having voting control is not sufficient to avoid consolidation. Digilog is exposed to variable returns because of possible losses and the convertibility option.

Example 4 considers asset impairments and restructuring charges and their implications.

EXAMPLE 4

Asset Impairments and Restructuring Charges

Two related topics that almost always require special consideration on the part of analysts are asset impairments and restructuring charges. Asset impairments are write-downs of assets required when circumstances indicate that the carrying amount of an asset is excessive compared with the expected future benefits.

The term "restructuring charge" is used under IFRS to indicate a sale or termination of a line of business, closure of business locations, changes in management structure, and/or a fundamental reorganization. All of these events could also give rise to the recognition of a liability (e.g., a commitment to make employee severance payments or to make a payment to settle a lease).

On 25 April 2013, Fuji Electric Co., Ltd, a Japanese company reporting under the GAAP of its home country, announced an impairment loss on land, buildings, structures, and leased assets employed in its "solar cell and module business" in the amount of ¥6.5 billion (Fuji Electric 2013). The entire loss was recorded in its 2012 fiscal year (ending 31 March). Assets and net income were reduced by ¥6.5 billion.

Elan Corporation, plc, a biotechnology company headquartered in Ireland, reported US$42.4 million in restructuring and other costs incurred during fiscal year 2012 related to its decision to close a research facility in San Francisco, with the loss of around 200 jobs, and to shift much of its operations back to Ireland because of changing business conditions. Some of these costs were associated with the obligation to make current and deferred employee severance payments (Leuty 2012).[7]

Recognizing an impairment loss and restructuring charges in a single period, although consistent with most GAAP, is *most likely* to overstate:

A   prior periods' net incomes.

B   current period's net income.

C   future periods' net incomes.

Solution:

A is correct. The impairment and the restructuring were likely the result of past activities and should be taken into account when evaluating past net incomes. The current period's net income, unless the impairment or restructuring is expected to be repeated, is understated. Future period net income may be overstated if reversals occur, but such behavior is not likely. Charging the entire impairment loss and restructuring charge in the current period are examples of conservative accounting principles.

An analyst would likely consider it probable that the events giving rise to Fuji Electric's impairment loss (evidently, declining activity and future prospects for its solar business) had actually occurred over a longer period than that single year. Similarly, an analyst might view the restructuring charge at Elan as relating to previous periods.

When faced with a restructuring charge, an impairment charge, or a combination of the two, an analyst should consider whether similar events occur regularly enough such that they should be factored into estimates of permanent earnings, or whether they should be regarded as one-off items that provide little information about the future earnings of the remaining activities of the company. If it is the former, then the

---

7 See also Elan Corporation, plc, Form 20-F, filed 12 February 2013.

analyst should attempt to "normalize" earnings by essentially spreading the current restructuring/impairment charge(s) over past periods as well as the current period. If an item is truly one-off—say, the financial effects of a natural disaster—then the analyst is justified in "normalizing" earnings by excluding the item from earnings. This process will require a significant amount of judgment, best informed by knowledge of the underlying facts and circumstances.

Items that are commonly encountered by analysts include the following:

- Revisions to ongoing estimates, such as the remaining economic lives of assets, may lead an analyst to question whether an earlier change in estimate would have been more appropriate.

- Sudden increases to allowances and reserves could call into question whether the prior estimates resulted in overstatement of prior periods' earnings instead of an unbiased picture of economic reality.

- Large accruals for losses (e.g., environmental or litigation-related liabilities) suggest that prior periods' earnings may have been overstated because of the failure to accrue losses earlier.

Management may use items such as reserves and allowances to manage or smooth earnings. The application of accounting standards illustrated in Examples 3 and 4 results in financial statements that may not reflect economic reality. Accounting standards may result in some economic assets and liabilities not being reflected in the financial statements. For example, a company may lease production equipment on an operating lease basis. The equipment will not appear on the company's balance sheet, and only the lease payments will appear on the income statement. Yet, the assets exist, are controlled by the company, and produce returns that are reflected on the income statement. The lease payments alone do not capture all of these economic effects. Another example is research and development (R&D) expense. Accounting standards do not permit the capitalization of expenditures for R&D expense, yet R&D produces assets that, in turn, produce future benefits. Accounting standards prohibit R&D's capitalization because of the difficulty in assessing which expenditures will actually produce future benefits and which expenditures will produce nothing. Accounting standards may also result in some information being reported in other comprehensive income rather than through net income. For example, classifying marketable securities as "available for sale" will result in their changes in fair value being reported in other comprehensive income. Contrast that reporting result against that for marketable securities classified as "trading": Their changes in fair value are reported in net income.

No basis of accounting can be expected to recognize all of the economic assets and liabilities for an entity. Consequently, figuring out what *is not* reported can be challenging. One frequently encountered example of an unrecognized asset is a company's sales order backlog. Under most GAAP, revenue is not recognized (and an asset is not created) until services have been performed and other criteria have been met. However, in certain industries, particularly large-scale manufacturing, such as airplane manufacturing, the order backlog can be a significant unrecognized asset. When the amount of backlog is significant, it is typically discussed in the management commentary, and an analyst can use this information to adjust reported amounts and to prepare forecasts.

Another dilemma for analysts is judging whether an item presented in other comprehensive income (OCI) should be included in their analysis as net income. Examples of items presented in OCI include the following:

- unrealized holding gains and losses on certain investments in equity securities,

- unrealized holding gains (and subsequent losses) on items of property and equipment for which the "revaluation option" is elected (IFRS only),

- effects on owners' equity resulting from the translation of the foreign currency-denominated financial statements of a foreign operation to the reporting currency of the consolidated entity,
- certain changes to net pension liability or asset, and
- gains and losses on derivative financial instruments (and certain foreign currency-denominated non-derivative financial instruments) accounted for as a hedge of future cash flows.

When an analyst decides that a significant item presented in OCI should be included in net income, the analyst can adjust reported and forecasted amounts accordingly.

EVALUATING THE QUALITY OF FINANCIAL REPORTS

Prior to beginning any financial analysis, an analyst should clarify the purpose and context and clearly understand the following:

- What is the purpose of the analysis? What questions will this analysis answer?
- What level of detail will be needed to accomplish this purpose?
- What data are available for the analysis?
- What are the factors or relationships that will influence the analysis?
- What are the analytical limitations, and will these limitations potentially impair the analysis?

In the context of evaluating the quality of financial reports, an analyst is attempting to answer two basic questions:

1 Are the financial reports GAAP-compliant and decision-useful?
2 Are the results (earnings) of high quality? Do they provide an adequate level of return, and are they sustainable?

General steps, which fit within the general framework just mentioned, are discussed first. Following these steps may help an analyst evaluate the quality of financial reports (answering the two basic questions). Then, quantitative tools for evaluating the quality of financial reports are discussed.

3.1 General Steps to Evaluate the Quality of Financial Reports

It is important to note that the steps presented here are meant to serve as a general guideline only. An analyst may choose to add steps, emphasize or deemphasize steps, or alter the order of the steps. Companies are unique, and variation in specific analytical projects will require specific approaches.

1 Develop an understanding of the company and its industry. Understanding the economic activities of a company provides a basis for understanding why particular accounting principles may be appropriate and why particular financial metrics matter. Understanding the accounting principles used by a company *and* its competitors provides a basis for understanding what constitutes the norm—and to assess whether a company's treatment is appropriate.

2 Learn about management. Evaluate whether the company's management has any particular incentives to misreport. Review disclosures about compensation and insider transactions, especially insiders' sales of the company's stock. Review the disclosures concerning related-party transactions.

3   Identify significant accounting areas, especially those in which management judgment or an unusual accounting rule is a significant determinant of reported financial performance.

4   Make comparisons:

A   Compare the company's financial statements and significant disclosures in the current year's report with the financial statements and significant disclosures in the prior year's report. Are there major differences in line items or in key disclosures, such as risk disclosures, segment disclosures, classification of specific expense, or revenue items? Are the reasons for the changes apparent?

B   Compare the company's accounting policies with those of its closest competitors. Are there significant differences? If so, what is the directional effect of the differences?

C   Using ratio analysis, compare the company's performance with that of its closest competitors.

5   Check for warnings signs of possible issues with the quality of the financial reports. For example,

- declining receivables turnover could suggest that some revenues are fictitious or recorded prematurely or that the allowance for doubtful accounts is insufficient;

- declining inventory turnover could suggest obsolescence problems that should be recognized; and

- net income greater than cash provided by operations could suggest that aggressive accrual accounting policies have shifted current expenses to later periods.

6   For firms operating in multiple segments by geography or product—particularly multinational firms—consider whether inventory, sales, and expenses have been shifted to make it appear that a company is positively exposed to a geographic region or product segment that the investment community considers to be a desirable growth area. An analyst may suspect that this shift is occurring if the segment is showing strong performance while the consolidated results remain static or worsen.

7   Use appropriate quantitative tools to assess the likelihood of misreporting.

The first six steps listed describe a qualitative approach to evaluating the quality of financial reports. In addition to the qualitative approach, quantitative tools have been developed to help in evaluating financial reports.

3.2 Quantitative Tools to Assess the Likelihood of Misreporting

This section describes some tools for assessing the likelihood of misreporting (Step 7 above). If the likelihood of misreporting appears high, an analyst should take special care in analyzing, including qualitatively analyzing, the financial reports of the company.

3.2.1 Beneish Model

Messod D. Beneish and colleagues conducted studies to identify quantitative indicators of earnings manipulation and to develop a model to assess the likelihood of misreporting (Beneish 1999; Beneish, Lee, and Nichols 2013). The following is the Beneish model and its variables. After the description of each variable, an intuitive explanation of why it is included is given.

The probability of manipulation (*M*-score) is estimated using a probit model:[8]

$$M\text{-score} = -4.84 + 0.920\,(DSR) + 0.528\,(GMI) + 0.404\,(AQI) + 0.892\,(SGI) +$$
$$0.115\,(DEPI) - 0.172\,(SGAI) + 4.670\,(Accruals) - 0.327\,(LEVI)$$

where

M-score = Score indicating probability of earnings manipulation

DSR (days sales receivable index) = $(Receivables_t/Sales_t)/(Receivables_{t-1}/Sales_{t-1})$.

Changes in the relationship between receivables and sales could indicate inappropriate revenue recognition.

GMI (gross margin index) = Gross margin$_{t-1}$/Gross margin$_t$.

Deterioration in margins could predispose companies to manipulate earnings.

AQI (asset quality index) = $[1 - (PPE_t + CA_t)/TA_t]/[1 - (PPE_{t-1} + CA_{t-1})/TA_{t-1}]$, where PPE is property, plant, and equipment; CA is current assets; and TA is total assets.

Change in the percentage of assets other than in PPE and CA could indicate excessive expenditure capitalization.

SGI (sales growth index) = Sales$_t$/Sales$_{t-1}$.

Managing the perception of continuing growth and capital needs from actual growth could predispose companies to manipulate sales and earnings.

DEPI (depreciation index) = Depreciation rate$_{t-1}$/Depreciation rate$_t$, where Depreciation rate = Depreciation/(Depreciation + PPE).

Declining depreciation rates could indicate understated depreciation as a means of manipulating earnings.

SGAI (sales, general, and administrative expenses index) = $(SGA_t/Sales_t)/(SGA_{t-1}/Sales_{t-1})$.

An increase in fixed SGA expenses suggests decreasing administrative and marketing efficiency, which could predispose companies to manipulate earnings.

Accruals = (Income before extraordinary items – Cash from operations)/Total assets.

Higher accruals can indicate earnings manipulation.

LEVI (leverage index) = Leverage$_t$/Leverage$_{t-1}$, where Leverage is calculated as the ratio of debt to assets.

Increasing leverage could predispose companies to manipulate earnings.

The *M*-score in the Beneish model is a normally distributed random variable with a mean of 0 and a standard deviation of 1.0. Consequently, the probability of earnings manipulation indicated by the model can be calculated by using the cumulative probabilities for a standard normal distribution or the NORMSDIST function in Excel. For example, *M*-scores of −1.49 and −1.78 indicate that the probability of earnings manipulation is 6.8% and 3.8%, respectively. Higher *M*-scores (i.e., less negative numbers) indicate an increased probability of earnings manipulation. The probability is given by the amount in the left side of the distribution.

---

8 Variables that are statistically significant in the empirical results of Beneish (1999) include the days sales receivable index, gross margin index, asset quality index, sales growth index, and accruals.

The use of the *M*-score to classify companies as potential manipulators depends on the relative cost of Type I errors (incorrectly classifying a manipulator company as a non-manipulator) and Type II errors (incorrectly classifying a non-manipulator as a manipulator). The cutoff value for classification minimizes the cost of misclassification. Beneish considered that the likely relevant cutoff for investors is a probability of earnings manipulation of 3.8% (an *M*-score exceeding −1.78).[9] Example 5 shows an application of the Beneish model.

EXAMPLE 5

Application of the Beneish Model

Exhibit 5 presents the variables and Beneish's *M*-Score for XYZ Corporation (a hypothetical company).

Exhibit 5 XYZ Corporation *M*-Score			
	Value of Variable	Coefficient from Beneish Model	Calculations
DSR	1.300	0.920	1.196
GMI	1.100	0.528	0.581
AQI	0.800	0.404	0.323
SGI	1.100	0.892	0.981
DEPI	1.100	0.115	0.127
SGAI	0.600	−0.172	−0.103
Accruals	0.150	4.670	0.701
LEVI	0.600	−0.327	−0.196
Intercept			−4.840
M-score			−1.231
Probability of manipulation			10.91%

1   Would the results of the Beneish model lead an analyst, using a −1.78 *M*-score as the cutoff, to flag XYZ as a likely manipulator?

2   The values of DSR, GMI, SGI, and DEPI are all greater than one. In the Beneish model, what does this indicate for each variable?

Solution to 1:

Yes, the model could be expected to lead an analyst to flag XYZ as a likely manipulator. The *M*-score is higher than the cutoff of −1.78, indicating a higher-than-acceptable probability of manipulation. For XYZ Corporation, the model estimates the probability of manipulation as 10.91%. Although the classification of companies as manipulators depends on the relative cost of Type I errors and Type II errors, the value of 10.91% greatly exceeds the cutoff of 3.8% that Beneish identified as the relevant cutoff.

---

9 See Beneish (1999) for an explanation and derivation of the cutoff values. Beneish et al. (2013) use an *M*-score exceeding −1.78 as the cutoff value.

> **Solution to 2:**
>
> Indications are as follows:
>
> **A** The value greater than one for DSR indicates that receivables as a percentage of sales have increased; this change may be an indicator of inappropriate revenue recognition. XYZ may have shipped goods prematurely and recognized revenues belonging in later periods. Alternatively, it may be caused by customers with deteriorating credit-paying ability—still a problem for the analyst of XYZ.
>
> **B** The value greater than one for GMI indicates that gross margins were higher last year; deteriorating margins could predispose companies to manipulate earnings.
>
> **C** The value greater than one for SGI indicates positive sales growth relative to the previous year. Companies could be predisposed to manipulate earnings to manage perceptions of continuing growth and also to obtain capital needed to support growth.
>
> **D** The value greater than one for DEPI indicates that the depreciation rate was higher in the prior year; a declining depreciation rate can indicate manipulated earnings.

3.2.2 *Other Quantitative Models*

Researchers have examined numerous factors that contribute to assessing the probability that a company is engaged in accounting manipulation. Variables that have been found useful for detecting misstatement include accruals quality; deferred taxes; auditor change; market-to-book value; whether the company is publicly listed and traded; growth rate differences between financial and non-financial variables, such as number of patents, employees, and products; accrual quality; and aspects of corporate governance and incentive compensation.[10]

3.2.3 *Limitations of Quantitative Models*

Accounting is a partial representation of economic reality. Consequently, financial models based on accounting numbers are only capable of establishing associations between variables. The underlying cause and effect can only be determined by a deeper analysis of actions themselves—perhaps through interviews, surveys, or investigations by financial regulators with enforcement powers.

An additional concern is that earnings manipulators are just as aware as analysts of the power of quantitative models to screen for possible cases of earnings manipulation. It is not surprising to learn, therefore, that Beneish et al.'s 2013 study found that the predictive power of the Beneish model is declining over time. Undoubtedly, many managers have learned to test the detectability of earnings manipulation tactics by using the model to anticipate analysts' perceptions. Thus, as useful as the Beneish model may be, the search for more powerful analytical tools continues. It is necessary for analysts to use qualitative, not just quantitative, means to assess quality.

---

10 A summary of research on predicting accounting misstatement is provided in Dechow, Ge, Larson, and Sloan (2011).

EARNINGS QUALITY

This section first discusses indicators of earnings quality and then describes how to evaluate the earnings quality of a company. Analytical tools related to identifying very poor earnings/results quality, such as quantitative approaches to assessing the probability of bankruptcy, are also discussed.

4.1 Indicators of Earnings Quality

In general, the term "earnings quality" can be used to encompass earnings, cash flow, and balance sheet quality. This section, however, focuses specifically on earnings quality. High earnings quality is often considered to be evidenced by earnings that are sustainable and represent returns equal to or in excess of the company's cost of capital.[11] High-quality earnings increase the value of the company more than low-quality earnings, and the term "high-quality earnings" assumes that reporting quality is high. In contrast, low-quality earnings are insufficient to cover the company's cost of capital and/or are derived from non-recurring, one-off activities. In addition, the term "low-quality earnings" can also be used when the reported information does not provide a useful indication of the company's performance.

A variety of alternatives have been used as indicators of earnings quality: recurring earnings, earnings persistence and related measures of accruals, beating benchmarks, and after-the-fact confirmations of poor-quality earnings, such as enforcement actions and restatements.

4.1.1 *Recurring Earnings*

When using a company's current and prior earnings as an input to forecast future earnings (for example, for use in an earnings-based valuation), an analyst focuses on the earnings that are expected to recur in the future. For example, earnings from subsidiaries that have been selected for disposal, which must be separately identified as "discontinued operations," are typically excluded from forecasting models. A wide range of other types of items may be non-recurring—for example, one-off asset sales, one-off litigation settlements, or one-off tax settlements. Reported earnings that contain a high proportion of non-recurring items are less likely to be sustainable and are thus considered lower quality.

Enron, an energy distribution company and a company famous for misreporting, presented non-recurring items, among other reporting issues, in such a way that they created an illusion of a solidly performing company. Example 6 shows aspects of Enron's reporting.

---

11 The residual income model of valuation is most closely linked to this concept of high earnings quality.

EXAMPLE 6

Non-Recurring Items

Enron Corp.

Exhibit 6	Excerpts from Enron and Subsidiaries Consolidated Income Statement, Year-Ended 31 December		
(In millions, except per share amounts)	2000	1999	1998
Total revenues	$100,789	$40,112	$31,260
Total costs and expenses	98,836	39,310	29,882
Operating income	$1,953	$802	$1,378
Other income and deductions			
Equity in earnings of unconsolidated equity affiliates	$87	$309	$97
Gains on sales of non-merchant assets	146	541	56
Gain on the issuance of stock by TNPC, Inc.	121	0	0
Interest income	212	162	88
Other income, net	–37	181	–37
Income before interest, minority interests, and income taxes	$2,482	$1,995	$1,582

1 How does the trend in Enron's operating income compare with the trend in its income after other income and deductions (i.e., Income before interest, minority interests, and income taxes)?

2 What items appear to be non-recurring as opposed to being a result of routine operations? How significant are these items?

3 The Enron testimony of short seller James Chanos before US Congress referred to "a number of one-time gains that boosted Enron's earnings" as one of the items that "strengthened our conviction that the market was mispricing Enron's stock" (Chanos 2002). What does Chanos's statement indicate about how Enron's earnings information was being used in valuation?

Solution to 1:

Enron's operating income varied dramatically from year to year, declining from 1998 to 1999 and then more than doubling in 2000. In contrast, Enron's income before interest, minority interests, and income taxes shows a smooth, upward trend with significant increases each year. The increases were 24% and 26% for 2000 and 1999 relative to 1999 and 1998, respectively.

Solution to 2:

Items that appear to be non-recurring are gains on sales of non-merchant assets and the gain on the issuance of stock by TNPC. Although gains from sales of non-merchant assets do recur in each year, this type of activity is not a part of Enron's energy distribution operations. In addition, two other non-operating items—the amount of equity in earnings from unconsolidated subsidiaries and the amount of other income—are highly variable. Two aspects of these items are significant. First, the smooth, upward trend in Enron's income is the direct result of these items. Second, these items collectively represent a significant percentage of the company's income before interest, minority interests, and income taxes, particularly in 1999 when these items represent 52% of the total: ($309 + $541+ $181)/ $1,995 = $1,031/$1,995.

Solution to 3:

Chanos's statement suggests that at least some market participants were mistakenly using Enron's reported income as an input to earnings-based valuation, without adjusting for non-recurring items.

Although evaluating non-recurring items for inclusion in operating metrics is important for making appropriate historical comparisons and for developing appropriate inputs in valuation, another aspect of non-recurring items merits mention. Because classification of items as non-recurring is a subjective decision, classification decisions can provide an opportunity to inflate the amount potentially identified by a user of the income statement as repeatable earnings—those earnings expected from the company's business operations, which investors label as "recurring" or "core" earnings. In the absence of special or one-time items (such as restructuring charges, employee separation costs, goodwill impairment charges, or gains on disposals of assets), operating income is representative of these kinds of earnings. So-called classification shifting, which does not affect total net income, can inflate the amount reported as recurring or core earnings. This could be accomplished by re-classifying normal expenses to special items or by shifting operating expenses to income-decreasing discontinued operations. Anecdotal evidence of classification shifting exists (see Exhibit 7), but the evidence only emerges after the fact.[12] From an analyst's perspective, after-the-fact evidence of earnings management is not particularly useful for anticipating issues with earnings quality. Although it may not be possible to identify whether a company might be engaging in classification shifting, an analyst should nonetheless give special attention to income-decreasing special items, particularly if the company is reporting unusually high operating earnings for the period or if the classification of the item enabled the company to meet or beat forecasts for operating earnings.

Exhibit 7   Anecdotal Evidence of Classification Shifting

- Borden, a food and chemicals company: The SEC determined that the company had classified $146 million of operating expenses as part of a special item (restructuring charges) when the expenses should have been included in selling, general, and administrative expenses (Hwang 1994).

- AmeriServe Food Distribution Inc., which declared bankruptcy only four months after completing a $200 million junk bond issuance: A bankruptcy court–appointed examiner found that the company's financial statements "classified substantial operating expenses... as restructuring charges," which "masked the company's serious financial underperformance and delayed recognition by all parties of the severity of the problems faced by the company (Sherer 2000)."

---

12 Archival evidence of classification shifting is presented in McVay (2006). McVay first models "expected core earnings" and then documents a relationship between reported-minus-expected core earnings and the number of special items. But in any given year, a company's management could attribute the unexpectedly high core earnings to economic improvements related to the special items; therefore, only the *ex post* evidence that unexpectedly high core earnings tend to reverse in the following year is suggestive of earnings management through classification shifting.

Exhibit 7 (Continued)

- Waste Management, which, in 1998, issued the then-largest restatement in SEC history: The enforcement documentation indicates that the company had improperly inflated operating income by netting non-operating gains from the sale of investments and discontinued operations against unrelated operating expenses (SEC 2001b).

- IBM: Revised disclosures, prompted by SEC scrutiny and analysts' requests, showed that the company had classified intellectual property income as an offset to selling, general, and administrative expenses. This classification resulted in an understatement of operating expenses and thus an overstatement of core earnings by $1.5 billion and $1.7 billion in 2001 and 2000, respectively (Bulkeley 2002).

Companies understand that investors differentiate between recurring and non-recurring items. Therefore, in addition to presenting components of income on the face of the income statement, many companies voluntarily disclose additional information to facilitate the differentiation between recurring and non-recurring items. Specifically, companies may disclose both total income and so-called *pro forma* income (or adjusted income, also referred to as non-GAAP measures, or non-IFRS measures if IFRS is applicable) that has been adjusted to exclude non-recurring items. Disclosures of *pro forma* income must be accompanied by a reconciliation between *pro forma* income and reported income. It is important to be aware, however, that determination of whether an item is non-recurring involves judgment, and some companies' managers may be motivated to consider an item non-recurring if it improves a performance metric relevant to investors. For example, Groupon, an online discount provider, included in its original initial public offering (IPO) filing a *pro forma* (i.e., non-GAAP) measure of operating income that excluded online marketing costs. The SEC determined that the measure was misleading and subsequently required the company to eliminate that measure as reported. Overall, although voluntarily disclosed adjustments to reported income can be informative, an analyst should review the information to ensure that excluded items are truly non-recurring.

4.1.2 *Earnings Persistence and Related Measures of Accruals*

One property of high earnings quality is earnings persistence—that is, sustainability of earnings excluding items that are obviously non-recurring and persistence of growth in those earnings. The assumption is that, for equity valuation models involving earnings forecasts, more persistent earnings are more useful inputs. Persistence can be expressed as the coefficient on current earnings in a simple model: [13]

$$\text{Earnings}_{t+1} = \alpha + \beta_1 \text{Earnings}_t + \varepsilon$$

A higher coefficient (β_1) represents more persistent earnings.

Earnings can be viewed as being composed of a cash component and an accruals component. The accrual component arises from accounting rules that reflect revenue in the period earned and expenses in the period incurred—not at the time of cash movement. For example, a sale of goods on account results in accounting income in the period the sale is made. If the cash collection occurs in a subsequent period, the difference between reported net income and cash collected constitutes an accrual. When earnings are decomposed into a cash component and an accruals component, research has shown that the cash component is more persistent (Sloan 1996). In the

---

[13] Descriptions of certain indicators in this section follow Dechow, Ge, and Schrand (2010).

following model, the coefficient on cash flow (β_1) has been shown to be higher than the coefficient on accruals (β_2), indicating that the cash flow component of earnings is more persistent:

$$\text{Earnings}_{t+1} = \alpha + \beta_1 \text{Cash flow}_t + \beta_2 \text{Accruals}_t + \varepsilon$$

Because of the greater persistence of the cash component, indicators of earnings quality evolved to measure the relative size of the accruals component of earnings. Earnings with a larger component of accruals would be less persistent and thus of lower quality.

An important distinction is between accruals that arise from normal transactions in the period (called "non-discretionary") and accruals that result from transactions or accounting choices outside the normal, which are possibly made with the intent to distort reported earnings (called "discretionary accruals"). Outlier discretionary accruals are an indicator of possibly manipulated—and thus low-quality—earnings. One common approach to identifying abnormal accruals is first to model companies' normal accruals and then to determine outliers. A company's normal accruals are modeled as a function of economic factors, such as growth in credit sales and the amount of depreciable assets. Growth in credit sales would be expected to result in accounts receivable growth, and depreciable assets would be associated with the amount of depreciation. To apply this approach, total accruals are regressed on the factors expected to give rise to normal accruals, and the residual of the regression would be considered a proxy for abnormal accruals.

This approach was pioneered by academics and subsequently adopted in practice.[14] The SEC describes its approach to modeling abnormal accruals:

> Our Accounting Quality Model extends the traditional approach [often based on the popular Jones Model or the Modified Jones Model] by allowing discretionary accrual factors to be a part of the estimation. Specifically, we take filings information across all registrants and estimate total accruals as a function of a large set of factors that are proxies for discretionary and non-discretionary components.... Discretionary accruals are calculated from the model estimates and then used to screen firms that appear to be managing earnings most aggressively. (Lewis 2012)

One simplified approach to screening for abnormal accruals is to compare the magnitude of total accruals across companies. To make a relevant comparison, the accruals would be scaled—for example, by average assets or by average net operating income. Under this approach, high amounts of accruals are an indicator of possibly manipulated and thus low-quality earnings.

A more dramatic signal of questionable earnings quality is when a company reports positive net income but negative operating cash flows. This situation is illustrated in Example 7.

---

14 See Jones (1991) and Dechow, Sloan, and Sweeney (1995). These seminal academic papers produced the Jones Model and the Modified Jones Model.

Discrepancy between Net Income and Operating Cash Flows

Allou Health & Beauty Care, Inc.

Allou Health & Beauty Care, Inc. was a manufacturer and distributor of hair and skin care products. Exhibit 8 presents excerpts from the company's financial statements from 2000 to 2002. Following the periods reported in these statements, Allou's warehouses were destroyed by fire, for which the management was found to be responsible. Allou was subsequently shown to have fraudulently inflated the amount of its sales and inventories in those years.

Exhibit 8 Illustration of Fraudulent Reporting in which Reported Net Income Significantly Exceeded Reported Operating Cash Flow, Annual Data 10-K for Allou Health & Beauty Care, Inc., and Subsidiaries

Years ended 31 March	2002	2001	2000
Excerpt from Income Statement			
Revenues, net	$564,151,260	$548,146,953	$421,046,773
Costs of revenue	500,890,588	482,590,356	367,963,675
Gross profit	$63,260,672	$65,556,597	$53,083,098
	⋮	⋮	⋮
Income from operations	27,276,779	28,490,063	22,256,558
	⋮	⋮	⋮
Income from continuing operations*	$6,589,658	$2,458,367	$7,043,548
Excerpt from Statement of Cash Flows			
Cash flows from operating activities:			
Net income from continuing operations	$6,589,658	$2,458,367	$7,043,548
Adjustments to reconcile net income to net cash used in operating activities:			
[Portions omitted]	⋮	⋮	⋮
Decrease (increase) in operating assets:			
Accounts receivable	(24,076,150)	(9,725,776)	(25,691,508)
Inventories	(9,074,118)	(12,644,519)	(40,834,355)
Net cash used in operating activities	$(17,397,230)	$(34,195,838)	$(27,137,652)

*The difference between income from operations and income from continuing operations included deductions for interest expense and provision for income taxes in each year and for a $5,642,678 loss on impairment of investments in 2001.

Referring to Exhibit 8, answer the following questions:

1 Based on the income statement data, evaluate Allou's performance over the period shown.

2 Compare Allou's income from continuing operations and cash flows from operating activities.

3 Interpret the amounts shown as adjustments to reconcile income from continuing operations to net cash used in operating activities.

Solution to 1:

Based on the income statement, the following aspects of Allou's performance are notable. Revenues grew in each of the past three years, albeit more slowly in the latest year shown. The company's gross margin declined somewhat over the past three years but has been fairly stable. Similarly, the company's operating margin declined somewhat over the past three years but has been fairly stable at around 5%. The company's income from continuing operations was sharply lower in 2001 as a result of an impairment loss. The company showed positive net income in each year. Overall, the company showed positive net income in each year, and its performance appears to be reasonably stable based on the income statement data.

Note: Gross margin is gross profit divided by revenues. For example, for 2002, $63,260,672 divided by $564,151,260 is 11.2%. The ratios for 2001 and 2000 are 12.0% and 12.6%, respectively.

Operating margin is income from operations divided by revenues. For example, for 2002, $27,276,779 divided by $564,151,260 is 4.8%. The ratios for 2001 and 2000 are 5.2% and 5.3%, respectively.

Solution to 2:

Allou reported positive income from continuing operations but negative cash from operating activities in each of the three years shown. Persistent negative cash from operating activities is not sustainable for a going concern.

Solution to 3:

The excerpt from Allou's Statement of Cash Flows shows that accounts receivable and inventories increased each year. This increase can account for most of the difference between the company's income from continuing operations and net cash used in operating activities. The company seems to be accumulating inventory and not collecting on its receivables.

Note: The statement of cash flows, prepared using the indirect method, adjusts net income to derive cash from operating activities. An increase in current assets is subtracted from the net income number to derive the cash from operating activities.

Similar to Allou, the quarterly data for Enron shown in Exhibit 9 shows positive net income but negative cash from operating activities in quarters that were subsequently shown to have been misreported.

Exhibit 9

Quarterly Data 10-Q: Enron and Subsidiaries

Three months ended 31 March ($ millions)	2001	2000
Net income	425	338
Net cash used in operating activities	(464)	(457)

Annual Data 10-K: Enron and Subsidiaries

Year ended 31 December ($ millions)	2000	1999	1998
Net income	979	893	703
Net cash provided by operating activities	4,779	1,228	1,640

An analyst might also question why net cash provided by operating activities was more than double that of net income in 1998, almost 50% greater than net income in 1999, and almost five times net income in 2000.

Although sizable accruals (roughly, net income minus operating cash flow) can indicate possibly manipulated and thus low-quality earnings, it is not necessarily the case that fraudulently reporting companies will have such a profile. For example, as shown in Exhibit 9, Enron's annual operating cash flows exceeded net income in all three years during which fraudulent financial reporting was subsequently revealed. Some of the fraudulent transactions undertaken by Enron were specifically aimed at generating operating cash flow. It is advisable for investors to explore and understand why the differences exist. The company's ability to generate cash from operations ultimately affects investment and financing within the company.

Similarly, as shown in Exhibit 10, WorldCom showed cash from operating activities in excess of net income in each of the three years shown, although the company was subsequently found to have issued fraudulent reports. WorldCom's most significant fraudulent reporting was improperly capitalizing (instead of expensing) certain costs. Because capital expenditures are shown as investing cash outflows rather than operating cash outflows, the company's fraudulent reporting had the impact of inflating operating cash flows.

Exhibit 10   Example of Fraudulent Reporting in which Reported Net Income Did Not Significantly Exceed Reported Operating Cash Flow, WorldCom Inc. and Subsidiaries ($ millions)

For the years ended 31 December	1999	2000	2001
Net income (loss)	$4,013	$4,153	$1,501
Net cash provided by operating activities	11,005	7,666	7,994

In summary, although accrual measures (i.e., differences between net income and operating cash flows) can serve as indicators of earnings quality, they cannot be used in isolation or applied mechanically. WorldCom shows how comparing cash-basis measures, such as cash provided by operating activities, with net income may provide a false sense of confidence about net income. Net income is calculated using subjective estimates, such as expected life of long-term assets, that can be easily manipulated. In each year shown in Exhibit 10, the cash provided by operations exceeded net income (earnings), suggesting that the earnings were of high quality; an analyst looking at this without considering the investing activities would have felt a false sense of security in the reported net income.

4.1.3 *Mean Reversion in Earnings*

A key analyst responsibility is to forecast earnings for the purpose of valuation in making investment decisions. The accuracy and credibility of earnings forecasts should increase when a company's earnings stream possesses a high degree of persistence. As already discussed, earnings can be viewed as being composed of a cash flow element plus an accruals element. Sustainable, persistent earnings are driven by the cash flow element of earnings, whereas the accruals element adds information about the company's performance. At the same time, the accruals component can detract from the stability and persistence of earnings because of the estimation process involved in calculating them.

Academic research has shown empirically what we already know intuitively: Nothing lasts forever. Extreme levels of earnings, both high and low, tend to revert to normal levels over time. This phenomenon is known as "mean reversion in earnings" and is a natural attribute of competitive markets. A company experiencing poor earnings performance will shut down or minimize its losing operations and replace inferior managers with ones capable of executing an improved strategy, resulting in improved earnings. At the other extreme, a company experiencing abnormally high profits will attract competition unless the barriers to entry are insurmountable. New competitors may reduce their prices to gain a foothold in an existing company's markets, thereby reducing the existing company's profits over time. Whether a company is experiencing abnormally high or low earnings, the net effect over time is that a return to the mean should be anticipated.

Nissim and Penman (2001) demonstrated that the mean reversion principle exists across a wide variety of accounting-based measures. In a time-series study encompassing companies listed on the New York Stock Exchange and the American Stock Exchange between 1963 and 1999, they tracked such measures as residual income, residual operating income, return on common equity, return on net operating assets, growth in common equity, core sales profit margins, and others. Beginning with data from 1964, they sorted the companies into 10 equal portfolios based on their ranking for a given measure and tracked the median values in each portfolio in each of the next five-year periods. At the end of each fifth year, the portfolios were re-sorted. The process was extended through 1994, yielding means of portfolio medians over seven rankings. The findings were similar across the metrics, showing a clear reversion to the mean over time.

For example, looking at the pattern for return on net operating assets (RNOA),[15] they found that the range of observed RNOAs was between 35% and –5% at the start of the observations but had compressed to a range of 22% to 7% by the end of the study. Their work illustrates the point that extremely strong or weak performance cannot be sustained forever. They also found that the RNOAs of the portfolios that were not outliers in either direction in Year 1—outperformance or underperformance—did not stray over time, staying constant or nearly so over the entire observation period.

---

15 Nissim and Penman define return on net operating assets as Operating income$_t$/Net operating assets$_{t-1}$. Net operating assets are operating assets (those assets used in operations) net of operating liabilities (those generated by operations).

The lesson for analysts is clear: One cannot simply extrapolate either very high or very low earnings into the future and expect to construct useful forecasts. In order to be useful, analysts' forecasts need to take into account normalized earnings over the relevant valuation time frame. As discussed, earnings are the sum of cash flows and accruals, and they will be more sustainable and persistent when the cash flow component dominates earnings. If earnings have a significant accruals component, it may hasten the earnings' reversion to the mean, even more so when the accrual elements are outliers relative to the normal amount of accruals in a company's earnings. In constructing their forecasts of future earnings, analysts need to develop a realistic cash flow model and realistic estimates of accruals as well.

4.1.4 *Beating Benchmarks*

Announcements of earnings that meet or exceed benchmarks, such as analysts' consensus forecasts, typically result in share price increases. However, meeting or beating benchmarks is not necessarily an indicator of high-quality earnings. In fact, exactly meeting or only narrowly beating benchmarks has been proposed as an indicator of earnings manipulation and thus low-quality earnings. Academic research has documented a statistically large clustering slightly above zero of actual benchmark differences, and this clustering has been interpreted by some as evidence of earnings management.[16] There is, however, disagreement about whether exactly meeting or only narrowly beating is an indicator of earnings manipulation.[17] Nonetheless, a company that consistently reports earnings that exactly meet or only narrowly beat benchmarks can raise questions about its earnings quality.

4.1.5 *External Indicators of Poor-Quality Earnings*

Two external indicators of poor-quality earnings are enforcement actions by regulatory authorities and restatements of previously issued financial statements. From an analyst's perspective, recognizing poor earnings quality is generally more valuable if it can be done before deficiencies become widely known and confirmed. Therefore, the external indicators of poor earnings quality are relatively less useful to an analyst. Nonetheless, even though it might be better to recognize poor earnings quality early, an analyst should be alert to external indicators and be prepared to re-evaluate decisions.

4.2 Evaluating the Earnings Quality of a Company (Cases)

The aim of analyzing earnings is to understand the persistence and sustainability of earnings. If earnings do not represent the financial realities faced by a company, then any forecast of earnings based on flawed reporting will also be flawed. Choices and estimates abound in financial reporting; and with those choices and estimates, the temptations for managers to improve their companies' performance by creative accounting are enormous. All too often, companies that appear to be extraordinary performers turn out to be quite ordinary or worse once their choice of accounting methods, including fraudulent choices, is uncovered by a regulator.

To avoid repeating the mistakes of the past, it may be helpful for analysts to learn how managers have used accounting techniques to enhance their companies' reported performance. Some cases provide useful lessons. In a study of 227 enforcement cases brought between 1997 and 2002, the SEC found that the most common accounting misrepresentation occurred in the area of revenue recognition (SEC 2003). Revenue is the largest single figure on the income statement and arguably the most important. Its sheer size and its effect on earnings, along with discretion in revenue recognition

---

16 See Brown and Caylor (2005); Burgstahler and Dichev (1997); and Degeorge, Patel, and Zeckhauser (1999).
17 See Dechow, Richardson, and Tuna (2003).

policies, have made it the most likely account to be intentionally misstated. For those reasons, investors should always thoroughly and skeptically analyze revenues. Too often, however, the chief concerns of analysts center on the quantitative aspects of revenues. They may ponder the growth of revenues and whether growth came from acquisitions or organically, but they rarely focus on the quality of revenues in the same way. A focus on the quality of revenues, including specifically on how it was generated, will serve analysts well. For example, was it generated by offering discounts or through bill-and-hold sales?

4.2.1 Revenue Recognition Case: Sunbeam Corporation

Premature/Fraudulent Revenue Recognition   Sunbeam Corporation was a consumer goods company focused on the production and sale of household appliances and outdoor products. In the mid- to late 1990s, it appeared that its new CEO, "Chainsaw Al" Dunlap, had engineered a turnaround at Sunbeam. He claimed to have done this through cutting costs and increasing revenues. The reality was different. Had more analysts performed basic but rigorous analysis of the financial statements in the earlier phases of Sunbeam's misreporting, they might have been more skeptical of the results produced by Chainsaw Al. Sunbeam engaged in numerous sales transactions that inflated revenues. Among them were the following:

- Sunbeam included one-time disposals of product lines in sales for the first quarter of 1997 without indicating that such non-recurring sales were included in revenues.

- At the end of the first quarter of 1997 (March), Sunbeam booked revenue and income from a sale of barbecue grills to a wholesaler. The wholesaler held the merchandise over the quarter's end without accepting ownership risks. The wholesaler could return the goods if it desired, and Sunbeam would pick up the cost of shipment both ways. All of the grills were returned to Sunbeam in the third quarter of 1997.

- Sunbeam induced customers to order more goods than they would normally through offers of discounts and other incentives. Often, the customers also had return rights on their purchases. This induced ordering had the effect of inflating current results by pulling future sales into the present. This practice is sometimes referred to as "channel stuffing." This policy was not disclosed by Sunbeam, which routinely made use of channel-stuffing practices at the end of 1997 and the beginning of 1998.

- Sunbeam engaged in bill-and-hold revenue practices. In a bill-and-hold transaction, revenue is recognized when the invoice is issued while the goods remain on the premises of the seller. These are unusual transactions, and the accounting requirements for them are very strict: The buyer must request such treatment, have a genuine business purpose for the request, and must accept ownership risks. Other criteria for justifying the use of this revenue recognition practice include the seller's past experience with bill-and-hold transactions, in which buyers took possession of the goods and the transactions were not reversed.

There was no real business purpose to the channel stuffing and bill-and-hold transactions at Sunbeam other than for the seller to accelerate revenue and for the buyers to take advantage of such eagerness without any risks on their part. In the words of the SEC, "these transactions were little more than projected orders disguised as sales" (SEC 2001a). Sunbeam did not make such transactions clear to analysts, and many of its disclosures from the fourth quarter of 1996 to the middle of 1998 were inadequate. Still, its methods of inflating revenue left indicators in the financial statements that should have alerted analysts to the low quality of its earnings and revenue reporting.

If customers are induced into buying goods they do not yet need through favorable payment terms or given substantial leeway in returning such goods to the seller, days' sales outstanding (DSO) may increase and returns may also increase. Furthermore, increases in revenue may exceed past increases and the increases of the industry and/or peers. Problems with and changes in collection, expressed through accounts receivable metrics, can give an analyst clues about the aggressiveness of the seller in making sales targets. Exhibit 11 contains relevant annual data on Sunbeam's sales and receivables from 1995 (before the misreporting occurred) through 1997 (when earnings management reached its peak level in the fourth quarter).

Exhibit 11 **Information on Sunbeam's Sales and Receivables, 1995–1997**			
($ millions)	**1995**	**1996**	**1997**
Total revenue	$1,016.9	$984.2	$1,168.2
Change from prior year	—	–3.2%	18.7%
Gross accounts receivable	$216.2	$213.4	$295.6
Change from prior year	—	–1.3%	38.5%
Receivables/revenue	21.3%	21.7%	25.3%
Change in receivables/revenue	0.7%	0.4%	3.6%
Days' sales outstanding	77.6	79.1	92.4
Accounts receivable turnover	4.7	4.6	4.0

Source: Based on information in original company 10-K filings.

What can an analyst learn from the information in Exhibit 11?

- Although revenues dipped 3.2% in 1996, the year the misreporting began, they increased significantly in 1997 as Sunbeam's various revenue "enhancement" programs were implemented. The important factor to notice—the one that should have given an analyst insight into the quality of the revenues—is the simultaneous, and much greater, increase in the accounts receivable balance. Receivables increasing faster than revenues suggests that a company may be pulling future sales into current periods by offering favorable discounts or generous return policies. As it turned out, Sunbeam offered all of these inducements.

- The percentage relationship of receivables to revenue is another way of looking at the relationship between sales and the time it takes a company to collect cash from its customers. An increasing percentage of receivables to revenues means that a lesser percentage of sales has been collected. The decrease in collection on sales may indicate that customers' abilities to repay have deteriorated. It may also indicate that the seller created period-end sales by shipping goods that were not wanted by customers; the shipment would produce documentation, which serves as evidence of a sale. Receivables and revenue would increase by the same absolute amount, which would increase the percentage of receivables to revenue. Customers would return the goods to the seller in the following accounting period. The same thing would happen in the event of totally fictitious revenues. Revenues from a non-existent customer would simultaneously increase receivables by the same amount. An increase in the relationship between revenue and receivables provides analysts with a clue that collections on sales have declined or that there is a possible issue with revenue recognition.

- The number of days sales outstanding [Accounts receivable/(Revenues/365)] increased each year, indicating that the receivables were not being paid on a timely basis—or even that the revenues may not have been genuine in the first place. DSO figures increasing over time indicate that there are problems, either with collection or revenue recognition. The accounts receivable turnover (365/DSO) tells the same story in a different way: It is the number of times the receivables converted into cash each year, and the figure decreased each year. A trend of slower cash collections, as exhibited by Sunbeam, shows increasingly inefficient cash collections at best and should alert an analyst to the possibility of questionable sales or revenue recognition practices.

- The accounts receivable showed poor quality. In 1997, it increased 38.5% over the previous year, while revenues gained 18.7%. The simple fact that receivables growth greatly outstripped the revenue growth suggests receivables collection problems. Furthermore, analysts who paid attention to the notes might have found even more tiles to fit into the mosaic of accounting manipulations. According to a note in the 10-K titled "Accounts Receivable Securitization Facility," in December 1997 Sunbeam had entered into an arrangement for the sale of accounts receivable. The note said that "At December 28, 1997, the Company had received approximately $59 million from the sale of trade accounts receivable." Those receivables were not included in the year-end accounts receivable balance. As the *pro forma* column in Exhibit 12 shows, the accounts receivable would have shown an increase of 66.1% instead of 38.5%; the percentage of receivables to sales would have ballooned to 30.4%, and the days' sales outstanding would have been an attention-getting 110.8 days. Had this receivables sale not occurred, and the receivables been that large, perhaps analysts would have noticed a problem sooner. Careful attention to the notes might have alerted them to how this transaction improved the appearance of the financial statements and ratios.

Exhibit 12	Information on Sunbeam's Sales and Receivables, 1995–1997, and *Pro Forma* Information, 1997			
($ millions)	1995	1996	1997	**1997 *Pro Forma***
Total revenue	$1,016.9	$984.2	$1,168.2	*$1,168.2*
Change from prior year	—	−3.2%	18.7%	*18.7%*
Gross accounts receivable	$216.2	$213.4	$295.6	*$354.6*
Change from prior year	—	−1.3%	38.5%	*66.1%*
Receivables/revenue	21.3%	21.7%	25.3%	*30.4%*
Change in receivables/revenue	0.7%	0.4%	3.6%	*8.7%*
Days' sales outstanding	77.7	79.2	92.3	*110.8*
Accounts receivable turnover	4.7	4.6	4.0	*3.2*

Source: Based on information in original company 10-K filings.

Analysts observing the trend in days' sales outstanding would have been rightly suspicious of Sunbeam's revenue recognition practices, even if they were observing the days' sales outstanding simply in terms of Sunbeam's own history. If they took the analysis slightly further, they would have been even more suspicious. Exhibit 13 compares Sunbeam's DSO and accounts receivable turnover with those of an industry median based on the numbers from a group of other consumer products companies—Harman International, Jarden, Leggett & Platt, Mohawk Industries, Newell Rubbermaid, and Tupperware Brands.

Exhibit 13	Comparison of Sunbeam and Industry Median, 1995–1997		
Sunbeam	**1995**	**1996**	**1997**
Days sales outstanding	77.7	79.2	92.3
Accounts receivable turnover	4.7	4.6	4.0
Industry median			
Days sales outstanding	44.6	46.7	50.4
Accounts receivable turnover	8.2	7.8	7.3
Sunbeam's underperformance relative to median			
Days sales outstanding	33.0	32.5	41.9
Accounts receivable turnover	(3.5)	(3.2)	(3.3)

Source: Based on information in company 10-K filings.

There was yet another clue that should have aroused suspicion in the analyst community. In the December 1997 annual report, the revenue recognition note had been expanded from the previous year's note:

> The Company recognizes revenues from product sales principally at the time of shipment to customers. *In limited circumstances, at the customer's request the Company may sell seasonal product on a bill and hold basis provided that the goods are completed, packaged and ready for shipment, such goods are segregated and the risks of ownership and legal title have passed to the customer. **The amount of such bill and hold sales at December 29, 1997 was approximately 3% of consolidated revenues.*** [Italics and emphasis added.]

Not only did Sunbeam hint at the fact that its revenue recognition policies included a method that was of questionable quality, a clue was dropped as to the degree to which it affected operations. That 3% figure may seem small, but the disclosure should have aroused suspicion in the mind of a thorough analyst. As shown in Exhibit 14, working through the numbers with some reasonable assumptions about the gross profit on the sales (28.3%) and the applicable tax rate (35%), an analyst would have seen that the bill-and-hold sales were significant to the bottom line.

Exhibit 14	Effect of Sunbeam's Bill-and-Hold Sales on Net Income ($ millions)
1997 revenue	$1,168.18
Bill-and-hold sales from note	3.0%

(continued)

Exhibit 14 (Continued)	
Bill-and-hold sales in 1997	$35.05
Gross profit margin	28.3%
Gross profit contribution	$9.92
After-tax earnings contribution	$6.45
Total earnings from continuing operations	$109.42
Earnings attributable to bill-and-hold sales	5.9%

An analyst questioning the genuineness of bill-and-hold sales and performing a simple test of the degree of exposure to their effects might have been disturbed to estimate that nearly 6% of net income depended on such transactions. This knowledge might have dissuaded an analyst from a favorable view of Sunbeam.

4.2.2 *Revenue Recognition Case: MicroStrategy, Inc.*

Multiple-Element Contracts   MicroStrategy, Inc. was a fast-growing software and information services company that went public in 1998. After going public, the company engaged in more complex revenue transactions than it had previously. Its revenue stream increasingly involved less outright sales of software and began tilting more to transactions containing multiple deliverables, including obligations to provide services.

Product revenue is usually recognized immediately, depending on the delivery terms and acceptance by customers, whereas service revenue is recognized as the services are provided. The relevant accounting standards for multiple-deliverable arrangements at the time permitted recognition of revenue on a software delivery only if the software sale could be separated from the service portion of the contract and only if the service revenues were in fact accounted for separately.

Analysts studying MicroStrategy's financial statements should have understood the effects of such accounting conventions on the company's revenues. MicroStrategy's revenue recognition policy in the accounting policies note of its 1998 10-K stated that the standards' requirements were, in fact, its practice:

> Revenue from product licensing arrangements is generally recognized after execution of a licensing agreement and shipment of the product, provided that no significant Company obligations remain and the resulting receivable is deemed collectible by management… Services revenue, which includes training and consulting, is recognized at the time the service is performed. The Company defers and recognizes maintenance revenue ratably over the terms of the contract period, ranging from 12 to 36 months. (p. 49)

MicroStrategy took advantage of the ambiguity present in such arrangements, however, to mischaracterize service revenues and recognize them earlier than they should have as part of the software sale. For example, in the fourth quarter of 1998, MicroStrategy entered into a $4.5 million transaction with a customer for software licenses and a broad array of consulting services. Most of the software licenses acquired by the customer were intended to be used in applications that MicroStrategy would develop in the future, yet the company recognized all of the $4.5 million as software revenue (SEC 2000).

Similarly, in the fourth quarter of 1999, MicroStrategy entered into a multiple-deliverable arrangement with another customer that included the provision for extensive services. Again, the company improperly allocated the elements of the contract, skewing them toward an earlier-recognized software element and improperly recognizing $14.1 million of product revenue in the quarter, which was material.

How could analysts have recognized this pattern of behavior? Without in-depth knowledge of the contracts, it is not possible to approve or disapprove of the revenue allocation with certainty. The company still left a trail that could have aroused the suspicion of analysts, had they been familiar with MicroStrategy's stated revenue recognition policy.

Exhibit 15 shows the mix of revenues for 1996, 1997, and 1998 based on the income statement in MicroStrategy's 1998 10-K:

Exhibit 15	MicroStrategy's Mix of Licenses and Support Revenues, 1996–1998 ($ millions)		
	1996	**1997**	**1998**
Licenses	$15,873	$36,601	$72,721
Support	6,730	16,956	33,709
Total	$22,603	$53,557	$106,430
Licenses	70.2%	68.3%	68.3%
Support	29.8	31.7	31.7
Total	100.0%	100.0%	100.0%

Between 1996 and 1997, the proportion of support revenues to total revenues increased slightly. It flattened out in 1998, which was the first year known to have mischaracterization between the support revenues and the software revenues. With perfect hindsight, had the $4.5 million of consulting services not been recognized at all, overall revenues would have been $101.930 million and support revenues would have been 33.1% of the total revenues. What could have alerted analysts that something was amiss, if they could not examine actual contracts?

Looking at the quarterly mix of revenues might have aroused analyst suspicions. Exhibit 16 shows the peculiar ebb and flow of revenues attributable to support services revenues.

Exhibit 16	MicroStrategy's Revenue Mix by Quarters, 1Q1998–4Q1999	
Quarter	**Licenses**	**Support**
1Q98	71.8%	28.2%
2Q98	68.3	31.7
3Q98	62.7	37.3
4Q98	70.7	29.3
1Q99	64.6	35.4
2Q99	68.1	31.9

(continued)

Exhibit 16   (Continued)

Quarter	Licenses	Support
3Q99	70.1	29.9
4Q99	73.2	26.8

The support services revenue climbed in the first three quarters of 1998 and dropped sharply in the fourth quarter—the one in which the company characterized the $4.5 million of revenues that should have been deferred as software license revenue. Subsequently, the proportion rose again and then continued a downward trend, most sharply in the fourth quarter of 1999 when the company again mischaracterized $14.1 million of revenue as software license revenue.

There is no logical reason that the proportion of revenues from licensing and support services should vary significantly from quarter to quarter. The changes should arouse suspicions and generate questions to ask management. Management's answers, and the soundness of the logic embedded in them, might have made investors more comfortable or more skeptical.

If an analyst knows that a company has a policy of recognizing revenues for contracts with elements of multiple-deliverable arrangements—something apparent from a study of the accounting policy note—then the analyst should consider the risk that misallocation of revenue can occur. Observing trends and investigating deviations from observed trends become important habits for an analyst to practice in order to isolate exceptions. Although a study of revenue trends may not pinpoint a manipulated revenue transaction, it should be sufficient to raise doubts about the propriety of the accounting for transactions.

Enhancing the recognition of revenue is a way for managers to increase earnings, yet it can leave indicators that can be detected by analysts vigilant enough to look for them. Exhibit 17 provides a summary of how to assess the quality of revenues.

Exhibit 17   Summary: Looking for Quality in Revenues

Start with the basics

The first step should be to fully understand the revenue recognition policies as stated in the most recent annual report. Without context for the way revenue is recognized, an analyst will not understand the risks involved in the proper reporting of revenue. For instance, analysts should determine the following:

- What are the shipping terms?
- What rights of return does a customer have: limited or extensive?
- Do rebates affect revenues, and if so, how are they accounted for? What estimates are involved?
- Are there multiple deliverables to customers for one arrangement? If so, is revenue deferred until some elements are delivered late in the contract? If there are multiple deliverables, do deferred revenues appear on the balance sheet?

Exhibit 17   (Continued)

Age matters

A study of DSO can reveal much about their quality. Receivables do not improve with age. Analysts should seek reasons for exceptions appearing when they

- Compare the trend in DSOs or receivables turnover over a relevant time frame.
- Compare the DSO of one company with the DSOs of similar competitors over similar time frames.

Is it cash or accrual?

A high percentage of accounts receivable to revenues might mean nothing, but it might also mean that channel-stuffing has taken place, portending high future returns of inventory or decreased demand for product in the future. Analysts should

- Compare the percentage of accounts receivable to revenues over a relevant time frame.
- Compare the company's percentage of accounts receivable to revenues with that of competitors or industry measures over similar time frames.

Compare with the real world when possible

If a company reports non-financial data on a routine basis, try relating revenues to those data to determine whether trends in the revenue make sense. Examples include

- Airlines reporting extensive information about miles flown and capacity, enabling an analyst to relate increases in revenues to an increase in miles flown or capacity.
- Retailers reporting square footage used and number of stores open.
- Companies across all industries reporting employee head counts.

As always, analysts should compare any relevant revenue-per-unit measure with that of relevant competitors or industry measures.

Revenue trends and composition

Trend analysis, over time and in comparison with competitors, can prompt analysts to ask questions of managers, or it can simply evoke discomfort with the overall revenue quality. Some relationships to examine include

- The relationships between the kinds of revenue recognized. For example, how much is attributable to product sales or licenses, and how much is attributable to services? Have the relationships changed over time, and if so, why?
- The relationship between overall revenue and accounts receivable. Do changes in overall revenues make sense when compared with changes in accounts receivable?

(continued)

Exhibit 17   (Continued)

Relationships

Does the company transact business with entities owned by senior officers or shareholders? This is a particularly sensitive area if the manager/
shareholder-owned entities are private and there are revenues recognized
from the private entity by a publicly owned company; it could be a dump-
ing ground for obsolete or damaged inventory while inflating revenues.

Overstating revenues is not the only way to enhance earnings; according to the SEC
study of enforcement cases brought between 1997 and 2002, the next most common
financial misreporting was improper expense recognition (SEC 2003). Improper expense
recognition typically involves understating expenses and has the same overstating
effects on earnings as improper revenue recognition. Understating expenses also
leaves indicators in the financial statements for the vigilant analyst to find and assess.

4.2.3 *Cost Capitalization Case: WorldCom Corp.*

Property/Capital Expenditures Analysis   WorldCom was a major global communica-
tions company, providing phone and internet services to both the business and consumer
markets. It became a major player in the 1990s, largely through acquisitions. To keep
delivering the earnings expected by analysts, the company engaged in the improper
capitalization of operating expenses known as "line costs." These costs were fees paid
by WorldCom to third-party telecommunications network providers for the right to
use their networks, and the proper accounting treatment for them is to classify them as
an operating expense. This improper treatment began in 1999 and continued through
the first quarter of 2002. The company declared bankruptcy in July 2002; restatements
of financial reports ensued.

The company was audited by Arthur Andersen, who had access to the company's
records. According to the findings of the special committee that headed the investigation of the failure (Beresford, Katzenbach, and Rogers 2003), Arthur Andersen failed
to identify the misclassification of line costs, among other things, because

Andersen concluded—mistakenly in this case—that, year after year, the
risk of fraud was minimal and thus it never devised sufficient auditing
procedures to address this risk. Although it conducted a controls-based
audit—relying on WorldCom's internal controls—it failed to recognize the
nature and extent of senior management's top-side adjustments through
reserve reversals with little or no support, highly questionable revenue
items, and entries capitalizing line costs. Andersen did not conduct tests
to corroborate the information it received in many areas. It assumed
incorrectly that the absence of variances in the financial statements and
schedules—in a highly volatile business environment—indicated there was
no cause for heightened scrutiny. Andersen conducted only very limited
auditing procedures in many areas where we found accounting irregular-
ities. Even so, Andersen still had several chances to uncover problems we
identify in this Report. (p. 230–231)

If auditors failed to detect fraud, could analysts really be expected to do better?
Analysts may not have been able to pinpoint what was going on at WorldCom, all
the way down to the under-reported line costs, but if they had focused on the company's balance sheet, they certainly could have been suspicious that all was not right.
If they were looking for out-of-line relationships between accounts—something that

the auditors would be expected to do—they might have uncovered questionable relationships that, if unsatisfactorily explained, should have led them to shun securities
issued by WorldCom.

For an operating expense to be under-reported, an offsetting increase in the balance of another account must exist. A simple scan of an annual time-series common-
size balance sheet, such as is shown in Exhibit 18, might identify the possibility that
capitalization is being used to avoid expense recognition. An analyst might not have
known that line costs were being under-reported, but simply looking at the time
series in Exhibit 18 would have shown that something unusual was going on in gross
property, plant, and equipment. The fraud began in 1999, and gross property, plant,
and equipment had been 30% and 31% of total assets, respectively, in the two prior
years. In 1999, property, plant, and equipment became a much more significant 37%
of total assets and increased to 45% in 2000 and 47% in 2001. The company had not
changed strategy or anything else to justify such an increase.

Exhibit 18	Common Size Asset Portion of Balance Sheet for WorldCom, 1997–2001				
	1997	**1998**	**1999**	**2000**	**2001**
Cash and equivalents	0%	2%	1%	1%	1%
Net receivables	5	6	6	7	5
Inventories	0	0	0	0	0
Other current assets	2	4	4	2	2
Total current assets	7%	12%	11%	10%	8%
Gross property, plant, and equipment	*30%*	*31%*	*37%*	*45%*	*47%*
Accumulated depreciation	3%	2%	5%	7%	9%
Net property, plant, and equipment	27%	29%	32%	38%	38%
Equity investments	NA	NA	NA	NA	1
Other investments	0	0	0	2	1
Intangibles	61	54	52	47	49
Other assets	5	5	5	3	3
Total Assets	100%	100%	100%	100%	100%

Note: NA is not available.
Source: Based on information from Standard & Poor's Research Insight database.

A curious analyst in 1999 might not have *specifically* determined that line costs
were being understated, but the buildup of costs in property, plant, and equipment
should have at least made the analyst suspicious that expenses were under-reported
somewhere in the income statement.

Capitalizing costs is not the only possible way of understating expenses. Exhibit 19
provides a summary of how to assess the quality of expense recognition, including
some things to consider.

Exhibit 19   Summary: Looking for Quality in Expense Recognition

Start with the basics

The first step should be to fully understand the cost capitalization policies as stated in the most recent annual report. Without context for the costs stored on the balance sheet, analysts will not be able to comprehend practice exceptions they may encounter. Examples of policies that should be understood include the following:

- What costs are capitalized in inventory? How is obsolescence accounted for? Are there reserves established for obsolescence that might be artificially raised or lowered?

- What are the depreciation policies, including depreciable lives? How do they compare with competitors' policies? Have they changed from prior years?

Trend analysis

Trend analysis, over time and in comparison with competitors, can lead to questions the analyst can ask managers, or it can simply evoke discomfort with overall earnings quality because of issues with expenses. Some relationships to examine include the following:

- Each quarter, non-current asset accounts should be examined for quarter-to-quarter and year-to-year changes to see whether there are any unusual increases in costs. If present, they might indicate that improper capitalization of costs has occurred.

- Profit margins—gross and operating—are often observed by analysts in the examination of quarterly earnings. They are not often related to changes in the balance sheet, but they should be. If unusual build-ups of non-current assets have occurred and the profit margins are improving or staying constant, it could mean that improper cost capitalization is taking place. Recall WorldCom and its improper capitalization of "line costs": Profitability was maintained by capitalizing costs that should have been expensed. Also, the overall industry environment should be considered: Are margins stable while balance sheet accounts are growing and the industry is slumping?

- Turnover ratio for total assets; property, plant, and equipment; and other assets should be computed (with revenues divided by the asset classification). Does a trend in the ratios indicate a slowing in turnover? Decreasing revenues might mean that the assets are used to make a product with declining demand and portend future asset write-downs. Steady or rising revenues and decreasing turnover might indicate improper cost capitalization.

- Compute the depreciation (or amortization) expense compared to the relevant asset base. Is it decreasing or increasing over time without a good reason? How does it compare with that of competitors?

- Compare the relationship of capital expenditures with gross property, plant, and equipment over time. Is the proportion of capital expenditures relative to total property, plant, and equipment increasing significantly over time? If so, it may indicate that the company is capitalizing costs more aggressively to prevent their recognition as current expenses.

Exhibit 19   (Continued)

Relationships

Does the company transact business with entities owned by senior officers or shareholders? This is a particularly sensitive area if the manager/shareholder-owned entities are private. Dealings between a public company and the manager-owned entity might take place at prices that are unfavorable for the public company in order to transfer wealth from the public company to the manager-owned entity. Such inappropriate transfers of wealth can also occur through excessive compensation, direct loans, or guarantees. These practices are often referred to as "tunneling" (Johnson, LaPorta, Shleifer, and Lopez-de-Silanes 2000).

In some cases, sham dealings between the manager-owned entity and the public company might be falsely reported to improve reported profits of the public company and thus enrich the managers whose compensation is performance based. In a different type of transaction, the manager-owned entity could transfer resources to the public company to ensure its economic viability and thus preserve the option to misappropriate or to participate in profits in the future. These practices are often referred to as "propping" (Friedman, Johnson, and Mitton 2003).

Assessing earnings quality should be an established practice for all analysts. Earnings quality should not automatically be accepted as "high quality" until accounting problems emerge and it is too late. Analysts should consider the quality of earnings before assigning value to the growth in earnings. In many cases, high reported earnings growth, which turned out to be fraudulent, preceded bankruptcy.

4.3 Bankruptcy Prediction Models

Bankruptcy prediction models address more than just the quality of a company's earnings and include aspects of cash flow and the balance sheet as well.[18] Various approaches have been used to quantify the likelihood that a company will default on its debt and/or declare bankruptcy.

4.3.1 *Altman Model*

A well-known and early model to assess the probability of bankruptcy is the Altman model (Altman 1968). The model is built on research that used ratio analysis to identify likely failures. An important contribution of the Altman model is that it provided a way to incorporate numerous financial ratios into a single model to predict bankruptcy. The model overcame a limitation of viewing ratios independently (e.g., viewing a company with poor profitability and/or solvency position as potentially bankrupt without considering the company's strong liquidity position).

---

18 Recall that the term "earnings quality" is used broadly to encompass the quality of earnings, cash flow, and/or balance sheet items.

Using discriminant analysis, Altman developed a model to discriminate between two groups: bankrupt and non-bankrupt companies. Altman's Z-score is calculated as follows:

$$Z\text{-score} = 1.2 \text{ (Net working capital/Total assets)} + 1.4 \text{ (Retained earnings/Total assets)} + 3.3 \text{ (EBIT/Total assets)} + 0.6 \text{ (Market value of equity/Book value of liabilities)} + 1.0 \text{ (Sales/Total assets)}$$

The ratios in the model reflect liquidity, profitability, leverage, and activity. The first ratio—net working capital/total assets—is a measure of short-term liquidity risk. The second ratio—retained earnings/total assets—reflects accumulated profitability and relative age because retained earnings accumulate over time. The third ratio—EBIT (earnings before interest and taxes)/total assets, which is a variant of return on assets (ROA)—measures profitability. The fourth ratio—market value of equity/book value of liabilities—is a form of leverage ratio; it is expressed as equity/debt, so a higher number indicates greater solvency. The fifth ratio—sales/total assets—indicates the company's ability to generate sales and is an activity ratio.

Note that Altman's discriminant function shown in his original article (1968) was

$$Z\text{-score} = 0.012X_1 + 0.014X_2 + 0.033X_3 + 0.006X_4 + 0.999X_5$$

with each of the X variables corresponding to the ratios just described. Altman (2000) explains that "due to the original computer format arrangement, variables X_1 through X_4 must be calculated as absolute percentage values. For instance, the company whose net working capital to total assets (X_1) is 10% should be included as 10.0% and not 0.10. Only variable X_5 (sales to total assets) should be expressed in a different manner: that is, a S/TA [sales/total assets] ratio of 200 percent should be included as 2.0" (p. 14). For this reason, the Z-score model is often expressed as shown in the first equation of this section.

The interpretation of the score is that a higher Z-score is better. In Altman's application of the model to a sample of manufacturing companies that had experienced losses, scores of less than 1.81 indicated a high probability of bankruptcy, scores greater than 3.00 indicated a low probability of bankruptcy, and scores between 1.81 and 3.00 were not clear indicators.

4.3.2 Developments in Bankruptcy Prediction Models

Subsequent research addressed various shortcomings in the Altman prediction model. One shortcoming is the single-period, static nature of the Altman model; it uses only one set of financial measures, taken at a single point in time. Shumway (2001) addressed this shortcoming by using a hazard model, which incorporates all available years of data to calculate each company's bankruptcy risk at each point in time.

Another shortcoming of the Altman model (and other accounting-based bankruptcy prediction models) is that financial statements measure past performance and incorporate the going-concern assumption. The reported values on a company's balance sheet assume that the company is a going concern rather than one that might be failing. An alternative is to use market-based bankruptcy prediction models. For example, market-based prediction models building on Merton's concept of equity as a call option on the company's assets infer the default probability from the company's equity value, amount of debt, equity returns, and equity volatility (Kealhofer 2003). Credit default swap data and corporate bond data can also be used to derive default probabilities. Other research indicates that the most effective bankruptcy prediction models include both accounting-based data and market-based data as predictor variables. For example, Bharath and Shumway (2008) model default probability based on market value of equity, face value of debt, equity volatility, stock returns relative to market returns over the previous year, and the ratio of net income to total assets to identify companies likely to default.

CASH FLOW QUALITY

Cash flow statements are free of some of the discretion embedded in the financial statements based on accrual accounting. As a result, analysts may place a great deal of importance and reliance on the cash flow statement. However, there are opportunities for management to affect the cash flow statement.

5.1 Indicators of Cash Flow Quality

Operating cash flow (OCF) is the cash flow component that is generally most important for assessing a company's performance and valuing a company or its securities. Therefore, discussions of cash flow quality typically focus on OCF.

Similar to the term "earnings quality," when reported cash flows are described as being of high quality, it means that the company's underlying economic performance was good (i.e., value enhancing) and it also implies that the company had high reporting quality (i.e., that the information calculated and disclosed by the company was a reasonable reflection of economic reality). Cash flow can be described as "low quality" either because the reported information correctly represents bad economic performance (poor results quality) or because the reported information misrepresents economic reality (poor reporting quality).

From an economic perspective, the corporate life cycle and industry profile affect cash flow and must be considered when analyzing the statement of cash flows. For example, a start-up company might be expected to have negative operating and investing cash flows, which would be funded from borrowing or from equity issuance (i.e., financing cash flows). In contrast, an established company would typically have positive operating cash flow from which it would fund necessary investments and returns to providers of capital (i.e., dividends, share repurchases, or debt repayments—all of which are investing cash flows).

In general, for established companies, high-quality cash flow would typically have most or all of the following characteristics:

- Positive OCF
- OCF derived from sustainable sources
- OCF adequate to cover capital expenditures, dividends, and debt repayments
- OCF with relatively low volatility (relative to industry participants)

As always, high quality requires not only high results quality, as in the previous list, but also high reporting quality. The reported cash flows should be relevant and faithfully represent the economic reality of the company's activities. For example, classifying a financing inflow as an operating inflow would misrepresent the economic reality.

From the perspective of cash flow reporting quality, OCF is generally viewed as being less easily manipulated than operating or net income. Large differences between earnings and OCF or increases in such differences can be an indication of earnings manipulation. The statement of cash flows can be used to highlight areas of potential earnings manipulation.

Even though OCF is viewed as being less subject to manipulation than earnings, the importance of OCF may create incentives for managers to manipulate the amounts reported. Therefore, quality issues with cash flow reporting can exist. One issue that arises with regard to cash flow reporting quality is timing. For example, by selling receivables to a third party and/or by delaying paying its payables, a company can boost OCF. An increase in such activities would be reflected as a decrease in the company's days' sales outstanding and an increase in the company's days of payables. Thus, an analyst can potentially detect management choices to decrease current assets or increase current liabilities, choices that will increase OCF, by looking at asset utilization (activity) ratios, changes in balance sheet accounts, and disclosures in notes to the financial statements. Another issue that arises with regard to cash flow reporting quality is related to classification of cash flows: Management may try to shift positive cash flow items from investing or financing activities to operating activities to inflate operating cash flows.

5.2 Evaluating Cash Flow Quality

Because OCF is viewed as being less subject to manipulation than earnings, the statement of cash flows can be used to identify areas of potential earnings manipulation. The financial fraud at Satyam Computer Services, an Indian information technology company, was described earlier in this reading. In that case, the use of a computer model based on accruals may have failed to detect the fraud. A *New York Times* article (Kahn 2009) provides anecdotal evidence:

> In September, [an analyst] used a computer model to examine India's 500 largest public companies for signs of accounting manipulation. He found that more than 20 percent of them were potentially engaged in aggressive accounting, but Satyam was not on the list. This is because the automated screens that analysts ... use to pick up signs of fraud begin by searching for large discrepancies between reported earnings and cash flow. In Satyam's case, the cash seemed to keep pace with profits.

In other words, a computer model that screened for companies with operating cash flow persistently lower than earnings would not have identified Satyam as a potential problem because its reported operating cash flow was relatively close to reported profits.

It may be helpful to examine pertinent indicators using a more qualitative approach. Exhibit 20 presents an excerpt from the statement of cash flows for Satyam for the quarter ended 30 June 2008.

Exhibit 20	Excerpt from Satyam's IFRS Consolidated Interim Cash Flow Statement (All amounts $ millions except per share data and as otherwise stated.)		
	Quarter ended 30 June 2008 (unaudited)	**Quarter ended 30 June 2007 (unaudited)**	**Year ended 31 March 2008 (audited)**
Profit before income tax	143.1	107.1	474.3
Adjustments for			
Share-based payment expense	4.3	5.9	23.0
Financial costs	1.3	0.8	7.0
Finance income	(16.2)	(16.4)	(67.4)
Depreciation and amortisation	11.5	9.3	40.3
(Gain)/loss on sale of premises and equipment	0.1	0.1	0.6

Exhibit 20   (Continued)

	Quarter ended 30 June 2008 (unaudited)	Quarter ended 30 June 2007 (unaudited)	Year ended 31 March 2008 (audited)
Changes in value of preference shares designated at fair value through profit or loss	0.0	0.0	(1.6)
Gain/(loss) on foreign exchange forward and option contracts	53.0	(21.1)	(7.4)
Share of (profits)/losses of joint ventures, net of taxes	(0.1)	0.0	(0.1)
	197.0	**85.7**	**468.7**
Movements in working capital			
— Trade and other receivables	(81.4)	(64.9)	(184.3)
— Unbilled revenue	(23.5)	(6.0)	(39.9)
— Trade and other payables	34.1	2.2	48.8
— Unearned revenue	5.8	2.4	11.4
— Other liabilities	(6.3)	30.3	61.2
— Retirement benefit obligations	3.7	1.3	17.8
Cash generated from operations	**129.4**	**51.0**	**383.7**
Income taxes paid	−3.8	−9.8	−49.4
Net cash provided by operating activities	**125.6**	**41.2**	**334.3**

Source: Based on information from Satyam's Form 6-K, filed 25 July 2008.

One item of note on this statement of cash flows is the $53 million non-cash item labeled "Gain/(loss) on foreign exchange forward and options contracts" (i.e., derivative instruments) in the quarter ended 30 June 2008. The item appears to be shown as a gain based on the labeling; however, it would not be correct to add back a gain in this calculation of operating cash flow because it is already included in profit before tax. When the company was asked about this item in the quarterly conference call with analysts, no answer was readily available. Instead, the company's manager said that he would "get back to" the questioner. The fact that the company's senior executives could not explain the reason for an item that represented almost 40% of the total pre-tax profit for the quarter ($53/$143.1 = 37%) is clearly a signal of potential problems. Refer to Exhibit 21 for an excerpt from the conference call.

Exhibit 21   Excerpt from Conference Call regarding Quarterly Results of Satyam, 18 July 2008

George Price, analyst at Stifel Nicolaus:	One question which is on the cash flow statement. You had a—you had $53 million in unrealized gain on derivative financial instruments in the quarter and it's a line item that just, on quick check, I don't think we've seen in past quarters. Can you comment on exactly what that is? ... On the comparison periods, there were more modest losses. What drove that large benefit? How should we think about timing of cash flow maybe over the next couple quarters? Any one-time issues like that?
Srinivas Vadlamani:	I—can you repeat that, please?

(continued)

Exhibit 21   (Continued)

| George Price: | Srinivas, there's was a $53 million unrealized gain in the cash flow statement, and I'm just wondering if you could explain that in a little bit more detail.... The magnitude is a little surprising. |
| Srinivas Vadlamani: | No, let me—let me check on that. I'll get back to you. |

Another item of note on the statement of cash flows is the steady growth in receivables. Analysts examine a company's ratios, such as days' sales outstanding. Exhibit 22 presents selected annual data for Satyam. The large jump in days' sales outstanding from 2006 to 2007 could cause concern. Furthermore, the management commentary in the company's Form 20-F indicated that "Net accounts receivable... increased... primarily as a result of an increase in our revenues and increase in collection period." An increase in the collection period of receivables raises questions about the creditworthiness of the company's customers, about the efficiency of the company's collection efforts, and about the quality of the revenue recognized. In addition, the allowance for doubtful debts consistently rises faster than sales.

Exhibit 22   Selected Annual Data on Accounts Receivable for Satyam, 2005–2008

($ millions)	2008	2007	2006	2005
Total revenue	$2,138.1	$1,461.4	$1,096.3	$793.6
% Change from previous year	*46.3%*	*33.3%*	*38.1%*	
Gross accounts receivable	$539.1	$386.9	$238.1	$178.3
% Change from previous year	*39.3%*	*62.5%*	*33.5%*	
Allowance for doubtful debts	$31.0	$22.8	$19.1	$17.5
% Change from previous year	*36.0%*	*19.4%*	*9.1%*	
Gross receivables/revenue	25.21%	26.47%	21.72%	22.47%
Change in receivables/revenue	*−4.8%*	*21.9%*	*−3.3%*	
Days' sales outstanding	92.0	96.6	79.3	82.0
Accounts receivable turnover	4.0	3.8	4.6	4.5

Source: Based on data from Satyam's 20-F filings.

A signal of problems related to cash, which would not have appeared on the statement of cash flows, was the purported use of the company's cash. Satyam reported increasing amounts invested in current accounts. On a conference call excerpted in Exhibit 23, an analyst asked for a specific reason why such large amounts would be held in non-interest-bearing accounts. Instead of providing a reason, the company officer instead stated that the amounts would be transferred to higher-earning accounts soon.

Exhibit 23	Excerpt from Conference Call regarding Quarterly Results for Satyam, 17 October 2008
Kawaljeet Saluja, analyst at Kotak Institutional Equities:	Hi, my questions are for Srinivas. Srinivas, any specific reason why you have $500m parked in current accounts which are not [gaining] any interest?
Srinivas Vadlamani:	No, that is basically—as on the quarter ending, but there is a statement to that [inaudible] to the deposit accounts. We have [inaudible] deposits now.
Kawaljeet Saluja:	But, Srinivas, if I look at the deposit accounts for the last four quarters, that number has remained absolutely flat. And most of the incremental cash that is parked in current accounts and this is not something which is this quarter changed. Would you highlight some of the reasons for it?
Srinivas Vadlamani:	No, basically, what will happen is these amounts will be basically in different countries. And then we will be bringing them to India based on the need. So we will be—basically, some of them are in overnight deposits and all that. So, now we have placing them into normal current deposits. So, next quarter onwards, we will see that as part of the deposits.

In Satyam CEO's January 2009 letter of resignation, he confessed that "the Balance Sheet carries as of September 30, 2008 [i]nflated (non-existent) cash and bank balances of Rs. 5,040 crore[19] (as against Rs. 5,361 crore reflected in the books)...."[20] In other words, of the amount shown as cash on the company's balance sheet, more than 90% was non-existent. It is suggested that some of the cash balances had existed but had been "siphoned off to a web of companies controlled by Mr. Raju and his family." (Kahn 2009)

Overall, the Satyam example illustrates how the statement of cash flows can suggest potential areas of misreporting. In Satyam's case, two items that raised questions were a large non-cash gain on derivatives and an increase in days' sales outstanding. Potential areas of misreporting can then be investigated by reference to the company's other financial reports. The following example illustrates how the statement of cash flows can highlight earnings manipulation and also illustrates how the cash flow information corresponds to information gleaned from analysis of the company's earnings.

Example 8 covers the application of cash flow evaluation to determine quality of earnings.

---

19 Crore is used in India to denote 10,000,000.
20 From Mr. B. Ramalinga Raju's resignation letter attached to Form 6-K that was filed with the SEC on 7 January 2009.

EXAMPLE 8

Sunbeam Statement of Cash Flows

As noted in the previous section, Sunbeam engaged in various improper accounting practices. Refer to the excerpt from Sunbeam's statement of cash flows in Exhibit 24 to answer the following questions:

1 One of the ways that Sunbeam misreported its financial statements was improperly inflating and subsequently reversing restructuring charges. How do these items appear on the statement of cash flows?

2 Another aspect of Sunbeam's misreporting was improper revenue recognition. What items on the statement of cash flow would primarily be affected by that practice?

Exhibit 24	Excerpt from Sunbeam's Consolidated Statement of Cash Flows, 1995–1997 ($ thousands)		
Fiscal Years Ended	**28 Dec. 1997**	**29 Dec. 1996**	**31 Dec. 1995**
Operating Activities:			
Net earnings (loss)	109,415	(228,262)	50,511
Adjustments to reconcile net earnings (loss) to net cash provided by (used in) operating activities:			
Depreciation and amortization	38,577	47,429	44,174
Restructuring, impairment, and other costs	—	154,869	—
Other non-cash special charges	—	128,800	—
Loss on sale of discontinued operations, net of taxes	13,713	32,430	—
Deferred income taxes	57,783	(77,828)	25,146
Increase (decrease) in cash from changes in working capital:			
Receivables, net	(84,576)	(13,829)	(4,499)
Inventories	(100,810)	(11,651)	(4,874)
Account payable	(1,585)	14,735	9,245
Restructuring accrual	(43,378)	—	—
Prepaid expenses and other current assets and liabilities	(9,004)	2,737	(8,821)
Income taxes payable	52,844	(21,942)	(18,452)
Payment of other long-term and non-operating liabilities	(14,682)	(27,089)	(21,719)
Other, net	(26,546)	13,764	10,805
Net cash provided by (used in) operating activities	(8,249)	14,163	81,516

Note: The reason that an increase in sales is shown as a negative number on the statement of cash flows prepared using the indirect method is to reverse any sales reported in income for which cash has not yet been received.

Solution to 1:

Sunbeam's statement of cash flows is prepared using the indirect method (i.e., the operating section shows a reconciliation between reported net income and operating cash flow). This reconciliation highlights that the amount of non-cash charges recorded in 1996 for restructuring, impairment, and other costs totaled about $284 million ($154.869 million + $128.8 million). In the following year, the reversal of the restructuring accrual was $43 million. By inflating and subsequently reversing restructuring charges, the company's income would misleadingly portray significant improvements in performance following the arrival of its new CEO in mid-1996.

Solution to 2:

The items on the statement of cash flows that would primarily be affected by improper revenue recognition include net income, receivables, and inventories. Net income and receivables would be overstated. The statement of cash flows, in which an increase in receivables is shown as a negative number, highlights the continued growth of receivables. In addition, Sunbeam's practice of recording sales that lacked economic substance—because the purchaser held the goods over the end of an accounting period but subsequently returned all the goods—is highlighted in the substantial increase in inventory in 1997.

An issue that arises with regard to cash flow reporting quality is classification shifting: shifting positive cash flow items from investing or financing to inflate operating cash flows. A shift in classification does not change the total amount of cash flow, but it can affect investors' evaluation of a company's cash flows and investors' expectations for future cash flows.

Flexibility in classification exists within accounting standards. For example, IFRS permits companies to classify interest paid either as operating or as financing. IFRS also permits companies to classify interest and dividends received as operating or as investing. In contrast, US GAAP requires that interest paid, interest received, and dividends received all be classified as operating cash flows. Thus, an analyst comparing an IFRS-reporting company to a US GAAP-reporting company would want to ensure comparable classification of interest and dividends and would adjust the reported amounts, if necessary. In addition, an analyst examining an IFRS-reporting company should be alert to any year-to-year changes in classification of interest and dividends. For example, consider an IFRS-reporting company that changed its classification of interest paid from operating to financing. All else equal, the company's operating cash flow would appear higher than the prior period even if no other activities occurred in the period.

As another example of the flexibility permitted by accounting standards, cash flows from non-trading securities are classified as investing cash flows, whereas cash flows from trading securities are typically classified as operating cash flows. However, each company decides what constitutes trading and non-trading activities, depending on how it manages its securities holdings. This discretion creates an opportunity for managers to shift cash flows from one classification to another.

Example 9 illustrates a shift of cash flows from investing to operating.

Classification of Cash Flows

Nautica Enterprises[21]

An excerpt from the statement of cash flows from the fiscal 2000 annual report of Nautica Enterprises, an apparel manufacturer, is shown as Exhibit 25. An excerpt from the statement of cash flows from the company's fiscal 2001 annual report is shown in Exhibit 26. Use these two excerpts to answer the questions below.

Exhibit 25　Excerpt from Nautica Enterprises' Consolidated Statement of Cash Flow from Annual Report, filed 27 May 2000 (amounts in thousands)

	Year ended 4 March 2000
Cash flows from operating activities	
Net earnings	$46,163
Adjustments to reconcile net earnings to net cash provided by operating activities, net of assets and liabilities acquired	
Minority interest in net loss of consolidated subsidiary	—
Deferred income taxes	(1,035)
Depreciation and amortization	17,072
Provision for bad debts	1,424
Changes in operating assets and liabilities	
Accounts receivable	(6,562)
Inventories	(3,667)
Prepaid expenses and other current assets	(20)
Other assets	(2,686)
Accounts payable: trade	(548)
Accrued expenses and other current liabilities	9,086
Income taxes payable	3,458
Net cash provided by operating activities	62,685
Cash flows from investing activities	
Purchase of property, plant, and equipment	(33,289)
Acquisitions, net of cash acquired	—
Sale (purchase) of short-term investments	21,116
Payments to register trademark	(277)
Net cash used in investing activities	(12,450)

21　Example adapted from Mulford and Comiskey (2005).

Exhibit 26	Excerpt from Nautica Enterprises' Consolidated Statements of Cash Flows from Annual Report, filed 29 May 2001 (amounts in thousands)	
	Year Ended 3 March 2001	**Year Ended 4 March 2000**
Cash flows from operating activities		
Net earnings	46,103	46,163
Adjustments to reconcile net earnings to net cash provided by operating activities, net of assets and liabilities acquired		
Minority interest in net loss of consolidated subsidiary	—	—
Deferred income taxes	(2,478)	(1,035)
Depreciation and amortization	22,968	17,072
Provision for bad debts	1,451	1,424
Changes in operating assets and liabilities		
Short-term investments	28,445	21,116
Accounts receivable	(17,935)	(768)
Inventories	(24,142)	(3,667)
Prepaid expenses and other current assets	(2,024)	(20)
Other assets	(36)	(2,686)
Accounts payable: trade	14,833	(548)
Accrued expenses and other current liabilities	7,054	3,292
Income taxes payable	3,779	3,458
Net cash provided by operating activities	78,018	83,801
Cash flows from investing activities		
Purchase of property, plant, and equipment	(41,712)	(33,289)
Acquisitions, net of cash acquired	—	—
Purchase of short-term investments	—	—
Payments to register trademark	(199)	(277)
Net cash used in investing activities	(41,911)	(33,566)

1 What amount does Nautica report as operating cash flow for the year ended 4 March 2000 in Exhibit 25? What amount does Nautica report as operating cash flow for the same year in Exhibit 26?

2 Exhibit 25 shows that the company had investing cash flows of $21,116 thousand from the sale of short-term investments for the year ended 4 March 2000. Where does this amount appear in Exhibit 26?

3 As actually reported (Exhibit 26), how did the company's operating cash flow for fiscal year 2001 compare with that for 2000? If Nautica had not changed the classification of its short-term investing activities, how would the company's operating cash flows for fiscal year 2001 have compared with that for 2000?

Solution to 1:

In Exhibit 25, Nautica reports operating cash flow for the year ended 4 March 2000 of $62,685 thousand. In Exhibit 26, Nautica reports operating cash flow for the same year of $83,801 thousand.

Solution to 2:

The $21,116 thousand (i.e., the difference between the amounts of operating cash flow reported in Exhibits 25 and 26) that appears in Exhibit 25 as investing cash flows from the sale of short-term investments for the year ended 4 March 2000 has been reclassified. In Exhibit 26, this amount appears under changes in operating assets and liabilities (i.e., as a component of operating cash flow).

Solution to 3:

As reported in Exhibit 26, the company's cash flows declined by 7% from fiscal year 2000 to fiscal year 2001 (= 78,018/83,801 − 1 = −7%). If Nautica had not changed the classification of its short-term investing activities, the company's operating cash flows for fiscal year 2001 would have been $49,573 thousand (=78,018 − 28,445), and would have shown a decline of 21% from fiscal year 2000 to fiscal year 2001 (= 49,573/62,685 − 1 = −21%).

An analyst could have identified Nautica's classification shift by comparing the statement of cash flows for 2000 in the fiscal year 2000 annual report with the statement in the fiscal year 2001 annual report. In general, comparisons of period-to-period reports issued by a company can be useful in assessing financial reporting quality. If a company restates prior years' financial statements (because of an error), recasts prior years' financial statements (because of a change in accounting policy), omits some information that was previously voluntarily disclosed, or adds some item, such as a new risk disclosure that was not previously disclosed, an analyst should aim to understand the reasons for the changes.

BALANCE SHEET QUALITY

With regard to the balance sheet, high financial *reporting* quality is indicated by completeness, unbiased measurement, and clear presentation. High financial *results* quality (i.e., a strong balance sheet) is indicated by an optimal amount of leverage, adequate liquidity, and economically successful asset allocation. Balance sheet strength is assessed using ratio analysis, including common-size financial statements, which is covered by the financial statement analysis readings. There are no absolute values for ratio analysis that indicate adequate financial strength; such analysis must be undertaken in the context of a firm's earnings and cash flow outlook, coupled with an understanding of the environment in which the firm operates. In this section, the focus is on high financial reporting quality.

An important aspect of financial reporting quality for the balance sheet is *completeness*. Significant amounts of off-balance-sheet obligations could be a concern for an analyst because exclusion of these obligations could understate the company's leverage. One common source of off-balance-sheet obligation is the use of operating leases (i.e., lease obligations that are not required to be shown on the balance sheet but are instead reflected in the financial statements only to the extent of the associated periodic rent expenses). Another type of off-balance-sheet obligation is purchase contracts, which may be structured as take-or-pay contracts. Analysts typically adjust reported financial statement information by constructively capitalizing operating lease obligations and, where material, purchase obligations. Constructive capitalization means that the analyst estimates the amount of the obligation as the present value of future lease (or purchase obligation) payments and then adds the amount of the obligation to the company's reported assets and liabilities.

The use of unconsolidated joint ventures or equity-method investees may reflect off-balance-sheet liabilities. In addition, certain profitability ratios (return on sales, also called "net profit margin") may be overstated because the parent company's consolidated financial statements include its share of the investee's profits but not its share of the investee's sales. If disclosures are adequate, an analyst can adjust the reported amounts to better reflect the combined amounts of sales, assets, and liabilities. A company operating with numerous or material unconsolidated subsidiaries for which ownership levels approach 50% could be a warning sign of accounting issues. Understanding why a company structures its operations in such a manner—industry practice or need for strategic alliances in certain businesses or geographies—can allay concerns.

Another important aspect of financial reporting quality for the balance sheet is *unbiased measurement*. Unbiased measurement is particularly important for assets and liabilities for which valuation is subjective. The following list presents several examples:

- As previously discussed, understatement of impairment charges for inventory; plant, property, and equipment; or other assets not only results in overstated profits on the income statement but also results in overstatement of the assets on the balance sheet. A company with substantial amounts of reported goodwill but with a market value of equity less than the book value of shareholders' equity may indicate that appropriate goodwill impairments have not been taken.

- Similarly, understatement of valuation allowance for deferred tax assets would understate tax expenses and overstate the value of the assets on the balance sheet. (Overstatement would have the opposite effect.) Significant, unexplainable variations in the valuation account can signal biased measurement.

- A company's investments in the debt or equity securities of another company would ideally be based on observable market data. For some investments, no observable market data exist and the valuation must be based solely on management estimates. The balance sheet of a company with a substantial portion of its assets valued using non-observable inputs likely warrants closer scrutiny.

- A company's pension liabilities require various estimates, such as the discount rate at which future obligations are present valued. If pension obligations exist, the level and changes for the discount rate should be examined.

Example 10 shows a company with overstated goodwill.

EXAMPLE 10

Goodwill

Sealed Air Corporation

In August 2012, a *Wall Street Journal* article listed six companies that were carrying more goodwill on their balance sheets than the companies' market values (Thurm 2012). At the top of the list was Sealed Air Corporation (NYSE: SEE), a company operating in the packaging and containers industry. Exhibit 27 presents an excerpt from the company's income statement for the following year, and Exhibit 28 presents an excerpt from the company's balance sheet.

Exhibit 27   Sealed Air Corporation and Subsidiaries Consolidated Statements of Operations ($ millions, except per share amounts)

Year ended 31 December	2012	2011	2010
Net sales	$7,648.1	$5,550.9	$4,490.1
Cost of sales	5,103.8	3,950.6	3,237.3
Gross profit	2,544.3	1,600.3	1,252.8
Marketing, administrative, and development expenses	1,785.2	1,014.4	699.0
Amortization expense of intangible assets acquired	134.0	39.5	11.2
Impairment of goodwill and other intangible assets	1,892.3	—	—
Costs related to the acquisition and integration of Diversey	7.4	64.8	—
Restructuring and other charges	142.5	52.2	7.6
Operating (loss) profit	(1,417.1)	429.4	535.0
Interest expense	(384.7)	(216.6)	(161.6)
Loss on debt redemption	(36.9)	—	(38.5)
Impairment of equity method investment	(23.5)	—	—
Foreign currency exchange (losses) gains related to Venezuelan subsidiaries	(0.4)	(0.3)	5.5
Net gains on sale (other-than-temporary impairment) of available-for-sale securities	—	—	5.9
Other expense, net	(9.4)	(14.5)	(2.9)
(Loss) earnings from continuing operations before income tax provision	(1,872.0)	198.0	343.4
Income tax (benefit) provision	(261.9)	59.5	87.5
Net (loss) earnings from continuing operations	(1,610.1)	138.5	255.9
Net earnings from discontinued operations	20.9	10.6	—
Net gain on sale of discontinued operations	178.9	—	—
Net (loss) earnings available to common stockholders	$(1,410.3)	$149.1	$255.9

Exhibit 28	**Excerpt from Sealed Air Corporation and Subsidiaries Consolidated Balance Sheets ($ millions, except share data)**		
Year Ended 31 December		**2012**	**2011**
ASSETS			
Current assets			
Cash and cash equivalents		$679.6	$703.6
Receivables, net of allowance for doubtful accounts of $25.9 in 2012 and $16.2 in 2011		1,326.0	1,314.2
Inventories		736.4	777.5
Deferred tax assets		393.0	156.2
Assets held for sale		—	279.0
Prepaid expenses and other current assets		87.4	119.7
Total current assets		$3,222.4	$3,350.2
Property and equipment, net		$1,212.8	$1,269.2
Goodwill		3,191.4	4,209.6
Intangible assets, net		1,139.7	2,035.7
Non-current deferred tax assets		255.8	112.3
Other assets, net		415.1	455.0
Total assets		$9,437.2	$11,432.0

1 SEE's financial statements indicate that the number of common shares issued and outstanding in 2011 was 192,062,185. The price per share of SEE's common stock was around $18 per share in December 2011 and around $14 in August 2012; the *Wall Street Journal* article (Thurm 2012) was written in 2012. What was the company's market value?

2 How did the amount of goodwill as of 31 December 2011 compare with the company's market value?

3 Why did the *Wall Street Journal* article state that goodwill in excess of the company's market value is "a potential clue to future write-offs"?

4 Based on the information in Exhibit 28, does the *Wall Street Journal* article statement appear to be correct?

Solution to 1:

SEE's market cap was about $3,457 million (= 192,062,185 shares × $18 per share) in December 2011 and around $2,689 million (= 192,062,185 shares × $14 per share) when the *Wall Street Journal* article was written in August 2012.

Solution to 2:

The amount of goodwill on SEE's balance sheet as of 31 December 2011 was $4,209.6 million. The amount of goodwill exceeded the company's market value. (Also note that goodwill and other intangible assets represented about 55% of SEE's total assets as of 31 December 2011.)

Solution to 3:

If the market capitalization exactly equaled the reported amount of goodwill, the value implicitly assigned to all the company's other assets would equal zero. In this case, because the market capitalization is less than the reported amount of goodwill, the value implicitly attributed to all the company's other assets is less than zero. This suggests that the amount of goodwill on the balance sheet is overvalued, so a future write-off is likely.

Solution to 4:

Yes, based on the information in Exhibit 28, the *Wall Street Journal* article statement appears correct. In the fiscal year ending 31 December 2012 after the article, SEE recorded impairment of goodwill and other intangible assets of $1,892.3 million.

Finally, *clear presentation* is also important for financial reporting quality for the balance sheet. Although accounting standards specify many aspects of what appears on the balance sheet, companies have discretion, for example, in determining which line items should be shown separately and which should be aggregated into a single total. For items shown as a single total, an analyst can usually consult the notes for information about the components. For example, in consulting the inventory note, an analyst may learn that inventory is carried on a last-in, first-out basis and that, consequently, in an inflationary environment, the inventory is carried on the balance sheet at a cost that is significantly lower than its current cost. This information would provide the analyst with comfort that the inventory is unlikely to be overstated.

7 SOURCES OF INFORMATION ABOUT RISK

A company's financial statements can provide useful indicators of financial, operating, or other risk. For example, high leverage ratios (or, similarly, low coverage ratios) derived from financial statement data can signal financial risk. As described in a previous section, analytical models that incorporate various financial data can signal bankruptcy risk, and others can predict reporting risks (i.e., the risk of a company misreporting). Operating risks can be indicated by financial data, such as highly variable operating cash flows or negative trends in profit margins. Additional information about risk can be obtained from sources other than the financial statements.

An audit opinion(s) covering financial statements (and internal controls over financial reporting, where required) can provide some information about reporting risk. However, the content of an audit opinion is unlikely to be a timely source of information about risk. A related item that is potentially a signal of problems (and thus potentially represents information about risk) is a discretionary change in auditor. For example, Allou Health & Beauty Care, discussed in Example 7, had a different auditor for 2000, 2001, and 2002.

The notes are an integral part of the financial statements. They typically contain information that is useful in understanding a company's risk. Beyond the information about risk that can be derived from a company's financial statements and notes, various other disclosures can provide information about financial, operating, reporting, or other risks. An important source of information is the management commentary, which provides management's assessment of the important risks faced by the company. Although risk-related disclosures in the management commentary sometimes overlap with disclosures contained in the financial statement notes or elsewhere in regulatory filings, the commentary should reveal the management perspective, and its content often differs from the note disclosures.

Other required disclosures that are specific to an event, such as capital raising, non-timely filing of financial reports, management changes, or mergers and acquisitions, can provide important information relevant to assessing risk. Finally, the financial press, including online media, if used judiciously, can be a useful source of information about risk.

7.1 Limited Usefulness of Auditor's Opinion as a Source of Information about Risk

An auditor's opinion is unlikely to be an analyst's first source of information about a company's risk. For financial statements, a clean audit opinion states that the financial statements present the information fairly and in conformity with the relevant accounting principles. For internal controls, a clean audit opinion states that the company maintained effective internal controls over financial reporting. A negative or going-concern audit opinion on financial statements or a report indicating an internal control weakness would clearly be a warning sign for an analyst. However, an audit opinion relates to historical information and would, therefore, typically not provide information on a timely enough basis to be a useful source of information about risk.

For example, Eastman Kodak Company filed for bankruptcy on 19 January 2012. The audit opinion for fiscal 2011 (dated 28 February 2012) is shown in Exhibit 29. The opinion is identical to the company's audit opinion for the prior fiscal year except for two differences: (1) the years have been updated, and (2) the paragraph highlighted in bold has been added. The added paragraph states that the financial statements were prepared under the "going-concern" assumption; the company has subsequently declared bankruptcy, which raises doubt about the company's ability to continue as a going concern; and the financial statements have not been adjusted to reflect the bankruptcy. An analyst would have learned about Eastman Kodak's bankruptcy on 19 January, so the audit opinion is not useful as a source of that information. In addition, the audit opinion addresses financial statements that had not been adjusted to reflect the bankruptcy, which would limit usefulness to an analyst.

Exhibit 29   Post-Bankruptcy Audit Opinion for Eastman Kodak

Report of Independent Registered Public Accounting Firm

To the Board of Directors and Shareholders of Eastman Kodak Company:

In our opinion, the consolidated financial statements listed in the index appearing under Item 15(a)(1) present fairly, in all material respects, the financial position of Eastman Kodak Company and its subsidiaries at December 31, 2011 and 2010, and the results of their operations and their cash flows for each of the three years in the period ended December 31, 2011 in conformity with accounting principles generally accepted in the United States of America. In addition, in our opinion, the financial statement schedule listed in the index appearing under Item 15(a)(2) presents fairly, in all material respects, the information set forth therein when read in conjunction with the related consolidated financial statements. Also in our opinion, the Company maintained, in all material respects, effective internal control over financial reporting as of December 31, 2011, based on criteria established in *Internal Control - Integrated Framework* issued by the Committee of Sponsoring Organizations of the Treadway Commission (COSO). The Company's management is responsible for these financial statements and financial statement schedule, for maintaining effective internal control over financial reporting and for its assessment of the effectiveness of internal control over financial reporting, included in Management's Report on Internal Control over

(continued)

Exhibit 29   (Continued)

Financial Reporting appearing under Item 9A. Our responsibility is to express opinions on these financial statements, on the financial statement schedule, and on the Company's internal control over financial reporting based on our integrated audits. We conducted our audits in accordance with the standards of the Public Company Accounting Oversight Board (United States). Those standards require that we plan and perform the audits to obtain reasonable assurance about whether the financial statements are free of material misstatement and whether effective internal control over financial reporting was maintained in all material respects. Our audits of the financial statements included examining, on a test basis, evidence supporting the amounts and disclosures in the financial statements, assessing the accounting principles used and significant estimates made by management, and evaluating the overall financial statement presentation. Our audit of internal control over financial reporting included obtaining an understanding of internal control over financial reporting, assessing the risk that a material weakness exists, and testing and evaluating the design and operating effectiveness of internal control based on the assessed risk. Our audits also included performing such other procedures as we considered necessary in the circumstances. We believe that our audits provide a reasonable basis for our opinions.

The accompanying financial statements have been prepared assuming that the Company will continue as a going concern. As more fully discussed in Note 1 to the financial statements, on January 19, 2012, the Company and its US subsidiaries filed voluntary petitions for relief under chapter 11 of the United States Bankruptcy Code. Uncertainties inherent in the bankruptcy process raise substantial doubt about the Company's ability to continue as a going concern. Management's plans in regard to these matters are also described in Note 1. The accompanying financial statements do not include any adjustments that might result from the outcome of this uncertainty.

A company's internal control over financial reporting is a process designed to provide reasonable assurance regarding the reliability of financial reporting and the preparation of financial statements for external purposes in accordance with generally accepted accounting principles. A company's internal control over financial reporting includes those policies and procedures that (i) pertain to the maintenance of records that, in reasonable detail, accurately and fairly reflect the transactions and dispositions of the assets of the company; (ii) provide reasonable assurance that transactions are recorded as necessary to permit preparation of financial statements in accordance with generally accepted accounting principles, and that receipts and expenditures of the company are being made only in accordance with authorizations of management and directors of the company; and (iii) provide reasonable assurance regarding prevention or timely detection of unauthorized acquisition, use, or disposition of the company's assets that could have a material effect on the financial statements.

Because of its inherent limitations, internal control over financial reporting may not prevent or detect misstatements. Also, projections of any evaluation of effectiveness to future periods are subject to the risk that controls may become inadequate because of changes in conditions, or that the degree of compliance with the policies or procedures may deteriorate.

/s/ PricewaterhouseCoopers LLP

PricewaterhouseCoopers LLP
Rochester, New York

Exhibit 29 (Continued)

February 28, 2012

Note: Bold-face type is added for emphasis.

In the case of Kodak, an analyst would not have obtained very useful information about risk from the auditor's report. Other sources of information—financial and market data—would have provided clear and timely indications of the company's financial difficulty.

Groupon provides another example of the timing of availability of information about risk in external auditors' reports. Exhibit 30 presents a timeline of events related to the company's material weakness in internal controls. Note that no negative external auditor opinion appeared before or during the time frame in which the weakness existed. No external opinion was required for the first annual filing, and the weakness had been remedied by the second annual filing.

Exhibit 30	Material Weaknesses in Internal Controls at Groupon
November 2011:	The company goes public (initial public offering)
March 2012:	The company revises financial results and discloses that management concluded there was a "material weakness" in internal controls over financial reporting, as of 31 December. Shares fall 17%. (Because of an exemption for newly public companies, no external auditor opinion on the effectiveness of internal controls was required.)
May 2012:	In its first-quarter filing, the company discloses that it is "taking steps" to correct the weaknesses but cannot provide assurance that internal controls will be considered effective by the end of the year.
August 2012:	Second-quarter filing includes a disclosure similar to that in first-quarter filing.
November 2012:	Third-quarter filing includes a disclosure similar to that in first-quarter filing.
February 2013:	Full-year filing indicates that the company "concluded that we have remediated the previously identified material weakness as of December 31, 2012." (As required for public companies, the filing includes Groupon's first external auditor opinion on the effectiveness of internal controls. The company received a clean opinion.)

In the case of Groupon, an analyst would not have obtained any useful information from the auditor's report. Other data would have given more useful indicators of the company's reporting difficulties. For example, the company was required to change its revenue recognition policy and to restate the amount of revenue reported in its IPO filing—clearly a sign of reporting difficulties. Another item of information providing a signal of likely reporting difficulties was the company's extensive number of acquisitions and explosive growth. Groupon's reported revenues for 2009 were more than 300 times the amount of 2008 reported revenues, and 2010 reported revenues were 23 times larger than 2009 revenues. As described in an August 2011 accounting blog (Catanach and Ketz 2011):

It is absolutely ludicrous to think that Groupon is anywhere close to having an effective set of internal controls over financial reporting having done 17 acquisitions in a little over a year. When a company expands to 45 countries, grows merchants from 212 to 78,466, and expands its employee base from 37 to 9,625 in only two years, there is little doubt that internal controls are not working somewhere.

The growth data, particularly coupled with disclosures in the IPO filing about management inexperience, are a warning sign of potential reporting risks. These reporting risks were observable many months before the company disclosed its internal control weakness, and the control weaknesses did not appear in an audit opinion.

Although the content of an audit opinion is unlikely to provide timely information about risk, a change in the auditor—and especially multiple changes in the auditor—can signal possible reporting problems. For example, one of the largest feeder funds for Bernie Madoff (the perpetrator of a multi-billion-dollar Ponzi scheme) had three different auditors for the three years from 2004 to 2006, a fact highlighted in testimony as a huge warning sign indicating "auditor shopping."[22] Similarly, the use of an auditor whose capabilities seem inadequate for the complexity of the company can indicate risk. For example, the accounting/auditing firm that audited Madoff's $50 billion operation consisted of three people (two principals and a secretary). The small size of the auditing firm relative to the size of Madoff's operations should have caused serious concern for any potential investor. In general, it is important to understand the relationship between the auditor and the firm. Any questions about the auditor's independence would be a cause for concern—for example, if the auditor and company management are particularly close or if the company represents a substantial portion of the auditing firm's revenue.

7.2 Risk-Related Disclosures in the Notes

The notes, an integral part of the financial statements, typically contain information that is useful in understanding a company's risk. For example, both IFRS and US GAAP require specific disclosures about risks related to contingent obligations, pension and post-employment benefits, and financial instrument risks.

Disclosures about contingent obligations include a description of the obligation, estimated amounts, timing of required payments, and related uncertainties.[23] Exhibit 31 shows excerpts from two of Royal Dutch Shell's financial statement notes disclosing information about provisions and contingencies. The year-to-year changes in management's estimated costs for items such as future decommissioning and restoration could have implications for risk evaluation. The disclosure also emphasizes the uncertain timing and amounts.

---

22 From the testimony of Harry Markopolos, CFA, given before the US House of Representatives Committee on Financial Services, 4 February 2009.
23 Contingent losses are recognized (i.e., reported on the financial statements) when it is probable the loss will occur and the amount can be reasonably estimated. Contingencies are disclosed (but not recognized) when the occurrence of a loss is less than probable but greater than remote and/or the amount cannot be reliably estimated. The concepts are similar under IFRS and US GAAP despite differences in terminology. IFRS makes a distinction between "provisions," which are recognized as liabilities because they meet the definition of a liability, and "contingent liabilities," which are disclosed but not recognized.

Exhibit 31   Disclosures about Contingent Obligations, Excerpt from Royal Dutch Shell's Note 19 and Note 25

19 Decommissioning and Other Provisions

	Current		Non-Current		Total	
	31 Dec 2012	31 Dec 2011	31 Dec 2012	31 Dec 2011	31 Dec 2012	31 Dec 2011
Decommissioning and restoration	1,356	894	14,715	13,072	16,071	13,966
Environmental	366	357	1,032	1,078	1,398	1,435
Redundancy	228	406	275	297	503	703
Litigation	390	256	307	330	697	586
Other	881	1,195	1,106	854	1,987	2,049
Total	3,221	3,108	17,435	15,631	20,656	18,739

The timing and amounts settled in respect of these provisions are uncertain and dependent on various factors that are not always within management's control. Additional provisions are stated net of reversals of provisions recognised in previous periods.

Of the decommissioning and restoration provision at December 31, 2012, an estimated $4,666 million is expected to be utilised within one to five years, $3,483 million within six to ten years, and the remainder in later periods.

Reviews of estimated decommissioning and restoration costs are carried out annually, which in 2012 resulted in an increase of $1,586 million ...

25 Legal Proceedings and Other Contingencies

Groundwater contamination

Shell Oil Company (including subsidiaries and affiliates, referred to collectively as SOC), along with numerous other defendants, has been sued by public and quasi-public water purveyors, as well as governmental entities. The plaintiffs allege responsibility for groundwater contamination caused by releases of gasoline containing oxygenate additives. Most of these suits assert various theories of liability, including product liability, and seek to recover actual damages, including clean-up costs. Some assert claims for punitive damages. Fewer than 10 of these cases remain. On the basis of court rulings in SOC's favour in certain cases claiming damages from threats of contamination, the claims asserted in remaining matters, and Shell's track record with regard to amounts paid to resolve varying claims, the management of Shell currently does not believe that the outcome of the remaining oxygenate-related litigation pending, as at December 31, 2012, will have a material impact on Shell.

Nigerian claims

Shell subsidiaries and associates operating in Nigeria are parties to various environmental and contractual disputes. These disputes are at different stages in litigation, including at the appellate stage, where judgments have been rendered against Shell. If taken at face value, the aggregate amount of these judgments could be seen as material. The management of Shell, however, believes that these matters will ultimately be resolved in a manner favourable to Shell. While no assurance can be provided as to the ultimate outcome of any litigation, these matters are not expected to have a material effect on Shell.

(continued)

Exhibit 31   (Continued)

Other

In the ordinary course of business, Shell subsidiaries are subject to a number of other loss contingencies arising from litigation and claims brought by governmental and private parties. The operations and earnings of Shell subsidiaries continue, from time to time, to be affected to varying degrees by political, legislative, fiscal and regulatory developments, including those relating to the protection of the environment and indigenous groups, in the countries in which they operate. The industries in which Shell subsidiaries are engaged are also subject to physical risks of various types. The nature and frequency of these developments and events, as well as their effect on future operations and earnings, are unpredictable.

Disclosures about pensions and post-employment benefits include information relevant to actuarial risks that could result in actual benefits differing from the reported obligations based on estimated benefits or investment risks that could result in actual assets differing from reported amounts based on estimates.

Disclosures about financial instruments include information about risks, such as credit risk, liquidity risk, and market risks that arise from the company's financial instruments, and how they have been managed.

EXAMPLE 11

Use of Disclosures

Use the excerpts from Royal Dutch Shell's note disclosing information about financial instruments in Exhibit 32 to answer the following questions:

1   Does Shell appear to take a centralized or decentralized approach to managing interest rate risk?

2   For the year ended 31 December 2012, Shell reported pre-tax income of $50,289 million. How significant is Shell's exposure to a 1% increase in interest rates?

3   For the year ended 31 December 2012, what would be the impact on Shell's pre-tax income of a 10% appreciation of the Australian dollar against the US dollar?

Exhibit 32   Disclosures about Financial Instruments, Excerpt from Royal Dutch Shell's Note 21

21 Financial Instruments and Other Derivative Contracts

A – Risks

In the normal course of business, financial instruments of various kinds are used for the purposes of managing exposure to interest rate, currency and commodity price movements.

....

Interest rate risk

Exhibit 32   (Continued)

Most debt is raised from central borrowing programmes. Interest rate swaps and currency swaps have been entered into to effectively convert most centrally issued debt to floating rate linked to dollar Libor (London Inter-Bank Offer Rate), reflecting Shell's policy to have debt principally denominated in dollars and to maintain a largely floating interest rate exposure profile. Consequently, Shell is exposed predominantly to dollar Libor interest rate movements. The financing of most subsidiaries is also structured on a floating-rate basis and, except in special cases, further interest rate risk management is discouraged.

On the basis of the floating rate net debt position at December 31, 2012, and assuming other factors (principally foreign exchange rates and commodity prices) remained constant and that no further interest rate management action were taken, an increase in interest rates of 1% would decrease pre-tax income by $27 million (2011: $146 million).

Foreign exchange risk

Many of the markets in which Shell operates are priced, directly or indirectly, in dollars. As a result, the functional currency of most Upstream companies and those with significant cross-border business is the dollar. For Downstream companies, the local currency is typically the functional currency. Consequently, Shell is exposed to varying levels of foreign exchange risk when it enters into transactions that are not denominated in the companies' functional currencies, when foreign currency monetary assets and liabilities are translated at the reporting date and as a result of holding net investments in operations that are not dollar-functional. The main currencies to which Shell is exposed are sterling, the Canadian dollar, euro and Australian dollar. Each company has treasury policies in place that are designed to measure and manage its foreign exchange exposures by reference to its functional currency.

Exchange rate gains and losses arise in the normal course of business from the recognition of receivables and payables and other monetary items in currencies other than individual companies' functional currency. Currency exchange risk may also arise in connection with capital expenditure. For major projects, an assessment is made at the final investment decision stage whether to hedge any resulting exposure.

Hedging of net investments in foreign operations or of income that arises in foreign operations that are non-dollar functional is not undertaken.

Assuming other factors (principally interest rates and commodity prices) remained constant and that no further foreign exchange risk management action were taken, a 10% appreciation against the dollar at December 31 of the main currencies to which Shell is exposed would have the following pre-tax effects:

(continued)

Exhibit 32 (Continued)				
	Increase (decrease) in income		Increase in net assets	
$ millions	2012	2011	2012	2011
10% appreciation against the dollar of:				
Sterling	(185)	(58)	1,214	1,042
Canadian dollar	131	(360)	1,384	1,364
Euro	30	458	1,883	1,768
Australian dollar	246	153	142	120

The above sensitivity information is calculated by reference to carrying amounts of assets and liabilities at December 31 only. The pre-tax effect on income arises in connection with monetary balances denominated in currencies other than the relevant entity's functional currency; the pre-tax effect on net assets arises principally from the translation of assets and liabilities of entities that are not dollar-functional.

Solution to 1:

Shell appears to take a centralized approach to managing interest rate risk based on its statements that most debt is raised centrally and that interest rate swaps and currency swaps have been used to convert most interest rate exposure to dollar Libor. In addition, Shell states that apart from structuring subsidiary financing on a floating-rate basis, it discourages subsidiary's further interest rate risk management.

Solution to 2:

For the year ended 31 December 2012, Shell's exposure to a 1% increase in interest rates is relatively insignificant. An increase in interest rates of 1% would decrease pre-tax income by $27 million, which is less than 0.1% of Shell's 2012 reported pre-tax income of $50,289 million.

Solution to 3:

The impact on Shell's pre-tax income of a 10% appreciation of the Australian dollar against the US dollar would be an increase of $246 million, which is about 0.5% of Shell's 2012 reported pre-tax income of $50,289 million.

These disclosures, along with expectations about future market conditions, can help an analyst assess whether the company's exposures to interest rate risk and foreign exchange risks pose a significant threat to the company's future performance.

7.3 Management Commentary (Management Discussion and Analysis, or MD&A)

The IFRS Practice Statement, *Management Commentary*, issued in December 2010, is a non-binding framework for commentary related to financial statements prepared in accordance with IFRS. One purpose of the commentary is to help users of the financial reports in understanding the company's risk exposures, approach to managing risks, and effectiveness of risk management. The practice statement includes five elements that should be contained in the commentary: (1) nature of the business; (2) objectives and strategies; (3) resources, risks, and relationships; (4) results and prospects; and (5) performance measures and indicators. The section on risks can be particularly useful (IFRS 2010).

> Management should disclose its principal strategic, commercial, operational, and financial risks, which are those that may significantly affect the entity's strategies and progress of the entity's value. The description of the principal risks facing the entity should cover both exposures to negative consequences and potential opportunities.... The principal risks and uncertainties can constitute either a significant external or internal risk to the entity. (p. 13)

Public US companies are required to include an MD&A as Item 7 of Form 10-K. The MD&A disclosures include information about (1) liquidity, (2) capital resources, (3) results of operations, (4) off-balance-sheet arrangements, and (5) contractual arrangements. Information about off-balance-sheet arrangements and contractual arrangements can enable an analyst to anticipate future impact on cash flow. Companies are required to present quantitative and qualitative information about the company's exposure to market risks as Item 7A of the 10-K. This disclosure should enable analysts to understand the impact of fluctuations in interest rates, foreign exchange, and commodity prices.[24]

The IFRS Practice Statement states specifically that companies should present only the principal risks and not list all possible risks and uncertainties. Similarly, the SEC Division of Corporation Finance's internal reference document, *Financial Reporting Manual*, states, "MD&A should not consist of generic or boilerplate disclosure. Rather, it should reflect the facts and circumstances specific to each individual registrant" (p. 296). In practice, disclosures do not always reflect the intent. One challenge faced by analysts is identifying important risks and distinguishing between risks that are generic and thus relevant to all companies and risks that are more specific to an individual company.

This challenge is illustrated by an excerpt from the "Key Risks and Uncertainties" section of Autonomy Corporation's 2010 Annual Report, its last annual report before it was acquired by Hewlett-Packard Company (HP) for $11.1 billion in 2011.[25] As shown in Exhibit 33, Autonomy's risk disclosures contain many items that are arguably generic, such as the inability to maintain the competitive value of its technology, loss of key executives, and continued unfavorable economic conditions. These types of risks would be faced by any technology company. This significant amount of generic commentary (two pages) could potentially distract a reader whose aim was to identify the specific and important risks faced by the company.

---

24 Although not part of the MD&A, disclosures about risk factors relevant to the company's securities are also required as Item 1A of Form 10-K.

25 HP subsequently took a multi-billion-dollar write-down on its investment, which it attributed to misreporting by Autonomy Corporation, stating that "the majority of this impairment charge is linked to serious accounting improprieties, disclosure failures and outright misrepresentations at Autonomy Corporation plc that occurred prior to HP's acquisition of Autonomy and the associated impact of those improprieties, failures and misrepresentations on the expected future financial performance of the Autonomy business over the long-term" (HP earnings announcement, 20 November 2012). Of course, HP's due diligence prior to purchasing the company would have gone far beyond the published financial reports; HP would have had access to all of the company's internal reporting as well.

Exhibit 33	Autonomy Corporation, Key Risks and Uncertainties		
Risk	**Description**	**Impact/Sensitivity**	**Mitigation/Comment**
Technology	Business depends on our core technology, and our strategy concentrates on developing and marketing software based on our proprietary technology.	Since substantially all of revenues derive from licensing our core technology, if unable to maintain and enhance the competitive value of our core technology, our business will be adversely affected.	Continue to invest heavily in research and development to maintain competitive advantage. Monitor market to maintain competitiveness. Apply core technology to new and additional vertical market applications.
Competition	Technology which significantly competes with our technology.	Could render our products out of date and could result in rapid loss of market share.	Invest heavily in new product development to ensure that we have products at various stages of the product life cycle.
Variability and visibility	There may be fluctuations in results due to quarterly reporting, and variability in results due to late-in-the-quarter purchasing cycles common in the software industry.	Although quarter-to-quarter results may not be meaningful due to the short periods, negative sentiment may arise based on interpretation of results. Due to late purchasing cycles common in the software industry, variability in closure rates could become exaggerated resulting in a negative effect on operations.	Close management of sales pipelines on a quarterly basis to improve visibility in results expectations. Close monitoring of macro and micro economic conditions to understand variability in closure rates. Annual and quarterly target setting to enable results achievement.
Margins	Expenditures increasing without a commensurate increase in revenues, and rapid changes in market conditions.	If increased expenses are not accompanied by increased revenues, we could experience decreased margins or operating losses.	Close monitoring by management of revenue and cost forecasts. Adjustment to expenditures in the event of anticipated revenue shortfalls.
Average selling prices	The average selling prices of our products could decrease rapidly.	May negatively impact revenues and gross margins.	Monitor market prices on an ongoing basis. Pricing responsibility at a senior level of management for deviations from standard.
Market conditions	The continuation of unfavourable economic and market conditions.	Could result in a rapid deterioration of operating results.	Regular monitoring of economic conditions. Adjustments to costs and product offerings to anticipate and match market conditions.
Resellers	Our ability to expand sales through indirect sellers and our general reliance on sales of our products by third parties.	Inability to recruit and retain resellers who can successfully penetrate their markets could adversely affect our business.	Invest in training resources for resellers. Close monitoring of reseller sales cycles. Investment in direct sales channel.
Management	The continued service of our executive directors.	The loss of any key member of management may affect the leadership of the company.	Establish succession plan. Maintain effective management training programme. Attract and retain senior personnel.
Hiring	The hiring and retention of qualified personnel.	Without the appropriate quality and quantity of skills throughout the organisation, it would be difficult to execute the business plans and grow.	Use of external recruiters and internal bonuses. Rigorous talent management plans and reviews. Provide competitive compensation packages. Ensure that work is challenging and rewarding.
Product errors	Errors or defects in our products.	Could negatively affect our revenues and the market acceptance of our products and increase our costs.	Invest in quality control programmes. Monitor integrity and effectiveness of software. Solicit and act on customer feedback.

Exhibit 33 (Continued)

Risk	Description	Impact/Sensitivity	Mitigation/Comment
Acquisitions	Problems encountered in connection with potential acquisitions.	We may not successfully overcome problems in connection with potential acquisitions, which could lead to a deterioration in our results.	Carefully evaluate transactions. Conduct thorough due diligence on all targets. Carefully plan for post-acquisition integration.
IP infringement	Claims by others that we infringe on their intellectual property rights.	If our technology infringed on other parties' intellectual property rights, we could be exposed to costs and injunctive relief.	Monitor market developments closely to identify potential violations of our patents, and by the company, and take action where necessary. Maintain a significant number of patents to support our business and protect competitive advantage.
Growth	Our ability to effectively manage our growth.	Expansion places demands on management, engineering, support, operations, legal, accounting, sales and marketing personnel, and other resources. Failure to manage effectively will impact business and financial results	Recruitment and retention of key personnel. Investment in corporate infrastructure, including support, operations, legal, and accounting personnel. Focus on internal controls.
International risks	Additional operational and financial risks as we continue to expand our international operations.	Exposure to movements in exchange rates and lack of familiarity with local laws could lead to infractions.	Pricing of contracts in US dollars to the extent possible to minimise exchange risk. Retention of local staff and local advisors, reporting to headquarters, to manage risk.
Security breaches	Any breach of our security measures and unauthorised access to a customer's or our data.	Could result in significant legal liability and negative publicity.	Establish and maintain strict security standards. Test security standards on a regular basis.

Source: Section from Autonomy Corporation's 2010 Annual Report.

7.4 Other Required Disclosures

Other required disclosures that are specific to an event, such as capital raising, non-timely filing of financial reports, management changes, or mergers and acquisitions, can provide important information relevant to assessing risk. In the United States, public companies would report such events to the SEC in a Form 8-K (and NT—"notification of inability to timely file"—when appropriate). Delays in filing are often the result of accounting difficulties. Such accounting difficulties could be internal disagreement on an accounting principle or estimate, the lack of adequate financial staff, or the discovery of an accounting fraud that requires further examination. In general, an NT filing is highly likely to signal problems with financial reporting quality.

For public companies in Europe, the Committee of European Securities Regulators (CESR) has published guidance concerning the types of inside information that must be disclosed on an ad hoc basis to the market. Examples of such information include changes in control; changes in management and supervisory boards; mergers, splits, and spinoffs; legal disputes; and new licenses, patents, and registered trademarks. Companies use the disclosure mechanisms specified by their relevant national authorities to make such disclosures. For example, in the United Kingdom, a company would release an announcement to the market via an approved regulatory information service.

In these cases, an examination of the information announced would be necessary to determine whether reporting quality would be affected. For example, an announcement of the sudden resignation of a company's most senior financial officer or external auditor would clearly be a warning sign of potential problems with financial reporting quality. As another example, an announcement of a legal dispute related to one of the company's important assets or products would warrant attention because it could negatively affect the company's future earnings. Announcements of mergers and acquisitions, although they might indicate future positive developments for the company, could also indicate changes in the company's risk profile, particularly during the transaction.

7.5 Financial Press as a Source of Information about Risk

The financial press can be a useful source of information about risk when, for example, a financial reporter uncovers financial reporting issues that had not previously been recognized. For example, a *Wall Street Journal* financial reporter, Jonathan Weil (2000), was one of the first people to identify problems with the accounting at Enron (and other companies that were using "gain-on-sale" accounting, an aggressive policy allowing immediate revenue recognition on long-term contracts). Indeed, the well-known investor James (Jim) Chanos cites an article by Weil as the catalyst of his investigation of Enron (Chanos 2002).

It is important to emphasize that even if an initial idea comes from a news article, further investigation is essential—first, by using definitive sources (i.e., regulatory filings) to confirm any accounting and financial disclosures and, second, by seeking supporting information from other sources, where available. For example, although a financial press article was the initial source of information for Chanos, the first step in his research was to analyze Enron's annual SEC filings (Form 10-K and 10-Q). In addition, Chanos obtained information about insider stock sales, the company's business strategy and tactics, and stock analysts' perspectives.

It is also important—and likely will become increasingly important as electronic media via the internet expands—to consider the source of any particular news article. Information reported by a well-known financial news provider is more likely to be factual than information from less-established sources. Similarly, stories or blogs written by financial journalists are more likely to be unbiased than those written by individuals with a related service or product to sell.

8   CONCLUSION

Assessing the quality of financial reports—both reporting quality and results quality—is an important analytical skill.

■ The quality of financial reporting can be thought of as spanning a continuum from the highest quality to the lowest.

■ Potential problems that affect the quality of financial reporting broadly include revenue and expense recognition on the income statement; classification on the statement of cash flows; and the recognition, classification, and measurement of assets and liabilities on the balance sheet.

■ Typical steps involved in evaluating financial reporting quality include an understanding of the company's business and industry in which the company is operating; comparison of the financial statements in the current period and the previous period to identify any significant differences in line items; an evaluation of the company's accounting policies, especially any unusual revenue and expense recognition compared with those of other companies in the same industry; financial ratio analysis; examination of the statement of cash flows with particular focus on differences between net income and operating cash flows; perusal of risk disclosures; and review of management compensation and insider transactions.

- High-quality earnings increase the value of the company more than low-quality earnings, and the term "high-quality earnings" assumes that reporting quality is high.

- Low-quality earnings are insufficient to cover the company's cost of capital and/or are derived from non-recurring, one-off activities. In addition, the term "low-quality earnings" can be used when the reported information does not provide a useful indication of the company's performance.

- Various alternatives have been used as indicators of earnings quality: recurring earnings, earnings persistence and related measures of accruals, beating benchmarks, and after-the-fact confirmations of poor-quality earnings, such as enforcement actions and restatements.

- Earnings that have a significant accrual component are less persistent and thus may revert to the mean more quickly.

- A company that consistently reports earnings that exactly meet or only narrowly beat benchmarks can raise questions about its earnings quality.

- Cases of accounting malfeasance have commonly involved issues with revenue recognition, such as premature recognition of revenues or the recognition of fraudulent revenues.

- Cases of accounting malfeasance have involved misrepresentation of expenditures as assets rather than as expenses or misrepresentation of the timing or amount of expenses.

- Bankruptcy prediction models, used in assessing financial results quality, quantify the likelihood that a company will default on its debt and/or declare bankruptcy.

- Similar to the term "earnings quality," when reported cash flows are described as being high quality, it means that the company's underlying economic performance was satisfactory in terms of increasing the value of the firm, and it also implies that the company had high reporting quality (i.e., that the information calculated and disclosed by the company was a good reflection of economic reality). Cash flow can be described as "low quality" either because the reported information properly represents genuinely bad economic performance or because the reported information misrepresents economic reality.

- For the balance sheet, high financial *reporting* quality is indicated by completeness, unbiased measurement, and clear presentation.

- A balance sheet with significant amounts of off-balance-sheet debt would lack the completeness aspect of financial reporting quality.

- Unbiased measurement is a particularly important aspect of financial reporting quality for assets and liabilities for which valuation is subjective.

- A company's financial statements can provide useful indicators of financial or operating risk.

- The management commentary (also referred to as the management discussion and analysis, or MD&A) can give users of the financial statements information that is helpful in assessing the company's risk exposures and approaches to managing risk.

- Required disclosures regarding, for example, changes in senior management or inability to make a timely filing of required financial reports can be a warning sign of problems with financial reporting quality.

- The financial press can be a useful source of information about risk when, for example, a financial reporter uncovers financial reporting issues that had not previously been recognized. An analyst should undertake additional investigation of any issue identified.

REFERENCES

"Ahold: Europe's Enron." 2003. *The Economist* (27 February).

Altman, Edward I. 1968. "Financial Ratios, Discriminant Analysis and the Prediction of Corporate Bankruptcy." *Journal of Finance*, vol. 23, no. 4 (September):589–609.

Altman, Edward I. 2000. "Predicting Financial Distress of Companies: Revisiting the Z-Score and Zeta® Models." Working paper (July).

Beneish, Messod D. 1999. "The Detection of Earnings Manipulation." *Financial Analysts Journal*, vol. 55, no. 5 (September/October):24–36.

Beneish, Messod D., Charles M.C. Lee, and D. Craig Nichols. 2013. "Earnings Manipulation and Expected Returns." *Financial Analysts Journal*, vol. 69, no. 2 (March/April):57–82.

Bens, Daniel A., Theodore H. Goodman, and Monica Neamtiu. 2012. "Does Investment-Related Pressure Lead to Misreporting? An Analysis of Reporting Following M&A Transactions." *Accounting Review*, vol. 87, no. 3 (May):839–865.

Beresford, Dennis R., Nicholas deB. Katzenbach, and C.B. Rogers, Jr. 2003. "Report of Investigation by the Special Investigative Committee of the Board of Directors of WorldCom, Inc." (31 March): www.sec.gov/Archives/edgar/data/723527/000093176303001862/dex991.htm.

Bharath, Sreedhar T., and Tyler Shumway. 2008. "Forecasting Default with the Merton Distance to Default Model." *Review of Financial Studies*, vol. 21, no. 3 (May):1339–1369.

Bhasin, Madan. 2012. "Corporate Accounting Frauds: A Case Study of Satyam Computers Limited." *International Journal of Contemporary Business Studies*, vol. 3, no. 10 (October):16–42.

Brown, Lawrence D., and Marcus L. Caylor. 2005. "A Temporal Analysis of Quarterly Earnings Thresholds: Propensities and Valuation Consequences." *Accounting Review*, vol. 80, no. 2 (April):423–440.

Bulkeley, W. 2002. "Questioning the Books: IBM Annual Report Shows Stronger Core Earnings." *Wall Street Journal* (12 March).

Burgstahler, D., and Ilia Dichev. 1997. "Earnings Management to Avoid Earnings Decreases and Losses." *Journal of Accounting and Economics*, vol. 24, no. 1 (December):99–126.

Catanach, Anthony H., and J. Edward Ketz. 2011. "Trust No One, Particularly Not Groupon's Accountants," Grumpy Old Accountants (August): http://blogs.smeal.psu.edu/grumpyoldaccountants.

Chanos, James. 2002. "Anyone Could Have Seen Enron Coming: Prepared Witness Testimony Given Feb. 6, 2002 to the House Committee on Energy and Commerce," *Wall $treet Week with FORTUNE* (http://www.pbs.org/wsw/opinion/chanostestimony.html).

Dechow, Patricia M., Richard G. Sloan, and Amy P. Sweeney. 1995. "Detecting Earnings Management." *Accounting Review*, vol. 70, no. 2 (April):193–225.

Dechow, Patricia M., Scott A. Richardson, and Irem Tuna. 2003. "Why Are Earnings Kinky? An Examination of the Earnings Management Explanation." *Review of Accounting Studies*, vol. 8, no. 2–3 (June):355–384.

Dechow, Patricia M., Weili Ge, and Catherine Schrand. 2010. "Understanding Earnings Quality: A Review of the Proxies, Their Determinants and Their Consequences." *Journal of Accounting and Economics*, vol. 50, no. 2–3 (December):344–401.

Dechow, Patricia, Seili Ge, Chad Larson, and Richard Sloan. 2011. "Predicting Material Accounting Misstatements." *Contemporary Accounting Research*, vol. 28, no. 1 (Spring):17–82.

Degeorge, François, Jayendu Patel, and Richard Zeckhauser. 1999. "Earnings Management to Exceed Thresholds." *Journal of Business*, vol. 72, no. 1 (January):1–33.

Fuji Electric. 2013. "Announcement of Impairment Losses on Noncurrent Assets (Extraordinary Losses)." memo (25 April): www.fujielectric.com/company/news/box/doc/130425_evaluation.pdf.

Erickson, Merle, and Shiing-wu Wang. 1999. "Earnings Management by Acquiring Firms in Stock for Stock Mergers." *Journal of Accounting and Economics*, vol. 27, no. 2 (April):149–176.

Erickson, M., S. Heitzman, and X.F. Zhang. 2012. "The Effect of Financial Misreporting on Corporate Mergers and Acquisitions." Working paper.

Friedman, Eric, Simon Johnson, and Todd Mitton. 2003. "Propping and Tunneling." *Journal of Comparative Economics*, vol. 31, no. 4 (December):732–750.

Hwang, S.L. 1994. "Borden to Reverse, Reclassify 40% of 1992 Charge." *Wall Street Journal* (22 March).

IASB. 2010. *Conceptual Framework for Financial Reporting 2010*. International Accounting Standards Board (September).

IFRS. 2010. *Management Commentary, A Framework for Presentation*. IFRS Practice Statement (December).

Johnson, S., R. LaPorta, A. Shleifer, and F. Lopez-de-Silanes. 2000. "Tunneling." *American Economic Review*, vol. 90, no. 2 (May):22–27.

Jones, Jennifer J. 1991. "Earnings Management during Import Relief Investigations." *Journal of Accounting Research*, vol. 29, no. 2 (Autumn):193–228.

Kahn, Jeremy. 2009. "In India, Clues Unfold to a Fraud's Framework." *New York Times* (26 January).

Kealhofer, Stephen. 2003. "Quantifying Credit Risk I: Default Prediction." *Financial Analysts Journal*, vol. 59, no. 1 (January/February):30–44.

Leuty, Ron. 2012. "Elan Will Shutter South S.F. Center as It Shifts R&D to New Company." *San Francisco Business Times* (5 October 2012): www.bizjournals.com/sanfrancisco/blog/biotech/2012/09/elan-neotope-onclave-alzheimers.html?page=all.

Lewis, Craig M. 2012. "Risk Modeling at the SEC: The Accounting Quality Model," Speech given at the Financial Executives International Committee on Finance and Information Technology (13 December): www.sec.gov/news/speech/2012/spch121312cml.htm.

McVay, Sarah E. 2006. "Earnings Management Using Classification Shifting: An Examination of Core Earnings and Special Items." *Accounting Review*, vol. 81, no. 3 (May):501–532.

Mulford, Charles W., and Eugene E. Comiskey. 2005. *Creative Cash Flow Reporting: Uncovering Sustainable Financial Performance*. Hoboken, NJ: John Wiley & Sons.

Nissim, Doron, and Stephen H. Penman. 2001. "Ratio Analysis and Equity Valuation: From Research to Practice." *Review of Accounting Studies*, vol. 6, no. 1 (March):109–154.

SEC. 2000. "Accounting and Auditing Enforcement, Release No. 1350." US Securities and Exchange Commission (14 December): www.sec.gov/litigation/admin/34-43724.htm.

SEC. 2001a "Accounting and Auditing Enforcement, Release No. 1393." US Securities and Exchange Commission (15 May): www.sec.gov/litigation/admin/33-7976.htm.

SEC. 2001b. "Accounting and Auditing Enforcement, Release No. 1405." US Securities and Exchange Commission (19 June): www.sec.gov/litigation/admin/34-44444.htm.

SEC. 2003. "Report Pursuant to Section 704 of the Sarbanes-Oxley Act of 2002" US Securities and Exchange Commission (24 January): www.sec.gov/news/studies/sox704report.pdf.

Sherer, P. 2000. "AmeriServe Examination Finds Financial Woes." *Wall Street Journal* (3 July).

Shumway, Tyler. 2001. "Forecasting Bankruptcy More Accurately: A Simple Hazard Model." *Journal of Business*, vol. 74, no. 1 (January):101–124.

Sloan, Richard G. 1996. "Do Stock Prices Fully Reflect Information in Accruals and Cash Flows about Future Earnings?" *Accounting Review*, vol. 71, no. 3 (July):289–315.

Thurm, Scott. 2012. "Buyers Beware: The Goodwill Games." *Wall Street Journal* (12 August).

Weil, Jonathan. 2000. "Energy Traders Cite Gains, But Some Math is Missing," *Wall Street Journal* (20 September).

PRACTICE PROBLEMS

The following information relates to Questions 1–4

Mike Martinez is an equity analyst who has been asked to analyze Stellar, Inc. by his supervisor, Dominic Anderson. Stellar exhibited strong earnings growth last year; however, Anderson is skeptical about the sustainability of the company's earnings. He wants Martinez to focus on Stellar's financial reporting quality and earnings quality.

After conducting a thorough review of the company's financial statements, Martinez concludes the following:

Conclusion 1   Although Stellar's financial statements adhere to generally accepted accounting principles (GAAP), Stellar understates earnings in periods when the company is performing well and overstates earnings in periods when the company is struggling.

Conclusion 2   Stellar most likely understated the value of amortizable intangibles when recording the acquisition of Solar, Inc. last year. No goodwill impairment charges have been taken since the acquisition.

Conclusion 3   Over time, the accruals component of Stellar's earnings is large relative to the cash component.

Conclusion 4   Stellar reported an unusually sharp decline in accounts receivable in the current year, and an increase in long-term trade receivables.

1   Based on Martinez's conclusions, Stellar's financial statements are *best* categorized as:

   A   non-GAAP compliant.

   B   GAAP compliant, but with earnings management.

   C   GAAP compliant and decision useful, with sustainable and adequate returns.

2   Based on Conclusion 2, after the acquisition of Solar, Stellar's earnings are *most likely*:

   A   understated.

   B   fairly stated.

   C   overstated.

3   In his follow-up analysis relating to Conclusion 3, Martinez should focus on Stellar's:

   A   total accruals.

   B   discretionary accruals.

   C   non-discretionary accruals.

4   What will be the impact on Stellar in the current year if Martinez's belief in Conclusion 4 is correct? Compared with the previous year, Stellar's:

   A   current ratio will increase.

> **B** days sales outstanding (DSO) will decrease.
>
> **C** accounts receivable turnover will decrease.

SOLUTIONS

1   B is correct. Stellar's financial statements are GAAP compliant (Conclusion 1) but cannot be relied upon to assess earnings quality. There is evidence of earnings management: understating and overstating earnings depending upon the results of the period (Conclusion 1), understated amortizable intangibles (Conclusion 2), and a high accruals component in the company's earnings (Conclusion 3).

2   C is correct. Martinez believes that Stellar most likely understated the value of amortizable intangibles when recording the acquisition of a rival company last year. Impairment charges have not been taken since the acquisition (Conclusion 2). Consequently, the company's earnings are likely to be overstated because amortization expense is understated. This understatement has not been offset by an impairment charge.

3   B is correct. Martinez concluded that the accruals component of Stellar's earnings was large relative to the cash component (Conclusion 3). Earnings with a larger component of accruals are typically less persistent and of lower quality. An important distinction is between accruals that arise from normal transactions in the period (called non-discretionary) and accruals that result from transactions or accounting choices outside the normal (called discretionary accruals). The discretionary accruals are possibly made with the intent to distort reported earnings. Outlier discretionary accruals are an indicator of possibly manipulated—and thus low quality earnings. Thus, Martinez is primarily focused on discretionary accruals, particularly outlier discretionary accruals (referred to as abnormal accruals).

4   B is correct. Because accounts receivable will be lower than reported in the past, Stellar's DSO [Accounts receivable/(Revenues/365)] will decrease. Stellar's accounts receivable turnover (365/days' sales outstanding) will increase with the lower DSO, giving the false impression of a faster turnover. The company's current ratio will decrease (current assets will decrease with no change in current liabilities).

Integration of Financial Statement Analysis Techniques

by Jack T. Ciesielski, Jr., CFA

Jack T. Ciesielski, Jr., CFA (USA).

LEARNING OUTCOMES

Mastery	The candidate should be able to:
☐	**a.** demonstrate the use of a framework for the analysis of financial statements, given a particular problem, question, or purpose (e.g., valuing equity based on comparables, critiquing a credit rating, obtaining a comprehensive picture of financial leverage, evaluating the perspectives given in management's discussion of financial results);
☐	**b.** identify financial reporting choices and biases that affect the quality and comparability of companies' financial statements, and explain how such biases may affect financial decisions;
☐	**c.** evaluate the quality of a company's financial data, and recommend appropriate adjustments to improve quality and comparability with similar companies, including adjustments for differences in accounting standards, methods, and assumptions;
☐	**d.** evaluate how a given change in accounting standards, methods, or assumptions affects financial statements and ratios;
☐	**e.** analyze and interpret how balance sheet modifications, earnings normalization, and cash flow statement related modifications affect a company's financial statements, financial ratios, and overall financial condition.

Note: New rulings and/or pronouncements issued after the publication of the readings in financial reporting and analysis may cause some of the information in these readings to become dated. Candidates are expected to be familiar with the overall analytical framework contained in the study session readings, as well as the implications of alternative accounting methods for financial analysis and valuation, as provided in the assigned readings. Candidates are not responsible for changes that occur after the material was written.

INTRODUCTION

It is important to keep in mind that financial analysis is the means to the end, and not the end itself. Rather than try to apply every possible technique and tool to every situation, it is more important for the investor to understand the proper type of analysis to apply in a given situation.

The primary reason for performing financial analysis is to facilitate an economic decision. Before making such decisions as whether to lend to a particular long-term borrower or to invest a large sum in a common stock, venture capital vehicle, or private equity candidate, an investor wants to put the odds of a successful outcome on his or her side. Rather than leaving outcomes to chance, financial analysis should identify potential losses and make the potential favorable outcomes more visible.

The purpose of this reading is to provide examples of the effective use of financial analysis in decision making. The framework for the analysis is shown in Exhibit 1. Each of the three case studies is set in a different type of company and has a different focus/purpose and context for the analysis. However, each case study follows the basic framework.

Exhibit 1	A Financial Statement Analysis Framework	
Phase	**Sources of Information**	**Examples of Output**
1 Define the purpose and context of the analysis.	■ The nature of the analyst's function, such as evaluating an equity or debt investment or issuing a credit rating ■ Communication with client or supervisor on needs and concerns ■ Institutional guidelines related to developing specific work product	■ Statement of the purpose or objective of analysis ■ A list (written or unwritten) of specific questions to be answered by the analysis ■ Nature and content of report to be provided ■ Timetable and budgeted resources for completion
2 Collect input data.	■ Financial statements, other financial data, questionnaires, and industry/economic data ■ Discussions with management, suppliers, customers, and competitors ■ Company site visits (e.g., to production facilities or retail stores)	■ Organized financial statements ■ Financial data tables ■ Completed questionnaires, if applicable
3 Process input data, as required, into analytically useful data.	■ Data from the previous phase	■ Adjusted financial statements ■ Common-size statements ■ Ratios and graphs ■ Forecasts
4 Analyze/interpret the data.	■ Input data and processed data	■ Analytical results

Exhibit 1 (Continued)		
Phase	**Sources of Information**	**Examples of Output**
5 Develop and communicate conclusions and recommendations (e.g., with an analysis report).	■ Analytical results and previous reports ■ Institutional guidelines for published reports	■ Analytical report answering questions posed in Phase 1 ■ Recommendation regarding the purpose of the analysis, such as whether to make an investment or grant credit
6 Follow-up.	■ Information gathered by periodically repeating above steps as necessary to determine whether changes to holdings or recommendations are necessary	■ Updated reports and recommendations

CASE STUDY 1: LONG-TERM EQUITY INVESTMENT

The portfolio manager for the food sector of a large public employee pension fund wants to take a long-term equity stake in a publicly traded food company, and has become interested in Nestlé S.A. (SWX Swiss Exchange: NESN and OTC [NY ADR]: NSRGY), a truly global company. In its 2007 management report, Nestlé's management outlined its long-term objectives for organic growth, continuous margin improvement, and improvement in return on invested capital. The management report indicated the following general strategic direction: "We continue to believe that our greatest opportunity to create value for our shareholders is through further transforming our Food and Beverages business into a Nutrition, Health, and Wellness offering and by improving its performance further." Those stated objectives captured the portfolio manager's attention, and the manager has become intrigued with Nestlé as an investment possibility. He commissions an analyst to evaluate Nestlé for consideration as a core holding. Before investing in the company, the portfolio manager has several concerns that he has conveyed to the analyst:

■ What are Nestlé's sources of earnings growth? How sustainable is Nestlé's performance? In other words, do the company's reported earnings represent economic reality? And if their performance is indeed robustly reported, will it be repeatable for, say, five to ten years while the pension fund treats the common stock as a core holding?

■ In determining the quality of earnings over a long-term time frame, the portfolio manager wants to understand the relationship of earnings to cash flow.

■ Having started out in the investment business as a lending officer, the portfolio manager wants to know how well Nestlé's balance sheet takes into account the company's full rights and obligations. Can the capital structure of the company support future operations and strategic plans? Even if the investor is primarily concerned with the earnings power of a possible investee, the balance sheet matters. For example, if asset write-downs or new legal liabilities cripple a company's financial standing, it is difficult for a company to sustain profitability if it has to repair its balance sheet. Worse still for an investor: If "repairing the balance sheet" means the issuance of dilutive stock, it can be even more costly to existing investors.

The analyst develops a plan of analysis to address the portfolio manager's concerns by following the framework in Exhibit 1. Phases 3 and 4 will be the focus of most of the work.

Phase 1: Define a Purpose for the Analysis

The analyst articulates the purpose and context of the analysis as isolating the factors that have driven the company's financial success and assessing their sustainability, while delineating and understanding the risks that may upset the sustainability of returns.

Phase 2: Collect Input Data

The analyst finds that Nestlé has an extensive library of financial statements on its website. After gathering several years of annual reports, he is ready to begin processing the data.

Phase 3: Process Data/Phase 4: Analyze/Interpret the Processed Data

The analyst intends to accomplish his purpose stated in Phase 1 through a series of financial analyses, including:

- A DuPont analysis;[1]
- An analysis of the composition of Nestlé's asset base;
- An analysis of Nestlé's capital structure;
- A study of the company's segments and the allocation of capital among them;
- An examination of the company's accruals in reporting as they affect earnings quality;
- A study of the company's cash flows and their adequacy for the company's continued operations and strategies; and
- Decomposition and analysis of the company's valuation.

While processing the input data consistent with the needs of the analyses above, the analyst plans to simultaneously interpret and analyze the resulting data. In his view, Phases 3 and 4 of the framework are best considered jointly.

DuPont Analysis

For several reasons, the analyst decides that the best way to first investigate Nestlé is through the lens of a DuPont analysis. The investment is expected to be in the company's common stock, and ultimately, the DuPont analysis isolates the components affecting the return on common equity. Furthermore, the disaggregation of ROE components leads to more threads to follow in assessing the drivers of Nestlé's performance. The analyst also intends to investigate the quality of the earnings and the underlying cash flows, as well as investigating the common shareholders' standing in the Nestlé capital structure.

---

1 A reminder to the reader: This case study is an example, and starting financial statement analysis with a DuPont analysis is not a mandate. Alternatively, another analyst might have preferred starting with a time-series common-size income statement. This analyst might be more interested in the trends of various income and expense categories as a financial statement analysis starting point than in the sources of returns on shareholder equity. It depends on the perspective of the individual analyst.

One basic premise underlying all research and analysis is to constantly look beneath the level of information presented—to constantly strive for disaggregation within information presented, whether it is a single line on a financial statement or within segments of an entire entity. This search for granularity can reveal the sources of a company's earnings drivers; it can also highlight weaker operations being masked by stronger ones in the aggregate. That premise of "seeking granularity" underlies DuPont analysis: By isolating the different components of return on equity, it helps the analyst find potential operational flaws and provides a springboard for dialogue with management about possible problems.

The analyst begins to process the data gathered in Phase 2 to assemble the information required for the DuPont analysis. Exhibit 2 shows the last three years of income statements for Nestlé; Exhibit 3 shows the last four years of Nestlé balance sheets. From his study of the income statement, the analyst notes that Nestlé has a significant amount of income from associates. In 2007, this amounted to CHF 1,280 million, or 11.2 percent, of Nestlé's net income (referred to by Nestlé as "profit for the period"). The income from associates[2] is a pure net income figure, after taxes and with no related revenue in the income statement. Much of the income relates to Nestlé's 30 percent stock ownership of L'Oreal, a cosmetics company.

The analyst's interest is to evaluate the company on a decomposed basis as much as possible in order to isolate any problem operations or to find misunderstood or unidentified opportunities. Including the net investments and returns of associates with full reported value of Nestlé's own assets and income would introduce noise into the analytical signals produced by the DuPont analysis. The returns earned by affiliates are not under the direct control of Nestlé's management as are the "pure Nestlé" operations and resources. To avoid making incorrect inferences about the profitability of Nestlé's operations, the analyst wants to remove the effects of the investments in associates from the balance sheet and income statement. Otherwise, DuPont analysis components such as net profit margin and total asset turnover will combine the impact of pure Nestlé operations with operations of associated companies. Conclusions drawn about Nestlé-only business would be based on flawed information.

The analyst restated the 2004 balance sheet from the published version to take into account several accounting changes Nestlé made as of 1 January 2005. Those adjustments would have affected 31 December 2004 balances if the financial statements had been restated for that year. In order to keep the DuPont analysis as logically consistent as possible throughout all the periods of study, he restated the 2004 balance sheet for those adjustments by isolating the 1 January 2005 adjustments from the 2005 financial statements, and restating the 31 December 2004 year end balances for them. They included changes for employee benefits plan accounting (IAS 19 adoption), lease classification (IFRIC 4 adoption), a reclassification of a warrants premium, and the cumulative effect on their investment of L'Oreal's first-time adoption of International Financial Reporting Standards. The revisions made by the analyst to the as-reported 2004 balance sheet are shown in Exhibit 4.

Exhibit 2	Nestlé S.A. Income Statements 2007–2005 (in Millions of CHF)		
	2007	**2006**	**2005**
Sales	107,552	98,458	91,115
Cost of goods sold	(45,037)	(40,713)	(37,917)
Distribution expenses	(9,104)	(8,244)	(7,402)

(continued)

---

2 Associates are companies in which Nestlé has the power to exercise a significant influence but does not exercise control. They are accounted for by the equity method.

Exhibit 2   (Continued)

	2007	2006	2005
Marketing and administration expenses	(36,512)	(34,465)	(32,421)
Research and development costs	(1,875)	(1,734)	(1,499)
EBIT before restructuring and impairments[a]	**15,024**	**13,302**	**11,876**
Net other income/(expenses)[b]	(590)	(516)	(920)
Profit before interest and taxes	14,434	12,786	10,956
Net financing cost			
Financial income	576	537	605
Financial expense	(1,492)	(1,218)	(1,192)
Profit before taxes and associates (EBT)	**13,518**	**12,105**	**10,369**
Taxes	(3,416)	(3,293)	(2,647)
Share of results of associates	1,280	963	896
Profit from continuing operations	**11,382**	**9,775**	**8,618**
Net profit/(loss) on discontinued operations	0	74	(14)
Profit for the period	**11,382**	**9,849**	**8,604**
of which attributable to minority interests	733	652	523
of which attributable to shareholders of the parent (Net profit)	10,649	9,197	8,081
Earnings per share from continuing operations			
Basic earnings per share	CHF 27.81	CHF 23.71	CHF 20.82
Diluted earnings per share	CHF 27.61	CHF 23.56	CHF 20.63

[a] Expenses include depreciation and amortization of 3,211; 3,061; and 2,728 for 2007, 2006, and 2005, respectively.
[b] Includes impairments of 482, 134, and 608 for 2007, 2006, and 2005, respectively.

Exhibit 3   Nestlé S.A. Balance Sheets 2007–2004 (in Millions of CHF)

	2007	2006	2005	2004 (Revised)
Assets				
Liquid assets				
Cash and cash equivalents	6,594	5,278	4,658	4,902
Short term investments	2,902	6,197	12,735	10,380
	9,496	11,475	17,393	15,282
Trade and other receivables	15,421	14,577	14,291	11,809
Assets held for sale	22	74	633	0
Inventories	9,272	8,029	8,162	7,025
Derivative assets	754	556	645	585
Prepayments and accrued income	805	594	641	584

Exhibit 3   (Continued)

	2007	2006	2005	2004 (Revised)
Total current assets	35,770	35,305	41,765	35,285
Non-current assets				
Net property, plant and equipment	22,065	20,230	18,990	17,208
Investments in associates	8,936	8,430	7,073	5,197
Deferred tax assets	2,224	2,433	2,466	2,173
Financial assets	4,213	2,778	2,513	2,410
Employee benefits assets	811	343	69	32
Goodwill	33,423	28,513	26,990	23,854
Intangible assets	7,217	3,773	2,852	2,028
Total non-current assets	78,889	66,500	60,953	52,902
Total assets	114,659	101,805	102,718	88,187
Liabilities and equity				
Current liabilities				
Trade and other payables	14,179	12,572	11,117	9,074
Liabilities directly associated with assets held for sale	7	0	38	0
Financial liabilities	24,541	15,494	18,841	14,722
Tax liabilities	856	884	705	584
Derivative liabilities	477	470	922	856
Accruals and deferred income	3,266	3,059	4,231	3,892
Total current liabilities	43,326	32,479	35,854	29,128
Non-current liabilities				
Financial liabilities	6,129	6,952	8,277	10,891
Employee benefits liabilities	5,165	5,415	5,747	5,704
Deferred tax liabilities	1,398	706	240	16
Other payables	1,091	366	185	327
Provisions	3,316	3,039	3,347	3,004
Total non-current liabilities	17,099	16,478	17,796	19,942
Total liabilities	60,425	48,957	53,650	49,070
Total equity attributable to shareholders of the parent	52,085	50,991	47,498	38,068
Minority interests	2,149	1,857	1,570	1,049
Total equity	54,234	52,848	49,068	39,117
Total liabilities and equity	114,659	101,805	102,718	88,187

Exhibit 4   Modifications to 2004 Balance Sheets (in Millions of CHF)

	As Reported	IAS 19 Effect (1)	IFRIC 4 Effect (2)	IAS 39 Warrant Premium Classification (3)	L'Oreal IFRS Adoption (4)	Revised
Assets						
Cash and cash equivalents	4,902					4,902
Short term investments	10,380					10,380
Liquid assets	15,282					15,282
Trade and other receivables	11,809					11,809
Inventories	7,025					7,025
Derivative assets	585					585
Prepayments and accrued income	584					584
Total current assets	35,285					35,285
Non-current assets						
Net property, plant and equipment	17,052		156			17,208
Investments in associates	4,091				1,106	5,197
Deferred tax assets	1,469	702	2			2,173
Financial assets	2,410					2,410
Employee benefits assets	928	(896)				32
Goodwill	23,854					23,854
Intangible assets	2,028					2,028
Total non-current assets	51,832	(194)	158		1,106	52,902
Total assets	87,117	(194)	158		1,106	88,187
Liabilities and equity						
Current liabilities						
Trade and other payables	9,074					9,074
Financial liabilities	14,722					14,722
Tax liabilities	584					584
Derivative liabilities	856					856
Accruals and deferred income	3,839			53		3,892
Total current liabilities	29,075					29,128
Non-current liabilities						
Financial liabilities	10,731		160			10,891
Employee benefits liabilities	3,234	2,470				5,704
Deferred tax liabilities	447	(431)				16
Other payables	327					327
Provisions	3,004					3,004
Total non-current liabilities	17,743					19,942
Total liabilities	46,818	2,039	160	53		49,070
Equity						

Exhibit 4 (Continued)

	As Reported	IAS 19 Effect (1)	IFRIC 4 Effect (2)	IAS 39 Warrant Premium Classification (3)	L'Oreal IFRS Adoption (4)	Revised
Total equity attributable to parent shareholders	39,236	(2,219)	(2)	(53)	1,106	38,068
Minority interests	1,063	(14)				1,049
Total equity	40,299	(2,233)				39,117
Total liabilities and equity	87,117	(194)	158	0	1,106	88,187

(1) IAS 19 was implemented in 2006, with comparative restatement made to January 1, 2005. The 1/1/05 adjustments were imposed on the 12/31/04 balance sheet by the analyst, taken from the Accounting Policies footnote of 2006 Annual Report, p. 21.

(2) IFRIC 4 required the company to recognize additional finance lease assets and obligations that were not previously considered to be lease arrangements. The 2005 adjustments were carried back to the end of 2004. The amounts were found in the Accounting Policies footnote of 2006 Annual Report, p. 21.

(3) IAS 39 changed the classification of premiums associated with Nestlé warrants included in a bond issue. The 1/1/05 adjustments were imposed on the 12/31/04 balance sheet by the analyst, taken from the Accounting Policies footnote of 2005 Annual Report, p. 23.

(4) L'Oreal adopted International Financial Reporting Standards as of 1/1/05. The cumulative effect was carried back to 12/31/04, as found in footnote d) to the 2005 Consolidated Statement of Changes in Equity, page 11.

The analyst draws the data shown in Exhibit 5 from Exhibits 2, 3 and 4 for the preparation of DuPont analysis:

Exhibit 5 Data Needed for DuPont Analysis (in Millions of CHF)

	2007	2006	2005	2004
Income Statement Data:				
Revenue	107,552	98,458	91,115	—
EBIT	14,434	12,786	10,956	—
EBT	13,518	12,105	10,369	—
Profit from continuing operations	11,382	9,775	8,618	—
Share of results of associates	1,280	963	896	—
Profit ex-associates	10,102	8,812	7,722	—
Balance Sheet Data:				
Total assets	114,659	101,805	102,718	88,187
Investments in associates	8,936	8,430	7,073	5,197
Total assets, ex-associates	105,723	93,375	95,645	82,990
Shareholders' equity	54,234	52,848	49,068	39,117

The five-way decomposition of ROE needs to be expanded to account for the presence of the investment in associates and the share of income they provide to Nestlé. Subtracting the investment from total assets results in a figure that more closely represents Nestlé's own asset base; subtracting the share of results of associates from the net income allows for the analysis of exclusively Nestlé profitability resulting from that exclusively Nestlé asset base. Exhibit 6 shows the results of expanding the DuPont analysis.

The net profit margin component and the asset turnover component require adjustments to remove the impact of the associates on the return on assets. To adjust the net profit margin component, the analyst subtracts the associates' income from the net income, and divides it by earnings before taxes. Recall that the number referred to as EBT is profit before taxes and associates (Exhibit 2). In 2007 terms, this was represented by (CHF 11,382 net income − 1,280 income from associates)/CHF 13,518 earnings before taxes = 74.73 percent. Interest burden and EBIT or operating profit margin are calculated as usual. Interest burden is calculated by dividing the profit before taxes and associates by the profit before interest and taxes: CHF 13,518/14,434 = 93.65 percent for 2007. The EBIT margin is simply the earnings before interest and taxes (operating profit or income) divided by sales: CHF 14,434/107,552 = 13.42 percent.

Multiplying the three components together produces the net profit margin of Nestlé—9.39 percent in 2007—excluding the associates' earnings. Calculating the net profit margin in the usual fashion—*with* the net income figure including the associates' earnings—yields 10.58 percent (CHF 11,382/107,552). That profit margin is not representative of the Nestlé-only operations. Dividing the net profit margin by the net profit margin *without* associates income (10.58%/9.39% = 112.67%) quantifies the magnifying effect of the associates' income on Nestlé's own margins. Where the "Nestlé-only" entity really earned 9.39 percent on every sales dollar, inclusion of the associates' income in net profit inflates the net profit margins by 12.67 percent (112.67% × 9.39% = 10.58%); a level that is not representative of what the Nestlé-only entity is capable of producing.

Exhibit 6	Expanded DuPont Analysis		
	2007	**2006**	**2005**
Tax burden (ex-associates)	74.73%	72.80%	74.47%
× Interest burden	93.65%	94.67%	94.64%
× EBIT margin	13.42%	12.99%	12.02%
= Net profit margin (ex-associates)	9.39%	8.95%	8.47%
× Associates' effect on net profit margin	112.67%	111.78%	111.43%
= Net Profit Margin	**10.58%**	**10.00%**	**9.44%**
Total asset turnover (ex-associates)	1.080	1.042	1.020
Effect of associates investments on turnover	(0.086)	(0.079)	(0.065)
× Total Asset Turnover	**0.994**	**0.963**	**0.955**
= Return on assets	10.52%	9.63%	9.02%
× Leverage	**2.02**	**2.01**	**2.16**
= Return on Equity	**21.25%**	**19.36%**	**19.48%**
Traditional ROE Calculation:			
Net income /	11,382	9,849	8,604
Average stockholders' equity	53,541	50,958	44,093
= Return on Equity	**21.26%**	**19.33%**	**19.51%**
(Differences in ROE calculations due to rounding)			

A similar picture of the net profit margin over time emerges from the DuPont analysis after neutralizing the effect of the associates' earnings. The margin would be greater in each year if the associates' earnings were included in net profit, as compared to looking at Nestlé alone. While Nestlé showed a consistent upward trend in the three years, the analysis excluding associates' earnings shows that the company's profit margins are not necessarily as large without the boost from associates' earnings.

To calculate a "Nestlé-only" total asset turnover, the asset base also needs to be neutralized for the amount of the investment in associates. In 2007, the adjusted total assets were CHF 105,723 (CHF 114,659 − 8,936 = 105,723); for 2006, the adjusted total assets were CHF 93,375 (CHF 101,805 − 8,430 = 93,375). Dividing the average of the two figures into 2007's sales yields a "Nestlé-only" total asset turnover rate of 1.080 (CHF 107,552/[(CHF 105,723 + 93,375)/2] = 1.080). Calculating the total asset turnover from the consolidated financial statements with amounts unadjusted for investments in associates yields a measure of 0.994 (CHF 107,552/[(CHF 114,659 + 101,805)/2] = 0.994). The difference between the asset turnover based on unadjusted financial statement amounts and the "Nestlé-only" asset turnover reveals the effect on total asset turnover of the investment in associates: a decrease of 0.087 in 2007.

The adjustments thus far have isolated the operational aspects of Nestlé performance and the assets that produced them from non-Nestlé operations. The resulting return on asset signal from the DuPont analysis is free from bias introduced by the affiliates' results, and the contribution to the overall return on assets from the non-Nestlé components is clearly identified.

The financial leverage ratio has not been adjusted by the analyst in similar fashion to profit margins and asset turnover. The DuPont components, profit margins and asset turnover, function fairly discretely: Nestlé assets produce a certain pretax return, as do the non-Nestlé assets. In the DuPont analysis, the assets are isolated from each other and it is possible to see the contributions of each to the aggregate performance. It might be tempting to likewise adjust the financial leverage ratio by subtracting the investment in associates from total assets and equity, but it would not improve the DuPont analysis. Without knowledge of how the investment in associates was financed—all debt, all from internally generated cash flow, or a blend—it would be arbitrary to erase the investment amount from the asset base and equity base to arrive at an adjusted financial leverage figure. If such information was available, the analyst might calculate separate financial leverage components as well. In Nestlé's case, such information is unavailable, and the analyst simply considers the investment to be part of the total assets supported by common equity. The inherent assumption is that a similar capital structure finances the associates' assets and the Nestlé-only assets.

From Exhibit 6, multiplying the three conventionally-calculated (including the effect of the associates) ROE components yields the return on equity shown in the top row of Exhibit 7. The return on equity exhibits a smooth, steadily increasing trend when examined without adjusting for investment in associates; however, the analyst wants to see the ROE for Nestlé alone and compare it to the aggregate ROE. Calculating the ROE on a "Nestlé-only" basis is done by multiplying the net profit margin ex-associates' investment by the total asset turnover ex-associates' investment by the financial leverage. For 2007, the Nestlé-only ROE was 20.48 percent (9.39% × 1.080 × 2.02 = 20.48%). Exhibit 7 shows the ROE prepared on the two bases and the contribution of the associates' investment to ROE. The trend is similar for the two ROE calculations, but the magnitudes of the ROE based on Nestlé only are lower.

Exhibit 7	ROE Performance Due to Investment in Associates		
	2007 (%)	2006 (%)	2005 (%)
Return on equity	21.25	19.36	19.48
Nestlé-only ROE	20.48	18.75	18.66
Associates' contribution to ROE	0.77	0.61	0.82

Although the analyst is satisfied with the trend and magnitude of the Nestlé return on equity, he is now aware that a significant amount of Nestlé's profitability is attributable to the investments in associates. He is convinced that in order to completely understand Nestlé's earnings drivers, he needs to understand these investments as well. He is somewhat concerned that the spread between "Nestlé-only" profit margins and the aggregate profit margins has widened over the past three years: Referring to Exhibit 6, the spread was 1.19 percent in 2007, higher than the 1.05 percent in 2006, which was higher than the 0.97 percent spread in 2005. In fact, the associate income for the past two years has made all the difference between double-digit net profit margins and single-digit profit margins. The analyst makes note to investigate the valuation aspects of the investment holdings later. For now, he is interested in learning more about the drivers of Nestlé's growth and revenues.

Asset Base Composition

The analyst examines the composition of the balance sheet over time, as shown in Exhibit 8.

Exhibit 8	Asset Composition as a Percentage of Total Assets			
	2007	2006	2005	2004
Cash and equivalents	5.8	5.2	4.5	5.6
Short-term investments	2.5	6.1	12.4	11.8
Trade and other receivables	13.4	14.3	13.9	13.4
Inventory	8.1	7.9	7.9	8.0
Other current	1.4	1.2	1.9	1.3
Total Current	**31.2**	**34.7**	**40.6**	**40.1**
PP&E, net	19.2	19.9	18.5	19.5
Intangibles	35.4	31.7	29.1	29.3
Other noncurrent	14.1	13.7	11.8	11.1
Total	**99.9***	**100.0**	**100.0**	**100.0**

*Does not add to 100 percent due to rounding.

While he expected significant investments in current assets, inventory, and physical plant assets—given that Nestlé is a food manufacturer and marketer—he is surprised to see so much investment in intangible assets, indicating that Nestlé's success may be due in part to successful acquisitions. The increasing proportion of the asset mix in intangibles and the reduction in short-term investments are consistent with growth through acquisition. The investing section of the statement of cash flows, Exhibit 9, supports this fact:

Exhibit 9	Nestlé Investing Activity, 2004–2007 (in Millions of CHF)				
Investing Activities	Total	2007	2006	2005	2004
Capital expenditure	(15,841)	(4,971)	(4,200)	(3,375)	(3,295)
Expenditure on intangible assets	(2,802)	(619)	(689)	(758)	(736)
Sale of property, plant and equipment	887	323	98	220	246
Acquisition of businesses	(19,329)	(11,232)	(6,469)	(995)	(633)
Disposal of businesses	1,362	456	447	193	266
Cash flows with associates	1,047	264	323	259	201
Other investing cash flows	(229)	26	(30)	(202)	(23)
Total investing cash flow	(34,905)	(15,753)	(10,520)	(4,658)	(3,974)
Acquisitions % of total investing activities	55.4%	71.3%	61.5%	21.4%	15.9%

For the four-year period, the acquisition of businesses was a significant part of the total resources dedicated to investment activities—over half for the entire time frame. In the largest acquisition year, 2007, Nestlé acquired Gerber and Novartis Medical Nutrition; the two purchases accounted for 85 percent (CHF 9,535/11,232) of the total cash invested in 2007 for business acquisitions.

Capital Structure Analysis

The analyst then examined Nestlé's long-term capital structure by constructing a chart on a common-size basis, displayed in Exhibit 10 below.

Although the DuPont analysis indicated that the company had de-leveraged somewhat over the last three years—financial leverage decreased from 2.16 in 2005 to 2.02 in 2007—the leverage ratio alone does not show much about the *nature* of the leverage. For example, the financial burden imposed by bond debt is more onerous and bears more consequences in the event of default than does restructuring provisions or employee benefit plan obligations. A look at Exhibit 10 reveals that Nestlé has been making its capital structure substantially less financially risky over the last five years. Not only is the proportion of the less risky equity financing rising—from 66.2 percent in 2004 to 76.0 percent in 2007—the more risky long-term financial liabilities have become a significantly smaller part of the capital mix, dropping to 8.6 percent in 2007 from 18.4 percent in 2004. Meanwhile, the "other long-term liabilities" (primarily employee benefit plan obligations and provisions) have remained at nearly the same proportion of the financing mix over the period.

Exhibit 10	Percent of Long-Term Capital Structure			
	2007	2006	2005	2004
Long-term financial liabilities	8.6	10.0	12.4	18.4
Other long-term liabilities	15.4	13.7	14.2	15.3
Total equity	76.0	76.2	73.4	66.2
Total long-term capital	**100.0**	**99.9***	**100.0**	**99.9***

*Does not add to 100 percent due to rounding.

Given the de-leveraging occurring in the long-term capital structure, the analyst wonders if there has been any offsetting change in the company's working capital accounts. He decides to examine Nestlé's liquidity situation; and from the financial statements in Exhibits 2 and 3, he constructs the table shown in Exhibit 11.

Exhibit 11	Nestlé Working Capital Accounts and Ratios, 2004–2007			
	2007	**2006**	**2005**	**2004**
Current ratio	0.83	1.09	1.16	1.21
Quick ratio	0.58	0.80	0.88	0.93
Defensive interval ratio*	100.7	114.4	149.4	
Days' sales outstanding (DSO)	50.9	53.5	52.3	
Days on hand of inventory (DOH)	70.1	72.6	73.1	
Number of days payables	−105.5	−106.5	−94.4	
Cash conversion cycle	15.5	19.6	31.0	

*For 2007, the daily cash expenditure = [45,037 + 9,104 + 36,512 + 1,875 − 3,211 + (590 − 482) + (1492 − 576)]/365 = 247.5. The defensive interval ratio is 24,917/247.5 = 100.7.

A significant increase in the current portion of the financial liabilities is responsible for the current ratio's deterioration between 2006 and 2007. He notes that the company's quick ratio and defensive interval ratio have also deteriorated in the last few years. The company seems to be responding by more aggressively managing its receivables and inventories; both receivables DSOs and inventory DOHs have improved in 2007 over 2006. While the decline in the actual working capital ratios is a concern, it is mitigated by the improvement in the management of receivables, inventory, and payables. Those improvements provide evidence that the company's managers are moving in the right direction on the management of working capital.

Segment Analysis/Capital Allocation

To understand any geopolitical investment risks, as well as the economies in which Nestlé operates, the analyst wants to know which geographic areas are of the greatest importance to the company. One issue the analyst confronts is the fact that Nestlé reports segment information by management responsibility and geographical area (hereafter referred to as "segment"), not by segments based exclusively on geographic areas. From the segment information in Exhibit 12, he notes that the European business, while still growing, is a lesser part of the revenue stream than two years ago; Nestlé Americas and Asia, Oceania, and Africa sectors show a similar decline as a percentage of revenues. All of the geographic sectors are growing in terms of absolute amount of revenues and EBIT, but they appear proportionally smaller each year because of the way Nestlé displays its Waters, Nutrition, and Other Food and Beverage segments: Their operations are not segmented geographically, but are shown on a global basis. Not only are they not included in the geographic information, they have also grown significantly in the last several years through acquisition: As pointed out earlier, the company acquired Gerber and Novartis Medical Nutrition in 2007. Those acquisitions, included into the non-geographic categories, make the three geographic categories look less material in the aggregate, from year to year. Nevertheless, the Americas sector appears to be the single most significant segment in terms of size and growth of both sales and EBIT.

Because of a realignment of segments in 2006 and the lack of complete restated data, the analyst cannot make meaningful comparisons to years before 2005.

The analyst is curious about the company's capital allocation decisions based on the geographic segments. Exhibit 13 shows the segment information regarding Nestlé's capital expenditures and assets.

Exhibit 12 Sales and EBIT by Segment (in Millions of CHF)

Sales	2007	% total	2006	% total	2005	% total	Year-to-Year % Change 2007	2006
Europe	28,464	26.5	26,652	27.1	25,599	28.1	6.8	4.1
Americas	32,917	30.6	31,287	31.8	28,956	31.8	5.2	8.1
Asia, Oceania, and Africa	16,556	15.4	15,504	15.7	14,296	15.7	6.8	8.4
Nestlé Waters	10,404	9.7	9,636	9.8	8,787	9.6	8.0	9.7
Nestlé Nutrition	8,434	7.8	5,964	6.1	5,270	5.8	41.4	13.2
Other Food and Beverage	3,458	3.2	2,728	2.8	2,245	2.5	26.8	21.5
Pharma	7,319	6.8	6,687	6.7	5,962	6.5	9.5	12.2
	107,552		98,458		91,115			
EBIT								
Europe	3,412	22.7	3,109	23.4	3,082	26.0	9.7	0.9
Americas	5,359	35.7	4,946	37.2	4,364	36.7	8.4	13.3
Asia, Oceania, and Africa	2,697	18.0	2,571	19.3	2,334	19.7	4.9	10.2
Nestlé Waters	851	5.7	834	6.3	709	6.0	2.0	17.6
Nestlé Nutrition	1,447	9.6	1,009	7.6	932	7.8	43.4	8.3
Other Food and Beverage	548	3.6	371	2.8	273	2.3	47.4	35.9
Pharma	2,435	16.2	2,136	16.0	1,833	15.4	14.0	16.5
Unallocated Items	(1,725)	–11.5	(1,674)	–12.6	(1,651)	–13.9		
	15,024		13,302		11,876			

Using the information from Exhibit 12 to calculate EBIT margins, and using the information about the asset and capital expenditure distribution from Exhibit 13, the analyst constructs the table in Exhibit 14, ranked by descending order of EBIT profitability.

Although the segmentation is not purely geographical, the analyst can still make some judgments about the allocation of capital. On the premise that the largest investments in assets will require a similar proportion of capital expenditures, he calculates a ratio of capital expenditures proportion to total asset proportion for the last three years, and compares them to the current EBIT profitability ranking. The resulting table is shown in Exhibit 15.

Exhibit 13 Asset and Capital Expenditure Segment Information (in Millions of CHF)

	Assets*			Capital Expenditures		
	2007	2006	2005	2007	2006	2005
Europe	15,794	15,566	14,387	932	812	797
Americas	19,503	19,191	19,228	1,371	1,125	908
Asia, Oceania, and Africa	9,153	8,741	8,153	675	588	546

(continued)

Exhibit 13   (Continued)

	Assets*			Capital Expenditures		
	2007	**2006**	**2005**	**2007**	**2006**	**2005**
Nestlé Waters	9,298	8,884	8,468	1,043	923	601
Nestlé Nutrition	13,990	3,774	2,577	271	194	134
Other Food and Beverage	1,792	1,473	1,011	269	141	86
Pharma	7,120	6,028	4,978	276	286	209
	76,650	63,657	58,802	4,837	4,069	3,281

*Assets do not equal total assets on the balance sheet due to unallocated and non-segment assets.

Exhibit 14   EBIT Margins, Asset, and Capital Expenditure Proportions by Segment

	EBIT Margins			% of Total Assets			% of Total Cap Ex		
	2007	**2006**	**2005**	**2007**	**2006**	**2005**	**2007**	**2006**	**2005**
Pharma	33.27	31.94	30.74	9.3	9.5	8.5	5.7	7.0	6.4
Nestlé Nutrition	17.16	16.92	17.69	18.3	5.9	4.4	5.6	4.8	4.1
Asia, Oceania, and Africa	16.29	16.58	16.33	11.9	13.7	13.9	14.0	14.5	16.6
Americas	16.28	15.81	15.07	25.4	30.1	32.7	28.3	27.6	27.7
Other Food and Beverage	15.85	13.60	12.16	2.3	2.3	1.7	5.6	3.5	2.6
Europe	11.99	11.67	12.04	20.6	24.5	24.5	19.3	20.0	24.3
Nestlé Waters	8.18	8.66	8.07	12.1	14.0	14.4	21.6	22.7	18.3
				100.0	100.0	100.0	100.0	100.0	100.0

Exhibit 15   Ratio of Capital Expenditures Percent to Total Asset Percent Ranked by EBIT Margin

	2007 EBIT	**2007**	**2006**	**2005**
Pharma	33.27	0.61	0.74	0.75
Nestlé Nutrition	17.16	0.31	0.81	0.93
Asia, Oceania, and Africa	16.29	1.18	1.06	1.19
Americas	16.28	1.11	0.92	0.85
Other Food and Beverage	15.85	2.43	1.52	1.53
Europe	11.99	0.94	0.82	0.99
Nestlé Waters	8.18	1.79	1.62	1.27

A ratio of 1 indicates that the segment's proportion of capital expenditures is the same as its proportion of total assets. A ratio *below* 1 indicates that the segment is being allocated a lesser proportion of capital expenditures than its proportion of total assets; if a trend develops, the segment will become less significant over time.

A ratio *above* 1 indicates the company is growing the segment. Comparing the ratio to the EBIT margin percentage gives the analyst an idea of whether the company is investing its capital in the most profitable segments.

Pharma, by the nature of the business, has significant research and development expenses and yet has the highest margins. It requires little in the way of invested assets and maintenance capital expenditures. Nutrition has similar characteristics, but to a lesser degree. The two are the highest EBIT margin segments, yet Nestlé has invested in both of them at a less aggressive rate, judging by the ratio of capital expenditures proportions to total assets proportions. The Nutrition segment, however, received significant investment in 2007 through the acquisition of Novartis Medical Nutrition and Gerber. The Pharma segment, consisting largely of US eye care company Alcon, is extremely profitable but is an outlier in terms of Nestlé's current portfolio. Given the differences in the food and pharmaceutical businesses, it would seem unlikely that the world's largest food company would elect to seriously grow the pharmaceutical segment. However, investment in Pharma is consistent with the objective stated in the management report to be recognized as a leader in Nutrition, Health, and Wellness. It was the strategy of transformation that initially appealed to the portfolio manager.

Investments in the Asia, Oceania, and Africa and the Americas segments have typically been in "growth" mode over the last three years; the proportion of capital expenditures to the proportion of total assets in each of these two segments is typically slightly above 1 annually. Given that these are large and well-margined segments, the capital allocation decisions appear reasonable.

The Other Food and Beverage segment appears problematic: While its EBIT margin is on almost the same level as the Asia, Oceania, and Africa and Americas segments, it is still the third lowest segment in terms of profitability. Yet the capital expenditures devoted to it over the last three years are in a rapid growth mode. It may be that the segment is a catch-all, or it may be the development of another line of business that will become more visible in the future; for now, the analyst notes that while it could be a problem or a promise, it is a small part of Nestlé's asset base, revenues, and EBIT and thus not of great concern at this time.

The Nestlé Waters segment is a much greater concern to the analyst. Its EBIT margin is about two-thirds of the next highest-ranked segment; and at 8.18 percent, it is well below the 13.42 percent company-wide EBIT margin (see Exhibit 6). Even after allowing for the fact that the Waters segment was charged with a CHF 210 million goodwill write-down in 2007, the segment's EBIT margin was only 10.20 percent—still well below the other segments. The fact that the Waters segment was the source of a goodwill write-down is also a sign that operating weaknesses might be present; otherwise, the cash flow assumptions used in the goodwill testing might have been high enough to prevent the write-down. Nestlé Waters is a significant part of the asset base at 12.1 percent in 2007, and it appears to be a high-maintenance operation. In each of the last three years, the ratio of capital expenditures proportion to total assets proportion shows the segment to be in a growth mode, with a ratio of 1.79, 1.62, and 1.27 in 2007, 2006, and 2005, respectively. In 2007 and 2006, the only segment to have greater absolute dollar capital expenditures was the more highly profitable Americas segment; in 2005, Nestlé Waters was outranked in terms of capital expenditures only by the Americas and Europe segments. In a worst-case scenario, if the company were to continue to allocate capital towards the lowest-margined businesses, the overall Nestlé-only returns might be impacted negatively. As a result, Nestlé might become more dependent on its investment in associates to sustain performance.

The analyst decides to look at Nestlé from a product group standpoint as well. The sales and EBIT information are shown in Exhibit 16.

To further examine capital allocation decisions, the analyst garners the asset and capital expenditure information by product group from the financial statements, as shown in Exhibit 17. The total assets and capital expenditures differ between the presentations by segment and product group. Nestlé presents its assets for the product groups on an *average* basis rather than on a year-end basis as it does for the segment reporting. Further, a significant amount of assets is unallocated to segments, but there is no unallocated amount by product groups. Capital expenditures by segment and product group represent additional investments in PP&E during the year, but the unallocated amount of capital expenditures is far greater by product group.

Exhibit 16   Sales and EBIT Segment Information by Product Group (in Millions of CHF)

Sales	2007	% of Total	2006	% of Total	2005	% of Total	Year to Year % Change 2007	2006
Beverages	28,245	26.3	25,882	26.3	23,842	26.2	9.1	8.6
Milk Products, Nutrition, and Ice cream	29,106	27.1	25,435	25.8	23,275	25.5	14.4	9.3
Prepared Dishes and Cooking Aids	18,504	17.2	17,635	17.9	16,673	18.3	4.9	5.8
Confectionery	12,248	11.4	11,399	11.6	10,794	11.8	7.4	5.6
Pet Care	12,130	11.3	11,420	11.6	10,569	11.6	6.2	8.1
Pharmaceutical Products	7,319	6.8	6,687	6.8	5,962	6.5	9.5	12.2
	107,552	100.0	98,458	100.0	91,115	100.0	9.2	8.1
EBIT								
Beverages	4,854	32.3	4,475	33.6	4,131	34.8	8.5	8.3
Milk Products, Nutrition, and Ice cream	3,744	24.9	3,003	22.6	2,598	21.9	24.7	15.6
Prepared Dishes and Cooking Aids	2,414	16.1	2,323	17.5	2,176	18.3	3.9	6.8
Confectionery	1,426	9.5	1,309	9.8	1,257	10.6	8.9	4.1
Pet Care	1,876	12.5	1,730	13.0	1,532	12.9	8.4	12.9
Pharmaceutical Products	2,435	16.2	2,136	16.1	1,833	15.4	14.0	16.5
	16,749	111.5	14,976	112.6	13,527	113.9	11.8	10.7
Unallocated Items	(1,725)	–11.5	(1,674)	–12.6	(1,651)	–13.9		
	15,024	100.0	13,302	100.0	11,876	100.0		

Exhibit 17   Asset and Capital Expenditure Segment Information by Product Group (in Millions of CHF)

	Assets			Capital Expenditures		
	2007	2006	2005	2007	2006	2005
Beverages	17,937	16,640	15,105	1,409	1,105	752
Milk Products, Nutrition, and Ice cream	23,047	17,970	15,516	933	702	689
Prepared Dishes and Cooking Aids	10,959	10,553	9,386	305	272	261
Confectionery	6,663	6,319	5,745	316	258	194

Exhibit 17   (Continued)

	Assets			Capital Expenditures		
	2007	2006	2005	2007	2006	2005
Pet Care	15,652	15,763	15,030	402	345	274
Pharmaceutical Products	6,704	5,492	4,538	155	122	97
	80,962	72,737	65,320	3,520	2,804	2,267

Using the information from Exhibit 16 to calculate EBIT margins and the information about the asset and capital expenditure distribution from Exhibit 17, the analyst constructs the table in Exhibit 18, ranked by descending order of EBIT profitability in 2007.

Exhibit 18   EBIT Margins, Assets, and Capital Expenditures Proportions by Product Group

	EBIT Margins			% of Total Assets			% of Cap Ex		
	2007	2006	2005	2007	2006	2005	2007	2006	2005
Pharmaceutical Products	33.27	31.94	30.74	8.3	7.6	6.9	4.4	4.4	4.3
Beverages	17.19	17.29	17.33	22.2	22.9	23.1	40.0	39.4	33.2
Pet Care	15.47	15.15	14.50	19.3	21.7	23.0	11.4	12.3	12.1
Prepared Dishes and Cooking Aids	13.05	13.17	13.05	13.5	14.5	14.4	8.7	9.7	11.5
Milk Products, Nutrition, and Ice cream	12.86	11.81	11.16	28.5	24.7	23.8	26.5	25.0	30.4
Confectionery	11.64	11.48	11.65	8.2	8.7	8.8	9.0	9.2	8.6
				100.0	100.0	100.0	100.0	100.0	100.0

He again prepares a schedule of the proportions of capital expenditures and the proportion of total assets for each of the product groups, and calculates the ratio of capital expenditure proportions to total asset proportions, ranked by the 2007 EBIT margin. The resulting table is shown in Exhibit 19.

Exhibit 19   Ratio of Capital Expenditures Percent to Total Asset Percent Ranked by EBIT Margin

	2007 EBIT Margin	2007	2006	2005
Pharmaceutical Products	33.27	0.53	0.58	0.62
Beverages	17.19	1.80	1.72	1.44
Pet Care	15.47	0.59	0.57	0.53
Prepared Dishes and Cooking Aids	13.05	0.64	0.67	0.80
Milk Products, Nutrition, and Ice cream	12.86	0.93	1.01	1.28
Confectionery	11.64	1.10	1.06	0.98

Exhibit 20	EBIT Margin of Beverages with and without Waters (Millions of CHF)		
	Beverages	**Waters**	**Beverages ex-Waters**
Total Beverage Sales	28,245	10,404	17,841
EBIT	4,854	851	4,003
EBIT %	17.19%	8.18%	22.44%

Exhibit 21	Ratio of Capital Expenditures Percent to Total Asset Percent Ex-Nestlé Waters, Ranked by EBIT Margin			
	2007 EBIT Margin	**2007**	**2006**	**2005**
Pharmaceutical Products	33.27	0.67	0.76	0.73
Beverages	22.44	1.22	0.81	0.78
Pet Care	15.47	0.74	0.74	0.62
Prepared Dishes and Cooking Aids	13.05	0.80	0.88	0.95
Milk Products, Nutrition, and Ice cream	12.86	1.17	1.33	1.52
Confectionery	11.64	1.38	1.38	1.15

The analyst uses this information to make some important observations:

■ The Beverages product group has a significantly higher EBIT margin than Nestlé Waters EBIT margin of 8.18 percent. Because Nestlé Waters is contained within the Beverages product group, the EBIT margins of the other products within the product group category—primarily soluble coffee, according to Nestlé's 2007 Management Report—must be much greater. The analyst removes the Waters sales and EBIT from the total product group (Exhibit 20) and finds that the remaining business is by far the most profitable segment after pharmaceuticals.

■ The analyst reworks the ratios presented in Exhibit 19 excluding the assets and capital expenditures for the Nestlé Waters segment. The result in Exhibit 21 shows that management is allocating its capital expenditures to the Beverages business on a growth basis the last year but at a lower rate than for Beverages with Waters. Given the margins of the product group without Waters, this is a favorable discovery, but the amount allocated to Waters is problematic.

■ Less favorable to note under either the original or revised exhibits: The two lowest-ranked product groups—Milk Products, Nutrition, and Ice cream and Confectionery—have been allocated capital expenditures at a "growth mode" rate for each of the last three years. If the trend continues and margins in these segments do not grow, Nestlé's company-wide margins could suffer. Further, the allocation to Pharmaceutical Products, the most profitable segment, is cause for concern.

Accruals and Earnings Quality

The consistent profitability exhibited by Nestlé is a desirable attribute, as hoped for and expected of a company operating primarily in the food industry where the demand for the product is typically not cyclical. However, the analyst wants to understand how important a role accruals may play in the company's performance; he is concerned in case the consistency is a result of earnings management. He decides to examine the balance-sheet-based accruals and cash-flow-based accruals over the last few years. From the Nestlé financial statements, he assembles the information and intermediate calculations shown in Exhibit 22.

Exhibit 22	Selected Balance Sheet and Statement of Cash Flows Information (in Millions of CHF)				
	2007	2006	2005	2004	2003
Balance Sheet Accrual Info:					
Total assets	114,659	101,805	102,718	88,187	89,561
Cash and short-term investments	9,496	11,475	17,393	15,282	15,128
Operating assets (A)	105,163	90,330	85,325	72,905	74,433
Total liabilities	60,425	48,957	53,650	49,070	51,738
Long-term debt	6,129	6,952	8,277	10,891	15,419
Debt in current liabilities	24,541	15,494	18,841	14,722	14,064
Operating liabilities (B)	29,755	26,511	26,532	23,457	22,255
Net Operating Assets (A) – (B)	75,408	63,819	58,793	49,448	52,178
Balance-sheet-based aggregate accruals (YTY Δ in NOA)	11,589	5,026	9,345	(2,730)	1,587
Average net operating assets	69,614	61,306	54,121	50,813	51,385
Statement of Cash Flows Accrual Info:					
Profit from continuing operations	11,382	9,775	8,618	7,031	6,593
Operating cash flow	(13,439)	(11,676)	(10,205)	(10,412)	(10,125)
Investing cash flow	15,753	10,520	4,658	3,974	4,728
Cash-flow-based aggregate accruals	13,696	8,619	3,071	593	1,196

The accruals ratios for the last five years are shown in Exhibit 23.

Exhibit 23	Accruals Ratios (in Millions of CHF)				
	2007	2006	2005	2004	2003
B/S aggregate accruals (YTY Δ in NOA)	11,589	5,026	9,345	(2,730)	1,587
Divided by: Average net operating assets	69,614	61,306	54,121	50,813	51,385
Balance-sheet-based accruals ratio	**16.6%**	**8.20%**	**17.3%**	**−5.4%**	**3.1%**
Cash-flow-based aggregate accruals	13,696	8,619	3,071	593	1,196

(continued)

Exhibit 23   (Continued)

	2007	2006	2005	2004	2003
Divided by: Average net operating assets	69,614	61,306	54,632	51,324	51,385
CF accruals ratio	19.7%	14.1%	5.6%	1.2%	2.3%

The analyst notes that the absolute level of accruals present in the balance sheet is not extremely high, but it is much higher in the most recent year than in the earlier years. Furthermore, the balance-sheet-based accruals ratio has fluctuated significantly. The analyst's concern with the accruals ratio fluctuations is that they could indicate the use of accruals to "time" earnings.

A slightly different, but no less concerning, trend exists for the cash-flow-based accrual ratio. The accruals ratio is low in the early years of the analysis and increases steadily over time. In 2007 and 2006, they are significantly higher than in the earlier years, indicating a higher degree of accruals present in the company's earnings.

Cash Flow Relationships

Given his concerns about the possible use of accruals to manage earnings, the analyst decides to study the company's cash flow and its relationship to net income. He begins his analysis with the compilation of Nestlé's statements of cash flows shown in Exhibit 24.

Exhibit 24   Nestlé Statements of Cash Flows, 2003–2007 (in Millions of CHF)

	2007	2006	2005	2004	2003
Operating activities:					
Profit from continuing operations	11,382	9,775	8,618	7,031	6,593
Less share of results of associates	(1,280)	(963)	(896)	(1,588)	(593)
Depreciation of property, plant, and equipment	2,620	2,581	2,382	2,506	2,408
Impairment of property, plant, and equipment	225	96	360	130	148
Amortisation of goodwill	NA	NA	NA	1,599	1,571
Impairment of goodwill	251	38	218	0	0
Depreciation of intangible assets	591	480	346	278	255
Impairment of intangible assets	6	0	30	0	74
Increase/(decrease) in provisions and deferred taxes	162	(338)	(526)	55	312
Decrease/(increase) in working capital	82	348	(315)	227	(688)
Other operating cash flows	(600)	(341)	(12)	174	45
Operating cash flow	13,439	11,676	10,205	10,412	10,125
Investing activities:					
Capital expenditure	(4,971)	(4,200)	(3,375)	(3,295)	(3,337)
Expenditure on intangible assets	(619)	(689)	(758)	(736)	(682)
Sale of property, plant and equipment	323	98	220	246	244
Acquisition of businesses	(11,232)	(6,469)	(995)	(633)	(1,950)
Disposal of businesses	456	447	193	266	725

Exhibit 24 (Continued)					
	2007	**2006**	**2005**	**2004**	**2003**
Cash flows with associates	264	323	259	201	208
Other investing cash flows	26	(30)	(202)	(23)	64
Investing cash flow	(15,753)	(10,520)	(4,658)	(3,974)	(4,728)
Financing activities:					
Dividend paid to shareholders of the parent	(4,004)	(3,471)	(3,114)	(2,800)	(2,705)
Purchase of treasury shares	(5,455)	(2,788)	(1,553)	(715)	(318)
Sale of treasury shares	980	906	1,295	573	660
Cash flows with minority interests	(205)	(191)	5	(189)	(197)
Bonds issued	2,023	1,625	1,617	558	2,305
Bonds repaid	(2,780)	(2,331)	(2,443)	(903)	(693)
Increase in other non-current financial liabilities	348	134	279	162	0
Decrease in other non-current financial liabilities	(99)	(289)	(207)	(845)	(134)
Increase/(decrease) in current financial liabilities	9,851	(14)	(492)	(1,204)	(2,930)
Decrease/(increase) in short-term investments	3,238	6,393	(1,910)	(2,564)	(2)
Other financing cash flows	0	(4)	2	0	0
Financing cash flow	3,897	(30)	(6,521)	(7,927)	(4,014)
Translation differences on flows	(64)	(360)	336	(494)	(457)
Increase/(decrease) in cash and cash equivalents	1,519	766	(638)	(1,983)	926
Cash and cash equivalents at beginning of year	5,278	4,658	4,902	7,074	6,338
Effects of exchange rate changes on opening balance	(203)	(146)	394	(189)	(190)
Cash and cash equivalents retranslated at beginning of year	5,075	4,512	5,296	6,885	6,148
Cash and cash equivalents at end of period	6,594	5,278	4,658	4,902	7,074
Cash interest paid	788	599	437	578	532
Cash taxes paid	3,072	2,811	2,540	2,523	2,267

The analyst's most pressing concern: Are Nestlé's operating earnings backed by cash flow, or does the pattern presented by the accrual measures above indicate that the operating earnings may be more of an accounting result? To convince himself of the genuineness of the Nestlé earnings, he first compares the operating cash flow before interest and taxes to the operating income, adjusted for accounting changes as shown in Exhibit 25.

Exhibit 25 Operating Cash Flow to Operating Income, 2003–2007 (in Millions of CHF)					
	2007	**2006**	**2005**	**2004**	**2003**
Operating cash flow	13,439	11,676	10,205	10,412	10,125
Cash interest paid	788	599	437	578	532
Cash taxes paid	3,072	2,811	2,540	2,523	2,267
Operating cash flow before interest and taxes	17,299	15,086	13,182	13,513	12,924
Operating income, equalized:					
Profit before interest and taxes	14,434	12,786	10,956	8,487	8,901

(continued)

Exhibit 25	(Continued)				
	2007	2006	2005	2004	2003
Amortisation of goodwill	—	—	—	1,599	1,571
Operating income, adjusted for accounting changes	14,434	12,786	10,956	10,086	10,472
Operating cash flow before interest and taxes/ Operating income	**1.20**	**1.18**	**1.20**	**1.34**	**1.23**

To keep the comparisons between cash flow and earnings symmetrical, the analyst added the cash paid for interest and taxes to the operating cash flow. The resulting operating cash flow before interest and taxes is the relevant operating cash flow for comparison to the operating income. This revision makes the cash from operations more directly comparable to accrual basis operating income; it is effectively the operating income (profit before interest and taxes or EBIT) on a cash basis. In another adjustment to make all comparisons analogous, the analyst added goodwill amortisation to the 2003 and 2004 operating income amounts. International Financial Reporting Standard 3, "Business Combinations," suspended the amortisation of goodwill after 31 March 2004; to subtract the amortisation in just two years of operating earnings would result in a misleading trend in the ratio of the relevant operating cash flow to operating earnings.

The analyst is encouraged by the fact that the operating cash flow before interest and taxes substantially exceeded the operating earnings in 2007, and in fact, for each of the last five years. With the exception of 2004, the ratio of the relevant operating cash flow to operating earnings has consistently been around 1.20.

Knowing that Nestlé has made a number of acquisitions, the analyst decides to examine the relationship between operating cash flow and total assets. The total assets reflect the sum total of management's resource allocations. The relationship is shown in Exhibit 26.

Exhibit 26	Operating Cash Flow to Total Assets, 2003–2007 (in Millions of CHF)				
	2007	2006	2005	2004	2003
Operating cash flow	13,439	11,676	10,205	10,412	10,125
Average total assets	108,232	102,262	95,453	88,874	88,457
Cash return on total assets	12.4%	11.4%	10.7%	11.7%	11.4%

The 2007 cash return on total assets is the highest in the five-year span and fairly consistent during the entire period. A similar pattern of returns, albeit of a higher magnitude, results if operating cash flow before interest and taxes is used. Nevertheless, the analyst is encouraged to do more cash flow analysis due to the results of the accruals analysis, coupled with the slight volatility in the relationship between operating cash flow and operating income. He decides to compare cash flow to reinvestment, debt, and debt-servicing capacity, as shown in Exhibit 27.

The current cash flow measures for each metric are strong: Reinvestment needs have been covered by cash flow by a factor of 2.40 in 2007 and 2.39 in 2006, indicating ample resources for the company's reinvestment program. Those two measures are only slightly lower than the cash flow reinvestment coverage of the prior three years. The decrease is the result of higher amounts of capital expenditures in the recent years compared to the earlier years.

The 2007 cash flow to total debt ratio of 55.5 percent indicates that the company is not highly leveraged. The ratio is high enough to indicate additional borrowing could be arranged should an investment opportunity arise. Further, the analyst notes that Nestlé has the capacity to pay off its debt in approximately four years even while maintaining its current reinvestment policy [31,147/(13,439 − 5,590)].

Exhibit 27	Operating Cash Flow to Reinvestment, Debt, and Debt-Servicing Capacity, 2003–2007 (in Millions of CHF)				
	2007	**2006**	**2005**	**2004**	**2003**
Cash flow to reinvestment:					
Operating cash flow	13,439	11,676	10,205	10,412	10,125
Capital expenditures	4,971	4,200	3,375	3,295	3,337
Expenditures on intangible assets	619	689	758	736	682
	5,590	4,889	4,133	4,031	4,019
Cash flow to reinvestment	**2.40**	**2.39**	**2.47**	**2.58**	**2.52**
Cash flow to total debt:					
Operating cash flow before interest and taxes	17,299	15,086	13,182	13,513	12,924
Current debt (Short-term financial liabilities)	24,541	15,494	18,841	14,722	15,419
Current derivative liabilities	477	470	922	856	846
Long-term debt (Long-term financial liabilities)	6,129	6,952	8,277	10,891	14,064
	31,147	22,916	28,040	26,469	30,329
Cash flow to total debt	**55.5%**	**65.8%**	**47.0%**	**51.1%**	**42.6%**
Cash flow interest coverage:					
Operating cash flow before interest and taxes	17,299	15,086	13,182	13,513	12,924
Interest paid	788	599	437	578	532
Cash flow interest coverage	**22.0**	**25.2**	**30.2**	**23.4**	**24.3**

Finally, the cash flow interest coverage ratio indicates more than satisfactory financial strength in the current year, with cash flow 22.0 times the interest paid. Like the cash flow to total debt ratio, it indicates that the company actually has plenty of financial capacity to add more debt if there is an investment reason. However, the current cash flow to interest is much lower than it was only two years ago at 30.2 times. The analyst is not overly concerned given the recent acquisitions by Nestlé.

Decomposition and Analysis of the Company's Valuation

At this point, the analyst believes he has obtained sufficient information about the company's sources of earnings and returns on shareholder equity, its capital structure, the results of its capital allocation decisions, and its earnings quality. Before he makes his report to the portfolio manager, he wants to study the company's market valuation. During his reading of the annual report, he noted that Nestlé owns significant equity stakes in Alcon (NYSE:ACL), a US ophthalmic products company (77.4 percent), and L'Oreal (Paris exchange: OR), a French cosmetics company (30.0 percent). By virtue of majority ownership in Alcon, Nestlé consolidates the company in its own financial statements, while L'Oreal is handled in the financial statements as an investment, because Nestlé's ownership stake does not give it control. While these companies contribute to the earnings of Nestlé as a whole, they also are valued in the public markets separately and their discrete valuations may be very different from a pure Nestlé valuation. To determine the value that the market is placing solely on Nestlé operations, the analyst first removes the value of the Alcon and L'Oreal holdings from the Nestlé market value, as shown in Exhibit 28.

Exhibit 28	Nestlé Market Value without Alcon and L'Oreal as of 31 December 2007 (Currency in Millions, except Share Prices)
L'Oreal Value:	
12/31/2007 share price	€97.98
Shares held by Nestlé (millions)	178.381
L'Oreal holding value	€17,478
12/31 euro: CHF rate	1.657
L'Oreal holding value in Swiss francs	CHF 28,961
Alcon Value:	
12/31/2007 share price	$140.78
Shares held by Nestlé (millions)	230.250
Alcon holding value	$32,415
12/31 USD: CHF rate	1.126
Alcon holding value in Swiss francs	CHF 36,499
Nestlé Market Value, with and without holdings	
Nestlé 12/31/2007 share price	CHF 497.77
Shares outstanding (millions)	393.073
Nestlé market capitalization	CHF 195,661
Value of L'Oreal holding	(28,961)
Value of Alcon holding	(36,499)
Implied value of Nestlé operations	CHF 130,201
Pro rata market value:	
L'Oreal	14.8%
Alcon	18.7%
Nestlé	66.5%
	100.0%

The value of the L'Oreal and Alcon holdings is approximately one-third of the value of Nestlé's market capitalization. The analyst now wants to remove their earnings from the earnings of the combined entity (Exhibit 29) so as to make price/earnings comparison for Nestlé earnings alone. For L'Oreal, this is simple: L'Oreal and Nestlé both report on an IFRS basis and Nestlé discloses in its annual report that L'Oreal has contributed CHF 1,302 to the current year earnings.

It is a more complicated, and less precise, exercise to remove the Alcon earnings from the consolidated whole. Alcon's financial statements are filed in the United States and are prepared on a US GAAP basis. Although Alcon is responsible for providing Nestlé with information on an IFRS basis, there is no publicly available reconciliation showing differences in reported earnings. The analyst can only estimate the amount of Alcon net earnings embedded in Nestlé's earnings on an IFRS basis. In reading the 2007 Management Review of Nestlé, he noted a mention of Alcon's sales and EBIT for 2007: CHF 6,700 and 2,300, respectively. Referencing the 2007 consolidated statement of earnings found in the US 20-F filing, he retrieves the other post-EBIT items and converts them into Swiss franc amounts using the average rate for 2007, found in the Nestlé 2007 financial statements. Those amounts are then combined with the EBIT; the resulting pretax figure is taxed at the Nestlé effective rate.

The estimate is crude, because it implicitly assumes the four non-EBIT item amounts, pulled from the US financial statements, would be the same under IFRS. The analyst does note, however, that the revenues on an IFRS basis were nearly the same amount as on a US basis, when converted into Swiss francs at the average 2007 exchange rate. The Management Review mentioned that Alcon had 2007 revenues of CHF 6,700 million; converted into US dollars at an average rate of 1.196, the dollar equivalent revenues are $5,602 million compared to the $5,599 million presented in the Alcon 20-F. Apparently, no significant difference exists between the revenues on an IFRS basis or US GAAP basis. Applying the same exercise to the IFRS-based EBIT of CHF 2,300 million mentioned in the Management Review, the US dollar equivalent is $1,923 million, compared to the 20-F amount of $1,892 million. The analyst excludes the US GAAP charge for in-process R&D from the 20-F EBIT amount; in-process R&D is capitalized under IFRS. The difference in the EBIT figures is minor, only about 2 percent, giving the analyst some comfort that the two bases of accounting produce much the same results for a large part of the reported Alcon earnings.

After isolating the different earnings sources, the analyst prepares the table shown in Exhibit 30, which compares the different market values and price/earnings ratios.

Exhibit 29	Calculation of Nestlé Earnings without Alcon and L'Oreal as of 12/31/2007 (All Currency in Millions)		
		In US $	In CHF
Calculation of Alcon estimated IFRS earnings:			
EBIT			2,300.0
Gain from foreign currency, net		$11.2	13.4
Interest income		69.3	82.9
Interest expense		(50.0)	(59.8)
Other, net		15.4	18.4
Total after-EBIT items			54.9
Earnings before income taxes			2,354.9
Income taxes at 25.3% (Nestlé's effective tax rate)			595.8
Estimated Alcon contribution to net income			1,759.1
Minority interest percentage: (1–77.4%)			22.6%
Portion allocable to minority interest			397.6
Portion allocable to Nestlé group shareholders			1,361.5
Calculation of non-Alcon minority interest:			
Reported profit attributable to minority interests			733.0

(continued)

Exhibit 29	(Continued)		
		In US $	In CHF
Less: Alcon-related portion			(397.6)
Non-Alcon minority interest			335.4
Calculation of Nestlé stand-alone earnings:			
Nestlé consolidated earnings			11,382.0
Less: L'Oreal earnings			(1,302.0)
Less: Estimated Alcon contribution to net income			(1,759.1)
Nestlé stand-alone earnings			8,320.9
Non-Alcon minority interest			(335.4)
Nestlé stand-alone earnings to shareholders			7,985.5

From Alcon 20-F, Restated into CHF at Average 2007 CHF/USD Exchange Rate of 1.196

At the time of the analysis (early 2008), Nestlé's common stock traded at a price/earnings multiple of 18.4 based on its year-end stock price and trailing earnings: a discount of 17 percent to the price/earnings multiple of 22.2 for the S&P 500 at year end 2007. Yet once earnings and available market value of the non-Nestlé holdings are taken out of the price/earnings valuation, the shares of the "Nestlé-only" company are selling on an even more discounted basis: at 16.3 times earnings, the discount to the overall market's price/earnings multiple was a steeper 27 percent. The analyst believes the discount is inappropriate for a company with the demonstrated cash flow and low financial leverage of Nestlé; it also seems severe in terms of the company's returns on equity. The analyst concludes that Nestlé shares may be undervalued relative to the market.

At this time, the analyst believes that he has processed and analyzed the data sufficiently to pull together his findings and make his report to the portfolio manager.

Exhibit 30	Comparison of Decomposed Nestlé Earnings and Price/Earnings Ratios (CHF in Millions)		
	Market Values	Earnings (Group Shareholder Level)	Respective P/Es:
Alcon	36,499	1,361.5	26.8
L'Oreal	28,961	1,302.0	22.2
Implied Nestlé-only	130,201	7,985.5	16.3
Actual	195,661	10,649.0	18.4
Recap in %:	Market Value (%)	Earnings (%)	
L'Oreal	14.8	12.8	
Alcon	18.7	12.2	
Nestlé	66.5	75.0	
	100.0	100.0	

Phase 5: Develop and Communicate Conclusions and Recommendations (e.g., with an Analysis Report)

As a result of the analyses performed, the analyst has gathered sufficient evidence regarding many of the operational and financial characteristics of Nestlé and believes he is able to address the concerns initially expressed by the portfolio manager. Summary points he will cover in his report are divided into two classes: support for an investment in Nestlé shares and causes for concern.

Support for an Investment in Nestlé Shares

- Nestlé's earnings growth and returns have come from its own operations, acquisitions, and investments in associates. Nestlé has the financial stability to fund growth in its existing operations and carry out its growth-by-acquisition strategy. The company's current liquidity and cash flows are more than adequate for future operating and investment purposes. The company has low leverage, and the capital structure is capable of supporting future operations and strategic plans.

- The company's margins and ROE have been consistently positive and generally have exhibited an upward trend. The disaggregation of the effects of income from associates on margins and ROE indicates that the investment in associates has improved ROE and margins but has not been the primary driver of ROE or margins. Nestlé's performance appears sustainable.

- The operating cash flows have consistently exceeded the operating earnings. The ratio of operating cash to operating income has been fairly consistent, approximately 1.20, and gives confidence in the quality of the earnings. Measures comparing cash flows to reinvestment, debt, and debt-servicing capacity indicate strength in financial capacity.

- Nestlé has been increasing its size by acquisitions, evidenced by the growth of goodwill in its asset mix, and its cash return on assets has been increasing over the last three years. The current cash return on total assets is the highest in the five-year span. The acquisitions appear to be generating the required cash to justify the acquisitions.

- Decomposing the earnings into Nestlé-only, L'Oreal, and Alcon and considering the respective P/Es, it appears that the implied Nestlé-only portion is undervalued. The implied Nestlé-only portion has a far lower P/E than Alcon, L'Oreal, or the market. This should be considered an opportunity, given Nestlé's demonstrated cash flows and low financial leverage.

Causes for Concern

- The increases in balance-sheet-based and cash flow accrual ratios raised the possible issue of earnings management. However, this concern was alleviated by the comparison of operating cash flows with various measures as noted above.

- The company has some unusual priorities in the allocation of capital expenditures. The low-margined Waters business seems to be taking in an inordinate amount of the company's capital expenditures. This will be an area of constant monitoring if the company makes an investment in Nestlé common stock.

- The research department's monitoring cost, in terms of time and effort, for an investment in Nestlé common stock may require an analyst to follow two additional companies. While Nestlé is viewed by the market as just one company, the presence of Alcon and L'Oreal are important separable components that reflect considerably on the aggregate Nestlé performance. If an investment in Nestlé stock requires an analyst to follow two additional companies, there is less analytical capacity available for other investments to be evaluated or to be monitored on a continuing basis.

The analyst concludes that Nestlé represents a good investment opportunity and recommends it as such.

Phase 6: Follow-up

Because of the discounted value of Nestlé shares and the financial strength and stability of the company, the portfolio manager decides to commit the pension fund to a core investment holding of Nestlé common stock. The portfolio manager is somewhat troubled with the resource allocation within the company, and wants to continually re-evaluate the holding. Unproductive capital spending may be a trigger for eliminating the holding. The analyst is charged with updating his findings in the initial research report at each reporting period, with a particular emphasis on the company's progress and continued investment in the Waters segment; the quality measures expressed by the accruals tests; and the cash flow support of earnings, with particular regard to returns on assets.

3 · CASE STUDY 2: OFF-BALANCE SHEET LEVERAGE FROM OPERATING LEASES

The quantitative analyst for a large equity mutual fund has become concerned that the fund's research analysts may not be looking for off-balance sheet financing as much as they should. While the fund's investment philosophy has always been rooted in understanding the fundamentals of an investee company, the accounting scandals of the early 2000s and the more recent credit crisis in the United States has convinced the quantitative analyst the fund should be focusing more efforts on determining the unseen financial leverage that companies may be employing. Due to the nature of the fund's investments in service industries, there has been little concern with unseen financial leverage.

The fund's investment philosophy has always led them to invest in service industries, with little operating leverage or inventory risk, and to avoid industries with high financial and operating leverage, such as the airline and retail industries. The companies in the latter industries are capital-intensive and typically have highly leveraged balance sheets, and also employ off-balance sheet leverage in the form of operating leases. Investors in those industries, as a result, are inclined to look for off-balance sheet financing. However, because the fund invests in service industries, off-balance sheet financing is assumed to be a nonissue. The quantitative analyst wonders if this is in fact true.

Phase 1: Define a Purpose for the Analysis

As a result of this concern, the quantitative analyst decides to look for companies in the fund's holdings where off-balance sheet financing may be an issue. He decides to focus on identifying companies with potentially unrecorded capital leases. The objective is not to come up with a point estimate of unrecorded leases or other sources of off-balance sheet financing, but rather to discover any companies in the fund's portfolio that might have hidden leverage and, if in fact such leverage exists, to analyze the impact of the leverage.

Phase 2: Collect Input Data

To identify companies with potentially unrecorded leases, the quantitative analyst filters the fund's holdings using a financial database. He compares the ratio of 7.4 times the current rent (operating lease) expense to total assets with a threshold percentage of 5 percent. 7.4 is the present value factor on a ten-year constant payment discounted at 6 percent; multiplying 7.4 times the rental expense generates an estimate of the incremental assets and debt under a ten-year capital lease discounted at 6 percent. While there is no way of knowing the actual terms of all the leases held by companies in the fund's holdings, the analyst assumes a ten-year lease is representative of current-lease terms.

The ratio of the estimated incremental assets and liabilities to total assets is compared to 5 percent. The quantitative analyst is only concerned with major understatements of assets and liabilities due to off-balance sheet treatment of operating leases and selects a 5 percent understatement threshold for further investigation of portfolio companies. If the ratio of "hidden" assets to total assets exceeds 5 percent for any of the companies in the fund's holdings, that company's information will be subjected to further analysis to see if in fact there are significant assets and liabilities that could be justifiably capitalized on the balance sheet.

Phase 3: Process Data/Phase 4: Analyze/Interpret the Processed Data

The screening process, shown in Exhibit 31, identifies a company that surprises the quantitative analyst: French advertising company Publicis Groupe (Euronext Paris: PUB).

Exhibit 31	Publicis Groupe: Operating Lease Expense Capitalized at 7.4 Times
2007 lease expense	€189.0
Lease multiplier	7.40
Estimated incremental assets and debt	€ 1,398.6
2007 total assets	€12,244.0
Estimated incremental assets to total reported assets	11%

The quantitative analyst is puzzled: Not only does the company lack heavy machinery or retail outlets to finance invisibly through operating leases, but even for a service company it is highly people-intensive. According to the Publicis Groupe annual report, there were 43,808 employees at the end of 2007; it has large office space needs to accommodate those employees. Publicis Groupe does business in virtually every country in the world and owns few offices, primarily leasing.

At 11 percent of total reported assets, the situation demands closer investigation by the analyst responsible for covering Publicis Groupe (the PG analyst). The PG analyst consults the 2007 annual report and finds that Publicis Groupe has significant long-term lease obligations through 2012, with another €455 million beyond that. He assumes that the post-2012 lease payments will be the same amount as in 2012, extinguishing the entire amount of the €455 million by 2016. From a scan of the company's debt schedule, he sees that the company has issued a Eurobond due in 2012 with an effective interest rate of 4.3 percent. He then assumes that the lease borrowing rate that Publicis Groupe would bear on the operating leases if they were capitalized might approximate 4.5 percent. From the payment schedule, he constructs the estimated present value of discounted lease payments shown in Exhibit 32.

Exhibit 32   Publicis Groupe: Operating Lease Payments and Present Value (in Millions)

Operating Lease Payments	At 12/31/2007	PMT PV
2008	€215	€206
2009	186	170
2010	160	140
2011	141	118
2012	136	109
2013	136	104
2014	136	100
2015	136	96
2016	47	32
	€1,293	€1,075

With the refined estimate of incremental asset basis and debt, the PG analyst revises balance sheet amounts and ratios with the new information on a pro forma basis, as shown in Exhibit 33.

Regardless of the leverage measure under scrutiny, Publicis Groupe becomes significantly more leveraged in the capitalization of the operating lease pro forma scenario than under the present operating lease reporting. In Exhibit 34, the analyst examines the impact on interest coverage if the operating leases are capitalized.

While Publicis Groupe still has ample interest coverage, the ratio presents a far different picture of financial strength than the as-reported figures. The PG analyst consults with the mutual fund's internal strategist, who is forecasting an economic slowdown. The PG analyst concludes that this will reduce advertising spending, which will adversely affect Publicis Groupe.

Exhibit 33   Publicis Groupe: 2007 Leverage Ratios after Capitalizing Operating Leases

	As Reported	Pro Forma
Financial leverage:		
Total assets	€12,244	
Total assets including estimated incremental assets based on capitalizing operating Leases		€13,319
Total equity	€2,225	€2,225
Financial leverage	**5.50**	**5.99**
Debt to equity:		
Estimated incremental liability based on capitalizing operating leases	—	€1,075
Long-term financial debt	1,293	1,293
Total long-term financial debt	€1,293	€ 2,368

Exhibit 33   (Continued)

	As Reported	Pro Forma
Long-term financial debt to equity:	**58.1%**	**106.4%**
Debt to long-term capital:		
Long-term financial debt	€1,293	€2,368
Total equity	2,225	2,225
Long-term capital (L-T financial debt + equity)	€3,518	€4,593
Long-term financial debt to long-term capital	**36.8%**	**51.6%**

Exhibit 34   Publicis Groupe: 2007 Interest Coverage Ratio without and with Capitalizing Operating Leases

	As Reported	Pro Forma
Earnings before interest and taxes	€746	€746
Average rent expense (2007 and 2006)		191
Estimated depreciation expense on newly recognized assets (€1,075.3M/9 years, the estimated lease term)		(119)
Revised EBIT		**€818**
Average interest rate on debt		4.5%
Interest expense as reported	€73.0	€73.0
Assumed interest expense on leases (4.5% × 1075.3)		48.4
Adjusted interest expense		**€121.4**
Interest coverage	**10.2**	**6.7**

Phase 5: Develop and Communicate Conclusions and Recommendations (e.g., with an Analysis Report)

The financial strength of the company, as evidenced by the debt and interest coverage ratios, does not appear as great when the operating leases are capitalized. Further, the PG analyst is concerned with the possible market response to a change in accounting for operating leases. In the most recent update of their Memorandum of Understanding for achieving accounting standard convergence, completed 11 September 2008, the FASB and the IASB agreed to develop a new lease standard by 2011. One likely reform is that all leases, including those currently defined as operating leases, might be required to be capitalized.

If Publicis Groupe was required to capitalize its lease obligations, then the balance sheet of Publicis Groupe would show far less available capacity for adding debt than currently. The ratios would deteriorate as shown by the pro forma information. While it is possible that bankers, bond investors, and shareholders make such adjustments in their lending decisions and in valuing the equity, the PG analyst is not convinced of the market's efficiency and is concerned with a decline in value when the hidden leverage is shown on the balance sheet. Given the significant hidden leverage within Publicis Groupe and a negative macroeconomic outlook, the PG analyst recommends that the fund decrease its holding in Publicis Groupe.

Phase 6: Follow-up

The quantitative analyst and PG analyst will continue to observe the value of Publicis Groupe to get feedback on the decision. Accounting pronouncements and changes will be monitored for potential impact on financial statements. They are both watching for and ready to assess the impact of a change in the accounting treatment of operating leases, should it occur, on the value of companies with significant hidden leverage.

CASE STUDY 3: ANTICIPATING EFFECTS OF CHANGES IN ACCOUNTING STANDARDS

The quantitative analyst of the large equity mutual fund, consistent with his mandate to monitor accounting pronouncements and changes, decides to look further at the technical plans on the websites of the International Accounting Standards Board and the Financial Accounting Standards Board.[3] In looking at the websites, he becomes aware of some very near-term efforts at the FASB in the United States to change the accounting for securitizations.

Currently under Statement 140, a company can remove financial assets from its balance sheet by placing them into a qualified special purpose entity, which then issues securities representing interests in those assets. If carried out in accordance with Statement 140 accounting, this transaction results in the recognition of a sale of the assets and their elimination from the balance sheet. The qualified special purpose entity, and the securities issued by it, does not appear on the seller's balance sheet. The combination of asset removal and non-recognition of liabilities may have a powerfully beneficial effect on financial leverage presented in the balance sheet.

The FASB has considered eliminating the concept of a "qualified" special purpose entity from the securitization accounting contained in Statement 140, and requiring consideration of such vehicles under the accounting requirements of FASB Interpretation 46, Revised (FIN 46(R)). The revised accounting standards would make a sale treatment of financial instruments—such as mortgage loans, accounts receivable, or credit card receivables—through a securitization much less likely. Companies could still securitize financial assets, but they would not be as easily removed from the balance sheet as under Statement 140. Liabilities issued in connection with the securitizations would also be likely to be shown on the company's balance sheet.

If the FASB's plans come to pass, then the United States accounting for securitizations would be closer to the accounting contained in International Accounting Standard 39, Financial Instruments: Recognition and Measurement. If the proposed accounting changes are to be applied to *existing* securitization transactions, it will probably cause companies to reconsolidate assets onto their balance sheets, along with associated liabilities, that had previously been accounted for as being sold. That could cause drastic changes in the leverage of companies that had been securitizing financial assets.

---

3 www.iasb.org and www.fasb.org, respectively.

Knowing that the mutual fund has holdings in several financial institutions that frequently securitize assets, the quantitative analyst contacted the financial analyst responsible for the financial institutions and advised him to look into the potential changes.

Phase 1: Define a Purpose for the Analysis

The financial analyst's objective is to identify financial institutions with securitizations that might be susceptible to the potential new accounting treatment, to analyze the effect this would have on reported leverage, and to consider the consequences of the reported leverage.

The financial analyst realized that the mutual fund's large holding in Discover Financial Services (NYSE: DFS) could be at risk from the possible accounting changes. She knows that the SEC requires companies to disclose the anticipated effects of new accounting pronouncements in the Management's Discussion and Analysis (MD&A) section of the 10-K filing. However, this disclosure does not occur until after a standard had been issued, and occurs with varying degrees of diligence by companies affected by a particular accounting pronouncement. Rather than waiting for the FASB to issue the pronouncement, and perhaps finding adequate disclosure of the effects of it in the 2008 10-K issued in early 2009, she decides to use existing disclosures to estimate the impact of the FASB's intended changes in securitization accounting. She considers it far more important to estimate the direction of changes in balance sheet leverage now, rather than wait for an exact amount.

Phase 2: Collect Input Data

She obtains the current 2008 10-Q filings and the 2007 10-K filing for Discover Financial Services (Discover Financial), and notices that the MD&A section and the segment information footnote presents certain financial data on a "managed basis." On this basis, the information is presented as if Discover Financial's sale treatment of credit card receivables had never occurred; instead the financial data is shown as if the securitization had been treated as a secured borrowing, with the assets remaining on the balance sheet and also including the securitization liabilities on the balance sheet.

Phase 3: Process Data/Phase 4: Analyze/Interpret the Processed Data

Using the balance sheets and the "managed basis" data related to securitization adjustments, she revises the reported balance sheet as of year end 30 November 2007 to a managed basis as shown in Exhibit 35.

Exhibit 35	Discover Financial Services: Removing Effects of "Sale" Treatment Securitizations ($ in Thousands)		
Assets	**Reported**	**Securitization Adjustments**	**Managed Basis**
Cash and cash equivalents	$8,787,095		$8,787,095
Available-for-sale securities	420,837		420,837
Held-to-maturity securities	104,602		104,602
Loans receivable:			
Loan portfolio:			

(continued)

Exhibit 35　(Continued)

Assets	Reported	Securitization Adjustments	Managed Basis
Credit card	23,468,965	$28,599,309	52,068,274
Commercial loans	234,136		234,136
Other consumer loans	251,194		251,194
Total loan portfolio	23,954,295		52,553,604
Total loan receivables	23,954,295	$28,599,309	52,553,604
Allowance for loan losses	(916,844)		(916,844)
Net loan receivables	23,037,451		51,636,760
Accrued interest receivable	139,414		139,414
Amounts due from asset securitization	3,093,472		3,093,472
Premises and equipment, net	658,492		658,492
Goodwill	255,421		255,421
Intangible assets, net	98,043		98,043
Other assets	781,278		781,278
Assets of discontinued operations	0		0
Total assets	$37,376,105	$28,599,309	$65,975,414
Liabilities and Stockholders' Equity			
Total liabilities	$31,776,683	$28,599,309	$60,375,992
Total stockholders' equity	5,599,422		5,599,422
Total liabilities and equity	$37,376,105	$28,599,309	$65,975,414

The managed basis information indicates that loan receivables and total assets have increased by $28.6 billion; the analyst assumes that the increase relates solely to the credit card loan portfolio. No additional information is provided that describes how the short-term and long-term liabilities would be affected by the inclusion of the securities resulting from the application of the managed basis. Therefore, the analyst adjusts for the impact under the heading of "total liabilities," implicitly assuming that the liabilities recognized would be the same as the assets recognized.

The adjustments have a significant impact on the balance sheet. Total assets increase 77 percent; total liabilities increase 90 percent. She then applies the same adjustment to the balance sheets as of 29 February 2008 and 31 May 2008 using information from the respective MD&A sections of the filings, and produces the schedule shown in Exhibit 36. The presentation shows 30 November 2007 on the left and 31 May 2008 on the right.

On an as-reported basis, the company appears to have become less leveraged over the last six months. Financial leverage (total assets divided by total equity) was 6.67 at 30 November 2007 and decreased to 5.85 by 31 May 2008. Discover Financial's application of Statement 140 treated its securitizations of receivables as if they were asset sales instead of secured borrowings. This has the effect of decreasing overall leverage. When calculating the financial leverage ratio on a pro forma managed basis—as if the securitized receivables were still the assets of the company—Discover Financial shows higher leverage but similar improvement over the same period. On a managed basis, the financial leverage was 11.78 at 30 November 2007 and decreased

Exhibit 36 Discover Financial Services: Revised Balance Sheets and Leverage Ratios ($ in Thousands)

Discover Financial Assets	30 Nov 2007		29 Feb 2008		31 May 2008	
	Reported	Managed Basis	Reported	Managed Basis	Reported	Managed Basis
Cash and cash equivalents	$8,787,095	$8,787,095	$8,286,290	$8,286,290	$8,765,384	$8,765,384
Available-for-sale securities	420,837	420,837	792,979	792,979	958,784	958,784
Held-to-maturity securities	104,602	104,602	99,527	99,527	96,371	96,371
Loans receivable:						
Loans held for sale	0	0	349,072	349,072	714,632	714,632
Loan portfolio:						
Credit card	23,468,965	52,068,274	19,895,527	46,353,256	18,683,242	46,022,670
Commercial loans	234,136	234,136	312,211	312,211	387,540	387,540
Other consumer loans	251,194	251,194	485,871	485,871	716,649	716,649
Total loan portfolio	23,954,295	52,553,604	20,693,609	47,151,338	19,787,431	47,126,859
Total loan receivables	23,954,295	52,553,604	21,042,681	47,500,410	20,502,063	47,841,491
Allowance for loan losses	(916,844)	(916,844)	(860,378)	(860,378)	(846,775)	(846,775)
Net loan receivables	23,037,451	51,636,760	20,182,303	46,640,032	19,655,288	46,994,716
Accrued interest receivable	139,414	139,414	122,765	122,765	131,388	131,388
Amounts due from asset securitization	3,093,472	3,093,472	2,935,494	4,192,534	2,705,638	2,705,638
Premises and equipment, net	658,492	658,492	567,475	567,475	556,030	556,030
Goodwill	255,421	255,421	255,421	255,421	255,421	255,421
Intangible assets, net	98,043	98,043	57,900	57,900	56,030	56,030
Other assets	781,278	781,278	922,578	922,578	839,911	839,911
Assets of discontinued operations	0	0	3,105,327	3,105,327	213,297	213,297
Total Assets	$37,376,105	$65,975,414	$37,328,059	$65,042,828	$34,233,542	$61,572,970
Liabilities and stockholders' equity						
Total liabilities	$31,776,683	$60,375,992	$31,673,718	$59,388,487	$28,383,851	$55,723,279
Total stockholders' equity	5,599,422	5,599,422	5,654,341	5,654,341	5,849,691	5,849,691
Total liabilities and equity	$37,376,105	$65,975,414	$37,328,059	$65,042,828	$34,233,542	$61,572,970
Financial leverage	6.67	11.78	6.60	11.50	5.85	10.53
Incremental leverage	5.11		4.90		4.67	
Understatement of leverage	–43%		–43%		–44%	
Liabilities as percent of capital	85.0%	91.5%	84.9%	91.3%	82.9%	90.5%

to 10.53 by 31 May 2008. The Statement 140 sale treatment understated leverage by 43 percent (11/30/07), 43 percent (2/29/08), and 44 percent (5/31/08) in the three respective periods.

Another measure of financial leverage, liabilities as a percentage of total assets, shows the as-reported liabilities would be 82.9 percent of total capital at 31 May 2008. That proportion is 90.5 percent in a calculation based on managed basis figures. While financial leverage on either basis (as-reported or managed) shows a lessening of leverage over the six-month period, that decline is less on a managed basis. Further, the absolute level of leverage would be significantly increased in a standard change like the one contemplated by the FASB.

The financial analyst then looks to the MD&A for information on the effects the managed basis would have on the income statement. While net interest income, provision for loan losses, and other income would change, the net income would be unaffected. It appears that the balance sheet impacts are those of concern.

Phase 5: Develop and Communicate Conclusions and Recommendations (e.g., with an Analysis Report)

The balance sheet effects concern the financial analyst on several levels. First, she is concerned that the current accounting treatment for securitizations masks the company's true leverage. Second, she is concerned that expected changes by standard setters will force Discover Financial to present a balance sheet that is more highly leveraged than investors have come to expect. That may raise concerns among other market participants about the company's financial standing, possibly weakening the company's valuation. Third, she is concerned that the company may try to offset the effects of the anticipated accounting change by raising equity, which would dilute the company's ownership and also possibly weaken the company's valuation.

She believes it is highly probable that the FASB will act on the project to change Statement 140 accounting and that it can only portend negative effects for the company's holding in Discover Financial Services. She recommends that the company reduce its holdings in Discover Financial Services.

Phase 6: Follow-up

Specifically, the quantitative analyst and financial analyst will continue to observe the value of Discover Financial Services to get feedback on the decision. Generally, accounting pronouncements and changes will be monitored for potential impact on financial statements and on company valuation.

SUMMARY

The three case studies demonstrate the use of financial analysis in decision making. Each case is set in a different type of industry: manufacturing, service, and financial service. The different focus, purpose, and context for each analysis result in different techniques and tools being applied to the analysis. However, each case demonstrates the use of a common financial statement analysis framework. In each case, an economic decision is arrived at; this is consistent with the primary reason for performing financial analysis: to facilitate an economic decision.

The following information relates to Questions 1–8

Sergei Leenid, CFA, is a long-only fixed income portfolio manager for the Parliament Funds. He has developed a quantitative model, based on financial statement data, to predict changes in the credit ratings assigned to corporate bond issues. Before applying the model, Leenid first performs a screening process to exclude bonds that fail to meet certain criteria relative to their credit rating. Existing holdings that fail to pass the initial screen are individually reviewed for potential disposition. Bonds that pass the screening process are evaluated using the quantitative model to identify potential rating changes.

Leenid is concerned that a pending change in accounting rules could affect the results of the initial screening process. One current screen excludes bonds when the financial leverage ratio (equity multiplier) exceeds a given level and/or the interest coverage ratio falls below a given level for a given bond rating. For example, any "A" rated bond of a company with a financial leverage ratio exceeding 2.0 or an interest coverage ratio below 6.0 would fail the initial screening. The failing bonds are eliminated from further analysis using the quantitative model.

The new accounting rule would require substantially all leases to be capitalized on a company's balance sheets. To test whether the change in accounting rules will affect the output of the screening process, Leenid collects a random sample of "A" rated bonds issued by companies in the retail industry, which he believes will be among the industries most affected by the change.

Two of the companies, Silk Road Stores and Colorful Concepts, recently issued bonds with similar terms and interest rates. Leenid decides to thoroughly analyze the potential effects of the change on these two companies and begins by gathering information from their most recent annual financial statements (Exhibit 1).

After examining lease disclosures, Leenid estimates the average lease term for each company at 8 years with a fairly consistent lease expense over that time. He believes the leases should be capitalized using 6.5 percent, the rate at which both companies recently issued bonds.

Exhibit 1	Selected Financial Data for Silk Road Stores and Colorful Concepts	
	Silk Road	**Colorful Concepts**
Revenue	3,945	7,049
EBIT	318	865
Interest expense	21	35
Income taxes	121	302
Net income	176	528
Average total assets	2,075	3,844

(continued)

	Silk Road	Colorful Concepts
Exhibit 1 **(Continued)**		
Average total equity	1,156	2,562
Lease expense	213	406

While examining the balance sheet for Colorful Concepts, Leenid also discovers that the company has a 204 ending asset balance (188 beginning) for investments in associates, primarily due to its 20 percent interest in the equity of Exotic Imports. Exotic Imports is a specialty retail chain and in the most recent year reported 1,230 in sales, 105 in net income, and had average total assets of 620.

1 If the accounting rules were to change, Silk Road's assets would increase by approximately:

A 1,297.

B 1,576.

C 1,704.

2 If the accounting rules were to change, Silk Road's interest coverage ratio would be *closest* to:

A 3.03.

B 3.50.

C 5.04.

3 If the accounting rules were to change, Silk Road's financial leverage ratio would be *closest* to:

A 1.37.

B 1.79.

C 2.92.

4 Will the change in accounting rules impact the result of the initial screening process for Colorful Concepts?

A It passes the screens now, but will not pass if the accounting rules change.

B It passes the screens now and will continue to pass if the accounting rules change.

C It fails the screens now and will continue to fail if the accounting rules change.

5 Based on Leenid's analysis of the results of the initial screening, relative to Colorful Concepts the bond rating of Silk Road should be:

A lower.

B higher.

C the same.

6 Ignoring the potential impact of any accounting change and excluding the investment in associates, the net profit margin for Colorful Concepts would be *closest* to:

A 6.0%.

B 7.2%.

C 7.5%.

7 Ignoring the impact of any accounting change, the asset turnover ratio for Colorful Concepts excluding the investments in associates would:

   A   stay the same.

   B   increase by 0.10.

   C   decrease by 0.10.

8 Excluding the investments in associates would result in the interest coverage ratio for Colorful Concepts being:

   A   lower.

   B   higher.

   C   the same.

The following information relates to Questions 9–15

Quentin Abay, CFA, is an analyst for a private equity firm interested in purchasing Bickchip Enterprises, a conglomerate. His first task is to determine the trends in ROE and the main drivers of the trends using DuPont analysis. To do so he gathers the data in Exhibit 1.

Exhibit 1	Selected Financial Data for Bickchip Enterprises (€ Thousands)		
	2009	**2008**	**2007**
Revenue	72,448	66,487	55,781
Earnings before interest and tax	6,270	4,710	3,609
Earnings before tax	5,101	4,114	3,168
Net income	4,038	3,345	2,576
Asset turnover	0.79	0.76	0.68
Assets/Equity	3.09	3.38	3.43

After conducting the DuPont analysis, Abay believes that his firm could increase the ROE without operational changes. Further, Abay thinks that ROE could improve if the company divested segments that were generating the lowest returns on capital employed (total assets less non-interest-bearing liabilities). Segment EBIT margins in 2009 were 11 percent for Automation Equipment, 5 percent for Power and Industrial, and 8 percent for Medical Equipment. Other relevant segment information is presented in Exhibit 2.

Exhibit 2	Segment Data for Bickchip Enterprises (€ Thousands)					
	Capital Employed			**Capital Expenditures (Excluding Acquisitions)**		
Operating Segments	**2009**	**2008**	**2007**	**2009**	**2008**	**2007**
Automation Equipment	10,705	6,384	5,647	700	743	616
Power and Industrial	15,805	13,195	12,100	900	849	634
Medical Equipment	22,870	22,985	22,587	908	824	749
	49,380	42,564	40,334	2,508	2,416	1,999

Abay is also concerned with earnings quality, so he intends to calculate Bickchip's cash-flow-based accruals ratio and the ratio of operating cash flow before interest and taxes to operating income. To do so, he prepares the information in Exhibit 3.

Exhibit 3	Earnings Quality Data for Bickchip Enterprises (€ Thousands)		
	2009	**2008**	**2007**
Net income	4,038	3,345	2,576
Net cash flow provided by (used in) operating activity[a]	9,822	5,003	3,198
Net cash flow provided by (used in) investing activity	(10,068)	(4,315)	(5,052)
Net cash flow provided by (used in) financing activity[b]	(5,792)	1,540	(2,241)
Average net operating assets	43,192	45,373	40,421
[a] includes cash paid for taxes of:	(1,930)	(1,191)	(1,093)
[b] includes cash paid for interest of:	(1,169)	(596)	(441)

9 Over the three-year period presented in Exhibit 1, Bickchip's return on equity is *best* described as:

   A   stable.

   B   trending lower.

   C   trending higher.

10 Based on the DuPont analysis, Abay's belief regarding ROE is *most likely* based on:

   A   leverage.

   B   profit margins.

   C   asset turnover.

11 Based on Abay's criteria, the business segment *best* suited for divestiture is:

   A   medical equipment.

   B   power and industrial.

   C   automation equipment.

12 Bickchip's cash-flow-based accruals ratio in 2009 is *closest* to:

   A   9.9%.

B 13.4%.

C 23.3%.

13 The cash-flow-based accruals ratios from 2007 to 2009 indicate:

A improving earnings quality.

B deteriorating earnings quality.

C no change in earnings quality.

14 The ratio of operating cash flow before interest and taxes to operating income for Bickchip for 2009 is *closest* to:

A 1.6.

B 1.9.

C 2.1.

15 Based on the ratios for operating cash flow before interest and taxes to operating income, Abay should conclude that:

A Bickchip's earnings are backed by cash flow.

B Bickchip's earnings are not backed by cash flow.

C Abay can draw no conclusion due to the changes in the ratios over time.

The following information relates to Questions 16–21

Michael Wetstone is an equity analyst covering the software industry for a public pension fund. Prior to comparing the financial results of Software Services Inc. and PDQ GmbH, Wetstone discovers the need to make adjustments to their respective financial statements. The issues preventing comparability, using the financial statements as reported, are the sale of receivables and the impact of minority interests.

Software Services sold $267.5 million of finance receivables to a special purpose entity. PDQ does not securitize finance receivables. An abbreviated balance sheet for Software Services is presented in Exhibit 1.

Exhibit 1	Abbreviated Balance Sheet for Software Services ($ 000)
Year Ending:	**31 December 2009**
Total current assets	1,412,900
Total assets	3,610,600
Total current liabilities	1,276,300
Total liabilities	2,634,100
Total equity	976,500

A significant portion of PDQ's net income is explained by its 20 percent minority interest in Astana Systems. Wetstone collects certain data (Exhibit 2) related to both PDQ and Astana in order to estimate the financials of PDQ on a stand-alone basis.

Exhibit 2	Selected Financial Data Related to PDQ and Astana Systems	
	PDQ (€ in 000)	Astana ($ in 000)
Earnings before tax (2009)	41,730	15,300
Income taxes (2009)	13,562	5,355
Net income (2009)	28,168	9,945
Market capitalization (recent)	563,355	298,350
Average $/€ exchange rate in 2009	1.55	
Current $/€ exchange rate	1.62	

16 Compared to holding securitized finance receivables on the balance sheet, treating them as sold had the effect of reducing Software Services' reported financial leverage by:

A 6.8%.

B 7.4%.

C 9.2%.

17 Had the securitized finance receivables been held on the balance sheet, Software Services' ratio of liabilities to total capital would have been *closest* to:

A 73.0%.

B 74.8%.

C 80.4%.

18 How much of PDQ's value can be explained by its equity stake in Astana?

A 6.5%.

B 10.6%.

C 20.0%.

19 On a "solo" basis, PDQ's P/E ratio is *closest* to:

A 19.6.

B 21.0.

C 24.5.

20 The adjusted financial statements were created during which phase of the financial analysis process?

A Data collection.

B Data processing.

C Data interpretation.

21 The estimate of PDQ's solo value is crude because of:

A the potential differences in accounting standards used by PDQ and Astana.

B the differing risk characteristics of PDQ and Astana.

C differences in liquidity and market efficiency where PDQ and Astana trade.

SOLUTIONS

1 A is correct. The capitalized value of Silk Road's leases, the amount by which assets would increase, is estimated as the present value of the operating lease expense (payments). The present value of 8 payments of 213 at 6.5 percent is 1,297.

2 B is correct. Adjusted EBIT = EBIT + Lease expense – Adjustment to depreciation = 318 + 213 – (1,297/8) = 369. Adjusted interest expense = Interest expense + Assumed interest expense on leases = 21 + (0.065 × 1,297) = 105.3. Adjusted interest coverage ratio = 369/105.3 = 3.50.

3 C is correct. The capitalized value of the leases is added to assets and liabilities but does not impact equity. On an adjusted basis, Silk Road's financial leverage ratio = (2,075 + 1,297)/1,156 = 2.92.

4 A is correct. Without the accounting change, Colorful Concepts has a financial leverage ratio = 3,844/2,562 = 1.50 and an interest coverage ratio = 865/35 = 24.71. These are both passing ratios. With the accounting change, the capitalized value of Colorful Concept's leases is 2,472. The financial leverage ratio = (3,844 + 2,472)/2,562 = 2.46 and the interest coverage ratio = [865 + 406 – (2,472/8)]/[35 + (2,472 × 0.065)] = 4.91. These are both failing ratios. The change in interest rate coverage is particularly dramatic.

5 A is correct. Silk Road has higher unadjusted and adjusted financial leverage ratios and lower unadjusted and adjusted interest coverage ratios than Colorful Concepts. Silk Road is riskier based on the financial leverage and interest coverage ratios, so it should have a lower bond rating.

6 B is correct. The investment in Exotic Imports is accounted for using the equity method and 20 percent of Exotic Import's net income is included in the net income of Colorful Concepts. The net profit margin excluding the investment in Exotic Imports is (528 – 21)/7,049 = 7.2 percent. (If the investment in Exotic Imports is included, net profit margin is 7.5 percent.)

7 B is correct. The asset turnover ratio (sales/average total assets) without adjustment is 7,049/3,844 = 1.83. To compute the asset turnover ratio excluding investments in associates, the average investment in associates [(204 + 188)/2 = 196] is deducted from average total assets. The adjusted asset turnover ratio is 7,049/(3,844 – 196) = 1.93. The asset turnover ratio increased by 0.10.

8 C is correct. The calculation for interest coverage is EBIT/interest expense, neither of which is affected by the investment in associates.

9 C is correct. The ROE has been trending higher. ROE can be calculated by multiplying (net profit margin) × (asset turnover) × (financial leverage). Net profit margin is net income/sales. In 2007 the net profit margin was 2,576/55,781 = 4.6% and the ROE = 4.6% × 0.68 × 3.43 = 10.8%. Using the same method, ROE was 12.9 percent in 2008 and 13.6 percent in 2009.

10 A is correct. The DuPont analysis shows that profit margins and asset turnover have both increased over the last three years, but leverage has declined. The reduction in leverage offsets a portion of the improvement in profitability and turnover. Thus, ROE would have been higher if leverage had not decreased.

11 B is correct. The Power and Industrial segment has the lowest EBIT margins but uses about 31 percent of the capital employed. Further, Power and Industrial's proportion of the capital expenditures has increased from 32 percent to 36 percent over the three years. Its capital intensity only looked to get worse, as the segment's percentage of total capital expenditures was higher than its percentage of total capital in each of the three years. If Abay is considering divesting segments that do not earn sufficient returns on capital employed, this segment is most suitable.

12 A is correct. The cash-flow-based accruals ratio = [NI − (CFO + CFI)]/(Average NOA) = [4,038 − (9,822 − 10,068)]/43,192 = 9.9%.

13 A is correct. The cash-flow-based accruals ratio falls from 11.0 percent in 2007 to 5.9 percent in 2008, and then rises to 9.9 percent in 2009. However, the change over the three-year period is a net modest decline, indicating a slight improvement in earnings quality.

14 B is correct. Net cash flow provided by (used in) operating activity has to be adjusted for interest and taxes, as necessary, in order to be comparable to operating income (EBIT). Bickchip, reporting under IFRS, chose to classify interest expense as a financing cash flow so the only necessary adjustment is for taxes. The operating cash flow before interest and taxes = 9,822 + 1,930 = 11,752. Dividing this by EBIT of 6,270 yields 1.9.

15 A is correct. Operating cash flow before interest and taxes to operating income rises steadily (not erratically) from 1.2 to 1.3 to 1.9. The ratios over 1.0 and the trend indicate that earnings are supported by cash flow.

16 A is correct. The leverage ratio is measured as total assets/total equity. As reported, this was $3,610,600/$976,500 = 3.70. Had the securitized receivables been held on the balance sheet, assets would have been $267,500 higher, or $3,878,100, and equity would have been unchanged. The ratio would then have been 3.97. The ratio of 3.70 as reported is 6.8 percent less than 3.97: 1 − 3.7/3.97 = 0.068.

17 B is correct. If the receivables had been held on the balance sheet, both assets and liabilities would have been $267,500 higher: $2,901,600/$3,878,100 = 74.8%.

18 A is correct. PDQ owns 20 percent of Astana (0.2 × 298,350 = $59,670). Translated at the current exchange rate of $1.62 per euro that is €36,833. 36,833/563,355 = 0.0654 or 6.5%.

19 A is correct. PDQ's solo market capitalization is 563,355 − 36,833 = 526,522. To calculate its solo net income, because Astana is accounted for using the equity method, 20 percent of Astana's net income of $9,945 is translated at the average exchange rate of $1.55/€ and deducted from PDQ's net income to produce €26,884 in adjusted net income for PDQ. P/E = 526,522/26,884 = 19.6.

20 B is correct. Adjusted financial statements are created during the data processing phase of the financial analysis process.

21 A is correct. Estimates of Astana's impact on PDQ's financial statements are crude due to the potential differences in accounting standards used by the two firms. Based on the currencies each reports in, Astana is likely using US GAAP and PDQ is likely using IFRS. Pricing (market capitalization) should reflect the other potential differences.

Glossary

Abandonment option The ability to terminate a project at some future time if the financial results are disappointing.

Abnormal earnings See *residual income*.

Abnormal return The return on an asset in excess of the asset's required rate of return; the risk-adjusted return.

Absolute convergence The idea that developing countries, regardless of their particular characteristics, will eventually catch up with the developed countries and match them in per capita output.

Absolute valuation model A model that specifies an asset's intrinsic value.

Absolute version of PPP The extension of the law of one price to the broad range of goods and services that are consumed in different countries.

Accounting estimates Estimates used in calculating the value of assets or liabilities and in the amount of revenue and expense to allocate to a period. Examples of accounting estimates include, among others, the useful lives of depreciable assets, the salvage value of depreciable assets, product returns, warranty costs, and the amount of uncollectible receivables.

Acquirer The company in a merger or acquisition that is acquiring the target.

Acquiring company The company in a merger or acquisition that is acquiring the target.

Acquisition The purchase of some portion of one company by another; the purchase may be for assets, a definable segment of another entity, or the purchase of an entire company.

Active factor risk The contribution to active risk squared resulting from the portfolio's different-than-benchmark exposures relative to factors specified in the risk model.

Active return The return on a portfolio minus the return on the portfolio's benchmark.

Active risk The standard deviation of active returns.

Active risk squared The variance of active returns; active risk raised to the second power.

Active specific risk The contribution to active risk squared resulting from the portfolio's active weights on individual assets as those weights interact with assets' residual risk.

Add-on interest A procedure for determining the interest on a bond or loan in which the interest is added onto the face value of a contract.

Adjusted funds from operations Funds from operations (FFO) adjusted to remove any non-cash rent reported under straight-line rent accounting and to subtract maintenance-type capital expenditures and leasing costs, including leasing agents' commissions and tenants' improvement allowances.

Adjusted present value (APV) As an approach to valuing a company, the sum of the value of the company, assuming no use of debt, and the net present value of any effects of debt on company value.

Adjusted R^2 A measure of goodness-of-fit of a regression that is adjusted for degrees of freedom and hence does not automatically increase when another independent variable is added to a regression.

Administrative regulations or administrative law Rules issued by government agencies or other regulators.

Agency costs Costs associated with the conflict of interest present when a company is managed by non-owners. Agency costs result from the inherent conflicts of interest between managers and equity owners.

Agency costs of equity The smaller the stake that managers have in the company, the less is their share in bearing the cost of excessive perquisite consumption or not giving their best efforts in running the company.

Agency issues Conflicts of interest that arise when the agent in an agency relationship has goals and incentives that differ from the principal to whom the agent owes a fiduciary duty. Also called *agency problems* or *principal–agent problems*.

Agency problem A conflict of interest that arises when the agent in an agency relationship has goals and incentives that differ from the principal to whom the agent owes a fiduciary duty.

Alpha The return on an asset in excess of the asset's required rate of return; the risk-adjusted return.

American Depositary Receipt A negotiable certificate issued by a depositary bank that represents ownership in a non-US company's deposited equity (i.e., equity held in custody by the depositary bank in the company's home market).

American option An option that can be exercised at any time until its expiration date.

Amortizing and accreting swaps A swap in which the notional principal changes according to a formula related to changes in the underlying.

Analysis of variance (ANOVA) The analysis of the total variability of a dataset (such as observations on the dependent variable in a regression) into components representing different sources of variation; with reference to regression, ANOVA provides the inputs for an *F*-test of the significance of the regression as a whole.

Arbitrage 1) The simultaneous purchase of an undervalued asset or portfolio and sale of an overvalued but equivalent asset or portfolio, in order to obtain a riskless profit on the price differential. Taking advantage of a market inefficiency in a risk-free manner. 2) The condition in a financial market in which equivalent assets or combinations of assets sell for two different prices, creating an opportunity to profit at no risk with no commitment of money. In a well-functioning financial market, few arbitrage opportunities are possible. 3) A risk-free operation that earns an expected positive net profit but requires no net investment of money.

Arbitrage-free models Term structure models that project future interest rate paths that emanate from the existing term structure. Resulting prices are based on a no-arbitrage condition.

Arbitrage-free valuation An approach to valuation that determines security values that are consistent with the absence of arbitrage opportunities.

Arbitrage opportunity An opportunity to conduct an arbitrage; an opportunity to earn an expected positive net profit without risk and with no net investment of money.

Arbitrage portfolio   The portfolio that exploits an arbitrage opportunity.

Arrears swap   A type of interest rate swap in which the floating payment is set at the end of the period and the interest is paid at that same time.

Asset-backed securities   A type of bond issued by a legal entity called a *special purpose vehicle* (SPV), on a collection of assets that the SPV owns. Also, securities backed by receivables and loans other than mortgage loans.

Asset-based approach   Approach that values a private company based on the values of the underlying assets of the entity less the value of any related liabilities.

Asset-based valuation   An approach to valuing natural resource companies that estimates company value on the basis of the market value of the natural resources the company controls.

Asset beta   The unlevered beta; reflects the business risk of the assets; the asset's systematic risk.

Asset purchase   An acquisition in which the acquirer purchases the target company's assets and payment is made directly to the target company.

Asymmetric information   The differential of information between corporate insiders and outsiders regarding the company's performance and prospects. Managers typically have more information about the company's performance and prospects than owners and creditors.

At-the-money   An option in which the underlying value equals the exercise price.

Autocorrelation   The correlation of a time series with its own past values.

Autoregressive model (AR)   A time series regressed on its own past values, in which the independent variable is a lagged value of the dependent variable.

Available-for-sale investments   Debt and equity securities not classified as either held-to-maturity or fair value through profit or loss securities. The investor is willing to sell but not actively planning to sell. In general, available-for-sale securities are reported at fair value on the balance sheet.

Backward integration   A merger involving the purchase of a target ahead of the acquirer in the value or production chain; for example, to acquire a supplier.

Backwardation   A condition in the futures markets in which the benefits of holding an asset exceed the costs, leaving the futures price less than the spot price.

Bankruptcy   A declaration provided for by a country's laws that typically involves the establishment of a legal procedure that forces creditors to defer their claims.

Basic earnings per share   (EPS) Net earnings available to common shareholders (i.e., net income minus preferred dividends) divided by the weighted average number of common shares outstanding during the period.

Basis swap   1) An interest rate swap involving two floating rates. 2) A swap in which both parties pay a floating rate.

Basis trade   A trade based on the pricing of credit in the bond market versus the price of the same credit in the CDS market. To execute a basis trade, go long the "underpriced" credit and short the "overpriced" credit. A profit is realized when the price of credit between the short and long position converges.

Bear hug   A tactic used by acquirers to circumvent target management's objections to a proposed merger by submitting the proposal directly to the target company's board of directors.

Benchmark   A comparison portfolio; a point of reference or comparison.

Benchmark value of the multiple   In using the method of comparables, the value of a price multiple for the comparison asset; when we have comparison assets (a group), the mean or median value of the multiple for the group of assets.

Bill-and-hold basis   Sales on a bill-and-hold basis involve selling products but not delivering those products until a later date.

Binomial model   A model for pricing options in which the underlying price can move to only one of two possible new prices.

Binomial tree   The graphical representation of a model of asset price dynamics in which, at each period, the asset moves up with probability p or down with probability $(1 - p)$.

Blockage factor   An illiquidity discount that occurs when an investor sells a large amount of stock relative to its trading volume (assuming it is not large enough to constitute a controlling ownership).

Bond indenture   A legal contract specifying the terms of a bond issue.

Bond option   An option in which the underlying is a bond; primarily traded in over-the-counter markets.

Bond yield plus risk premium method   An estimate of the cost of common equity that is produced by summing the before-tax cost of debt and a risk premium that captures the additional yield on a company's stock relative to its bonds. The additional yield is often estimated using historical spreads between bond yields and stock yields.

Bonding costs   Costs borne by management to assure owners that they are working in the owners' best interest (e.g., implicit cost of non-compete agreements).

Book value   Shareholders' equity (total assets minus total liabilities) minus the value of preferred stock; common shareholders' equity.

Book value of equity   Shareholders' equity (total assets minus total liabilities) minus the value of preferred stock; common shareholders' equity.

Book value per share   The amount of book value (also called carrying value) of common equity per share of common stock, calculated by dividing the book value of shareholders' equity by the number of shares of common stock outstanding.

Bootstrapping   A statistical method for estimating a sample distribution based on the properties of an approximating distribution.

Bottom-up approach   With respect to forecasting, an approach that usually begins at the level of the individual company or a unit within the company.

Bottom-up investing   An approach to investing that focuses on the individual characteristics of securities rather than on macroeconomic or overall market forecasts.

Breakup value   The value derived using a sum-of-the-parts valuation.

Breusch–Pagan test   A test for conditional heteroskedasticity in the error term of a regression.

Broker   1) An agent who executes orders to buy or sell securities on behalf of a client in exchange for a commission. 2) *See* Futures commission merchants.

Brokerage   The business of acting as agents for buyers or sellers, usually in return for commissions.

Buy-side analysts   Analysts who work for investment management firms, trusts, and bank trust departments, and similar institutions.

Call   An option that gives the holder the right to buy an underlying asset from another party at a fixed price over a specific period of time.

Callable bond   Bond that includes an embedded call option that gives the issuer the right to redeem the bond issue prior to maturity, typically when interest rates have fallen or when the issuer's credit quality has improved.

Cannibalization   Cannibalization occurs when an investment takes customers and sales away from another part of the company.

Cap   1) A contract on an interest rate, whereby at periodic payment dates, the writer of the cap pays the difference between the market interest rate and a specified cap rate if, and only if, this difference is positive. This is equivalent to a stream of call options on the interest rate. 2) A combination of interest rate call options designed to hedge a borrower against rate increases on a floating-rate loan.

Cap rate   See *capitalization rate.*

Capital charge   The company's total cost of capital in money terms.

Capital deepening   An increase in the capital-to-labor ratio.

Capital rationing   A capital rationing environment assumes that the company has a fixed amount of funds to invest.

Capital structure   The mix of debt and equity that a company uses to finance its business; a company's specific mixture of long-term financing.

Capitalization of earnings method   In the context of private company valuation, valuation model based on an assumption of a constant growth rate of free cash flow to the firm or a constant growth rate of free cash flow to equity.

Capitalization rate   The divisor in the expression for the value of perpetuity. In the context of real estate, the divisor in the direct capitalization method of estimating value. The cap rate equals net operating income divided by value.

Capitalized cash flow method   In the context of private company valuation, valuation model based on an assumption of a constant growth rate of free cash flow to the firm or a constant growth rate of free cash flow to equity. Also called *capitalized cash flow model.*

Capitalized cash flow model   In the context of private company valuation, valuation model based on an assumption of a constant growth rate of free cash flow to the firm or a constant growth rate of free cash flow to equity. Also called *capitalized cash flow method.*

Capitalized income method   In the context of private company valuation, valuation model based on an assumption of a constant growth rate of free cash flow to the firm or a constant growth rate of free cash flow to equity.

Caplet   Each component call option in a cap.

Capped floater   Floating-rate bond with a cap provision that prevents the coupon rate from increasing above a specified maximum rate. It protects the issuer against rising interest rates.

Capped swap   A swap in which the floating payments have an upper limit.

Carried interest   A share of any profits that is paid to the general partner (manager) of an investment partnership, such as a private equity or hedge fund, as a form of compensation designed to be an incentive to the manager to maximize performance of the investment fund.

Carrying costs   The costs of holding an asset, generally a function of the physical characteristics of the underlying asset.

Cash available for distribution   Funds from operations (FFO) adjusted to remove any non-cash rent reported under straight-line rent accounting and to subtract maintenance-type capital expenditures and leasing costs, including leasing agents' commissions and tenants' improvement allowances.

Cash-generating unit   The smallest identifiable group of assets that generates cash inflows that are largely independent of the cash inflows of other assets or groups of assets.

Cash offering   A merger or acquisition that is to be paid for with cash; the cash for the merger might come from the acquiring company's existing assets or from a debt issue.

Cash settlement   A procedure used in certain derivative transactions that specifies that the long and short parties engage in the equivalent cash value of a delivery transaction.

Catalyst   An event or piece of information that causes the marketplace to re-evaluate the prospects of a company.

CDS spread   A periodic premium paid by the buyer to the seller that serves as a return over Libor required to protect against credit risk.

Chain rule of forecasting   A forecasting process in which the next period's value as predicted by the forecasting equation is substituted into the right-hand side of the equation to give a predicted value two periods ahead.

Cheapest-to-deliver   The debt instrument that can be purchased and delivered at the lowest cost yet has the same seniority as the reference obligation.

Clean surplus accounting   Accounting that satisfies the condition that all changes in the book value of equity other than transactions with owners are reflected in income. The bottom-line income reflects all changes in shareholders' equity arising from other than owner transactions. In the absence of owner transactions, the change in shareholders' equity should equal net income. No adjustments such as translation adjustments bypass the income statement and go directly to shareholders equity.

Clean surplus relation   The relationship between earnings, dividends, and book value in which ending book value is equal to the beginning book value plus earnings less dividends, apart from ownership transactions.

Clientele effect   The preference some investors have for shares that exhibit certain characteristics.

Club convergence   The idea that only rich and middle-income countries sharing a set of favorable attributes (i.e., are members of the "club") will converge to the income level of the richest countries.

Cobb–Douglas production function   A function of the form $Y = K^\alpha L^{1-\alpha}$ relating output (Y) to labor (L) and capital (K) inputs.

Cointegrated   Describes two time series that have a long-term financial or economic relationship such that they do not diverge from each other without bound in the long run.

Commercial real estate properties   Income-producing real estate properties, properties purchased with the intent to let, lease, or rent (in other words, produce income).

Common size statements   Financial statements in which all elements (accounts) are stated as a percentage of a key figure such as revenue for an income statement or total assets for a balance sheet.

Company fundamental factors   Factors related to the company's internal performance, such as factors relating to earnings growth, earnings variability, earnings momentum, and financial leverage.

Company share-related factors   Valuation measures and other factors related to share price or the trading characteristics of the shares, such as earnings yield, dividend yield, and book-to-market value.

Comparables   Assets used as benchmarks when applying the method of comparables to value an asset. Also called *comps, guideline assets,* or *guideline companies.*

Compiled financial statements   Financial statements that are not accompanied by an auditor's opinion letter.

Comprehensive income   All changes in equity other than contributions by, and distributions to, owners; income under clean surplus accounting; includes all changes in equity during a period except those resulting from investments by owners and distributions to owners; comprehensive income equals net income plus other comprehensive income.

Comps   Assets used as benchmarks when applying the method of comparables to value an asset.

Conditional convergence   The idea that convergence of per capita income is conditional on the countries having the same savings rate, population growth rate, and production function.

Conditional heteroskedasticity   Heteroskedasticity in the error variance that is correlated with the values of the independent variable(s) in the regression.

Conglomerate discount   The discount possibly applied by the market to the stock of a company operating in multiple, unrelated businesses.

Conglomerate merger   A merger involving companies that are in unrelated businesses.

Consolidation   The combining of the results of operations of subsidiaries with the parent company to present financial statements as if they were a single economic unit. The assets, liabilities, revenues and expenses of the subsidiaries are combined with those of the parent company, eliminating intercompany transactions.

Constant dividend payout ratio policy   A policy in which a constant percentage of net income is paid out in dividends.

Constant maturity swap   A swap in which the floating rate is the rate on a security known as a constant maturity treasury or CMT security.

Constant maturity treasury (CMT)   A hypothetical US Treasury note with a constant maturity. A CMT exists for various years in the range of 2 to 10.

Constant returns to scale   The condition that if all inputs into the production process are increased by a given percentage, then output rises by that same percentage.

Contango   A situation in a futures market where the current futures price is greater than the current spot price for the underlying asset.

Contingent consideration   Potential future payments to the seller that are contingent on the achievement of certain agreed on occurrences.

Continuing earnings   Earnings excluding nonrecurring components. Also referred to as *core earnings, persistent earnings,* or *underlying earnings.*

Continuing residual income   Residual income after the forecast horizon.

Continuing value   The analyst's estimate of a stock's value at a particular point in the future.

Continuous time   Time thought of as advancing in extremely small increments.

Control premium   An increment or premium to value associated with a controlling ownership interest in a company.

Convenience yield   The nonmonetary return offered by an asset when the asset is in short supply, often associated with assets with seasonal production processes.

Conventional cash flow   A conventional cash flow pattern is one with an initial outflow followed by a series of inflows.

Conversion factor   An adjustment used to facilitate delivery on bond futures contracts in which any of a number of bonds with different characteristics are eligible for delivery.

Conversion period   For a convertible bond, the period during which bondholders have the right to convert their bonds into shares.

Conversion price   For a convertible bond, the price per share at which the bond can be converted into shares.

Conversion ratio   For a convertible bond, the number of shares of common stock that a bondholder receives from converting the bond into shares.

Conversion value   For a convertible bond, the value of the bond if it is converted at the market price of the shares. Also called *parity value.*

Convertible bond   Bond with an embedded conversion option that gives the bondholder the right to convert their bonds into the issuer's common stock during a pre-determined period at a pre-determined price.

Core earnings   Earnings excluding nonrecurring components. Also referred to as *continuing earnings, persistent earnings,* or *underlying earnings.*

Corporate governance   The system of principles, policies, procedures, and clearly defined responsibilities and accountabilities used by stakeholders to overcome the conflicts of interest inherent in the corporate form.

Corporate raider   A person or organization seeking to profit by acquiring a company and reselling it, or seeking to profit from the takeover attempt itself (e.g., greenmail).

Corporation   A legal entity with rights similar to those of a person. The chief officers, executives, or top managers act as agents for the firm and are legally entitled to authorize corporate activities and to enter into contracts on behalf of the business.

Correlation analysis   The analysis of the strength of the linear relationship between two data series.

Cost approach   Approach that values a private company based on the values of the underlying assets of the entity less the value of any related liabilities. In the context of real estate, this approach estimates the value of a property based on what it would cost to buy the land and construct a new property on the site that has the same utility or functionality as the property being appraised.

Cost of carry   The cost associated with holding some asset, including financing, storage, and insurance costs. Any yield received on the asset is treated as a negative carrying cost.

Cost-of-carry model   A model for pricing futures contracts in which the futures price is determined by adding the cost of carry to the spot price.

Cost of debt   The cost of debt financing to a company, such as when it issues a bond or takes out a bank loan.

Cost of equity   The required rate of return on common stock.

Covariance stationary   Describes a time series when its expected value and variance are constant and finite in all periods and when its covariance with itself for a fixed number of periods in the past or future is constant and finite in all periods.

Covered interest arbitrage   A transaction executed in the foreign exchange market in which a currency is purchased (sold) and a forward contract is sold (purchased) to lock in the exchange rate for future delivery of the currency. This transaction should earn the risk-free rate of the investor's home country.

Covered interest rate parity   Relationship among the spot exchange rate, forward exchange rate, and the interest rates in two currencies that ensures that the return on a hedged (i.e., covered) foreign risk-free investment is the same as the return on a domestic risk-free investment.

Cox–Ingersoll–Ross model   A partial equilibrium term structure model that assumes interest rates are mean reverting and interest rate volatility is directly related to the level of interest rates.

Credit correlation   The correlation of credits contained in an index CDS.

Credit curve   The credit spreads for a range of maturities of a company's debt; applies to non-government borrowers and incorporates credit risk into each rate.

Credit default swap   A derivative contract between two parties in which the buyer makes a series of cash payments to the seller and receives a promise of compensation for credit losses resulting from the default.

Credit derivative   A derivative instrument in which the underlying is a measure of the credit quality of a borrower.

Credit event   The outcome that triggers a payment from the credit protection seller to the credit protection buyer.

Credit protection buyer   One party to a credit default swap; the buyer makes a series of cash payments to the seller and receives a promise of compensation for credit losses resulting from the default.

Credit protection seller   One party to a credit default swap; the buyer makes a series of cash payments to the seller and receives a promise of compensation for credit losses resulting from the default.

Credit ratings   Ordinal rankings of the credit risk of a company, government (sovereign), quasi-government, or asset-backed security.

Credit risk   The risk that the borrower will not repay principal and interest. Also called *default risk*.

Credit scoring   Ordinal rankings of a retail borrower's credit riskiness. It is called an *ordinal ranking* because it only orders borrowers' riskiness from highest to lowest.

Credit spreads   The difference between the yields on default-free and credit risky zero-coupon bonds.

Currency option   An option that allows the holder to buy (if a call) or sell (if a put) an underlying currency at a fixed exercise rate, expressed as an exchange rate.

Current credit risk   The risk associated with the possibility that a payment currently due will not be made.

Current exchange rate   For accounting purposes, the spot exchange rate on the balance sheet date.

Current rate method   Approach to translating foreign currency financial statements for consolidation in which all assets and liabilities are translated at the current exchange rate. The current rate method is the prevalent method of translation.

Curvature   One of the three factors (the other two are level and steepness) that empirically explain most of the changes in the shape of the yield curve. A shock to the curvature factor affects mid-maturity interest rates, resulting in the term structure becoming either more or less hump-shaped.

Curve trade   Buying a CDS of one maturity and selling a CDS on the same reference entity with a different maturity.

Cyclical businesses   Businesses with high sensitivity to business- or industry-cycle influences.

Daily settlement   See *marking to market*.

Data mining   The practice of determining a model by extensive searching through a dataset for statistically significant patterns.

Day trader   A trader holding a position open somewhat longer than a scalper but closing all positions at the end of the day.

"Dead-hand" provision   A poison pill provision that allows for the redemption or cancellation of a poison pill provision only by a vote of continuing directors (generally directors who were on the target company's board prior to the takeover attempt).

Debt ratings   An objective measure of the quality and safety of a company's debt based upon an analysis of the company's ability to pay the promised cash flows, as well as an analysis of any indentures.

Decision rule   With respect to hypothesis testing, the rule according to which the null hypothesis will be rejected or not rejected; involves the comparison of the test statistic to rejection point(s).

Deep-in-the-money   Options that are far in-the-money.

Deep-out-of-the-money   Options that are far out-of-the-money.

Default intensity   Gives the probability of default over the next instant $[t, t + \Delta]$ when the economy is in state X_t.

Default probability   See *probability of default*.

Default risk   See *credit risk*.

Definition of value   A specification of how "value" is to be understood in the context of a specific valuation.

Definitive merger agreement   A contract signed by both parties to a merger that clarifies the details of the transaction, including the terms, warranties, conditions, termination details, and the rights of all parties.

Delivery   A process used in a deliverable forward contract in which the long pays the agreed-upon price to the short, which in turn delivers the underlying asset to the long.

Delivery option   The feature of a futures contract giving the short the right to make decisions about what, when, and where to deliver.

Delta   The relationship between the option price and the underlying price, which reflects the sensitivity of the price of the option to changes in the price of the underlying.

Dependent variable   The variable whose variation about its mean is to be explained by the regression; the left-hand-side variable in a regression equation.

Depository Trust and Clearinghouse Corporation   A US-headquartered entity providing post-trade clearing, settlement, and information services.

Depreciated replacement cost   In the context of real estate, the replacement cost of a building adjusted different types of depreciation.

Derivative   A financial instrument whose value depends on the value of some underlying asset or factor (e.g., a stock price, an interest rate, or exchange rate).

Descriptive statistics   The study of how data can be summarized effectively.

Diff swaps   A swap in which the payments are based on the difference between interest rates in two countries but payments are made in only a single currency.

Diluted earnings per share   (diluted EPS) Net income, minus preferred dividends, divided by the weighted average number of common shares outstanding considering all dilutive securities (e.g., convertible debt and options); the EPS that would result if all dilutive securities were converted into common shares.

Dilution   A reduction in proportional ownership interest as a result of the issuance of new shares.

Diminishing marginal productivity   When each additional unit of an input, keeping the other inputs unchanged, increases output by a smaller increment.

Direct capitalization method   In the context of real estate, this method estimates the value of an income-producing property based on the level and quality of its net operating income.

Direct financing leases   A type of finance lease, from a lessor perspective, where the present value of the lease payments (lease receivable) equals the carrying value of the leased asset. The revenues earned by the lessor are financing in nature.

Discount   To reduce the value of a future payment in allowance for how far away it is in time; to calculate the present value of some future amount. Also, the amount by which an instrument is priced below its face value.

Discount factor   The present value or price of a risk-free single-unit payment when discounted using the appropriate spot rate.

Discount for lack of control   An amount or percentage deducted from the pro rata share of 100 percent of the value of an equity interest in a business to reflect the absence of some or all of the powers of control.

Discount for lack of marketability   An amount of percentage deducted from the value of an ownership interest to reflect the relative absence of marketability.

Discount function   Discount factors for the range of all possible maturities. The spot curve can be derived from the discount function and vice versa.

Discount interest   A procedure for determining the interest on a loan or bond in which the interest is deducted from the face value in advance.

Discount rate   Any rate used in finding the present value of a future cash flow.

Discounted abnormal earnings model   A model of stock valuation that views intrinsic value of stock as the sum of book value per share plus the present value of the stock's expected future residual income per share.

Discounted cash flow (DCF) analysis   In the context of merger analysis, it is an estimate of a target company's value found by discounting the company's expected future free cash flows to the present.

Discounted cash flow method   Income approach that values an asset based on estimates of future cash flows discounted to present value by using a discount rate reflective of the risks associated with the cash flows. In the context of real estate, this method estimates the value of an income-producing property based by discounting future projected cash flows.

Discounted cash flow model   A model of intrinsic value that views the value of an asset as the present value of the asset's expected future cash flows.

Discrete time   Time thought of as advancing in distinct finite increments.

Discriminant analysis   A multivariate classification technique used to discriminate between groups, such as companies that either will or will not become bankrupt during some time frame.

Diversified REITs   REITs that own and operate in more than one type of property; they are more common in Europe and Asia than in the United States.

Divestiture   The sale, liquidation, or spin-off of a division or subsidiary.

Dividend coverage ratio   The ratio of net income to dividends.

Dividend discount model   (DDM) A present value model of stock value that views the intrinsic value of a stock as present value of the stock's expected future dividends.

Dividend displacement of earnings   The concept that dividends paid now displace earnings in all future periods.

Dividend imputation tax system   A taxation system which effectively assures that corporate profits distributed as dividends are taxed just once, at the shareholder's tax rate.

Dividend payout ratio   The ratio of cash dividends paid to earnings for a period.

Dividend policy   The strategy a company follows with regard to the amount and timing of dividend payments.

Dividend rate   the annualized amount of the most recent dividend.

Dominance   An arbitrage opportunity when a financial asset with a risk-free payoff in the future must have a positive price today.

Double taxation system   Corporate earnings are taxed twice when paid out as dividends. First, corporate earnings are taxed regardless of whether they will be distributed as dividends or retained at the G-13 corporate level, and second, dividends are taxed again at the individual shareholder level.

DOWNREIT   A variation of the UPREIT structure under which the REIT owns more than one partnership and may own properties at both the REIT level and the partnership level.

Downstream   A transaction between two related companies, an investor company (or a parent company) and an associate company (or a subsidiary) such that the investor company records a profit on its income statement. An example is a sale of inventory by the investor company to the associate or by a parent to a subsidiary company.

Due diligence   Investigation and analysis in support of a recommendation; the failure to exercise due diligence may sometimes result in liability according to various securities laws.

Dummy variable   A type of qualitative variable that takes on a value of 1 if a particular condition is true and 0 if that condition is false.

Duration   A measure of an option-free bond's average maturity. Specifically, the weighted average maturity of all future cash flows paid by a security, in which the weights are the present value of these cash flows as a fraction of the bond's price. A measure of a bond's price sensitivity to interest rate movements.

Dutch disease   A situation in which currency appreciation driven by strong export demand for resources makes other segments of the economy (particularly manufacturing) globally uncompetitive.

Dynamic hedging A strategy in which a position is hedged by making frequent adjustments to the quantity of the instrument used for hedging in relation to the instrument being hedged.

Earnings surprise The difference between reported EPS and expected EPS. Also referred to as *unexpected earnings*.

Earnings yield EPS divided by price; the reciprocal of the P/E ratio.

Economic growth The expansion of production possibilities that results from capital accumulation and technological change.

Economic obsolescence In the context of real estate, a reduction in value due to current economic conditions.

Economic profit See *residual income*.

Economic sectors Large industry groupings.

Economic value added (EVA®) A commercial implementation of the residual income concept; the computation of EVA® is the net operating profit after taxes minus the cost of capital, where these inputs are adjusted for a number of items.

Economies of scale A situation in which average costs per unit of good or service produced fall as volume rises. In reference to mergers, the savings achieved through the consolidation of operations and elimination of duplicate resources.

Edwards–Bell–Ohlson model A model of stock valuation that views intrinsic value of stock as the sum of book value per share plus the present value of the stock's expected future residual income per share.

Effective convexity Sensitivity of duration to changes in interest rates.

Effective duration Sensitivity of the bond's price to a 100 bps parallel shift of the benchmark yield curve, assuming no change in the bond's credit spread.

Embedded options Contingency provisions found in a bond's indenture or offering circular representing rights that enable their holders to take advantage of interest rate movements. They can be exercised by the issuer, by the bondholder, or automatically depending on the course of interest rates.

Enterprise value (EV) Total company value (the market value of debt, common equity, and preferred equity) minus the value of cash and investments.

Enterprise value multiple A valuation multiple that relates the total market value of all sources of a company's capital (net of cash) to a measure of fundamental value for the entire company (such as a pre-interest earnings measure).

Entry price The price paid to acquire an asset.

Equilibrium The condition in which supply equals demand.

Equity carve-out A form of restructuring that involves the creation of a new legal entity and the sale of equity in it to outsiders.

Equity charge The estimated cost of equity capital in money terms.

Equity forward A contract calling for the purchase of an individual stock, a stock portfolio, or a stock index at a later date at an agreed-upon price.

Equity options Options on individual stocks; also known as stock options.

Equity REIT A REIT that owns, operates, and/or selectively develops income-producing real estate.

Error autocorrelation The autocorrelation of the error term.

Error term The portion of the dependent variable that is not explained by the independent variable(s) in the regression.

Estimated parameters With reference to a regression analysis, the estimated values of the population intercept and population slope coefficient(s) in a regression.

Eurodollar A dollar deposited outside the United States.

European option An option that can only be exercised on its expiration date.

Ex ante version of PPP Hypothesis that expected changes in the spot exchange rate are equal to expected differences in national inflation rates. An extension of relative purchasing power parity to expected future changes in the exchange rate.

Ex-dividend Trading ex-dividend refers to shares that no longer carry the right to the next dividend payment.

Ex-dividend date The first date that a share trades without (i.e., "ex") the dividend.

Ex-dividend price The price at which a share first trades without (i.e., "ex") the right to receive an upcoming dividend.

Excess earnings method Income approach that estimates the value of all intangible assets of the business by capitalizing future earnings in excess of the estimated return requirements associated with working capital and fixed assets.

Exchange for physicals (EFP) A permissible delivery procedure used by futures market participants, in which the long and short arrange a delivery procedure other than the normal procedures stipulated by the futures exchange.

Exchange ratio The number of shares that target stockholders are to receive in exchange for each of their shares in the target company.

Exercise The process of using an option to buy or sell the underlying. Also called *exercising the option*.

Exercise price The fixed price at which an option holder can buy or sell the underlying. Also called *strike price*, *striking price*, or *strike*.

Exercise rate The fixed rate at which the holder of an interest rate option can buy or sell the underlying. Also called *strike rate*.

Exercise value The value of an asset given a hypothetically complete understanding of the asset's investment characteristics; the value obtained if an option is exercised based on current conditions. Also called *intrinsic value*.

Exercising the option The process of using an option to buy or sell the underlying. Also called *exercise*.

Exit price The price received to sell an asset or paid to transfer a liability.

Expanded CAPM An adaptation of the CAPM that adds to the CAPM a premium for small size and company-specific risk.

Expected holding-period return The expected total return on an asset over a stated holding period; for stocks, the sum of the expected dividend yield and the expected price appreciation over the holding period.

Expected loss The probability of default multiplied by the loss given default; the full amount owed minus the expected recovery.

Expiration date The date on which a derivative contract expires.

Exposure to foreign exchange risk The risk of a change in value of an asset or liability denominated in a foreign currency due to a change in exchange rates.

Extendible bond Bond with an embedded option that gives the bondholder the right to keep the bond for a number of years after maturity, possibly with a different coupon.

External growth   Company growth in output or sales that is achieved by buying the necessary resources externally (i.e., achieved through mergers and acquisitions).

External sustainability approach   An approach to assessing the equilibrium exchange rate that focuses on exchange rate adjustments required to ensure that a country's net foreign-asset/GDP ratio or net foreign-liability/GDP ratio stabilizes at a sustainable level.

Factor   A common or underlying element with which several variables are correlated.

Factor betas   An asset's sensitivity to a particular factor; a measure of the response of return to each unit of increase in a factor, holding all other factors constant.

Factor portfolio   See *pure factor portfolio.*

Factor price   The expected return in excess of the risk-free rate for a portfolio with a sensitivity of 1 to one factor and a sensitivity of 0 to all other factors.

Factor risk premium   The expected return in excess of the risk-free rate for a portfolio with a sensitivity of 1 to one factor and a sensitivity of 0 to all other factors. Also called *factor price.*

Factor sensitivity   See *factor betas.*

Failure to pay   When a borrower does not make a scheduled payment of principal or interest on any outstanding obligations after a grace period.

Fair market value   The market price of an asset or liability that trades regularly.

Fair value   The amount at which an asset (or liability) could be bought (or incurred) or sold (or settled) in a current transaction between willing parties, that is, other than in a forced or liquidation sale; as defined in IFRS and US GAAP, the price that would be received to sell an asset or paid to transfer a liability in an orderly transaction between market participants at the measurement date.

Fiduciary call   A combination of a European call and a risk-free bond that matures on the option expiration day and has a face value equal to the exercise price of the call.

Finance lease   Essentially, the purchase of some asset by the buyer (lessee) that is directly financed by the seller (lessor). Also called *capital lease.*

Financial contagion   A situation where financial shocks spread from their place of origin to other locales; in essence, a faltering economy infects other, healthier economies.

Financial distress   Heightened uncertainty regarding a company's ability to meet its various obligations because of lower or negative earnings.

Financial futures   Futures contracts in which the underlying is a stock, bond, or currency.

Financial risk   The risk that environmental, social, or governance risk factors will result in significant costs or other losses to a company and its shareholders; the risk arising from a company's obligation to meet required payments under its financing agreements.

Financial transaction   A purchase involving a buyer having essentially no material synergies with the target (e.g., the purchase of a private company by a company in an unrelated industry or by a private equity firm would typically be a financial transaction).

First-differencing   A transformation that subtracts the value of the time series in period $t - 1$ from its value in period t.

First-in, first-out (FIFO)   The first in, first out, method of accounting for inventory, which matches sales against the costs of items of inventory in the order in which they were placed in inventory.

First-order serial correlation   Correlation between adjacent observations in a time series.

Fitted parameters   With reference to a regression analysis, the estimated values of the population intercept and population slope coefficient(s) in a regression.

Fixed-rate perpetual preferred stock   Nonconvertible, noncallable preferred stock with a specified dividend rate that has a claim on earnings senior to the claim of common stock, and no maturity date.

Flip-in pill   A poison pill takeover defense that dilutes an acquirer's ownership in a target by giving other existing target company shareholders the right to buy additional target company shares at a discount.

Flip-over pill   A poison pill takeover defense that gives target company shareholders the right to purchase shares of the acquirer at a significant discount to the market price, which has the effect of causing dilution to all existing acquiring company shareholders.

Floor   A combination of interest rate put options designed to hedge a lender against lower rates on a floating-rate loan.

Floor traders   Market makers that buy and sell by quoting a bid and an ask price. They are the primary providers of liquidity to the market.

Floored floater   Floating-rate bond with a floor provision that prevents the coupon rate from decreasing below a specified minimum rate. It protects the investor against declining interest rates.

Floored swap   A swap in which the floating payments have a lower limit.

Floorlet   Each component put option in a floor.

Flotation cost   Fees charged to companies by investment bankers and other costs associated with raising new capital.

Forced conversion   For a convertible bond, when the issuer calls the bond and forces bondholders to convert their bonds into shares, which typically happens when the underlying share price increases above the conversion price.

Foreign currency transactions   Transactions that are denominated in a currency other than a company's functional currency.

Forward contract   An agreement between two parties in which one party, the buyer, agrees to buy from the other party, the seller, an underlying asset at a later date for a price established at the start of the contract.

Forward curve   The term structure of forward rates for loans made on a specific initiation date.

Forward dividend yield   A dividend yield based on the anticipated dividend during the next 12 months.

Forward integration   A merger involving the purchase of a target that is farther along the value or production chain; for example, to acquire a distributor.

Forward P/E   A P/E calculated on the basis of a forecast of EPS; a stock's current price divided by next year's expected earnings.

Forward price or forward rate   The fixed price or rate at which the transaction scheduled to occur at the expiration of a forward contract will take place. This price is agreed on at the initiation date of the contract.

Forward pricing model   The model that describes the valuation of forward contracts.

Forward rate   An interest rate that is determined today for a loan that will be initiated in a future time period.

Forward rate agreement (FRA) A forward contract calling for one party to make a fixed interest payment and the other to make an interest payment at a rate to be determined at the contract expiration.

Forward rate model The forward pricing model expressed in terms of spot and forward interest rates.

Forward swap A forward contract to enter into a swap.

Franking credit A tax credit received by shareholders for the taxes that a corporation paid on its distributed earnings.

Free cash flow The actual cash that would be available to the company's investors after making all investments necessary to maintain the company as an ongoing enterprise (also referred to as free cash flow to the firm); the internally generated funds that can be distributed to the company's investors (e.g., shareholders and bondholders) without impairing the value of the company.

Free cash flow hypothesis The hypothesis that higher debt levels discipline managers by forcing them to make fixed debt service payments and by reducing the company's free cash flow.

Free cash flow method Income approach that values an asset based on estimates of future cash flows discounted to present value by using a discount rate reflective of the risks associated with the cash flows.

Free cash flow to equity The cash flow available to a company's common shareholders after all operating expenses, interest, and principal payments have been made, and necessary investments in working and fixed capital have been made.

Free cash flow to equity model A model of stock valuation that views a stock's intrinsic value as the present value of expected future free cash flows to equity.

Free cash flow to the firm The cash flow available to the company's suppliers of capital after all operating expenses (including taxes) have been paid and necessary investments in working and fixed capital have been made.

Free cash flow to the firm model A model of stock valuation that views the value of a firm as the present value of expected future free cash flows to the firm.

Friendly transaction A potential business combination that is endorsed by the managers of both companies.

Functional currency The currency of the primary economic environment in which an entity operates.

Functional obsolescence In the context of real estate, a reduction in value due to a design that differs from that of a new building constructed for the intended use of the property.

Fundamental factor models A multifactor model in which the factors are attributes of stocks or companies that are important in explaining cross-sectional differences in stock prices.

Fundamentals Economic characteristics of a business such as profitability, financial strength, and risk.

Funds available for distribution Funds from operations (FFO) adjusted to remove any non-cash rent reported under straight-line rent accounting and to subtract maintenance-type capital expenditures and leasing costs, including leasing agents' commissions and tenants' improvement allowances.

Funds from operations Accounting net earnings excluding (1) depreciation charges on real estate, (2) deferred tax charges, and (3) gains or losses from sales of property and debt restructuring.

Futures commission merchants (FCMs) Individuals or companies that execute futures transactions for other parties off the exchange.

Futures contract A variation of a forward contract that has essentially the same basic definition but with some additional features, such as a clearinghouse guarantee against credit losses, a daily settlement of gains and losses, and an organized electronic or floor trading facility.

FX carry trade An investment strategy that involves taking on long positions in high-yield currencies and short positions in low-yield currencies.

Gamma A numerical measure of how sensitive an option's delta is to a change in the underlying.

Generalized least squares A regression estimation technique that addresses heteroskedasticity of the error term.

Going-concern assumption The assumption that the business will maintain its business activities into the foreseeable future.

Going-concern value A business's value under a going-concern assumption.

Goodwill An intangible asset that represents the excess of the purchase price of an acquired company over the value of the net identifiable assets acquired.

Gross domestic product A money measure of the goods and services produced within a country's borders over a stated time period.

Gross lease A lease under which the tenant pays a gross rent to the landlord who is responsible for all operating costs, utilities, maintenance expenses, and real estate taxes relating to the property.

Growth accounting equation The production function written in the form of growth rates. For the basic Cobb–Douglas production function, it states that the growth rate of output equals the rate of technological change plus α times the growth rate of capital plus $(1 - \alpha)$ times the growth rate of labor.

Growth capital expenditures Capital expenditures needed for expansion.

Growth option The ability to make additional investments in a project at some future time if the financial results are strong. Also called *expansion option*.

Guideline assets Assets used as benchmarks when applying the method of comparables to value an asset.

Guideline companies Assets used as benchmarks when applying the method of comparables to value an asset.

Guideline public companies Public-company comparables for the company being valued.

Guideline public company method A variation of the market approach; establishes a value estimate based on the observed multiples from trading activity in the shares of public companies viewed as reasonably comparable to the subject private company.

Guideline transactions method A variation of the market approach; establishes a value estimate based on pricing multiples derived from the acquisition of control of entire public or private companies that were acquired.

Harmonic mean A type of weighted mean computed by averaging the reciprocals of the observations, then taking the reciprocal of that average.

Hazard rate The probability that an event will occur, given that it has not already occurred.

Hazard rate estimation A technique for estimating the probability of a binary event, such as default/no default, mortality/no mortality, and prepay/no prepay.

Health care REITs   REITs that invest in skilled nursing facilities (nursing homes), assisted living and independent residential facilities for retired persons, hospitals, medical office buildings, or rehabilitation centers.

Hedge ratio   The relationship of the quantity of an asset being hedged to the quantity of the derivative used for hedging.

Hedging   A general strategy usually thought of as reducing, if not eliminating, risk.

Held for trading investments   Debt or equity securities acquired with the intent to sell them in the near term.

Held-to-maturity investments   Debt (fixed-income) securities that a company intends to hold to maturity; these are presented at their original cost, updated for any amortization of discounts or premiums.

Herfindahl–Hirschman Index (HHI)   A measure of market concentration that is calculated by summing the squared market shares for competing companies in an industry; high HHI readings or mergers that would result in large HHI increases are more likely to result in regulatory challenges.

Heteroskedastic   With reference to the error term of regression, having a variance that differs across observations.

Heteroskedasticity   The property of having a nonconstant variance; refers to an error term with the property that its variance differs across observations.

Heteroskedasticity-consistent standard errors   Standard errors of the estimated parameters of a regression that correct for the presence of heteroskedasticity in the regression's error term.

Historical exchange rates   For accounting purposes, the exchange rates that existed when the assets and liabilities were initially recorded.

Ho–Lee model   The first arbitrage-free term structure model. The model is calibrated to market data and uses a binomial lattice approach to generate a distribution of possible future interest rates.

Holding period return   The return that an investor earns during a specified holding period; a synonym for total return.

Homoskedasticity   The property of having a constant variance; refers to an error term that is constant across observations.

Horizontal merger   A merger involving companies in the same line of business, usually as competitors.

Hostile transaction   An attempt to acquire a company against the wishes of the target's managers.

Hotel REITs   REITs that own hotel properties but, similar to health care REITs, in many countries they must refrain from operating their properties themselves to maintain their tax-advantaged REIT status.

Human capital   The accumulated knowledge and skill that workers acquire from education, training, or life experience.

Hybrid approach   With respect to forecasting, an approach that combines elements of both top-down and bottom-up analysis.

Hybrid REITs   REITs that own and operate income-producing real estate and invest in mortgages as well; REITs that have positions in both real estate assets and real estate debt.

I-spreads   Shortened form of "interpolated spreads" and a reference to a linearly interpolated yield.

Illiquidity discount   A reduction or discount to value that reflects the lack of depth of trading or liquidity in that asset's market.

Impairment   Diminishment in value as a result of carrying (book) value exceeding fair value and/or recoverable value.

Impairment of capital rule   A legal restriction that dividends cannot exceed retained earnings.

Implied repo rate   The rate of return from a cash-and-carry transaction implied by the futures price relative to the spot price.

Implied volatility   The volatility that option traders use to price an option, implied by the price of the option and a particular option-pricing model.

In-sample forecast errors   The residuals from a fitted time-series model within the sample period used to fit the model.

In-the-money   Options that, if exercised, would result in the value received being worth more than the payment required to exercise.

Income approach   Valuation approach that values an asset as the present discounted value of the income expected from it. In the context of real estate, this approach estimates the value of a property based on an expected rate of return; the estimated value is the present value of the expected future income from the property, including proceeds from resale at the end of a typical investment holding period.

Incremental cash flow   The cash flow that is realized because of a decision; the changes or increments to cash flows resulting from a decision or action.

Indenture   A written contract between a lender and borrower that specifies the terms of the loan, such as interest rate, interest payment schedule, maturity, etc.

Independent projects   Independent projects are projects whose cash flows are independent of each other.

Independent regulators   Regulators recognized and granted authority by a government body or agency. They are not government agencies per se and typically do not rely on government funding.

Independent variable   A variable used to explain the dependent variable in a regression; a right-hand-side variable in a regression equation.

Index amortizing swap   An interest rate swap in which the notional principal is indexed to the level of interest rates and declines with the level of interest rates according to a predefined schedule. This type of swap is frequently used to hedge securities that are prepaid as interest rates decline, such as mortgage-backed securities.

Index CDS   A type of credit default swap that involves a combination of borrowers.

Indexing   An investment strategy in which an investor constructs a portfolio to mirror the performance of a specified index.

Industrial REITs   REITs that hold portfolios of single-tenant or multi-tenant industrial properties that are used as warehouses, distribution centers, light manufacturing facilities, and small office or "flex" space.

Industry structure   An industry's underlying economic and technical characteristics.

Information ratio   (IR) Mean active return divided by active risk; or alpha divided by the standard deviation of diversifiable risk.

Informational frictions   Forces that restrict availability, quality, and/or flow of information and its use.

Initial margin requirement   The margin requirement on the first day of a transaction as well as on any day in which additional margin funds must be deposited.

Initial public offering   (IPO) The initial issuance of common stock registered for public trading by a formerly private corporation.

Inter-temporal rate of substitution the ratio of the marginal utility of consumption *s* periods in the future (the numerator) to the marginal utility of consumption today (the denominator).

Interest rate call An option in which the holder has the right to make a known interest payment and receive an unknown interest payment.

Interest rate cap A series of call options on an interest rate, with each option expiring at the date on which the floating loan rate will be reset, and with each option having the same exercise rate. A cap in general can have an underlying other than an interest rate.

Interest rate collar A combination of a long cap and a short floor, or a short cap and a long floor. A collar in general can have an underlying other than an interest rate.

Interest rate floor A series of put options on an interest rate, with each option expiring at the date on which the floating loan rate will be reset, and with each option having the same exercise rate. A floor in general can have an underlying other than the interest rate. Also called *floor*.

Interest rate option An option in which the underlying is an interest rate.

Interest rate parity A formula that expresses the equivalence or parity of spot and forward rates, after adjusting for differences in the interest rates.

Interest rate put An option in which the holder has the right to make an unknown interest payment and receive a known interest payment.

Interest rate risk Risk that interest rates will change such that the return earned is not commensurate with returns on comparable instruments in the marketplace.

Internal rate of return (IRR) Rate of return that discounts future cash flows from an investment to the exact amount of the investment; the discount rate that makes the present value of an investment's costs (outflows) equal to the present value of the investment's benefits (inflows).

Internal ratings Credit ratings developed internally and used by financial institutions or other entities to manage risk.

International Fisher effect Proposition that nominal interest rate differentials across currencies are determined by expected inflation differentials.

Intrinsic value The value of an asset given a hypothetically complete understanding of the asset's investment characteristics; the value obtained if an option is exercised based on current conditions. The difference between the spot exchange rate and the strike price of a currency.

Inverse price ratio The reciprocal of a price multiple, e.g., in the case of a P/E ratio, the "earnings yield" E/P (where P is share price and E is earnings per share).

Investment objectives Desired investment outcomes; includes risk objectives and return objectives.

Investment strategy An approach to investment analysis and security selection.

Investment value The value to a specific buyer, taking account of potential synergies based on the investor's requirements and expectations.

ISDA Master Agreement A standard or "master" agreement published by the International Swaps and Derivatives Association. The master agreement establishes the terms for each party involved in the transaction.

Judicial law Interpretations of courts.

Justified (fundamental) P/E The price-to-earnings ratio that is fair, warranted, or justified on the basis of forecasted fundamentals.

Justified price multiple The estimated fair value of the price multiple, usually based on forecasted fundamentals or comparables.

Key rate durations Sensitivity of a bond's price to changes in specific maturities on the benchmark yield curve. Also called *partial durations*.

kth order autocorrelation The correlation between observations in a time series separated by *k* periods.

Labor force Everyone of working age (ages 16 to 64) that either is employed or is available for work but not working.

Labor force participation rate The percentage of the working age population that is in the labor force.

Labor productivity The quantity of real GDP produced by an hour of labor. More generally, output per unit of labor input.

Labor productivity growth accounting equation States that potential GDP growth equals the growth rate of the labor input plus the growth rate of labor productivity.

Lack of marketability discount An extra return to investors to compensate for lack of a public market or lack of marketability.

Last-in, first-out (LIFO) The last in, first out, method of accounting for inventory, which matches sales against the costs of items of inventory in the reverse order the items were placed in inventory (i.e., inventory produced or acquired last are assumed to be sold first).

Law of one price Hypothesis that (1) identical goods should trade at the same price across countries when valued in terms of a common currency, or (2) two equivalent financial instruments or combinations of financial instruments can sell for only one price. The latter form is equivalent to the principle that no arbitrage opportunities are possible.

Leading dividend yield Forecasted dividends per share over the next year divided by current stock price.

Leading P/E A P/E calculated on the basis of a forecast of EPS; a stock's current price divided by next year's expected earnings.

Legal risk The risk that failures by company managers to effectively manage a company's environmental, social, and governance risk exposures will lead to lawsuits and other judicial remedies, resulting in potentially catastrophic losses for the company; the risk that the legal system will not enforce a contract in case of dispute or fraud.

Legislative and regulatory risk The risk that governmental laws and regulations directly or indirectly affecting a company's operations will change with potentially severe adverse effects on the company's continued profitability and even its long-term sustainability.

Lessee The party obtaining the use of an asset through a lease.

Lessor The owner of an asset that grants the right to use the asset to another party.

Level One of the three factors (the other two are steepness and curvature) that empirically explain most of the changes in the shape of the yield curve. A shock to the level factor changes the yield for all maturities by an almost identical amount.

Leveraged buyout (LBO) A transaction whereby the target company management team converts the target to a privately held company by using heavy borrowing to finance the purchase of the target company's outstanding shares.

Leveraged recapitalization A post-offer takeover defense mechanism that involves the assumption of a large amount of debt that is then used to finance share repurchases;

the effect is to dramatically change the company's capital structure while attempting to deliver a value to target shareholders in excess of a hostile bid.

Libor–OIS spread The difference between Libor and the over-night indexed swap (OIS) rate.

Limit down A limit move in the futures market in which the price at which a transaction would be made is at or below the lower limit.

Limit move A condition in the futures markets in which the price at which a transaction would be made is at or beyond the price limits.

Limit up A limit move in the futures market in which the price at which a transaction would be made is at or above the upper limit.

Linear association A straight-line relationship, as opposed to a relationship that cannot be graphed as a straight line.

Linear regression Regression that models the straight-line relationship between the dependent and independent variable(s).

Linear trend A trend in which the dependent variable changes at a constant rate with time.

Liquidation To sell the assets of a company, division, or subsidiary piecemeal, typically because of bankruptcy; the form of bankruptcy that allows for the orderly satisfaction of creditors' claims after which the company ceases to exist.

Liquidation value The value of a company if the company were dissolved and its assets sold individually.

Liquidity preference theory A term structure theory that asserts liquidity premiums exist to compensate investors for the added interest rate risk they face when lending long term.

Liquidity premium The premium or incrementally higher yield that investors demand for lending long term.

Liquidity risk The risk that a financial instrument cannot be purchased or sold without a significant concession in price due to the size of the market.

Local currency The currency of the country where a company is located.

Local expectations theory A term structure theory that contends the return for all bonds over short time periods is the risk-free rate.

Locals Market makers that buy and sell by quoting a bid and an ask price. They are the primary providers of liquidity to the market.

Locational obsolescence In the context of real estate, a reduction in value due to decreased desirability of the location of the building.

Locked limit A condition in the futures markets in which a transaction cannot take place because the price would be beyond the limits.

Lockout period Period during which a bond's issuer cannot call the bond.

Log-linear model With reference to time-series models, a model in which the growth rate of the time series as a function of time is constant.

Log-log regression model A regression that expresses the dependent and independent variables as natural logarithms.

Logit model A qualitative-dependent-variable multiple regression model based on the logistic probability distribution.

London interbank offered rate (Libor) Collective name for multiple rates at which a select set of banks believe they could borrow unsecured funds from other banks in the London interbank market for different currencies and different borrowing periods ranging from overnight to one year.

Long The buyer of a derivative contract. Also refers to the position of owning a derivative.

Long/short trade A long position in one CDS and a short position in another.

Long-term equity anticipatory securities (LEAPS) Options originally created with expirations of several years.

Look-ahead bias A bias caused by using information that was not available on the test date.

Loss given default The amount that will be lost if a default occurs.

Lower bound The lowest possible value of an option.

Macroeconomic balance approach An approach to assessing the equilibrium exchange rate that focuses on exchange rate adjustments needed to close the gap between the medium-term expectation for a country's current account balance and that country's normal (or sustainable) current account balance.

Macroeconomic factor model A multifactor model in which the factors are surprises in macroeconomic variables that significantly explain equity returns.

Macroeconomic factors Factors related to the economy, such as the inflation rate, industrial production, or economic sector membership.

Maintenance capital expenditures Capital expenditures needed to maintain operations at the current level.

Maintenance margin requirement The margin requirement on any day other than the first day of a transaction.

Managerialism theories Theories that posit that corporate executives are motivated to engage in mergers to maximize the size of their company rather than shareholder value.

Margin The amount of money that a trader deposits in a margin account. The term is derived from the stock market practice in which an investor borrows a portion of the money required to purchase a certain amount of stock. In futures markets, there is no borrowing so the margin is more of a down payment or performance bond.

Marginal investor An investor in a given share who is very likely to be part of the next trade in the share and who is therefore important in setting price.

Mark-to-market The revaluation of a financial asset or liability to its current market value or fair value.

Market approach Valuation approach that values an asset based on pricing multiples from sales of assets viewed as similar to the subject asset.

Market conversion premium per share For a convertible bond, the difference between the market conversion price and the underlying share price, which allows investors to identify the premium or discount payable when buying a convertible bond rather than the underlying common stock.

Market conversion premium ratio For a convertible bond, the market conversion premium per share expressed as a percentage of the current market price of the shares.

Market efficiency A finance perspective on capital markets that deals with the relationship of price to intrinsic value. The **traditional efficient markets formulation** asserts that an asset's price is the best available estimate of its intrinsic value. The **rational efficient markets formulation** asserts that investors should expect to be rewarded for the costs of information gathering and analysis by higher gross returns.

Market timing   Asset allocation in which the investment in the market is increased if one forecasts that the market will outperform T-bills.

Market value   The estimated amount for which a property should exchange on the date of valuation between a willing buyer and a willing seller in an arm's-length transaction after proper marketing wherein the parties had each acted knowledgeably, prudently, and without compulsion.

Market value of invested capital   The market value of debt and equity.

Marking to market   A procedure used primarily in futures markets in which the parties to a contract settle the amount owed daily. Also known as the *daily settlement*.

Mature growth rate   The earnings growth rate in a company's mature phase; an earnings growth rate that can be sustained long term.

Mean reversion   The tendency of a time series to fall when its level is above its mean and rise when its level is below its mean; a mean-reverting time series tends to return to its long-term mean.

Merger   The absorption of one company by another; two companies become one entity and one or both of the pre-merger companies ceases to exist as a separate entity.

Method based on forecasted fundamentals   An approach to using price multiples that relates a price multiple to forecasts of fundamentals through a discounted cash flow model.

Method of comparables   An approach to valuation that involves using a price multiple to evaluate whether an asset is relatively fairly valued, relatively undervalued, or relatively overvalued when compared to a benchmark value of the multiple.

Minority Interest   The proportion of the ownership of a subsidiary not held by the parent (controlling) company.

Mispricing   Any departure of the market price of an asset from the asset's estimated intrinsic value.

Mixed offering   A merger or acquisition that is to be paid for with cash, securities, or some combination of the two.

Model specification   With reference to regression, the set of variables included in the regression and the regression equation's functional form.

Molodovsky effect   The observation that P/Es tend to be high on depressed EPS at the bottom of a business cycle, and tend to be low on unusually high EPS at the top of a business cycle.

Momentum indicators   Valuation indicators that relate either price or a fundamental (such as earnings) to the time series of their own past values (or in some cases to their expected value).

Monetary assets and liabilities   Assets and liabilities with value equal to the amount of currency contracted for, a fixed amount of currency. Examples are cash, accounts receivable, accounts payable, bonds payable, and mortgages payable. Inventory is not a monetary asset. Most liabilities are monetary.

Monetary/non-monetary method   Approach to translating foreign currency financial statements for consolidation in which monetary assets and liabilities are translated at the current exchange rate. Non-monetary assets and liabilities are translated at historical exchange rates (the exchange rates that existed when the assets and liabilities were acquired).

Monetizing   The conversion of the value of a financial transaction into currency.

Moneyness   The relationship between the price of the underlying and an option's exercise price.

Monitoring costs   Costs borne by owners to monitor the management of the company (e.g., board of director expenses).

Mortgage-backed securities   Asset-backed securitized debt obligations that represent rights to receive cash flows from portfolios of mortgage loans.

Mortgage REITs   REITs that invest the bulk of their assets in interest-bearing mortgages, mortgage securities, or short-term loans secured by real estate.

Mortgages   Loans with real estate serving as collateral for the loans.

Multi-family/residential REITs   REITs that invest in and manage rental apartments for lease to individual tenants, typically using one-year leases.

Multicollinearity   A regression assumption violation that occurs when two or more independent variables (or combinations of independent variables) are highly but not perfectly correlated with each other.

Multiple linear regression   Linear regression involving two or more independent variables.

Multiple linear regression model   A linear regression model with two or more independent variables.

Mutually exclusive projects   Mutually exclusive projects compete directly with each other. For example, if Projects A and B are mutually exclusive, you can choose A or B, but you cannot choose both.

n-Period moving average   The average of the current and immediately prior $n - 1$ values of a time series.

Naked credit default swap   A position where the owner of the CDS does not have a position in the underlying credit.

Negative serial correlation   Serial correlation in which a positive error for one observation increases the chance of a negative error for another observation, and vice versa.

Net asset balance sheet exposure   When assets translated at the current exchange rate are greater in amount than liabilities translated at the current exchange rate. Assets exposed to translation gains or losses exceed the exposed liabilities.

Net asset value   The difference between assets and liabilities, all taken at current market values instead of accounting book values.

Net asset value per share   Net asset value divided by the number of shares outstanding.

Net lease   A lease under which the tenant pays a net rent to the landlord as well as an additional amount based on the tenant's pro rata share of the operating costs, utilities, maintenance expenses, and real estate taxes relating to the property.

Net liability balance sheet exposure   When liabilities translated at the current exchange rate are greater assets translated at the current exchange rate. Liabilities exposed to translation gains or losses exceed the exposed assets.

Net operating income   Gross rental revenue minus operating costs, but before deducting depreciation, corporate overhead, and interest expense. In the context of real estate, a measure of the income from the property after deducting operating expenses for such items as property taxes, insurance, maintenance, utilities, repairs, and insurance but before deducting any costs associated with financing and before deducting federal income taxes. It is similar to earnings before interest, taxes, depreciation, and amortization (EBITDA) in a financial reporting context.

Net operating profit less adjusted taxes (NOPLAT) A company's operating profit with adjustments to normalize the effects of capital structure.

Net present value (NPV) The present value of an investment's cash inflows (benefits) minus the present value of its cash outflows (costs).

Net realisable value Estimated selling price in the ordinary course of business less the estimated costs necessary to make the sale.

Net regulatory burden The private costs of regulation less the private benefits of regulation.

Net rent A rent that consists of a stipulated rent to the landlord and a further amount based on their share of common area costs for utilities, maintenance, and property taxes.

Netting When parties agree to exchange only the net amount owed from one party to the other.

Network externalities The impact that users of a good, a service, or a technology have on other users of that product; it can be positive (e.g., a critical mass of users makes a product more useful) or negative (e.g., congestion makes the product less useful).

No-growth company A company without positive expected net present value projects.

No-growth value per share The value per share of a no-growth company, equal to the expected level amount of earnings divided by the stock's required rate of return.

Node Each value on a binomial tree from which successive moves or outcomes branch.

Non-cash rent An amount equal to the difference between the average contractual rent over a lease term (the straight-line rent) and the cash rent actually paid during a period. This figure is one of the deductions made from FFO to calculate AFFO.

Non-convergence trap A situation in which a country remains relative poor, or even falls further behind, because it fails to t implement necessary institutional reforms and/or adopt leading technologies.

Non-monetary assets and liabilities Assets and liabilities that are not monetary assets and liabilities. Non-monetary assets include inventory, fixed assets, and intangibles, and non-monetary liabilities include deferred revenue.

Non-renewable resources Finite resources that are depleted once they are consumed; oil and coal are examples.

Nonconventional cash flow In a nonconventional cash flow pattern, the initial outflow is not followed by inflows only, but the cash flows can flip from positive (inflows) to negative (outflows) again (or even change signs several times).

Nondeliverable forwards (NDFs) Cash-settled forward contracts, used predominately with respect to foreign exchange forwards.

Nonearning assets Cash and investments (specifically cash, cash equivalents, and short-term investments).

Nonlinear relation An association or relationship between variables that cannot be graphed as a straight line.

Nonstationarity With reference to a random variable, the property of having characteristics such as mean and variance that are not constant through time.

Normal backwardation The condition in futures markets in which futures prices are lower than expected spot prices.

Normal contango The condition in futures markets in which futures prices are higher than expected spot prices.

Normal EPS The EPS that a business could achieve currently under mid-cyclical conditions. Also called *normalized EPS*.

Normalized earnings The expected level of mid-cycle earnings for a company in the absence of any unusual or temporary factors that affect profitability (either positively or negatively).

Normalized EPS The EPS that a business could achieve currently under mid-cyclical conditions. Also called *normal EPS*.

Normalized P/E P/E based on normalized EPS data.

Notional amount The amount of protection being purchased in a CDS.

NTM P/E Next twelve months P/E: current market price divided by an estimated next twelve months EPS.

Off-market FRA A contract in which the initial value is intentionally set at a value other than zero and therefore requires a cash payment at the start from one party to the other.

Off-the-run A series of securities or indexes that were issued/created prior to the most recently issued/created series.

Office REITs REITs that invest in and manage multi-tenanted office properties in central business districts of cities and suburban markets.

Offsetting A transaction in exchange-listed derivative markets in which a party re-enters the market to close out a position.

On-the-run The most recently issued/created series of securities or indexes.

One-sided durations Effective durations when interest rates go up or down, which are better at capturing the interest rate sensitivity of bonds with embedded options that do not react symmetrically to positive and negative changes in interest rates of the same magnitude.

Operating lease An agreement allowing the lessee to use some asset for a period of time; essentially a rental.

Operating risk The risk attributed to the operating cost structure, in particular the use of fixed costs in operations; the risk arising from the mix of fixed and variable costs; the risk that a company's operations may be severely affected by environmental, social, and governance risk factors.

Operational risk The risk of loss from failures in a company's systems and procedures, or from external events.

Opportunity cost The value that investors forgo by choosing a particular course of action; the value of something in its best alternative use.

Optimal capital structure The capital structure at which the value of the company is maximized.

Option A financial instrument that gives one party the right, but not the obligation, to buy or sell an underlying asset from or to another party at a fixed price over a specific period of time. Also referred to as contingent claims.

Option-adjusted spread (OAS) Constant spread that, when added to all the one-period forward rates on the interest rate tree, makes the arbitrage-free value of the bond equal to its market price.

Option premium The amount of money a buyer pays and seller receives to engage in an option transaction.

Option price The amount of money a buyer pays and seller receives to engage in an option transaction.

Orderly liquidation value The estimated gross amount of money that could be realized from the liquidation sale of an asset or assets, given a reasonable amount of time to find a purchaser or purchasers.

Organic growth Company growth in output or sales that is achieved by making investments internally (i.e., excludes growth achieved through mergers and acquisitions).

Other comprehensive income Changes to equity that bypass (are not reported in) the income statement; the difference between comprehensive income and net income.

Out-of-sample forecast errors The differences between actual and predicted value of time series outside the sample period used to fit the model.

Out-of-the-money Options that, if exercised, would require the payment of more money than the value received and therefore would not be currently exercised.

Overnight index swap (OIS) A swap in which the floating rate is the cumulative value of a single unit of currency invested at an overnight rate during the settlement period.

Pairs trading An approach to trading that uses pairs of closely related stocks, buying the relatively undervalued stock and selling short the relatively overvalued stock.

Par curve A hypothetical yield curve for coupon-paying Treasury securities that assumes all securities are priced at par.

Par swap A swap in which the fixed rate is set so that no money is exchanged at contract initiation.

Parameter instability The problem or issue of population regression parameters that have changed over time.

Partial equilibrium models Term structure models that make use of an assumed form of interest rate process. Underlying risk factors, such as the impact of changing interest rates on the economy, are not incorporated in the model.

Partial regression coefficients The slope coefficients in a multiple regression. Also called *partial slope coefficients*.

Partial slope coefficients The slope coefficients in a multiple regression. Also called *partial regression coefficients*.

Partnership A business owned and operated by more than one individual.

Payer swaption A swaption that allows the holder to enter into a swap as the fixed-rate payer and floating-rate receiver.

Payoff The value of an option at expiration.

Payout amount The payout ratio times the notional.

Payout policy The principles by which a company distributes cash to common shareholders by means of cash dividends and/or share repurchases.

Payout ratio An estimate of the expected credit loss.

Pecking order theory The theory that managers take into account how their actions might be interpreted by outsiders and thus order their preferences for various forms of corporate financing. Forms of financing that are least visible to outsiders (e.g., internally generated funds) are most preferable to managers and those that are most visible (e.g., equity) are least preferable.

PEG The P/E-to-growth ratio, calculated as the stock's P/E divided by the expected earnings growth rate.

Perfect capital markets Markets in which, by assumption, there are no taxes, transactions costs, or bankruptcy costs, and in which all investors have equal ("symmetric") information.

Performance appraisal The evaluation of risk-adjusted performance; the evaluation of investment skill.

Periodic inventory system An inventory accounting system in which inventory values and costs of sales are determined at the end of the accounting period.

Perpetual inventory system An inventory accounting system in which inventory values and costs of sales are continuously updated to reflect purchases and sales.

Perpetuity A perpetual annuity, or a set of never-ending level sequential cash flows, with the first cash flow occurring one period from now.

Persistent earnings Earnings excluding nonrecurring components. Also referred to as *core earnings*, *continuing earnings*, or *underlying earnings*.

Pet projects Projects in which influential managers want the corporation to invest. Often, unfortunately, pet projects are selected without undergoing normal capital budgeting analysis.

Physical deterioration In the context of real estate, a reduction in value due to wear and tear.

Physical settlement Involves actual delivery of the debt instrument in exchange for a payment by the credit protection seller of the notional amount of the contract.

Plain vanilla swap An interest rate swap in which one party pays a fixed rate and the other pays a floating rate, with both sets of payments in the same currency.

Poison pill A pre-offer takeover defense mechanism that makes it prohibitively costly for an acquirer to take control of a target without the prior approval of the target's board of directors.

Poison puts A pre-offer takeover defense mechanism that gives target company bondholders the right to sell their bonds back to the target at a pre-specified redemption price, typically at or above par value; this defense increases the need for cash and raises the cost of the acquisition.

Pooling of interests method A method of accounting in which combined companies were portrayed as if they had always operated as a single economic entity. Called pooling of interests under US GAAP and uniting of interests under IFRS. (No longer allowed under US GAAP or IFRS).

Portfolio balance approach A theory of exchange rate determination that emphasizes the portfolio investment decisions of global investors and the requirement that global investors willingly hold all outstanding securities denominated in each currency at prevailing prices and exchange rates.

Position trader A trader who typically holds positions open overnight.

Positive serial correlation Serial correlation in which a positive error for one observation increases the chance of a positive error for another observation, and a negative error for one observation increases the chance of a negative error for another observation.

Potential credit risk The risk associated with the possibility that a payment due at a later date will not be made.

Potential GDP The maximum amount of output an economy can sustainably produce without inducing an increase in the inflation rate. The output level that corresponds to full employment with consistent wage and price expectations.

Preferred habitat theory A term structure theory that contends that investors have maturity preferences and require yield incentives before they will buy bonds outside of their preferred maturities.

Premise of value The status of a company in the sense of whether it is assumed to be a going concern or not.

Premium The amount of money a buyer pays and seller receives to engage in an option transaction.

Premium leg The series of payments the credit protection buyer promises to make to the credit protection seller.

Present value model A model of intrinsic value that views the value of an asset as the present value of the asset's expected future cash flows.

Present value of growth opportunities The difference between the actual value per share and the no-growth value per share. Also called *value of growth*.

Present value of the expected loss   Conceptually, the largest price one would be willing to pay on a bond to a third party (e.g., an insurer) to entirely remove the credit risk of purchasing and holding the bond.

Presentation currency   The currency in which financial statement amounts are presented.

Price limits   Limits imposed by a futures exchange on the price change that can occur from one day to the next.

Price momentum   A valuation indicator based on past price movement.

Price multiples   The ratio of a stock's market price to some measure of value per share.

Price-setting option   The operational flexibility to adjust prices when demand varies from forecast. For example, when demand exceeds capacity, the company could benefit from the excess demand by increasing prices.

Priced risk   Risk for which investors demand compensation for bearing (e.g., equity risk, company-specific factors, macroeconomic factors).

Principal–agent problem   A conflict of interest that arises when the agent in an agency relationship has goals and incentives that differ from the principal to whom the agent owes a fiduciary duty.

Principal components analysis   (PCA) A non-parametric method of extracting relevant information from high-dimensional data that uses the dependencies between variables to represent information in a more tractable, lower-dimensional form.

Principle of no arbitrage   In well-functioning markets, prices will adjust until there are no arbitrage opportunities.

Prior transaction method   A variation of the market approach; considers actual transactions in the stock of the subject private company.

Private market value   The value derived using a sum-of-the-parts valuation.

Probability of default   The probability that a bond issuer will not meet its contractual obligations on schedule.

Probability of survival   The probability that a bond issuer will meet its contractual obligations on schedule.

Probit model   A qualitative-dependent-variable multiple regression model based on the normal distribution.

Procedural law   The body of law that focuses on the protection and enforcement of the substantive laws.

Production-flexibility   The operational flexibility to alter production when demand varies from forecast. For example, if demand is strong, a company may profit from employees working overtime or from adding additional shifts.

Project sequencing   To defer the decision to invest in a future project until the outcome of some or all of a current project is known. Projects are sequenced through time, so that investing in a project creates the option to invest in future projects.

Prospective P/E   A P/E calculated on the basis of a forecast of EPS; a stock's current price divided by next year's expected earnings.

Protection leg   The contingent payment that the credit protection seller may have to make to the credit protection buyer.

Protective put   An option strategy in which a long position in an asset is combined with a long position in a put.

Proxy fight   An attempt to take control of a company through a shareholder vote.

Proxy statement   A public document that provides the material facts concerning matters on which shareholders will vote.

Prudential supervision   Regulation and monitoring of the safety and soundness of financial institutions to promote financial stability, reduce system-wide risks, and protect customers of financial institutions.

Purchasing power gain   A gain in value caused by changes in price levels. Monetary liabilities experience purchasing power gains during periods of inflation.

Purchasing power loss   A loss in value caused by changes in price levels. Monetary assets experience purchasing power loss during periods of inflation.

Purchasing power parity (PPP)   The idea that exchange rates move to equalize the purchasing power of different currencies.

Pure expectations theory   A term structure theory that contends the forward rate is an unbiased predictor of the future spot rate. Also called the *unbiased expectations theory*.

Pure factor portfolio   A portfolio with sensitivity of 1 to the factor in question and a sensitivity of 0 to all other factors.

Put   An option that gives the holder the right to sell an underlying asset to another party at a fixed price over a specific period of time.

Put–call–forward parity   The relationship among puts, calls, and forward contracts.

Put–call parity   An equation expressing the equivalence (parity) of a portfolio of a call and a bond with a portfolio of a put and the underlying, which leads to the relationship between put and call prices.

Putable bond   Bond that includes an embedded put option, which gives the bondholder the right to put back the bonds to the issuer prior to maturity, typically when interest rates have risen and higher-yielding bonds are available.

Qualitative dependent variables   Dummy variables used as dependent variables rather than as independent variables.

Quality of earnings analysis   The investigation of issues relating to the accuracy of reported accounting results as reflections of economic performance; quality of earnings analysis is broadly understood to include not only earnings management, but also balance sheet management.

Random walk   A time series in which the value of the series in one period is the value of the series in the previous period plus an unpredictable random error.

Rational efficient markets formulation   See *market efficiency*.

Real estate investment trusts (REITS)   Tax-advantaged entities (companies or trusts) that typically own, operate, and—to a limited extent—develop income-producing real estate property.

Real estate operating companies   Regular taxable real estate ownership companies that operate in the real estate industry in countries that do not have a tax-advantaged REIT regime in place or are engaged in real estate activities of a kind and to an extent that do not fit within their country's REIT framework.

Real exchange rate   The relative purchasing power of two currencies, defined in terms of the *real* goods and services that each can buy at prevailing national price levels and nominal exchange rates. Measured as the ratio of national price levels expressed in a common currency.

Real interest rate parity   The proposition that real interest rates will converge to the same level across different markets.

Real options   Options that relate to investment decisions such as the option to time the start of a project, the option to adjust its scale, or the option to abandon a project that has begun.

Receiver swaption   A swaption that allows the holder to enter into a swap as the fixed-rate receiver and floating-rate payer.

Reconstitution   When dealers recombine appropriate individual zero-coupon securities and reproduce an underlying coupon Treasury.

Recovery rate   The percentage of the loss recovered.

Reduced form models   Models of credit analysis based on the outputs of a structural model but with different assumptions. The model's credit risk measures reflect changing economic conditions.

Reference entity   The borrower on a single-name CDS.

Reference obligation   A particular debt instrument issued by the borrower that is the designated instrument being covered.

Regime   With reference to a time series, the underlying model generating the times series.

Regression coefficients   The intercept and slope coefficient(s) of a regression.

Regulatory arbitrage   Entities identify and use some aspect of regulations that allows them to exploit differences in economic substance and regulatory interpretation or in foreign and domestic regulatory regimes to their (the entities) advantage.

Regulatory burden   The costs of regulation for the regulated entity.

Regulatory capture   Theory that regulation often arises to enhance the interests of the regulated.

Regulatory competition   Regulators may compete to provide a regulatory environment designed to attract certain entities.

Relative-strength indicators   Valuation indicators that compare a stock's performance during a period either to its own past performance or to the performance of some group of stocks.

Relative valuation models   A model that specifies an asset's value relative to the value of another asset.

Relative version of PPP   Hypothesis that changes in (nominal) exchange rates over time are equal to national inflation rate differentials.

Renewable resources   Resources that can be replenished, such as a forest.

Rental price of capital   The cost per unit of time to rent a unit of capital.

Replacement cost   In the context of real estate, the value of a building assuming it was built today using current construction costs and standards.

Replacement value   The market value of a swap.

Reporting unit   For financial reporting under US GAAP, an operating segment or one level below an operating segment (referred to as a component).

Reputational risk   The risk that a company will suffer an extended diminution in market value relative to other companies in the same industry due to a demonstrated lack of concern for environmental, social, and governance risk factors.

Required rate of return   The minimum rate of return required by an investor to invest in an asset, given the asset's riskiness.

Residential properties   Properties that provide housing for individuals or families. Single-family properties may be owner-occupied or rental properties, whereas multi-family properties are rental properties even if the owner or manager occupies one of the units.

Residual autocorrelations   The sample autocorrelations of the residuals.

Residual dividend policy   A policy in which dividends are paid from any internally generated funds remaining after such funds are used to finance positive NPV projects.

Residual income   Earnings for a given time period, minus a deduction for common shareholders' opportunity cost in generating the earnings. Also called *economic profit* or *abnormal earnings*.

Residual income method   Income approach that estimates the value of all intangible assets of the business by capitalizing future earnings in excess of the estimated return requirements associated with working capital and fixed assets.

Residual income model   (RIM) A model of stock valuation that views intrinsic value of stock as the sum of book value per share plus the present value of the stock's expected future residual income per share. Also called *discounted abnormal earnings model* or *Edwards–Bell–Ohlson model*.

Residual loss   Agency costs that are incurred despite adequate monitoring and bonding of management.

Restructuring   Reorganizing the financial structure of a firm.

Retail REITs   REITs that invest in such retail properties as regional shopping malls or community/neighborhood shopping centers.

Return on capital employed   Operating profit divided by capital employed (debt and equity capital).

Return on invested capital   A measure of the after-tax profitability of the capital invested by the company's shareholders and debt holders.

Reviewed financial statements   A type of non-audited financial statements; typically provide an opinion letter with representations and assurances by the reviewing accountant that are less than those in audited financial statements.

Rho   The sensitivity of the option price to the risk-free rate.

Riding the yield curve   A maturity trading strategy that involves buying bonds with a maturity longer than the intended investment horizon. Also called *rolling down the yield curve*.

Risk-neutral probabilities   Weights that are used to compute a binomial option price. They are the probabilities that would apply if a risk-neutral investor valued an option.

Risk-neutral valuation   The process by which options and other derivatives are priced by treating investors as though they were risk neutral.

Risk reversal   An option position that consists of the purchase of an out-of-the-money call and the simultaneous sale of an out-of-the-money put with the same "delta," on the same underlying currency or security, and with the same expiration date.

Robust standard errors   Standard errors of the estimated parameters of a regression that correct for the presence of heteroskedasticity in the regression's error term.

Roll   When an investor moves from one series to a new one.

Rolling down the yield curve   A maturity trading strategy that involves buying bonds with a maturity longer than the intended investment horizon. Also called *riding the yield curve*.

Root mean squared error (RMSE)   The square root of the average squared forecast error; used to compare the out-of-sample forecasting performance of forecasting models.

Sales comparison approach   In the context of real estate, this approach estimates value based on what similar or comparable properties (comparables) transacted for in the current market.

Sales-type leases   A type of finance lease, from a lessor perspective, where the present value of the lease payments (lease receivable) exceeds the carrying value of the leased asset. The revenues earned by the lessor are operating (the profit on the sale) and financing (interest) in nature.

Scaled earnings surprise   Unexpected earnings divided by the standard deviation of analysts' earnings forecasts.

Scalper   A trader who offers to buy or sell futures contracts, holding the position for only a brief period of time. Scalpers attempt to profit by buying at the bid price and selling at the higher ask price.

Scatter plot   A two-dimensional plot of pairs of observations on two data series.

Scenario analysis   Analysis that involves changing multiple assumptions at the same time.

Screening   The application of a set of criteria to reduce a set of potential investments to a smaller set having certain desired characteristics.

Seasonality   A characteristic of a time series in which the data experiences regular and predictable periodic changes, e.g., fan sales are highest during the summer months.

Seats   Memberships in a derivatives exchange.

Securities offering   A merger or acquisition in which target shareholders are to receive shares of the acquirer's common stock as compensation.

Security selection risk   See *active specific risk*.

Segmented markets theory   A term structure theory that contends yields are solely a function of the supply and demand for funds of a particular maturity.

Self-regulating organizations   Private, non-governmental organizations that both represent and regulate their members. Some self-regulating organizations are also independent regulators.

Sell-side analysts   Analysts who work at brokerages.

Sensitivity analysis   Analysis that shows the range of possible outcomes as specific assumptions are changed; involves changing one assumption at a time.

Serially correlated   With reference to regression errors, errors that are correlated across observations.

Settlement   In the case of a credit event, the process by which the two parties to a CDS contract satisfy their respective obligations.

Settlement date   The date on which the parties to a swap make payments. Also called *payment date*.

Settlement period   The time between settlement dates.

Settlement price   The official price, designated by the clearinghouse, from which daily gains and losses will be determined and marked to market.

Shaping risk   The sensitivity of a bond's price to the changing shape of the yield curve.

Shareholders' equity   Total assets minus total liabilities.

Shark repellents   A pre-offer takeover defense mechanism involving the corporate charter (e.g., staggered boards of directors and supermajority provisions).

Shopping center   REITs that invest in such retail properties as regional shopping malls or community/neighborhood shopping centers.

Short   The seller of a derivative contract. Also refers to the position of being short a derivative.

Single-name CDS   Credit default swap on one specific borrower.

Sinking fund bond   A bond which requires the issuer to set aside funds over time to retire the bond issue, thus reducing credit risk.

Sole proprietorship   A business owned and operated by a single person.

Speculative value   The difference between the market price of the option and its intrinsic value, determined by the uncertainty of the underlying over the remaining life of the option. Also called *time value*.

Spin-off   A form of restructuring in which shareholders of a parent company receive a proportional number of shares in a new, separate entity; shareholders end up owning stock in two different companies where there used to be one.

Split-off   A form of restructuring in which shareholders of the parent company are given shares in a newly created entity in exchange for their shares of the parent company.

Split-rate tax system   In reference to corporate taxes, a split-rate system taxes earnings to be distributed as dividends at a different rate than earnings to be retained. Corporate profits distributed as dividends are taxed at a lower rate than those retained in the business.

Spot curve   The term structure of spot rates for loans made today.

Spot rate   The interest rate that is determined today for a risk-free, single-unit payment at a specified future date.

Spot yield curve   The term structure of spot rates for loans made today.

Spurious correlation   A correlation that misleadingly points toward associations between variables.

Stabilized NOI   In the context of real estate, the expected NOI when a renovation is complete.

Stable dividend policy   A policy in which regular dividends are paid that reflect long-run expected earnings. In contrast to a constant dividend payout ratio policy, a stable dividend policy does not reflect short-term volatility in earnings.

Standard deviation   The positive square root of the variance; a measure of dispersion in the same units as the original data.

Standard of value   A specification of how "value" is to be understood in the context of a specific valuation.

Standardized beta   With reference to fundamental factor models, the value of the attribute for an asset minus the average value of the attribute across all stocks, divided by the standard deviation of the attribute across all stocks.

Standardized unexpected earnings   (SUE) Unexpected earnings per share divided by the standard deviation of unexpected earnings per share over a specified prior time period.

Static trade-off theory of capital structure   A theory pertaining to a company's optimal capital structure; the optimal level of debt is found at the point where additional debt would cause the costs of financial distress to increase by a greater amount than the benefit of the additional tax shield.

Statistical factor model   A multifactor model in which statistical methods are applied to a set of historical returns to determine portfolios that best explain either historical return covariances or variances.

Statistically significant   A result indicating that the null hypothesis can be rejected; with reference to an estimated regression coefficient, frequently understood to mean a result indicating that the corresponding population regression coefficient is different from 0.

Statutes   Laws enacted by legislative bodies.

Statutory merger   A merger in which one company ceases to exist as an identifiable entity and all its assets and liabilities become part of a purchasing company.

Steady state rate of growth   The constant growth rate of output (or output per capita) which can or will be sustained indefinitely once it is reached. Key ratios, such as the capital–output ratio, are constant on the steady-state growth path.

Steepness   One of the three factors (the other two are level and curvature) that empirically explain most of the changes in the shape of the yield curve. A shock to the steepness factor changes short-term yields more than long-term yields.

Sterilized intervention   A policy measure in which a monetary authority buys or sells its own currency to mitigate undesired exchange rate movements and simultaneously offsets the impact on the money supply with transactions in other financial instruments (usually money market instruments).

Stock purchase   An acquisition in which the acquirer gives the target company's shareholders some combination of cash and securities in exchange for shares of the target company's stock.

Storage costs   The costs of holding an asset, generally a function of the physical characteristics of the underlying asset.

Storage REITs   REITs that own and operate self-storage properties, sometimes referred to as mini-warehouse facilities.

Straight bond   An underlying option-free bond with a specified issuer, issue date, maturity date, principal amount and repayment structure, coupon rate and payment structure, and currency denomination.

Straight-line rent   The average annual rent under a multiyear lease agreement that contains contractual increases in rent during the life of the lease. For example if the rent is $100,000 in Year 1, $105,000 in Year 2, and $110,000 in Year 3, the average rent to be recognized each year as revenue under straight-line rent accounting is ($100,000 + $105,000 + $110,000)/3 = $105,000.

Straight-line rent adjustment   See *non-cash rent.*

Strategic transaction   A purchase involving a buyer that would benefit from certain synergies associated with owning the target firm.

Strike   See *exercise price.*

Strike price   See *exercise price.*

Strike rate   The fixed rate at which the holder of an interest rate option can buy or sell the underlying. Also called *exercise rate.*

Striking price   See *exercise price.*

Stripping   A dealer's ability to separate a bond's individual cash flows and trade them as zero-coupon securities.

Structural models   Structural models of credit analysis build on the insights of option pricing theory. They are based on the structure of a company's balance sheet.

Subsidiary merger   A merger in which the company being purchased becomes a subsidiary of the purchaser.

Substantive law   The body of law that focuses on the rights and responsibilities of entities and relationships among entities.

Succession event   A change of corporate structure of the reference entity, such as through a merger, divestiture, spinoff, or any similar action, in which ultimate responsibility for the debt in question is unclear.

Sum-of-the-parts valuation   A valuation that sums the estimated values of each of a company's businesses as if each business were an independent going concern.

Sunk cost   A cost that has already been incurred.

Supernormal growth   Above average or abnormally high growth rate in earnings per share.

Survivorship bias   Bias that may result when failed or defunct companies are excluded from membership in a group.

Sustainable growth rate   The rate of dividend (and earnings) growth that can be sustained over time for a given level of return on equity, keeping the capital structure constant and without issuing additional common stock.

Swap curve   The term structure of swap rates.

Swap rate   The interest rate for the fixed-rate leg of an interest rate swap.

Swap rate curve   The term structure of swap rates.

Swap spread   The difference between the fixed rate on an interest rate swap and the rate on a Treasury note with equivalent maturity; it reflects the general level of credit risk in the market.

Swaption   An option to enter into a swap.

Synthetic call   The combination of puts, the underlying, and risk-free bonds that replicates a call option.

Synthetic CDO   Created by combining a portfolio of default-free securities with a combination of credit default swaps undertaken as protection sellers.

Synthetic forward contract   The combination of the underlying, puts, calls, and risk-free bonds that replicates a forward contract.

Synthetic lease   A lease that is structured to provide a company with the tax benefits of ownership while not requiring the asset to be reflected on the company's financial statements.

Synthetic put   The combination of calls, the underlying, and risk-free bonds that replicates a put option.

Systematic risk   Risk that affects the entire market or economy; it cannot be avoided and is inherent in the overall market. Systematic risk is also known as non-diversifiable or market risk.

Systemic risk   The risk of failure of the financial system.

Takeover   A merger; the term may be applied to any transaction, but is often used in reference to hostile transactions.

Takeover premium   The amount by which the takeover price for each share of stock must exceed the current stock price in order to entice shareholders to relinquish control of the company to an acquirer.

Tangible book value per share   Common shareholders' equity minus intangible assets reported on the balance sheet, divided by the number of shares outstanding.

Target   The company in a merger or acquisition that is being acquired.

Target capital structure   A company's chosen proportions of debt and equity.

Target company   The company in a merger or acquisition that is being acquired.

Target payout ratio   A strategic corporate goal representing the long-term proportion of earnings that the company intends to distribute to shareholders as dividends.

Technical indicators   Momentum indicators based on price.

TED spread   A measure of perceived credit risk determined as the difference between Libor and the T-bill yield of matching maturity.

Temporal method   A variation of the monetary/non-monetary translation method that requires not only monetary assets and liabilities, but also non-monetary assets and liabilities that are measured at their current value on the balance sheet date to be translated at the current exchange rate. Assets and liabilities are translated at rates consistent with the timing of their measurement value. This method is typically used when the functional currency is other than the local currency.

Tender offer A public offer whereby the acquirer invites target shareholders to submit ("tender") their shares in return for the proposed payment.

Term premium The additional return required by lenders to invest in a bond to maturity net of the expected return from continually reinvesting at the short-term rate over that same time horizon.

Terminal price multiples The price multiple for a stock assumed to hold at a stated future time.

Terminal share price The share price at a particular point in the future.

Terminal value of the stock The analyst's estimate of a stock's value at a particular point in the future. Also called *continuing value of the stock*.

Termination date The date of the final payment on a swap; also, the swap's expiration date.

Theta The rate at which an option's time value decays.

Time series A set of observations on a variable's outcomes in different time periods.

Time to expiration The time remaining in the life of a derivative, typically expressed in years.

Time value The difference between the market price of the option and its intrinsic value, determined by the uncertainty of the underlying over the remaining life of the option. Also called *speculative value*.

Time value decay The loss in the value of an option resulting from movement of the option price towards its payoff value as the expiration day approaches.

Tobin's q The ratio of the market value of debt and equity to the replacement cost of total assets.

Top-down approach With respect to forecasting, an approach that usually begins at the level of the overall economy. Forecasts are then made at more narrowly defined levels, such as sector, industry, and market for a specific product.

Top-down investing An approach to investing that typically begins with macroeconomic forecasts.

Total factor productivity (TFP) A multiplicative scale factor that reflects the general level of productivity or technology in the economy. Changes in total factor productivity generate proportional changes in output for any input combination.

Total invested capital The sum of market value of common equity, book value of preferred equity, and face value of debt.

Total return swap A swap in which one party agrees to pay the total return on a security. Often used as a credit derivative, in which the underlying is a bond.

Tracking error The standard deviation of the differences between a portfolio's returns and its benchmark's returns; a synonym of active risk. Also called *tracking risk*.

Tracking risk The standard deviation of the differences between a portfolio's returns and its benchmark's returns; a synonym of active risk. Also called *tracking error*.

Trailing dividend yield Current market price divided by the most recent annualized dividend.

Trailing P/E A stock's current market price divided by the most recent four quarters of EPS (or the most recent two semi-annual periods for companies that report interim data semi-annually.) Also called *current P/E*.

Tranche CDS A type of credit default swap that covers a combination of borrowers but only up to pre-specified levels of losses.

Transaction exposure The risk of a change in value between the transaction date and the settlement date of an asset of liability denominated in a foreign currency.

Trend A long-term pattern of movement in a particular direction.

Triangular arbitrage An arbitrage transaction involving three currencies which attempts to exploit inconsistencies among pair wise exchange rates.

Unbiased expectations theory A term structure theory that contends the forward rate is an unbiased predictor of the future spot rate. Also called the *pure expectations theory*.

Unconditional heteroskedasticity Heteroskedasticity of the error term that is not correlated with the values of the independent variable(s) in the regression.

Uncovered interest rate parity The proposition that the expected return on an uncovered (i.e., unhedged) foreign currency (risk-free) investment should equal the return on a comparable domestic currency investment.

Underlying An asset that trades in a market in which buyers and sellers meet, decide on a price, and the seller then delivers the asset to the buyer and receives payment. The underlying is the asset or other derivative on which a particular derivative is based. The market for the underlying is also referred to as the spot market.

Underlying earnings Earnings excluding nonrecurring components. Also referred to as *continuing earnings, core earnings*, or *persistent earnings*.

Unexpected earnings The difference between reported EPS and expected EPS. Also referred to as an *earnings surprise*.

Unit root A time series that is not covariance stationary is said to have a unit root.

Uniting of interests method A method of accounting in which combined companies were portrayed as if they had always operated as a single economic entity. Called pooling of interests under US GAAP and uniting of interests under IFRS. (No longer allowed under US GAAP or IFRS).

Unlimited funds An unlimited funds environment assumes that the company can raise the funds it wants for all profitable projects simply by paying the required rate of return.

Unsterilized intervention A policy measure in which a monetary authority buys or sells its own currency to mitigate undesired exchange rate movements and does not offset the impact on the money supply with transactions in other financial instruments.

Upfront payment The difference between the credit spread and the standard rate paid by the protection if the standard rate is insufficient to compensate the protection seller. Also called *upfront premium*.

Upfront premium See *upfront payment*.

UPREITs An umbrella partnership REIT under which the REIT owns an operating partnership and serves as the general partner of the operating partnership. All or most of the properties are held in the operating partnership.

Upstream A transaction between two related companies, an investor company (or a parent company) and an associate company (or a subsidiary company) such that the associate company records a profit on its income statement. An example is a sale of inventory by the associate to the investor company or by a subsidiary to a parent company.

Valuation The process of determining the value of an asset or service on the basis of variables perceived to be related to future investment returns, or on the basis of comparisons with closely similar assets.

Value additivity   An arbitrage opportunity when the value of the whole equals the sum of the values of the parts.

Value at risk (VAR)   A money measure of the minimum value of losses expected during a specified time period at a given level of probability.

Value of growth   The difference between the actual value per share and the no-growth value per share.

Variance   The expected value (the probability-weighted average) of squared deviations from a random variable's expected value.

Variation margin   Additional margin that must be deposited in an amount sufficient to bring the balance up to the initial margin requirement.

Vasicek model   A partial equilibrium term structure model that assumes interest rates are mean reverting and interest rate volatility is a constant.

Vega   The relationship between option price and volatility.

Venture capital investors   Private equity investors in development-stage companies.

Vertical merger   A merger involving companies at different positions of the same production chain; for example, a supplier or a distributor.

Visibility   The extent to which a company's operations are predictable with substantial confidence.

Weighted average cost   An inventory accounting method that averages the total cost of available inventory items over the total units available for sale.

Weighted average cost of capital   (WACC) A weighted average of the after-tax required rates of return on a company's common stock, preferred stock, and long-term debt, where the weights are the fraction of each source of financing in the company's target capital structure.

Weighted harmonic mean   See *harmonic mean*.

White-corrected standard errors   A synonym for robust standard errors.

White knight   A third party that is sought out by the target company's board to purchase the target in lieu of a hostile bidder.

White squire   A third party that is sought out by the target company's board to purchase a substantial minority stake in the target—enough to block a hostile takeover without selling the entire company.

Winner's curse   The tendency for the winner in certain competitive bidding situations to overpay, whether because of overestimation of intrinsic value, emotion, or information asymmetries.

Write-down   A reduction in the value of an asset as stated in the balance sheet.

Yield curve factor model   A model or a description of yield curve movements that can be considered realistic when compared with historical data.

Z-spread   The constant basis point spread that needs to be added to the implied spot yield curve such that the discounted cash flows of a bond are equal to its current market price.

Zero   A bond that does not pay a coupon but is priced at a discount and pays its full face value at maturity.

Zero-cost collar   A transaction in which a position in the underlying is protected by buying a put and selling a call with the premium from the sale of the call offsetting the premium from the purchase of the put. It can also be used to protect a floating-rate borrower against interest rate increases with the premium on a long cap offsetting the premium on a short floor.

Zero-coupon bond   A bond that does not pay a coupon but is priced at a discount and pays its full face value at maturity.

Index